Lecture Notes in Computer Science 16319

Founding Editors

Gerhard Goos
Juris Hartmanis

Ludger Hagedorn · Ute Schmid · Susan Winter ·
Stefan Woltran
Editors

Digital Humanism

First Interdisciplinary Science and Research Conference, DIGHUM 2025

Vienna, Austria, November 20–21, 2025

Proceedings

 Springer

Editors
Ludger Hagedorn
IWM
Vienna, Austria

Ute Schmid
University of Bamberg
Bamberg, Germany

Susan Winter
University of Maryland
College Park, MD, USA

Stefan Woltran
Technische Universität Wien
Vienna, Austria

ISSN 0302-9743   ISSN 1611-3349 (electronic)
Lecture Notes in Computer Science
ISBN 978-3-032-11107-4   ISBN 978-3-032-11108-1 (eBook)
https://doi.org/10.1007/978-3-032-11108-1

Preface

Technology and digitalization profoundly shape the world we live in, and the stakes are high. The recent rise of AI has further triggered a heightened awareness of the far-reaching impact of digital technologies, ranging from numerous beneficial uses to worrisome concerns for open democratic societies and the lives of their citizens. Technological change is expanding the boundaries of what is possible. There are strong reasons to be concerned about the enormous concentration of power, resources, and the prioritization of future AI R&D directions in the hands of very few players.

We understand Digital Humanism as an approach that describes, analyzes, and — most importantly — influences this complex interplay of technology and humankind for a better society and life, fully respecting universal human rights. The papers collected in this volume take up this challenge and contribute to the understanding of the fundamental changes our world is undergoing at this moment. They examine new opportunities enabled by technological advances as well as the tremendous risks inherent in digitalization, envisaging the prospects for a better life in the digitalized era.

Issues addressed by the papers revolve around digitalization and its entanglement with contemporary social, political, economic, and cultural developments — from algorithmic governance and regulation to the role of AI in popular culture, and to the ever-increasing permeation of our lives by digital devices. Addressing these challenges requires interdisciplinary collaboration between a wide range of domains, from computer science to the humanities. Accordingly, the contributions assembled here explore multiple scientific aspects of the complex interplay between humans and machines in the digitalized age. Different research methodologies and approaches attest to the capacity of Digital Humanism research to break disciplinary silos and reflect on digitalization's impact on the world of today and possibly tomorrow.

All papers in this volume were presented at the first *Digital Humanism – Interdisciplinary Science and Research Conference*, held in Vienna, Austria, on November 20–21, 2025. We received 98 submissions, of which 42 were accepted after a careful peer-review process. One paper was withdrawn after acceptance.

The peer reviewing was double blind with submissions receiving three reviews each, on average. 81 Program Committee Members from different disciplines contributed to the in-depth reviewing process. We are deeply grateful for their help and insights. We received 68 full papers, of which 32 were accepted, and 30 short papers, of which 10 were accepted. PC members were excluded from the reviewing process for papers that they had contributed to as authors or co-authors and for all papers that were authored or co-authored by close collaborators or members of the same faculty.

In addition, we invited three speakers to deliver keynotes at the conference. These invited talks were given by Gry Hasselbalch: "Human Power — A Politics for the AI Machine Age", Julian Nida-Rümelin: "Philosophical Foundations of Digital Humanism", and Hannes Werthner: "The Role of Computer Science in the Age of AI (or Digital Humanism?)".

For this volume, we present the papers in four main chapters: 1) "Digital Humanism Reshaping Computer Science", 2) "Digital Humanism: Ethical and Legal Aspects", 3) "Digital Humanism in Political and Social Sciences", and 4) "Breaking Disciplinary Silos: Digital Humanism Across Disciplines". The order within the invidual chapters is alphabetical by last names with short papers following after full papers.

We thank all authors and reviewers for their support and contributions. The realisation of the conference and the corresponding volume was made possible due to a close collaboration of the Institute for Human Sciences (IWM), Vienna, and the Vienna University of Technology (TU Wien). Special thanks go to the Federal Ministry for Innovation, Mobility, and Infrastructure (BM IMI), Republic of Austria, for its kind support of the Digital Humanism Fellowship program run by the IWM in cooperation with TU Wien. We also would like to acknowledge the support from the Digital Humanism Association and the Faculty of Informatics of TU Wien. Further thanks go to the Vienna Science and Technology Fund (WWTF) and the European Digital Humanism Initiative (EUDHIT) for the joint organization of the reception event. Last but not least, we thank Marie-Louise Lackner for her competent and dedicated technical support.

The organizational work for the conference and the proceedings was facilitated by the use of EasyChair.

October 2025

Ludger Hagedorn
Ute Schmid
Susan Winter
Stefan Woltran

Organization

Program Chairs

Ludger Hagedorn	Institute for Human Sciences / IWM, Austria
Ute Schmid	University of Bamberg, Germany
Susan Winter	University of Maryland, USA
Stefan Woltran	TU Wien, Austria

Program Committee

Hans Akkermans	Vrije Universiteit Amsterdam, The Netherlands
Daniel Arp	TU Wien, Austria
Ricardo Baeza-Yates	AI Institute, Barcelona Supercomputing Center, Spain
Christoph Benzmüller	Universität Bamberg, Germany
Domenico Bianculli	University of Luxembourg, Luxembourg
Anna Bon	Vrije Universiteit Amsterdam, The Netherlands
Antonio Casilli	Polytechnic Institute of Paris, France
Claudia Chiavarino	Istituto Universitario Salesiano Torino, Italy
Stefania Costantini	Università degli Studi dell'Aquila, Italy
Virginia Dignum	Umeå University, Sweden
Gordana Dodig Crnkovic	Chalmers University of Technology, Sweden
Georg Dorffner	Medical University Vienna, Austria
Verena Dorner	WU Vienna, Austria
Hannes Fellner	University of Vienna, Austria
Gerlinde Fellner-Röhling	WU Vienna, Austria
Carlo Ghezzi	Politecnico di Milano, Italy
Davide Grossi	University of Groningen, The Netherlands
Dario Guarascio	Sapienza University of Rome, Italy
Claudio Gutierrez	Universidad de Chile, Chile
Thomas Haigh	University of Wisconsin-Milwaukee, USA
Adrian Haret	LMU Munich, Germany
Manfred Hauswirth	TU Berlin & Fraunhofer FOKUS, Germany
Marlien Herselman	CSIR, South Africa
Elisabeth Hoffberger-Pippan	Peace Research Institute Frankfurt, Germany
Andrea Hrckova	Kempelen Institute of Intelligent Technologies, Slovakia

Brigitte Huber	Internationale Hochschule München, Germany
Paola Inverardi	Gran Sasso Science Institute, Italy
Damir Isovic	Mälardalen University, Sweden
Éva Kaczkó	Johannes Kepler University Linz, Austria
Peter Knees	TU Wien, Austria
Laura Koesten	University of Vienna, Austria & Mohamed bin Zayed University of Artificial Intelligence, United Arab Emirates
Sabine Theresia Koeszegi	TU Wien, Austria
Anastasia Kordoni	Trilateral Research & Lancaster University, UK
Jeff Kramer	Imperial College London, UK
Brigitte Krenn	Austrian Research Institute for Artificial Intelligence, Austria
Bernhard Krüpl-Sypien	Became AI, Austria
Marie-Louise Lackner	TU Wien, Austria
Martin Lackner	FH St.Pölten, Austria
Monika Lanzenberger	European Commission, Belgium
James Larus	EPFL, Switzerland
Sophie Lecheler	University of Vienna, Austria
Mark Levine	Lancaster University, UK
Nadia Magnenat-Thalmann	University of Geneva, Switzerland
Stavros Makris	University College London, UK
Katja Mayer	University of Vienna, Austria
Sunimal Mendis	Tilburg University, The Netherlands
Matúš Mesarčík	Kempelen Instititute of Intelligent Technologies, Slovakia
Irina Nalis	Johannes Kepler University Linz, Austria
Enrico Nardelli	Università di Roma Tor Vergata
Julia Neidhardt	TU Wien, Austria
Wolfgang Nejdl	Leibniz Universität Hannover & Forschungszentrum L3S, Germany
Clara Neppel	IEEE, Austria
Bashar Nuseibeh	The Open University, UK
Jürgen Pfeffer	Technical University of Munich, Germany
Barbara Prainsack	University of Vienna, Austria
Dimitri Prandner	Johannes Kepler University Linz, Austria
Erich Prem	eutema GmbH, Austria
Peter Reichl	University of Vienna, Austria
Francesco Ricci	Free University of Bozen-Bolzano, Italy
Marc Rotenberg	Center for AI and Digital Policy, USA
Francis Saa-Dittoh	University for Development Studies, Ghana
Marta Sabou	WU Vienna, Austria

Klara Sandor	University of Szeged, Hungary
Viola Schiaffonati	Politecnico di Milano, Italy
Alex Schmoelz	FH BFI Wien, Austria
Tim Sprenger	Friedrich-Alexander-Universität Erlangen-Nürnberg, Germany
Eugenia Stamboliev	University of Vienna, Austria
Klaus Staudacher	bidt, Germany
Paul Timmers	University of Leuven, Belgium & European University, Cyprus
Paloma Krõõt Tupay	University of Tartu, Estonia
Núria Vallès Peris	Artificial Intelligence Research Institute, Spanish National Research Council & Universitat Autònoma de Barcelona, Spain
Kees van Berkel	TU Wien, Austria
Toby Walsh	University of New South Wales, Australia
Christiane Wendehorst	University of Vienna, Austria
Hannes Werthner	TU Wien, Austria
Dorothea Winter	Humanistische Hochschule Berlin, Germany
Andrea Zisman	The Open University, UK

Additional Reviewers

Breuer, Nils
Eichinger, Anita
Harikrishnan, Sri
Markschies, Lisa
Nardi, Oliviero
Normann, Philipp
Qua, Kenneth
Ruiz Moreno, Johan Santiago
Schmude, Timothée
Sun, Fei
Vestrucci, Andrea

Sponsors

The organization of the Digital Humanism - Interdisciplinary Science and Research Conference as well as the Open Access publication of these proceedings was supported by the Austrian Federal Ministry of Innovation, Mobility and Infrastructure (BMIMI).

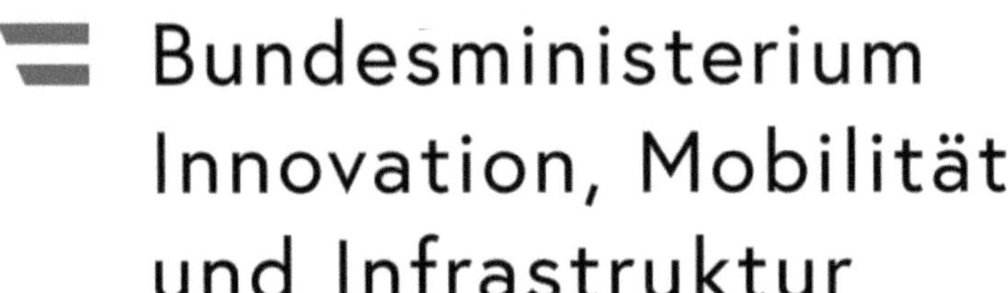

We received additional funding towards the Open Access publication of the proceedings from the Digital Humanism Association.

Invited Talks

Gry Hasselbalch DataEthics.eu

Human Power — A Politics for the AI Machine Age

The rapid and tumultuous introduction of AI into our everyday lives has triggered a self-exploratory public debate about what it means to be human. What are our human potential, talents, and powers – what essentially is our place in the modern world? Are we nothing but outdated machines in dire need of a technological fix?

The keynote is based on the book Human Power — Seven Traits for the Politics of the AI Machine Age (CRC Press, 2025) and reflects on the shifting power dynamics between humans and the AI-powered technologies and their industrial complexes increasingly shaping our world. Exploring the distinctiveness of human power, it argues for a new foundation of the politics that is needed in the AI Machine Age.

Julian Nida-Rümelin, MU München

Philosophical Foundations of Digital Humanism

The core of humanism in general is human agency — its anthropological preconditions and its ethical, social and political implications. Digital humanism is the application of it to the challenges of digital transformation. This talk will present the main arguments in favor of (1) humanism in general and (2) digital humanism specifically. It will focus on the philosophical foundations of digital humanism and exemplify their relevance by discussing some of its practical implications.

Literature: Julian Nida-Rümelin & Nathalie Weidenfeld: Digital Humanism (Springer, Open Access).

Hannes Werthner, TU Wien

The Role of Computer Science in the Age of AI (or Digital Humanism?)

Developments in the field of sub-symbolic AI, which are no longer quite so new, continue to surprise us with new insights and results. It is no longer just about text generation and automatic real-time translation (which was very difficult or even impossible in the past), but now problems at doctoral level are already being solved or it is even targeting NP-complete problems such as the SAT problem (with the results surpassing those developed by humans who won the competitions). In this context it is also interesting to note that AI as a field is inherently undefined, highlighting the absence of a universally accepted definition and the resulting ambiguity in what should or should not be classified as artificial intelligence.

The potential is enormous, but it also raises massive social issues (energy, economic concentration, even the question of "What is humanity and its role?"). As never before, computer science is now at the center of public discussion – right up to the political level of geopolitics and global regulation. What does this mean for computer science, which pragmatically focuses on problem solving – and on a theoretical level (based on formal models) on correctness, certainty and provability – this is now being replaced by uncertain statements based on probability.

At the same time, there are immense implications where interaction with (or even integration of methods from) the social and human sciences is required, almost as if it were becoming a social science itself. Computer science is thus challenged methodologically from "inside" and "outside" by its implications.

How should we deal with this situation? Does digital humanism provide a framework?

Contents

Digital Humanism in Political and Social Sciences

Breaking Disciplinary Silos: Digital Humanism Across Disciplines

Digital Humanism Reshaping Computer Science

Heuristic Search and Constraint Verification for Value-Centric Electrification Planning

William Berglund[1] and Andreas Brännström[2]($\boxtimes$)

[1] Iteract AB, Umeå, Sweden
`william@iteract.se`
[2] Department of Computing Science, Umeå University, Umeå, Sweden
`andreasb@cs.umu.se`

Abstract. Expanding electrification infrastructure demands route planning tools that optimize feasibility while respecting legal, environmental, and stakeholder constraints. We present a hybrid system for value-centric electrification planning that combines heuristic search with logic-based verification. A modified A* algorithm explores alternatives using expert-informed heuristics, while an Answer Set Programming (ASP)-based rule set evaluates stakeholder constraint compliance. This separation of planning and evaluation supports transparency and explainability. Expert feedback highlights the system's value in early-stage decision support, and statistical analysis suggests that it consistently identifies technically feasible routes with reduced private land intrusion.

Keywords: Heuristic search · Logic Programming · Electrification planning · Value alignment · Knowledge elicitation

1   Introduction

Expanding energy infrastructure is a vital enabler of sustainable development, underpinning the electrification of homes, industries, and transport networks [3,19]. While significant attention has been devoted to extending electricity access in underserved regions, planning infrastructure routes remains one of the most complex and contested phases of implementation [24]. Routing decisions must navigate a dense web of constraints, including rugged terrain [7,21], legal protections on land use [8], and socio-political sensitivities tied to landowner conflict and public resistance [1]. These challenges are exacerbated by fragmented data systems, limited modeling transparency, and weak integration of stakeholder values into decision-making processes.

In practice, electrification routing is still dominated by manual geographic information system (GIS) inspection, aided by domain experts and shaped by institutional knowledge [2,11]. While this approach is flexible, it lacks scalability and consistency, and often fails to produce traceable justifications for

L. Hagedorn et al. (Eds.): DIGHUM 2025, LNCS 16319, pp. 3–18, 2026.
https://doi.org/10.1007/978-3-032-11108-1_1

planning choices. Many algorithmic solutions have emerged to optimize electrification at regional scales, often focusing on cost minimization or technology deployment-such as hybrid microgrids or off-grid solar systems-through clustering algorithms [27,32], mixed-integer linear programming (MILP) [25], and demand-driven simulation [3,29]. While electrification planning has advanced significantly in terms of technical modeling-optimizing for least-cost rollout, demand coverage, and infrastructure feasibility-many tools fall short in systematically addressing, verifying, and providing explanations for, whether the resulting routes are socially, legally, or environmentally acceptable [8,15]. Limited stakeholder involvement has been linked to poor performance in rural electrification initiatives [26] (a study performed in Uganda), while broader energy planning studies show that public opposition often arises from perceived procedural injustice and lack of transparency in siting decisions [30]. Environmental risks remain under-addressed: when electrification aligns with household practices and land use, it can mitigate deforestation, but ignoring these dynamics may lead to ecological harm [22]. These examples highlights the need for planning systems that integrate stakeholder concerns and land-use constraints as foundational criteria.

This need for more socially aligned infrastructure planning connects with broader concerns in the Artificial Intelligence (AI) and decision-support communities. Early-stage design is increasingly seen as critical for aligning system behavior with legal, ethical, and functional constraints under Trustworthy AI principles [9]. Yet existing methods are often generic or inconsistently applied. A recent survey shows that although ICT practitioners frequently use standard techniques such as interviews and stakeholder meetings, few report applying elicitation methods tailored to the unique challenges of AI systems-including those related to fairness, explainability, and data governance [31], and ethical concerns such as accountability are often overlooked in early development [17].

To move beyond current limitations, more expressive and transparent planning mechanisms are required. Moreover, methods for capturing expert knowledge and stakeholder values into electrification planning and verification are needed. Heuristic search methods such as A* pathfinding are well-suited for scalable spatial exploration, as they can incorporate terrain and infrastructure cost surfaces into route scoring [16]. However, heuristic methods alone cannot provide guarantees about compliance with non-spatial or socially derived constraints. In contrast, logic-based reasoning frameworks, such as based on logic programming, are ideal for declaratively encoding complex regulations and stakeholder rules, enabling the systematic verification of whether candidate routes uphold all specified constraints and values [14].

In this paper, we propose Hybrid Heuristic Search and Constraint Verification for Electrification Planning (HHSCV-EP); a planning system that combines the scalability of A* pathfinding with the expressiveness of logic-based verification via Answer Set Programming (ASP) [13]. Expert knowledge is elicited to inform the heuristic cost model and the constraint rules. Geospatial data and stakeholder values and constraints are integrated into a unified pipeline that generates and verifies electrification route alternatives. The result is a transparent decision-support tool that produces technically feasible and value-aligned plans.

The remainder of this paper is structured as follows: Sect. 2 reviews related work. Section 3 introduces the methodological foundations. Section 4 outlines the knowledge elicitation process. Section 5 presents the proposed system. Section 6 reports a user evaluation. Section 7 reports a statistical evaluation. Section 8 discusses limitations, strengths, and directions for future work.

2   Related Work

A wide range of algorithmic approaches have been developed to support electrification planning, particularly in rural and infrastructure-scarce contexts, such as [1–3, 18–20, 24]. These works cover geographic information system (GIS)-based visualization tools, demand simulation, graph-theoretic planning, mixed-integer optimization, clustering algorithms, and multi-criteria evaluation-each contributing to scalable and cost-effective electrification strategies.

Early tools such as Banks et al. [2] provided scenario-based assessments by scoring demographic and economic benefits and applying Kruskal's algorithm to compute cost-efficient connection trees. Such models proved useful for rapid policy prototyping, but had limited flexibility to model technical constraints or topological complexity. Subsequent GIS-based systems added spatial granularity to network and off-grid technology siting, as seen in Mentis et al. [24] and Kemausuor et al. [19], facilitating broader national planning efforts.

Simulation frameworks have since played a major role in evaluating long-term investment mixes [3, 20]. Blechinger et al. [3] integrate spatial planning with energy demand forecasts to identify least-cost technology blends. Open-access data and tools have further democratized electrification modeling, as shown by Korkovelos et al. [20], who applied the open-source OnSSET platform in Malawi to evaluate technology options in line with the United Nations Sustainable Development Goal 7 (SDG7) on clean energy access. Moreover, clustering and graph-based methods offer scalable alternatives for realistic topological modeling. Parreno et al. [27] use spatial clustering to reduce problem complexity before layout generation. Gadelha et al. [11] model electrification as a graph problem with terrain-aware routing, yielding network structures more faithful to physical environments. Caminiti et al. [6] present a modular planning framework that integrates demand growth models and terrain analysis to co-design technical and socio-geographic aspects. Torres-Pérez et al. [32] embed clustering into a techno-economic planning pipeline, enabling fine-grained allocation of load centers. Luchmaya et al. [21] were among the first to incorporate digital terrain models directly into route planning logic.

Despite these advances, stakeholder-centric concerns, such as landowner resistance, regulatory exceptions, or protected terrain, are rarely encoded as first-class planning constraints. Most systems focus on cost-optimal or coverage-maximizing solutions, often lacking transparency about trade-offs and rule violations. While existing methods for constrained heuristic search, e.g., [10, 23], are inspirational for our approach, these are not specific for electrification planning. Our work responds to the aforementioned gaps by integrating knowledge-informed heuristic search with logic-based evaluation, offering a verifiable and constraint-transparent tool for value-centric electrification route planning.

3   Preliminaries

This section covers the basic concepts in the methodologies used in this work considering heuristic search and answer set programs.

Heuristic Search and A* (star) Algorithm [16]: The A* is a graph search algorithm that finds a least-cost path from a start node s to a goal node t in a graph $G = (V, E)$ with non-negative edge costs $c : E \to \mathbb{R}_{\geq 0}$. For each node $n \in V$, the evaluation function is $f(n) = g(n) + h(n)$, where $g(n)$ is the cost of the shortest known path from s to n, and $h(n)$ is a heuristic estimate of the cost from n to t. A* expands nodes in order of increasing f-value. If h is admissible $(\forall n, \ h(n) \leq h^*(n))$ and consistent $(\forall (n, n') \in E, \ h(n) \leq c(n, n') + h(n'))$, then A* is complete and optimal.

Answer Set Programs [5]: A logic program P is a finite set of rules of the form $a \leftarrow b_1, \ldots, b_k, \ not \ c_1, \ldots, not \ c_l$, where a, b_i $(1 \leq i \leq k)$, c_j $(1 \leq j \leq l)$ are atoms, and not denotes negation as failure. A rule with empty head is a constraint; a rule with empty body is a fact. A literal is an atom or its strong negation $\neg a$. A default literal is an atom or $not \ a$. The ground instantiation $\mathrm{gr}(P)$ replaces variables with ground terms. The GelfondLifschitz reduct P^I of P under interpretation I removes all rules with $not \ c$ in the body where $c \in I$, and removes all remaining default literals. A stable model (answer set) is an interpretation I that is the minimal model of P^I.

Integrating A* with ASP combines the goal-directed, heuristic-driven efficiency of A* with the expressive, constraint-based reasoning capabilities of ASP, enabling spatial planning that is both computationally scalable and formally grounded in logic. This integration supports our aim of finding not just any shortest path, but alternatives that satisfies expert-informed constraints.

4   Elicitation of Stakeholder Values and Constraints

To inform the modeling and implementation, we conducted semi-structured interviews with five stakeholders involved in energy infrastructure planning (see Table 1). The participants were identified through collaboration with a local company specializing in geographic data, and their contacts in electrification planning. We consider them representative of relevant expertise, spanning technical, geospatial, and economic perspectives. The interview data was then analyzed using thematic analysis, following established practices for eliciting human perspectives into computational models [4,28]. The resulting themes guided the modeling of stakeholder-informed spatial and regulatory constraints.

A thematic analysis on the transcribed interviews revealed consistent planning priorities (see Table 2). In particular: [Terrain and land characteristics],

Table 1. Participant profiles for the knowledge elicitation phase

Code	Role	Professional Background
P1	Planning Engineer	Works at a regional energy utility. Specializes in routing of new lines and preparing permitting documentation.
P2	Network Development Manager	Oversees long-term infrastructure strategy and prioritization at a utility organization. Involved in high-level planning and coordination with stakeholders.
P3	GIS Specialist	Expert in geospatial analysis for infrastructure and environmental planning. Supports routing and risk analysis using GIS data and tools.
P4	GIS Consultant	Managing director of a GIS consultancy. Develops decision support systems for infrastructure clients and public agencies. Experience integrating cost, land use, and regulation.
P5	Compensation Catalog Manager	Senior representative from a national industry body. Maintains the EBR economic models used to estimate project costs and landowner compensation.

Table 2. Thematic analysis; Experts expressing similar views are highlighted.

Code	[Theme]: {categories}	Representative Quote	Experts
T1	[Terrain as constraint]: {wetlands, steep slopes, natural obstacles, terrain class, rerouting risk, topographic suitability}	"Wetlands or steep slopes change everything; you can't just draw a line through them." (P1)	P1, P3, P5
T2	[Soft vs hard ground]: {rock excavation, digging cost, geological difficulty, underground cable feasibility, construction effort}	"You don't want to dig in rock unless you absolutely have to." (P4)	P1, P4
E1	[Restricted environments]: {protected zones, nature reserves, archaeological sites, crossing minimization, public sensitivity, regulatory exceptions}	"If you absolutely have to cross a protected area, you cut the corner, never run straight through." (P3)	P1, P3, P5
I1	[Private land avoidance]: {landowner intrusion, route delays, social acceptability, legal conflict potential, ease of negotiation}	"Avoiding private landowners when possible makes the whole process faster." (P5)	P2, P4, P5
I2	[Landowner dialogue]: {transparency, justification of route, conflict prevention, procedural fairness, feedback expectations}	"You have to expect complaints if people don't understand why a line goes where it goes." (P1)	P1, P5
C1	[Spatial cost variation]: {land type-dependent cost, farmland vs protected land, compensation variation, terrain-driven pricing, construction modifiers}	"It costs differently depending on where you are – farmland is one thing, nature reserve is another." (P5)	P2, P3, P5
C2	[Administrative overhead]: {permit time, zoning complexity, legal processing burden, jurisdictional fragmentation}	"Permits take longer if the land is zoned differently or if many owners are involved." (P2)	P2, P5
R1	[Avoiding sharp turns]: {angle penalties, route straightness, engineering simplicity, pole placement logic, visual clarity}	"You really want to go straight. Every angle is a cost and a risk." (P3)	P1, P3, P4
B1	[Building proximity restriction]: {15 m buffer, construction safety, building integrity, fixed exclusion zones}	"You always need to stay 15 m away from any building edge. That's non-negotiable." (P2)	P1, P2, P5
M1	[Need for automation]: {automated proposals, time savings, initial drafts, repeatable logic, early-stage support tools}	"We'd love to see proposals generated automatically to avoid wasting time." (P4)	P2, P3, P4
M2	[Flexibility required]: {iterative refinement, manual adjustment, contextual overrides, feedback integration, changing constraints}	"The first draft is never the final route it always changes based on feedback." (P2)	P1, P2, P5

including rock, wetlands, and agricultural areas, were described as primary constraints (Codes T1, T2), influencing both routing feasibility and the choice between overhead lines and underground cables. Participants stressed that early identification of such terrain is crucial to avoid costly rerouting later. Concerns about [intrusion and land ownership] were also prominent: minimizing disruption to private landowners (I1) was seen as essential for avoiding delays, and several experts highlighted the importance of explaining and justifying route choices to prevent formal objections (I2).

Reliable [cost estimation] was seen as essential, since construction and compensation costs vary with land type and legal context (C1, C2), and poor early estimates risk infeasible or over-budget plans. Route geometry also mattered: minimizing [turns] reduces technical complexity and negotiation overhead (R1), while strict [building buffers], especially the 15-meter rule, were described as non-negotiable (B1). [Protected areas] required routes to "cut corners" or minimize crossings to avoid ecological disruption and opposition (E1). Participants also wanted [automation] to generate transparent alternatives (M1), but stressed the need for [flexibility] to adapt routes as new input and conditions arise (M2). These insights highlight the need for tools that embed technical, legal, and stakeholder constraints from the outset.

Table 3. Synthesis on guiding principles and their implementation targets

Code	Guiding Principle	Rules and Heuristics Specifications (samples)	System
T1	Terrain as constraint	Add terrain-based cost weights in raster grid	A*
T1	Terrain as constraint	Mark wetlands, water, and unstable ground as no-step	A*,ASP
T2	Avoid steep slopes	Flag segments exceeding slope threshold	ASP
I1	Private land avoidance	Apply cost gradient from parcel edges inward	A*, ASP
I1	Private land avoidance	Penalize deep crossings more than edge-skimming	A*
I2	Minimize land conflict	Flag routes with high private intrusion ratio	ASP
E1	Protected areas	Add cost decay near edges; reject full crossing	A*, ASP
E1	Protected areas	Penalize repeated transitions in protected areas	ASP
B1	15 m building buffer	Mark nearby cells to buildings as no-step	A*
R1	Avoid sharp turns	Add turn penalty for large direction changes	A*
R1	Avoid sharp turns	Flag high turn density over route length	ASP
C1	Land class affects cost	Assign base traversal cost by land use type	A*
C2	Respect zoning rules	Disqualify routes in restricted categories	ASP
M1	Generate alternatives	Rerun A* with spatial noise to vary paths	A*
M2	Flexible automation	ASP flags + multiple A* runs for adaptability	App feature
M2	Flexible automation	Allow stakeholder-based adjustments without rerouting	App feature

As summarized in Table 3, expert insights were distilled into guiding principles for route planning, reflecting spatial and regulatory concerns such as land avoidance [I1], protected areas [E1], turn reduction [R1], and building buffers [B1], as well as needs for flexibility and alternatives [M1, M2]. This step provides the basis for encoding stakeholder priorities into algorithms and logic rules for value-centric electrification planning.

5   System for Value-Centric Electrification Planning

The proposed system is structured as a modular geospatial reasoning pipeline comprising three interconnected modules: 1) spatial preprocessing, 2) a directional routing engine, and 3) a logic-based evaluation backend. Each module operationalizes expert-derived planning knowledge via mathematically grounded transformations, spatial heuristics, and declarative rule checking.

An implementation is available online[1], composed of standalone microservices that demonstrate a complete pipeline for route analysis.

5.1   Spatial Preprocessing

The spatial preprocessing module converts raw geospatial data into structured raster layers for routing and constraint evaluation. This involves rasterization, classification, feature intersection, and per-cell cost computation. The system operates within a planning region defined by a user-supplied line or polygon, expanded by a default $2000\,\mathrm{m}$ buffer to support flexible rerouting around constraints.

Raster Grid Generation. The planning region is discretized into a uniform raster grid with resolution $r \in \{5\,\mathrm{m}, 10\,\mathrm{m}\}$, depending on the resolution of the input data. Each raster cell (x, y) is assigned a numeric traversal cost $C(x, y) \in \mathbb{R}_{\geq 0}$, which reflects the accumulated planning resistance at that location.

Spatial Feature Encoding. Each input polygon $A_i \subset \mathbb{R}^2$, representing a spatial feature (e.g., forest, building, water), is assigned an *influence mode* that defines how it contributes to cell cost or constraints for each grid cell $(x, y) \in G$:

1. **Inside:** Adds cost to all cells within A_i; decays near the polygon boundary.
2. **Edge:** Applies cost outside A_i, decreasing with distance to its boundary.
3. **No-go:** Treats all cells inside A_i as fully blocked (e.g., buildings).
4. **No-step:** Permits crossing A_i, but disallows start or end in it (e.g., water).

Cost Function Construction. The overall traversal cost at cell (x, y) is:

$$C(x, y) = \sum_{i=1}^{n} w_i \cdot \delta_i(x, y)$$

where $w_i \in \mathbb{R}_{\geq 0}$ is the cost weight assigned to the i-th spatial layer, determined based on expert preference or planning guidelines, and $\delta_i(x, y) \in \{0, 1\}$ or $[0, 1]$ is the influence value from layer i at cell (x, y), based on its influence mode and geometric proximity. Each layer contributes a spatially bounded region of influence. For inside mode, $\delta_i(x, y) = 1$ if inside the polygon, and possibly decays linearly toward the edge. For edge mode, $\delta_i(x, y)$ decreases with Euclidean distance d from the boundary: $\delta_i(x, y) = \max(0, 1 - d/d_{\mathrm{max}})$. The decay width d_{max} is calibrated per feature type.

---

[1] https://github.com/will-smed/HHSCV (Implementation repository).

No-Step and No-Go Masking. A binary mask is generated where: $\mathtt{no\_go}$(x,y) is true if cell (x, y) lies within a restricted area and must not be entered, and $\mathtt{no\_step}$(x,y) is true if (x, y) is traversable but not valid as a start or end point of a segment. These masks are stored alongside the cost grid and referenced during pathfinding.

Noise-Based Rerun Preparation. To support generation of multiple alternatives under uncertain planning preferences (Code M1), a Perlin noise field $N_\alpha(x, y)$ is precomputed and added to the base cost grid with varying amplitude α (see Fig. 1). The perturbed cost grid is:

$$C'(x, y) = C(x, y) + N_\alpha(x, y), \quad \alpha \in \{0, 5, 10, 20\}$$

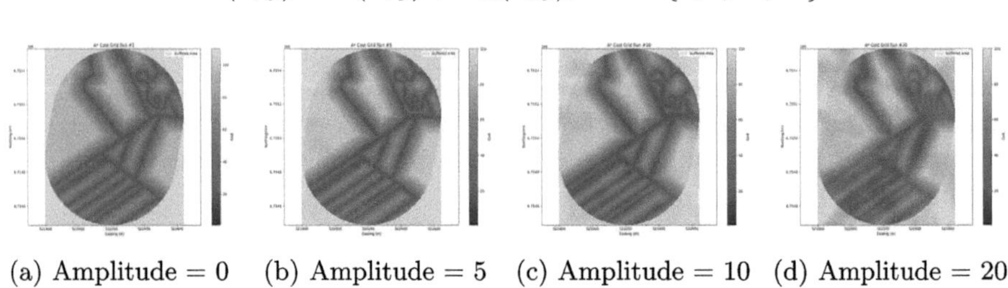

(a) Amplitude $= 0$ (b) Amplitude $= 5$ (c) Amplitude $= 10$ (d) Amplitude $= 20$

Fig. 1. Cost layers with increasing Perlin noise distortion. Higher amplitudes encourage route variation by simulating uncertain or changing planning conditions.

The output consists of a 2D cost array $C(x, y)$ and noise-augmented versions $C'(x, y)$; no-go and no-step binary masks; and planning metadata for each raster cell, including contributing features and constraint flags. This module operationalizes planning constraints from Codes T1, B1, E1, C1, and I1, enabling downstream modules to reason about terrain, access, regulatory, and societal constraints in a quantifiable and extensible form.

5.2   Directional A* Routing

The routing engine implements a directional variant of the A* algorithm, adapted for the constraints and geometry of overhead line infrastructure planning. The objective is to generate cost-efficient, constructible routes that minimize directional changes, respect legal exclusions, and align with expert-derived criteria. Each route is computed over a preprocessed cost surface (Subsect. 5.1), with optional perturbation for variation. The search is performed in both forward and reverse directions to increase coverage. The movement model samples direction vectors at $3°$ intervals within a forward-facing arc (typically $120°180°$), generating segments of approximately $100\,\mathrm{m}$ in length.

Each candidate segment is evaluated by line rasterization (using Bresenham algorithm [12]) to accumulate cost across traversed cells. The cost function guiding the search is defined as:

$$f(s) = g(s) + h(s) + P_{\text{turn}}(s)$$

where s denotes a candidate segment with defined start and direction, $g(s)$ is the cumulative cost from the start node to the current segment endpoint, $h(s)$ is the heuristic cost to the goal, defined as straight-line Euclidean distance. Finally, $P_{\mathrm{turn}}(s)$ is a directional penalty applied if the segment deviates significantly from the previous direction, given by:

$$P_{\mathrm{turn}} = \begin{cases} \lambda \cdot \theta, & \theta > \theta_{\min} \\ 0, & \text{otherwise} \end{cases}$$

where θ is the angular deviation between the current segment and its predecessor (in degrees), $\theta_{\min}$ is a threshold below which no penalty is applied (e.g., 5°), and λ is a tunable scaling factor that controls the weight of the penalty in the overall cost.

Segments are rejected if they cross cells marked with a **no-step** constraint (Sect. 5.1). Prior to expanding the search tree, the algorithm performs a direct line-of-sight check from the current node to the goal. If the path is unblocked and remains under a defined cost threshold, it is accepted immediately as the solution. Otherwise, the A* search continues until the goal is reached or a proximity radius (e.g., 150 m) is met.

The output of the module is a path composed of ordered segments, along with metadata for each segment including angle, cumulative cost, intersected land types, and any encountered constraint zones. This information is exported as structured route descriptors, which serve as input to the logic-based verification system introduced next.

This module encodes routing principles corresponding to expert guidance on directional simplicity (Code R1), safety and exclusion zones (Code B1), and supports scenario variation for planning flexibility (Code M2).

5.3   ASP-Based Evaluation

The final evaluation stage checks each route candidate for compliance with domain constraints encoded in Answer Set Programming (ASP).

Each candidate route $r = \langle p_0, p_1, \ldots, p_n \rangle$, with points $p_i = (x_i, y_i) \in \mathbb{R}^2$ is encoded as a grounded logic program $P_r = F_r \cup R$, where F_r is a route-specific fact base and R is a fixed set of rules. The fact base F_r consists of:

$$\begin{aligned} F_r = {} & \{\, \texttt{height}(i, h_i) \mid i \in \{0, \ldots, n\},\ h_i = \lfloor 10 \cdot H(x_i, y_i) \rfloor \,\} \\ & \cup \{\, \texttt{intrusion}(k) \mid k = \lfloor 100 \cdot \tfrac{L_{\mathrm{priv}}}{L_{\mathrm{total}}} \rfloor \,\} \\ & \cup \{\, \texttt{turns}(T),\ \texttt{points}(P) \mid T = |\{i \in \{1, \ldots, n-1\} \mid \theta_i > \theta_{\min}\}|,\ P = n+1 \,\} \\ & \cup \{\, \texttt{crosses}(z) \mid z \in \mathcal{Z},\ \exists i \in \{0, \ldots, n\} : p_i \in \Omega_z \,\} \end{aligned}$$

where $H(x, y)$ is the elevation at (x, y) from the rasterized height model; L_{priv} is the total length of route segments intersecting private parcels; L_{total} is the total route length; θ_i is the angular deviation at point p_i between adjacent segments; $\theta_{\min}$ is a fixed angle threshold (e.g., 5°); $\mathcal{Z}$ is the set of protected zone types; and $\Omega_z \subset \mathbb{R}^2$ is the spatial extent of zone z.

Let $R = P_{\text{slope}} \cup P_{\text{intrusion}} \cup P_{\text{turns}} \cup P_{\text{protected}}$ be the rule set evaluated over the route fact base F_r. A violation atom is derived if a rule condition is satisfied. Rules in R are defined by the following subprograms:

Slope Constraint (Code T2). This rule flags a violation if the elevation difference between any two route points exceeds a threshold.

Let $P = \langle p_0, \ldots, p_n \rangle$ be the route with elevation values given by $H : P \to \mathbb{N}$ in decimeters. Let $\texttt{max\_slope} \in \mathbb{N}$ be the maximum allowed difference. Define:

$$P_{\text{slope}} = \{\ \texttt{violation("steep\_gradient")} \leftarrow \texttt{height}(i,\ H_i),\ \texttt{height}(j,\ H_j),$$
$$d = |H_i - H_j|,\ d > \texttt{max\_slope} \mid i, j \in P,\ H_i, H_j \in \mathbb{Z}\ \}$$

where $\texttt{height}(i,\ H_i)$ assigns height H_i to point p_i, and d is the absolute height difference. We set $\texttt{max\_slope} = 50$, reflecting expert judgment that height gaps over $5\,\text{m}$ require special construction or pose environmental risk.

Private Land Intrusion (Code I2). This rule flags a violation if a route overlaps private land beyond an acceptable ratio.

Let $P = \langle p_0, \ldots, p_n \rangle$ be the route, and let $\Omega_{\text{priv}} \subset \mathbb{R}^2$ be the set of private parcels. Let L_{priv} be the total length on private land, and L_{total} the total length, and $k = \left\lfloor 100 \cdot \frac{L_{\text{priv}}}{L_{\text{total}}} \right\rfloor$. Define:

$$P_{\text{intrusion}} = \{\ \texttt{violation("high\_intrusion")} \leftarrow \texttt{intrusion}(k),$$
$$k > \texttt{max\_intrusion} \mid k \in \mathbb{N}\ \}$$

where $\texttt{intrusion}(k)$ encodes the private intrusion ratio. Based on expert input that higher ratios are likely to result in project delays or stakeholder pushback, we set $\texttt{max\_intrusion} = 40$.

Turn Density Penalty (Code R1). This rule flags routes that contain too many directional changes relative to their total length.

$$P_{\text{turns}} = \{\ \texttt{violation("turn\_density")} \leftarrow \texttt{turns}(t),\ \texttt{points}(p),$$
$$d = t \cdot 100/p,\ d > \texttt{max\_t} \mid t, p \in \mathbb{N}\ \}$$

where $\texttt{turns}(t)$ and $\texttt{points}(p)$ give the number of turns and points in the route, respectively. The derived value d computes turn density as a percentage. We set $\texttt{max\_t} = 35$, as experts noted that excessive turning increases construction complexity and weakens route credibility.

Protected Zone Crossing (Code E1). This rule flags any route that intersects a protected area. Let $\mathcal{Z}$ be the set of zone identifiers, and let $\texttt{crosses}(z)$ denote that the route intersects zone $z \in \mathcal{Z}$. Let $\texttt{sensitive\_zone}(z)$ indicate that z is classified as protected. Define:

$$P_{\text{protected}} = \{\ \texttt{violation("sensitive\_zone")} \leftarrow \texttt{crosses}(z),$$
$$\texttt{sensitive\_zone}(z) \mid z \in \mathcal{Z}\ \}$$

where `sensitive_zone`(z) is true for zones requiring legal or ecological protection. In our implementation, this includes `protected_nature`, based on expert guidance that even partial crossings of such zones should be avoided unless justified by exceptional planning need.

If any `violation(Label)` atom is derived in the answer set, the route is flagged as non-compliant. An answer set is a stable model that contains a set of ground atoms (facts and conclusions) that hold under the logic program:

```
{..., height(0,3210), height(1,3280), intrusion(0.87),
violation("steep_gradient"), violation("high_intrusion"), ...}
```

This component operationalizes rules grounded in expert guidance (e.g., Codes T2, I1, I2, E1, R1), enabling systematic verification of each route alternative against formalized planning constraints.

6   Expert Evaluation

We presented four route alternatives to three infrastructure experts to assess alignment between expert judgment and encoded rules. Each route was generated under distinct spatial cost configurations. Figure 2 presents the routes and their quantitative attributes; Table 4 summarizes the results of the evaluations.

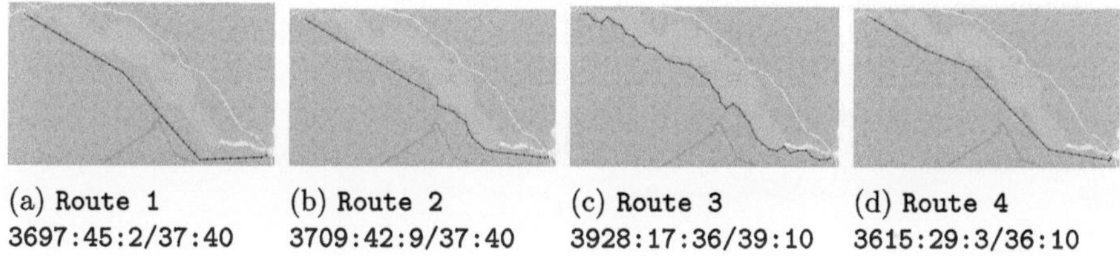

Fig. 2. Visual comparison of routes generated between the same origin and destination under varying planning conditions by terrain, geometry, and property constraints. Data: `[Le:In:T/P:He]` where `[Le]` Length (m), `[In]` Intrusion (m), `[T/P]` Turns/Points, `[He]` Height diff. (m).

Across all four generated routes, the constraint-based ASP evaluation matched expert judgments in identifying feasibility issues. Routes 1 − 3 triggered violations (e.g., `steep_gradient`, `turn_density`, `high_intrusion`) and were consistently rejected by participants due to steep slopes, fragmentation, or expected conflicts. Route 4, with no triggered violations, was approved by all experts. This indicates alignment between the ASP-based verification and the experts' reasoning. Moreover, it suggests that the modified A* algorithm can generate feasible routes. In the following section, we present a statistical evaluation to further assess the system's validity as an early-stage screening tool.

Table 4. Expert evaluation of routes. Data: [Le:In:T/P:He] where [Le]Length (m), [In]Intrusion (m), [T/P]Turns/Points, [He]Height diff. (m).

	Route 1	Route 2	Route 3	Route 4
Data	`3697:45:2/37:40`	`3709:42:9/37:40`	`3928:17:36/39:10`	`3615:29:3/36:10`
P1	"Too steep"	"Cable OK"	"Too complex"	"Acceptable"
P2	"Costly"	"Fragmented"	"Too risky"	"No concerns"
P3	"Crosses path"	"Unacceptable"	"Unrealistic"	"Compliant"
ASP	`steep_gradient, high_intrusion`	`turn_density, high_intrusion`	`turn_density, steep_gradient`	None

7   Statistical Evaluation

We evaluated private land intrusion across 2294 matched pairs of real and generated routes, selected from a GIS-dataset[2] using two criteria: (1) route length difference within $\pm 5\%$, and (2) similarity score ≥ 0.5, based on terrain type, elevation change, and number of crossed properties. The mean intrusion was 136.88 for real routes and 134.13 for generated ones; the mean difference was 2.75, with a median of 2.00 and standard deviation 12.83. Among all pairs, 1281 (56%) of the generated routes showed lower intrusion, 931 (41%) were higher, and 82 (4%) were equal.

Paired t-test ($t = 10.26$, $p < 0.0001$), and Wilcoxon signed-rank test ($p < 0.0001$) confirmed a significant reduction. The effect size was small ($d = 0.01$, 95% CI: [2.22, 3.27]), but consistently favored generated routes.

Figure 3a shows that most points fall below the diagonal, indicating lower intrusion in generated routes. Figure 3b shows that the differences are concentrated above zero. In particular, the distribution of intrusion was more concentrated for generated routes, with lower median (134.1 vs. 136.9) and reduced variability (SD 12.8), and over half (56%) of the pairs, showing improvement.

(a) Tendency for lower values in [G]

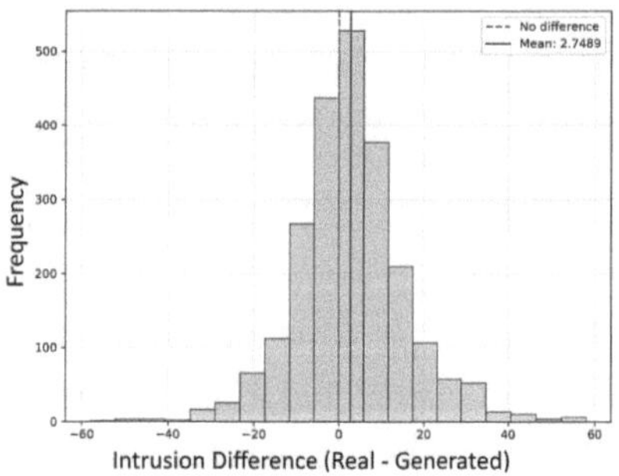

(b) Intrusion diff skewed toward [R]

Fig. 3. Intrusion comparison across 324 [R]eal and [G]enerated routes.

---

[2] https://geotorget.lantmateriet.se/dokumentation/GEODOK/51/latest.html.

Intrusion changes ranged from -58 to $+58$ m^2, reflecting cases where optimization conflicted with real-world constraints. Generated routes significantly reduced intrusion while preserving terrain and length similarity.

8 Discussion and Future Work

This work demonstrates how stakeholder constraints, captured in heuristics and in logic-based rules, can provide value-centric electrification planning. By combining GIS data, A* search, and logic-based verification, the system identifies alternatives that meet technical constraints while significantly reducing private land use, as suggested by the user evaluation and statistical analysis. The hybrid architecture, integrating A* with ASP, provides the goal-directed, heuristic-driven efficiency of A* with the expressive, constraint-based reasoning capabilities of ASP, enabling spatial planning that is both computationally scalable and formally grounded in logic. This integration supports our aim of finding not just any shortest path, but alternatives that satisfies expert-informed constraints. Moreover, rather than automating decisions, the system provides logic-based verification details—answer sets—that supports traceable trade-off analysis.

Notable limitations in the proposed hybrid approach regard the static coordination between components: A* explores routes based on expert-informed cost signals, and ASP filters complete routes post hoc. A direction for future work is to develop methods for localized and incremental evaluation; introducing segment-wise or rolling evaluation could enable earlier detection of infeasible solutions during search. This would allow route generation to avoid problematic areas proactively, rather than filtering after the fact. Another direction for future work concerns the limitations of static rule sets. In spatial planning, rules alone are not sufficient to capture situated knowledge, tacit reasoning, and evolving priorities. Future work should leverage the nonmonotonic reasoning capabilities of ASP to handle exceptions and context-dependent rules, and explore methods for dynamically adjusting constraints or incorporating local input during the planning process. ASP can also support alternative route generation.

Further potential lies in generalizing the rule base into modular, reusable components for rapid adaptation to different regulatory or geographic contexts. More broadly, this work advances the development of transparent and interpretable decision-support systems for public infrastructure, enabling traceable, contestable, and value-aligned planning processes. This contributes to the broader agenda of trustworthy AI and ICT development [9,17,31], where transparency, contextual reasoning, and modular system design are essential for aligning digital tools with public values and long-term societal goals.

Acknowledgments. This work was partially supported by the Wallenberg AI, Autonomous Systems and Software Program (WASP) funded by the Knut and Alice Wallenberg Foundation.

Disclosure of Interests. The authors have no relevant financial or non-financial interests to disclose.

References

1. Abdul-Salam, Y., Phimister, E.: How effective are heuristic solutions for electricity planning in developing countries. Socioecon. Plann. Sci. **55**, 14–24 (2016)
2. Banks, D., Mocke, F., Jonck, E., Labuschagne, E., Eberhard, R.: Electrification planning decision support tool. In: Cape Town: Domest. Use Energy Conf (2000)
3. Blechinger, P., Cader, C., Bertheau, P.: Least-cost electrification modeling and planning-a case study for five Nigerian federal states. Proc. IEEE **107**(9), 1923–1940 (2019)
4. Brännström, A., Wester, J., Nieves, J.C.: A formal understanding of computational empathy in interactive agents. Cogn. Syst. Res. **85**, 101203 (2024)
5. Brewka, G., Eiter, T., Truszczyński, M.: Answer set programming at a glance. Commun. ACM **54**(12), 92–103 (2011)
6. Caminiti, C.M., et al.: The gisele framework: innovations in rural electrification planning. In: 2024 IEEE International Humanitarian Technologies Conference (IHTC), pp. 1–7. IEEE (2024)
7. Dimovski, A., Corigliano, S., Edeme, D., Merlo, M.: Holistic milp-based approach for rural electrification planning. Energ. Strat. Rev. **49**, 101171 (2023)
8. Elkadeem, M., Younes, A., Sharshir, S.W., Campana, P.E., Wang, S.: Sustainable siting and design optimization of hybrid renewable energy system: a geospatial multi-criteria analysis. Appl. Energy **295**, 117071 (2021)
9. European Commission: Ethics guidelines for trustworthy AI (2019). https://ec.europa.eu/digital-single-market/en/news/ethics-guidelines-trustworthy-ai
10. Fox, M.S., Sadeh, N., Baykan, C.: Constrained heuristic search. In: Proceedings of the Eleventh International Joint Conference on Artificial Intelligence, pp. 309–315 (1989)
11. Gadelha Filho, T., Silvia, C., Aleksandar, D., Massimo, B., Marco, M.: Rural electrification planning based on graph theory and geospatial data: a realistic topology oriented approach. Sustain. Energy Grids Netw. **28**, 100525 (2021)
12. Gaol, F.L.: Bresenham algorithm: implementation and analysis in raster shape. J. Comput. **8**(1), 69–78 (2013)
13. Gebser, M., Kaminski, R., Kaufmann, B., Schaub, T.: Answer Set Solving in Practice. Morgan and Claypool Publishers (2012)
14. Gelfond, M., Kahl, Y.: Knowledge Representation, Reasoning, and the Design of Intelligent Agents. Cambridge University Press (2014)
15. Hafeznia, H., Stojadinović, B.: Resilience-based decision support system for installing standalone solar energy systems to improve disaster resilience of rural communities. Energ. Strat. Rev. **54**, 101489 (2024)
16. Hart, P.E., Nilsson, N.J., Raphael, B.: A formal basis for the heuristic determination of minimum cost paths. IEEE Trans. Syst. Sci. Cybern. **4**(2), 100–107 (1968)
17. Jobin, A., Ienca, M., Vayena, E.: The global landscape of AI ethics guidelines. Nat. Mach. Intell. **1**(9), 389–399 (2019)
18. Kamal, M.M., Ashraf, I., Fernandez, E.: Efficient two-layer rural electrification planning and techno-economic assessment integrating renewable sources. Energy Storage **4**(3), e314 (2022)
19. Kemausuor, F., Adkins, E., Adu-Poku, I., Brew-Hammond, A., Modi, V.: Electrification planning using network planner tool: the case of ghana. Energy Sustain. Dev. **19**, 92–101 (2014)
20. Korkovelos, A., Khavari, B., Sahlberg, A., Howells, M., Arderne, C.: The role of open access data in geospatial electrification planning and the achievement of sdg7. an onsset-based case study for Malawi. Energies **12**(7), 1395 (2019)

21. Luchmaya, A., Dwolatzky, B., Meyer, A.: Using terrain information in an electrification planning tool. In: 2001 IEEE/PES Transmission and Distribution Conference and Exposition. Developing New Perspectives (Cat. No. 01CH37294), vol. 1, pp. 456–460. IEEE (2001)
22. Ly, A., Chakir, R., Creti, A.: Electrification or deforestation? Evidence from household practices in côte d'ivoire. Energy Econ. **128**, 107717 (2024). https://doi.org/10.1016/j.eneco.2024.107717
23. Malburg, J., Fraser, G.: Combining search-based and constraint-based testing. In: 2011 26th IEEE/ACM International Conference on Automated Software Engineering (ASE 2011), pp. 436–439. IEEE (2011)
24. Mentis, D., et al.: A gis-based approach for electrification planning-a case study on Nigeria. Energy Sustain. Dev. **29**, 142–150 (2015)
25. Moretti, L., Astolfi, M., Vergara, C., Macchi, E., Pérez-Arriaga, J.I., Manzolini, G.: A design and dispatch optimization algorithm based on mixed integer linear programming for rural electrification. Appl. Energy **233**, 1104–1121 (2019)
26. Mpangwire, V., Ainomugisha, S., Musiita, B.: Stakeholder involvement and team capacity on the performance of rural electrification projects in Southwestern Uganda. J. Econ. Behav. Stud. **16**(1), 109–117 (2024)
27. Parreno, R.P., Jr., Del Mundo, R.: Clustering algorithm as a planning support tool for rural electrification optimization. Int. J. Sci. Technol. Res. **4**(12), 112–120 (2015)
28. Pidgeon, N.F., Turner, B.A., Blockley, D.I.: The use of grounded theory for conceptual analysis in knowledge elicitation. Int. J. Man Mach. Stud. **35**(2), 151–173 (1991)
29. Riva, F., Sanvito, F.D., Tonini, F.T., Colombo, E., Colombelli, F.: Modelling long-term electricity load demand for rural electrification planning. In: 2019 IEEE Milan PowerTech, pp. 1–6. IEEE (2019)
30. Roddis, P., Carver, S., Dallimer, M., Norman, P., Ziv, G.: The role of community acceptance in planning outcomes for onshore wind and solar farms: an energy justice analysis. Appl. Energy **226**, 353–364 (2018)
31. de Sousa Silva, A.F., Ramos Sousa Silva, G., Canedo, E.D.: Requirements elicitation techniques and tools in the context of artificial intelligence. In: Brazilian Conference on Intelligent Systems (BRACIS), pp. 15–29. Springer (2022). https://doi.org/10.1007/978-3-031-21686-2_2
32. Torres-Pérez, M., Domínguez, J., Arribas, L., Amador, J., Ciller, P., González-García, A.: A geospatial clustering algorithm and its integration into a techno-economic rural electrification planning model. Eng. Appl. Artif. Intell. **137**, 109249 (2024)

A System Prototype for Food Sales Forecasting and Optimization to Reduce Food Waste for Short-Shelf-Life Products

Lukas Grasmann[(✉)] and Nysret Musliu

Institute of Logic and Computation, TU Wien, 192/2, Favoritenstraße 9-11,
1040 Vienna, Austria
{lukas.grasmann,nysret.musliu}@tuwien.ac.at

Abstract. The reduction of food waste is one of the major challenges of today for retailers and wholesalers. Large amounts of food are thrown away on the retail and wholesale level per year. Since globally available resources are limited, preventing food waste is a very important way to reduce the carbon footprint and even help protect the environment because the production of goods consumes both large amounts of energy and land. Preventing food waste is intertwined with the related problem of order generation. The generation of orders depends on accurate forecasts provided to the users. In this paper, we present a system description of a prototype that significantly improves forecasts to facilitate the reduction of food waste through the use of machine learning to provide a basis for subsequent order optimization. Our system has been developed in cooperation with Austrian retailers and wholesalers who provide both real-world data and valuable insights into the inner workings of Austrian grocers. We present an overview of the system and the technologies utilized to achieve our goals. In addition, we also discuss the constraints and ethical considerations encountered. Our evaluation shows that our system can help achieve the goals of reducing food waste while being very useful to our project partners and, therefore, workable in the real world.

Keywords: Sales Forecasting · Machine Learning · User Interaction · Food Waste Reduction

1 Introduction

The waste of perishable food products is a very critical socio-economical problem due to the limitation of global resources. Every year, around 1.3 billion tons of still edible food are discarded in the retail and wholesale industry or by consumers [12]. Preventing food waste can improve the utilization of available resources to reduce world hunger. Due to this massive importance, the reduction of food waste is also codified as Goal 12 of the United Nation's *Sustainable Development Goals* [32]. At the same time, food waste also causes monetary losses for

© The Author(s) 2026

L. Hagedorn et al. (Eds.): DIGHUM 2025, LNCS 16319, pp. 19–34, 2026.
https://doi.org/10.1007/978-3-032-11108-1_2

the retail industry, which results in an interest in its prevention by grocers. For retailers and wholesalers, significant food waste is directly caused by inaccurate ordering procedures that result in overordering of products that subsequently go out of date or spoil without being sold on time. Such overordering usually occurs when there is insufficient knowledge about the expected demand and sales or when a too large safety stock is used to prevent lost sales due to potential out-of-stock situations. Reduction of waste, when closely integrated, can lead to optimized manufacturing plans [29]. Forecasting expected demand as accurately as possible is therefore critical to improving the ordering process and reducing waste generation in all retail, wholesale, and similar environments.

Artificial Intelligence (AI) in general and *Machine Learning* (ML) in particular are very useful tools that can be used in different forecasting applications, including, but not limited to, different kinds of forecasting of demand and sales. Existing approaches to demand and sales forecasting work with limited data sets [20,24] or are tailored to related but different problems such as water demand forecasting [6] or demand for construction machinery [1]. None of sales forecasting approaches make use of a complete and extensive set of data or long-term real-world data from retail and wholesale environments. Some potentially helpful (contextual and other) feature sets like days before and after a holiday or window days are also not considered in the literature. Tying together the extensive real-world data sets with state-of-the-art algorithms is also not trivial in practice, since most of the approaches are also optimized to single scenarios and in many cases even single locations.

In this paper, we present a system description of a prototype that helps with waste reduction through improved forecasting by using machine learning approaches. We describe how the forecasting can then be used as a basis for the subsequent order optimizations in an integrated system. In addition, we describe the challenges we have encountered when designing and implementing this system, as well as the lessons derived from the implementation process. We also illustrate the use case and usefulness of our system through an example.

Our system is based on the use of state-of-the-art Machine Learning (ML) techniques which produce forecasts to be subsequently used for order optimization. For this, we first process the data from different sources, including from different grocers in a uniform way. Then we train machine learning models that are capable of predicting the sales of individual days. These forecasts are subsequently used to generate order suggestions, but can also be used to (semi)manually adjust the order suggestions. By generating significantly improved orders through improved forecasting, food waste can be reduced to a significant degree while also keeping lost sales of our grocer project partners limited.

Our multiyear work is part of the APPETITE research project that aims to incorporate new technologies to implement a system that helps optimize the ordering process and reduce the waste of perishable products. We work together with different **project partners**. These include Spar, Austria's largest retailer, and Metro and Kastner, two of the biggest Austrian wholesalers. Through this close collaboration, we have access to real-world data and expertise, allowing us to craft a prototype that satisfies the requirements of the real world. This ensures our results are usable in the real world and our grocer partners can use the insights generated through our work in practice. The system prototype has been developed in cooperation with Fraunhofer Austria Research GmbH, the Vienna University of Economics and Business Administration (WU Wien), and IT-Power Services GmbH. Additional prototyping support and input data were provided by INVENIUM Data Insights GmbH.

Our paper is structured as follows. In Sect. 2 we describe the current state of the art as well as a selection of related research. Subsequently, we describe our system design in Sect. 3. This section is divided into the description of the acquisition and processing of the input data in Sect. 3.1, the forecasting module in Sect. 3.2, the order optimization module in Sect. 3.3, and the user dashboard and user interaction in Sect. 3.4. We also describe the deployment and evaluation of our system and the lessons learned from this in Sect. 4. Finally, we conclude our paper in Sect. 5 and give potential future work.

2   Related Work

Currently, our grocer project partners rely largely on statistical tools to calculate simple and complex metrics that the ordering is then based on. Such metrics include average sales for the past few days, deviations, preorders, and others. One of our project partners also uses an external company to generate the forecasts for products that must be ordered weeks in advance.

Earlier designs and concepts for our project were published by Birkmaier et al. [4,5]. Based on this, our paper introduces a functional prototype as has been devised as a continuation of the APPETITE project. We include details on the data used, the forecasting module, other components related to user interaction, feedback from domain experts who tested the system, and the lessons learned.

There are some very closely related examples in the literature for our use case. The first is a forecasting project for a Japanese supermarket chain conducted by Liu et al. [21]. Here, we find both a similar use case and similar product categories. However, this research does not provide any data or code directly, making direct comparisons impossible. It also does not describe how the forecasts themselves can then be used for order optimization in practice. Also closely related in terms of the use case is the Chinese e-commerce forecasting presented in [20] that focuses on the time series themselves. Demand forecasting is also considered in [24]. Other works with similar scenarios include the master theses [30] and [27].

Different data sources and data processing have also been used in the literature. In [28], promotional data are used to improve the forecasting of sales time series. Other works using promotional data are [2] and [26]. Contextual data can be found in [30] which also provided the basis for our own list of contextual data together with [21]. For the Japanese supermarket chain mentioned above, weather data have been successfully used [21]. The success may not always transfer because different countries encounter different climate and weather impacts.

Movement data retrieved from cell towers is a novel addition to our system which is not encountered in the literature. Our system is also novel insofar as it combines multiple different retailers and wholesales into a single system despite differences in their internal processes and data handling. We also have a large data set that encompasses multiple years and thousands of products available to us, which are also not found in the literature. Due to our close cooperation with our grocer project partners, we also have access to a wide array of qualitative feedback to improve our system to make it usable in practice.

Other research in the area has mainly focused on the forecasting part of our system instead of the design of the system itself. There exist two surveys of sales of forecasting perishable product by Tsoumakas [31] and Mavani et al. in [22] where the latter is both more recent and more comprehensive. Previous work using *artificial neural networks* includes [1,7,33], and [9]. Long Short-Term Memory (LSTM) networks are also common in our use case and are used in [30] and [21] with varying performance. Support vector machines have been used successfully for related forecasting tasks in [1] and in [6] and for sales forecasting in [26]. Other examples found in the literature include linear regression [11] and Bayesian networks [2,11] for both of which the performance may vary depending on the type of demand the product exhibits. *Lasso* regression, *Ridge* regression, and *Elastic Net* regression [11] have also been used in the past. As seen in [14], it is also possible to combine different approaches.

3   System Design

We now give an outline of the system design of our prototype, which is an evolution of the system presented in [4]. We focus on our implementation of the forecasting module and the user interaction with regard to it including derived information and how it can be used for order suggestions. All other components are described briefly but not in depth. A schematic overview of the system can be found in Fig. 1 which is a modified version of the overview presented in [4] focusing more on input data and clarity of user input.

In Fig. 1, we outline three distinct modules that work together for our system prototype. The order optimization module takes the internal and external data sets as input and generates a forecast result to pass on to the order optimization module. In the order optimization step, more detailed stock data and logistics data are also considered when generating an order suggestion that is passed to the dashboard. Users can interact directly with the dashboard where they can view information about the products (including stock level), view order suggestions, and generate orders by (optionally) modifying the order suggestions. Based on the order suggestion and the user's interaction, the dashboard then generates modified orders. Not depicted in our system overview is the simulation environment which was used for evaluation of the prototype discussed in this work. The simulation environment primarily serves as a way to simulate the progression of days based on real-world historical sales data.

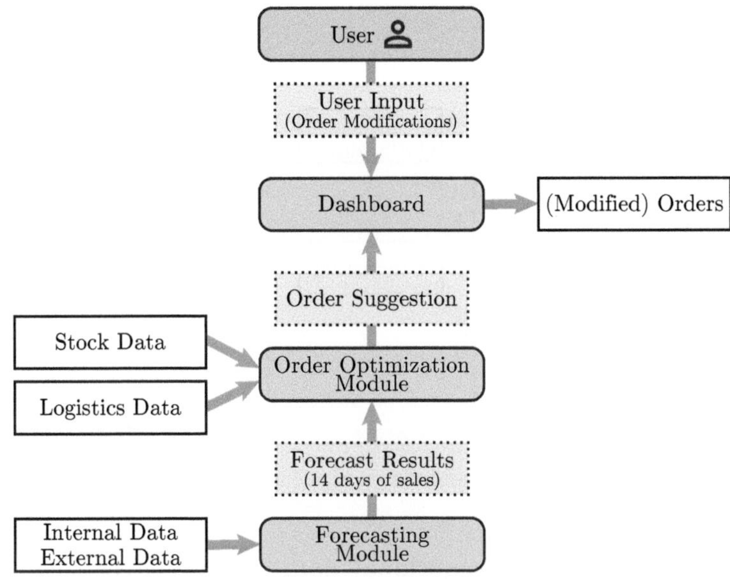

Fig. 1. System overview of all individual components (modified from [4])

3.1   Input Data

We now describe the data acquisition and processing, as well as ethical and data protection considerations encountered.

An overview of the data collection and its sources can be found in Fig. 2. We divide the acquired data into *internal* and *external* data sets. The primary difference is that *internal* data is provided by the grocers and consists of general data (e.g., the names of the articles and their dimensions) and historical data (e.g., sales history and associated promotions). We further subdivide the internal and external data as outlined in the following subsections.

Internal Data. This refers to all data provided by our grocer project partners. We distinguish between *general, sales, logistics,* and *other historical* data.

The first subdivision contains **general internal data** such as product and customer information, as well as data on sales locations, distribution centers, and outlets. In addition, information relevant to logistics, such as potential order dates and delivery dates, is also part of this subdivision.

The largest subdivision contains the **(historical) sales** and **(historical) logistics data**. This encompasses all data about sales and logistics (e.g., deliveries and distribution of wares). These are made available at different levels of aggregation depending on the partners. In general, sales are available at least on a per-product per-day basis for each location, but may also be available as individual transactions including the corresponding customers.

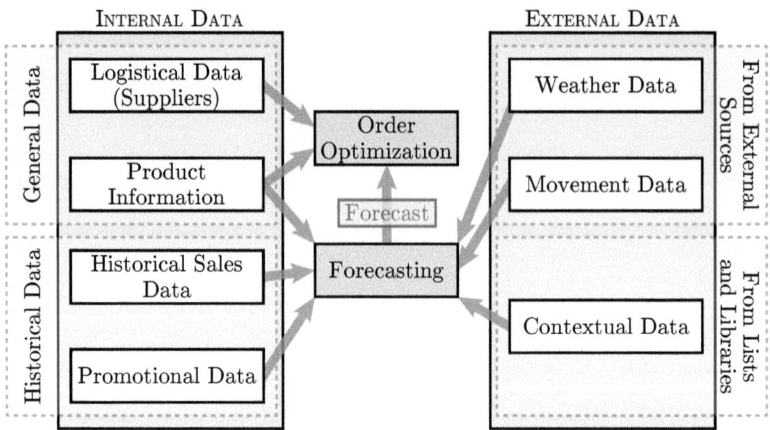

Fig. 2. Overview and Categorization of Data Sources.

Lastly, the **historical promotional data** subdivision contains historical data related to the promotions that were run at the given sales times. This includes promotional material in print or digital form, as well as discounts and other marketing campaigns that have had an impact on sales. What promotional data are available and the granularity of those data heavily depends on the individual grocer providing the data.

External Data. External data are provided by external sources instead of the grocers. Our external data include *weather*, *movement*, and *contextual* data. The data is provided via APIs and similar data sources (weather and contextual data) or collaborating external project partners (movement data).

Weather data are provided by external weather forecasts and historical weather data. For this, multiple different providers can be used that offer differing granularities and forecasting areas. For our project, we have chiefly employed the *Global Forecasting System* (GFS) and *Integrated Nowcasting through Comprehensive Analysis* (INCA). The former is a global system for weather forecasts, while the latter is a specialized Austrian solution developed by the Austrian Central Institute for Meteorology and Geodynamics [13]. An detailed overview of the features included in the weather data can be found in Table 1.

Movement data are obtained from cell towers and have been provided for this project by INVENIUM Data Insights GmbH. It is usually connected by the cell phone service providers that operate the individual towers. The aggregated and evaluated data are then collected and provided by specialized firms. A detailed overview of the dimensions included in the movement data can be found in Table 2. The placeholder **XX** denotes a two-digit time in a 24 h format, i.e., 00 through 23.

Table 1. Overview Weather Data

	Description	Unit
T2M	Air temp.	$°C$
TD2M	Dew point temp.	$°C$
RH2M	Relative humidity	%
PO	Mean sea level pressure	Pa
GL	Global radiation	W/m^2
UU	Wind speed in eastwards direction	m/s
VV	Wind speed in northwards direction	m/s
RR	Precipitation sum (1h)	kg/m^2

Table 2. Overview Movement Data

	Description	Type
residents	Number of residents on a specific date	Integer
visits	Number of visits in the area (visitors may visit multiple times per day)	Integer
visitors	Number of unique visitors (not counting duplicate visitors)	Integer
load_XX	Total number of persons at time XX	Integer

Contextual data provide the context for each data point used for training or forecasting. This encompasses, for example, the day of the week, the season, and whether or not a day is a holiday or falls on a weekend. As such, contextual data differ from the rest of the "external" data sets insofar as no dedicated external provider is necessary since all contextual data can instead be retrieved using default libraries or date lists (for example, for public and school holidays). An overview of the contextual data features can be found in Table 3.

Table 3. Overview Contextual Data

	Description	Type
isHoliday	Whether a day is a (public) holiday	Boolean
isBeforeHoliday	Whether a day is directly before a public holiday	Boolean
isAfterHoliday	Whether a day is directly after a public holiday	Boolean
isSchoolHoliday	Whether a day is a school holiday	Boolean
isWeekend	Whether a day is part of the weekend (Sat, Sun)	Boolean
isWeekday	Whether a day is part of the weekdays (Mon - Fri)	Boolean
weekday	Day of the week	Categorical
dayOfYear	Day of the year	Integer
month	Month of the year	Integer
season	(Meteorological) season	Categorical

Data Processing. In this section, we discuss the challenges and procedures involved in the handling of the data. We will also pay special attention to the associated ethical and data protection considerations. An overview of internal data processing steps, excluding grocer-specific and highly proprietary sanitization steps, can be found in Fig. 3.

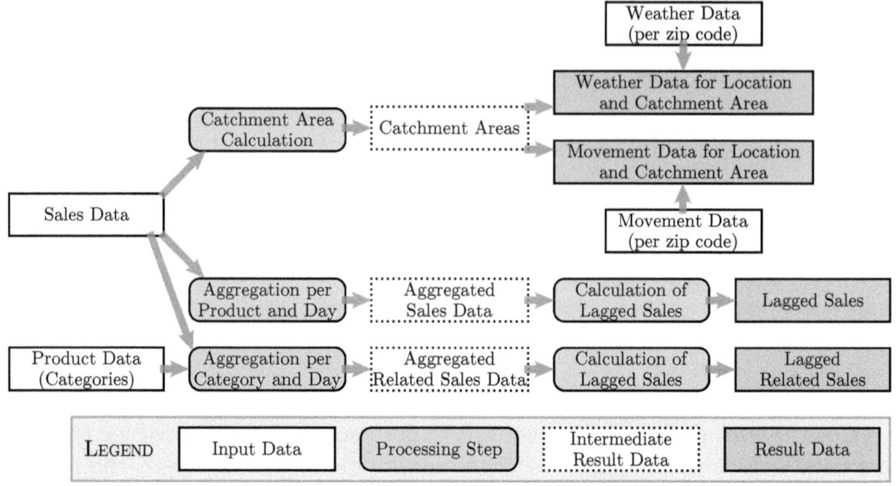

Fig. 3. Overview Data Processing Steps.

As part of the project, we have created a uniform format for sales data that can be computed for all retailers and subsequently used for both the forecasts based on machine learning and the visualizations via the dashboard. We aggregate all sales data on a per-day, per-product basis since they are provided with different time granularities depending on the internal systems of the grocer project partners. This is also the granularity of the output of the forecasts. For our use cases, orders are placed once per day at the end of the day, making finer granularities unnecessary.

Ethical and Data Protection Considerations. Primarily, all internal data are subject to confidentiality within each grocer. The need for confidentiality is primarily due to the potential competitive advantages that other grocers could gain by having access to historical sales data and promotional strategies employed by each individual grocer. As such, we must ensure that data from different project partners do not bleed into other data sets or systems. We mitigate that by, while having a largely uniform data format which allows for reusability of program components, having distinctly separate storages for the data that can only be accessed by the respective project partners and the developers needing access. Both data sets and models are stored for each grocer individually in containers where each can only be accessed by the grocers that have originally provided the internal data. Our data sets were also kept strictly separate during the development process for all internal data.

We also take care to process a minimal amount of personal data or customer-specific data. Individual transactions are only used to generate the aggregated input format for machine learning techniques and to determine catchment areas for individual locations. For sales data aggregation, the data are aggregated on a per-product basis, completely eliminating individual customer data in favor of total sales. In the latter case, data are additionally aggregated by zip code of the customer. Customer-specific data are never used as inputs when training or using ML methods, which also means that customer data or individual transactions cannot be extracted using adversarial AI or similar means. Through these mitigations, there is no risk of exposing confidential or protected customer data by the system through the input data themselves or the trained models.

For external data, there are also potential privacy concerns for cell tower data. Here, we also use only aggregated data on a zip-code basis with up to hourly granularity. As such, there are also no privacy and data protection concerns on an individual level. However, due to legal restrictions, these data are kept strictly confidential and not distributed outside of the system itself in any nonanonymized fashion. This also includes restricting access from the grocers themselves. The raw data are only used as basis for the inputs for the forecasting methods.

3.2   Forecasting Module

The forecasting module has been developed primarily by the authors of this contribution and is designed to generate forecasts for future sales that can be used as input to the order optimization module seen in Fig. 1. To generate these forecasts, we use different ML approaches. The choice of ML approach depends on each individual product. Currently, multiple models are trained and then the best one is selected in the prototype since the number of products is limited. The best performing forecasts for a test data set are used in the simulations to evaluate the "real-world" capabilities of our approach.

We select among *Linear Regression* (LR) [10,11], *Elastic Net Regularization* (EN) [34], *Random Forest* (RF) [15,16], *eXtreme Gradient Boosting* (XGB) [8], *Light Gradient Boosting Method* (LGB) [19,23], *Long Short-Term Memory Networks* (LSTM) [17], *eXtended Long Short Term Memory Networks* (xLSTM) [3], and the *Tree-based Pipeline Optimization Tool* (TPOT) [25].

Both LR and EN are linear models that might not be suitable for products where sales cannot be approximated by any linear models. RF represents a very successful approach in the literature among tree- and forest-based models. Since gradient boosting is also very successful in the literature, we use both XGB and LGB here where LGB can be considered a modified variant of XGB developed by Microsoft that performs better in some scenarios. For neural networks, we use LSTM and the novel xLSTM which perform well, especially for some hard to predict products. We also use an AutoML approach with TPOT that takes up much more resources than the other approaches but is capable of finding unusual configurations for some of the products where the wide array of optimized settings of or prototype does not work.

From discussions with our grocer project partners, we have determined that 14 days is the forecast horizon needed for our applications. This is due to the fact that fresh produce must be ordered in rough quantities up to 14 days in advance from central suppliers. To maximize performance, we use *direct* forecasting to generate predictions for 14 days. We train multiple models $\mathcal{M} = \{m_t\}$ where t is the step and m_t is a model for step t. Given a forecast horizon of 14 days, it follows that $\mathcal{M}$ contains 14 models for each product.

3.3   Order Optimization Module

The order optimization module was developed primarily by the WU Wien team and is described in [18] (preprint). We keep the description brief, as it was implemented by our project partner. It takes the outputs from the forecasts as input and generates a suggestion for the orders at a specific ordering date. Orders are only generated on days where ordering from the individual product's suppliers is possible. To minimize the amount of foodstuffs ordered, the order optimization component takes into account the order date, the expected delivery date, the next possible date for the subsequent order, and the delivery date for the subsequent order. As such, one of the basic assumptions of the order optimization module for reducing food waste is that smaller orders are placed whenever possible and necessary (i.e., there are expected sales for the sales period).

3.4   User Dashboard and Interaction

The user interface has been developed primarily by IT-Power Services GmbH and consists of three parts.

- The first part provides **general information** about the product in question. This includes product number, group, price, delivery days, and similar information as well as current stock levels.
- Following the general information section, the results of the **order optimization** process are displayed. This also includes the system-generated order recommendation based on future order and delivery dates, the forecast, and the current stock level. Here, the expected stock level curve can also be used to gauge the safety level of the stock kept back to avoid out-of-stock situations. A brief overview of this component can be found in Fig. 4.
- At the bottom, the **forecasts** for the next 14 days are displayed next to the sales and forecast history. An example can be found in Fig. 5.

In Fig. 4, the blue curve shows the historical stock level before the current date, which is marked by a blue-filled dot. The red continuation of the curve shows the predicted stock levels with a given order suggestion. For this example, we see that there is a relatively high level of safety for the stock level such that out-of-stock situations and lost sales should not occur. The two solid vertical lines mark the next two opportunities to order, including the current one for which the order is generated. Both corresponding delivery dates are marked by the dashed lines to the right of their individual potential order dates. We note that a delivery date may also be after the next opportunity to order, which does not affect the inner workings of the order optimization.

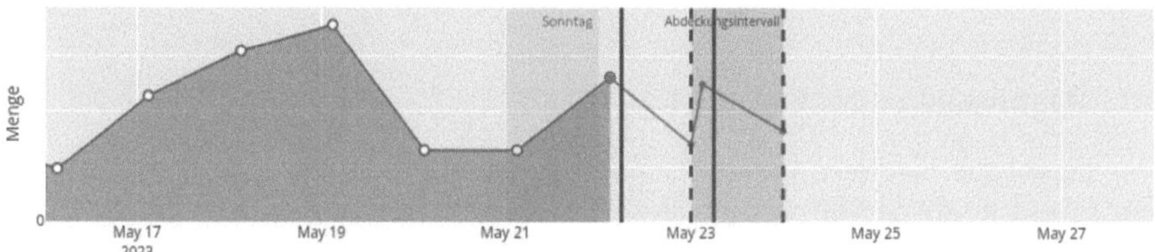

Fig. 4. System Order Optimization Visualization. (Color figure online)

Figure 5 shows a visualization of the forecasting. The two upper series of bars show the historical sales progressions observed in the previous years. The third series of bars shows the historical sales progressions (dark blue) up to the current date, which is a solid vertical line. After that, the system displays the results of the sales forecasts (lighter blue with marked confidence intervals). This can be used to check and evaluate the order suggestion.

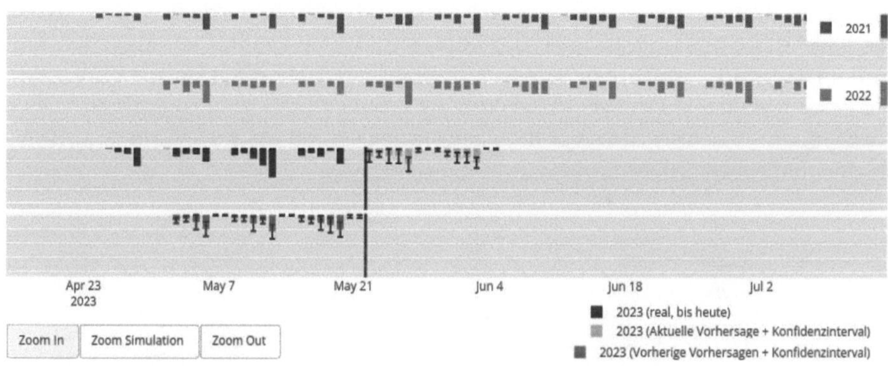

Fig. 5. System Forecasting Visualization. (Color figure online)

User interactions in the system are currently limited to the ordering process itself. The system gives the users the ability to adjust the order suggestions which were automatically generated to save time. Order suggestions are generated when ordering from the suppliers is possible. Any suggestion can either be accepted or rejected by modifying the amount.

4   Evaluation of System Prototype Deployment

In this section, we discuss the deployment of our prototype, the potential and observed impacts, and the lessons learned from the development, testing, and feedback received from our grocer partners.

4.1   Deployment and Impact

Our prototype has been deployed in a test environment with selected products and tested by dispatchers and ordering managers from our grocer project partners with designated simulation instances. For this, a period of Mai and June of 2023 was replayed with models being trained and evaluated exclusively using data before these dates. Feedback from domain experts was retrieved as verbal experience reports, questionnaires, and in the form of quantitative changes to the order suggestions with the corresponding reasons. Currently, the system is in the state of a working prototype that demonstrates its core capabilities. For deployment into production, future modifications are still necessary to accommodate the specific individual existing ordering and logistics systems and workflows.

In Fig. 6, we show the impact of our system with an example encountered during our prototype testing phase. This figure includes two weeks of simulation versus reality for a product where waste has occurred in reality. The stock is a dotted line, while waste is recorded as the red bar at the bottom of the chart. The simulation keeps a more sensible stock level and, despite not losing sales, avoids the large write-offs present in reality almost fully. As seen in the orange left bars (order suggestion) and green bars (order quantity), only slight interventions were performed by the specialist testing the prototype which has brought stock level dangerously close to lost sales. It follows that our system is capable of having a sizable and measurable impact on waste reduction.

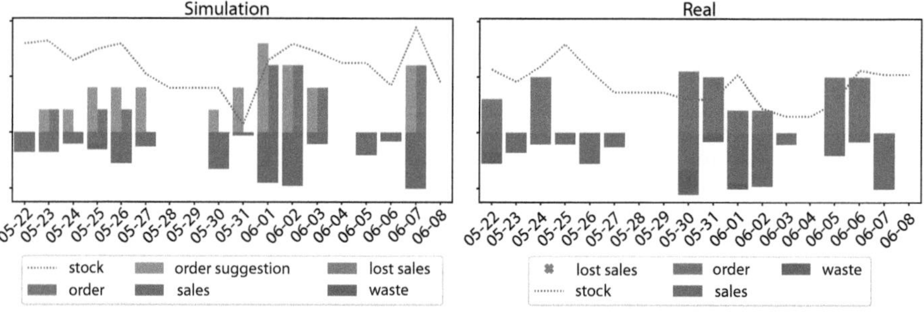

Fig. 6. Example for impact of our prototype on waste reduction.

4.2 Lessons Learned and Feedback

One of the primary lessons learned during prototype deployment and testing is that, while our system can speed up and simplify ordering, significant familiarization time is necessary to use the system. Evaluating a single product also required multiple minutes instead of previous estimations of seconds.

Generally, our prototype was received very positively by the grocers, who praised that the information was displayed very clearly and the predictions were also clearly understandable. In particular, it was praised that the prototype makes it clear which products were hard to predict and as such needed extra human attention to fix potential misestimations. In particular, the expected error bars of the confidence intervals were highly praised as being helpful in gauging individual order suggestions. For the representation of this, the testers were split between whether a plot-based interface as currently provided was superior to a corresponding table of numbers. It was also pointed out that the prototype can significantly improve the ordering process by supplying the forecasts and order optimization as new components to aid the existing logistics system, which is most often largely based on performance indexes instead of actual forecasts.

5 Conclusion and Future Work

In this work, we have presented the design of a prototype for a system that uses ML forecasts to generate orders for perishable foodstuffs in real-world retail and wholesale environments. We have described the data acquisition and processing used by the system in detail and also addressed the ethical considerations that come with processing these data. Subsequently, we have also described the general design of the system in-depth with a focus on the forecasting component. We have described the testing and evaluation of our system here, including the lessons learned from testing and the impact the prototype can have on the reduction of waste for perishable goods.

Our prototype has shown great potential for reducing food waste in real-world retail and wholesale environments during testing and evaluation. It has been well-received by our project partners and has been found to be usable in the real world pending some future work to integrate it into the production systems used for logistics management at the individual partners. We have also managed to obtain important feedback both general to the system and proprietary to the individual grocers to aid with further development.

Future work extends towards full integration of logistics and supplier optimizations. This includes optimizing loading and routes, but also should take into account different factors such as vendor reliability, spoilage risks, and risk of delivery failures. A more in-depth evaluation of individual plots and performance metrics used for decision making is also sensible due to the different experiences with the user interface reported during testing. Another field worth exploring in more depth is explainable artificial intelligence. All project partners have expressed interest in being able to gauge the underlying predictions based on how they were generated. However, this limits the range of feasible ML methods.

Acknowledgments. This research is carried out in the context of the project "APPETITE" funded by the Federal Ministry for Climate Action, Environment, Energy, Mobility, Innovation and Technology as part of the program "ICT of the future", Grant No. 887547 and managed by the Austrian Research Promotion Agency FFG.

Disclosure of Interests. The authors have no competing interests to declare that are relevant to the content of this article.

References

1. Aktepe, A., Yanık, E., Ersöz, S.: Demand forecasting application with regression and artificial intelligence methods in a construction machinery company. J. Intell. Manuf. **32**(6), 1587–1604 (2021). https://doi.org/10.1007/s10845-021-01737-8
2. Ali, Ö.G., Sayin, S., Woensel, T.V., Fransoo, J.: SKU demand forecasting in the presence of promotions. Expert Syst. Appl. **36**(10), 12340–12348 (2009)
3. Beck, M., Pöppel, K.: XLSTM: extended long short-term memory (2024). https://github.com/NX-AI/xlstm
4. Birkmaier, A., Imeri, A., Reiner, G.: Improving supply chain planning for perishable food: data-driven implications for waste prevention. J. Bus. Econ. **94**(6), 1–36 (2024)
5. Birkmaier, A., Imeri, A., Riester, M., Reiner, G.: Preventing waste in food supply networks - a platform architecture for AI-driven forecasting based on heterogeneous big data. Procedia CIRP **120**, 708–713 (2023). https://doi.org/10.1016/j.procir.2023.09.063
6. Brentan, B.M., Luvizotto, E., Jr., Herrera, M., Izquierdo, J., Pérez-García, R.: Hybrid regression model for near real-time urban water demand forecasting. J. Comput. Appl. Math. **309**, 532–541 (2017)
7. Çetinkaya, Z., Erdal, E.: Daily food demand forecast with artificial neural networks: Kırıkkale university case. In: 2019 4th CSEIT (UBMK), pp. 1–6. IEEE, New York, NY, USA (2019). https://doi.org/10.1109/UBMK.2019.8907105
8. Chen, T., Guestrin, C.: Xgboost: a scalable tree boosting system. In: Krishnapuram, B., Shah, M., Smola, A.J., Aggarwal, C.C., Shen, D., Rastogi, R. (eds.) Proceedings 22nd ACM SIGKDD, pp. 785–794. ACM, New York, NY, USA (2016)
9. Doganis, P., Alexandridis, A., Patrinos, P., Sarimveis, H.: Time series sales forecasting for short shelf-life food products based on artificial neural networks and evolutionary computing. J. Food Eng. **75**(2), 196–204 (2006)
10. Freedman, D.: Statistical Models: Theory and Practice. Cambridge University Press, Cambridge, second edn (2009)
11. Garre, A., Ruiz, M.C., Hontoria, E.: Application of machine learning to support production planning of a food industry in the context of waste generation under uncertainty. Oper. Res. Perspect. **7**, 100147 (2020)
12. Gustavsson, J., Cederberg, C., Sonesson, U.: Global food losses and food waste - extent causes and prevention (2021). https://www.fao.org/3/mb060e/mb060e00.htm. Accessed 23 Nov 2023

13. Haiden, T., Kann, A., Pistotnik, G., Stadlbacher, K., Wittmann, C.: Integrated nowcasting through comprehensive analysis (INCA)-system description. ZAMG Rep **61** (2009)
14. Harshini, K., Madhira, P.K., Chaitra, S., Reddy, G.P.: Enhanced demand forecasting system for food and raw materials using ensemble learning. In: 2021 International Conference on AIMV, pp. 1–6. IEEE, New York, NY, USA (2021). https://doi.org/10.1109/AIMV53313.2021.9671005
15. Ho, T.K.: Random decision forests. In: Third ICDAR, 1995, Volume I, pp. 278–282. IEEE Computer Society, New York, NY, USA (1995)
16. Ho, T.K.: The random subspace method for constructing decision forests. IEEE TPA **20**(8), 832–844 (1998)
17. Hochreiter, S., Schmidhuber, J.: Long short-term memory. Neural Comput. **9**(8), 1735–1780 (1997)
18. Imeri, A., Reiner, G.: A myopic ordering policy for fixed shelf-life products under non-stationary demand in the grocery sector. SSRN (2025). https://doi.org/10.2139/ssrn.5394323
19. Ke, G., et al.: LightGBM: a highly efficient gradient boosting decision tree. In: Advances in NIPS, vol. 30. Curran Associates, Inc., New York, NY, USA (2017)
20. Li, M., Ji, S., Liu, G.: Forecasting of Chinese e-commerce sales: an empirical comparison of arima, nonlinear autoregressive neural network, and a combined arima-narnn model. Math. Probl. Eng. **2018**(1), 6924960 (2018)
21. Liu, X., Ichise, R.: Food sales prediction with meteorological data - A case study of a Japanese chain supermarket. In: Tan, Y., Takagi, H., Shi, Y. (eds.) 2nd DMBD, Proceedings. Lecture Notes in Computer Science, vol. 10387, pp. 93–104. Springer, New York, NY, USA (2017). https://doi.org/10.1007/978-3-319-61845-6_10
22. Mavani, N.R., Ali, J.M., Othman, S., Hussain, M.A., Hashim, H., Rahman, N.A.: Application of artificial intelligence in food industry–a guideline. Food Eng. Rev. **14**(1), 134–175 (2022)
23. microsoft: LigthGBM (2017). https://github.com/microsoft/LightGBM
24. Mukherjee, S., Shankar, D., Ghosh, A., Tathawadekar, N., Kompalli, P., Sarawagi, S., Chaudhury, K.: ARMDN: associative and recurrent mixture density networks for eretail demand forecasting. CoRR arXiv:1803.03800 (2018)
25. Olson, R.S., Bartley, N., Urbanowicz, R.J., Moore, J.H.: Evaluation of a tree-based pipeline optimization tool for automating data science. In: GECCO 2016, Proceedings of the GECCO Conference 2016, pp. 485–492. ACM, New York, NY, USA (2016)
26. Di Pillo, G., Latorre, V., Lucidi, S., Procacci, E.: An application of support vector machines to sales forecasting under promotions. 4OR **14**(3), 309–325 (2016). https://doi.org/10.1007/s10288-016-0316-0
27. Sarvi, T.: Predicting product sales in retail store chain. Master's thesis, Aalto University. School of Science (2020). http://urn.fi/URN:NBN:fi:aalto-2020122056353
28. Sroginis, A.: The use of contextual information in demand forecasting. Dissertation, Lancaster University (2021). https://doi.org/10.17635/lancaster/thesis/1445
29. Tang, X., He, Y., Salling, M.: Optimal pricing and production strategies for two manufacturers with industrial symbiosis. IJPE **235** (2021)
30. Tiainen, M.: Forecasting seasonal demand at the product level in grocery retail. Master's thesis, Aalto University. School of Science (2021). http://urn.fi/URN:NBN:fi:aalto-202105236892
31. Tsoumakas, G.: A survey of machine learning techniques for food sales prediction. Artif. Intell. Rev. **52**(1), 441–447 (2018). https://doi.org/10.1007/s10462-018-9637-z

32. UNSDG: Responsible consumption and production (2015). https://www.undp.org/sustainable-development-goals/responsible-consumption-and-production. Accessed 19 Feb 2024
33. Yang, C., Sutrisno, H.: Short-term sales forecast of perishable goods for franchise business. In: 10th International Conference on KST. KST 2018, pp. 101–105. IEEE, New York, NY, USA (2018)
34. Zou, H., Hastie, T.: Regularization and variable selection via the elastic net. J. R. Stat. Soc. Ser. B Stat Methodol. **67**(2), 301–320 (2005)

Schedules Need to be Fair Over Time
Position Paper

Marie-Louise Lackner[✉]

DBAI, TU Wien, Favoritenstrasse 9-11, 1040 Vienna, Austria
`marie-louise.lackner@tuwien.ac.at`

Abstract. Fairness is essential to ensure long-term satisfaction and engagement of employees, users, and clients—particularly in systems that rely on automated decisions such as scheduling. In this position paper, we argue that fairness in scheduling must be understood as a property over time: treating each scheduling decision in isolation—without considering how often agents have been favored or disadvantaged in the past—can lead to persistent unfairness. We propose a framework for fairness over time in repeated scheduling scenarios that captures individual utilities across a history of decisions and can be adapted to multiple applications and fairness concepts. We hope this framework will encourage further research and will serve as a foundation for both theoretical exploration and the development of practical scheduling systems that promote fairness over time.

Keywords: Scheduling · Fairness · Fairness Over Time · Combinatorial Optimization · Employee Scheduling · Production Scheduling

1   Why Do We Need Fairness over Time?

Consider the problem of generating a weekly work schedule for a group of employees. The schedule must satisfy a set of constraints—such as maximum daily working hours, total weekly workload, and required shift coverage. Within these constraints, employees may express preferences regarding when and how much they wish to work. However, due to conflicting preferences and limited flexibility, it is typically impossible to fulfill all individual wishes.

To evaluate the quality of a schedule, objective functions are defined [3,34]. These might measure service quality, adherence to preferences, workload balance, or other operational goals. The scheduling problem can then be formulated as a constraint optimization problem [36], and solved using exact methods to find an optimal schedule—that is, one that minimizes the objective function. Scheduling problems are typically computationally hard (often NP-hard), which means enumerating all solutions is infeasible. Instead, advanced algorithms—ranging from constraint programming to metaheuristics—are used to find high-quality schedules. For illustration, we assume an optimal solution is known.

© The Author(s) 2026

L. Hagedorn et al. (Eds.): DIGHUM 2025, LNCS 16319, pp. 35–50, 2026.
https://doi.org/10.1007/978-3-032-11108-1_3

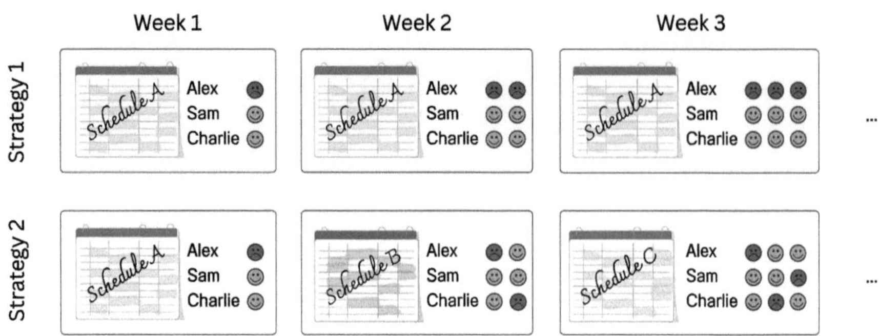

Fig. 1. Illustration of the key concept of fairness over time in scheduling scenarios. Solving scheduling instances in an isolated fashion–as illustrated by strategy 1 in the top part of the figure–can lead to an increasingly unfair distribution of burdens over time. On the other hand, taking into consideration satisfaction levels of past decisions–as illustrated by strategy 2 in the lower part of the figure–enables a fairer distribution of burdens and leads to *fairness over time*.

Now suppose that, in such an optimal solution, one employee—say, Alex—receives a less favorable assignment than the others. If the same scheduling instance is solved again the following week using the same method (and assuming deterministic behavior), the same optimal solution will be returned. Once again, Alex will receive the less desirable outcome. And this may happen repeatedly, week after week. See the top part of Fig. 1 for an illustration of this example.

From a technical standpoint, this is not a flaw in the model. Each scheduling instance is treated independently, and the solver has no knowledge of past outcomes or accumulated dissatisfaction. Yet, from a fairness perspective, the repetition of suboptimal treatment for Alex is clearly problematic. Schedule A might be acceptable for Alex every now and then, but not every week. Moreover, another optimal schedule might exist in which a different employee—say, Charlie—takes on the less desirable assignment, allowing for a fairer rotation of burdens. But without knowledge of past satisfaction levels, the model has no reason to prefer that alternative. An alternative outcome for the described example, which could be achieved by taking previous satisfaction levels into account, is illustrated in the bottom part of Fig. 1.

This simple example illustrates a key challenge: fairness is a longitudinal property. It cannot be fully captured by solving each scheduling instance in isolation—which, nonetheless, remains the standard practice. In reality, scheduling decisions are rarely one-off events; instead, they are made repeatedly and regularly, whether weekly, monthly, or at other intervals depending on the context. We are thus convinced that incorporating fairness into scheduling requires a broader view that considers the distribution of favorable and unfavorable assignments over time:

> Organizations that truly care about the long-term satisfaction of their members, clients, or users need to keep track of how individual satisfaction evolves across past scheduling decisions and adopt mechanisms that ensure *fairness over time*. Accordingly, researchers and practitioners developing algorithmic scheduling models must recognize fairness over time as a key design objective and integrate it as a central component of their solutions.

We argue that developing algorithmic scheduling frameworks that ensure fairness over time offers a range of important benefits. Such frameworks can help maintain individual engagement and satisfaction, which is particularly crucial in settings where long-term participation is desired or where sustained cooperation is needed. Moreover, fairness over time can foster group cohesion, as the system is more likely perceived as just and inclusive when fairness is consistently upheld. If the underlying fairness criteria are made transparent, this enhances the explainability of automated decisions and strengthens trust as well as acceptance of automated decision-making processes.

Content of the Paper. In the following section, we propose a flexible framework for *fairness over time in repeated scheduling scenarios*. In Sect. 3, we point to previous work that considers fairness issues for scheduling problems and to related work that deals with fairness over time. In Sect. 4, we list possible directions for future work in the area of fair scheduling over time.

2   Developing a Framework for Fairness in Repeated Scheduling

We propose a framework for *fairness over time in repeated scheduling scenarios*. A schematic overview of this framework is given in Fig. 2. Its individual components can flexibly be adapted to different application domains of scheduling problems. In what follows, we do not distinguish between employees, members, clients, or users; instead we refer to the individuals whom the schedule applies to and toward whom fairness should be achieved as *agents*.

We formulate five questions that need to be answered when designing such a framework for a specific scheduling application:

- Q1: Toward whom do we want to achieve fairness, i.e., who are the agents? This question is addressed in Sect. 2.1.
- Q2: How does one define the satisfaction level or utility of an agent for a given schedule? This question is addressed in Sect. 2.2.
- Q3: How does one aggregate utilities for past decisions for a given agent? This question is also addressed in Sect. 2.2.
- Q4: How does one define fairness over time? Possible fairness criteria are proposed in Sect. 2.3.
- Q5: How can one integrate fairness in the optimization process, i.e., how can one include the chosen fairness criteria in existing optimization problems? Possible routes are sketched in Sect. 2.4.

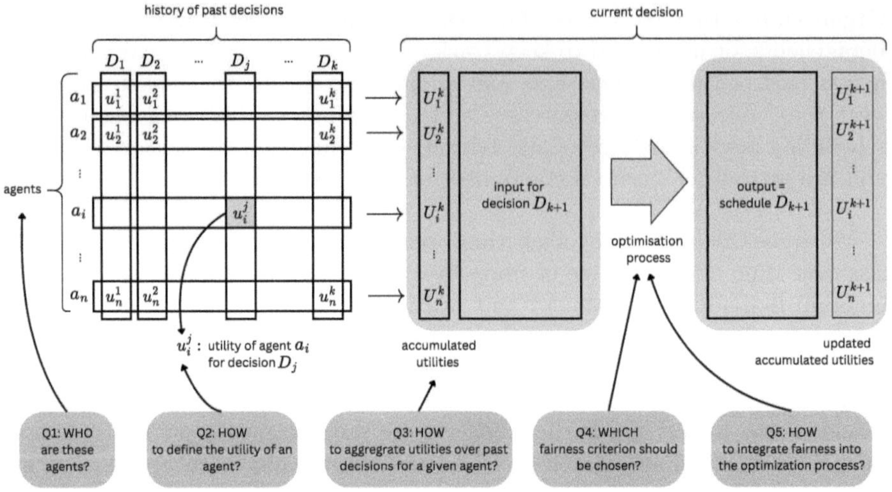

Fig. 2. Overview of the proposed framework for fair scheduling decisions over time.

In the remainder of this paper, we use the following notation: The set of *agents* toward whom fairness should be achieved is denoted by $\mathcal{A} = \{a_1, \ldots, a_n\}$ for some $n \in \mathbb{N}$. Moreover, a *history of scheduling decisions* $D_1, D_2, \ldots D_k$ is given for some $k \geq 1$. The history of scheduling decisions corresponds to the sequence of outputs, i.e. schedules, obtained by solving k instances of the scheduling problem at hand, one after the other. For simplicity, we assume that all previous decisions concern the same set of agents. The current decision that needs to be taken is denoted by D_{k+1}. We denote by $u_i^j \in \mathbb{R}$ the satisfaction or *utility* of agent $a_i \in \mathcal{A}$ with a given decision/schedule D_j with $1 \leq j \leq k$. Note that negative utilities are possible. Furthermore, U_i^j denotes the *accumulated utility* of agent $a_i \in \mathcal{A}$ across all previous decisions $D_1, D_2, \ldots D_j$ with $j \leq k$.

2.1 Fairness for Whom? Agents in Scheduling Contexts

Depending on the specific scheduling application, the *agents* toward whom fairness should be achieved can vary widely. The following outlines several important application domains, without attempting to be exhaustive.

Employees. One of the most prominent domains where fairness plays a critical role is employee scheduling—also referred to as workforce or personnel scheduling. In this setting, the agents toward whom fairness is directed are the employees themselves. Scheduling problems arise in many sectors that require continuous or variable coverage, including healthcare, emergency services, transportation, manufacturing, and customer support. A wide range of problem variants have been studied, from assigning employees to predefined shifts to designing shifts under complex constraints such as legal regulations and contractual agreements. These problems are typically captured under the umbrella of the General

Employee Scheduling Problem [22]. Comprehensive overviews of this area are provided in the surveys on staff scheduling and rostering [15], general personnel scheduling [3], skill-based workforce planning [11], and nurse rostering [7,31].

Customers or Jobs. Another important perspective on fairness in scheduling arises in production and manufacturing contexts, where the agents toward whom fairness is directed are the jobs themselves. When customers submit multiple jobs, fairness can also be considered at the customer level, aggregating satisfaction across all their submitted jobs. Here, the objective is to schedule a set of jobs or tasks on one or multiple machines, subject to a use-case-specific objective and a range of constraints. These constraints may include release dates, due dates, processing times, setup times, machine capacities, secondary resource requirements, precedence relations, and machine eligibility. A schedule determines the start and end times of each job (or of a selected subset, if not all can be accommodated), thereby inducing varying degrees of satisfaction or dissatisfaction across the set of jobs. A wide variety of scheduling problems have been studied in this domain, including environments with a single machine or identical, uniform or unrelated machines in parallel, (flexible) flow shop and job shop scheduling, project scheduling, and batch scheduling, in both deterministic and stochastic settings. Foundational overviews and models are provided in the textbooks by Pinedo [34] and Blazewicz et al. [5], as well as in the more recent review on production scheduling in the context of Industry 4.0 [32].

Similar considerations apply to scheduling in distributed and parallel computing environments such as cloud platforms, high-performance computing clusters, or grid systems [39]. Here, fairness toward the *users* who submit jobs for execution is desirable. While the technical setting resembles production scheduling, key differences arise in the dynamic and multi-tenant nature of these systems. Moreover, jobs are often short-lived and numerous, and the focus is on fair sharing of infrastructure rather than detailed scheduling of each task.

Machines or Resources. In production scheduling, fairness can also be directed toward the resources—both human and non-human—that execute the scheduled jobs. These include machines, tools, workstations, or employees treated as renewable resources. While resources are typically modeled as constraints, they can also be viewed as agents affected by the distribution of workload, utilization levels, and idle times. Fairness in this context concerns the balanced allocation of work across resources, which is crucial for preventing overuse, underutilization, or bottlenecks. This perspective is closely related to classical objectives such as load balancing [37] and to fairness-driven resource allocation in parallel computing and production systems [27].

In some applications, fairness may need to be ensured simultaneously with respect to multiple types of agents—for example, employees and customers, or customers and resources.

2.2 How to Measure Satisfaction? Defining and Aggregating Individual Utilities

This section addresses two central design choices of the framework: first, how to define the utility u_i^j of an agent a_i for an individual decision D_j, and second, how to aggregate these utilities over a history of decisions.

Utilities for Individual Decisions. Given a decision D_j, i.e., the schedule resulting from solving the j-th instance of the scheduling problem, the utility u_i^j should reflect the satisfaction of agent a_i with the part of the schedule relevant to them, i.e., the assignment of that employee, the start and end times of their job(s), or the allocation of resources they are associated with.

Utilities may be derived from explicitly stated agent preferences or from performance metrics relevant to the specific scheduling context. The criteria that determine individual satisfaction—whether based on preferences or objective measures—need to be clearly defined prior to making scheduling decisions. Ideally, this should be done in direct consultation with the agents involved.[1] Depending on the use case, examples include:

- **Preferences of employees:** Individual preferences are often expressed as temporal preferences such as "prefer not to work on Fridays", "prefer night over early shifts", "want weekends off". Other types of preferences may concern interpersonal relationships (e.g., "prefer not to work with employee X"), work locations or task roles.
  Utilities can be calculated using a weighted sum of preference violations and satisfactions, where satisfied preferences contribute positively and violations negatively to the overall score.
- **Job- or customer-centered metrics:** completion time, maximal completion time of a customer's set of jobs, flow time, (maximal) tardiness or lateness, or the number of scheduled jobs per customer, see the textbook by Pinedo [34] for details.
- **Resource-centered metrics:** deviation from an ideal workload, idle time, frequency of usage. For instance, the utility of a machine or human resource may be negatively impacted by overload or excessive idle time.
- **User-centered metrics in computing environments:** waiting time in queues, turnaround time, or share of allocated resources.

In the case of employee preferences, it is evident that these reflect individual, agent-specific priorities that can vary significantly across the set of agents. To some extent, the same holds for other types of agents—such as jobs, customers, users, or resources. For example, in a production scheduling context, a job with a strict delivery deadline might be best evaluated using tardiness, which penalizes late completion. In contrast, for a job where earlier completion is always preferable—regardless of a due date—completion time or lateness may be more

---

[1] In some practical settings, simply enabling agents to express individual preferences may already represent a significant improvement over the status quo.

appropriate metrics. This illustrates that the choice of utility metric depends not only on the broader scheduling context, but also on the specific needs or preferences of each agent. As a result, it may be both necessary and reasonable to define utilities using different metrics for different agents within the same scheduling instance.

Note that, unlike the simplified setup in Sect. 1 (where the same instance is repeatedly solved across multiple decisions, see Fig. 1), the problem instances and agent preferences can also vary over time. Agents are thus allowed to revise their preferences over time.

Interpersonal comparison of utilities poses a challenge, especially when utility ranges differ across agents. For example, some agents may have inherently harder-to-satisfy preferences due to structural constraints. One way to address this is to define each agent's utility relative to their individual optimum—that is, the best utility they could achieve if the instance were solved for them alone.

Accumulated Utilities of an Agent over a History of Decisions. The aggregated utility U_i^j captures an agent's overall experience across multiple scheduling decisions $D_1, \ldots, D_j$. Several aggregation schemes are possible:

- **Cumulative sum:** $U_i^j = \sum_{t=1}^{j} u_i^t$ gives equal weight to all past decisions.
- **Moving window:** Aggregate only the most recent l decisions: $U_i^j = \sum_{t=\max(1,j-l+1)}^{j} u_i^t$.
- **Discounted sum:** Past utilities decay geometrically over time: $U_i^j = \sum_{t=1}^{j} \gamma^{j-t} u_i^t$ for some $0 < \gamma < 1$. This reflects the idea that more recent experiences matter more.

If the set of agents changes over time (e.g., due to new employees or departing users), it may be appropriate to weight an agent's aggregated utility by the number of decisions the agent participated in.

2.3 Fairness Objectives: Aggregating Individual Utilities to Achieve Fairness

In this section, we present fundamental fairness objectives from the social choice literature that are based on aggregating individual utilities.[2] For comprehensive references, we refer to Moulin's *Axioms of Cooperative Decision Making* [29] and the part on Fair Allocation in the *Handbook of Computational Social Choice* [6].

In our context, fairness is assessed based on the utilities that agents accumulate across a sequence of scheduling decisions. Aggregation thus occurs on two levels: first, for each individual agent across time; and second, across agents to assess the overall fairness of the process. The different fairness objectives introduced below reflect distinct philosophical views and normative principles. The choice of which objective to pursue should be guided by the specific application domain and the fairness notion most appropriate to it.

---

[2] Other fairness concepts not grounded in utility aggregation—such as envy-freeness or axiomatic fairness notions—are also common in the social choice literature; we briefly discuss some of them as future research directions in Sect. 4.

Max-Min Fairness. The sole goal of *Max-Min Fairness* is to maximize the minimum utility, i.e., to ensure that the worst-off agent is as well-off as possible:

$$\text{maximize} \ \min_{i=1\ldots n} u_i$$

This definition of fairness captures a strongly egalitarian view, as formulated by John Rawls [35]. In the case of allocation of divisible resources, Max-Min Fairness leads to every agent receiving the same share. Max-Min Fairness is well-suited for scenarios in which minimum guarantees should be given to all agents. However, since it prioritizes lifting up the worst-off agent, overall inefficiency is a possible drawback. Moreover, Max-Min Fairness does not take into consideration the distribution of utilities beyond the minimal utility. It is often extended to *LexiMin* (lexicographic minimax) [38], which first aims at maximizing the minimal utility; then, among all options that maximize the minimal utility, it chooses the one that maximizes the second-smallest utility, etc.

Nash Social Welfare. The *Nash social welfare* objective [8,10], defined as maximizing the product of individual utilities,

$$\text{maximize} \ NSW = \prod_{i=1}^{n} u_i$$

strikes a balance between efficiency and fairness by favoring allocations that improve the well-being of worse-off agents while still rewarding overall utility gains. Nash social welfare thus achieves a compromise between egalitarian goals (as given by Max-Min Fairness) and utilitarian ones, where the sum of utilities is maximized but the distribution of utilities among agents is irrelevant.

Taking the logarithm transforms this into the sum of log utilities, linking it closely to proportional fairness [21]. Maximizing NSW ensures Pareto efficiency, meaning no individual can be made better off without making someone else worse off. However, NSW is only defined for non-negative utilities and is highly sensitive to zero utilities—any agent receiving zero utility nullifies the entire product—thus ruling out such allocations. Extensions such as *Constrained Nash Welfare* introduce utility floors to mitigate this sensitivity.

Alpha-Fairness. α-fairness (alpha-fairness) is a parametrized family of fairness objectives that smoothly interpolates between different fairness ideals using the single real-valued parameter $\alpha \geq 0$. The concept of α-fairness originates from network bandwidth allocation [28] and economics but is now widely used in AI fairness, scheduling, and social choice theory.

Given the aggregated utilities U_i^j for all agents $a_i \in \mathcal{A}$–aggregated for a history of decisions D_1 up to D_j, the alpha-fair utility function is defined as:

$$U_\alpha(U_i^j) = \begin{cases} \frac{(U_i^j)^{1-\alpha}}{1-\alpha} & \text{if } \alpha \neq 1 \\ \log(U_i^j) & \text{if } \alpha = 1 \end{cases}$$

Then, the goal of alpha-fairness is to maximize the total alpha-fair utility:

$$\text{maximize} \sum_{i=1}^{n} U_\alpha(U_i^j)$$

The following are special cases of alpha-fairness:

- $\alpha = 0$: Utilitarian philosophy, i.e., maximize total utility.
- $\alpha = 1$: Proportional fairness (see previous paragraph on Nash Social Welfare)
- $\alpha \to \infty$: Max-min fairness/egalitarian fairness (see paragraph on Max-Min fairness)

The value of α can thus be interpreted as follows: the smaller α is, the higher the priority is on total efficiency; the larger α is, the higher the priority is on establishing egalitarian fairness.

OWA Functions. Ordered Weighted Averaging functions, or OWA functions for short, were introduced by Ronald Yager in 1988 [40], who proposed them as a tool in decision making. OWA-functions are wiedely used in the context of social welfare functions, e.g., for multiple referenda and multiwinner elections [2]. These functions enable a flexible emphasis on different parts of ordered utilities, making it possible to explicitly emphasize or de-emphasize extreme values.

Given a sequence of utilities $(U^j) = U_1^j, U_2^j, \ldots, U_n^j$, the individual utilities are first rearranged in non-increasing order, such that

$$U_{(1)}^j \geq U_{(2)}^j \geq \cdots \geq U_{(n)}^j)$$

An OWA function aggregates these sorted utilities using weights $w_1, w_2, ..., w_n$ where $w_i \geq 0$ and $\sum_{i=1}^{n} w_i = 1$:

$$OWA(U^j) = \sum_{i=1}^{n} w_i \cdot U_{(i)}^j$$

and the fairness objective is to maximize the OWA function. Some simple examples of OWA functions are the following:

- If all weight is on the highest value, i.e., $w_1 = 1, w_i = 0$ for $i > 1$, the OWA function behaves like a max operator.
- If all weight is on the lowest value, i.e., $w_n = 1, w_i = 0$ for $i < n$, it behaves like a min operator.
- If weights are uniform, it becomes the average (mean).
- If weights are distributed evenly among the first $m < n$ entries, i.e., $w_1 = w_2 = \ldots = w_m = 1/m$ and $w_i = 0$ for $i > m$, the goal is to maximize the averaged utility of the m worst-off agents.

2.4   Integrating Fairness into the Optimization Process

Let us assume that an appropriate fairness objective for fairness over time has been selected (see Sect. 2.3). The next challenge is to incorporate this objective into the optimization process used to solve the underlying scheduling problem.[3] In most practical settings, fairness is not the sole goal, but must be balanced against classical performance objectives—such as minimizing total completion time, maximizing throughput, or respecting resource utilization targets—as well as objectives specific to the application domain, for instance, ensuring coverage requirements, minimizing understaffing, or adhering to legal or contractual constraints in employee scheduling. It is therefore usually unrealistic to assume that fairness can replace existing objectives entirely.

A first possible strategy is to include the fairness objective as an additional term in the objective function, using a weighted sum to balance fairness and the other objectives. In this case, care must be taken to normalize the individual components to ensure that the trade-off is meaningful and interpretable. Alternatively, lexicographic optimization [12, 25] can be employed: fairness is prioritized as the primary objective, and traditional scheduling goals are optimized only among fairness-optimal solutions.

Another strategy is to enforce fairness via explicit constraints. For instance, one can require a minimum aggregated utility for each agent (thus enforcing a certain degree of Max-Min Fairness over time), limit the disparity in utilities across agents, or bound the maximum deviation from an ideal fairness profile. In situations where such constraints may render the problem infeasible, penalty terms can be introduced to softly enforce fairness, allowing constraint violations at a cost.

In some cases, it may be beneficial to combine multiple fairness formulations. For example, one might minimize the maximum deviation from fairness constraints within each decision, while simultaneously optimizing a cumulative fairness measure such as time-discounted α-fairness across all past decisions. This layered approach can be handled, for instance, via lexicographic multi-objective optimization, where fairness over time is prioritized over fairness within a single instance, or vice versa.

3   Related Literature

We briefly review related literature that considers fairness issues for scheduling problems and related work dealing with fairness over time that provides helpful directions for the research proposed in Sect. 2.

Fairness in (Repeated) Scheduling Decisions. A recent and highly relevant contribution is the work by Hermelin et al. [19], who study fairness in repetitive scheduling problems. This work is among the first to explicitly address fairness

---

[3] We focus on optimization-based scheduling problems here, but the framework can be extended to satisfaction problems in a straightforward way.

as an evolving objective in a repetitive scheduling context. In their model, a set of clients submits one job per instance over a sequence of scheduling periods, and fairness is defined over the entire decision history. The objective is to minimize the maximum cumulative dissatisfaction across clients, measured according to individual dissatisfaction functions applied to each scheduled job. The authors provide complexity results for single-machine settings, analyze the price of fairness, and explore both classical and parameterized algorithmic techniques. A key assumption in their framework is that the full sequence of scheduling instances is known in advance, allowing the optimizer to plan globally over time. While this assumption simplifies the analysis and design of scheduling policies, it is often unrealistic in practical applications, where scheduling decisions must be made sequentially and under uncertainty. Moreover, their model is tailored to job scheduling settings with one job per client per instance and does not extend directly to more complex scenarios such as employee scheduling. Finally, while their fairness objective focuses on minimizing maximum dissatisfaction (which is equivalent to maximizing the minimum utility in our setting), we propose a broader framework that supports a variety of fairness objectives.

A related early contribution is the work by Ajtai et al. [1], which addresses fairness in repetitive scheduling in a car-sharing context. Each client is both a requester and a resource provider, and the goal is to construct a schedule over a finite time horizon such that all clients receive an equal share of resource usage.

Apart from these two works, we are not aware of any other studies that consider fairness in scheduling decisions as a property over time. Fairness within individual scheduling decisions has been studied more extensively. A notable example is the literature on nurse rostering and healthcare staff scheduling [7,15,31] (see also Sect. 2.1). Another related perspective is offered by Wierman and Zwart [39], who study fairness in single-server queues and discuss various scheduling disciplines with respect to their fairness-efficiency tradeoffs. For further examples from different scheduling domains, we refer the interested reader to the references cited in Hermelin et al. [19].

Rotating Workforce Problem. Another strand of research, particularly in healthcare and workforce management, deals with fairness through rotation schemes [30]. The rotating workforce problem reflects a more rigid and predefined notion of fairness. Here, fairness is achieved by enforcing cyclic schedules that rotate employees through different shift types in a fixed pattern, often independently of their individual preferences. Although this approach can be practical as individual shifts are known a long time in advance and a formal kind of long-term equity is ensured, it allows little flexibility in adapting to specific preferences or dynamic scheduling requirements. Moreover, note that assigning the same shifts to all agents (over time) does not necessarily guarantee that utilities are distributed evenly across agents.

Fairness over Time in Computational Social Choice. Computational social choice offers rich formalizations of fairness [6,26,29] that can inform repeated scheduling decisions. Most work on repeated decisions and fairness as a property over time focuses on voting-based formalisms [9,13,14,23,24]; some work has also been done on repeated fair allocations [20]. Closest to our setting is the work by Freeman et al. [17] which studies a dynamical setting in which an alternative is chosen each round according to reported utility functions. The goal is to maximize long-term Nash social welfare. Different rules are proposed for this setting and their properties are analyzed.

While most studies in social choice address resource allocation and voting rather than scheduling, there is growing crossover—for instance, the work by Pascual et al. concerning collective schedules [33] that integrate agents' ranked preferences over ordered tasks with durations.

4   Conclusion and Outlook on Fairness Over Time in Scheduling

In this paper, we argue that fairness in scheduling should be understood as a property that unfolds over time. Rather than treating scheduling decisions in isolation, we advocate for a perspective that considers the cumulative effects of a sequence of decisions on the agents involved—be they employees, users, clients, or resources. To support this perspective, we have introduced a flexible framework that captures fairness across time and can be instantiated in various scheduling domains. We hope that this conceptualization will inspire further research in scheduling that integrates fairness over time as a central component.

Several research directions emerge in the context of fair scheduling over time:

First, it is important to understand the practical implications of adding fairness considerations to established solution approaches. How do such fairness constraints or objectives affect solution quality, computational efficiency, or feasibility? Moreover, it remains an open question how costly fairness is in terms of classical scheduling objectives—a trade-off often referred to as the price of fairness [4].

A second key research question concerns the information setting. How does the integration of fairness objectives differ between offline settings—where all scheduling instances are known in advance (as studied by Hermelin et al. [19])—and online settings like ours, where decisions are made sequentially with access only to past data? To assess the fairness achieved by different approaches for a specific scheduling problem—whether in an offline or online setting, and under varying fairness objectives—it would be valuable to use diagnostic tools such as the Gini coefficient, utility spread measures, or other inequality indices. These tools could also be integrated into optimization processes as part of feedback or evaluation loops. Moreover, to assess how fairness evolves over time in a practical setting, tools for visualizing satisfaction levels and fairness metrics could be integrated into scheduling systems.

Beyond objective functions and constraints, it may be worthwhile to investigate whether stronger fairness guarantees can be achieved through mechanism design. This includes, for instance, ensuring fairness properties such as bounded "dry spells" [23] (i.e., long sequences of unfavorable outcomes for an agent) or proportional access to high-quality assignments. In this context, techniques from social choice theory could be used to guide the prioritization of agents—drawing on methods such as those by Frege [18] or Thiele [16] to balance long-term satisfaction, or applying voting-inspired rules to decide which agents should receive preferential treatment at each step.

In a similar spirit, future work could explore extensions of classical fairness concepts such as envy-freeness to the scheduling domain. Although envy-freeness might be difficult to guarantee in constrained scheduling settings, it may be possible to define relaxed versions of envy that hold over time or within rolling windows. Work in this direction could take inspiration from Igarashi et al. [20], who study envy-free mechanisms for repeated fair allocation of indivisible items.

Fairness over time toward groups is another underexplored area. How can we ensure equitable treatment of demographic groups (e.g., by gender or skill level), customer types (e.g., small vs. large clients), or user categories in shared computing platforms? This may require group-level utility tracking and the introduction of new fairness metrics relating to proportionality, inspired by characterizations from social choice theory [13, 24].

Finally, learning-based approaches could be employed to infer agent preferences from past outcomes. If data on satisfaction or acceptance of past schedules is available, machine learning methods could help refine utility models and personalize fairness-aware scheduling even further. Machine learning methods could also be employed to help elicit preferences or individual scheduling constraints.

Taken together, these directions offer a rich landscape for future exploration. Our hope is that by placing fairness over time at the heart of scheduling research, we can develop methods that not only optimize system performance, but also support long-term trust, satisfaction, and sustainability in the systems and organizations we design.

Disclosure of Interests. The author has no competing interests to declare that are relevant to the content of this article.

References

1. Ajtai, M., Aspnes, J., Naor, M., Rabani, Y., Schulman, L.J., Waarts, O.: Fairness in scheduling. J. Algorithms **29**(2), 306–357 (1998). https://doi.org/10.1006/JAGM.1998.0953
2. Amanatidis, G., Barrot, N., Lang, J., Markakis, E., Ries, B.: Multiple referenda and multiwinner elections using hamming distances: Complexity and manipulability. In: Proceedings of the 2015 International Conference on Autonomous Agents and Multiagent Systems, AAMAS 2015, Istanbul, Turkey, 4–8 May 2015, pp. 715–723. ACM (2015)
3. Van den Bergh, J., Beliën, J., De Bruecker, P., Demeulemeester, E., De Boeck, L.: Personnel scheduling: a literature review. Eur. J. Oper. Res. **226**(3), 367–385 (2013)
4. Bertsimas, D., Farias, V.F., Trichakis, N.: The price of fairness. Oper. Res. **59**(1), 17–31 (2011). https://doi.org/10.1287/OPRE.1100.0865

5. Błażewicz, J., Ecker, K.H., Pesch, E., Schmidt, Günter Sterna, M., Weglarz, J.: Handbook on Scheduling: From Theory to Practice. Springer, Cham (2019)
6. Brandt, F., Conitzer, V., Endriss, U., Lang, J., Procaccia, A.D. (eds.): Handbook of Computational Social Choice. Cambridge University Press (2016)
7. Burke, E.K., De Causmaecker, P., Berghe, G.V., Van Landeghem, H.: The state of the art of nurse rostering. J. Sched. **7**, 441–499 (2004)
8. Caragiannis, I., Kurokawa, D., Moulin, H., Procaccia, A.D., Shah, N., Wang, J.: The unreasonable fairness of maximum Nash welfare. In: Proceedings of the 2016 ACM Conference on Economics and Computation (EC), pp. 305–322. ACM (2016)
9. Chandak, N., Goel, S., Peters, D.: Proportional aggregation of preferences for sequential decision making. In: Proceedings of the AAAI Conference on Artificial Intelligence, vol. 38, no. 9, pp. 9573–9581 (2024). https://doi.org/10.1609/aaai.v38i9.28813
10. Cole, R., Gkatzelis, V.: Approximating the Nash social welfare with indivisible items. In: Proceedings of the 47th Annual ACM Symposium on Theory of Computing (STOC), pp. 371–380. ACM (2015). https://doi.org/10.1145/2746539.2746584
11. De Bruecker, P., Van den Bergh, J., Beliën, J., Demeulemeester, E.: Workforce planning incorporating skills: state of the art. Eur. J. Oper. Res. **243**(1), 1–16 (2015). https://doi.org/10.1016/j.ejor.2014.10.038
12. Ehrgott, M., Gandibleux, X.: A survey and annotated bibliography of multiobjective combinatorial optimization. OR Spectr. **22**(4), 425–460 (2000). https://doi.org/10.1007/S002910000046
13. Elkind, E., Neoh, T.Y., Teh, N.: Temporal elections: welfare, strategyproofness, and proportionality. In: ECAI 2024 - 27th European Conference on Artificial Intelligence, Santiago de Compostela, Spain, 19–24 October 2024, vol. 392, pp. 3292–3299. IOS Press (2024). https://doi.org/10.3233/FAIA240877
14. Elkind, E., Obraztsova, S., Teh, N.: Temporal fairness in multiwinner voting. In: Proceedings of the AAAI Conference on Artificial Intelligence, vol. 38, no. 20, pp. 22633–22640 (2024). https://doi.org/10.1609/aaai.v38i20.30273
15. Ernst, A., Jiang, H., Krishnamoorthy, M., Sier, D.: Staff scheduling and rostering: a review of applications, methods and models. Eur. J. Oper. Res. **153**(1), 3–27 (2004). https://doi.org/10.1016/S0377-2217(03)00095-X
16. Faliszewski, P., Skowron, P., Slinko, A., Talmon, N.: Multiwinner voting: a new challenge for social choice theory. In: Endriss, U. (ed.) Trends in Computational Social Choice, chap. 2, pp. 27–47. AI Access (2017)
17. Freeman, R., Zahedi, S.M., Conitzer, V.: Fair and efficient social choice in dynamic settings. In: Proceedings of the 26th International Joint Conference on Artificial Intelligence (IJCAI-2017), pp. 4580–4587. ijcai.org (2017)
18. Harrenstein, P., Lackner, M.L., Lackner, M.: A mathematical analysis of an election system proposed by Gottlob Frege. Erkenntnis **87**(6), 2609–2644 (2022)
19. Hermelin, D., Molter, H., Niedermeier, R., Pinedo, M.L., Shabtay, D.: Fairness in repetitive scheduling. Eur. J. Oper. Res. **323**(3), 724–738 (2025). https://doi.org/10.1016/J.EJOR.2024.12.052
20. Igarashi, A., Lackner, M., Nardi, O., Novaro, A.: Repeated fair allocation of indivisible items. In: Proceedings of the 38th AAAI Conference on Artificial Intelligence (AAAI 2024), pp. 9781–9789. AAAI Press (2024)
21. Kelly, F.P.: Charging and rate control for elastic traffic. Eur. Trans. Telecommun. **8**(1), 33–37 (1997). https://doi.org/10.1002/ett.4460080106
22. Kletzander, L., Musliu, N.: Solving the general employee scheduling problem. Comput. Oper. Res. **113** (2020). https://doi.org/10.1016/J.COR.2019.104794

23. Lackner, M.: Perpetual voting: fairness in long-term decision making. In: Proceedings of the 34th AAAI Conference on Artificial Intelligence (AAAI 2020), pp. 2103–2110. AAAI Press (2020)
24. Lackner, M., Maly, J.: Proportional decisions in perpetual voting. In: Proceedings of the 37th AAAI Conference on Artificial Intelligence (AAAI 2023), pp. 5722–5729. AAAI Press (2023)
25. Lai, L., Fiaschi, L., Cococcioni, M., Deb, K.: Pure and mixed lexicographic-paretian many-objective optimization: state of the art. Nat. Comput. $22(2)$, 227–242 (2023). https://doi.org/10.1007/S11047-022-09911-4
26. Lan, T., Kao, D.T.H., Chiang, M., Sabharwal, A.: An axiomatic theory of fairness in network resource allocation. In: INFOCOM 2010. 29th IEEE International Conference on Computer Communications, San Diego, CA, USA, 15–19 March 2010, pp. 1343–1351. IEEE (2010). https://doi.org/10.1109/INFCOM.2010.5461911
27. Li, B., Jamin, S., Shin, K.G.: Fair resource allocation in computing systems. J. Comput. Inf. Technol. $13(3)$, 203–216 (2005)
28. Mo, J., Walrand, J.: Fair end-to-end window-based congestion control. In: Lai, W.S., Cooper, R.B. (eds.) Performance and Control of Network Systems II, vol. 3530, pp. 55 – 63. International Society for Optics and Photonics, SPIE (1998). https://doi.org/10.1117/12.325891
29. Moulin, H.: Axioms of Cooperative Decision Making. Econometric Society Monographs. Cambridge University Press (1988)
30. Musliu, N., Gärtner, J., Slany, W.: Efficient generation of rotating workforce schedules. Discrete Appl. Math. $118(1)$, 85–98 (2002). https://doi.org/10.1016/S0166-218X(01)00258-X. Special Issue devoted to the ALIO-EURO Workshop on Applied Combinatorial Optimization
31. Ngoo, C.M., Goh, S.L., Sabar, N.R., Abdullah, S., Kendall, G., et al.: A survey of the nurse rostering solution methodologies: the state-of-the-art and emerging trends. IEEE Access 10, 56504–56524 (2022)
32. Parente, M., Figueira, G., Amorim, P., Marques, A.: Production scheduling in the context of industry 4.0: review and trends. Int. J. Prod. Res. $58(17)$, 5401–5431 (2020). https://doi.org/10.1080/00207543.2020.1718794
33. Pascual, F., Rzadca, K., Skowron, P.: Collective schedules: scheduling meets computational social choice. In: Proceedings of the 17th International Conference on Autonomous Agents and MultiAgent Systems, AAMAS 2018, Stockholm, Sweden, 10–15 July 2018, pp. 667–675 (2018)
34. Pinedo, M.L.: Scheduling: Theory, Algorithms, and Systems, 6 edn. Springer, Cham (2022). Accessed 14 Dec 2022, 698 pages
35. Rawls, J.: A Theory of Justice. Harvard University Press, Cambridge (1971)
36. Rossi, F., van Beek, P., Walsh, T. (eds.): Handbook of Constraint Programming, Foundations of Artificial Intelligence, vol. 2. Elsevier (2006)
37. Schwiegelshohn, U.: Approximation algorithms for machine scheduling: 20 years of recent progress. ACM Comput. Surv. (CSUR) $55(2)$, 1–38 (2022)
38. Sen, A.: Collective Choice and Social Welfare. Holden-Day, San Francisco (1970)
39. Wierman, A.: Fairness and scheduling in single server queues. Surv. Oper. Res. Manag. Sci. $16(1)$, 39–48 (2011). https://doi.org/10.1016/j.sorms.2010.07.002
40. Yager, R.R.: On ordered weighted averaging aggregation operators in multicriteria decisionmaking. Man Cybern. IEEE Trans. Syst. (1988)

A Bayesian View of the Result Model

Yoann Morello[(✉)] and Agata Ciabattoni[(✉)]

Vienna University of Technology (TU Wien), Vienna, Austria
yoann.morello@gmail.com, agata@logic.at

Abstract. Real-world datasets often contain inconsistencies that challenge traditional case-based reasoning models. Building upon the result model, a well-established formal representation of case base reasoning in law, we propose a Bayesian reinterpretation that effectively addresses such inconsistencies. Our Bayesian enhancement quantifies the reliability of precedents and encapsulates principled, explainable predictions even in the presence of conflict, representing a meaningful step forward in using these models to design AI agents.

Keywords: Case-based reasoning · Bayesian inference · Legal AI · Inconsistency · Explainability · Normative AI Agents

1 Introduction

A central challenge in machine ethics, the area of Artificial Intelligence (AI) focused on building systems capable of normative reasoning, lies in acquiring and representing normative information in a form that is both implementable and transparent. Symbolic methods, such as rule-based systems, provide transparency, but lack flexibility. Conversely, approaches based on black-box machine learning lack reliability and explainability. A hybrid approach inspired by common law reasoning has been introduced in [6] and is based on the *reason model* [11]; the approach aims to bridge this divide: norms are learned from particular cases (bottom-up) but represented symbolically (top-down). Indeed, in common law, norms arise not from statute but from precedents—that is, actions or decisions that serve as justification or support for future actions or decisions. As decisions accumulate, a body of normative expectations emerges, and constrain future decisions. The *reason model* formalizes this idea by requiring new decisions to be consistent with precedents and by integrating additional information provided by the judge in the form of explicit reasons justifying each decision. However, in many contexts, such as the DIAS (Drug-Interdiction Auto-Stop) dataset [9], such reasons are often unavailable. In these cases, the *result model*, a minimal symbolic framework introduced in [1] (see also [10]), enables normative inference directly from case outcomes and fact patterns. To connect these frameworks for formalizing common law to machine ethics, consider a hypothetical robot whose decision-making relies on questionnaires administered to users, each capturing a specific situation. The responses to these questionnaires serve as precedents, and the robot's future decisions in new situations should be

L. Hagedorn et al. (Eds.): DIGHUM 2025, LNCS 16319, pp. 51–66, 2026.
https://doi.org/10.1007/978-3-032-11108-1_4

constrained by them. Last but not least, the robot must provide explanations for its decisions.

Yet, when applying such frameworks to systems like our hypothetical robot, a key limitation becomes evident: most approaches rely on the assumption that the set of precedents is consistent. In other words, they assume that the dataset does not impose contradictory decisions for the same or stronger fact situations. However, this assumption is unrealistic.

Inconsistencies can indeed arise for several reasons. First, different users may hold divergent normative intuitions and provide conflicting judgments. Second, borderline cases may genuinely be ambiguous, leading even a single user to choose different sides in similar contexts. Third, the factors used to describe cases may fail to capture critical distinctions, resulting in substantively different situations being treated as equivalent in the dataset. These inconsistencies are not rare exceptions. They are, in fact, common features of real-world legal and ethical corpora, as illustrated by the DIAS dataset [8,9].

Two distinct approaches to accommodating inconsistencies have recently been proposed in [5,14,15]. The first, developed in the context of the reason model, provides a logically sound framework for reasoning under conflicting precedents. However, it does not leverage the statistical information that the case database reveals about the reliability of the constraints we aim to derive from precedent decisions. Our first contribution is to adapt this framework to the result model, yielding two predictive variants that we refer to as the *Strict Binary* and *Binary Majority* models. The second approach [14,15], designed for models based on dimensions and a different notion of precedent, introduces the concept of *authoritativeness* to resolve conflicts. Our main contribution, the *Bayesian model*, extends this idea by learning a distribution over authoritativeness directly from data, thereby capturing both the strength of a precedent and the uncertainty surrounding its application.

Unlike previous approaches, the Bayesian model reinterprets the result model *probabilistically*, allowing it to handle inconsistencies in real case datasets while providing epistemic confidence in each prediction. It thus represents a promising *hybrid* between symbolic legal reasoning and data-driven inference: it retains the transparency and traceability of rule-based methods while making principled use of data to assess the reliability of conclusions.

The three predictive models presented in this paper: the *Strict Binary, Binary Majority,* and *Bayesian* models lay the groundwork for subsequent experimental evaluation.

2   Preliminaries

We provide essential contextual information for understanding the paper.

2.1   The Result Model in a Nutshell

The result model [1] is a highly conservative approach to precedential reasoning: it formalizes which types of inferences from prior cases are admissible—namely, that only weaker precedents can constrain new decisions. The result model is governed by the principle that:

> "To follow precedent, a constrained court must decide its case for the party analogous to the winner in the precedent case if the constrained case is as strong or stronger a case for that result than the precedent case was for its result".

To formalize this idea: according to [16] a factor is a consideration a decision maker must or may take into account to determine an outcome. Let F be the set of factors, partitioned into F^π (favoring the plaintiff) and F^δ (favoring the defendant), so that $F = F^\pi \cup F^\delta$.

Definition 1. *A case is a tuple $\langle X, s \rangle$, where $X \subseteq F$ is the set of present factors[1] and $s \in \{\pi, \delta\}$ is the side that won. We define $X^s = X \cap F^s$ as the factors in X that favor side s. We write $\bar{s}$ to denote the side opposite to s, so that $\bar{\pi} = \delta$ and $\bar{\delta} = \pi$.*

Definition 2 (Strength Ordering). *Given two fact situations X and Y, we say that X is* stronger for side s *than Y, written $X \succcurlyeq_s Y$, if*

$$X^s \supseteq Y^s \quad and \quad X^{\bar{s}} \subseteq Y^{\bar{s}}.$$

Example 1. Let $\{f_1^\pi, f_2^\pi\}$ the set F^π favoring the plaintiff and $F^\delta = \{f_1^\delta\}$, the set favoring the defendant. Consider two cases with the following sets of factors:

- $X = \{f_1^\pi, f_1^\delta\}$
- $Y = \{f_1^\pi, f_2^\pi\}$

The relevant sets are:

$$X^\delta = \{f_1^\delta\}, \quad Y^\delta = \emptyset \quad \Rightarrow \quad X^\delta \supseteq Y^\delta$$

$$X^\pi = \{f_1^\pi\}, \quad Y^\pi = \{f_1^\pi, f_2^\pi\} \quad \Rightarrow \quad X^\pi \subseteq Y^\pi$$

Therefore, $X \succcurlyeq_\delta Y$, that is case X is stronger for the defendant than Y, because it contains more factors supporting the defendant and fewer factors supporting the plaintiff.

Definition 3 (Case base). *A case base is a finite set of cases.*

Definition 4 (Consistency). *A case base is consistent if there do not exist $c = \langle X, \delta \rangle$ and $c' = \langle Y, \pi \rangle$ such that $X \succcurlyeq_\pi Y$.*

This condition can be equivalently stated in terms of the *a fortiori* constraint, which governs the admissibility of new decisions based on prior ones.

---

[1] Following Horty's factor-based account of precedent [11], we treat a *factor* as a legally salient pattern of facts that invariably favors one litigant. For illustration, the DIAS dataset contains pro-government factors such as LEGAL INDICATIONS OF DRUG USE and VEHICLE CONTENTS SUGGEST DRUGS.

Definition 5 (A Fortiori Constraint). *Let $c = \langle X, s \rangle$ be a new case and let $c' = \langle Y, s \rangle$ be a past case in the case base. The a fortiori constraint requires that if $X \succcurlyeq_s Y$, then the decision in c must also be in favor of s.*

That is, no weaker case should be decided for a side if a stronger one was not.

Under this principle, consistency means that the case base contains no pair of cases violating the a fortiori constraint.

Example 2 (Violation of the a fortiori constraint). Consider the two cases:

$$c_1 = \langle X_1, \pi \rangle \quad \text{and} \quad c_2 = \langle X_2, \delta \rangle,$$

where the factor sets are:

$$X_1 = \{f_1^\pi, f_1^\delta\} \quad \text{and} \quad X_2 = \{f_1^\pi, f_2^\pi\}.$$

We observe that:

$$X_1^\pi = \{f_1^\pi\} \subseteq X_2^\pi = \{f_1^\pi, f_2^\pi\}, \quad X_1^\delta = \{f_1^\delta\} \supseteq X_2^\delta = \emptyset.$$

Hence, by definition, $X_2 \succcurlyeq_\pi X_1$, meaning c_2 is stronger than c_1 for the plaintiff. However, c_1 is decided for the plaintiff, while c_2 is decided for the defendant. This contradicts the *a fortiori* principle: if a weaker case is decided for the plaintiff, a stronger one should be as well.

We can identify several potential sources of such inconsistencies in the data, including:

1. **Suboptimal factor design.** In some cases, the factors used to describe legal situations may conflate distinct evidentiary strengths. For instance, in the DIAS dataset [8,9], one can find cases[2] judged for the plaintiff with only the factor $f_1^\pi =$ *"Vehicle contents suggest drugs"*, while other cases containing this same factor along with several additional plaintiff-favoring factors are judged for the defendant. Upon examining the textual descriptions, it becomes evident that in the cases judged for the plaintiff, f_1^π refers to strong indicators (e.g., a strong smell of marijuana, or visible white powder on the driver), whereas in cases judged for the defendant, it refers to weaker signs (e.g., faint odor, presence of syringes). Splitting this factor into two levels of evidentiary strength, or modeling it using a dimensional approach, would likely eliminate the observed inconsistency.
2. **Value pluralism across judges.** Different judges may apply the same legal principles in different ways due to divergent normative priorities.
3. **Indeterminacy in borderline cases.** When a case is near the boundary of legal ambiguity, even the same judge may decide in different directions on different occasions, essentially choosing between two well-balanced alternatives.

---

[2] Most of these inconsistencies might be attributable to divergent practices across different jurisdictions in categorizing cases.

Remark 1. Introduced by Horty [11], the *reason model* refines the result model by associating each decision with an explicit *reason*, that is, a subset of factors identified by the judge as justifying the outcome. The same principle of a fortiori reasoning can be recovered if we replace each real case by a counterfactual one, where the full set of winning-side factors is replaced by the stated reason. Under this transformation, analogical constraints can be applied as in the result model. The reason model improves on the result model by resolving certain inconsistencies and enabling a broader range of predictions. However, it is only applicable when judges explicitly provide reasons for their decisions.

2.2   Bayesian Framework

We briefly recall the core concepts of Bayesian statistics necessary to evaluate how reliably the *a fortiori* principle is supported by empirical data. Bayesian statistics models uncertainty about unknown quantities—such as the reliability of a legal constraint—by treating them as random variables described by probability distributions. As new data is observed, beliefs about these quantities are updated using *Bayes' theorem*. For a more comprehensive introduction, see [7]. Bayes' theorem relates our prior beliefs about a parameter θ (the *prior distribution*) to our updated beliefs after observing data (the *posterior distribution*):

$$p(\theta, \text{data}) = p(\theta \mid \text{data})\, p(\text{data}) = p(\text{data} \mid \theta)\, p(\theta).$$

Rewriting it in proportional form:

$$p(\theta \mid \text{data}) \propto p(\text{data} \mid \theta)\, p(\theta)$$

where

- $p(\theta)$ is the *prior distribution*, encoding our belief about θ before observing any data;
- $p(\text{data} \mid \theta)$ is the *likelihood*, measuring how likely the observed data is under parameter value θ, and
- $p(\theta \mid \text{data})$ is the *posterior distribution*, our updated belief incorporating the data.

The proportionality symbol ($\propto$) indicates that $p(\text{data})$ acts as a normalization constant independent of θ.

In the context of our work, we consider how often the *a fortiori* constraint holds between pairs of cases. Each such observation is a binary outcome: either the constraint is satisfied or violated. This suggests modeling constraint application as a Bernoulli trial.

Definition 6 (Bernoulli Distribution). *The Bernoulli distribution models binary outcomes and is parameterized by a probability $\theta \in [0, 1]$, which in our setting corresponds to the unknown reliability of the* a fortiori *constraint. For a given observation $x \in \{0, 1\}$, the probability mass function is:*

$$\mathrm{Bern}(x; \theta) = \begin{cases} \theta & \text{if } x = 1, \\ 1 - \theta & \text{if } x = 0. \end{cases}$$

In our context, $x = 1$ indicates that the a fortiori *constraint is satisfied between a pair of cases, while $x = 0$ indicates a violation.*

Definition 7 (Uniform Distribution). *The uniform distribution on the interval $[0, 1]$ is defined by the constant probability density:*

$$\mathrm{Uniform}(\theta) = 1 \quad for\ \theta \in [0, 1].$$

It represents a non-informative prior, *expressing total ignorance: all values of θ are considered equally plausible before observing any data.*

Remark. The uniform distribution over $[0, 1]$ is a special case of the Beta distribution, specifically Beta$(1, 1)$. This provides a smooth transition into using the Beta family as a prior in our Bayesian analysis.

Bayesian inference yields not a single point estimate of θ but a full posterior distribution, reflecting the degree of certainty or uncertainty in our beliefs after observing data.

To perform Bayesian inference for a Bernoulli parameter θ, we choose a prior distribution over $[0, 1]$. An expressive family of priors is the Beta distribution:

Definition 8 (Beta Distribution). *The Beta distribution with parameters $\alpha > 0$ and $\beta > 0$ has density:*

$$\mathrm{Beta}(\theta; \alpha, \beta) = \frac{\theta^{\alpha-1}(1-\theta)^{\beta-1}}{B(\alpha, \beta)},$$

where the Beta function $B(\alpha, \beta)$ is defined as:

$$B(\alpha, \beta) = \int_0^1 t^{\alpha-1}(1-t)^{\beta-1}dt.$$

Conjugacy. The Beta distribution is the *conjugate prior* to the Bernoulli distribution. This means that if we use a Beta prior and observe data from a Bernoulli process, the posterior distribution is also a Beta distribution, but with updated parameters. Conjugate priors are useful as they allow posterior distributions to be computed analytically, avoiding the need for numerical approximation.

More concretely, if $\theta \sim \mathrm{Beta}(\alpha, \beta)$ and we observe n binary outcomes with k successes ($x_i = 1$) and $n - k$ failures ($x_i = 0$), the posterior distribution is:

$$\theta \mid \mathrm{data} \sim \mathrm{Beta}(\alpha + k, \beta + n - k).$$

Interpretation. The parameters α and β of the Beta distribution are often called *pseudo-counts* because they act like prior observations, even though no real data has been seen yet.

- For instance, a prior Beta$(1, 1)$ is uniform over $[0, 1]$, but it behaves as if we had seen one success and one failure before collecting any real data.

- When we later observe r actual successes and s actual failures, the posterior becomes Beta($\alpha+r, \beta+s$). So the prior contributes *as if* it had already added α successes and β failures to the total.
- This allows Bayesian inference to start with a prior belief and then update it smoothly as data is observed.

This property makes the Beta distribution especially suitable for our setting, where we wish to quantify how often the *a fortiori* constraint is upheld versus violated. A precedent that is frequently followed with few violations yields a Beta distribution sharply concentrated near 1. In contrast, if its constraint is often violated or rarely tested, the resulting posterior remains broad, reflecting greater uncertainty. Thus, each precedent can be associated with a specific Beta distribution that captures our empirical confidence in its normative force.

3   Predictive Models

Several works have attempted to model prediction using precedents; a comprehensive survey is given in [3]. Most of these approaches rely on analogical similarity measures between cases rather than enforcing normative reasoning rules such as those encoded in the result model. An application of a fortiori reasoning can be found in [19], though it applies to numerical (or many-valued) rather than binary data. It is worth noting that a fortiori reasoning is just another name for the result model, while its adaptation to continuous or multi-level attributes is typically called *the result model with dimensions.*

By contrast, our focus is on the binary setting, in which attributes/factors are either present or absent. We explicitly target inconsistency, and we describe below three predictive models. The first two models adapt established literature rules (strict abstention or majority tie-breaking), while our Bayesian model adds a principled, reliability-based treatment to make predictions under conflict; the latter employs Bayesian statistics to quantify the degree of confidence the data warrants in each prediction made via the result model.

The section is organized as follows: Sect. 3.1 recalls a strict binary model that only allows prediction in the absence of conflicting precedents; Sect. 3.2 presents the model minimizing inconsistency proposed by [5], which we reformulate as a voting mechanism inspired by social choice theory; Section 3.3 introduces our Bayesian model, which quantifies uncertainty and weights precedents by reliability.

3.1   Strict Binary Result Model

This model predicts an outcome only if all applicable precedents agree. If any conflict is found among applicable constraints, the model abstains. This reflects the definition of constraints under inconsistencies defined by [5] for the reason model. To make this precise, we adapt below Canavotto's definitions (from the reason model) to the setting of the result model.

Definition 9 (Supporting and Conflicting Precedents). *Let $c = \langle X, s \rangle$ be a new case. Define*

$$\text{supporting}_s(c) \ = \ \{\, c' \in \mathcal{C} \mid \text{outcome}(c') = s \,\wedge\, c \succcurlyeq_s c' \,\},$$

$$\text{conflicting}_s(c) \ = \ \{\, c' \in \mathcal{C} \mid \text{outcome}(c') = \overline{s} \,\wedge\, c \succcurlyeq_{\overline{s}} c' \,\}.$$

Proposition 1 (Strict Decision Criterion). *Under the result-model adaptation, the strict binary result model decides c as follows:*

$$\text{If supporting}_s(c) = \emptyset \text{ and supporting}_{\overline{s}}(c) \neq \emptyset, \quad \text{then decide } c \text{ for } \overline{s}.$$

Otherwise, the model abstains.

Proof (Sketch). By definition, $\text{supporting}_{\overline{s}}(c) = \text{conflicting}_s(c)$. Thus

$$\text{supporting}_s(c) = \emptyset \quad \wedge \quad \text{conflicting}_s(c) \neq \emptyset$$

means there is no precedent enforcing s but at least one enforcing $\overline{s}$, forcing the decision $\overline{s}$, with abstention in all other cases. $\qquad\square$

This principle of enforcing a decision only when precedents are one-sided was connected in [4] to standard deontic logic SDL, whose deontic operators of permission and obligation are interpreted, respectively, as existential and universal quantifiers over a set of possible worlds [20]. The name *Strict Binary* reflects the model's rigid enforcement criteria: it permits a binary prediction only in the absence of conflicting precedents, thereby adhering strictly to the normative force of the *a fortiori* constraint. The model abstains as soon as ambiguity arises, which contrasts with more permissive approaches that tolerate conflict by aggregating information from competing precedents.

Example 3. Consider the following three cases with factors drawn from $F^\pi = \{f_1^\pi\}$, and $F^\delta = \{f_1^\delta\}$:

- $c_1 = \langle \{f_1^\pi, f_1^\delta, f_2^\delta\}, \pi \rangle$ (a precedent for the plaintiff),
- $c_2 = \langle \{f_1^\pi, f_2^\pi, f_1^\delta\}, \delta \rangle$ (a precedent for the defendant),
- $c_3 = \langle \{f_1^\pi, f_1^\delta\}, ? \rangle$ (a new case to be decided).

We observe:

$$\{f_1^\pi, f_1^\delta\} \succcurlyeq_\pi \{f_1^\pi, f_1^\delta, f_2^\delta\}, \quad \text{and} \quad \{f_1^\pi, f_1^\delta\} \succcurlyeq_\delta \{f_1^\pi, f_2^\pi, f_1^\delta\}.$$

Thus, c_1 and c_2 both act as applicable precedents for c_3, but they enforce opposite outcomes. Since the strict binary model abstains whenever there are conflicting applicable precedents, it will refrain from making a prediction for c_3.

3.2   The Binary Majority Vote Model

The Binary Strict model makes predictions only when there are precedents supporting a decision and none supporting the opposite. It abstains both when no applicable precedent exists and when precedents for both outcomes are found. As the number of inconsistencies in the case database increases, the number of such conflicts typically grows, leading the model to abstain on more and more test cases.

To address this issue, [5] proposed a refined framework (for the reason model): when faced with conflicting precedents, select the decision that conflicts with the smallest number of precedents in the database.

Inspired by social choice theory [12], we reformulate the minimal number of conflicts principle as a voting rule:

Proposition 2. *Minimizing the number of conflicts is equivalent to assigning each π-precedent of the new case a vote of $+1$, and each δ-precedent a vote of -1. The case is predicted as π if the total sum is strictly positive, as δ if strictly negative, and left unclassified in case of a tie.*

Proof. Choosing a decision s for a new case introduces $\#$(precedents for $\bar{s}$) conflicts, as each such precedent supports the opposite side. Comparing the number of conflicts introduced by choosing s versus $\bar{s}$ amounts to checking the sign of:

$$\#\text{precedents for } \pi - \#\text{precedents for } \delta.$$

$\square$

Example 4 (Majority Vote Resolution). The case c_3 from the example 3 would also not be predicted by the *Binary Majority* model, as there is an equal number of applicable precedents supporting each side: one for π (namely c_1) and one for δ (namely c_2). Now consider adding a new case:

$$c_4 = \langle \{f_1^\pi, f_1^\delta, f_2^\delta\}, \pi \rangle,$$

which is identical to c_1. Then both c_1 and c_4 support the plaintiff and are applicable to c_3, while only c_2 supports the defendant.

In this case, the *Binary Majority* model identifies a majority of applicable precedents supporting π, and therefore predicts c_3 for the plaintiff.

While this model improves coverage, it still assumes all precedents have equal authority in enforcing the *a fortiori* constraint. Yet not all precedents are equally reliable. Some cases may frequently violate their expected influence over stronger or weaker cases, suggesting they should be trusted less.

This observation invites us to revisit the foundational motivation for the constraint itself. The *a fortiori* principle expresses a form of normative reasoning from precedent: if a weaker case is decided for the plaintiff, then a stronger one should be as well—and symmetrically for the defendant. Inconsistencies in the dataset can then be interpreted as uncertainty about the applicability of this principle in particular contexts.

3.3   The Bayesian Result Model

The considerations at the end of the previous section leads to a more refined question: can we use the data to quantify our confidence in the *a fortiori* constraint? A natural starting point is to measure the proportion of case pairs that satisfy the constraint versus those that violate it. Intuitively, the more often the constraint is upheld, the stronger our belief in its normative force. This proportion-based idea was explicitly adopted by [14], who defines a precedent's *authoritativeness* as the fraction of times the expected constraint that one associates to it is respected in the dataset.

While our approach, like [14], aims to quantify the normative strength of precedents, it differs in two essential respects. First, we identify applicable precedents directly through the *a fortiori* constraint defined by the result model—that is, by comparing fact patterns via subset inclusion—whereas [14,15] rely on a distance-based similarity metric over dimensional case representations. Their approach is more closely aligned with the HYPO framework [2], a pioneering and influential model of legal case-based reasoning that uses analogical arguments built from precedents estimated to be similar to the case at hand.

Second, whereas they assign each precedent a scalar *authoritativeness* score (which, under certain assumptions, corresponds to the mean of our Beta posterior), our Bayesian framework yields a full probability distribution. This richer representation encapsulates not only the expected strength of a precedent but also the uncertainty around that estimate, enabling principled reasoning under epistemic uncertainty in downstream decisions.

These considerations motivate the probabilistic framework we introduce below. We begin by observing that the *a fortiori* principle is not a single global rule, but rather a scheme of local constraints—one associated with each case c in the training set. Each c acts as a potential precedent and defines its own individual constraint:

Definition 10 (Individual *a fortiori* Constraint for a Case c). *Let c be a case in the training set.*

- *If $decision(c) = \pi$, then c enforces that any case c' with $c' \succcurlyeq c$ must also be decided for π.*
- *If $decision(c) = \delta$, then c enforces that any case c' with $c \succcurlyeq c'$ must also be decided for δ.*

This formulation provides the basis for our Bayesian treatment of precedent reliability. Rather than treating all precedents equally, we learn a distributional confidence for each case's individual constraint—allowing us to model varying degrees of normative strength among precedents.

Inconsistencies in the dataset imply that the *a fortiori* constraint for a case is only stochastically applied. Since the application of such a constraint is a binary (0/1) observation, it is natural to model this uncertainty using a Bernoulli distribution with an unknown success parameter θ_c. To estimate this parameter, we place a Beta prior over each θ_c, resulting in a posterior distribution:

$$\theta_c \sim \mathrm{Beta}(r_c + 1, s_c + 1),$$

where r_c is the number of successful applications of the constraint in the training data (i.e., pairs where the constraint applies and is satisfied), and s_c is the number of observed violations. We use a uniform prior $\mathrm{Beta}(1,1)$ to model lack of prior knowledge, as discussed in Sect. 2.2. From the definition of the Beta distribution, this yields the posterior in closed form due to conjugacy. While we suggest here the uniform prior $\mathrm{Beta}(1,1)$, we note that alternative prior choices are possible and will return to this discussion in Sect. 3.3.

This use of Bayesian statistics differs significantly from prior work in rule learning. For instance, [13,18] apply Bayesian methods to discover symbolic rules or logical clauses from labeled data. Their goal is to induce rule structure. By contrast, we do not attempt to learn the constraint itself—it is fixed and justified on normative grounds. Instead, we use Bayesian inference to assess how confidently each instance of the constraint (i.e., each precedent) should be applied, based on empirical evidence from the case base.

This framework also aligns with the theoretical ideal of normative consistency: as the empirical evidence supporting a constraint grows, so too does our confidence in its validity. In particular, a high number of supporting instances r_c relative to violations s_c, combined with a large overall sample size, yields a posterior increasingly concentrated near 1. In the limiting case of a perfectly consistent and infinite dataset—where the constraint has never been violated—we recover full certainty: With $\theta_c \sim \mathrm{Beta}(r_c + 1, 1)$, we have $\theta_c \to 1$ in probability as $r_c \to \infty$; thus the limiting law is the degenerate distribution at 1 (i.e., all probability mass is concentrated at a single point), representing an idealized belief that the variable equals 1 with certainty.

At prediction time, each precedent c casts a probabilistic vote for the side it supports via the *a fortiori* relation. This vote is drawn from a Bernoulli distribution with success parameter $\theta_c \sim \mathrm{Beta}(r_c + 1, s_c + 1)$. Precedents with strong empirical support will more reliably contribute to the vote, while noisy or ambiguous ones may abstain.

Because the voting is stochastic, we simulate the prediction process using Monte Carlo sampling [17]. For each simulation run:

1. Sample θ_c from the learned Beta distribution for each precedent.
2. Sample a Bernoulli variable with parameter θ_c to decide whether the precedent casts a vote (1) or abstains (0).
3. Sum all votes to determine a predicted side.

Repeating this procedure many times yields an empirical probability mass function over vote sums. As the vote sum is integer-valued, we work with a probability mass function (pmf) rather than a density. We approximate this pmf by Monte Carlo sampling. We can then quantify prediction confidence by computing the proportion of simulations where the total vote aligns with the predicted decision. Let $f(v)$ denote the empirical probability mass function over total vote sums v. If the predicted decision corresponds to the sign of the sum (positive for π, negative for δ), these are:

$$\mathrm{Conf} = \begin{cases} \sum_{v>0} f(v), & \text{if the predicted side is } \pi, \\ \sum_{v<0} f(v), & \text{if the predicted side is } \delta . \end{cases}$$

This confidence score refines binary predictions with epistemic insight and allows selective decision-making under uncertainty.

What an Explanation Looks Like in the Bayesian Model. Consider a synthetic case where two precedents support the plaintiff (π) and one supports the defendant (δ), yet judgment favors the defendant. We simulate this by assigning Beta posteriors $\mathrm{Beta}(r_c+1, s_c+1)$ to each precedent—treating r_c as confirmations and s_c as violations of its *a fortiori* constraint—and sampling votes via Monte Carlo.

Figure 1 displays two visualizations: the left shows the Beta distributions representing the authority (i.e., reliability of the *a fortiori* constraint) for each precedent; the right shows the results of a Monte Carlo simulation combining these votes. The figure explains a δ prediction *despite* a majority of π precedents; as panel (a) makes clear, the δ precedent is more reliable than the π precedents (peak farther right and narrower), which explains the outcome; (b) shows the *four* possible outcomes when combining the *three* opposing precedents: the left rectangle (-1) means the defendant (δ) wins, the middle rectangle (0) means tie/abstention, and the right rectangles ($+1$, $+2$) means the plaintiff (π) wins. The height of each rectangle is the relative frequency of that outcome across Monte Carlo runs. There are four rectangles because the δ precedent can contribute either 0 or -1, the π precedents can each contribute either 0 or $+1$, so their sum can only be -1, 0, $+1$ or $+2$.

We observe that even when more precedents support one side, their influence is modulated by empirical reliability; by contrast, the Binary Majority model ignores reliability and counts all precedents equally. In this example, the δ-precedent, being more authoritative (with a Beta distribution sharply peaked near 1), overrides both π-precedents, which exhibit low mean and high variance. As a result, the model predicts a decision in favor of the defendant. However, the confidence in this prediction is relatively low, as shown by the relatively small area in the hatched region in Fig. 1b.

Note that the *Binary Majority Vote Model*, which weights all precedents equally, would have favored the plaintiff, based solely on the count of precedents. This contrast shows how the Bayesian model considers not just the number but also the reliability of precedents.

Furthermore, the model's confidence score derived from the proportion of simulations favoring the predicted side can support downstream tasks such as aggregating predictions across models or deferring low-confidence cases, thereby enhancing reliability.

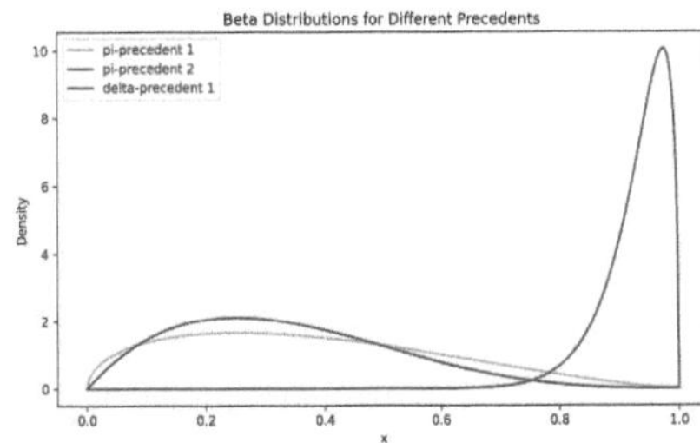

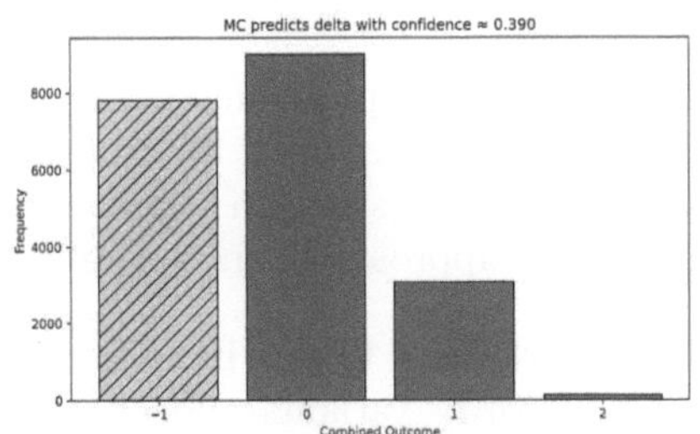

(a) Beta distributions: π-precedents have low expected authority and high variance (mass spread leftward), while the δ-precedent has a high mean and low variance (narrow peak near 1).

(b) Monte Carlo estimate of the vote pmf: The shaded bar marks the predicted side. Its height indicates the model's confidence in the predicted outcome.

Fig. 1. Illustrative output of the Bayesian Result Model for a synthetic case with two π-precedents and one δ-precedent.

Discussion on Prior Choice. We have so far adopted the uniform prior $(\mathrm{Beta}(1,1))$ to model complete ignorance about precedent reliability. As in any Bayesian framework, this choice is somewhat arbitrary. Several alternatives are possible; here we outline two simple options; one is to compute *aggregate* parameters for the *a fortiori* constraint across the case base. Specifically, by considering all pairs of cases (c, c') with $c \succeq_\pi c'$, we may count

$$r_{\mathrm{tot}} = \#\{\text{pairs where both decisions agree}\},$$
$$s_{\mathrm{tot}} = \#\{\text{pairs where the weaker favors } \pi \text{ and the stronger } \delta\}.$$

A prior of the form $\mathrm{Beta}(r_{\mathrm{tot}}, s_{\mathrm{tot}})$ then encodes a global tendency for the constraint to hold, leading to posteriors of the form

$$\theta_c \mid \mathrm{data} \sim \mathrm{Beta}(r_{\mathrm{tot}} + r_c, s_{\mathrm{tot}} + s_c).$$

An alternative is to maintain two separate priors, one for π-precedents and one for δ-precedents, computed in the same way.

Both approaches combine individual evidence about each case with pooled information from the entire case base, which may be advantageous when many cases are precedents for only a few others. However, they also dilute case-specific information. In a large case base where sufficient evidence is typically available for each precedent, the uninformative prior $\mathrm{Beta}(1,1)$ may then be preferable.

Caveat: Many Weak Precedents. A limitation of all our models, only partly mitigated in the Bayesian one, is that many *weak* precedents can outweigh a single *strong* precedent. While the Bayesian model accounts for reliability (downweighting weak precedents), a substantial imbalance in their number can still dominate the outcome.

Future work should address this.

4 Conclusions and Future Work

We introduced a probabilistic extension of the result model that handles inconsistency while preserving the transparency of rule-based approaches. Our framework models the strength of precedents based on their observed reliability in the data. This approach offers several advantages:

1. **Uncertainty Quantification.** While classical models like the strict binary or majority variants appear to provide deterministic outputs, they in fact ignore uncertainty from data inconsistencies. The Bayesian model makes this uncertainty explicit, allowing predictions to be accompanied by meaningful confidence estimates derived from observed precedent behavior.
2. **Extension to Other Normative Modes.** Although we have focused on the *a fortiori* constraint, our approach can accommodate any admissible mode of reasoning over precedents. For example, one could assign learned weights to hypothetical analogies, rhetorical moves such as downplaying opposing factors, or domain-specific argument patterns. Each such normative mode could contribute a probabilistic "vote" toward a decision, encapsulating its strength and reliability as calibrated from data.
3. **Flexibility and Modularity.** The Bayesian framework is flexible and can incorporate application-specific beliefs about how precedents should be trusted. These priors can encode normative stances or policy constraints, enabling the system to adapt its reasoning to different institutional or legal settings.
4. **Extensibility to Richer Models.** Our framework can be naturally extended to the more expressive reason model, as well as to variants involving dimensional fact representations or explicit factor hierarchies. The probabilistic structure can incorporate rule-based justifications and reason-strength comparisons in a unified framework.

In summary, our Bayesian approach represents a promising hybrid between symbolic legal reasoning and data-driven inference. It offers a transparent and traceable decision procedure while making principled use of data to assess the reliability of conclusions. This positions it as a compelling foundation for building interpretable AI systems that reason under normative uncertainty.

We also plan to evaluate our model using the DIAS dataset [9], which contains court opinions addressing whether police officers in the U.S. possess the requisite constitutional suspicion to make a prolonged detention of a motorist suspected of trafficking or possessing drugs. The dataset includes 264 annotated vehicle inspection decisions. For benchmarking, we will implement the Strict Binary Result Model and Binary Majority Vote Model, and compare them against our approach and a finely tuned random forest classifier. Given the class imbalance, macro-averaged F1 will serve as our primary evaluation metric. Finally, we will conduct a qualitative analysis of conflict cases to assess how different models resolve inconsistencies in practice.

Acknowledgments. Work supported by WWTF [Grant ID: 10.47379/ICT23030].

Disclose or Interests. The authors have no disclosing interests to declare that are relevant to the content of this article.

References

1. Alexander, L.: Constrained by precedent. South. Calif. Law Rev. **63**, 1 (1989)
2. Ashley, K.D.: Reasoning with cases and hypotheticals in hypo. Int. J. Man Mach. Stud. **34**(6), 753–796 (1991)
3. Badra, F., Lesot, M.J.: Case-based prediction – a survey. Int. J. Approx. Reason. **158**, 108920 (2023)
4. Canavotto, I.: Inconsistent precedents and deontic logic. In: Maranhão, J., Peterson, C., Straßer, C., van der Torre, L. (eds.) 16th International Conference, DEON 2023, pp. 317–333. College Publications (2023)
5. Canavotto, I.: Reasoning with inconsistent precedents. Artif. Intell. Law **33**, 1–30 (2023)
6. Canavotto, I., Horty, J.F.: Piecemeal knowledge acquisition for computational normative reasoning. In: AIES 2022, pp. 171–180. ACM (2022)
7. Gelman, A., Carlin, J.B., Stern, H.S., Rubin, D.B.: Bayesian Data Analysis. Chapman and Hall/CRC (1995)
8. Gray, M., Savelka, J., Oliver, W., Ashley, K.: Toward automatically identifying legally relevant factors. In: Legal Knowledge and Information Systems, pp. 53–62. IOS Press (2022)
9. Gray, M., Savelka, J., Oliver, W., Ashley, K.: Empirical legal analysis simplified: reducing complexity through automatic identification and evaluation of legally relevant factors. Philos. Trans. Royal Soc. A **382** (2024)
10. Horty, J.F.: The result model of precedent. Leg. Theory **10**(1), 19–31 (2004)
11. Horty, J.F.: Rules and reasons in the theory of precedent. Leg. Theory **17**(1), 1–33 (2011)
12. Kelly, J.S.: Social Choice Theory: An Introduction. Springer, Singapore (2013). https://doi.org/10.1007/978-981-16-9661-9
13. Letham, B., Rudin, C., McCormick, T.H., Madigan, D.: Interpretable classifiers using rules and Bayesian analysis. Ann. Appl. Stat. **9**(3) (2015)
14. Peters, J.G., Bex, F.J., Prakken, H.: Model-and data-agnostic justifications with a fortiori case-based argumentation. In: Proceedings of the Nineteenth International Conference on Artificial Intelligence and Law, pp. 207–216 (2023)
15. Peters, J.G., Bex, F.J., Prakken, H., et al.: Justifications derived from inconsistent case bases using authoritativeness. In: Proceedings of ArgXAI 2022, vol. 3209, pp. 1–13. CEUR WS (2022)
16. Rempell, S.: Factors. 70 Buff. L. Rev. 1755 (2022)
17. Robert, C.P., Casella, G., Casella, G.: Monte Carlo Statistical Methods, vol. 2. Springer, New York (1999). https://doi.org/10.1007/978-1-4757-3071-5
18. Schoenmackers, S., Davis, J., Etzioni, O., Weld, D.S.: Learning first-order horn clauses from web text. In: Proceedings of the 2010 Conference on Empirical Methods in Natural Language Processing, pp. 1088–1098 (2010)
19. van Woerkom, W., Grossi, D., Prakken, H., Verheij, B.: A fortiori case-based reasoning: from theory to data. J. Artif. Intell. Res. **81**, 401–441 (2024)
20. von Wright, G.H.: Deontic logics. Am. Philos. Q. **4**(2), 136–143 (1967)

Towards Fair AI Systems: An Insurance Case Study to Identify and Mitigate Discrimination

Annabel Resch[(✉)] and Allan Hanbury[ID]

Data Science Research Unit, TU Wien, Favoritenstraße 9-11, 1040 Vienna, Austria
annabelresch@gmail.com, allan.hanbury@tuwien.ac.at
https://informatics.tuwien.ac.at/orgs/e194-04

Abstract. We investigate potential gender-based discrimination in a real-world insurance machine learning model designed to identify claims likely to "explode" in compensation costs. With the EU AI Act and Austrian legal frameworks requiring non-discriminatory algorithmic systems, ensuring fairness in insurance claim prediction models has become critically important. The research examines whether a Light Gradient Boosting Machine (LGBM) model used by an Austrian insurance company exhibits gender discriminatory behavior and explores methods to mitigate such bias. This study analyzed a dataset of 450,000 insurance claims provided by an Austrian insurance company.

The baseline analysis revealed significant discrimination against female claimants compared to male claimants. While mitigation methods successfully improved fairness metrics, these improvements came at a cost to predictive performance.

Keywords: Algorithmic Fairness · Discrimination · Insurance

1 Introduction

The insurance industry represents a critical domain for the application and evaluation of fair AI systems. On the one hand, insurance providers offer essential services to modern societies. Motor insurance facilitates mobility, health insurance provides access to medical care, and property insurance protects against catastrophic losses. These services fulfill essential social needs and contribute to broader social welfare. On the other hand, most insurers are commercial entities with profit-oriented objectives. They must carefully calculate reserves, manage risk pools, and maintain financial viability to continue providing their services. This commercial imperative necessitates sophisticated risk assessment and pricing mechanisms, increasingly powered by AI and machine learning technologies. Fair AI systems in insurance must navigate this duality, ensuring non-discrimination while preserving the actuarial principles that enable insurers to operate sustainably.

© The Author(s) 2026
L. Hagedorn et al. (Eds.): DIGHUM 2025, LNCS 16319, pp. 67–82, 2026.
https://doi.org/10.1007/978-3-032-11108-1_5

The field of algorithmic fairness, which emerged approximately fifteen years ago, has rapidly evolved in response to the growing recognition of the potential harms that biased AI systems can inflict [18]. A concrete example of algorithmic discrimination comes from the Austrian insurance sector, where AI systems used for risk assessment have been found to encode socioeconomic biases [12]. These systems were found to discriminate against individuals from lower-income neighborhoods or with specific migration backgrounds when calculating premiums.

Recent legal regulations, like the EU AI Act explicitly require companies to not only design new AI systems with fairness considerations but also to retrospectively evaluate existing systems for potential discrimination [26]. This creates an implementation gap: insurance companies are legally obligated to prevent discrimination but lack clear guidance on how to operationalise fairness in their AI systems. In response to this challenge, an Austrian insurance company has provided a case study from 2019, including a baseline model and dataset, which is currently implemented in their business processes. This case study, called 'Explosive Claims', employs machine learning to identify insurance claims that ultimately result in significantly higher compensation costs than initially calculated. Claims were classified as "explosive" if they required reserve increases exceeding €100,000 or if reserve amounts grew by a factor of ten or more within one month of initial reporting.

The amount of published scientific literature on discrimination in AI systems has expanded considerably in recent years, yet significant challenges persist in developing solutions that are both robust and generalizable to real-world applications. A fundamental limitation in this field is the scarcity of comprehensive benchmark datasets that mirror real-world insurance complexity [22]. This dependence on simplified data questions the external validity of research findings [28], creating uncertainty about whether fairness strategies will effectively translate from research to production environments.

The literature on algorithmic fairness presents numerous fairness metrics, each embodying different philosophical and mathematical conceptualizations of fairness [3]. Even among computer scientists there remains a lack of consensus about which constraints are most appropriate [22]. This theoretical fragmentation creates significant barriers for insurance practitioners seeking to implement fairness-aware systems in compliance with regulations.

Another evaluation challenge is the methodological question about bias mitigation approaches. Insurance companies face the daunting task of selecting from numerous bias mitigation techniques without clear guidance on their comparative efficacy in insurance-specific contexts [27]. A critical shortcoming in current fairness literature is the frequent neglect of model performance considerations. In real-world AI systems, particularly in the insurance sector where predictive accuracy directly impacts business outcomes and customer experiences, maintaining high model performance is non-negotiable. The literature frequently presents fairness as a constraint to be satisfied, initially resulting in accuracy degradation [20]. Commonly used strategies typically minimize discrimination by adding penalty terms to loss functions, which restricts the model's ability to use all available information for prediction [9,16,35]. Scientific work has advanced to better understanding these tradeoffs, with some research challenging the assumption that fairness necessarily reduces accuracy [10]. Despite this progress, it remains unclear what constitutes the optimal balance between fairness and accuracy objectives in real-world applications.

In conclusion, it is unclear whether the 'Explosive Claims' algorithm (negligently) currently discriminates, how discrimination can be measured, and which measures can be taken to mitigate discrimination.

From this problem statement, the research questions are derived:

RQ1: To what extent does the current baseline model discriminate in the context of this case study?

RQ2: To what extent can fairness be improved through discrimination mitigation techniques in comparison to the baseline?

RQ3: To what extent does the predictive performance decrease by introducing the above-mentioned mitigation techniques, compared to baseline?

A more detailed version of this work, in particular additional results on nationality and the use of post-processing discrimination mitigation methods, can be found in the master's thesis [29].

2   Fairness, Bias, and Discrimination

Computer scientists aim to mitigate discrimination by promoting algorithmic fairness and ensuring that AI applications operate impartially. Two primary sources of unfairness are often identified: bias within the data itself and bias within the design of the algorithm [22]. Bias refers to the (un)intentional skewing of AI systems, which can arise at various stages, including biased training data, flawed algorithmic design, or the misinterpretation of model outcomes [24]. Bias is both a cause and a source of discrimination in AI systems [31].

Most existing studies on algorithmic fairness in insurance focus on actuarial fairness, primarily investigating discrimination risks in underwriting [4,19,34]. Others explore how fairness principles from insurance pricing can be applied to machine learning, given the shared challenges of managing uncertainty, fairness, and accountability [13]. Additionally, moral trade-offs between non-discrimination and predictive accuracy in risk prediction have been examined, highlighting the complexity of balancing fairness with actuarial precision [21]. Beyond fairness in underwriting, further studies have analyzed broader challenges arising from AI-driven insurance models, including emerging regulatory concerns and technological shifts [23]. The dilemma of choosing a suitable fairness metric is demonstrated in a fictional example about fraud detection in insurance claims [30].

The EU places significant emphasis on trustworthy AI, resulting in a comprehensive regulatory landscape [32]. While discrimination can manifest in structural, systemic, and statistical forms, EU legislation explicitly prohibits two specific forms: direct and indirect discrimination [7].

- **Direct discrimination** occurs "where one person [or a group of people] is treated less favorably than another is, has been, or would be treated in a comparable situation on grounds of" a protected attribute [7].

- **Indirect discrimination** occurs when "an apparently neutral provision, criterion, or practice would put persons of a protected group at a particular disadvantage compared with other persons, unless that provision, criterion, or practice is objectively justified by a legitimate aim and the means of achieving that aim are appropriate and necessary" [7]. In other words, indirect discrimination occurs when decisions based on seemingly neutral attributes disproportionately disadvantage protected groups.

EU law establishes *protected attributes* (also known as sensitive attributes), which cannot legally be used as grounds for discrimination. Such discrimination remains illegal even when unintentional. The European Union's non-discrimination directives collectively prohibit discrimination based on six protected attributes: **age, disability, gender, religion or belief, racial or ethnic origin, and sexual orientation** [5,7,8].

Insurance companies operate on the principle of risk classification to generate profit. Consequently, in the insurance sector, EU non-discrimination directives only strictly prohibit discrimination based on **gender and ethnicity**, without allowing any exceptions [6,7].

EU legislation explicitly mandates that insurance AI systems must not discriminate based on protected attributes like gender and ethnicity while requiring transparency and continuous monitoring of these systems. However, the regulatory framework notably lacks quantifiable metrics or mathematical definitions of fairness [32]. This absence creates a significant implementation gap when translating legal anti-discrimination principles into algorithmic contexts. Developers and insurers must therefore navigate between imprecise legal standards and the mathematical precision required for technical implementation in AI systems.

3   Algorithmic Fairness Metrics

When properly designed, algorithmic systems can enhance our ability to detect discriminatory patterns [17], as they enable the application of well-defined metrics that formalize and quantify fairness [22]. A systematic literature review identified 33 objective metrics for ethical AI [25]. Metrics that describe the fairness performance of an AI system are referred to as fairness definitions or non-discrimination criteria [2]. We will therefore use the terms "fairness metric" and "fairness definition" synonymously.

3.1   Fundamentals

The following widely used statistical measures are used in this paper:

Prevalence (Prev) is the proportion of actual positives relative to the total dataset.

True Positive Rate (TPR), also called recall or sensitivity, describes the proportion of correctly predicted positives relative to all actual positives.

False Negative Rate (FNR) describes the proportion of actual positives, which were misclassified as negative, relative to all actual positives. FNR and TPR are complementary, as they together account for all actual positives.

True Negative Rate (TNR) also called specificity, describes the proportion of correctly predicted negatives relative to all actual negatives.

False Positive Rate (FPR) also called type 1 error, describes the proportion of actual negatives, which were misclassified as positive, relative to all actual negatives. TNR and FPR are complementary, as they together account for all actual negatives.

False Omission Rate (FOR) describes the proportion of actual positives that were incorrectly predicted as negatives, relative to all predicted negatives.

Negative Predictive Value (NPV) describes the proportion of correctly predicted negatives, relative to all predicted negatives. FOR and NPV are complementary, as they together account for all predicted negatives.

False Discovery Rate (FDR) describes the proportion of actual negatives that were incorrectly predicted as positives, relative to all predicted positives.

Positive Predicted Value (PPR) also called precision, describes the proportion of correctly predicted positives, relative to all predicted positives. FDR and PPV are complementary, as they together account for all predicted positives.

Acceptance Rate is the proportion of all predicted positives relative to the total dataset.

Group fairness aims to treat different groups, which are defined by one or several distinct values of a sensitive attribute, equally [31]. Therefore, the above-described classification performance metrics need to be equal across all groups [25]. The comparison of metrics across all groups can be done using either (absolute) differences or ratios [15,25]. Ratios and relative values allow to determine the direction of the discrimination and to account for extreme class imbalances. For any of the above-mentioned classification performance metrics, the respective ratio R is calculated as follows:

$$\text{Ratio R} = \frac{rate_{S=b}}{rate_{S=a}} \tag{1}$$

Throughout this analysis, ratios are consistently calculated with Group A (majority group) in the denominator and Group B (minority group) in the numerator.

The direction of discrimination revealed by these metrics depends critically on their contextual interpretation. When $TPRR < 1$, a clear disadvantage exists for the minority group, the model identifies their positive outcomes less accurately than those of the majority group. Conversely, the implications of $FPRR < 1$ require nuanced evaluation. Whether a lower score FPR for the minority group represents preferential treatment or systematic disadvantage hinges entirely on the specific domain context and the consequences of false classifications within that environment. $R = 1$ represents perfect parity, therefore perfect fairness [27].

3.2   Fairness Evaluation Metrics

This section presents the metrics applied during the fairness assessment and details the discrimination mitigation methods implemented to improve fair outcomes. The following fairness metrics are computed and evaluated:

Treatment Equality is achieved when the ratio of false negatives to false positives is equal for both groups [27].

Statistical Parity, also known as **demographic parity**, seeks to establish equivalent acceptance rates across both groups [30].

Equalized Odds aims for equal true positive rates (TPR) and equal false positive rates (FPR) for both groups [14]. **Average Odds Difference** can be used to calculate how far a model deviates from achieving equalized odds.

The initial exploratory data analysis has revealed an extreme class imbalance in the dataset. Certain fairness metrics expose significant bias only after **normalization**, highlighting the impact of class imbalance [15]. For all basic statistical measures discussed in Sect. 3.1, their normalized variants are also computed. For any ratio R (see Eq. 1), the normalization is computed as follows:

$$\text{Normalized Ratio} = \frac{R}{R+1} \tag{2}$$

The normalization of ratio values maps the original unbounded ratios to the interval $[0, 1]$, where 0.5 indicates equal rates between groups and values closer to the extremes indicate greater disparity in rates. It is important to note that the interpretation of normalized values depends on the specific metric being evaluated. The same normalized value (e.g., 0.8) can have opposite fairness implications depending on whether TPRR is examined (where higher values for the minority group may indicate better performance) versus FORR (where higher values for the minority group may indicate harmful bias). This context-dependent interpretation must be considered when analyzing results across different fairness metrics.

4   Discrimination Mitigation Techniques

Discrimination mitigation methods in real-world business scenarios should be carefully chosen to maximize profit for the company [2]. Unfortunately, the Austrian insurance company did not indicate quantitative amounts for the cost of false positives or the reward for true positives. Therefore, it is difficult to calculate the optimal trade-off threshold.

In order to decide which mitigation technique is most suitable, it is necessary to analyze the meaning of false positives and negatives in the case study once more. False positives, as well as false negatives, represent tangible costs to satisfy popular notions of algorithmic fairness, which need to be weighed against each other. In this case study, false positives mean that the model unnecessarily flags a low-risk claim as high-risk. This might lead to undesirable actions, such as avoidable costs for medical treatments and more workload for insurance employees. The policyholder enjoys better caretaking on the other hand.

False negatives mean that the model fails to identify a high-risk claim that is likely to explode. This results in high, unforeseen costs for the insurance company and worse long-term conditions for the insured person.

Overall, false negatives result in worse consequences for both insurance company and policyholder. Thus, the mitigation techniques should result in equal (low) false negative rates, which means similar (high) true positive rates.

In-processing methods aim to improve fairness directly during the model training [33]. Because the baseline is a Light Gradient Boosting Machine (LGBM), currently used by the insurance company, we concentrate on a widely used in-processing approach: the Fair Gradient-Boosting Machine (FairGBM or FGBM). FGBM extends traditional gradient boosting by incorporating fairness constraints directly into the gradient boosting model training [9]. This approach is known as a dual ascent learning framework. The algorithm converges to a solution that satisfies both the performance objective and the fairness constraints. This dual ascent approach allows FGBM to effectively navigate the trade-off between prediction accuracy and fairness requirements.

An advantage of FGBM is the possibility to implement global constraints alongside fairness constraints in the model. When dealing with class-imbalanced datasets where achieving high overall accuracy might be misleading, particular performance targets can be specified instead. For instance, in this case study the aim is to achieve equal opportunity (equal TPR rates) while keeping false positives under control. This allows building models that balance overall performance metrics with group-specific fairness considerations [9].

FGBM was applied in the following two configurations: **(1) FGBM using same parameters as the baseline model:** FGBM should be especially suitable for imbalanced datasets [9]. To test the statement, the baseline LGBM model was replaced with the FGBM model. While all core LGBM parameters remain unchanged, FGBM requires the definition of certain constraint parameters[1]. In other words, the fairness constraint is to optimize TPR ratio with at most a 1% FPR ratio. The constraint parameters were chosen in good faith to achieve the fairest model possible.

(2) FGBM using hyperparameter tuning: To investigate whether different parameter settings result in even better fairness and accuracy trade-off, comprehensive hyperparameter tuning (HPT) and selection were conducted. The process was suggested by the authors of FGBM[2] and adapted for this case study. The HPT ran for 4 h. While the algorithm was tasked to maximize the overall recall score, it was simultaneously penalized if the TPRR (comparison of recall per subgroup) was below a generous threshold of 0.5. The optuna hyperparameter optimization was used [1].

Post-processing approaches are covered in [29]. Although pre-processing mitigation methods fall outside the scope of this paper, the 'fairness through

---

[1] https://github.com/feedzai/fairgbm, visited on 05/14/25.

[2] https://pypi.org/project/hyperparameter-tuning/, visited on 05/13/25.

Table 1. Baseline model performance on gender test set

	Absolute frequencies				Relative frequencies (%)			
	TN	FP	FN	TP	TN	FP	FN	TP
Male	26,269	167	10	13	99.13	0.63	0.04	0.05
Female	15,766	90	6	4	99.39	0.57	0.04	0.03
Unknown	15,639	96	9	8	99.31	0.61	0.06	0.05

unawareness' (FTU) approach is incorporated into the analysis. FTU describes a simple pre-processing approach that involves removing protected attributes and their obvious proxies from the dataset before model training [22]. The approach is based on the assumption that if a classifier cannot access protected attribute values, it cannot directly discriminate based on them. While the baseline LGBM model uses both gender and nationality as input features, all models in the fairness analysis exclude these protected attributes from the training data. To distinguish between the effects attributable to FTU and those resulting from other mitigation techniques, it is essential to evaluate FTU independently. Solely using this method for discrimination mitigation is widely criticized. It fails to prevent indirect discrimination, as models can still infer the eliminated protected attributes from other seemingly neutral features [11,31].

5   Results

This section describes the results of the fairness assessment on the explosive claims case study. First, the baseline model is analyzed, and relevant fairness metrics, as well as disadvantaged subgroups, are determined. Afterwards, the implementation of different discrimination mitigation methods is evaluated based on the fairness metrics. Finally, the impact of fairness strategies on the predictive performance is analyzed. The Python scripts, including all relevant code, are available on GitHub[3] for reproducibility.

5.1   Baseline Model

The confusion matrix values are shown in Table 1. These show that all groups have at least some true explosive claims in the test set. But since the group sizes and base rates are imbalanced, fairness metrics are essential to evaluate parity.

To decide which metrics are problematic in terms of discrimination, it is necessary to compare them group-wise. Figure 1 shows the statistical measure ratios for the two subgroups, male vs. female. The blue graph describes the original ratios, where values close to 1 indicate parity. The green values describe the normalized ratios, where values close to 0.5 indicate parity. The dotted graphs describe the respective parity.

---

[3] https://github.com/AnnabelRe/FairnessAnalysis, visited on 05/15/25.

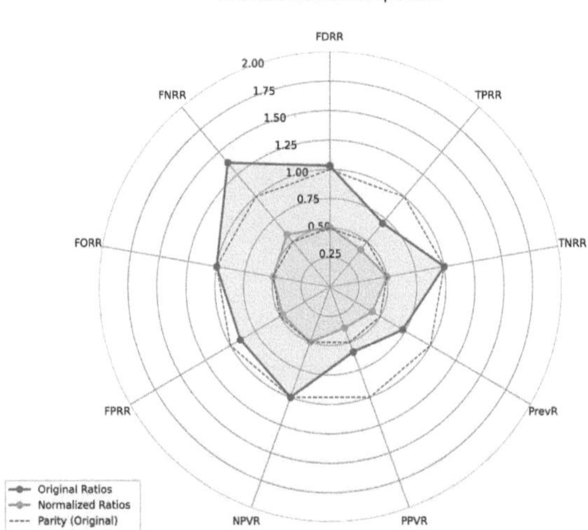

Fig. 1. Fairness ratios male vs. female subgroup, baseline model.

The key findings are:

- PPVR, which compares the precision per group, reveals potential discrimination against the female subgroup. That means that the proportion of positive predictions that are actually correct is smaller for the female subgroup.
- FNRR, which compares the proportion of false negatives per group, is much higher for the female subgroup, which means that actual positives are much more likely to be misclassified as negatives.
- TPRR, which describes the correctly classified positives, is lower for the female subgroup. As FNR and TPR are complementary, this means that the model fails to predict actual positives for the female subgroup as well as for the male subgroup.
- The male subgroup has a higher prevalence (positive base rate) than the female subgroup in the test set, which indicates an imbalance in the underlying distribution of positives.

Figure 2 shows the impact on the chosen fairness metrics. The key findings are:

- The normalization of values significantly emphasizes the disparity for all three metrics.
- The positive treatment equality value shows that the female group receives more false negatives than the male group.
- The original statistical parity difference is insignificant. Only when normalizing the values does a moderate disparity show. It indicates that the female group has a 13% lower probability of receiving a favorable outcome compared to the male group. This suggests that overall decision outcomes are skewed in favor of the male group.

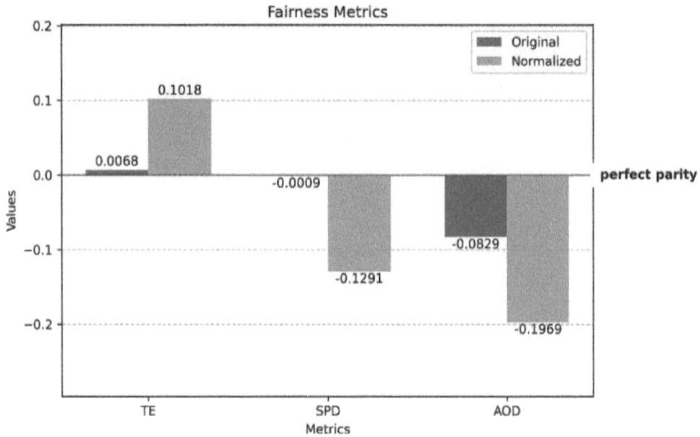

Fig. 2. Comparison of treatment equality, statistical parity difference, and average odds difference for male vs. female subgroup, baseline model.

- The average odds difference of -0.0829 indicates that the female subgroup has a lower chance of receiving a true or false positive prediction compared to the male subgroup.

The equal selection parity is -86.0, which means that the male subgroup has a total of 86 more positively predicted claims. This conforms with the previous findings, like disparity in base rates.

5.2   Discrimination Mitigation Methods

In-processing methods are implemented by replacing the baseline LGBM model with appropriate fair models. Besides the selected in-processing method, the comparison also includes one pre-processing mitigation method: FTU. The comparison is essential for a comprehensive understanding of the different strategies, since all of the mitigation methods are based on the FTU outcome. Post-processing methods are considered in [29].

Figure 3 provides an overview of the adjusted fairness ratios per mitigation method. It shows that especially the FGBM model with hyperparameter tuning achieves fairness scores close to the perfect parity value of 1.0 for unnormalized values, and 0.5 for normalized values. Generally, the normalized values highlight the improved performance of all fair models compared to the baseline model. The FTU method shows only very little variance from the baseline model, thus their graphs are overlapping. Figure 4 confirms that both FGBM versions perform significantly better than the FTU mitigation, which barely shows any improvement from the baseline model.

In conclusion, when considering fairness metrics alone (such as ratios and differences), both versions of FGBM demonstrate significantly superior performance compared to the baseline model. Thus, the in-processing mitigation strategies are successful.

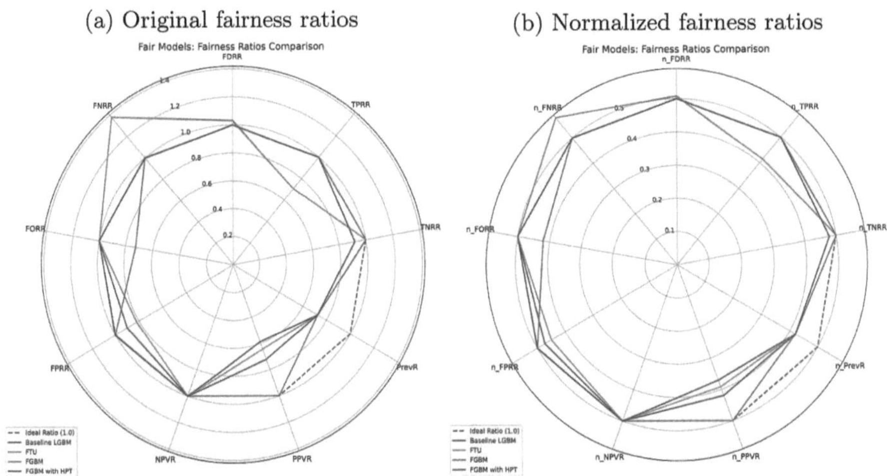

Fig. 3. Fairness ratios male vs. female subgroup after mitigation methods.

5.3 Performance Evaluation

This section compares the predictive output of the baseline LGBM model to the modified outputs of the mitigation strategies. The aim is to identify the effect of the improvement in fairness on the predictive performance.

Due to the highly imbalanced nature of the dataset (0.01% positive cases), standard accuracy can be misleading as it may appear artificially high by simply predicting the majority class for all instances. Instead, the following performance metrics are used. *Balanced accuracy* is the average of true negative rate (TNR) and true positive rate (TPR), which provides equal weight to performance on both classes regardless of their prevalence. *Recall* (TPR) is the proportion of actual positives correctly identified. *Precision* (PPV) is the proportion of positive predictions that are actually correct. The *F1 score* is the harmonic mean of

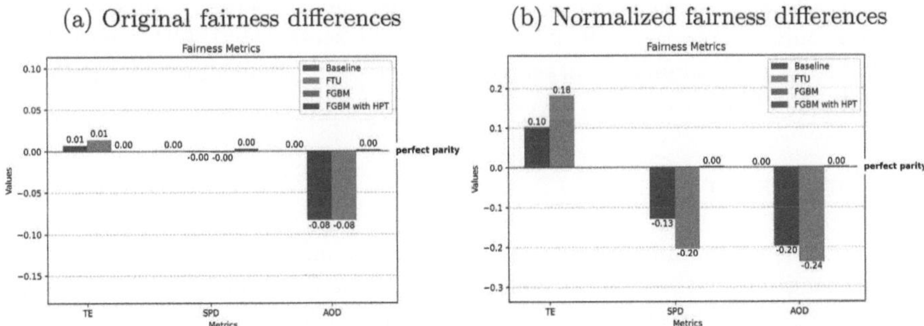

Fig. 4. Comparison of treatment equality, statistical parity difference, and average odds difference for male vs. female subgroup after mitigation.

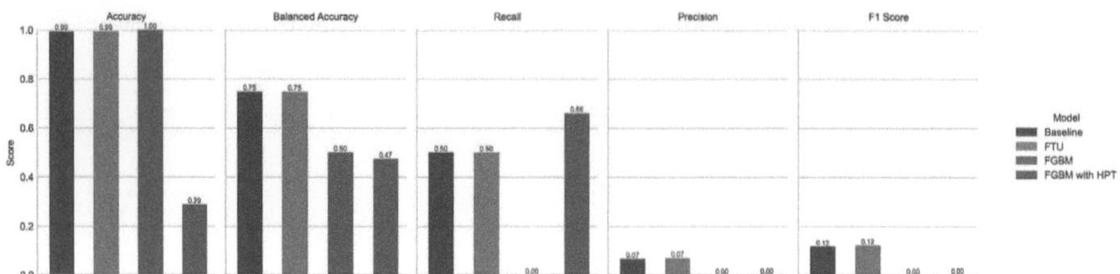

Fig. 5. Performance metrics by model type for gender.

precision and recall, providing a single metric that balances both considerations. All performance metrics described above range from 0 to 1, with 1 describing the best possible performance.

The baseline model employs a classification threshold of 0.5, where prediction scores above this value yield a positive label (1), while scores at or below this threshold result in an negative label (0). The baseline model achieves an accuracy score of 99.35%, which is not necessarily informative in datasets with high class imbalance, though. Thus, the other performance metrics provide better insights. Especially the recall score should not drop lower than the baseline model result of 50%, since already half of the very few positives are misclassified as negative. Only 6.61% of predicted positives of the baseline model are actually positive, indicating many false positives and a very low precision score. Consequently, the F1 score also shows poor overall performance (11.68%). However, in this case study, false negatives impose higher costs on the insurance company than false positives. In conclusion, despite the high overall accuracy, the model's performance on the positive class is poor, as evidenced by the modest balanced accuracy, low precision, and particularly weak F1 score. This serves as an indication that the model struggles with the extreme class imbalance.

Figure 5 shows the predictive performance of the mitigation strategies applied to optimize fairness between the male and female gender groups. FTU performs identically or at least very similarly to the baseline model. The FGBM model shows a recall of 0, which indicates no correctly predicted positives. In fact, this model predicts the negative class for all claims, which results in almost perfect accuracy but very poor recall, precision, and F1 score. The FGBM with HPT achieves a desirable higher recall score than the baseline model by over-predicting the explosive claims class.

6   Conclusion

We discussed algorithmic fairness and discrimination, and a real-world machine learning model from the insurance industry was tested for gender discrimination. The answers to the research questions are in the following paragraphs:

RQ1: The baseline evaluation demonstrated that metrics based on absolute differences, such as balance and equal selection parity, prove inadequate when analyzing datasets characterized by significant class imbalance. Furthermore, binary fairness criteria that demand exact parity (like equalized odds or conditional use accuracy equality) yield only binary satisfaction states, limiting their interpretability and actionability. As a result, this research found that relative measures expressed as ratios or proportional differences provide the most interpretable and practically applicable framework for assessing algorithmic fairness in this context, as they enable direct comparison of disparities across different demographic groups regardless of baseline rate variations.

RQ2: The FGBM model with baseline parameters successfully modifies the predictions during model training so that the most valuable fairness metrics, like equalized opportunity, are satisfied for all 6 group pairings of this fairness analysis. When hyperparameter tuning is applied to the FGBM, equalized opportunity is only satisfied for the male vs. female subgroup comparison. In addition, fairness metrics that measure proportional differences generally showed a much closer value to 0 for both FGBM versions when optimized for the gender attribute.

RQ3: The baseline model has a recall score of 50%, which should not decrease any further by implementing fairness measures, according to the insurance company. None of the mitigation methods lead to an improvement in the predictive performance. At most, they do not become worse. In conclusion, mitigation methods were found that significantly improve the fairness and mitigate discrimination. However, the negative impact on the predictive performance was too serious to select a strategy for the future. Nevertheless, the FTU mitigation method should definitely be implemented, even if there was no change in fairness or performance metrics. Using protected attributes during model training should be avoided.

The dataset characteristics represent significant challenges. The high class imbalance makes accurate interpretation of fairness and performance metrics difficult. Continuous monitoring and analysis of new claims data would provide more robust insights over time.

This research did not define acceptable tolerance ranges for fairness metrics like equalized odds. As a result, many of the metrics demanded perfect parity, which is rarely achievable in real-world scenarios. For future work, we recommend establishing reasonable thresholds around the ideal parity score of 1, allowing fairness criteria to be considered satisfied even when results show minor deviations from perfect equality. While resource-intensive approaches like individual fairness assessment may be impractical in business contexts, group fairness metrics should be evaluated with appropriate caution. The insurance industry's potential to impact individuals' financial and health outcomes makes non-discrimination particularly critical, not only ethically but also financially, given potential regulatory penalties.

Disclosure of Interests. The authors have no competing interests to declare that are relevant to the content of this article.

References

1. Akiba, T., Sano, S., Yanase, T., Ohta, T., Koyama, M.: Optuna: a next-generation hyperparameter optimization framework. In: Proceedings of the 25th ACM SIGKDD International Conference on Knowledge Discovery & Data Mining, pp. 2623–2631. ACM (2019)
2. Barocas, S., Hardt, M., Narayanan, A.: Fairness and Machine Learning: Limitations and Opportunities. MIT Press (2023)
3. Castelnovo, A., Crupi, R., Greco, G., Regoli, D., Penco, I.G., Cosentini, A.C.: A clarification of the nuances in the fairness metrics landscape. Sci. Rep. **12**(1), 4209 (2022)
4. Charpentier, A., Hu, F., Ratz, P.: Mitigating discrimination in insurance with Wasserstein barycenters. In: Meo, R., Silvestri, F. (eds.) ECML PKDD 2023. CCIS, vol. 2133, pp. 161–177. Springer, Cham (2025). https://doi.org/10.1007/978-3-031-74630-7_11
5. Charter of Fundamental Rights of the Europea: Union. Off. J. Eur. Union **C**(326), 391–407 (2012)
6. European Commission: Guidelines on the application of council directive 2004/113/EC to insurance, in the light of the judgment of the court of justice of the European union in case c-236/09 (test-achats). Off. J. Eur. Union **C**(11), 1–11 (2012)
7. Council of the Europea: Union: Council directive 2000/43/ec implementing the principle of equal treatment between persons irrespective of racial or ethnic origin. Off. J. **180** (2000)
8. Council of the Europea: Union: Council directive 2004/113/ec implementing the principle of equal treatment between men and women in the access to and supply of goods and services. Offic. J. Eur. Union (2004)
9. Cruz, A.F., Belém, C., Jesus, S., Bravo, J., Saleiro, P., Bizarro, P.: FAIRGBM: gradient boosting with fairness constraints. In: The Eleventh International Conference on Learning Representations (2023)
10. Dutta, S., Wei, D., Yueksel, H., Chen, P.Y., Liu, S., Varshney, K.R.: Is there a trade-off between fairness and accuracy? A perspective using mismatched hypothesis testing. In: Proceedings of the 37th International Conference on Machine Learning, ICML 2020. JMLR.org (2020)
11. Dwork, C., Hardt, M., Pitassi, T., Reingold, O., Zemel, R.: Fairness through awareness. In: Proceedings of the 3rd Innovations in Theoretical Computer Science Conference, pp. 214–226. ACM (2012)
12. Favaretto, M., De Clercq, E., Elger, B.S.: Big data and discrimination: perils, promises and solutions. a systematic review. J. Big Data **6**(1), 12 (2019)
13. Fröhlich, C., Williamson, R.C.: Insights from insurance for fair machine learning. In: Proceedings of the 2024 ACM Conference on Fairness, Accountability, and Transparency, pp. 407–421. ACM (2024)
14. Hardt, M., Price, E., Srebro, N.: Equality of opportunity in supervised learning. In: Proceedings of the 30th International Conference on Neural Information Processing Systems, pp. 3323–3331. Curran Associates (2016)
15. Kamalaruban, P., et al.: Evaluating fairness in transaction fraud models: fairness metrics, bias audits, and challenges. In: Proceedings of the 5th ACM International Conference on AI in Finance, pp. 555–563. ACM (2024)
16. Kamishima, T., Akaho, S., Asoh, H., Sakuma, J.: Fairness-aware classifier with prejudice remover regularizer. In: Flach, P.A., De Bie, T., Cristianini, N. (eds.)

ECML PKDD 2012. LNCS (LNAI), vol. 7524, pp. 35–50. Springer, Heidelberg (2012). https://doi.org/10.1007/978-3-642-33486-3_3

17. Kleinberg, J., Ludwig, J., Mullainathan, S., Sunstein, C.R.: Discrimination in the age of algorithms. J. Legal Anal. **10**, 113–174 (2019)

18. Lenders, D., Oloo, A.: 15 years of algorithmic fairness - scoping review of interdisciplinary developments in the field. CoRR **abs/2408.01448** (2024)

19. Lindholm, M., Richman, R., Tsanakas, A., Wüthrich, M.V.: Discrimination-free insurance pricing. ASTIN Bull. J. IAA **52**(1), 55–89 (2022)

20. Liu, S., Vicente, L.N.: Accuracy and fairness trade-offs in machine learning: a stochastic multi-objective approach. CMS **19**, 513–537 (2022)

21. Loi, M., Christen, M.: Choosing how to discriminate: navigating ethical trade-offs in fair algorithmic design for the insurance sector. Philos. Technol. **34**(4), 967–992 (2021). https://doi.org/10.1007/s13347-021-00444-9

22. Mehrabi, N., Morstatter, F., Saxena, N., Lerman, K., Galstyan, A.: A survey on bias and fairness in machine learning. ACM Comput. Surv. (CSUR) **54**(6), 1–35 (2021)

23. Oletzky, T., Reinhardt, A.: Herausforderungen der regulierung von und der aufsicht über den einsatz künstlicher intelligenz in der versicherungswirtschaft. Zeitschrift für die gesamte Versicherungswissenschaft **111**(4), 495–513 (2022)

24. Oneto, L., Chiappa, S.: Fairness in machine learning. In: Oneto, L., Navarin, N., Sperduti, A., Anguita, D. (eds.) Recent Trends in Learning From Data. SCI, vol. 896, pp. 155–196. Springer, Cham (2020). https://doi.org/10.1007/978-3-030-43883-8_7

25. Palumbo, G., Carneiro, D., Alves, V.: Objective metrics for ethical AI: a systematic literature review. Int. J. Data Sci. Anal. (2024)

26. European Parliament and of the Council: Regulation (EU) 2024/1689 laying down harmonised rules on artificial intelligence (artificial intelligence act). Off. J. Eur. Union **OJ L**, 1–201 (2024)

27. Pessach, D., Shmueli, E.: A review on fairness in machine learning. ACM Comput. Surv. **55**(3), 51:1–51:44 (2022)

28. Quy, T.L., Roy, A., Iosifidis, V., Zhang, W., Ntoutsi, E.: A survey on datasets for fairness-aware machine learning. WIREs Data Mining Knowl. Discov. **12**(3) (2022)

29. Resch, A.: Towards fair AI systems: an insurance case study to identify and mitigate discrimination. Master's thesis, TU Wien (2025)

30. Ruf, B., Detyniecki, M.: Towards the right kind of fairness in AI. CoRR (2021)

31. Strotherm, J., Müller, A., Hammer, B., Paaßen, B.: Fairness in KI-systemen. In: Vertrauen in Künstliche Intelligenz, pp. 163–183. Springer, Wiesbaden (2024)

32. Wachter, S., Mittelstadt, B., Russell, C.: Bias preservation in machine learning: the legality of fairness metrics under EU non-discrimination law. West Virginia Law Rev. **123**(3), 735 (2021)

33. Wan, M., Zha, D., Liu, N., Zou, N.: In-processing modeling techniques for machine learning fairness: a survey. ACM Trans. Knowl. Discov. Data **17**(3), 35:1–35:27 (2023)

34. Xin, X., Huang, F.: Antidiscrimination insurance pricing: regulations, fairness criteria, and models. North Am. Act. J. **28**(2), 285–319 (2024)

35. Zafar, M.B., Valera, I., Gomez-Rodriguez, M., Gummadi, K.P.: Fairness constraints: a flexible approach for fair classification. J. Mach. Learn. Res. **20**(75), 1–42 (2019)

TiBaLLi: Internet Inclusion Through Artificial Intelligence

Francis Saa-Dittoh[1]([envelope])[iD], Anna Bon[2][iD], André Baart[3], and Gossa Lô[4][iD]

[1] University for Development Studies, Tamale, Ghana
`fdittoh@uds.edu.gh`
[2] Vrije Universiteit Amsterdam, Amsterdam, The Netherlands
`a.bon@vu.nl`
[3] Babafla, Amsterdam, The Netherlands
`andre@babafla.com`
[4] Amsterdam, The Netherlands

Abstract. In recent years, Artificial Intelligence has aided in the development of many solutions around the world in numerous fields and it has become imperative to ask how advanced AI methods like Machine Learning and Natural Language Processing can be reconstructed so as to make the Internet more inclusive practically, for communities in low-resource environments in the Global South. This paper outlines the project in Ghana, which utilizes a Participatory Action Research approach to build a local voice-based Automatic Speech Recognition system to provide domain-focused web-based information to local communities in Dagbani (a local Ghanaian language). We look at the methodology, and how it utilized insights from community engagement to build an inclusive system. We also look at what broader implications of this design process for the Web and AI in the context of decolonization of the Internet.

Keywords: low-resource environments · web inclusion · indigenous languages · artificial intelligence · natural language processing · participatory action research

1 Introduction

The digital divide refers to the gap between those who have ready access to computers and the internet and those who do not. This divide exists between countries, particularly the Global North-South, but also within countries (an Urban-Rural divide) which is more pronounced in the Global South and is significantly impacting social and economic development [1].

United Nations' SDG 9.c seems to suggest that the main issue concerning the Digital Divide is having universal and affordable access to the Internet. While this is indeed an important factor in the Global South, the starting point and hypothesis underlying this project is that more variables/factors are involved, in particular: (i) the local content, relevance and salience of offered Internet

L. Hagedorn et al. (Eds.): DIGHUM 2025, LNCS 16319, pp. 83–93, 2026.
https://doi.org/10.1007/978-3-032-11108-1_6

information; (ii) the local language(s) and their modality (speech; given high levels of illiteracy) in which Internet information is provided.

Decolonizing the Internet, connecting the unconnected, and closing the digital divide, does not just reside in having affordable Internet access everywhere. It is also in the ability (i) to provision locally important information (ii) in the languages and modalities people are familiar with. The project undertakes to address both variables/factors (i) and (ii). We do so by participatory field experimentations in collaboration with rural communities in northern Ghana. The project's focus is: (i) communications to and from people on highly relevant local domains such as weather/climate or market price information as pertaining to farming in the Sahel; (ii) delivering such information via local-language voice-based systems in a domain-focused speech vocabulary that is crowd-sourced from rural communities themselves.

This suggests the use of Artificial Intelligence (AI), which in recent years, has aided in the development of many solutions around the world in numerous fields. It has therefore become imperative to investigate how AI can make impact in resource-constrained environments. In this paper, we therefore look at an innovative and practical example of how AI can be leveraged for digital information access in resource-constrained environments and explain why the concept of stakeholder and community participation is imperative right from the ideating phase.

2   Methodology

The research adapts a Participatory Action Research (PAR) methodology where individuals and communities are conceived of as first-class partners in a co-creation. This is in contrast to certain social science approaches whereby people (whether called objects, subjects, or even research participants) are in fact considered as "observed entities" by a value-neutral academic "spectator" researcher, as for example is the case in empiricist variable-oriented hypothesis-testing [2,3]. A general overview of PAR is found, e.g., in [4]. As a methodological paradigm, PAR has a long history and tradition of emancipatory aims and roots [5,6] and so fits well into critical indigenous [7] and decolonizing methodologies [8,9]. With respect to the design and deployment, we employ Design Science methodology for Information Systems and Software Engineering as explicated in [10] that is concerned with constructing, testing and evaluating ICT/IS artefacts in interaction with their real-world context. This methodology is central and key to the research, as failures in ICT implementations in the Global South have shown that a human-centered approach is not only helpful but imperative to successful design, adoption and use [11–13].

In this research, we begin this process by way of stakeholder meetings with community members, community leaders, farmers, agricultural extension workers, agricultural researchers, climate experts, linguistics experts, AI experts, etc. The various meetings and engagements led to a stakeholder workshop where, with the end-users (farmers from the targeted communities) as the main focus, we delved into the various aspects of the research question. Day 1 of the workshop had participants formed into break-out sessions consisting of a combination of expertise. A typical group contained about 9 members including 2 farmers (one male, one female), a moderator and scribe (mostly a core team member), and about 5 others ranging from ICT4D Researchers, AI Experts, Linguists, etc. Day 2 had a different structure; groups were structured based on expertise; 2 AI Groups (AI Experts, AI Enthusiasts, Programmers,....), 1 Language Group (Linguistic Experts, Media Experts, Native Dagbanli Speakers,...), 2 Climate and Farmer Group (Meteo Experts, Agriculture Experts, Farmers,....).

This further led to a larger community engagement at the communities, where the team held focus group discussions (FGDs) with almost 100 community members in three separate groups; Men, Women and Youth. These focus group discussions centred on the same concepts from the workshop; ICTs, Farming, Climate and Language, but broken down for the understanding of a wider audience for discussion. For the most part, these discussions reiterated the accuracy of the information that was teased out during the sessions. In addition to the knowledge gleaned for the continuation of the project, the FGDs were recorded and kept for future use.

The result of these in-depth deliberations was a detailed road-map resulting from the research question, but most importantly, in context of the local situation and centered on the end-users and stakeholders.

3   Implementation and Intermediary Results

To realize the project's goal of implementing a domain-focused Automatic Speech Recognition (ASR) model for a small indigenous language (Dagbani, spoken by approximately 3 Million people in the Northern Region of Ghana), it was required to 1) obtain recorded fragments for words in the selected domain (we began with numbers 0 to 10, "yes" and "no"), 2) using Machine Learning, build a Natural Language Processing (NLP) model for our dataset, 3) incorporate our NLP model into a system that is usable by the local community.

For the first step, team members worked together with people within the target communities to build a crowdsourcing app[1] that permits users to record people pronouncing local words. These recordings will serve as training data for the machine learning model that will accurately convert Dagbani speech to text. The mobile application is developed with React Native and Expo. It offers an intuitive interface for capturing and submitting audio samples of local words. Utilizing the capabilities of mobile devices, the application ensures high-quality recordings. The app allows for the recording of voice fragments. A list of words are provided (currently; "yes", "no" and the numbers 1 to 10) which the user can select and then prompt a willing participant to record said word in a local language. The recorded fragments are stored (temporarily) on the device and can be later uploaded to our server (Firebase). Figure 1a shows a screenshot of the App.

---

[1] Source code will be linked.

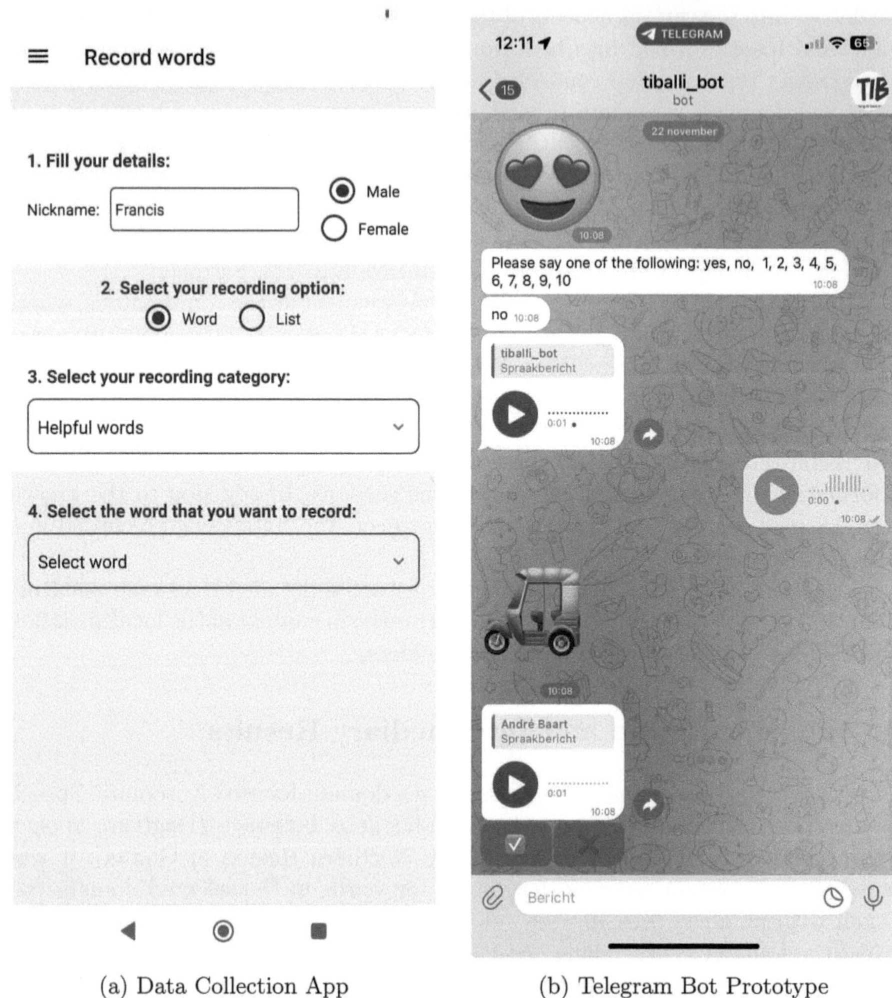

(a) Data Collection App	(b) Telegram Bot Prototype

Fig. 1. Screenshots of the tools developed.

This simple, but effective tool is used by enumerators to take recordings from community members. During the first iteration of the model, almost 4000 voice fragments were gathered in roughly 4 months with only a small data-collection team of about 8 users. The process of building this app was not trivial, especially in terms of PAR; ensuring that the end-users and stakeholders are involved in the process so as to iteratively build a solution that really works both technically and contextually in the local setting. The concept of a localized app, built with contributions for local communities and used by actual community members for crowd-sourcing in itself is quite novel in the context of resource-constrained communities and came about due to the user-centric, community-based, participatory mindset resulting from the methodologies learnt and used over the years [14].

AI Model Build Process. With the gathered training data of approximately 4000 utterances of Dagbani words, an AI model was trained. The base model used was Wav2Vec Massively Multilingual Speech, by Meta [15]. This is a model based on the well-known wav2vec2 architecture that is pre-trained on 1100 languages. We fine-tuned this model, using the training data of our limited initial vocabulary (yes, no, 0 through 10). This resulted in a model that is tuned to these specific words and will only give back results that fall in this vocabulary.

Telegram Bot and Test. In order to test the model, we built a Telegram bot that 'parrots back' the user. We chose Telegram as it is well suited for rapid development of prototypes. The prototype bot expects a voice message from the user, containing one of the words in the vocabulary. This message is then processed by the ASR model, which results in a written version of what the user said. This text is then converted back to speech (using the slot-and-filler method [16]) and sent as a voice-message back to the user. The user can then listen to the response of the bot, and confirm whether the result was correct or not. We included two rapid-response buttons, a green checkmark (correct) and a red cross (incorrect), which the user can use to indicate the quality of the result. The result is stored and can be used (together with the user input) as additional training data to improve the accuracy of the model in a later stage. Figure 1b shows a screenshot of the Telegram Bot.

The prototype was tested, as seen in Fig. 2 in the Tingoli community, which resulted in a near-perfect accuracy through the diverse population (young, old, male, female, etc.).

4   Lessons Learned and Reflections

The project's successes, so far (successful corpus collection, development of AI Model, implementation into a test system, testing in the field), shows us that the question of advanced AI methods (ML, NLP) being reconstructed so as to make the Internet more inclusive for communities in low-resource environments in the Global South, is doable, especially in a considerably short amount of time. The high accuracy of the AI model shows that it is not required to have an overly large dataset for successful ASR in small languages.

4.1   Insights from Community Engagement

The methodology employed in this research requires collaboration with many entities which all should focus on the community. Not surprisingly, there is little to no opposing needs or priorities shown within our select communities, nor between communities and stakeholders. This is because collaboration with these various stakeholders (farmers, agricultural institutes, Universities, Ministry of Agriculture, linguists, etc.) did not by any means start with us. These groups

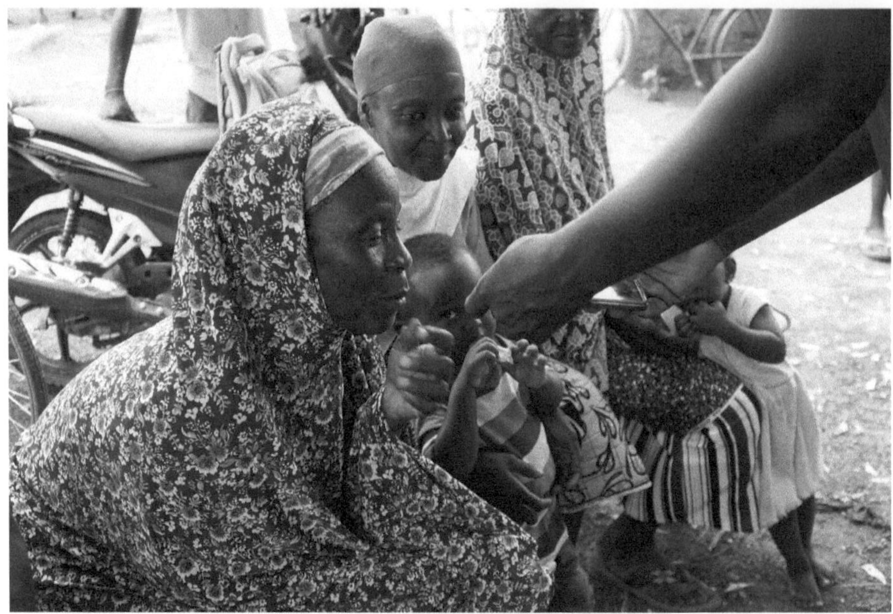

Fig. 2. Prototype under testing in the community.

(although perhaps not the same communities and individuals) have worked hand in hand for a long time in developmental issues especially pertaining to agriculture. Due to this, their challenges and needs have been clear to them over time.

This existing relationship enabled easier community engagement and collaboration between all involved entities. This led to very insightful information from the communities which aided the ongoing successes of this project. The nuances of dialects (which as "outsiders", we may have overlooked), the complexities of numbering (some numbers - e.g. 1 - have more than one word), the complexities of currencies (numbering for currencies is completely different, and more complicated, than counting), the traditional nuance in the non-word "Zero", which does not exist as a number, are some examples of intricacies that community engagement did not just bring to light, but helped to posit solutions for.

Beyond this, community members played a major role in iterative feedback for the design and build of the data collection app, select members were trained and handled the data collection process in the field, and large groups of community members participated in testing the ASR implementation.

We see from this experience (in addition to lessons learnt from numerous failed and successful ICT4D implementations) that the involvement of the intended users of solutions for low-resource environments is imperative. Regardless of the methodology used, there should be constant community and stakeholder involvement; remember, we are "plugging in" our innovation into their ecosystem to solve a problem they have identified together with us. The lifecycle of the solution development must therefore include end-user and stakeholder engagement, with prototyping where they can utilize the modules of your solution to see if they fit in with what they require and are inclined to use.

4.2   Inclusivity

The project was especially particular in ensuring the collective voice (literally and figuratively) of men, women and youth. Community engagement was structured to ensure that all opinions were heard. Moreover, the success of the ASR model required voice fragments from all genders and diverse age groups. For the most part, the opinions, challenges and suggested solutions were similar across genders and age groups. However, there are, of course, some areas of interest pertaining especially to men, women and youth respectively; while men and youth are mostly concerned with staple and cash crops (maize, rice, yam, etc.), women are more concerned with vegetables (pepper, tomatoes, green leafy vegetables, etc.) which tend to have different informational needs in terms of farming practices, market prices and climate. This, luckily, is not a huge challenge in this project, since there is available information on for all these crops and climate information provided can cater for all crops. It must however be ensured that any system built, for agriculture, is not biased towards crops that are of interest to a particular gender or age group, especially since at the onset, a few specific crops may be selected for the system.

4.3   Participant Benefits, Skills, and Ownership

The PAR-based methodology of the project enabled local data gathering, which involved local enumerators with financial remuneration to go out, record short voice bits, check the quality and write down what participants say. They also benefit from learning how to use a phone for recording, how to tag information, and how to fix simple technical problems. In the workshops, the volunteers saw how to run the little audio tool themselves and check the recordings. At the same time, students from the University for Development Studies gain from integration of aspects of the project to build and test the tools in their assignments and mini projects. This ensures that some technical skills are passed on after the pilot is over. Finally, the open Dagbani dataset [17] lists the Tingoli and Nyankpala communities as coauthors (with permission), operationalizing community credit and citation in perpetuity; this is a form of ownership that remains with the corpus and any future reuse.

4.4   Sustainability

Keeping the project alive requires several pieces. First is the technical aspect, which is sometimes overlooked. However, technical choices can have a huge impact on sustainability. The system runs on GSM-based IVR instead of heavy data apps, so it works on cheap phones and needs almost no Internet. The next step will use a small plug computer that does phonetic matching and a tiny speech recognizer, hosted at a local place like UDS/ISOC Ghana and looked after by Ghanaian IT staff, which cuts the need for big cloud services. Second, the partnership with UDS, ISOC Ghana, and SARI gives the project a solid home for hardware, data, and model files once the pilot is over. That makes it credible and gives logistical help. Third, the financial side remains stable by keeping the paid recorder jobs and turning some of them into local AI-tech apprenticeships, so people move from just collecting data to also testing and analyzing it. The whole tool chain – a tiny ReactNative plus Firebase app, a Docker container for speech matching, and simple bot fronts – is rolled out at the start of the rainy season, which helps repeat the work in new places.

4.5   Technical Challenges and Solutions

Our biggest technical challenge interestingly is not from Artificial Intelligence, as one may expect in this attempt to use advanced technologies in low-resource environments, but as a result of the initial information type selected for the use-case; climate. During the research, it was revealed that due to the lack of sufficient ground weather stations in Ghana, there is extremely low accuracy in weather prediction and as such it is not trusted by local farmers [18]. This meant that the information being delivered, if we attempted climate information in its current state, would be inaccurate and would result in mistrust of the system. To mitigate this, and also to continue the main aim of the project; using advanced AI methods (ML, NLP) to make the Internet more inclusive for communities in low-resource environments, we did two things; 1) launch a sub-project on improving climate information by resourcing local weather information and 2) focus on readily available and more accurate, but also very relevant information; market prices.

4.6   Broader Implications for Web and AI

The same principles that have governed the successful ICT solutions in low-resource environments that provide information from the web (example in [19]) thus far are largely the same principles required for successful use of AI for solutions in low-resource environments, but even to a much larger extent. The fathers of the Internet have at recent times mentioned how colonized their invention has become and how on hindsight it would have been better to have certain voices at the start, which was not the case. The same "mistake" should not be repeated in the AI revolution, especially in solutions for marginalized communities.

The successes of this project thus far shows us that community involvement is as paramount as the technical skills needed to build these solutions. More so, it is imperative that the technical designers of these solutions have a good understanding of the local context, which comes from the communities and stakeholders, inherently forming an inter-disciplinary team albeit not necessarily an academic one. This leads to a human system, literally built by the people, for the people.

Lastly, the idea of a participatory design process focused in the field directly promotes decolonization. In this project, the idea is local, the sourced voice data is local, the voice data collection process is local, the NLP model is based on this local data, testing and evaluations are done locally in the field. The data to be shared may be local or not, but again, this is based on the needs and wants of the communities. This already combats issues like bias in our AI model. There is of course still reliance on external servers and LLM architecture which in time can also be localized. We wish to gradually shift the dependence on large technology companies on the road to decolonization [20].

5   Future Work

The project will build a larger corpus on numbering, currencies and crops. This will follow the same methodology and will result in a local-based ASR system that community members can interact with to obtain web-based market prices of crops from different parts of the country. Future directions will also involve a look at alternative methods of building ASR. One promising direction is the concept of phonetic-based ASR methods which will greatly reduce the need for large datasets for building ASRs for small languages.

Acknowledgments. This work was supported by the Internet Society Foundation (https://www.isocfoundation.org/), the CSIR-Savanna Agriculture Research Institute, Ghana (https://csir-sari.org/) and the Web Alliance for Regreening in Africa (W4RA) (https://w4ra.org/), with deep gratitude to Wilhelm Nomu Kutah, Gideon Amakama Ali, Bram Kreuger, Chris van Aart, Hans Akkermans, members of the Internet Society Ghana Chapter (https://isoc.gh/), and the people of Tingoli and Nyankpala in the Tolon District of Ghana for their enthusiastic participation and insights.

References

1. Ragnedda, M., Muschert, G.: The Digital Divide: The Internet and Social Inequality in International Perspective (2013)
2. Robson, C., McCartan, K.: Real World Research, 4th edn. Wiley, Chichester, UK (2016)
3. Johnson, C.W., Parry, D.C.: Fostering Social Justice Through Qualitative Inquiry. Taylor & Francis Group (2022)
4. Reason, P., Bradbury, H.: Handbook of Action Research. Sage Publications Ltd. (2006)
5. Freire, P.: Pedagogy of the Oppressed. Continuum (2000)
6. Borda, O.F.: Investigating reality in order to transform it: the Colombian experience. Dialectical Anthropol. 4(1), 33–55 (1979). http://www.jstor.org/stable/29789952
7. Denzin, N.K.: Handbook of Critical and Indigenous Methodologies. SAGE (2008)

8. Kovach, M.: Indigenous Methodologies: Characteristics, Conversations, and Contexts. University of Toronto Press (2010)
9. Smith, L.T.: Decolonizing Methodologies: Research and Indigenous Peoples (2012)
10. Wieringa, M.: What to account for when accounting for algorithms: a systematic literature review on algorithmic accountability. In: Proceedings of the 2020 Conference on Fairness, Accountability, and Transparency (2020). https://doi.org/10.1145/3351095.3372833
11. Benjamin, P.: Community development and democratisation through information technology. In: Reinventing Government in the Information Age. Routledge (1999)
12. Tettey, W.: The media and democratization in Africa: contributions, constraints and concerns of the private press. Media Cult. Soc. **23**(1), 5–31 (2000)
13. Sharma, V.V., Rao, K.V.: Bridging the digital divide: information kiosks in rural India. In: Rural India: Achieving Millennium Development Goals and Grassroots Development, vol. 383 (2009)
14. Panayiotou, A., Saa-Dittoh, F., Bon, A.: Resourcing small indigenous languages in the field – designing a user-centered data collection method for automatic speech recognition. In: Proceedings of ICT4SD 2023, vol. 3, Goa, India (2023)
15. Pratap, V., et al.: Scaling speech technology to 1,000+ languages. arXiv:2305.13516 [cs.CL] (2023)
16. Baart, A., Bon, A., de Boer, V., Dittoh, F., Tuijp, W., Akkermans, H.: Affordable voice services to bridge the digital divide: presenting the Kasadaka platform. In: Escalona, M.J., Domínguez Mayo, F., Majchrzak, T.A., Monfort, V. (eds.) WEBIST 2018. LNBIP, vol. 372, pp. 195–220. Springer, Cham (2019). https://doi.org/10.1007/978-3-030-35330-8_10
17. Francis Saa-Dittoh and Tingoli and Nyankpala Communities of the Northern Region of Ghana. Recordings of spoken Dagbani for the letters zero to ten and the words yes and no. Zenodo (2024). https://doi.org/10.5281/zenodo.13284004
18. Nyadzi, E., Werners, S.E., Biesbroek, R., Ludwig, F.: Towards weather and climate services that integrate indigenous and scientific forecasts in Ghana. Environ. Dev. **42**, 100698 (2022). https://doi.org/10.1016/j.envdev.2021.100698
19. Dittoh, F., Akkermans, H., de Boer, V., Bon, A., Tuyp, W., Baart, A.: Tibaŋsim: Information access for low-resource environments. In: Yang, X.-S., Sherratt, S., Dey, N., Joshi, A. (eds.) Proceedings of Sixth International Congress on Information and Communication Technology. LNNS, vol. 235, pp. 675–683. Springer, Singapore (2022). https://doi.org/10.1007/978-981-16-2377-6_62
20. Wieringa, M.: What to account for when accounting for algorithms: a systematic literature review on algorithmic accountability. In: Proceedings of the 2020 Conference on Fairness, Accountability, and Transparency (2020). https://doi.org/10.1145/3442188.3445885

Normative Challenges in Europe's Digital Infrastructure: A Transdisciplinary Exploration of Smart Meter Data Sharing

Nikolas Zechner[1]([✉]) [iD], Florian Güldenpfennig[1,2] [iD], and Michael Funk[1] [iD]

[1] Faculty of Computer Science, University of Vienna, Vienna, Austria
`nikolas.zechner@univie.ac.at` , `florian.gueldenpfennig@univie.ac.at` ,
`michael.funk@univie.ac.at`
[2] German University of Applied Sciences (DHAW), Potsdam, Germany

Abstract. With its digital strategy "Shaping Europe's Digital Future", the EU is decisively pursuing the goal of building an innovative data economy. The central building blocks of this strategy are interoperable data spaces, which are intended to enable the sovereign and trustworthy exchange of data across application sectors and national borders. However, despite explicitly formulated regulatory principles, it remains unclear how these can be made tangible in concrete implementation. This paper offers a conceptual contribution to the design of data spaces by examining the diverse perspectives involved and the value conflicts that arise between them. Drawing on our experience as designers in an EU energy data space project, we use the notion of trustworthiness as an entry point to explore these tensions: How can systems be designed in ways that meet users' expectations of trust, while also aligning with ethical, legal, economic, technical, and political demands? To ground our reflection, we complement it with empirical insights from a survey (n = 24) and qualitative interviews with potential users. In our analysis, we follow basic principles of Green Technology and Digital Humanism. Rather than offering solutions, this paper aims to clarify the conceptual problem space and support critical reflection in future design and governance processes.

Keywords: Energy Data Space · Smart Meter · Energy Transition · Prosumer Economy · User Perspective · Ethics · Digital Capitalism

1 Introduction

Towards European Data Spaces. A few years ago, digital *data spaces* were proclaimed the central infrastructure of the European data economy [5]. A data space refers to a decentralized data ecosystem in which participants can securely share, access, and use data based on common rules and standards, without relinquishing control over their data [2] – an endeavor that deeply resonates with the aims of Digital Humanism, which similarly seeks to establish guiding rules and

L. Hagedorn et al. (Eds.): DIGHUM 2025, LNCS 16319, pp. 94–109, 2026.
https://doi.org/10.1007/978-3-032-11108-1_7

standards for technology design in order to aid the people [34]. With initiatives such as GAIA-X [18] and the provision of legal frameworks such as the Data Governance Act [6] and the Data Act [11], the European Union (EU) aims to enable trustworthy and sovereign handling of data. This political strategy is guided by principles such as Human-Centeredness and Transparency. These values are echoed in related regulatory efforts, such as the Ethics Guidelines for Trustworthy AI [19], and most recently the AI Act [15], both of which emphasize accountability, fairness, and respect for fundamental rights in the design of digital systems. Ultimately, the EU's goal is to create (digital) data space infrastructures that are both technologically powerful and based on European values. This anchoring in European values is a core concern of Digital Humanism, a concept prominently expressed by Julian Nida-Rümelin, who emphasizes the fundamental role of the Enlightenment and humanistic ideals in shaping the digital transformation in a human-centered way [26,27].

Different Data Space Domains. Data spaces are typically specialized in a particular type of data, such as the Agriculture Data Space [8] or Health Data Space [7]. In this paper, we will focus specifically on the energy sector, directing our analysis and considerations toward this critical infrastructure. Its importance is particularly heightened in the context of the European Green Deal [4] and the transition to green energy, which require efficient data sharing frameworks.

Normative Considerations from the Outset. We argue, in line with the principles of Digital Humanism, for the need to engage with normative considerations from the very outset, rather than addressing ethical issues only retrospectively. Tackling the complex challenges involved in data space design, requires a transdisciplinary approach at the intersection of various fields like computer science/technology, social sciences, and Philosophy. Therefore, this paper follows/probes an integrative and iterative research strategy that includes technical design practice, engineering, an empirical survey, and an ethical assessment (as will be discussed later with reference to Fig. 4). This goal can be substantiated, among other things, by the fact that decisive factors in data space design are underdetermined. While their objectives are clearly formulated, the specific approach for implementing the proclaimed principles remains open.

Different Roles and Interests in the Design of Data Spaces. How, for example, data sovereignty and trustworthiness can actually be made tangible for people in practical application depends on the skill of the operators and developers of data spaces and corresponding applications. Taking a further step back to gain a clearer view of the situation quickly reveals that things are even more complex or more 'messy'. Numerous roles and interests in are intertwined in the design of data spaces. Just to mention the most generic and obvious ones (see also Figs. 1 and 3, introduced later in the paper):

– *Philosophers* have been thinking critically about Europe's digital infrastructure for quite some time [32] as evidenced, for example, by the Ethics Guidelines for Trustworthy AI [19].

- *Legislators* want to provide a framework for creating data spaces that are trustworthy for citizens. Among many other reasons, this is important in order to ensure the transition to a sustainable energy economy.
- From a plain *technical perspective*, mechanisms must then be developed that allow this large-scale project to be efficiently implemented in accordance with the necessary technical security standards. Compliance with data protection must be guaranteed so that there can be no data breaches, for example, and thus no damage or loss of trust.
- The *developers and operators* of data spaces naturally also want to gain the trust of their users, not least in order to be able to earn money.
- Thus, the legal framework must allow data to be used in an *economically viable* way. Data protection that prevents any business ideas from being realized would make the whole endeavor impossible. At this point at the latest, critics from the field of Digital Humanism will point to the concept of *Surveillance Capitalism* [16,36] – the systemic commercialization of personal data under the guise of innovation and user benefit. Ultimately, the decision of whether to trust or not rests with the *individual*. However, it also depends on the societal context of individual actions, including humanistic values, legal legislation, and cultural habits [17]. Trust in technology depends on various factors [21, 29]. This makes the mix of involved perspectives complex, to say the least.

Research Question and Contributions of the Present Paper. Against this broader backdrop, this paper turns to a concrete and technically relevant application: energy data spaces, with a particular focus on smart meter infrastructures. These systems hold significant potential for supporting Europe's energy transition, yet they also bring to the surface tensions between individual data sovereignty and collective sustainability goals. At the same time, the economic viability of data-driven services must be balanced with privacy concerns and user autonomy. This raises our central research question:

> *What are the main normative challenges in designing energy data spaces, especially in the context of smart meter implementations?*

To explore this, we build on our practical experience in a European data space project in the energy domain. We enrich this perspective through preliminary empirical findings from a survey and user interviews, which reveal insights into trust and consent, and perceived risks. In addition, we draw on philosophical reasoning (combining ethical guidance with critical reflection) to illuminate the normative foundations of responsible infrastructures.

The paper proceeds as follows: Sect. 2 introduces the political and technical context of energy data spaces, with a focus on smart meters and EU regulation. Section 3 presents conceptual work, discussing the intersection of Digital Capitalism and the energy transition. Section 4 outlines our empirical approach and highlights insights from user surveys and interviews. Section 5 offers a broader discussion of normative tensions across individual, political, and economic perspectives. Finally, Sect. 6 concludes the paper.

2   Smart Meters and the Role of Energy Data Spaces in the EU

The European Union (EU) has introduced regulatory frameworks such as the directive 2009/72/EC and directive (EU) 2019/944 which were set up to change and liberalize the Union's energy market and promoting the energy transition of the EU [12,14]. These liberalization policies of energy markets have shown over the years that they have effectively reduced CO2-emissions, particularly in European high-income countries by promoting renewable energy and eliminating trade barriers [28]. Directive 2019/944 further emancipates the member state's energy consumers in the energy market by establishing an "Active Customer"- someone who can participate in the internal energy market, thus enabling a "Prosumer Economy" [30]. The directive also states that the absence of real-time or near real-time information on consumers' energy consumption has prevented them from being active participants in the market. As a result, energy consumers and their households must be equipped with smart meters that can record and provide this data.

These meters are also beneficial for the grid, as distribution system operators (DSOs) and transmission system operators (TSOs) can better monitor the current energy load demand for energy distribution and transmission [13,25]. Additionally, the collected data should be transparent and easily accessible to end users, enabling them to share or transfer it to third parties in line with their right to data portability under EU data protection regulations [14]. However, the directives do not clearly specify how data sharing and accessibility should be implemented.

Therefore, the European strategy for data has resulted in the creation of "Common European Data Spaces" that aim to ensure that data will become available for the economy and society while maintaining that the individual who created the data will remain in control of it [10]. The concept and key features of European data spaces include the open participation of all individuals, a secure and privacy-ensuring infrastructure, clearly defined access rules, respect for EU laws and values, the ability for data holders to share information, and empowerment to make data available for reuse, either for free or against compensation. [9]. Nagel et al. defined four design principles for European data spaces to be built on, which are data sovereignty, data level playing field, decentralized infrastructure and public-private governance. Furthermore, building blocks can be categorized into technical which deal with the data exchange and governance blocks for access policies ensuring trustworthy exchange [24].

In terms of energy-related data spaces, the main idea is that making data more available will increase the efficiency of energy systems and operations. Consequentially, through the smart meter rollout, this data can also be integrated into data spaces which further enable unique use cases such as predictive maintenance or energy management for buildings [1]. There are many European projects such as IntNET, OMEGA-X and EDDIE [9] that are creating various energy related data spaces for specific use cases within this sector and enable data exchange across national borders [9]. Within these projects, energy data exchange is a core component and functionality. As a result, various perspectives—such as economic, legal, and user viewpoints—often come into conflict. We identified a gap in how the user perspective is addressed within energy data spaces and argue that the user's role in data exchange should be approached more thoughtfully.

3   Smart Meter Data: Usage in the Context of the Energy Transition and Digital Capitalism

As discussed, there is a challenge within the EU's data strategy, particularly in the creation of data spaces and in meeting the expectations of various perspectives, including legal, economic, user-centric viewpoints etc. On one hand, privacy and trust must be secured; on the other, data should be available for the economy, thus enabling novel service ideas for the energy market and advancing green and sustainable technology for the energy transition, for instance.

How Smart Meter Data Reveal Behavior. However, with these services relying so heavily on data and profiting from it, it is unclear how else this data can be used beyond its original use case once it is in the company's possession. Energy data from smart meters, for example, is very sensitive and can reveal a lot about a household, such as which devices are used, when tenants are home, and their usage patterns, which can shed light on their behavior [3]. This can uncover what Shoshana Zuboff calls "behavioral surplus", referring to the additional data collected beyond what is necessary for the service [36]. As a consequence, there are immense privacy issues to consider when sharing this information, as energy data has the potential for further intrusive data mining and collection practices for commercial gain, similar to those of social media companies. Through "Surveillance Capitalism", these services can profit even more from customers' energy data [22]. As a consequence, from a user perspective, these immense data-hungry services could feel overwhelming for a typical European household, as their personal data is a gold mine, an analogy used by Zuboff [36] as well.

Regulating the Digital Energy Economy. At the same time, Allison Stanger [31] argues that Big Tech companies are not as powerful as they appear, as there is a difference between voluntary and involuntary surveillance. These companies may only seem to have total information control if citizens allow them to commercialize their personal data. The primary danger appears when initially consented data is sold to third parties by the data-driven service. Furthermore, Stanger argues that the problem lies not with Big Data technology or the use of personal data for behavior change itself, but rather with whether it is used for positive or negative purposes and without the user's consent or knowledge. Therefore, as the GDPR (General Data Protection Regulation) and DSA (Digital Service Act) have laid the first steps for promoting a fair playground for a modern digital economy, third-party markets for personal data should be further regulated.

Consequentially, Paul Timmers [33] mentions that in the digital age, a central problem in developing policies for sovereignty lies in the way digital technologies are advancing in collecting information from citizens and interacting with them. He argues that in this new era, policies for sovereignty must equally take geopolitical and technological perspectives into account. This highlights a transformation in traditional policymaking, as the unique speed, scale, and impact of digital technologies are increasingly influencing the focus on achieving digital strategic autonomy.

Müller and Kettemann [23] further highlight the European Union's growing regulatory response to the societal and economic power of digital platforms through legal instruments such as the GDPR, DSA, DMA (Digital Markets Act), and the proposed AI Act. These regulations aim to balance innovation and data-driven services with the protection of fundamental rights, such as privacy, freedom of expression, and contractual freedom. A key aspect of their analysis is the EU's attempt to enforce a form of horizontal fundamental rights accountability, where private tech platforms—especially those with systemic influence—are increasingly obligated to respect users' rights. In the context of energy data, this regulatory trajectory is crucial, as it seeks to prevent the unchecked commodification of personal data while enabling innovation for sustainability.

Furthermore, the political and economic perspectives are also seeking to advance Green Technology to transition to a sustainable economy, as seen with the mentioned EU directives and the deployment of smart meters. However, the desired energy transition is highly complex, with social, legal, economic, and climatic factors playing a role. Aleksander Jakimowicz [20] writes that with the active customer-which is now enabled through the EU regulations- playing a vital role, such a "Prosumer" economic system would also involve performing free labor for a system that benefits from it at the expense of personal freedoms and privacy. This highlights the need to critically examine how participatory roles in digital energy systems are structured, and to what extent they align with broader goals of autonomy, fairness, and transparency.

Navigating Competing Values. It therefore remains questionable whether these data-driven services, the sharing of sensitive data (e.g., energy data from smart meters) and the Prosumer Economy are the right approaches to tackling climate change and improving energy economy with novel innovations and efficiency, especially when sacrificing user perspectives in terms of privacy and sovereignty. It is also unclear how the various perspectives should be weighed to advance the green energy transition, which is being implemented through policies such as the European Green Deal (see Sect. 5). This includes balancing individual user rights, the perspective of progressing the green energy transition with sustainability as a guiding principle, and the Digital Capitalism perspective, which involves collecting information on energy usage behavior to provide solutions for the collective energy transition. Figure 1 provides an overview of the normative problem area to illustrate the challenges of technical development and applied Digital Humanism.

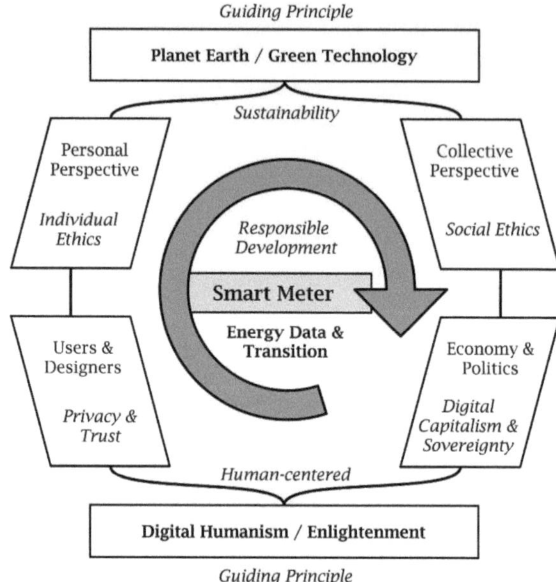

Fig. 1. Problem area of smart meters and energy data, highlighting tensions between ethics and societal frameworks within Green Technology and Digital Humanism.

To further understand the different views, as well as the interplay and potential clash of interests, additional research is needed. Therefore, we explored the user perspective in a practical, empirical way in terms of what is more important for the individual while sharing smart meter data: an innovative, novel service that helps change energy behavior by providing data analytical insights from the smart meter data, thus saving energy and using it more efficiently for a sustainable energy system, or the protection of personal rights such as privacy.

4   Insights from Practice: Context and User Voices

During our work on an EU project on energy data spaces, we encountered the issue of *users' trust* in our designed system on numerous occasions (see [35] for a description of the design process). Specifically, our task was to import our users' electricity data from their smart meters through a data space to a service that processes the data for visualizations and data analytical functionalities[1]. With their consent, we were able to create relatively simple but effective visualizations of the consumption data. This enabled them, among other things, to track their electricity consumption, estimate their costs, view forecasts for the future, and

---

[1] Technically, the data space is designed as a foundational framework that aggregates users' data from diverse sources. With the users' consent, third parties can access this data to develop their own applications that make use of it. The application mentioned in this paper thus represents a third-party use case within the data space.

even estimate their ecological footprint: all potentially useful functions for which the user must give their consent to share their energy data with our system or data space.

From a technical perspective, a lower layer of the data space took some of the work off our hands. We were able to use a ready-made mechanism that obtained the user's consent via a small web mask and then automatically retrieved the data from the user's respective energy consumer. The system also managed how long this consent was valid for us, and once it expired, no more data would flows to us. It was our responsibility to process the energy data as soon as it was available in the data space and, of course, not to pass it on or use it inappropriately. We were also responsible for designing the user interface that informs the user about the consent form and the subsequent processing steps; this gave us a great deal of freedom in the design, which had a significant impact on user trust.

In numerous discussions in the context of the project and interviews with potential users, the topic of trust came up repeatedly. For example, when asked for feedback on a concept, one person said: *"Well, I don't know if I really need it. Your app is certainly interesting, but it's also interesting to see when I'm not at home. And what else are you trying to sell me with it?"* This statement certainly reflected a healthy skepticism about the loss of control over one's own data. For example, if the wrong people get hold of consumption patterns, they can potentially deduce when the house is unoccupied from the electricity consumption, according to the interviewee's assumption (see Sect. 3). This and similar statements prompted us to deepen our research by designing a survey and conducting targeted interviews.

4.1 Survey and Interviews

Survey: To better understand whether and under what conditions potential users would trust and adopt the system, we introduced it to 24 individuals and walked them through a detailed demonstration of the web interface. Subsequently, we invited them to complete a 14-item survey designed to encourage honest and low-pressure responses. They received no financial compensation, and data was processed anonymously. The questions focused on a) functionality, b) trust in the system, and c) whether they would use it or even pay for it. As usual, they were formulated as statements, and participants had to indicate on a five-point Likert scale how much they agreed with them, ranging from 1 (strongly disagree) to 5 (strongly agree).

In the following, we will focus on the questions (statements) concerning part b – trust. These are shown in Fig. 2 with abbreviated designations. In addition, the questions from part c and one exemplary question from part a are included in this figure. This latter question from part a – "Visualization is useful"[2] – was included into the figure to provide the readers with an impression of whether

---

[2] Full statement in survey: "The visualization of my historical energy consumption in kWh is useful.".

the system was considered useful by the respondents. With an average response across genders of M = 4.21 (SD = 0.83), this result clearly favors our application.

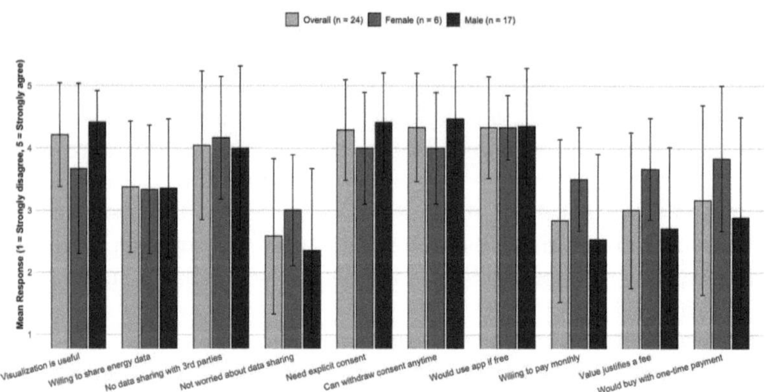

Fig. 2. Mean agreement ratings (±1 SD) across ten statements on energy data usage and app adoption, by gender (Female, Male) and total sample (Overall). Higher values indicate stronger agreement (1 = Strongly disagree, 5 = Strongly agree).

Figure 2 presents mean agreement ratings and standard deviations (SD) for all ten statements concerning the use of energy data and app-related attitudes. Results are reported separately for female (n = 6) and male (n = 17) respondents, as well as for the overall sample (n=24) including all gender identities[3]. We go on to highlight trust-related results.

Willingness to share energy data showed similar values across groups, with the overall mean at 3.38 (SD = 1.06), females at 3.33 (SD = 1.03), and males slightly higher at 3.35 (SD = 1.11). The demand for *no data sharing with third parties* was generally high, especially among females (M = 4.17, SD = 0.98), while males and the overall sample averaged 4.00 and 4.04 (SD = 1.32 and 1.20, respectively). Conversely, when asked whether they were *not worried about data sharing*, agreement was lower overall (M = 2.58 SD = 1.25), with females reporting slightly more agreement (M = 3.00, SD = 0.89) than males (M = 2.35, SD = 1.32). The importance of *giving explicit consent before data is processed* received high agreement across all groups, with an overall mean of 4.29 (SD = 0.81), females scoring slightly lower (M = 4.00, SD = 0.89), and males higher (M = 4.41, SD = 0.80). Agreement was similarly high regarding the *ability to withdraw consent at any time*, with an overall mean of 4.33 (SD = 0.87), females at 4.00 (SD = 0.89), and males at 4.47 (SD = 0.87).

Overall, the findings suggest a general skepticism toward sharing energy data, with participants placing high importance on privacy and control. Agreement

---

was particularly strong for explicit consent and the ability to withdraw it at any time. Opposition to third-party data sharing was also high, while few agreed they were unconcerned about data sharing. Due to the small sample size, comparisons remain descriptive and should not be interpreted as statistically significant.

Interviews: Throughout the project, we further conducted numerous interviews with the same target group to gather feedback on our system's design. We were interested in many aspects, such as users' attitudes toward environmental protection (a key objective of our app) and its overall usability. However, what stood out most were the numerous curious and at times skeptical to even heated reactions regarding the topic of data sharing.

During the analysis of the interviews, participants' statements frequently clustered into five distinct groups that emerged inductively from the data: *Resisters*, who reject or avoid the technology; *Suspicious Users*, who are not categorically opposed but remain highly cautious and alert to potential risks; *Strategic Users*, who weigh benefits and drawbacks before engaging; *Fine-Print Readers*, who carefully scrutinize terms and conditions; and *Anonymous Users*, who seek to prevent traceability by obscuring their identity[4].

Resisters, for example, rejected the idea behind data spaces outright and made this clear through statements such as: "I don't like the idea of surveilling nor the thought of control."[5] Table 1 presents illustrative quotes from all groups. Note, the categorization is intended as an exploratory analytical tool to help structure and interpret the data. It does not imply clear-cut typologies, as individual respondents may express views that span multiple categories.

4.2   Pulling the Empirical Insights Together

While the empirical impressions presented here do not claim to be generalizable, they do provide interesting insights into the concerns that preoccupy users of data spaces. The above statements indicate that one of the target groups of energy data spaces (young people with an affinity for technology) have many questions about data security, *etc.*. They stated that they attach great importance to being able to determine exactly who can access their data, for what purpose, and for how long. Through our empirical survey, we observed a willingness to share energy data; however, there are concerns regarding privacy. Consequently, a trustworthy environment is needed, as seen from the quotes from the interviews. Data-driven energy services and the underlying data space used for data transmission should be designed in such a way that people are aware of where their data is going, what it is used for, and have control over who can access it.

---

[4] The user type labels are deliberately descriptive and somewhat exaggerated to illustrate the salient characteristics observed in the data. They serve as analytical tools rather than definitive classifications.

[5] The interviews were conducted in German and translated into English for this paper.

Table 1. Overview of different kinds of users as emerged from explorative interviews

User Group	Representative Quote
Resister	"I don't like the idea of surveilling nor the thought of control."
Suspicious User	"Yes, I would … if I don't then start getting 10 messages from my electricity supplier like: 'We've seen this and that, would you like to change your tariff?' So, only if it's not connected to that kind of thing."
Fine-Print Reader	"Yes, I would share my data. I would carefully read where exactly my data is being stored and whether it remains stored locally."
Strategic User	"It really depends on the exchange … on what I get in return for sharing my data."
Anonymous User	"Yes, as long as it's not personalized and is shared anonymously."

5 Discussion

This section systematically structures the complex problem area of energy data spaces and examines the inherent normative conflicts of values from different perspectives. It therefore provides some answers to our initial question: *What are the main normative challenges in designing energy data spaces, especially in the context of smart meter implementations?* Fig. 1 in Sect. 3 illustrates an overview of the problem area, flanked by the normative principles of Human-Centeredness and Green Technology. Previous sections have shown that the main normative challenges arise at the intersection of a) personal practice (individual ethics), including the perspectives of designers and users, and b) societal embedding (social ethics), including legal regulation, the economy, and political power (Fig. 3).

Some of the main challenges arise at the intersection of individual users and the economy: Earning money (Digital Capitalism) versus individual autonomy (privacy and user trust). Technical developers, including designers, engineers, etc., also run into a normative conflict with legal regulation when it comes to the freedom of technological innovation. Note that these conflicts are somewhat generic and cannot be reduced to energy data management or smart meters. However, they are intertwined at the central nexus of shifting from energy consumers to Prosumers (see the central box in Fig. 3). On the one hand, the shift towards independent energy producers who engage in reliable technical practices could be considered the ideal of Digital Humanism and the guiding principle of Human-Centeredness. On the other hand, Prosumers gain joint responsibility for the energy infrastructure, which extends beyond individual freedom of energy consumption. With this, citizens are placed at the intersection of political power and data monopolies. They become increasingly important players in terms of critical infrastructure and digital sovereignty. In short: One of the main

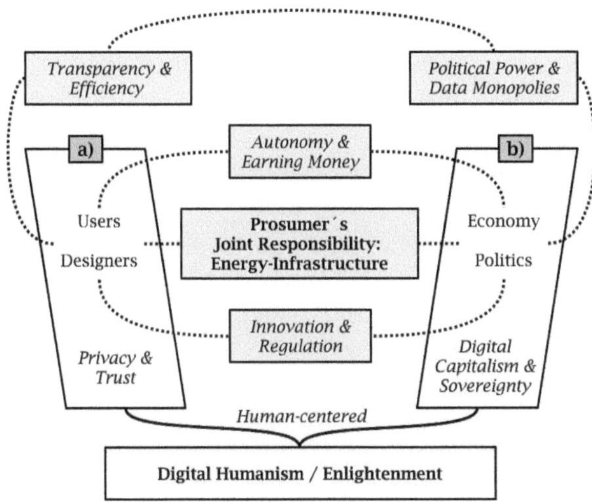

Fig. 3. Systematic structure of normative conflicts in using smart meters, showing prosumers' responsibility amid competing values.

challenges that needs further transdisciplinary investigation is reconciling the conflicting values of prosuming freedom in energy consumption and prosuming responsibility for critical infrastructure (the energy market).

Rather than offering definitive solutions, this discussion aims to stimulate thought and identify initial points for future normative analyses and design decisions. The conceptual analysis applied here allows us to differentiate the various relationships within the problem area more precisely. Some follow-up questions could be: How can we negotiate the design of human-centered, sustainable energy data spaces in a technological way? How can technical development, public interest, and individual user requirements be combined in the case of smart meter technologies and energy data services? Do we need the kind of producers that we have, and do we have the producers that we need from an ethical point

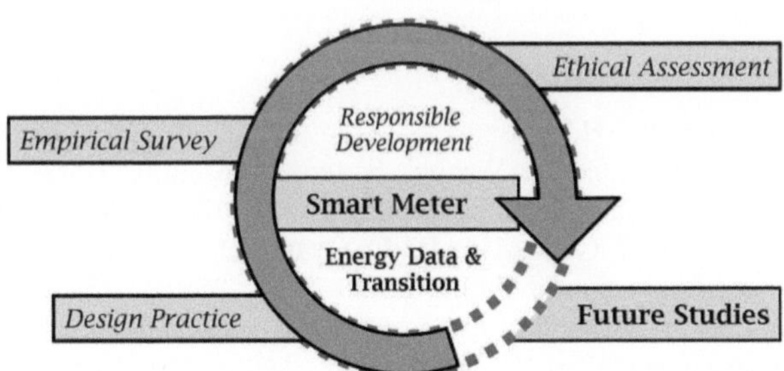

Fig. 4. Transdisciplinary integration toward ethically grounded design of smart meters and energy data spaces.

of view? How can transdisciplinary approaches and empirical user perspectives help address these tensions in practice? To shed more light on these issues, we encourage iterative and integrative research (Fig. 4).

6   Conclusion

During our work on energy data spaces, questions about data protection arose regularly. Potential users consistently expressed high expectations regarding data security. As developers, we were confronted with the challenge of translating these requirements into technical solutions. This ongoing confrontation with value-laden demands led us to a deeper inquiry into the normative foundations and ethical tensions involved in shaping digital infrastructures for the energy sector, particularly in the highly sensitive context of smart meter technology.

We approached this exploration through the guiding principles of Digital Humanism and Green Technology. Our specific methodology involved moving from empirical observations, gathered through surveys and interviews, toward philosophical reflection. This paper thus provides not only preliminary empirical data (Sect. 4) but also a conceptual mapping of the problem space that emerges around energy data spaces and smart meters (Fig. 1). It highlights how this space is structured by differing roles or perspectives and how it is framed by broader value systems. In addition, we outlined potential normative conflicts inherent in this field (Fig. 3). To support our analysis, we draw on the concept of Digital Capitalism, among other things (Sect. 3). We concluded with a sketch of transdisciplinary working processes (Fig. 4), an approach we are actively engaged in ourselves, that may offer a path toward more measured and ethically grounded design and implementation of smart meters and energy data spaces.

Acknowledgements. This work is conducted under the ambit of EDDIE—'European Distributed Data Infrastructure for Energy', co-funded by the European Union's Horizon Innovation Actions under grant agreement No.101069510. Funded by the European Union.

References

1. Berkhout, V., Frey, C., Hertweck, P., Nestle, D., Wickert, M.: Energy data space. In: Otto, B., ten Hompel, M., Wrobel, S. (eds.) Designing Data Spaces, pp. 329–341. Springer, Cham (2022). https://doi.org/10.1007/978-3-030-93975-5_20
2. Braud, A., Fromentoux, G., Radier, B., Le Grand, O.: The road to European digital sovereignty with Gaia-X and IDSA. IEEE Netw. **35**(2), 4–5 (2021). https://doi.org/10.1109/MNET.2021.9387709
3. Chen, D., Bovornkeeratiroj, P., Irwin, D., Shenoy, P.: Private memoirs of IoT devices: safeguarding user privacy in the IoT era. In: Proceedings of ICDCS, pp. 1327–1336 (2018). https://doi.org/10.1109/ICDCS.2018.00133
4. European Commission: The European Green Deal (2019). https://eur-lex.europa.eu/legal-content/EN/TXT/?uri=CELEX%3A52019DC0640

5. European Commission: Shaping Europe's digital future (2020). https://digital-strategy.ec.europa.eu/en. Accessed 08 July 2025

6. European Commission: European Data Governance Act (2022). https://digital-strategy.ec.europa.eu/en/policies/data-governance-act, regulation (EU) 2022/868 of 30 May 2022; entered into force on 23 June 2022, applicable since 24 September 2023

7. European Commission: Proposal for a Regulation on the European Health Data Space (2022). https://eur-lex.europa.eu/legal-content/EN/TXT/?uri=CELEX:52022PC0197, cOM(2022) 197 final

8. European Commission: Policy Brief – Rolling out the Common European Agricultural Data Space (2024). https://digital-strategy.ec.europa.eu/en/news/policy-brief-rolling-out-common-european-agricultural-data-space

9. European Commission: Common European Data Spaces (2025). https://digital-strategy.ec.europa.eu/en/policies/data-spaces. Accessed 8 July 2025

10. European Commission: European Strategy for Data (2025). https://digital-strategy.ec.europa.eu/en/policies/strategy-data. Accessed 8 July 2025

11. European Commission: The Data Act (2025). https://digital-strategy.ec.europa.eu/en/policies/data-act. Accessed 8 July 2025

12. European Parliament and the Council of the EU: Directive 2009/72/EC of the European Parliament and of the Council of 13 July 2009 concerning common rules for the internal market in electricity and repealing Directive 2003/54/EC (2009). https://eur-lex.europa.eu/legal-content/EN/TXT/?uri=CELEX:32009L0072. Accessed 07 July 2025

13. European Parliament and the Council of the EU: Directive (EU) 2019/944 of the EU Parliament and of the Council of 5 June 2019 on common rules for the internal market for electricity and amending Directive 2012/27/EU (2019). https://eur-lex.europa.eu/legal-content/EN/LSU/?uri=oj:JOL_2019_158_R_0004. Accessed 07 July 2025

14. European Parliament and the Council of the European Union: Directive (EU) 2019/944 of the EU Parliament and of the Council of 5 June 2019 on common rules for the int. Market for electricity and amending Directive 2012/27/EU (2019). https://eur-lex.europa.eu/eli/dir/2019/944/oj/eng. Accessed 07 July 2025

15. European Union: Regulation (EU) 2024/1689 of the European Parliament and of the Council of 13 June 2024 laying down harmonised rules on artificial intelligence (Artificial Intelligence Act). https://eur-lex.europa.eu/legal-content/EN/TXT/?uri=CELEX%3A32024R1689 (2024)

16. Fuchs, C.: Der digitale Kapitalismus: Arbeit. Entfremdung und Ideologie im Informationszeitalter. Arbeitsgesellschaft im Wandel, Beltz Juventa, Weinheim (2023)

17. Funk, M., Dieber, B., Pichler, H., Coeckelbergh, M.: Gamification of trust in HRI? In: Nørskov, M., Seibt, J., Quick, O.S. (eds.) Culturally Sustainable Social Robotics: Proceedings of Robophilosophy 2020; 18–21 August 2020, Aarhus University and online. Front. Artif. Intell. Appl. **335**, 632–642. IOS Press, Amsterdam, Berlin (2020)

18. GAIA-X AISBL: GAIA-X: A Federated Data Infrastructure for Europe (2020). https://www.gaia-x.eu. Accessed 08 July 2025

19. High-Level Expert Group on AI: Ethics Guidelines for Trustworthy AI (2019). https://digital-strategy.ec.europa.eu/en/library/ethics-guidelines-trustworthy-ai. accessed 10 July 2025

20. Jakimowicz, A.: The energy transition as a super wicked problem: the energy sector in the era of prosumer capitalism. Energies **15**(23), 9109 (2022)

21. Lankton, N.K., McKnight, D.H., Tripp, J.: Technology, humanness, and trust: rethinking trust in technology. J. Assoc. Inf. Syst. **16**(10), 880–918 (2015). https://doi.org/10.17705/1jais.00411
22. Levenda, A.M., Mahmoudi, D., Sussman, G.: The neoliberal politics of "smart": electricity consumption, household monitoring, and the enterprise form. Can. J. Commun. **40**(4), 615–636 (2015)
23. Müller, M., Kettemann, M.C.: European approaches to the regulation of digital technologies. In: Werthner, H., et al. (eds.) Introduction to Digital Humanism: A Textbook, pp. 623–637. Springer, Cham (2024). https://doi.org/10.1007/978-3-031-45304-5_39
24. Nagel, L., Lycklama, D.: How to build, run, and govern data spaces. In: Otto, B., ten Hompel, M., Wrobel, S. (eds) Designing Data Spaces, pp. 17–28. Springer, Cham (2022)
25. Neenan, B., Hemphill, R.C.: Societal benefits of smart metering investments. Electr. J. **21**(8), 32–45 (2008)
26. Nida-Rümelin, J., Weidenfeld, N.: Was kann und darf künstliche Intelligenz? Ein Plädoyer für digitalen Humanismus. Piper, München (2023)
27. Nida-Rümelin, J., Winter, D.: Humanism and enlightenment. In: Werthner, H., et al. (eds.) Introduction to Digital Humanism, pp. 3–16. Springer, Cham (2024). https://doi.org/10.1007/978-3-031-45304-5_1, first online: 21 December 2023
28. Ponce, P., Oliveira, C., Álvarez, V., de la Cruz del Río-Rama, M.: The liberalization of the internal energy market in the European Union: evidence of its influence on reducing environmental pollution. Energies **13**(22), 6116 (2020)
29. Schwaninger, I., Güldenpfennig, F., Weiss, A., Fitzpatrick, G.: What do you mean by trust? Establishing shared meaning in interdisciplinary design for assistive technology. Int. J. Soc. Robot. **13**(8), 1879–1897 (2021)
30. Schweiger, G., et al.: Active consumer participation in smart energy systems. Energy Build. **227**, 110359 (2020)
31. Stanger, A.: The real cost of surveillance capitalism: digital humanism in the United States and Europe. In: Werthner, H., Prem, E., Lee, E.A., Ghezzi, C. (eds.) Perspectives on Digital Humanism, pp. 33–40. Springer, Cham (2022). https://doi.org/10.1007/978-3-030-86144-5_5
32. Thürmel, S.: Von Cyberphysikalischen Systemen zu intelligenten Infrastrukturen. In: Mainzer, K. (ed.) Philosophisches Handbuch Künstliche Intelligenz, pp. 639–650. Springer, Wiesbaden (2024)
33. Timmers, P.: Sovereignty in the digital age. In: Werthner, H., et al. (eds.) Introduction to Digital Humanism: A Textbook, pp. 571–592. Springer, Cham (2024). https://doi.org/10.1007/978-3-031-45304-5_36
34. Werthner, H., Lee, E.A., Akkermans, H., Vardi, M., et al.: Wiener Manifest für Digitalen Humanismus / Vienna Manifesto on Digital Humanism. Online-Publikation (2019). https://www.informatik.tuwien.ac.at/dighum/wp-content/uploads/2019/07/Vienna_Manifesto_on_Digital_Humanism_DE.pdf
35. Zechner, N., Güldenpfennig, F., Thalmann, L., Zeiß, J.: Towards a conscious use of energy: designing a web application for leveraging insights from energy-data analytics. In: Mensch und Computer 2024 - Workshopband. Gesellschaft für Informatik e.V., Karlsruhe (2024)
36. Zuboff, S.: Surveillance capitalism and the challenge of collective action. New Labor Forum **28**(1), 10–29 (2019). https://doi.org/10.1177/1095796018819461

Catastrophic Computation. On the Impossibility of Sustainable Artificial Intelligence

Rainer Rehak[1,2]([envelope]) [ORCID]

[1] Weizenbaum Institute for the Networked Society, 10623 Berlin, Germany
[2] WZB Berlin Social Science Center, 10785 Berlin, Germany
rainer.rehak@weizenbaum-institut.de
https://www.weizenbaum-institut.de

Abstract. Artificial intelligence (AI) is currently considered a sustainability "game-changer" within and outside of academia. I argue that while there are indeed many sustainability-related use cases for AI, they are likely to have more overall drawbacks than benefits. To substantiate this claim, I differentiate three 'AI materialities' of the AI supply chain: first the literal materiality (e.g. water, cobalt, lithium, energy consumption etc.), second, the informational materiality (e.g. lots of data and centralised control necessary), and third, the social materiality (e.g. exploitative data work, communities harm by waste and pollution). In all materialities, effects are especially devastating for the global south while benefiting the global north. A second strong claim regarding sustainable AI circles around so-called apolitical optimisation (e.g. regarding city traffic), however the optimisation criteria (e.g. cars, bikes, emissions, commute time, health) are purely political and have to be collectively negotiated before applying AI optimisation. Hence, sustainable AI, in principle, cannot break the glass ceiling of transformation and might even distract from necessary societal change. To address that I propose to stop 'unformation gathering' and to apply the 'small is beautiful' principle. This aims to contribute to an informed academic and collective negotiation on how to (not) integrate AI into the sustainability project while avoiding to reproduce the status quo by serving hegemonic interests between useful AI use cases, techno-utopian salvation narratives, technology-centred efficiency paradigms, the exploitative and extractivist character of AI and concepts of digital degrowth. In order to discuss sustainable AI, this article draws from insights by critical data and algorithm studies, STS, transformative sustainability science, critical computer science, and public interest theory.

Keywords: Sustainability · Artificial Intelligence · Efficiency · Narratives · Digital Decolonialism · Digital Degrowth · Tiny Models · Critical Data Infrastructure Studies

L. Hagedorn et al. (Eds.): DIGHUM 2025, LNCS 16319, pp. 110–118, 2026.
https://doi.org/10.1007/978-3-032-11108-1_8

1   Introduction

Two of the existential issues of our time are the climate catastrophe and the dramatic loss of biodiversity. They are existential in the way that our human livelihood depends on functioning ecosystems [15]. Therefore, calls for ecological sustainability are in fact calls for protecting human life, democratic societies, and their institutions, such as public interest infrastructures in a globally fair and equitable fashion. The decline of ecological systems directly entails the accelerating magnification of long known political problems like global inequality, poverty, hunger, or war. Increased scarcity of life-sustaining resources, even concerning habitable areas, fuel conflict and injustice [2].

In light of the herculean endeavour of shaping sustainable societies (e.g. see the UN Sustainable Development Goals), where the needs of all present human beings as well as future generations are met within the planetary ecological boundaries [34], promising approaches and solutions are desperately needed. The search especially includes the use of digital tools like artificial intelligence (AI), which is currently considered a "game-changer" and "revolutionary" technology in the fight against climate change by many, even the UN itself [41].

While AI is not one single technology but a large bouquet of related digital methods, there are indeed use cases for sustainability-oriented AI systems like circular economy optimisation [43], reduction of resource and energy consumption [18], local CO2 emission reduction [3], smart city optimisation [11], sustainable mobility [42], waste separation and disposal [44], and new ways of information gathering like environmental pollution detection [31] or radically improved approaches to earth observation [5]. Calling these and other concrete examples a sustainability game-changer discloses a very reduced understanding of the sustainability project, as well as of AI technology, because it ignores the political and economic context of AI applications and even its own resource demand. I therefore want to argue that centering any AI technology in the sustainability struggle will, if continuing on the current path, very likely do more harm than good and might even be a distraction from the actually relevant societal tasks of a sustainability transformation. I advocate for moving forward in a problem- and goal-oriented manner and not in a technology- or even AI-driven one. AI might eventually play a role in societal sustainability transitions, although a very small one.

In this short paper I extensively draw from insights by critical data and algorithm studies, STS, transformative sustainability science, critical computer science, and, more remotely, public interest theory. I will first outline some core properties of AI systems, then socially contextualise and critically discuss these regarding their sustainability implications. I will make constructive remarks concerning a sensible use of certain kinds of AI in combating problems like climate change and conclude the piece.

2   AI Materialities

AI, like all digital tools, has specific common materialities. While the concept of materiality traditionally refers to physical properties, I will use it in a more abstract sense underlining its resourceness. This includes physical characteristics, but also informational properties and limitations, and even inner and outer social dynamics [39].

On the physical level it is important to focus on the ecological implications. While there are many possible sustainability-related use cases of AI, the concrete technologies residing under this umbrella term have an astronomically high consumption of material resources like water, cobalt lithium, or energy (e.g., [12,25]), whose production and disposal has major ecological impacts, especially in the global south. Overall, the use of AI skyrockets all indicators of current and future estimated digital ecological impact [40]. Major tech companies like Microsoft and Google just reported rises in resource uses previously unheard of, stopped carbon offsetting, and announced that they would miss their already loose [19] sustainability pledges, precisely because of their large scale AI roll-out (e.g. [26,27,33]). Although there are attempts to minimise AI resource use [30,45], their success is very limited, and efficiency gains will very likely be eaten up by the usual digital rebound effects [6,14,23].

Regarding the informational materiality, AI systems can be differentiated between discriminative and generative systems. The former can detect patterns in input data (e.g. categorisation, grouping), the latter can produce patterns (e.g., text, images) related to input data. However both are based on advanced statistics and provide heuristic (not precise) results. This makes AI systems applicable for specific use cases where clearly defined and precise results are not needed, but AI is in no way a "general purpose"technology [4]. In addition, AI systems require large amounts of up-to-date valid data to be preconfigured for tasks. This implies a tendency towards centralisation as well as fundamental limits regarding practicability and usefulness [35].

And concerning the aspect of social materiality, the global AI supply chain has to be taken into focus. AI inherits the general implications of the digital supply chain, but in a much more intense way. Not only do AI technologies consume vast amounts of materials, lots of them from conflict-torn regions (e.g. conflict minerals, with the mining mainly commissioned by western corporations) and are disposed of in equally problematic e-waste sites heavily affecting the health and freedom of the workers and communities involved. Furthermore, many AI systems require complex and exploitative global networks [29] of data workers gathering, sorting, categorising, and labelling data in precarious and disempowered work arrangements [28], again especially in the global south.

3   The Purpose of (Sustainable) AI

After having briefly outlined some key characteristics of AI, we can now reflect further on its current use and its general potential, beyond the ecology-oriented applications mentioned above. A current hot topic in public and academic AI discourse is how to use "AI technology" for the common good. While the transition from focusing on the values being inscribed into AI systems to focusing more on AI governance itself by applying public interest theory seems very promising for specific public service use cases [46], a sustainability perspective has to take an overall net impact stance. From this point of view of limited resources, we need to choose wisely where to (not) use AI.

The current overpromises regarding sustainable AI could not be explained by small claims like sorting trash better or optimising the length of machinery use by predictive maintenance alone, but rather by impressive claims like mega city traffic optimisation or global fair resource distribution, meaning: really hard societal problems. But while AI is actually quite useful for sorting trash and predictive maintenance [20, 44], the latter two are, in fact, no technical problems to be calculated, but social problems of collectively agreeing on the very meaning of optimality in the given case.

The example of city traffic optimisation exemplifies that there first has to be a decision on what to optimise for, before then using AI based optimisation systems. Traffic could be optimised for cars, bikes or pedestrians, for low emissions, short commute time, good citizen health, or any other parameter or mix of potentially contradicting parameters. AI cannot make this decision, since it has neither agency nor is it neutral [32, 35, 36]. It cannot produce objectively good solutions agreeable by everyone. I leave the task to the reader to apply this thought experiment to the case of global resource distribution.

The main claim of AI, that it could technically produce a result, which is in fact the social precondition necessary to meaningfully apply AI, is clearly just circular reasoning. This misjudgement explains why AI can not be the "game changer" being able to break the glass ceiling of transformation [17]: AI systems can only implement what we as society have decided so far and are always created under the current, fundamentally unsustainable framework conditions. AI therefore currently, and under current conditions, only helps to carry on with business as usual (cf. [21]), and sustainable AI only works as change placebo resulting in placebo change; or to put it more concisely in Schütze's words: "sustainable AI is the technical solution to the climate crisis from a techno-solutionist vantage point simply reproducing the status quo. The enthusiasm for sustainable AI primarily serves hegemonic interests" [38]

The necessary societal and political negotiations cannot be automated [13], and for the sake of sustainability it is crucial to decenter technological thinking and focus on questions of power and social change [10, 39].

4   A Sustainable Path Forward

If we do not want to employ sustainability-related or humanist reasons to ban AI altogether, because we still want to harness the impressive results it can have in some areas, two guiding principles should be seriously discussed and taken into account in policy discourse, better sooner than later.

4.1 Stop Unformation Gathering

Many new sustainability-related AI applications promise to generate new insights, may it be regarding forest health, biodiversity indicators or crop quality. Yet, in most cases of possible protective climate or biodiversity action we as humanity already have sufficient scientific actionable insight. Getting more information is never bad, but the grave implications of AI use might not justify mere theoretical curiosity. Such research could even have a delaying effect, if decision-makers use it to wait for more detailed but practically meaningless results. I call these kinds of results, i.e. the information produced by an obsessive focus on getting more data – without taking action on the sufficient knowledge already available – *unformation*, which must be called out and prevented, especially when used as pretext for inaction.

4.2 Small is Beautiful

The larger an AI system, the more devastating are the sustainability-related effects as described above. Although there is much talk currently regarding large language models (LLMs) like ChatGPT, BART, and the like, the field of AI itself is already nearly 70 years old and has also, together with adjacent disciplines such as statistics, produced all kinds of rather lightweight approaches (e.g. [16]). Those small systems are usually really good for one specific use case, like water usage optimisation or visual bike detection. They are not only environmentally lightweight, but also do not promote power centralisation like LLMs necessarily do [39]; small AI is beautiful AI. Furthermore, currently all kinds of purposes are being pursued utilising powerful AI systems. However, in many areas it has been proven that with a bit of development effort, similarly usable results can be achieved using conventional and lightweight non-AI data processing methods, such as traditional statistics (e.g. [9]). If this is possible, AI must not be used. So let's focus on lightweight systems [37] and call for digital degrowth [1, 22].

5 Collective Conclusion

The currently hyped kinds of AI-like LLMs-are among the resource hungriest digital technologies we humans have ever developed and they depend on exceptionally exploitative and destructive AI supply chains, e.g. the broad introduction of AI drives the construction of one hyper-scaler data centre after the other [26] in a neo-colonial fashion [7, 24] and by taking away renewable energy, resources and water from other uses. From a sustainability point of view such technology needs an extremely well argued case for still being deployed today. Merely increasing profit for a few is no such case and given the fact that LLMs are largely used for misinformation, surveillance, and desire creation [8], it is hard to see why such systems should exist at all. There are indeed some benefits, but are they really worth it?

No single person can answer that, so this clearly is a topic for collective negotiation, preferably as a conviviality issue and preferably without AI stakeholders.

Acknowledgments. The article processing charge was funded by the German Federal Ministry of Research, Technology and Space (BMFTR), grant no. 16DII131.

Disclosure of Interests. The author declared to have no competing interests.

References

1. Aanestad, M.: Digital degrowth - beyond solutionism. In: Jones, M.R., Mukherjee, A.S., Thapa, D., Zheng, Y. (eds.) IFIPJWC 2023. IFIP AICT, vol. 696, pp. 55–60. Springer, Cham (2023). https://doi.org/10.1007/978-3-031-50154-8_6
2. Abel, G.J., Brottrager, M., Crespo Cuaresma, J., Muttarak, R.: Climate, conflict and forced migration, **54**, 239–249. https://doi.org/10.1016/j.gloenvcha.2018.12.003
3. Alli, Y.A., et al.: Photocatalysts for CO2 reduction and computational insights, **344**, 12810. https://doi.org/10.1016/j.fuel.2023.128101
4. Bender, E.M., Gebru, T., McMillan-Major, A., Shmitchell, S.: On the dangers of stochastic parrots: can language models be too big? In: Proceedings of the 2021 ACM Conference on Fairness, Accountability, and Transparency, pp. 610–623. ACM. https://doi.org/10.1145/3442188.3445922
5. Bereta, K., Koubarakis, M., Manegold, S., Stamoulis, G., Demir, B.: From big data to big information and big knowledge: the case of earth observation data. In: Proceedings of the 27th ACM International Conference on Information and Knowledge Management, pp. 2293–2294. ACM. https://doi.org/10.1145/3269206.3274270
6. Bergman, N., Foxon, T.J.: Drivers and effects of digitalization on energy demand in low-carbon scenarios **23**(3), 329–342. https://doi.org/10.1080/14693062.2022.2145260
7. Brodie, P.: Data infrastructure studies on an unequal planet, **10**(1), 2053951723118240. https://doi.org/10.1177/20539517231182402. Accessed 20 Nov 2024
8. Castor, A., Gerard, D.: Pivot to AI: pay no attention to the man behind the curtain. amycastor.com (2023). https://amycastor.com/2023/09/12/pivot-to-ai-pay-no-attention-to-the-man-behind-the-curtain/
9. Cerasa, A., et al.: Predicting outcome in patients with brain injury: differences between machine learning versus conventional statistics, **10**(9), 2267. https://doi.org/10.3390/biomedicines10092267
10. Creutzig, F., et al.: Digitalization and the anthropocene **47**(1), 479–50. https://doi.org/10.1146/annurev-environ-120920-100056
11. Cugurullo, F.: Urban artificial intelligence: from automation to autonomy in the smart city, **2**, 3. https://doi.org/10.3389/frsc.2020.00038
12. De Vries, A.: The growing energy footprint of artificial intelligence **7**(10), 2191–219https://doi.org/10.1016/j.joule.2023.09.004
13. Eyert, F., Lopez, P.: Rethinking transparency as a communicative constellation. In: 2023 ACM Conference on Fairness, Accountability, and Transparency, pp. 444–454. ACM. https://doi.org/10.1145/3593013.3594010
14. Freitag, C., Berners-Lee, M., Widdicks, K., Knowles, B., Blair, G.S., Friday, A.: The real climate and transformative impact of ICT: a critique of estimates, trends, and regulations, **2**(9), 100340. https://doi.org/10.1016/j.patter.2021.100340

15. German Advisory Council on Global Change (WBGU): Towards our common digital future. WBGU. https://www.wbgu.de/en/publications/publication/towards-our-common-digital-future
16. Hansen, E.B., Iftikhar, N., Bøgh, S.: Concept of easy-to-use versatile artificial intelligence in industrial small & medium-sized enterprises, **51**, 1146–115. https://doi.org/10.1016/j.promfg.2020.10.161
17. Hausknost, D.: The environmental state and the glass ceiling of transformation, **29**(1), 17–37. https://doi.org/10.1080/09644016.2019.1680062
18. Himeur, Y., Ghanem, K., Alsalemi, A., Bensaali, F., Amira, A.: Artificial intelligence based anomaly detection of energy consumption in buildings: a review, current trends and new perspectives, **287**, 116601. https://doi.org/10.1016/j.apenergy.2021.116601
19. Hoffmann, M.L.: eine praktische evaluation und visualisierung der reaktionen von unternehmen auf den klimawandel#03 climate pledge rating: a hands-on evaluation and visualization of companies' responses to climate change .https://doi.org/10.14279/DEPOSITONCE-18624, publisher: Technische Universität Berlin
20. Kamel, H.: Artificial intelligence for predictive maintenance, **2299**(1), 01200. https://doi.org/10.1088/1742-6596/2299/1/012001
21. Kwet, M.: Digital colonialism: South Africa's education transformation in the shadow of silicon valley. https://doi.org/10.2139/ssrn.3496049
22. Kwet, M.: Digital Degrowth: Technology in the Age of Survival. Pluto Press, London (2024). https://www.plutobooks.com/product/digital-degrowth/, paperback publication August 2024, also available as eBook
23. Lange, S., Pohl, J., Santarius, T.: Digitalization and energy consumption. Does ICT reduce energy demand? **176**, 106760. https://doi.org/10.1016/j.ecolecon.2020.106760
24. Lehdonvirta, V., Wú, B., Hawkins, Z.: Compute north vs. compute south: the uneven possibilities of compute-based AI governance around the globe, **7**, 828–83. https://doi.org/10.1609/aies.v7i1.31683
25. Li, P., Yang, J., Islam, M.A., Ren, S.: Making AI less "thirsty": uncovering and addressing the secret water footprint of AI models. https://doi.org/10.48550/ARXIV.2304.03271, version Number: 5
26. Marx, P.: Generative AI is a climate disaster – tech companies are abandoning emissions pledges to chase AI market share. Disconnect.blog. https://disconnect.blog/generative-ai-is-a-climate-disaster/
27. Metz, R.: Google's emissions shot up 48% over five years due to AI. https://www.bloomberg.com/news/articles/2024-07-02/google-s-emissions-shot-up-48-over-five-years-due-to-ai
28. Miceli, M., Posada, J.: The data-production dispositif, **6**, 1–37. https://doi.org/10.1145/3555561
29. Mühlhoff, R.: Human-aided artificial intelligence: or, how to run large computations in human brains? toward a media sociology of machine learning, **22**(10), 1868–188. https://doi.org/10.1177/1461444819885334
30. Nenno, S.: Potentials and limitations of active learning: for the reduction of energy consumption during model training, **4**(1). https://doi.org/10.34669/WI.WJDS/4.1.3, publisher: Weizenbaum Institute
31. Pouyanfar, N., et al.: Artificial intelligence-based microfluidic platforms for the sensitive detection of environmental pollutants: recent advances and prospects, **34**, e0016. https://doi.org/10.1016/j.teac.2022.e00160
32. Prietl, B.: Big data: inequality by design? https://doi.org/10.34669/WI.CP/2.11, publisher: Weizenbaum Institute Version Number: 1

33. Rathi, A., Bass, D.: Microsoft's AI push imperils climate goal as carbon emissions jump 30%. Bloomberg (2024). https://www.bloomberg.com/news/articles/2024-05-15/microsoft-s-ai-investment-imperils-climate-goal-as-emissions-jump-30

34. Raworth, K.: A safe and just space for humanity: can we live within the doughnut? Oxfam. https://www-cdn.oxfam.org/s3fs-public/file_attachments/dp-a-safe-and-just-space-for-humanity-130212-en_5.pdf

35. Rehak, R.: AI narrative breakdown. A critical assessment of power and promise. In: Proceedings of the 2025 ACM Conference on Fairness, Accountability, and Transparency, pp. 1250–1260. ACM. https://doi.org/10.1145/3715275.3732083

36. Rehak, R.: The language labyrinth: constructive critique on the terminology used in the AI discourse. In: Verdegem, P. (ed.) AI for Everyone? Critical Perspectives, pp. 87–102. University of Westminster Press. https://doi.org/10.16997/book55.f

37. Rehak, R., Ullrich, A., Vladova, G.: Contesting openness in AI. reflections on the transformative value and participatory potential of open source AI. In: International Conference on Information Technology for Social Good (ACM GoodIT '25), pp. 1–9. ACM. https://doi.org/10.1145/3748699.3749795

38. Schütze, P.: The problem of sustainable AI: a critical assessment of an emerging phenomenon. Weizenbaum J. Digit. Soc. **4**(1). https://doi.org/10.34669/WI.WJDS/4.1.4

39. Steig, F., et al.: Sustainability powered by digitalization? (re-)politicizing the debate, **21**(1), 252118. https://doi.org/10.1080/15487733.2025.2521181

40. Taddeo, M., Tsamados, A., Cowls, J., Floridi, L.: Artificial intelligence and the climate emergency: opportunities, challenges, and recommendations, **4**(6), 776–77. https://doi.org/10.1016/j.oneear.2021.05.018

41. United Nations Office of the High Commissioner for Human Rights (UN-OHCHR): Artificial intelligence: A game-changer for sustainable development. https://www.ohchr.org/en/stories/2024/06/artificial-intelligence-game-changer-sustainable-development

42. Vermesan, O., et al.: Automotive intelligence embedded in electric connected autonomous and shared vehicles technology for sustainable green mobility, **2**, 688482. https://doi.org/10.3389/ffutr.2021.688482

43. Wilson, M., Paschen, J., Pitt, L.: The circular economy meets artificial intelligence (AI): understanding the opportunities of AI for reverse logistics, **33**(1), 9–2. https://doi.org/10.1108/MEQ-10-2020-0222

44. Wilts, H., Garcia, B.R., Garlito, R.G., Gómez, L.S., Prieto, E.G.: Artificial intelligence in the sorting of municipal waste as an enabler of the circular economy, **10**(4), 2. https://doi.org/10.3390/resources10040028

45. Wu, C.J., et al.: Sustainable AI: environmental implications, challenges and opportunities. https://doi.org/10.48550/ARXIV.2111.00364, version Number: 2

46. Züger, T., Asghari, H.: AI for the public. How public interest theory shifts the discourse on AI, **38**(2), 815–828. https://doi.org/10.1007/s00146-022-01480-5

Adaptive Alignment of Human Values in Cyber-Physical Supply Chains

Thomas Welsh[1]([✉]) [iD], Diane Hassett[2], Bashar Nuseibeh[3] [iD],
and Andrea Zisman[3] [iD]

[1] University of Iceland, Reykjavík, Iceland
`tomwelsh@hi.is`
[2] University of Limerick, Limerick, Ireland
[3] The Open University, Milton Keynes, UK
`{bashar.nuseibeh,andrea.zisman}@open.ac.uk`

Abstract. Supply chains are fundamental to the economic functioning of society, through the assembly and transport of essential goods such as food, clothes and medicine. Technological advancements have driven supply chains to become increasingly automated, to optimise for efficiency and cost, and to respond to disturbances. However, optimising for social concerns is less prevalent. Increasing consumer preferences towards purchasing goods whose production is more aligned with those consumers' values (such as sustainability), requires values-management capabilities within supply chain software. Such capabilities include tracing, monitoring, and verifying values-alignment between end-consumers and stakeholders. In this paper, we advocate for adaptive values-alignment between end-consumers and stakeholders in cyber-physical supply chains. We motivate this by means of an example of a coffee supply chain, which in turn surfaces social and technical challenges to values-alignment. We then propose a distributed, locally adaptive values-alignment approach. We implement this approach within a software framework and quantitatively illustrate its impact in increasing alignment from two competing perspectives: supply chain stakeholders and end-consumers. We show that end-consumer bias performs better by reducing values-misalignment by up to 85%. We also find that the homogeneity of stakeholders' values is not correlated with an increase in values-alignment with end-consumers and that mixed values-alignment across the supply chain may be beneficial for supporting stakeholder engagement.

Keywords: human values · system adaptation · cyber-physical supply chain · adaptive alignment

1 Introduction

Society is functionally dependent upon supply chains to produce and deliver goods and services. Global issues such as climate change and the COVID-19 pandemic, have prompted a shift in supply chain goals. Traditionally, such goals

L. Hagedorn et al. (Eds.): DIGHUM 2025, LNCS 16319, pp. 119–134, 2026.
https://doi.org/10.1007/978-3-032-11108-1_9

focused on maximising profit through managing *value*. Now, a greater focus is upon prioritising social needs according to *human values* [7]. Environmental, economic and social events are driving changes in consumer preferences and product availability. The framework of environmental, social and corporate governance (ESG) [20] has become an important part of many organisations' strategies. Supply chains must adapt to these changes to ensure operational persistence [12].

The increasing dependence on software systems has driven the emergence of *cyber-physical supply chains*, in which computational, physical, communication and control capabilities are integrated alongside interactions with humans. As part of future industry paradigms, software components monitor the supply chain, to reason and adapt, and to support real-time optimisation [13]. In order to accommodate complex social concerns, cyber-physical supply chains need to be *socio-technically values-aligned*, ensuring that systems are representative and inclusive of diverse *human values*. Monitoring and tracing human values may highlight *values-misalignment* between end-consumer and supply chain stakeholders and, thus, reduce purchases by an end-consumer. For example, a values-misalignment will occur when a consumer requires values sustainable production, but one or more producers in the supply chain does not meet their standards. Therefore, *personalisation* [3] of goods according to a consumer's values can reduce values-misalignment and increase engagement.

While software is inherently able to manage quantitative concepts such as financial value, managing social value is still in its infancy. The software engineering community has identified the *operationalisation of human values* [14] in software as a key priority - values need to be embedded in the software we all use, so that the outcomes of using the software better reflect societal values.

Cyber-physical supply chains consist of a dynamic pool of consumers and producers of goods with integrated software components, organisations, resources and assets. The distribution characteristic of cyber-physical supply chains across geographical, organisational, linguistic and cultural boundaries ensures they are managed and used by different and diverse stakeholders. This diversity characteristic causes the operationalisation of values within software to fall short in cyber-physical supply chains. Novel approaches to managing values[1] within cyber-physical supply chains are necessary.

In this paper, we contribute to the research in operationalisation of values [2,14] by presenting a novel *adaptive approach to support values-alignment* between stakeholders (consumers and producers) in cyber-physical supply chains. Our approach considers the dynamism, complexity, and diversity characteristics of cyber-physical supply chains. In this context, we define *values-alignment* as *the ability to support identifying and ameliorating discrepancies among values of stakeholders*. We note that while locality supports values-alignment between neighbouring stakeholders, values-alignment with end-consumers requires traceability techniques to identify discrepancies among val-

---

[1] For simplicity, we will use the term *values* instead of *human values* from this point onwards in the paper.

ues, and distributed approaches to align them. We also note that given a large pool of supply chain stakeholders with diverse and dynamic values-alignment, understanding the impact of the adaptive approaches upon distributing values-alignment across the supply chain is important. However, observability of supply chains is challenging given their large, diverse and dynamic structure. To mitigate this, our approach uses network-theoretic modelling and analysis of the supply chain. Values visibility and alignment capabilities are critical for enabling human agency in increasingly automated supply chains. Therefore, we believe our approach is consistent with digital humanism principles [18].

This paper is structured as follows. In Sect. 2 we discuss how the characteristics of cyber-physical supply chains create challenges to realising values-alignment, and we illustrate these through a coffee cyber-physical supply chain. In Sect. 3 we present a distributed adaptive software approach to values-alignment in cyber-physical supply chains. Section 4 presents a simulated method, results and analysis of the adaptive approach. In Sect. 5 we discuss the results, impact, limitations and future research. In Sect. 6 we highlight some related work. Finally, in Sect. 7 we conclude our work and describe some future plans.

2   Motivating Example and Challenges

Coffee supply chains feature physical, cyber and social layers. Consider coffee beans grown in South America, harvested, processed, and then exported for roasting and blending. Coffee is prepared into various end states (beans, pods, granules) for onward sale to retailers and consumers worldwide. Coffee sources can range from niche (e.g., female producers, prisoner roasters) to large scale operations which oversee the entire supply chain (e.g., Starbucks, Nestle). Coffee supply chain incorporates various stakeholders and organisations: growers, farmers, intermediaries (government bodies, NGO's), buyers, exporters and roasters - all of whom play a role in values creation within the supply chain. The values of each participant will likely vary, often in relation to distribution. Ensuring the values of all participants are respected and aligned is important for the continued overall operation of the supply chain.

The production of coffee is focused on fairtrade, ethical, and organic certification and practices. Other issues such as climate change and increasing population, threaten the land available for growing coffee heightening need for sustainable supply chains. Given the complexity and dispersed nature of coffee supply chains, cyber-physical technologies such as Industrial Internet of Things (IIoT) to monitor the production and distribution processes; blockchain to track and trace the coffee from source to retailer); mobile apps to connect consumers to growers; drones to monitor crop and land; and AI to monitor and provide feedback of quality of beans can be used to support maintaining coffee supply chains. However, cyber-physical supply chains pose challenges towards managing values within software. These challenges are *social* as a result of their distribution across diverse cultures; and *technical* as a result of interconnecting diverse cyber-physical components across different organisations. We discuss below these challenges.

Heterogenous Values. The values stakeholders deem important may be diverse as a result of their physical location causing differences in culture and legislation. For example, coffee growers may value self-direction in managing their schedule and techniques, while buyers or distributors may value power in controlling how coffee beans are processed. Sometimes, their understanding of values may be *inconsistent*. For example, western countries may value conformity to quality standards for processing coffee beans, whereas in other countries these standards may not be prioritised due to their negative impact upon cost. This diversity and inconsistency ensures values may *conflict*.

Values-based software requires capabilities to elicit and monitor values to understand their diversity, and to support conflict management.

Evolving Values. Stakeholders' values are subject to change and are impacted by political, societal, or environmental events which are non-trivial to predict. For example, an increased concern for environmental sustainability, as a result of climate change, may cause consumers to only purchase coffee if the supply chain is transparent and sustainability assured. A change in the economic climate where coffee beans are grown, may cause coffee bean growers to seek a higher price to ensure their own security; while the changing economic climate in wealthier countries may mean consumers accept a lower quality product.

Values-based software will need to incorporate adaptative techniques to support changes in values, and reason about the most appropriate course of action to ensure alignment of values.

Limited Observability. The structure of supply chains is inherently complex due to frequent subcontracting, sheer large scale and the multidimensional nature of cyber-physical systems. Consequently, supply chain stakeholders may only be aware of those in their local vicinity (up and downstream nodes in the supply chain). For example, a coffee bean grower may be unaware of who is distributing their coffee and to where it is being distributed. Consumers may be unaware of the values of the growers and be unsure whether their benevolence choices, according to price paid or project purchased, are fulfilled. Factors surrounding data (e.g., protection, volatility and proprietary formats) make observability of values non-trivial. For example, supermarkets may value their privacy and security and, thus, be unwilling to divulge data needed for values management. The *alignment* of values is directly impacted by these observability constraints.

Automated approaches to values-alignment requires values to be visible and also traceable across the whole supply chain; yet decisions must be made locally to account for the limited global observability.

Values-Alignment and Local Cost Trade Off. Making values visible in supply chains will provide opportunities to manage conflicts through *values-alignment* and thus sustain relationships and transactions. However, aligning values will require adjustments to production processes which may increase the cost of production. For example, aligning more strongly with sustainability may require an investment in more energy efficient machines. Individual supply chain actors will need to balance an increase in transactions in the longer term with potential higher costs associated with values-alignment.

Values-alignment tools must support trade off analysis when adjusting production processes to reduce values conflicts.

Integration of Diverse Cyber-Physical Systems. Cyber-physical supply chains require the *integration* of diverse cyber-physical systems (e.g., for tracking and tracing of assets). This integration is a component of smart-manufacturing paradigms, but also for *monitoring* human values. Enabling technologies (e.g. block chains and IIoT) have security properties such as confidentiality and immutability. Therefore, their capability for values-alignment is uncertain. Due to cultural differences there will be disparities in the way humans interact with technologies and the data they collect, store and process. For example, IIoT may be employed to support transparency as deemed important to the consumer and distributor. Farmers may be less inclined to use these technologies as they may reduce their self-direction or increase cost, reducing their efficacy overall.

Values-based software must consider the interoperability of heterogeneous systems and data within confidentiality constraints to support monitoring of values.

3   Adaptive Values-Alignment

To address the challenges above, we propose an approach to support values-alignment in cyber-physical supply chains. Our approach provides functionality to adaptively identify, monitor and trace values across the supply chain, handling their change and diversity and supporting trade off analysis through quantification of misalignment. To achieve global values-alignment in the presence of observability constraints, our approach is based on a collective local values-alignment adaptation process, for each node in a supply chain. The local adaptation process follows the Monitor Analyse Plan Execute-Knowledge (MAPE-K) approach [19] in each node of a chain: in order to allow values-alignment to be collectively achieved across the supply chain.

We consider definitions of *cyber-physical supply chain, actor* and *end-consumer*. We replace the previously used concept of stakeholder to distinguish between the different types of stakeholder (actors and end-consumer). A cyber-physical supply chain is modelled as a linear process, in which a sequence of *actors* manipulate goods as consumers and producers, until the goods reach an *end-consumer* as a product. A product will not be used by end-consumers if their values do not align with the values of the actors involved in the production process. Our approach presents algorithms for adapting values-alignment according to end-consumers and adapting to those in an actor's local neighbourhood. Our network theoretic model of a cyber-physical supply chain supports statistics, such as assortativity which indicates the tendency of nodes to be connected to those with a similar number of edges or attributes and thus can describe global distribution of values-alignment [8].

As previously proposed [2], our approach assumes that distinct values types are defined in terms of attributes related to the production context and these attributes can be instantiated by actors and end-users. These attributes may be elicited through behaviour monitoring or more direct methods such as surveys. Using production-related attributes supports values analysis in the cyber-physical production systems used. For example, sustainability values type can be defined by attributes *level of energy consumption, recyclable packaging, travel distance.* Moreover, these attributes and their instantiations can be adjusted during the production process to improve values-alignment between actors and end-consumers. As shown in Fig. 1, an end-consumer defines their values preferences which will be traced through the supply chain from the point of sale to the raw products, and confirm if their attribute preferences agree with the preferences of each actor in the supply chain.

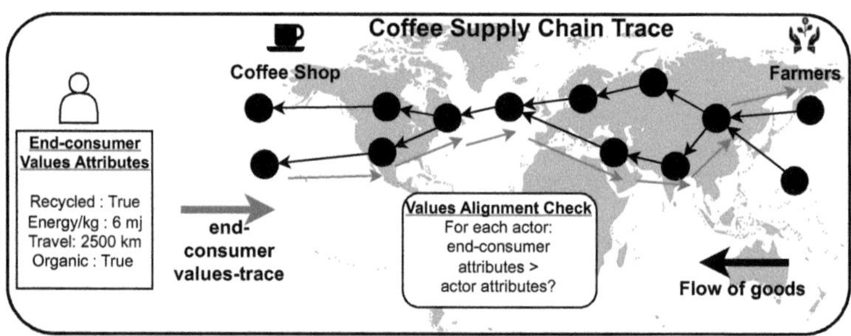

Fig. 1. An end-consumer traces their values attributes from the point of purchase to the harvesting of raw materials. Attributes are compared against those of each supply chain actor and the resulting values-alignment stored.

Figure 2 illustrates the architecture of our approach. As shown in the figure, nodes in the supply chain involved in the production process of a good are traced from the end-consumer. For each traced node, values from actors and end-consumers represented in the **knowledge base** are **monitored**. The monitoring stage of the architecture is distributed [19] across all actors. Each supply chain actor locally monitors their attributes which are then stored in the global knowledge-base, accessed by the end-consumer or other supply chain actors. This allows local adaptation over shared values-alignment knowledge, to achieve global values-alignment collectively. As adaptation to achieve alignment occurs independently, for each supply chain actor, the alignment stages occur locally at each actor site. The values and their attributes stored globally are then **analysed** locally for each actor for discrepancies. If discrepancies are detected, an alignment for a values type is then **planned** and **executed** by incremental adjustments in the attributes and instances of that values type (e.g., reduction of energy consumption, change of sustainable packaging).

Monitoring and Analysing Values. Our approach supports monitoring the values of all the actors associated with the nodes in the production process of a good, and the values of the end-consumer. Monitoring values of actors and end-consumers is important because their stated values may not always be reflected in their actions and because they may diverge.

In our approach, for each node in the trace of the production process of a good, the values of the actors in the nodes are monitored against the values of an end-consumer. The cyber-physical supply chain is modelled as a Directed Acylic Graph where the nodes in the graph represent the actors, and the edges represent the direction in which the goods flow. In this study, we monitor and trace a singular values type, e.g. sustainability, but note that this approach may be scaled to monitor a set of other values types.

Fundamentally, supply chains model the connectivity between interacting actors of relevance to a particular good or service. In our work, it is essential to model this connectivity to understand values observability and conflicts. Therefore, we employ a network-theoretic model to describe the cyber-physical supply chain and the values-alignment of its actors and end-consumers. Formally, in our approach, a cyber-physical supply chain is modelled as a tuple $SC = (A, E, V, S, \delta, C)$ where:

- A is a set of actors in the chain: $\{1.Farmers, 2.Exporters, 3.Roasters, ...\}$;
- E is a list of relations, representing the order of the production process, between the actors ($E \subseteq A \times A$);
- V is a set representing values (e.g. self-direction) of the actors in the chain;
- S is an attribute specification for each value which defines the available types and their parameters (described below);
- δ is a mapping between actors, the attribute specification and their values attributes, $\delta : A \times S \rightarrow V$. For example, the energy attributes of a supply chain actor (farmer) could be defined as $\delta(farmer, energy) = \{4.1\}$;
- C is a set of end-consumers with their values attributes, defined in the same way as the supply chain actors.

In our approach, we currently denote attributes with wide ranges such as energy in MJ/kg or travel in 1000 KMs, represented as a probability distribution, where the first value indicates the mean and the second the standard deviation. This is to allow adaptation of these attributes according to the standard deviation. Binary attributes such as *organic* are represented as either True or False. Other attributes can be represented across some finite set such as the types of recyclable plastics are represented as 1-PET, 2-HDPE, 3-PVC. For example, a sustainability attribute specification could be defined as in Eq. 1.

$$S = \{(energy, \{5.0, 0.5\}), (travel, \{1.5, 0.25\}),$$
$$(organic, \{False, True\}), (packaging, \{Card, Plastic\}),$$
$$(recycling, \{PET, HDPE, PVC\})\}$$

$$(1)$$

During the monitor stage the end-consumer traces through each actor a in the chain and compares their values $\delta(a, s)$ with the values of an end-consumer *c.* Each end-consumer attribute is compared against the corresponding actor's attribute. Whether higher or lower is better is context dependent. For sustainability lower is often better (e.g., lower energy cost). However, it is important that the template is organised consistently to accommodate this fact. For example, the sets of possible recycling options are ranked from lower (better) to higher (worse). We define $\phi_c(v)$ as the alignment verification for an end-consumer c against actor values v in Eq. 2.

$$\phi_c(v) = \begin{cases} -1 & \text{if } v < c \\ 1 & \text{if } v \geq c \end{cases} \tag{2}$$

The knowledge base K stores the sum of the result of alignment verification for each actor and attribute, where $K_a(s) = K_a(s) + \phi_c(\delta(a, s))$. This result can be used for planning new attribute adjustments in the production context, in order to reduce values-misalignment later.

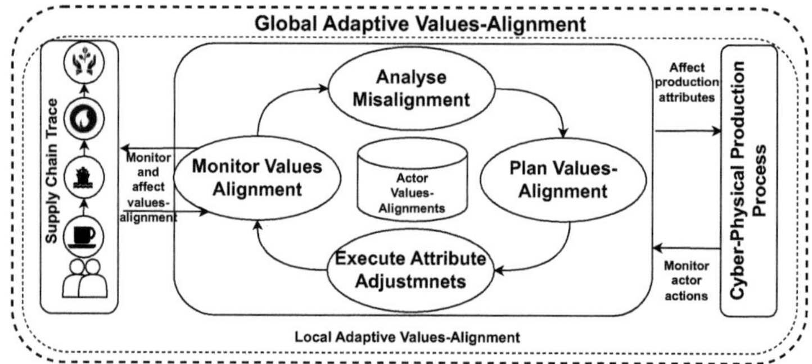

Fig. 2. Adaptive supply chain values-alignment using the MAPE-K model.

The **analysis** phase identifies the differences between the alignment of the values of an end-consumer and all actors in the chain. The end-consumer can determine whether there is values-misalignment with all the actors they have traced through the supply chain (e.g. to purchase the product), by determining if the sum of all alignment checks is equal to the number of actors they have traced. Therefore, Eq. 3 is 0 or *false* for values-misalignment; otherwise, Eq. 3 is 1 or *true* for alignment.

$$\pi(c) = \begin{cases} 1 & \text{if } \sum_{a=1}^{|A|} \sum_{s=1}^{|S|} \phi_c(\delta(a, s)) \leq |A| \times |S| \\ 0 & \text{otherwise} \end{cases} \tag{3}$$

Planning and Executing Values-Alignment. The alignment of values of actors with end-consumer is achieved by adjusting the attributes and instances of the actors' values. In this work we compare two different approaches and evaluate their combined performance, as follows. (1) Where actors adapt their values to other actors in their neighbourhood; i.e., those to which they are directly connected. This is a realistic scenario for current supply chains as actors deal only with immediate actors in the supply chain. (2) Where actors adapt their values to the recorded end-consumer values-misalignment in the knowledge base.

1) Neighbourhood Adaptation. In this approach, actors attempt to increment their attributes closer to the neighbourhood mean (Eq. 5). In our approach, θ denotes an adjustment coefficient for the attributes such as 1% or 10%; neighbourhood for an actor a, or the set of all adjacent actors, is $N_a = a \in A : n \sim a$. Equation 4 presents the mean of a particular attribute s in neighbourhood N_a.

$$\mu(a, s) = \frac{\sum_{j=1}^{|N_a|} \delta(a_j, s)}{|N_a|} \tag{4}$$

$$\forall a \in A, \forall s \in S : \begin{cases} \delta(a, s) \leftarrow \delta(a, s) + \theta & \text{if } \delta(a, s) < \mu \\ \delta(a, s) \leftarrow \delta(a, s) - \theta & \text{if } \delta(a, s) > \mu \end{cases} \tag{5}$$

2) End-Consumer values-misalignment adaptation. In this approach, the actor analyses values-misalignment recorded for every end-consumer and modifies their attributes to reduce values-misalignment for the global pool of end-consumers. For each conflicting values type in the knowledge base, this will adjust the attributes and instances of the respective values type. The actor's resulting alignment accounts for varying end-consumer alignment both positively and negatively (Eq. 6).

$$\forall a \in A, \forall s \in S : \begin{cases} \delta(a, s) \leftarrow \delta(a, s) + \theta & \text{if } K_a(s) < 0 \\ \delta(a, s) \leftarrow \delta(a, s) - \theta & \text{if } K_a(s) > 0 \end{cases} \tag{6}$$

4   Simulation and Results

In order to evaluate the work, we implemented a simulation to measure the effectiveness of the adaptive values-alignment approach in reducing values-misalignment of multiple end-consumers in a supply chain. Simulation was necessary to evaluate our approach due to the complexity of supply chains, the lack of an available test bed, and the high recruitment challenge of large numbers of supply chain actors to participate in an evaluation. The code and resulting datasets can be found on GitHub[2]. We firstly present our methodology and then the results and analysis of reducing values-misalignment for different scenarios.

4.1   Methodology

In the simulations, firstly a supply chain model of size $|A|$ is generated as a growing network due to its structural properties being similar to a supply chain [17]. Secondly, an attribute specification is defined (as in Eq. 1) and the values

---

[2] https://github.com/tomwelsh/Adaptive-Values-Alignment-in-SupplyChains.

and their attributes for all actors $a \in A$ and end-consumers $c \in C$ are initiated following a normal distribution. Finally, a loop of the adaptive values-alignment framework from Sect. 3 occurs for T iterations of the MAPE-K loop to compute $\pi(c)$, whereby each end-consumer $c \in C$ traces through each actor a, to determine the number of values-misalignment (Eq. 3). We measure the *values-misalignment index* as the mean of the values-misalignment of all consumers (Eq. 7).

$$Misalignment\ Index_t = \frac{1}{|C|} \sum_{c=1}^{|C|} \pi_t(c) \tag{7}$$

The values-misalignment index indicates the performance of each adaptation approach. Where 0 indicates that no values-misalignment occurs for all end-consumers across all iterations, and 1 indicates that values-misalignment occurs at every possible stage for all end-consumers. We also measured *assortativity*, or the homogeneity of values-alignment across the supply chain [8]. Where 1 indicates homophily - homogeneous values-alignment, -1 heterophily - heterogeneous values-alignment, while 0 is equally mixed. Independent variables simulate supply chain dynamics: the *end-consumer change-rate* and *actor change-rate* measured as a percentage of change. In all experiments end-rates were fixed at end-consumer 50% and actor 10%, respectively to isolate the results of adaptation. For example, a 10% change-rate causes 10% of randomly selected actors to have new values at the start of the iteration. Which could indicate a new production process, an actor joining the chain, or simply a change in the alignment of values. Understanding and investigating realistic change rates is important future work.

4.2   Validation with Consumer Tolerance

We consider that consumers may have a tolerance to the number of attributes they require for values-alignment. For example, a 0% tolerance would require 4 of 4 attributes. We tested the mean values-misalignment against consumer tolerances from 0% to 100%. At 100% end-consumer tolerance no values-misalignment occurred, with an increase in values-misalignment as the tolerance reduces. At 50% tolerance, values-misalignment occurred in all cases. These results validate the simulation. As the goal of our approach is to strongly align values between end-consumers and actors, consumer tolerance of 50% is the target for the rest of the analysis in this paper.

4.3   Values-Misalignment and Assortativity Trends

Figure 3 shows a time series of values-misalignment and assortativity of a single supply chain where the running time (MAPE iterations) of the simulation $T = 1000$. The high rates (10%), converged rapidly to a low values-misalignment, although higher rates will create greater costs for the actor (e.g. instigating sustainable packaging). Low-rate adaptation (1%) converged slowly to a low values-misalignment. Combined updates settled at a higher values-misalignment when

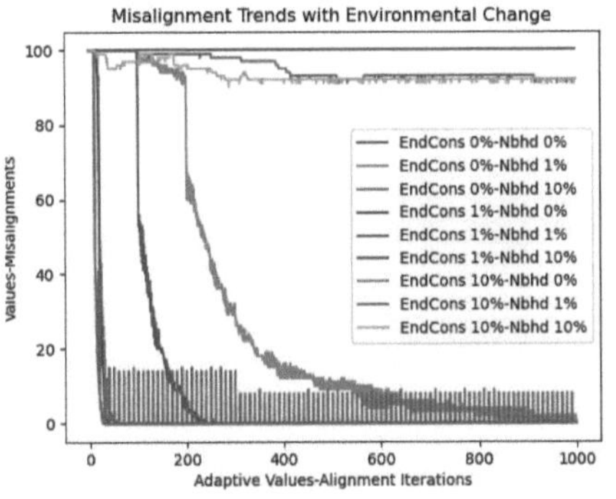
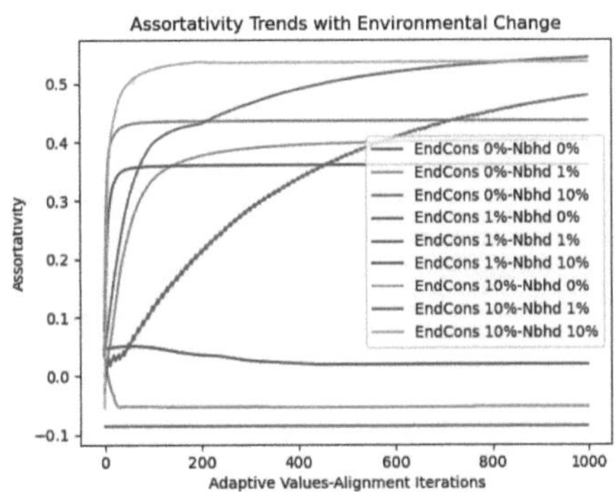

Fig. 3. Time-series of values-misalignment and assortativity for one supply chain (T=1000). The series captions refer to EndCons - End Consumer Adaptation and NBhd - Neighbourhood Adaptation with the corresponding adaptation rate. High adaptation rates (10%) achieves rapid alignment. Low rates (1%) converge to alignment slower. Mixed rates converge to values-misalignment when the same but to low alignment when mixed. There is limited correlation between assortativity and the values-misalignment performance, although the majority of techniques converge early in the simulations.

the rates were the same whereas when mixed they were balanced against speed. The assortativity indicates that, in general, the networks converged to a global values-alignment early. The outlier was End-Consumer 10% Neighbourhood 1% with oscillating values-misalignment throughout the simulation and a continuously increasing homophily. These results represent a single supply chain, not the overall performance, as each test case is subject to variation due to the stochastic and complexity properties of the system e.g. the initial starting conditions.

4.4   Large-Scale Simulation

We consider that actors need to reduce values-misalignment in a short time-frame to maintain end-consumer engagement. We tested each adaptation approach for 100 iterations, over 1000 randomly generated supply chains (50 actors and 100 end-consumers with normally distributed values alignment) producing 216,000 test cases. We show a subset of these results where end-consumer and actor change rates are 50% and 10%, respectively, selected from a preliminary study for both realism and impact upon misalignment. Figure 4 presents the mean of the values-misalignment index for the results. The results highlight the end-consumer high adaption (10%) was the best performing in reducing values-misalignment. To understand the values homophily, we tested the correlation between the mean of assortativity and values-misalignment across the 9 adaptation approaches and found no evidence of a linear correlation ($r = -0.065, p = 0.7036$). Therefore, Fig. 4 presents a heatmap of the mean assortativity broken down by adaptation approach, highlighting the most successful end-consumer approach creates a mixed values-alignment.

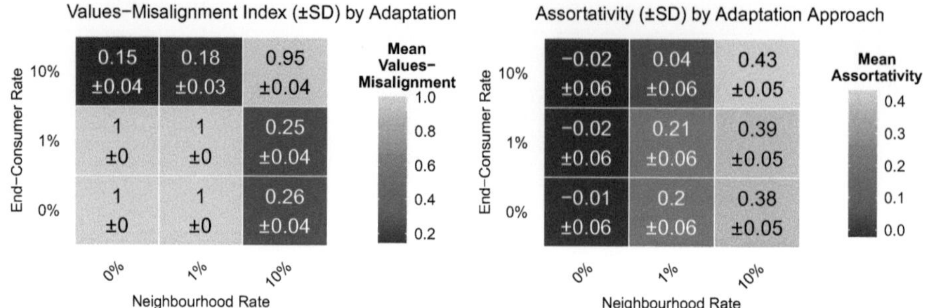

Fig. 4. Heatmap of mean values-misalignment for 1000 supply chains where $T = 100$. High adaptation (10%) and mixed rate combinations were the best performing. The performance of lower rates (1%) was equal to no adaptation. Neighbourhood adaptation drove the network towards homophily while the end-consumer adaptation trended towards a mixed values-alignment.

5   Discussion and Limitations

We discuss below the implications of the adaptive values-alignment approach and future research challenges.

Adaptive Values-Alignment simulated results have shown that adaptation is necessary with total end-consumer cyber-physical supply chain visibility so that actors can reduce alignment conflicts. Taking a locally adaptive values-alignment approach achieved global collective values-alignment. Adapting in response to end-consumer misalignment was the most successful, although only at higher (10%) increments, in the shorter time scale. Adapting values-alignment at a local level drives the supply chain towards a global alignment, as can be seen in the assortativity trends (Fig. 3). Although no linear correlation between the different adaptation approaches was observed, the most successful, end-consumer adaptation, maintained a mixed values-homophily. This suggests that supply chains which adapt continuously to diverse end-consumer values may be more successful in maintain customer engagement. This is in contrast to maintaining a high level towards one particular value.

Values at scale observability can be enabled by the distributed alignment monitoring shown in this approach. It could allow strategic insight concerning trends through *monitoring* and *tracing* values across societal sectors and geographical regions, highlighting *values boundaries*. Understanding values from a group perspective can protect the privacy of the individual through abstraction. This might present novel research opportunities due to the dataset describing trends in values over wide geographical areas. Such trends could then be used to make more accurate and informed *planning* within adaptation, considering different supply chain domains and real-world disruptive events such as geo-political or climate change which impact end-consumer purchase trends.

Scalable and adaptive reasoning approaches to values-alignment will be necessary to handle change in end-consumers, actors and the supply chain structure overall. Future work will require approaches which enable enhanced domain and context-specific knowledge to better understand trends and shifting values boundaries. This will allow learning approaches [16] to learn and operate through interaction within a changing multi-agent system. Further decentralisation of the adaptive approach could enable agents to represent a distinct supply chain system of a stakeholder or organisation. This allows local perspectives to be represented in different scales. Such *adaptive reasoning* could be achieved locally, globally, or between arbitrary boundaries, based on the needs or change in values of different societal groups.

Data models representing values will be the foundation for values-management. Values data models should be computable and unambiguous. The averaging approaches used in this paper may obscure scenarios whereby stakeholders have multiple conflicting values and therefore segmenting them according to related values would be more realistic. They will have wider benefits such as mediating technical interoperability across diverse supply chain systems. Enabling interoperability may mitigate observability challenges, allowing values representations to be exchanged across geographical, technical, and cultural boundaries, potentially reducing conflicts where values definitions vary between cultures. This allows moving between local and global perspectives across the entire supply chain, ensuring values observability at different scales.

Threats To Validity Internal threats to validity arise from the use of pseudorandom numbers for the attribute values and the end-consumer and actors selected for change. These threats were mitigated through the use of a normal distribution for the attribute and production values and through running each test case over 1000 supply chains. The mean of the values-misalignment index and assortativity was then selected to mitigate outliers. It should, therefore, be noted that these results show the comparative performance of each test case over exact performance values. External threats to validity centre around the supply chain models and the number of end-consumers relative to the supply chain size. Such models are useful for evaluating our approach but not validated as representing real-world supply chains. In addition, the end-consumer and actor models would benefit from greater granularity and complexity in terms of decision making related to the business costs and consumer willingness when deciding to adapt their values.

6   Related Work

Values-based supply chains have been studied in agriculture literature, where the aim to preserve the values of those who produce and process products and to ensure values-alignment with consumers [7]. These approaches tend to focus on values of sustainability, fairness, resilience and transparency. They typically aim to uncover barriers to operation and adoption [5]; optimise for consumer personalisation [21]; or differentiate products and processes through sustainable social and environmental business practices [11]. These approaches lack technological solutions to manage values. Human values have been studied during software development [9]; in requirements engineering activities [10]; to uncover values embedded in software systems [15]; identify desirable and important values in use feedback to reflect upon within future design activities [15], and also highlight values misalignment [9]. In AI literature, *Values-based reasoning* can been used to make decisions in the presence of values [1]. Ensuring that decisions do not conflict with the values of their users or society requires solving the *value-alignment problem* [16]. To the best of our knowledge, values-based reasoning and values-alignment has not been studied for cyber-physical supply chains. These capabilities require values to be managed across the supply chain (distributed), at run-time and adapt in response to the supply chain and consumer dynamics. Opinion dynamics literature has previously examined iterative convergence of opinions between agents [4,6]. In contrast, our approach provides continuous adaptation to dynamically evolving end-consumer values over time, as opposed to convergence. In addition, we provide a novel metric: *values-misalignment index* to track evolving values and also present a novel application of assortativity, to measure the distribution of values alignment. These metrics move from formal mathematical consensus to socio-technical metrics which are more strongly aligned with digital humanism principles.

7   Conclusion

In this paper, we presented an adaptive approach to support values-alignment between supply chain stakeholders. Our approach is based on the adjustments of values between actors involved in the production process of a product and end-consumers of the product. The values adjustments occur locally in each node involved in the production process, following the MAPE-K loop, in order to achieve global values-alignment in the cyber-physical supply chain. Our approach was evaluated to show how observability in the supply chain impacts values-alignment for end-consumers. Values visibility and alignment capabilities are critical for enabling human agency in increasingly automated supply chains. Therefore, we believe our approach is consistent with digital humanism principles [18]. Future work will develop our approach to support multiple values, larger scale supply chains with a greater number of consumers, real-world applications in continuous time, and further understanding the impact of different parameters for adjusting attributes.

Acknowledgments. The authors acknowledge UKRI for their ongoing support.

Disclosure of Interests. The authors declare that they have no competing interests.

References

1. Atkinson, K., Bench-Capon, T.: Taking account of the actions of others in value-based reasoning. Artifi. Intell. **254** (2018)
2. Bennaceur, A., Hassett, D., Nuseibeh, B., Zisman, A.: Values@ runtime: An adaptive framework for operationalising values. In: 2023 IEEE/ACM 45th International Conference on Software Engineering: Software Engineering in Society (ICSE-SEIS), pp. 175–179. IEEE (2023)
3. Chandra, S., Verma, S., Lim, W.M., Kumar, S., Donthu, N.: Personalization in personalized marketing: trends and ways forward. Psychol. Marketing **39**(8) (2022)
4. DeGroot, M.H.: Reaching a consensus. J. Am. Statist. Associat. **69**(345) (1974)
5. Gutiérrez, J.A., Macken-Walsh, Á.: Ecosystems of collaboration for sustainability-oriented innovation: the importance of values in the agri-food value-chain. Sustainability **14**(18) (2022)
6. Hegselmann, R.: Opinion dynamics and bounded confidence: models, analysis and simulation. J. Artifi. Societies Soc. Simulat. (2015)
7. Lerman, T.: A review of scholarly literature on values-based supply chains. Agricultural Sustainability Institute, University of California, Davis, Sustainable Agriculture Research and Education Program (2012)
8. Newman, M.E.J.: Assortative mixing in networks. Phys. Rev. Lett. **89**, 208701 (2002)
9. Nurwidyantoro, A., et al.: Human values in software development artefacts: a case study on issue discussions in three android applications. Inform. Soft. Tech. **141** (2022)
10. Perera, H., et al.: The impact of considering human values during requirements engineering activities. IEEE Trans. Softw. Eng. (2021)
11. Pullman, M.E., Dillard, J.: Values based supply chain management and emergent organizational structures. Inter. J. Operat. Product. Manag. (2010)
12. Qader, G., Junaid, M., Abbas, Q., Mubarik, M.S.: Industry 4.0 enables supply chain resilience and supply chain performance. Technol. Forecasting Soc. Change **185** (2022)
13. Raut, R.D., Gotmare, A., Narkhede, B.E., Govindarajan, U.H., Bokade, S.U.: Enabling technologies for industry 4.0 manufacturing and supply chain: concepts, current status, and adoption challenges. IEEE Eng. Manag. Rev. **48**(2) (2020). https://doi.org/10.1109/EMR.2020.2987884
14. Shahin, M., Hussain, W., Nurwidyantoro, A., Perera, H., Shams, R., Grundy, J., Whittle, J.: Operationalizing human values in software engineering: a survey. IEEE Access **10** (2022). https://doi.org/10.1109/ACCESS.2022.3190975
15. Shams, R.A., Hussain, W., Oliver, G., Nurwidyantoro, A., Perera, H., Whittle, J.: Society-oriented applications development: investigating users' values from bangladeshi agriculture mobile applications. In: 2020 IEEE/ACM 42nd International Conference on Software Engineering: Software Engineering in Society (ICSE-SEIS). IEEE (2020)
16. Szabo, J., Such, J., Pacheco, N.C., Modgil, S.: Integrating quantitative and qualitative reasoning for value alignment. In: The 19th European Conference on Multi-Agent Systems (2022)
17. Welsh, T., Alrimawi, F., Farahani, A., Hassett, D., Zisman, A., Nuseibeh, B.: Topology-aware adaptive inspection for fraud in i4. 0 supply chains. IEEE Trans. Indust. Inform. **19**(4) (2022)

18. Werthner, H., et al.: Introduction to digital humanism: A textbook. springer nature (2024)
19. Weyns, D., et al.: On patterns for decentralized control in self-adaptive systems. In: de Lemos, R., Giese, H., Müller, H.A., Shaw, M. (eds.) Software Engineering for Self-Adaptive Systems II. LNCS, vol. 7475, pp. 76–107. Springer, Heidelberg (2013). https://doi.org/10.1007/978-3-642-35813-5_4
20. Xie, J., Nozawa, W., Yagi, M., Fujii, H., Managi, S.: Do environmental, social, and governance activities improve corporate financial performance? Business Strategy Environ. **28**(2) (2019)
21. Yao, J., Shi, H., Liu, C.: Optimising the configuration of green supply chains under mass personalisation. Inter. J. Product. Res. **58**(24) (2020)

Digital Humanism: Ethical and Legal Aspects

Beyond the Digital Judge: Legal Reasoning in Compliance Checking and Compliance Choices

Marcello Ceci[(⊠)] and Domenico Bianculli

University of Luxembourg, Luxembourg, Luxembourg
`marcello.ceci@uni.lu, domenico.bianculli@uni.lu`

Abstract. This paper investigates the practical reasoning involved in compliance-related decisions, distinguishing between two scenarios where a state of affairs is evaluated in the light of applicable norms: *ex post* compliance checking and *ex ante* compliance choices. While the literature in legal reasoning representation is exclusively focused on compliance checking scenarios, i.e., simulating a *digital judge*, different factors seem to play a role in the *inner deliberation* of compliance choices. In this paper we investigate how human agents are influenced in their compliance choices by their own value ranking and risk assessment and how, in turn, the choice affects their preference among alternative interpretations of the law. We contend that contributions from the literature such as the value-based argumentation framework, while focused on *ex post* judgments, may be able to provide a comprehensive framework for *ex ante* compliance decisions. The main goal of the research behind this work is to achieve a comprehensive representation of legal reasoning that can be used as a reference for the explanation of automated compliance decisions.

Keywords: AI and Law · Compliance · Digital Justice · Legal Reasoning · Human Decision Making · Value-based Argumentation

1 Introduction

The ever-advancing process of automation is stepping into the area of decision making, including legal decisions affecting the personal freedom of individuals. As technological advancements go, it comes with its own dangers and inevitable learning curves. For example, a decision support software[1], used for decades in courts to automate the parole system, has been criticized on multiple occasions for racial bias [1,5]. While the bias in this case is to be attributed to historical data, the risk of biased decisions is further increased for generative models, where the factors leading to a decision are even more opaque. Moreover, while important, the decision on parole concerns the execution of the penalty, and as such is not the most important decision in a legal process: other,

---

[1] Correctional Offender Management Profiling for Alternative Sanctions (COMPAS) is a case management and decision support software used in some U.S. courts to assess the likelihood of a defendant becoming a recidivist.

© The Author(s) 2026
L. Hagedorn et al. (Eds.): DIGHUM 2025, LNCS 16319, pp. 137–152, 2026.
https://doi.org/10.1007/978-3-032-11108-1_10

more important decisions are likely to be automated in the future, such as the judgment of being guilty of breaching the law.

The prospect of Artificial Intelligence being applied not only as *digital judges* in courts of law, but also as *digital agents* in decisional processes that are subject to regulations[2] poses a critical question regarding our capability to formally represent and thus evaluate those types of decisions. Thus, there is a need to *represent the reasoning of digital agents faced with a compliance-related decision.*

Let us consider two cases, regarding natural and legal persons respectively, inspired by real-life events but anonymized due to privacy concerns:

- *Euthanasia:* a doctor assists consensual patients in performing euthanasia in a country where the practice constitutes a crime *unless its sole purpose is to reduce pain.* The doctor is arrested and tried several times: at first acquitted, then eventually convicted for second-degree murder.
- *Anti-money laundering (AML):* a cryptocurrency firm willingly facilitates transactions from sanctioned groups such as ransomware hackers, and is eventually fined for a hefty sum by the competent AML public authority.

As we will see, the research in AI and Law has done considerable advancements in the representation of the reasoning involved in those judges' decisions, but did not pay as much attention to the representation of the reasoning that may have led the doctor (in the euthanasia case) and the crypto firm (in the AML one) to act the way they did. However, scenarios relegated to science fiction just a few years ago, such as a digital doctor autonomously performing end-of-life choices in an automated healthcare institution or a nonhuman entity autonomously facilitating transactions, are not hard to imagine nowadays, and are likely to become reality in the near future [22]. A formalization and representation of these reasoning processes is paramount to achieve a framework against which compliance-related decisions of digital agents can be coherently explained and thus evaluated.

In this paper we investigate compliance-related decisions, i.e., decisions between alternative actions in the presence of normative restrictions. We do so from the perspective of legal knowledge representation and a focus on practical reasoning[3], with the purpose of examining the capability of the state-of-the-art to represent such reasoning for software applications and automation. In other words, we aim to understand whether our representation of the *digital judge* is on par with that of the *digital agent.* The reasoning involved in compliance choices is in fact different from that involved in other legal reasoning such as the one aimed at resolving conflicts between norms, which rely on rule priorities[4]: compliance decisions are influenced by several factors, including the *context* of the action and the *value ranking* of the agent.

---

[2] Many decisions are already automated, e.g., granting a loan in banking services. Future scenarios go way beyond that: Gervais and Nay [22] envision a *legal singularity* where nonhuman entities that are not directed by humans may enter the legal system as a new *species* of legal subjects, leading to an *interspecific* legal system.

[3] Practical reasoning is an approach to action selection proposed by Raz [42].

[4] Examples of priorities are *lex superior, lex posterior, lex specialis.*

To investigate the differences in legal reasoning, we introduce the two scenarios of *compliance checking* (an *ex post* judgment on a case) and *compliance choice* (an *ex ante* decision on which action to take in a situation). The state-of-the-art in checking the compliance of an autonomous system with regulations, focusing on *ex post* approaches, tends to neglect the fact that breaking the law is sometimes desirable [7]. On the contrary, an autonomous system unable to understand the factors that influence a compliance choice will treat all breaches of the law in the same way, a dangerous scenario especially as the world become less democratic, with freedom of expression, deliberation, rule of law and elections in net decline in the last decade [26]. An automated compliance approach aiming for blind application of the law, neglecting its principles and the values shared by its subjects, has the potential to trigger a feedback loop [40] towards thoughtless, conformance-driven dystopias, whereas democratic systems aim to elicit rule-following on the basis of shared legal principles and values.

The rest of the paper is structured as follows. We begin our investigation into the representation of compliance decisions by presenting (Sect. 2) the recent advancements in the representation of legal reasoning. We then introduce (Sect. 3) the two scenarios of *ex post* and *ex ante* compliance decisions, successively focusing on the *inner deliberation* process of *ex ante* compliance choices and its relation with the preference among alternative interpretations of the law. We further show (Sect. 4) how additional factors seem to play a role in compliance choices, in a defeasible meta-argumentative process related to the (expressed) preference among alternative interpretations of a norm. We finally show (Sect. 5) how such a process can be represented via an argumentation framework, to support practical reasoning.

2   Background: The Representation of Legal Reasoning

In this section, we present the most important contributions in the representation of legal reasoning from the fields of AI and Law and Requirements Engineering (RE).

Models for Representing Legal Concepts. The field of AI and Law provides approaches for legal compliance checking based on modeling deontic norms, representing peculiarities of legal knowledge such as norm defeasibility or multiple interpretations [20]. In the field of RE, models such as the taxonomy of semantic metadata of legal provisions [46] or the approach for deriving business processes from the law [15] are attempts to tame the complexity of the legal domain with task-automation objectives in mind. However, those models use a high-level, often generic, representation of the provisions and exhibit a weak relationship to the real-life states of affairs [29].

Rule Languages for Representing Norms. In AI and Law, semantic markup languages (e.g., LegalRuleML) or open formats [20], and representations of the norms complexities [2] have been widely investigated. Complex normative structures have been studied also in RE, to support the precise definition of software requirements. While earlier attempts at rule-based formalizations lack consideration for legal peculiarities [13], more recent approaches such as Legal GRL by Ghavanati et al. [23] and Nòmos by Ingolfo et al. [27] account for aspects such as Hohfeldian relations and alternative representations of legal norms. Legal GRL represents legal requirements in the context of goal-based reasoning, thus integrating aspects of practical reasoning; however, while successfully representing the elements of legal reasoning applied to software engineering, the approach lacks consideration of the dynamics of it, as shown by Ghavanati et al.'s [23] assumption that "when a legal goal is of type *Obligation*, it must be satisfied completely". As we will see in Sect. 3.2, this is not always the case.

Legal Reasoning. While the field of RE does not focus on the automated application of legal requirements through reasoning, contributions on the topic from AI and Law are many and diverse. The most comprehensive solution to representing legal reasoning while accounting for aspects such as alternative representations is considered to be the use of argumentation [9,10,31], whose formal study has played an important role within Artificial Intelligence for considerable time [35]. Dung's abstract argumentation framework [18] provided a standard approach for detecting conflicts of arguments, with a huge impact on AI and Law [6]. Further research by Modgil and Prakken [37] led to the development of an extended argumentation framework, allowing the resolution of such conflicts via a meta-argumentation layer prioritizing arguments *pro* or *con* a certain conclusion according to preferences. Walton et al. [49] introduced the concept of argumentation schemes, forms of argument that capture stereotypical patterns of human reasoning. These schemes allow for the defeasibility of arguments via critical questions, enabling the representation of a meta-argumentation layer where a certain value ranking may determine the preference among conflicting arguments. Normative reasoning has been also captured in constrained I/O logics [33], and recent efforts are trying to combine this approach with formal argumentation [8]. The above presented contributions however focus on a judgment perspective (*ex post* analysis), neglecting the agent's perspective, as we will see next.

3   Towards a General Legal Reasoning Framework

3.1   Legal Reasoning in *Ex Post* Compliance Checking vs. *Ex ante* Compliance Choices

The literature in legal reasoning representation deals with **ex post compliance decisions**, i.e., the application of the law to a *case*[5]. These are the decisions taken by judges in judgments (constituting the body of norms called *case law*) and by compliance officers in internal audits. *Ex post* decisions lead to a *judgment of action*: we will therefore call this activity **compliance checking**. Since these evaluations concern past facts and events whose truth is approximated according to the burden of proof, the legal reasoning performed therein does not involve uncertain information.

However, since the purpose of compliance checking is to evaluate a past state of affairs from a strictly legal viewpoint (i.e., to determine if an action or state of affairs

---

[5] *Case* here is meant as defined by Čyras and Lachmayer [17], as opposed to *situation*. Situations concern the future and are related with ex-ante analysis, whereas cases are related with ex-post, being concerned with the past; this implies that certain judgments (e.g., preliminary rulings) which are not taken *ex post* are not considered in the present work.

is in breach of applicable norms), with the exception of criminal trials[6] and theoretical work on argumentation frameworks (see Sect. 5), current conceptualizations of compliance are not concerned with understanding why the illegal action was taken nonetheless. We have no clue as to whether the action was due to a mistake, a wrong interpretation, an unlucky bet, or a deliberate choice. Furthermore, we do not know what a rational person would do if faced by the same choice. This knowledge lies in the realm of **compliance choices**, i.e., ***ex ante* compliance decisions** on which action to take in a specific *situation* [17]. Since those decisions have to be taken on the basis of incomplete information and uncertain outcomes, they imply practical reasoning, following one of two approaches: either an *actualist approach*, i.e., they can try to *actually* obtain the best reward, or a *possibilist approach*, i.e., they can try to maximize the potential reward, however unlikely that might be[7]. While, under a possibilist approach, an agent will try to comply to the maximum possible extent with normative restrictions, human agents are rather prone to adopt the actualist approach, which implies a different way to factor in normative restrictions, as we will see in the next subsection.

3.2 The Inner Deliberation

Current approaches to compliance tend to assume that people's (and companies') behavior is perfectly law-abiding and thus provide a vision of the world according to which the agent acts exclusively within the boundaries of the law. For example, in the field of Requirements Engineering (RE), legal requirements are specified as if all norms were equally sufficient in influencing behavior. In the RE literature there is no mention of norms that can be ignored or breached, and how to determine them and translate that evaluation into software requirements. In autonomous systems, prohibited actions tend to be downright unavailable [7]. But is that truly how our world works? Do we comply to all norms that are applicable to our situation? For example, do we read and understand all the terms and conditions before using a software? Studies suggest otherwise [32,47]. In fact, agents use a form of utility function to make decisions on whether to act in compliance or in breach of applicable norms, and normally choose the action which has the most favorable consequences *for themselves*.

Bench-Capon and Modgil [7] state that in some cases we know that a rule applies but we still do not conform. They go further, stating that unreflecting adherence to norms (i.e., blind rule conformance) is not what we expect from a genuinely moral reasoner: *rules are made to be broken*. This is indeed a step towards an *actualist* approach to compliance choices, where a deliberate breach of a norm is possible. In fact, when faced with a choice of action in the face of normative restrictions, we engage in an **inner deliberation**, an *actualist* dialogue juxtaposing conflicting arguments about whether to comply or not. Differently from compliance dialogues (discussed in the context of multi

---

[6] In the euthanasia case, the goals of the doctor are relevant to the judgment: the debate in court would revolve around whether the act had the *intent to relieve pain* as opposed to the *intent to cause death* (see Sect. 3.3). On the other hand, in the AML case, with AML being in the subdomain of corporate criminal liability, little to no importance is given to goals; in the example, the fact that illegal transactions were facilitated would alone justify the penalty.

[7] In value learning the two approaches are called *on-policy* and *off-policy*—see Christian [16].

agent systems by Rotolo [43]) and deliberation dialogues (described by Atkinson and Bench-Capon [4]), the dialogue of inner deliberation does not involve multiple agents (or audiences) with different goals (or value rankings), but rather involves different potentially conflicting factors arguing for alternative choices of action.

When dealing with how humans act in the face of normative restrictions, we are in the domain of decisions in the face of uncertain outcomes. This correspond to the domain of practical reasoning (or game theory when involving other agents), where we want to understand the possible implications in each choice, factoring the legal consequences (mainly, the risk of a penalty) with all other factors involved in decision making. The basic example to express the reward system in game theory considers that the cost of riding a bus without a ticket corresponds to the penalty for the violation multiplied by the enforcement probability: for example, if the fine for being caught without a valid ticket is 10€ and the chance of being caught is 10%, then riding ticketless is a rational choice if the price of a ticket exceeds 1€. In the world of legal compliance these considerations form part of *risk management*[8].

There is, however, more than risk management in a compliance choice, as greed is not the only reason for an agent to deliberately breach a norm. A breach may in fact be *necessary* in the situations when compliance to all applicable rules at once is impossible (e.g., because of a conflict of norms or jurisdictions). There are further cases, where the breach of a law is not simply a mistake, a bet, or an inevitable choice. For example, it can be a way to improve security: de Mattos et al. [34] report how 25% of surveyed papers consider breaches as *positive* (e.g., in improving work conditions and safety). In the euthanasia case, the doctor chose to assist people in causing their own death with the intention to do good (relieving pain, fulfilling a man's will): in fact, he never received any economic compensation for his services. After being prosecuted and acquitted several times in situations where he did not materially administer the lethal injection, he came to the point of administering it himself and publicly confessing his deed, practically requesting to be prosecuted, with the aim of seeing the lawfulness of any such acts sanctioned in a court of law. This configures as a blatant breach of a norm, i.e., a breach not caused by a mistake or a material impossibility to comply, and not done in secret in the hope to avoid legal scrutiny.

We have seen how laws can be breached intentionally, sometimes even deliberately. Before investigating further (in Sect. 4) the factors that lead a subject to choose to act in breach of a norm, we will now investigate the qualification of breaches: are they always acts of rebellion to the authority, or may they be something else? It turns out that behaviors judged as breaches are often not seen by the agents as deliberate violations, but rather as behaviors that are lawful, *under the agent's own interpretation of the norm.*

3.3   Arguing About Alternative Interpretations

There is always a limit to a norm's applicability: it cannot be overstretched to have effects that go against the principles behind it. These principles are often implicit, but can manifest themselves in the preamble of the law or through the so-called *final rules* (e.g., as theorized in Italy's legal system as *norme di chiusura*), whose function is to

---

[8] Compliance risk [19] is a subcategory of operational risk.

solve conflicts or gaps in the law. For example, in work safety law, even in the absence of specific norms, the foreman is still required to adopt caution and diligence in order to protect the physical integrity of workers[9]. Similar rules prevent legal norms to counteract the very principles they are meant to foster, e.g., if complying with a norm would harm the interest of third parties[10]. These norms constitute a particular kind of legal exceptions, whose effect is represented in AI and Law as rule *defeasibility* [10] rather than rule violation: from a legal-theoretical point of view, the agent is not breaching the norm but it is rather the norm's coercitive power to be defeated by an exception derived from legal principles. In case-based reasoning, an influential contribution by Berman and Hafner [9] argues that, in absence of precedent, the decision should be made according to which social purposes would be promoted by deciding for either part, choosing whichever would better serve the prevalent social values.

Not following an applicable norm is therefore not always an act of rebellion to the authority. It is more often performed by agents who, though they recognize the authority, they believe they can justify their action according to an interpretation of the legal text, driven by legal principles, that excludes their action from the red zone of legal prohibitions. In the euthanasia case, the law prohibited to *knowingly provide the physical means or participate in the act of suicide*, with the exception of acts whose *intent is to relieve pain*. In the example, the defense argued that the law did not apply to the doctor, whose aim was to eliminate suffering, with death occurring as a mere consequence of his goal. Here, the issue concerns the interpretation of the world *pain*, and the identification of the threshold of pain that would warrant the exception. During the first trials, the interpretation of the law made by the defense seemed to match that of the jury, as the doctor was repeatedly acquitted. Interestingly, the doctor would later be found guilty of second-degree murder. In that occasion however, two things were different: first, the doctor administered the lethal injection himself; second, he publicly admitted to his deed while exposing controversial beliefs about life and religion. These circumstances highlight the link between the interpretation of the law, the goals of the action and the agent's values in the context of law application.

We note how, in both cases of *ex post* compliance checking and *ex ante* compliance choices, **the decision is twofold**: we decide our preference among *alternative representations* of the law (mostly due to *alternative interpretations*) and at the same time we decide on *a (judgment of) action*. According to Hawkins [25], there are different decisional frames to a decision. While the choice of action may depend on any of these, in *ex post* justification the legal frame prevails: the agent is expected to try to justify their action before the law, by adopting an interpretation of the law that renders their action lawful (or as little illegal as possible), even if the agent does not share that interpretation. Judges on the other hand are not supposed to be influenced by their personal preferences when adopting an interpretation: they are supposed to be impartial, not choosing according to a desired outcome, such as seeing in jail someone they despise. Still, they will apply the legal interpretation that matches the values or principles of the

---

[9] Art. 2087 of the Italian Civil Code.

[10] See for example the Directive 2009/65/EC of the European Parliament and of the Council of 13 July 2009 on the coordination of laws, regulations and administrative provisions relating to undertakings for collective investment in transferable securities (UCITS).

law as understood by them. According to Atkinson and Bench-Capon [4], the reasoning behind judgments implies an inverted *direction of fit*[11] where the judge selects the interpretation of the norm to adapt it to its (alleged) principles. This seems to be even more the case for *ex ante* compliance choices with an *actualist* approach. In those situations, human agents do not always *conform*, i.e., adapt their actions to the law: often, they rather **adapt the interpretation of the law to the desired action**.

We have seen how, while in judgments the interpretation is aligned to the principles of the law as understood by the judge, in compliance choices the interpretation is often aligned to the subject's choice of action and justified according to values. In the next section, we outline the factors playing a role in the weighing of alternative actions in the context of a compliance choice.

4   The Factors of *ex ante* Compliance Choices

As we have seen, *ex ante* legal reasoning is shaped, to put it in the words of Leith [30], as "a process of guesswork and deductive justification". This implies that choices among interpretations are made after, and based on, the chosen action. In this latter choice, other factors come into play. Muthuri et al. [38] show how, for companies, legal choices are handled at a strategic level as a legal risk, and the interpretation of the law determines the preference among arguments in a legal dispute. Bench-Capon and Modgil [7] show how the **values** promoted/demoted by the norm play a fundamental role in determining our preference among actions as well as among alternative interpretations of a norm. For example, we do not accept an interpretation that would contravene the very principles behind the legal act that we are interpreting.

The approach of value-based reasoning seems an ideal base for any legal intelligent application dealing with *ex ante* decisions. However, as we have seen in the previous section, alternative actions and alternative interpretations are related but are not the same thing. In this section, we focus on the choice of action, trying to identify the factors that must be taken into account in order to provide a comprehensive model of compliance choices.

We identified two distinct dimensions influencing a compliance choice of action:

- The **desired state of affairs** (determined by the agent's **goals**, which in turn derive from their **value ranking** [7][12]). In the euthanasia case, the choice to assist in euthanasia would achieve a state where a person who is suffering is no more, which

---

[11] Discussions on principles and values have a different *direction of fit* than fact-based discussions (mind-to-world instead of world-to-mind). Notably, this allows for alternative solutions which are all equally rational [4]. The notion of *direction of fit* was introduced by John Searle in his work on practical reasoning. He wrote: "Assume universally valid and accepted standards of rationality, assume perfectly rational agents operating with perfect information, and you will find that rational disagreement will still occur; because, for example, the rational agents are likely to have different and inconsistent values and interests, each of which may be rationally acceptable" [45].

[12] Atkinson and Bench-Capon [3] define the argument scheme for practical reasoning as "In the circumstances R we should perform action A to achieve new circumstances S which will realise some goal G which will promote some value V".

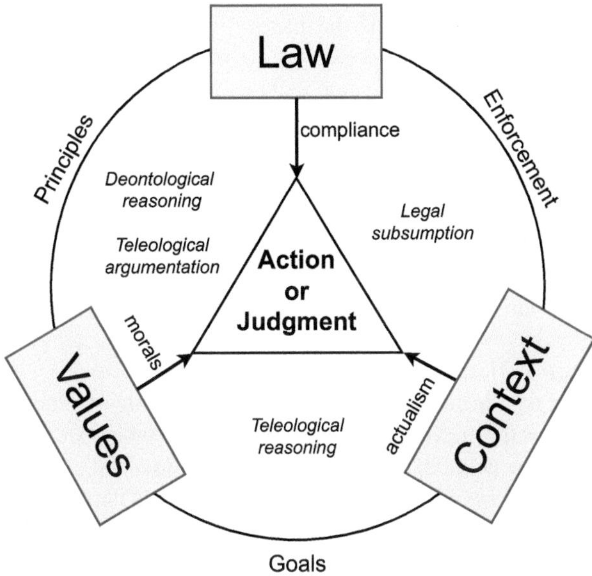

Fig. 1. The Deliberational Screwhead.

would fulfill the goal of reducing suffering, based on the value of caring for other individuals and freedom of individuals [44]. On the other side, a refusal would result in one more person being alive, compatible with the goals of maximising the working population; it would also avoid the creation of a caste of god-like purveyors of death; both of these goals pertain to the value of social security. In the AML case, the crypto firm's behaviour is aimed to have more clients, fulfilling the goal of maximizing profit, based on the value of power through resources; on the other hand, refusing transactions from sanctioned groups would result in those groups being weakened, compatible with the goal of reducing socially dangerous activities, a goal which—again—fosters the value of social security.

- The **risk** embedded in a certain behavior (mainly that of **enforcement and penalty** [41]). This factor is related to strategical thinking; however, other characteristics come into play: short of norms whose violators incur capital punishment (for which *Pascal's Wager* applies), the way in which humans see crime and punishment is a complex matter, and cannot be reduced to mere strategical thinking. As mentioned earlier, this aspect of choices is formalized in a business perspective in the discipline of risk management, and more specifically compliance risk. Regarding our examples, we can imagine how the risk of enforcement and penalty played little to no role into the doctor's choice in the euthanasia case, as he was actually looking for a prosecution in order to prove his point; at the same time, that risk/reward analysis must have played an important role in the crypto firm's choice, which later turned out to be an unlucky bet, but at the time of the decision must have seemed more likely to provide a positive economic outcome than a negative one.

The diagram in Fig. 1 represents the factors interacting in a compliance choice, which we call the *Deliberational Screwhead*; its main elements, as identified by Verheij [48] in the context of ethical decision making, are *law*, *context* and *values*.

- **Law** is intended as the sum of statutes, case-law, guidelines, and any other official document expressing norms. Resolution of legal conflicts and other formal legal reasoning is performed here, before the result in terms of applicable norms is carried on to influence the choice of action or judgement. Law influences the choice of *judgment* or *action* through **compliance**: to the extent to which an action (or judgement) is determined by the law, we can say that it is influenced by compliance.
- **Context** is intended as the contingent state of affairs (the facts) to be seen either as *case* or *situation* [17], depending on whether we are discussing *ex post* or *ex ante* (i.e., whether we decide on a *judgment* or an *action*). Context influences the choice of *judgment* or *action* through **actualism**: to the extent to which an action or judgement is determined by the context, we can say that it is influenced by actualism.
- **Values** are, in the words of Schwartz [44], "conceptions on the desirable that influence the way people select action and evaluate events". They influence a compliance decision through the so-called value ranking [4]. As noted previously, in the euthanasia case, the ranking would prioritize freedom of individuals in the case of a pro-euthanasia behavior, and the preservation of human life in the case of a contrary position. In Schwartz's value theory [44], a pro-euthanasia approach seems to prioritize *self direction (action)* over *societal security*, while the opposite applies to the contrary position. In the AML example, the values involved seem to be *power (resources)* vs. *societal security, norm conformance*, and *face* (i.e., avoiding the loss of reputation in case the breach was discovered). Unfortunately, we are currently unable to specify human goals and societal values in a way that reliably directs AI behavior [39]. Values influence the choice of *judgment* or *action* through **morals**: to the extent to which an action or judgement is determined by their values, we can say that it is influenced by morals.

A choice is hardly ever influenced by a single factor. In that sense, we can see how some concepts of legal compliance such as **legal principles**, **goals** and **enforcement** can be seen as a combination of factors (law and values, values and context, and context and law, respectively). Furthermore, these combinations of factors seem to imply different types of reasoning: reasoning on principles is related to deontological reasoning and teleological argumentation; reasoning on goals is related to teleological reasoning; and reasoning on enforcement is related to legal subsumption, a type of legal interpretation. An important question here is whether (and to what extent) these factors of compliance choices should be made explicit in the deliberation process. This question is related to whether we consider legal compliance as being limited to detect *rule conformance* or as encompassing *rule following*[13].

---

[13] While in *rule conformance* we limit our analysis to the compliance of the behavior with the norm, in *rule following* we also want to verify the congruence of the agent's intentions with the legal principles. The difference is important when drawing insights from observing an agent's behavior—see Galoob and Hill [21]. The first to argue for rule following was Kant [28].

The factors that we have outlined in this section work as prioritization criteria among alternatives of action. In the next section, we will investigate how such prioritization criteria can be implemented in an argumentation framework through a meta-argumentation layer.

5   Handling Compliance Decisions with Argumentation

The goal of Dung's abstract argumentation framework is to determine the acceptability of arguments. The framework is composed of only two elements: arguments and binary conflict-based attack relations [18]. For example, in the euthanasia case, the argument that *"the doctor acted with the purpose of economic profit"* is attacked by the argument that *"the doctor received no economic compensation for his action"*. Dung's abstract argumentation framework does not include a solution to solve conflicts between argument, i.e., arguments that attack each other reciprocally. For example the arguments *"causing death to remove pain is not murder"* and *"causing death is always murder"* are in conflict. To handle such conflicts, an **extended argumentation framework** with a meta-argumentation layer is necessary [12]. Modgil [35] proposed such a framework for value-based reasoning, prioritizing alternative interpretations of a norm according to the value ranking of the agent. Despite the framework being "usable in any situation in which reasoning about actions is required" (Atkinson and Bench-Capon [4]), when dealing with law as a domain-specific application, the literature focuses on *ex post* judgments, showing how value rankings lead to the preference among alternative interpretations of the law[14].

In the context of our example, Fig. 2 shows the arguments involved in the euthanasia case. The white circles represent arguments, and the arrows represent attack relations. Compared to Dung's abstract framework [18], we added a grey circle representing a meta-argument via value ranking. On the left-hand side, we see the conflict between the arguments *"causing death to remove pain is not murder"* and *"causing death is always murder"*. Here, the conflict can be resolved via a value ranking between social security and personal freedom. On the right-hand side, the value-based conflict is shown in details, following Modgil's extended argumentation framework [36]. Here, the two white circles represent the conflicting arguments. Their attack relations are themselves attacked by the two possible value preference arguments (grey circles), namely $v2>v1$ and $v1>v2$. Such value-based conflict is solved in a specific extension of the framework by determining the ranking of $v1$ and $v2$.

The application of practical reasoning to moral choices is investigated by Atkinson and Bench-Capon [3], but without taking into account the enforcement risk, and has not been adopted beyond theoretical research. Nevertheless, the framework for value-based reasoning seems fit for representing the inner deliberation of *ex ante* compliance choices: different value rankings would lead to different (and equally rational) choices of action and preferences among alternative interpretations. For example, we may see how choosing a prohibited action could derive from a deliberation involving a preference of value $v2$ over value $v1$, which made the agent prefer an action promoting value

---

[14] In Atkinson and Bench-Capon [4], the example concerns the analogy in case law, a typical use case for AI and Law in common law systems.

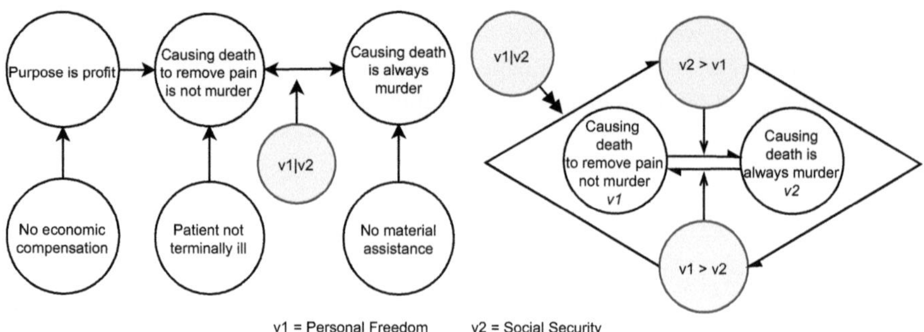

Fig. 2. *Left*: possible representation of the *ex post* judgment on the euthanasia case using Dung's abstract framework with the addition of meta-arguments (grey circle); *right*: value-based conflict in an extended argumentation framework, as given by Modgil and Bench-Capon [36].

v2 while the norm seems to promote value *v1*; we could then verify whether it exists an interpretation of the breached norm under the same value ranking *v2>v1* which would result in the same action being compliant to the norm.

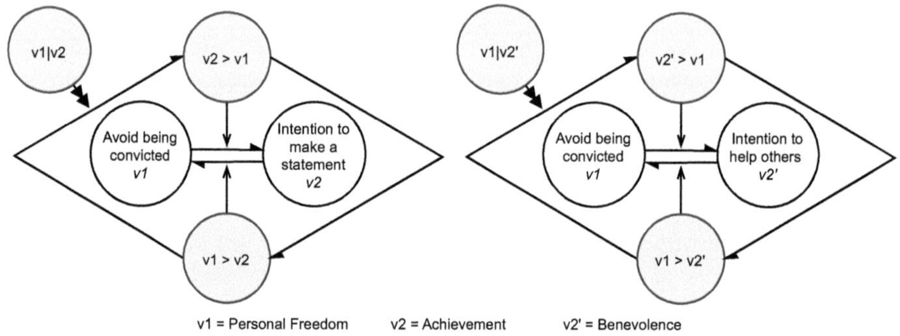

Fig. 3. Possible value-based conflicts in the *ex ante* choice on euthanasia.

The value-based conflicts in the euthanasia case are provided in Fig. 3. We can assume the desire of avoiding conviction as the main argument attacking the choice of assisting in euthanasia. This argument is in conflict with two possible intentions of the doctor, i.e., that of helping others and that of making a public statement and possibly gain renown. These conflicts can be solved via meta-arguments referring to the value ranking and the enforcement risk; however, in the example, the doctor was undeterred by the latter: he seemed convinced of his capability to avoid punishment, or ready to accept it, thus both instances of *v2* are preferred over *v1* in this case[15]. This is what characterizes, when referring to the diagram in Fig. 1, the choice of the doctor as a *moral*

---

[15] The value of *personal freedom* leads to an *ex post* judgment of euthanasia as lawful, while in an *ex ante* choice leads to abstaining from such an act. This difference further explains the importance of accurately modeling the factors of compliance decisions in both scenarios.

(rather than a *compliant* or *actualist*) choice. The two diagrams in Figs. 2 and 3 are related in that, after a choice in the inner deliberation of Fig. 3 has been taken, the argumentation of Fig. 2 represents the way in which the doctor (more precisely his attorney) will argue for the lawfulness of his (client's) action. Only a combination of the two diagrams can in fact explain the inter-relationship between choice of action and preference among interpretations (see § 3.3).

It seems that argumentation has a different task in the case of compliance choices: rather than to verify a complete set of facts (a *case* [17]) under alternative interpretations, the task concerns the analysis of different choices of action combined with different interpretations of the law in a specific *situation*. On that regard, ambiguity propagation logic [24] allows for exploring alternative conclusions in the presence of unknown or uncertain information on the acceptability of specific arguments.

6   Conclusions

In this paper, we have investigated the representation of compliance decisions from the perspective of both *digital judges* and *digital agents*. We discussed the state of the art in the representation of *ex ante* and *ex post* compliance decisions and tried to expand on the factors that lead to a *compliance choice*. We saw how compliance choices are related to different factors and how they influence the preference among alternative interpretations of a norm. While value-based argumentation [4] seems able to support *ex ante* reasoning, this framework is not adopted in practical applications, where instead a naive approach to compliance choices prevails, with agents supposed to spontaneously comply with all the rules applicable to their situation.

A fit model for digital judges would perform poorly for a digital agent if its motivations of action were built solely upon the justifications provided in court, ignoring the inner deliberation of *ex ante* compliance choices, and the relation between the choice of action and the (declared) preference among alternative interpretations. We showed how, in our euthanasia example, the two sargumentations are inherently different.

From this consideration arises an important concern on AI alignment [16]: automated agents should make compliance choices by contextualizing value(-based goal)s and normative restrictions in the specific situation, as a human would. In this paper, we have outlined how context and values shape not only the legal interpretation of the rules, but also the uncertainties of ethical decision making [48], which affect the utility functions of practical reasoning [14]. We argue that the research towards a general legal architecture for intelligent applications should extend legal case-based reasoning [3] and value-based argumentation [4] to encompass practical reasoning and game-theoretical aspects of *ex ante, actualist* compliance choices [11].

We need to represent human legal reasoning (i.e., practical reasoning) as it is, and not as we would like it to be (i.e., mere rules application), to avoid the risk that biased AIs, unaware of our inner deliberation due to an inaccurate representation of legal reasoning, reproduce an *ex post* bias which, in a feedback loop [40], has the potential to downplay the relationship of humans with law towards thoughtless rule conformance.

Acknowledgments. This research was funded in whole, or in part, by the Luxembourg National Research Fund (FNR), under grant number C24/IS/18894115/AGLAIA.

Disclosure of Interests. The authors have no competing interests to declare that are relevant to the content of this article.

References

1. Angwin, J., Larson, J., Mattu, S., Kirchner, L.: Machine bias. In: Ethics of Data and Analytics, pp. 254–264. Auerbach Publications (2022)
2. Anim, J., Robaldo, L., Wyner, A.Z.: A SHACL-based approach for enhancing automated compliance checking with RDF data. Information **15**(12) (2024)
3. Atkinson, K., Bench-Capon, T.: Addressing moral problems through practical reasoning. J. Appli. Logic **6**, 135–151 (2008)
4. Atkinson, K., Bench-Capon, T.J.: Value-based argumentation. FLAP **8**(6), 1543–1588 (2021)
5. Bahl, U., Topaz, C., Obermuller, L., Goldstein, S., Sneirson, M.: Algorithms in judges' hands: Incarceration and inequity in Broward County, Florida. UCLA L. Rev. Disc. **71** (2023)
6. Bench-Capon, T.: Before and after dung: argumentation in AI and Law. Argument Comput. **11**(1–2), 221–238 (2020)
7. Bench-Capon, T., Modgil, S.: Norms and value based reasoning: justifying compliance and violation. Artif. Intell. Law **25**(1), 29–64 (2017)
8. van Berkel, K., Straßer, C.: Reasoning with and about norms in logical argumentation. In: Computational Models of Argument, vol. 353. IOS Press (2022)
9. Berman, D.H., Hafner, C.D.: Representing teleological structure in case-based legal reasoning: the missing link. In: Proceedings of the 4th Int. Conf. in AI and Law, ICAIL 1993. Association for Computing Machinery, New York (1993)
10. Billi, M., et al.: Argumentation and defeasible reasoning in the law. J - Multidisciplinary Sci. J. **4**, 897–914 (2021)
11. Boella, G., van Der Torre, L.: A game-theoretic approach to normative multi-agent systems. Normative Multi-agent Systems (2007)
12. Boella, G., Gabbay, D.M., van der Torre, L., Villata, S.: Meta-argumentation modelling I: methodology and techniques. Stud. Logica. **93**(2), 297 (2009)
13. Boella, G., Humphreys, L., Muthuri, R., Rossi, P., van der Torre, L.: A critical analysis of legal requirements engineering from the perspective of legal practice. In: RELAW 2014 (2014)
14. Bradley, R., Drechsler, M.: Types of uncertainty. Erkenntnis **79**(6), 1225–1248 (2014)
15. Breaux, T.D., Antón, A.I., Doyle, J.: Semantic parameterization: a process for modeling domain descriptions. ACM Trans. Softw. Eng. Methodol. **18**(2), 5:1–5:27 (2008)
16. Christian, B.: The alignment problem: how can machines learn human values? Atlantic Books (2021)
17. Čyras, V., Lachmayer, F.: Situation versus case and two kinds of legal subsumption. In: Abstraction and Application. In: Proceedings of the 16th Int. Legal Informatics Symposium, IRIS (2013)
18. Dung, P.M.: On the acceptability of arguments and its fundamental role in nonmonotonic reasoning, logic programming and n-person games. Artifi. Intell. **77**(2) (1995)
19. Esayas, S., Mahler, T.: Modelling compliance risk: a structured approach. Artifi. Intell. Law **23**(3), 271–300 (2015). https://doi.org/10.1007/s10506-015-9174-x
20. Francesconi, E., Governatori, G.: Patterns for legal compliance checking in a decidable framework of linked open data. Artifi. Intell. Law **31**, 1–20 (2022)
21. Galoob, S.R., Hill, A.: Norms, attitudes and compliance. Tulsa Law Rev. **50**(2) (2015)

22. Gervais, D.J., Nay, J.J.: Artificial intelligence and interspecific law. Science **382**(6669), 376–378 (2023)
23. Ghanavati, S., Amyot, D., Rifaut, A.: Legal goal-oriented requirement language (legal GRL) for modeling regulations. In: MiSE 2014, pp. 1–6 (2014)
24. Governatori, G., Maher, M.J., Antoniou, G., Billington, D.: Argumentation semantics for defeasible logic. J. Log. Comput. **14**(5), 675–702 (2004)
25. Hawkins, K.: Enforcing regulation: working theories of compliance and punishment. In: Proc. of the Conference on the Enforcement of Regulation; Indecopi: Lima, Peru (2016)
26. Hellmeier, S., et al.: State of the world 2020: autocratization turns viral. Democratization **28**(6), 1053–1074 (2021)
27. Ingolfo, S., Siena, A., Susi, A., Perini, A., Mylopoulos, J.: Modeling laws with nomos 2. In: RELAW 2013, pp. 69–71 (2013)
28. Kant, I.: The Metaphysics of Morals. Cambridge University Press (1797)
29. Kosenkov, O., Unterkalmsteiner, M., Méndez, D., Fucci, D., Gorschek, T., Fischbach, J.: On developing an artifact-based approach to regulatory requirements engineering. In: MoDRE 2024, pp. 262–271 (2024)
30. Leith, P.: Logic, formal models and legal reasoning. Jurimetrics J. **24**, 334 (1983)
31. Longo, L.: Argumentation for knowledge representation, conflict resolution, defeasible inference and its integration with machine learning. ML Health Inform. (2016)
32. Luger, E., Moran, S., Rodden, T.: Consent for all: revealing the hidden complexity of terms and conditions. In: Proc. SIGCHI Conference on Human Factors in Computing Systems, CHI 2013, pp. 2687–2696. Association for Computing Machinery, New York (2013)
33. Makinson, D., Van Der Torre, L.: Constraints for input/output logics. J. Philos. Log. **30**, 155–185 (2001)
34. de Mattos, L.A., Rocha, R., de Castro, F.: Human error and violation of rules in industrial safety: a systematic literature review. Work **79**(3), 1237–1253 (2024)
35. Modgil, S.: Reasoning about preferences in argumentation frameworks. Artif. Intell. **173**(9–10), 901–934 (2009)
36. Modgil, S., Bench-Capon, T.: Integrating object and meta-level value based argumentation. COMMA **172**, 240–251 (2008)
37. Modgil, S., Prakken, H.: A general account of argumentation with preferences. Artif. Intell. **195**, 361–397 (2013)
38. Muthuri, R., Capecchi, S., Sulis, E., Amantea, I.A., Boella, G.: Integrating value modeling and legal risk management: an IT case study. Inform. Syst. e-Business Manag., 1–29 (2022)
39. Nay, J.J.: Law informs code: a legal informatics approach to aligning artificial intelligence with humans. Nw. J. Tech. & Intell. Prop. **20**, 309 (2022)
40. O'Hara, I.: Feedback loops: Algorithmic authority, emergent biases, and implications for information literacy. Pennsylvania Libraries: Res. Pract. **9**(1), 8–15 (2021)
41. Peeters, M., Denkers, A., Huisman, W.: Rule violations by SMEs: the influence of conduct within the industry, company culture and personal motives. Eur. J. Criminol. **17**(1), 50–69 (2020)
42. Raz, J. (ed.): Practical Reasoning. Oxford University Press, New York (1978)
43. Rotolo, A.: Norm compliance of rule-based cognitive agents. In: Proceedings of the 22nd International Joint Conference on AI, IJCAI 2011, vol. 3. AAAI Press (2011)
44. Schwartz, S.H.: The refined theory of basic values. In: Roccas, S., Sagiv, L. (eds.) Values and Behavior, pp. 51–72. Springer, Cham (2017). https://doi.org/10.1007/978-3-319-56352-7_3
45. Searle, J.R.: Rationality in action. MIT press (2003)
46. Sleimi, A., Sannier, N., Sabetzadeh, M., Briand, L., Ceci, M., Dann, J.: An automated framework for the extraction of semantic legal metadata from legal texts. Empir. Softw. Eng. **26**(3), 1–50 (2021). https://doi.org/10.1007/s10664-020-09933-5

47. Steinfeld, N.: "I agree to the terms and conditions": (How) do users read privacy policies online? An eye-tracking experiment. Comput. Hum. Behav. **55**, 992–1000 (2016)
48. Verheij, B.: Formalizing value-guided argumentation for ethical systems design. Artif. Intell. Law **24**(4), 387–407 (2016)
49. Walton, D., Reed, C., Macagno, F.: Argumentation schemes. Cambridge Univ, Press (2008)

Visual Neuroprosthetics, Digital Humans
and the Law of Evidence

Claudia González-Márquez[1,2(✉)] and Burkhard Schafer[3]

[1] School of Law, The University of Edinburgh, Edinburgh, UK
c.gonzalezmarquez@ed.ac.uk
[2] Edinburgh Futures Institute, Centre for Technomoral Futures, The University of Edinburgh,
Edinburgh, UK
[3] School of Law, The University of Edinburgh, Edinburgh, Scotland, UK

Abstract. The paper explores some of the evidential implications of neuro-implants that assist or restore vision from the perspective of evidence law. As people with disabilities are disproportionately victims of crime, and often experience secondary victimisation during trials where their credibility is often questioned, these technologies raise the question of how evidence law should treat "technologically mediated" witness accounts.

Keywords: neurotechnologies · eyewitness · evidence law

1 Introduction

Digital humanism is "the approach that describes, analyses, and, most importantly, influences the complex interplay between technology and humankind—striving for a better society while fully respecting universal human rights" [28]. Digital technologies that are intimately connected to a human wearer, so intimately indeed that it can become challenging to draw borders between them, force us to revisit some older concepts and conceptions of justice. It asks how we should accommodate technological transformation in a system that traditionally emphasised the human, while delegating technology to something "owned by" them, if these objects become so intimately connected to their wearers that separation is no longer effortlessly possible.

Vision-enhancing and vision-restoring neuro-implants, in particular, are becoming a reality. From the (now defunct) Orion/Argus systems by Second Sight to Neuralink's Blindsight, brain implants that translate images captured on a head-mounted video camera directly into neural stimulation of the visual cortex have been successfully trialled "in the wild" and provided their users, albeit limited, capabilities to experience "visual" representations of their surroundings [1].

For the law, these technologies represent largely uncharted territory, though the risks they pose if left unregulated—particularly to our physical well-being, privacy, and autonomy—are increasingly acknowledged. This paper aims to examine a specific challenge that has so far received little academic attention: how should evidence from a wearer of a vision-restoring or enhancing neuro-implant be treated in a criminal trial? Should

L. Hagedorn et al. (Eds.): DIGHUM 2025, LNCS 16319, pp. 153–168, 2026.
https://doi.org/10.1007/978-3-032-11108-1_11

they be regarded as eyewitnesses, subject to the rules governing eyewitness testimony, or should the equipment itself be considered an independent source of evidence, potentially introduced through expert witnesses? Alternatively, do we need to fundamentally rethink the traditional boundaries between established classifications of evidence and the procedural rules that govern them? While it will only offer a tentative solution, our goal is to map out the territory at least. This entails marking parts of the map with warnings of "here be dragons" for the journey into the legal unknown.

While our discussion uses mainly examples and illustrations from common law jurisdictions, we try as much as possible to be "jurisdiction neutral" and will also use concepts and proposals from other legal traditions. The aim is to highlight conceptual and normative problems that advances in neuro-implant technology will pose to all of them, albeit in subtly different forms.

In the next section, we prepare the ground for the discussion by introducing some key concepts from the law of evidence. In section two, we introduce some of the key technologies that underpin visual neuroprosthetics, and identify their legal salience.

In part three, we will put the question of technologically enhanced evidence in a much wider historical context. It is dangerous to be blinded by the apparent novelty of a scientific breakthrough, and to overlook that while technologies can change rapidly, humans and their desires, faults and problems are much more constant over time. Law as a tool to resolve these conflicts and maximize the chance for human flourishing can draw on centuries of experience, which is why we advocate also for a "methodological principle of conservatism in law reform" that mirrors the principle of epistemic entrenchment in the theory of belief revision [2]: optimizing informational economy requires doxastic and epistemic conservatism, (the "principle of minimum mutilation"), so that any legislative response to new facts or developments should leave as much of the existing system intact. Despite this methodological commitment, we will see that neuro-implants may be a good candidate for quite significant legal reform.

In part 4, we will draw on current legal, philosophical, and ethical discussions to outline some of the possible ways in which the law could develop. Our focus will be on the international human rights canon. How could law reform maximise and mediate between potentially conflicting rights, particularly the right to a fair trial, privacy rights, the right to equality—especially for citizens with disabilities—respect for autonomy, and dignity. We will specifically examine whether a "global" philosophical framework, such as the extended theory of mind, can aid us in navigating these challenges, or if more pragmatic ad-hoc solutions present a more promising approach.

2   Of Witnesses and Witnessing: When Seeing is Believing

This section introduces some concepts of the law of evidence that we will need later for our discussion of evidence created by the wearers of neuroprosthetics.

One of the most central concepts of the law of evidence is the concept of the "eyewitness" as the oldest, yet heavily contested, form of evidence in trials. In many jurisdictions, it is governed by complex rules that determine how it is introduced (e.g., the right of the accused to have the witness cross-examined) and assessed (e.g., instructions to the jury highlighting factors that can influence a witness's reliability) [3]. Historically, it was often regarded as a gold standard, and some legal systems required (or still require) either eyewitness- or confession evidence for a conviction [4].

For the purposes of this paper, we do not distinguish unless otherwise stated between evidence provided by bystanders, victim- and confession evidence, and most of the time, we use the term "eyewitness evidence" for all three. All are based on the direct sensory experience of the person testifying to them, and although the legal rules governing them can differ, they share many of the issues that "technologically enhanced or altered" senses pose for the law.

The very term "eyewitness evidence" reflects our reliance, as humans, on vision as the primary example of "sense evidence", and it is employed in many contexts to also refer to other forms of direct witness evidence, such as witnesses who testify to having heard a shot or smelled gas. Since this paper focuses on visual neuro-implants and therefore eyewitness evidence in the strict sense, we will use the term eyewitness evidence to encompass all forms of direct, sense-based evidence presented through witness testimony, to contrast it with expert witness evidence. However, we note that much of what we discuss is also likely applicable to neuroprosthetics that enhance or restore hearing, such as AI-supported cochlear implants like those described by Zhang et al. [5].

Despite the ongoing significance of eyewitness evidence, it has become somewhat less prominent in modern legal systems. From the 18th century onwards, the prominence of expert witness evidence increased alongside the growing influence of scientific disciplines. For legal doctrine, expert witnesses posed a challenge, particularly in common law countries. Conceptually, expert evidence is at least partly hearsay evidence, which would typically mean it should be excluded. After all, experts base their opinions on extensive training and reading academic literature—without the court being able to call in their instructors or authors for cross-examination [6]. To balance the defendant's right to challenge witnesses with the court's interest in using scientific evidence, complex rules were developed to create exemptions from the hearsay prohibition. In the US, for example, the Frye and Daubert standards establish frameworks that act as filters to prevent unreliable evidence from being admitted and provide guidance on how to assess the reliability and weight of the remaining evidence [7].

The interaction between scientific expert evidence and eyewitness evidence can be complex. There is, in particular, a growing body of knowledge from cognitive science, psychology, optics, and biology that helps us identify common sources of error in eyewitness evidence, along with an increasing understanding that even witnesses who are subjectively truthful can sometimes be mistaken. Despite this, it is generally not permitted to have a scientific expert assess the reliability and accuracy of a specific eyewitness, even though the advantages of doing so have been thoroughly argued [8]. However, there are exceptions to this rule. Children, and in some jurisdictions, adults with severe cognitive impairments, are sometimes evaluated by a psychologist or other suitable expert [9].

In the common law tradition, two legal principles explain this situation. The first is the division of work between the witness (expert or otherwise), who presents facts as they see them, and the jury or judge, who then assesses the witness's reliability and credibility. For example, a scientific expert evaluating the credibility of an eyewitness would encroach on the jury's role (see the court in United States v. Toledo, 985 F.2d 1462, 1470 (10th Cir.)). The second principle is that an expert witness should provide the fact-finder with knowledge they do not already possess. "Being judged by a jury of one's peers" also implies that they can, through an accepted legal fiction, rely on their own introspective understanding of their biases and cognitive limitations to assess experts who are sufficiently similar to them. This approach is not applicable when evaluating witnesses whose cognitive functions differ markedly.

The final category we need to briefly introduce is digital or computer evidence. It first emerged in the 1970s, but its significance grew rapidly with the invention of the Internet, and even more with the widespread use of mobile phones and other IoT devices. Digital evidence is often presented by experts and shares many qualities with other types of expert evidence. However, sometimes it can also be introduced as "real" evidence and shown directly to the judge or jury. An example of this is digital footage taken from a CCTV camera, which is shown directly to the jury.

While computer evidence can naturally fall into various established categories, the unique nature of the digital world has necessitated a re-evaluation of some fundamental legal terms and the creation of domain-specific legal rules. An example of the former, which will be relevant later in our discussion, is the concept of "original". Under the "best evidence rule," courts should utilize the highest quality version of any evidence, meaning the original of a document is usually preferred over a copy or photograph. While this is clear with physical documents, the very idea of an "original" becomes disputed when dealing with digital files that are reconstructed and subtly altered each time they are opened on a computer. An example of the latter is the highly problematic English law's "assumption of the correct working of a computer," which establishes a rebuttable evidential presumption for the accuracy of a digital file's content. While this presumption helps avoid costly and often unnecessary detailed investigations into a computer's inner workings every time a routine Word document is introduced as evidence in court, it has also been criticized for contributing to high-profile miscarriages of justice, such as the Post Office scandal [10].

We now possess the legal vocabulary needed to analyze testimony based on the "observations" of someone who sees with the aid of a neuro-implant. We can already glimpse some of the challenges this paper aims to highlight. If we treat the evidence of a neuro-implant user as ordinary eyewitness evidence, it would be impossible to introduce expert evidence regarding the proper functioning of the device that enabled their vision. Instead, it would be up to the judge or jury to determine the witness's credibility, with little additional guidance. Alternatively, we could bypass the wearer and focus solely on the data generated by the device. In this case, at least in English law for now, the presumption that computer evidence is accurate and reliable would guide its interpretation, giving the fact-finder less scope to question its trustworthiness than if it had been presented as eyewitness evidence. Or, we could broaden the concept of cognitive disability, present it as eyewitness evidence from a vulnerable witness, and allow experts to testify on the reliability of the human-computer entity, for example by asking the wearer to undergo standardized tests.

These are just three potential ways in which testimony by the wearer of a visual neuroprosthetic could be interpreted within the law, each with its own advantages and disadvantages, and with varying effects on the fundamental human rights of the witness (whether as a bystander or victim) and the suspect. We will see that other options are also available, but to fully understand their implications, it is necessary to examine in more detail the technology behind visual neuro-implants.

3 AIWitnesses: The Technology

Neural interfacing technologies have advanced significantly over recent decades, evolving from early experimental tools to highly sophisticated devices now embedded within the human body. Early developments—ranging from non-invasive options like smart glasses to retinal implants such as the Argus II—laid the groundwork for more advanced fully implanted systems [11–13]. Among these, AI-enabled neuro-prostheses have demonstrated remarkable progress in restoring sensory functions, especially in the area of vision [14].

Unlike devices that employ externally mounted cameras to capture environmental images, visual neuro-implant technology now integrates with the visual cortex (the pathway involved in visual information) itself, by direct subcortical implantation [15]. These modern visual neuroprosthetics bypass the ocular pathway by interfacing directly with neural tissues in the visual cortex or along the optic nerve [16], and directly stimulate neural circuits involved in visual processing—offering a form of "artificial vision" to individuals who are blind or severely visually impaired.

A distinctive aspect of these modern visual implants is the integration of artificial intelligence within the closed-loop system. Embedded AI algorithms continuously process and decode the brain's own light signals [17], converting them into precise electrical stimulation patterns that evoke visual perceptions. In other words, rather than capturing images via an external camera, the implant, through real-time AI processing, recognises patterns, incorporates internal light-sensitive elements, or enhances residual neural signals. These signals are delivered via an electrode array directly to the relevant neural circuits, prompting 'visual perceptions' that the brain learns to interpret as meaningful visual cues [18].

AI-mediation vision means that what the user "sees" is not a direct reproduction of the external environment but rather a computed, synthesised, subjective interpretation; an AI-generated translation of reality instead of a direct human experience. The implant's AI system continuously evaluates neural signals, determining which features or elements to emphasise or filter out. The user's view is filtered through AI: the implant might highlight obstacles, enhance contrasts, identify faces or attenuate redundant information to facilitate navigation. This process transforms raw visual data into an adaptable, user-focused experience, significantly supporting visual recognition and perception, although it remains inherently mediated by algorithmic processes.

AI-enabled visual neuroprosthetics demonstrate a pioneering merging of neural interfacing, machine learning, and neurostimulation technologies by combining internal sensory inputs with real-time AI processing, transforming sensory rehabilitation. However, the inherent subjectivity caused by AI mediation suggests that the user's perceptual experience is not a direct reflection of reality but an algorithmically filtered interpretation.

Current systems mimic conventional vision by translating data from a visual sensor, such as a camera, into signals that the brain perceives. This approach highlights the continuity with the traditional understanding of vision. However, we can easily envisage a future where this connection is severed. For example, the camera could incorporate not only the normal visual spectrum but also infrared sensing, or even more radically, combine audio and visual information. From the wearer's perspective, this would still be experienced as visual perception, such as seeing a large object to the right. The reason for this would be a combination of audio and visual data that the AI integrates before stimulating the relevant part of the visual cortex, which may be clear to an outside observer but hidden from the wearer. As noted above, the law generally does not distinguish between "eyewitnesses" and "earwitnesses", although jury instructions are sometimes tailored towards visual identification. In many common law systems, for instance, jurors are instructed to consider the lighting conditions present when the witness observed the event. Nonetheless, the unusual way sensors are used in this context may necessitate reconsidering this approach.

In this brief introduction to the technology, we highlighted its novelty and already hinted at some of the challenges to established legal categories that AI-enabled neuro-implants might pose. In the next section, we will, by contrast, emphasise the continuity of these technologies with other, much simpler, "technologically mediated" eye witnessing. The aim is to clarify our above commitment to "minimal legal disruption": ideally, we want to avoid ad hoc adjustments to the law that are highly specific to a particular technology, and instead develop a more stable framework that encompasses a broad range of similar past and future technologies.

4   The Long History of Assistive Visual Technology

Although AI-supported visual neuro-implants are a particularly impressive form of vision assistance, technologies that assist those with vision impairment are, of course, not new, and even much simpler versions can pose legal issues similar to those caused by more advanced devices.

An iconic early example comes from fiction, Henry Fonda's Juror 8 in Sidney Lumet's 1957 masterpiece *12 Angry Men*. Juror 8 questions the reliability of one eyewitness by pointing out that he was habitually dependent on glasses and unlikely to have worn them when observing the murder. This persuades some jurors to dismiss his evidence or at least assign it less probative value. While what we see in the film is legally flawed and highly speculative, a procedurally correct approach would have been for the defense solicitor to 'impeach" the witness in open court, questioning him about his eyesight and whether he was wearing glasses. As previously noted, it would not normally be possible to request the witness undergo an expert assessment of his vision or be compelled to surrender his glasses for inspection, although the jury could infer things from his level of cooperation. It would then be up to the jury to decide if the lack of a necessary visual aid rendered the identification unreliable.

In most common law jurisdictions, jurors are reminded of the importance of this fact through a mandatory jury instruction issued by the judge before they retire to consider their verdict [19]. This instruction reminds them to consider this factor, along with a fixed number of others, without guiding them on *how* to weigh it or what the outcome should be. Empirical studies have shown that, contrary to what is depicted in the film, jurors tend to trust eyewitness evidence highly even when they are told that the witness had some visual impairment and was not wearing glasses [8].

Glasses are purely passive aids that can also be easily detached from the wearer for a quick inspection, and are also "strictly deterministic": any set of glasses produced to the same specifications will produce identical effects on the wearer. In contrast, a technology that is nearing neuroprosthetics is SenseCam, a Microsoft product originally created for leisure activities such as lifelogging. However, it has found its main use in therapeutic settings to assist people with mild dementia or other memory issues [20].

SenseCam is a digital camera worn around the neck, equipped with built-in memory storage, various sensors for acceleration, temperature, and light conditions, and a basic AI that uses sensor data to decide when to activate the camera. It typically triggers when there is a change in the sensor-reported conditions. Acceleration can signify that the wearer has moved to a new environment, while a decrease in light may indicate someone approaching and casting a shadow over the lens. The camera then takes a still image, capturing a moment as if seen through the wearer's eyes. Recent models can create and store up to 4000 images in a single day.

In the therapeutic use case, the carer will review the images in the evening with the wearer, stimulating their memory recall. Research has shown that such a regime offers benefits for the patient that extend beyond recalling the specific recorded events, enhancing their overall memory, potentially even establishing a feedback loop between camera recordings and brain activity that causes changes detectable in a brain scan [21].

It is this more intimate, causal link between the brain of the wearer and the camera that could allow us to see them as a unity, rather than two entirely separate objects. However, this is not how the law is likely to treat them. We should note that, to the best of our knowledge, there have been no cases where a SenseCam user was involved as a witness in a trial, and our analysis can only make informed speculations. However, what would happen if a wearer was in the vicinity of a crime, either as a bystander or victim? Imagine this scenario: in the evening, a carer and patient review the images. The carer sees what looks like abuse of another patient (or the wearer) by a nurse. They ask the patient if they remember this, and when the answer is affirmative, they inform the police.

Unlike a typical eyewitness case, the prosecution now has two sources of evidence: the images stored on the camera and the memory or testimony of its wearer. The law, as mentioned earlier, treats them very differently. The images on the digital device could be admitted as "real evidence" and presented directly to the jury. While there is a presumption in England that the camera functioned correctly, it may be necessary to present expert evidence that the images were not tampered with, especially if the chain of custody from the time the image was taken until it was retrieved by the police cannot be established.

Here, we can see that the two evidence sources are not entirely independent: if an adversary had managed to interfere with the recording equipment *before* the wearer used them for their daily review and added or manipulated an image, this manipulation could easily create a false memory in a vulnerable user. Even without such third-party interference, we must note for legal purposes that the review process would have altered the wearer's memory, and if they were to testify, it would be difficult to distinguish between aided and unaided memory.

Finally, it may be necessary to introduce expert evidence regarding the functioning of the AI. This could be relevant if, for example, the fact that *no* image was captured is significant for the case. For instance, it could suggest that no one else entered the room during a certain period, as this would have produced a recording. In such cases, experts would need to "look under the hood" of the black-box AI, which may be protected by trade secret and commercial confidentiality laws, to verify the device's accuracy.

Once the data on the device is analyzed, the question arises whether the wearer should also testify as a second source of evidence. It is less problematic to call them to testify that, on that day, they were indeed wearing the device—something that may be necessary if they are the alleged victim, and the images show an attack on whoever was wearing the device. Beyond that, the prosecutor may be hesitant, both to prevent unnecessary distress to a cognitively impaired witness and because of an awareness that jurors may not give credence to a witness with dementia, even if such discounting is unwarranted in the case. Since the witness has a cognitive disability, it may be possible, exceptionally, to introduce expert evidence regarding their competence, which would also raise the novel question of whether the evaluation should focus on the witness's performance with or without the assistance of SenseCam.

One question that needs to be addressed is whether the two types of evidence are sufficiently independent. As mentioned earlier, it might be that the witness's memory is so heavily dependent on or created by what the camera recorded that they are effectively the same. This is especially significant in jurisdictions such as Scotland, which have a "corroboration requirement". Essentially, there must be two independent sources of evidence for each element of an offence. Would a testimony from a witness with dementia qualify as corroboration of their own observation and memory? The intuitive answer is yes, similarly to how a photographer would testify to what they saw when taking a photo, as would the photo itself, although questions remain about how the interaction between image and memory should be regarded.

Until now, our focus has been on the reliability of the evidence. However, assistive devices like SenseCam raise legal and evidential issues that go beyond mere reliability and could significantly affect other human rights. They can turn potentially vulnerable patients into mobile surveillance tools, raising data protection and privacy concerns for their carers, visitors, and other patients. This issue becomes especially evident if the "witness" is also the suspect. In many jurisdictions, the suspect cannot be compelled to testify against their own interests. In common law systems, this is known as the right against self-incrimination, which is also recognized in many civilian jurisdictions, including Germany, where there is a right to lie in one's own defense [22]. For our hypothetical dementia sufferer, this right is now severely compromised, as the prosecutor no longer needs their testimony—only the corresponding camera recording. A device intended to support disabled citizens in achieving equality could, through the operation of the law, have the opposite effect.

By the same token, excluding the wearer simply because "better" and "more objective" evidence is produced that would not exist *but for* their disability should also be a concern. While many people find testifying in court stressful, it can also be viewed as a form of civic participation. This is most evident in Duff's communicative theory of the trial, and to exclude an entire group from such a role, regardless of individual wishes, seems to deny them full civic participation. This is especially clear in the case of the victim-witness, who in this case is quite literally reduced to a mere supporting tool for the technology (providing its mobility) rather than the other way round, and becomes a passive bystander in a case that should primarily involve them.

All these issues could be prevented if, instead of viewing the camera/AI device and the person wearing it as separate, distinct objects, they are legally considered a single entity. Andy Clark's and David Chalmers' theory of the extended mind could underpin such an approach: he argued that if, for someone with a cognitive impairment, an external tool (his example being Post-it notes) performs the same function as our internal memory, then we should regard the external resource as "part of the mind" [23]. Although his concerns mainly focus on ontological and epistemological questions, the theory can also be interpreted morally: if an external tool endows a person with a disability with cognitive abilities typically associated with the internal workings of the mind, then the external tool should not be legally treated unfavourably compared to internal memories. Specifically, this would mean that data collected by SenseCam that incriminates its wearer should not be admissible without their consent.

Finally, we briefly mention Google Glasses (GG) and other augmented reality tools. While SenseCam simply aims to record the external world, just as an eye would, they use AI to enhance cognitive functions. For example, they could identify the person the wearer talks to and display their name in the wearer's visual field. What is a subtle and possibly negligible interaction between recorded and biological memory in SenseCam now becomes more significant: If a GG wearer observes a crime and their glasses suggest a name, displayed in a way that subtly or subliminally helps the user recognise the person, was it the AI or the wearer who, for legal purposes, made the identification?

AI-generated and directly perceived environments become even more intertwined. Can we be certain it was the wearer who made the identification? Is their testimony enough, or should we evaluate the accuracy of the AI separately? Should it matter if the use of GG was for medical necessity, as a therapeutic tool as in [25], or merely for entertainment? This could influence whether the device's use within the courtroom remains legitimate. Scots law, for instance, requires "dock identification": the witness must repeat their positive ID of a suspect (for example, after an identity parade) in open court. If the user relies on GG as a therapeutic tool, can they continue to wear it to participate, or does this undermine the purpose of dock identification?

With this last thought, we now have the conceptual tools needed to map out the problems and options that visual neuroprosthetics bring for the law of evidence.

5   The AIWitness and the Law

We have now laid the groundwork for our promised map of the legal landscape surrounding visual neuroprosthetics and evidence law. We introduced some key legal concepts and illustrated, through two older examples, the issues they can pose for the law. We also explored some of the functionality of visual neuroprosthetics, which allows us either to group them with older technologies or to argue for their distinctiveness, possibly requiring legislative action.

Consider the following scenario: X is effectively blind. He has a neural implant, as described above, that combines an external video recorder with an AI chip implanted in his brain, stimulating his visual cortex. Although it cannot enable him to recognise individuals, it allows for basic shape recognition. X was in a room where a crime occurred. For the police investigation, it would be crucial for him to confirm whether two people entered the room from the left, where the window opens to the garden, or a single person entered from the right, an office accessible only to staff. How should we regard his testimony?

One option is to treat the neuroimplant the same as a pair of glasses and disregard the technology entirely. He saw what he saw, albeit through a tool. The defense can cross-examine him and ask questions that challenge his credibility, but cannot subject him to testing and evaluation by a medical doctor or a technology expert. An alternative would be to create a new form of jury instructions that includes some relevant information for them, without pre-empting their credibility assessment. Either approach would enhance the equality aspect of assistive technologies, maintain the distinction between cognitive and other disabilities for the sake of evidence law, and maximise the protection of his privacy interests.

This would, however, raise significant concerns regarding the fairness of the trial. Unlike passive glasses or even SenseCam, where the senses are directly experienced, the subjective sense perception is now entirely mediated by and ontologically dependent on technology. There is no independent pathway from the external world to the witness's memory. He could not compare the experience created by a manipulated or simply malfunctioning AI with a "correct" representation of the external world. For example, it seems clear that a report of his visual experience could not, even in law, corroborate a video recording since they are essentially the same. Therefore, it appears necessary to have at least some means to examine the inner workings of the equipment.

Similarly, treating technology and the wearer as entirely separate entities, as we would with SenseCam, is equally problematic. While SenseCam can be easily detached from its wearer, who maintains full control over when to carry it and can be asked to remove it in sensitive contexts to protect others' privacy, a neuroimplant is an integral part of the body. Removal entails major surgery, and even remote access to the data would be categorically different from simply accessing someone's mobile phone. Unlimited exploitation of the data, even for trial purposes, reduces a human to a mobile CCTV, creating privacy risks for themselves and others, and significantly weakening procedural protections. From both equality and privacy perspectives, the costs are prohibitively high. Furthermore, unlike SenseCam, because the digital evidence is functionally identical to subjective visual perception, reliance on this data would lead to the exclusion of citizens in their own trials and diminish their civic participation rights.

This suggests that we tentatively conclude that neuroimplants indeed challenge established legal categories beyond simple solutions. They are not merely an extension of a process that began with glasses and continued with SenseCam; instead, they expose the problems with the compromises already created by these tools. The proposal would then be to recognise the neuro-enhanced observer as a new type of entity for evidence law, one that considers the biological and technological components as an inseparable whole. The current legal framework establishes two often incompatible regimes: neuroimplant evidence, depending on one's perspective, is either eyewitness or digital evidence, making the legal rules both too broad and too narrow. This presents significant risks for both the users of these devices and potentially for those who interact with them.

We mentioned earlier that Chalmers' and Clark's extended mind theory could serve as a conceptual basis for such a step, but on its own, it does not resolve the conflict among the various stakeholders—the witness, the suspect, the victim, and the privacy rights of all involved. However, it indicates a unified set of rules focused on the witness in all their *roles*: as victim, witness, or suspect; as active participants in the process of the trial; and also as private citizens with a legitimate interest in protecting their data. Reconciling these tensions then falls to the legislator, who must develop a unique set of rules for criminal trial evidence gathered from neuroimplants.

If we were to take this approach to the next level, we would get a mix of digital and biological constraints that the law now must align. The first two questions would therefore be:

"Is the technology used to compensate for a biological shortcoming of its wearer?"

And

"Is the assistance they receive as a result at or below the level of an unaided witness?"

Together, these rules ensure that *neuroenhancement,* that is, the use of neurotechnologies to get a better-than-expected result in comparison to the average human, is excluded. As a first hurdle, they safeguard that only medically required technologies fall under the set of rules that we are proposing. They also ensure that users with disability are treated as much as possible by the law as those who are not affected by an impairment of their optical senses.

In countries permitting a "trial within a trial", discussions regarding a witness's capacity to interpret visual stimuli and provide evidence could, in theory, be conducted privately and without the jury's involvement. In countries that do not differentiate between different roles for decision-makers, an alternative approach would need to be established. For either group, however, the decision of the wearer would remain central and should only be disregarded if the fact-finder concludes that the eyewitness statement is unnecessary.

The rules intentionally do not ask *why* the wearer perceives the environment the way they do. Going back to the argument made above, a camera that "sees", for example, mainly heat radiation would be treated exactly like one that "sees" in the visual spectrum. In theory, there could be a discussion at this point about whether the witness's vision "matches" that of an unaided person. However, our approach is to focus on the sense perception that the witness reports, rather than its cause. This is arguably the point where our proposal diverges significantly from other possible approaches. As long as the main intention behind the optical device is to restore, even partially, the wearer's ability, the law should, in our opinion, accept this at face value and organise itself around this idea.

There are two possible variations of this approach, depending on who the wearer of the technology is. The first, closer to what current systems allow, involves the third-party witness or victim. They may be aware of the limitations of the technology that was intended to give them abilities comparable to those of an unaided observer. The second involves the suspects, assuming, for now, that the technology enabled them to engage in a criminal activity. In either case, the legal response to their decision to *deny* access to the equipment is, in our approach so far, straightforward: there is no new legal burden that would permit discrimination against witnesses whose vision was assisted by a computational device.

More contentious could be the decision in the opposite case. In this scenario, either the witness or the suspect has seen something of direct relevance to the prosecution's case, and both are concerned that their statement might be disregarded by the jurors or, in continental European legal systems, the judge. They also hope that by providing access to the technology, they can overcome any hesitation on the part of the fact-finder. Our approach so far, however, would deny them this option and treat their statement more like a traditional observation made by a party.

This situation requires further consideration. Is the person using an advanced visual simulation device more similar to an ordinary witness, a witness whose abilities have been enhanced by a technical aid such as glasses, or should we regard them as a completely new third category? Treating them like a witness with eyeglasses seems to answer our questions in a natural way. The wearer can testify, but may face questioning from the opposition if their testimony conflicts with their hypothesis about the events. These questions, however, would be directed at the wearer and would not introduce a third party as an expert witness into the process.

Alternatively, we could permit the eyewitness to make all or part of the data available. Provided that the technology permits such a move, it might enable independent analysis of the collected data, for example, in the form of a video clip. We note that in this analysis, it does not matter whether the technology is externally located or part of the brain's "inner workings". The question is not "is this action possible?" but "to what extent does the action align with the user's preferences?" For this reason alone, it would not be permissible to obtain data from any device that the user did not authorise. This applies equally to data stored on devices owned by the eyewitness as well as data held on devices owned by third parties. The aim of this provision is to make the wearer of the eye implant as functioning a member of the justice system as possible; they *can* go further than current witnesses, but don't *have* to.

Both solutions are consistent with current legal practices. The first emphasises the attempts of the technology to create a level playing field for enhanced and ordinary witness statements. The second emphasises that despite this overarching effort, technology has been used to mitigate the disability of the witness, and the witness themselves can decide whether to make it available or not. Neither approach looks at the role of the witness in the trial. Prosecution and defence witnesses have the same rights in either solution, and either both are prevented from submitting also data from their equipment (Option 1) or are both allowed, but not compelled, to do so (Option 2).

Clark's and Chalmers' theory enabled us to "see" people using technology as functional equivalents of native brain functions to overcome brain deficiencies. For them, this means to "think in different ways", but ways that are the direct equivalent of other modes of cognition. We have arguably shifted their theory from a purely descriptive perspective to a normative one. However, we argue that this shift in emphasis is not just permitted by Clark and Chalmers but indeed required. In their book, Clark and Chalmers contrast Otto - Alzheimer sufferer with severe impairment of his memory functions - and Inga, who is not affected by this illness. Otto performs his daily functions with the aid of an external device that pins down his timetable and keeps notes of some major points of engagement for him. Inga, by contrast, relies exclusively on her mental capabilities.

Clark and Chalmers argue convincingly that the only difference between these two cases is that Inga's memory is being internally processed by the brain, while Otto's memory performs the very same functions through the notebook. Otto's mind has been "extended" to include the notebook as the source of his memory, because it is constantly and immediately accessible by its wearer, and his wearer only. In this sense, the notebook becomes a "fragile biological limb or organ" [23 p. 8] that Otto wants typically to shield from third-party access. By shifting the debate from an ontological to a normative context, we can see how it addresses some of the concerns that the wearer of the devises may encounter, while at the same time answering some of the questions that their thought experiment was raising.

One typical criticism is that the difference between Inga and Otto is that it denies the differences in memory construction between the two. Clark addresses this criticism in *Supersizing the Mind*:

[The] claim was not that the processes in Otto and Inga are identical, or even similar, in terms of their detailed implementation. It is simply that, with respect to the role that the long-term encodings play in guiding current response, both modes of storage can be seen as supporting dispositional beliefs. It is the way the information is poised to guide reasoning… And behavior that counts. [26, p. 99].

This and similar arguments work better in a normative context than an ontological one. The normative context allows us to balance out, to a degree, the shortcomings of the strict analysis, and the disadvantages for the pursuit of justice, while at the same time staying true to the overarching insight of the functional equivalence between different forms of knowledge production. In other words, while the model explains and justifies why we grant extensive protection and autonomy to the extended mind, we can also discuss additional measures that address any concerns we have regarding the pursuit of justice.

In particular, we recommend using generic, "boilerplate" instructions read to the jury, a variant of the "ADVOKATE" instructions they already receive in several cases [27]. These instructions do not introduce a new way of analysing the specific technology involved in the case. Instead, they provide the jury with independent guidance on the general issues and complexities that eyewitness identification may raise. Their use does not cast any doubt on the witness statements heard by the jury (or judge) during the trial. Rather, they assist jurors in reflecting on their own experiences and recognising issues that could give rise to doubts.

Typical examples could be:

"Consider the likelihood that the AI was manipulated at the point of attack."

"Consider the difficulty in expressing an observation made when using the AI to someone not familiar with this technology."

"Consider the possibility that the witness was not truthful in their account."

The combination of rules of evidence relating to individuals, along with those addressing known concerns of evidence categories, is one way to ensure that the benefits of brain technology are realised while potential worries are also managed.

6 Conclusion

We have presented a discussion of various forms of evidence that require, in varying degrees, technological assistance. This allowed us to see the current debate concerning AI-assisted vision as part of a broader chain of developments that also included ordinary glasses and SenseCam technologies. Clark's and Chalmers' theory of the extended mind enabled us to develop a model that reconnects the final step of this development with the original observer position.

We extended this analysis with a minimal external addition, the use of pre-formulated statements that fit those of the traditional eyewitness schema and remind the juror of the inherent fallibility of eyewitness reports. Together, they should enable us to reap the benefits of AI-enabled vision while protecting against its potential abuse. There have so far been no examples of wearers of the type of technology envisaged in this paper as witnesses in a trial. However, we hope to have convinced the reader that such an inclusion would be less problematic than one might have expected.

Disclosure of Interests.   Schafer was supported by UKRI grant EP/T022485/1, "DeCaDe".

References

1. Waisberg, E., Ong, J., Lee, A.: The potential to restore vision with Neuralink's "Blindsight" neural interface technology. The Pan-Am. J. Ophthalmol. **6**(3), 84 (2024)
2. Gärdenfors, P.: Epistemic importance and minimal changes of belief. Australas. J. Philos. **62**(2), 136–157 (1984)
3. See e.g. Cheng, E.K., Nunn, G.A.: Beyond the witness: bringing a process perspective to modern evidence law. Tex. L. Rev. **97**, 1077 (2018)
4. Damaska, M.: Evidentiary barriers to conviction and two models of criminal procedure: a comparative study. U. Pa. L. Rev. **121**, 506
5. Zhang, G., et al.: Artificial intelligence-enabled innovations in cochlear implant technology: advancing auditory prosthetics for hearing restoration. Bioeng. Transl. Med., e10752 (2025)
6. Mnookin, J.L.: Idealizing science and demonizing experts: an intellectual history of expert evidence. Vill. L. Rev. **52**, 763.-526 (2007)
7. Cheng, E.K., Yoon, A.H.: Does Frye or Daubert matter-a study of scientific admissibility standards. Va. L. Rev. **91**, 471 (2005)
8. Handberg, R.B.: Expert testimony on eyewitness identification: a new pair of glasses for the jury. Am. Crim. L. Rev. **32**, 1013 (1994)
9. Bull, R.: The investigative interviewing of children and other vulnerable witnesses: psychological research and working/professional practice. In: Investigating the Truth, pp. 126–146. Routledge (2018)
10. Bohm, N., et al.: The legal rule that computers are presumed to be operating correctly-unforeseen and unjust consequences. Digit. Evid. Elec. Signature L. Rev. **19**, 123 (2022)

11. Mirochnik, R.M., Pezaris, J.S.: Contemporary approaches to visual prostheses. Mil. Med. Res. **6**, 19 (2019)
12. Giansanti, D.: Advancements in ocular neuro-prosthetics: bridging neuroscience and information and communication technology for vision restoration. Biol. **14**, 134 (2025)
13. Mahadiuzzaman, A.S.M., others: Visual neuroprostheses for impaired human nervous system: state-of-the-art and future outlook. Int. J. Cell Biol. **2024**, 2651763 (2024)
14. Wu, K.Y., others: Retinal prostheses: engineering and clinical perspectives for vision restoration. Sensors **23**, 5782 (2023)
15. Yang, J.-W., others: An electroactive hybrid biointerface for enhancing neuronal differentiation and axonal outgrowth on bio-subretinal chip. Mater. Today Bio **14**, 100253 (2022)
16. Beyeler, M., Sanchez-Garcia, M.: Towards a smart bionic eye: AI-powered artificial vision for the treatment of incurable blindness. J. Neural Eng. **19**, 063001 (2022)
17. Stoddart, P.R., others: Nanoparticle-based optical interfaces for retinal neuromodulation: a review. Front. Cell. Neuroscience **18** (2024)
18. Pulicharla, M.R., Premani, V.: AI-powered neuroprosthetics for brain-computer interfaces (BCIs). World J. Adv. Eng. Technol. Sci. **12**, 109 (2024)
19. Helm, R.K.: Evaluating witness testimony: juror knowledge, false memory, and the utility of evidence-based directions. Int. J. Evid. Proof **25**(4), 264–285 (2021)
20. Browne, G., et al.: SenseCam improves memory for recent events and quality of life in a patient with memory retrieval difficulties. Memory **19**(7), 713–722 (2011)
21. Berry, E., et al.: The neural basis of effective memory therapy in a patient with limbic encephalitis. J. Neurol. Neurosurg. Psychiatry **80**(11), 1202–1205 (2009)
22. Walker, J.K.: A comparative discussion of the privilege against self-incrimination. NYL Sch. J. Int. Comp. L. **14**, 1 (1993)
23. Clark, A., Chalmers, D.: The extended mind. Analysis **58**(1), 7–19 (1998)
24. Bappaditya, M., et al.: A wearable face recognition system on google glass for assisting social interactions. In: Asian Conference on Computer Vision (2014)
25. Haber, N., Voss, V.C., Wall, D.: Making emotions transparent: Google Glass helps autistic kids understand facial expressions through augmented-reaiity therapy. IEEE Spectr. **57**(4), 46–52 (2020)
26. Clark, A.: Supersizing the Mind. Oxford University Press (2008)
27. Bromby, M., MacMillan, M., McKellar, P.: An examination of criminal jury directions in relation to eyewitness identification in commonwealth jurisdictions. Common Law World Rev. **36**(4), 303–336 (2007)
28. https://caiml.org/dighum/dighum-res/. Accessed 11 Feb 2025

Understanding the Humanist Notion of Trust in the Age of Generative AI

Pia-Zoe Hahne$^{(\boxtimes)}$ and Alexander Schmoelz

University of Applied Sciences BFI Vienna, Vienna, Austria
`pia.hahne@fh-vie.ac.at`

Abstract. This research stresses the humanist conceptualisation of trust rooted in human self-trust and communication which classifies trust as an ethical and epistemic condition for the possibility of cooperative life. Considering artificial intelligence (AI), we assess that AI should not meet the criteria to qualify for trust. We claim that the discussion of trust in AI is misguided and instead propose a digital humanist perspective on trust to allow for human agency in human- technology relations. From a digital humanist perspective, trust in artificial intelligence lacks the foundational communicative and ethical grounding that characterises humanistic trust. Instead, the relation between AI and humans should not exceed reliance as a trust relation between humans and AI systems would imply the moral agency of AI systems.

Keywords: digital humanism · trust · generative AI · communication · ethics

1 Introduction – Discussing Trust in Generative AI (GenAI)

Using trust to discuss human interactions with Generative AI (GenAI) systems such as ChatGPT has become a ubiquitous practice: Newspaper articles, blog posts and company announcements ponder on the question whether or not users should trust AI systems, stress the trustworthiness of specific GenAIs, or the potential of trusting information generated by AI [1–3]. However, the range of applications of the concept of trust in relation to AI also shows that GenAI is not only used to gather information – although that function already comes with severe problems such as hallucinations and misinformation – but the technology is also used as a therapist or for interpersonal guidance [2]. These interactions presuppose that the user trusts the GenAI, either in the sense that the user trusts the information given (epistemic) or in the sense that the user creates an almost personal relation with the GenAI (normative).

The concept of trust has a vast intellectual history. Trust is deeply social and is often seen as a foundational criterion of societal stability [4, 5]. The most simplistic definition of trust in interpersonal relations is a three-part relation: *A trusts B to do X because of p* [6–9], where A is the trustor, B the trustee, X the object or action that necessitates trust, and p the reason for trusting – their trustworthiness. This formula can be edited as well: For example, Baier [6] adds "with valued thing c" (p. 236) to stress the inherently normative character of trust. Laying out trust relations like this immediately suggests

L. Hagedorn et al. (Eds.): DIGHUM 2025, LNCS 16319, pp. 169–178, 2026.
https://doi.org/10.1007/978-3-032-11108-1_12

the difference between trust and trustworthiness: trust is the action between two agents while trustworthiness is the reason to trust. Trustworthiness therefore becomes the prerequisite for trust relations as it makes a moral judgement about the trustee: "in judging trustworthiness, in deciding whether to trust, we reach a sense of the whole person and his or her integrity and competence" (p. 18) [10]. Being trustworthy goes beyond being merely reliable; instead, reliability can only be understood as a feature of trustworthiness but extends reliability by actively considering the trustee and their interests [11]. Hence, "trustworthiness is more than reliability in that it is evaluative as well as descriptive" (p. 110) [11]. Trust in its simplest form always involves a relational perspective between the trustor and trustee: the potential of the trustor to assess the trustworthiness of the trustee – and therefore make an evaluative judgement of the trustee – requires a continuous interaction between the individual trustee and trustor.

The application of trust when discussing AI inadvertently also blurs the line between human and technological characteristics. In contrast to human actors, an AI system cannot be classified as a moral agent; it cannot have good or ill will, it is not free to act and can be held accountable for its actions [12]. The difference between AI and traditional technological applications concerning moral agency is that in contrast to traditional systems, AI is designed to appear as if it possesses the capacity for moral reasoning or emotions. To avoid the attribution of moral agency to artificial intelligence, a digital humanist perspective on trust and AI is necessary to further understand the theoretical implications of broadening the concept of trust to include artificial intelligence. In our position paper, we suggest a humanist understanding of trust that demonstrates the clear conceptual disconnect between trust and AI and instead can – in best-case scenarios – be relied upon.

2   The Humanist Model of Trust

General definitions of trust focus on the interpersonal relation between trustor and trustee; for interpersonal relations, this can easily be simplified to *A trusts B to do X because of p* [6–9]. While both the trustee and trustor in this definition of trust are human, it is not a humanistic model of trust. A humanistic model of trust centres the individual as inherently capable of ethical agency and self-knowing. The difference between general human trust, such as the trust between individuals, and an explicitly humanist trust is that at the basis of humanist trust lies the philosophical conviction that self-knowledge as a central human potential. As Cassirer [13] emphasized, self-knowledge has remained the enduring core of philosophical inquiry, even across the most sceptical traditions. True insight begins with an understanding of one's own being. In this light, the trust in the potential of self-knowledge becomes the prerequisite for self-realization, the condition under which individuals can live truthfully and meaningfully. Within a humanistic model of trust, this underscores the idea that trust is inseparable from the process of knowing, becoming and creating oneself. It is through trusting in our capacity for self-knowledge that we open the path to autonomy, dignity, authentic and ethical agency.

Drawing on humanistic psychology, this model understands trust not as a static state or a mere function of external reliability, but as a dynamic process of formation and "Bildung" rooted in the human's relationship to self, others, and the world. A foundational axiom of the humanistic perspective is that the inner core of the person has the potential to be good, trustworthy, and ethical. Trust, then, is not simply earned through behaviour or guaranteed by institutions; it is grounded in a foundational ethical orientation toward the self and others.

2.1 Trust as Self-Trust

At its foundation, humanistic trust begins with the individual's capacity for self-trust. This echoes Fromm's [14] critique of modern alienation, where he argues that the moral problem of our time is the human's indifference to themselves. Fromm highlights how individuals have lost a sense of their own significance and uniqueness, becoming alienated from their own powers and treating themselves as commodities. In such a condition, people lose trust in their own judgment and creative capacities, surrendering their conscience to collective norms. Humanistic self-trust thus entails reclaiming confidence in one's own inner authority and the courage to live authentically, even against the grain of social conformity. Maslow [15]—the founder of humanistic psychology—articulates this as the ability to rely on one's own "delight-criterion"—a personal sense of what is right, meaningful, or fulfilling. Self-trust enables autonomy, moral judgment, and authentic self-expression. It is an affirmation of one's inner authority and evaluative capacity, and it forms the basis for psychological health and growth.

Trust in the humanistic sense is not an innate fixed trait, but an achievement of Formation and "Bildung". It can be cultivated or eroded depending on early experiences, especially in childhood, personal relationships as well as societal circumstances. When relationships and circumstances are permissive, supportive, and loving, they foster trust in the self and in others. In contrast, authoritarian or fear-inducing relationships and circumstances teach individuals to distrust their inner self, leading to conformity, anxiety, and dependency on external validation. While self-trust is primary, it does not emerge in isolation. Human beings are relational, and trust develops in the context of lived and shared experiences. The humanistic model sees trust as a dynamic quality of relationships, shaped by mutual recognition, respect, and authenticity. Trusting oneself often arises in tandem with being trusted by others, and vice versa. Therefore, the relational matrix in which individuals grow profoundly influences their capacity for trust. Trust, in this context, is part of an open, accepting, and non-instrumental relationship to others and the world. It implies a willingness to let things be, to receive them without immediate categorization or control. This kind of trust supports experiences of wonder, insight, and wholeness. Trust allows a mode of perceiving reality without defensiveness, manipulation, or reductionism.

Consequentially, the humanistic model of trust is also an ethical stance: it affirms the dignity, autonomy, and value of the human person. To trust, in this view, is to commit to the possibility of growth, meaning, and authenticity—even in the face of uncertainty and risk. It requires courage and responsibility. Trust is not the absence of fear, but the decision to move forward despite it, grounded in the knowledge of the human potential. In sum, the humanistic model of trust reframes trust not as a mechanism of control or assurance, but as an existential and relational process. It is both an inward capacity and an outward orientation—a mode of being that sustains personal formation, ethical relationships, and meaningful engagement with society and the world.

2.2 Trust in the Research Method for the Pursuit of Knowledge

Carl Rogers [16, 17], a pioneer of humanistic psychology, emphasized the essential role of trust in the scientific process—not as confidence in static, objective facts, but as trust in a dynamic process of discovering truth through lived and shared experience. Science is not an impersonal, detached endeavour, but an open and authentic engagement with human meaning. A humanistic research paradigm integrates subjective, interpersonal, and objective forms of knowledge. The research process is an existential and ethical act, where the trustworthiness of knowledge depends on the integrity, openness, and authenticity of the persons involved. The research process builds on the trust in intuitive, phenomenological insight, regarding the researcher as an active, sensing participant whose inner experience is a valid and necessary instrument of discovery. This advocates for a science that includes the observation of inner processes, emotions, and meanings—integrating the personal and the intersubjective. Trust in the research process, then, entails confidence in the capacity of individuals to approach truth not merely through logic and measurement, but through empathic understanding and self-knowing. This demands a "granting attitude"—a posture of openness toward what emerges in the process, and a willingness to revise one's perspectives in the light of experience. Research is inherently value-laden, shaped by the goals, histories, and commitments of those who practice it. Thus, trust in research includes an ethical commitment: the recognition that both the researcher and the subject are persons whose dignity and perspectives matter. Authentic science, in this view, resists methodological dogmatism and welcomes a plurality of methods as long as they serve the pursuit of meaningful understanding and knowledge. Trust, therefore, is not placed in fixed outcomes or protocols, but in the process of inquiry itself—an unfolding, dialogical, and continually corrected search for insight that honours both subjectivity and shared human experience.

2.3 Trust and Truthfulness in Human Communication

In current humanistic philosophy [18], communication is foundationally framed as dependent on trust and truthfulness—without which meaningful dialogue and shared understanding are impossible. Truthfulness and trust are necessary to enable reliable communication. A baseline expectation exists that people will generally assert only what they themselves know to be true. While norms of truthfulness may vary, the underlying ethical expectation of trust persists, especially in more intimate or socially embedded interactions. In environments where the expectation of trust and trustfulness is confined, reliable communication, and thus stable trust, is restricted. The norms of trust and truthfulness are not solely moral imperatives; they function as stabilizing forces within systems of collective decision-making. They help prevent manipulative and strategic behaviour that can distort shared understanding and undermine rational public discourse. When individuals disclose and justify their preferences openly and transparently within a communicative community, the possibility for manipulation diminishes, and the prospects for achieving collective rationality improve. Thus, ethical norms of trust and truthfulness are essential not only for human relationships but also for sustaining the structural integrity of democratic deliberation and communal cooperation.

3 Humanistic Trust and Trust in AI

The relation between trust and AI has been discussed extensively, with varying outcomes for the conceptual relation between trust and AI. On one hand, scholars such as Brusseau, Pink et al., and Ryan categorically oppose the extension of the concept of trust to artificial intelligence as AI systems cannot enter in a reciprocal relation that is usually necessitated between trustor and trustee [19–21]. Since trusting another agent requires more than just dependable habits, i.e. an evaluative judgment of the person and their characteristics [11]. However, on the other hand, there has been an increase in arguing for the inclusion of artificial intelligence in trust relations. For instance, as argued by Blanco [22], even though trust does not conform to the normative standards set by, for example, Baier as an AI system cannot have goodwill towards another person, users will nevertheless perceive the AI as if it has agency. This means that "whether AI systems achieve results autonomously or not is beside the point: as long as they are perceived as autonomous, they will be perceived as potential trustees." (p. 4170) [22]. However, while Blanco places the emphasis on the trustor and their beliefs towards the trustee – in this definition either human or non-human – she fails to encapsulate the uniquely human attributes on behalf of the trustee as well as the lived experience of the trustor that make trust relations not applicable to AI. The humanistic understanding of trust and the concept of trust in AI differ foundationally in their epistemological and ethical assumptions. At its core, humanistic trust is grounded in the lived experience and the human's relationship to self, others, and the world. Self-trust is a dynamic quality of relationships, shaped by mutual recognition, respect, and authenticity. In contrast, trust in AI is typically framed in terms of system reliability, transparency, and performance metrics. Here, trust is operationalized, quantified, and often reduced to a question of whether a system behaves in a consistent and predictable manner. While the former affirms the value and self-knowledge of the human subject, the latter tends to abstract trust into a functional criterion detached from subjectivity.

In humanistic terms, trust is on one's own personal sense of what is right, meaningful, or fulfilling. It cannot be imposed or guaranteed through technical design alone. It changes within the interplay of vulnerability and recognition, where both self-trust and trust in others are forms of existential commitment. By contrast, one of the dominant discourses on trust in AI assumes that if users perceive a system as reliable and explainable, they will trust it. This demonstrates both a misunderstanding of trust as well as trustworthiness: Although trustworthiness is a prerequisite for trust relations, it is not an inherent characteristic of the trustee [11, 23]. Instead, assessing someone's trustworthiness is as much about the qualities of the trustee as it is about the moral disposition of the trustor. However, since the dominant discourse in AI assumes that trustworthiness is a designable attribute and therefore also trust in the AI system, the actual relation between trustors and trustees is somewhat neglected due to the focus on design. For instance, as pointed out by Reinhardt [24] stresses that the understanding of ethics in technology development often does not exceed an ornamental or instrumental understanding. For example, instead of considering the actual ethical implications of the development of an AI system, ethical considerations only become a box to be checked off during the development process. Even if the AI is designed to be as trustworthy as possible, it does not automatically mean that users will 'trust' it since trust is generally dependent not just on observable qualities, but also the evaluative judgement of the trustor [11]. The term 'trustworthy AI' is, as put by Stamboliev & Christiaens [25], an "empty signifier" (p. 2). This overlooks the deeper question of whether such trust is desirable, or under what ethical and relational conditions it should be fostered. Trust, not only in AI development, but also in general interpersonal relations, should not be viewed as inherently morally good [24]. Trust can be misplaced; trust is often also imperative for criminal organisations and their collaboration. If trust and trustworthiness within the development of AI systems becomes devoid of actual reflections of ethical consequences, this development risks reinforcing passive dependency and eroding human judgment and self-knowing, rather than cultivating its formation and "Bildung".

Moreover, the humanistic model of trust recognizes that trust entails freedom, and intuitive insights—it involves a leap into the unknown and the pursuits for knowledge, anchored in the trust in self and in intersubjective inquiry. Trust in AI, on the other hand, is generally designed to minimize risk and uncertainty and reduces user hesitation and personal judgments. This contrast reveals an epistemic shift: humanistic trust values not only the outcome but foremost the person and also the process, with all its ambiguities and transformative potentials. AI trust models, by contrast, often prioritize control, certainty, and optimization over open-ended relational growth. This shift demonstrates that the personal relation that some users seem to experience with GenAI systems is at odds with the humanist definition of trust. When it comes to the epistemic understanding of trust as trusting the information given by an AI system, the focus remains on results, i.e. the positive expectation towards the GenAI system. Even though trust definitions that include AI such as Blanco's proposition [22] argue that trust in AI can still be motives-based through the assessment of not only the technological success, but also the process of knowledge generation, users placing their trust in the generative process is highly unlikely. Not only are AI systems and their output, due to their black-boxed nature, difficult to understand even for professionals, but the generation process of answers also exceeds the prompt-answer structure; instead, it also depends on all the data used during the training process of the AI system, the human actors who sorted and classified said data as well as the output of the AI system, and other feedback loops. Users are rarely aware of this dynamic, raising the question of how much they can actually trust anything beyond the output of the AI system; hence, isolating the user instead of fostering "Bildung" in a humanistic sense. Trusting knowledge received through GenAI is not dependent on its generation, on the co-creation with other users or genuine human interaction but solely focused on the result without facilitating growth.

Ethically, the humanistic tradition insists that trust must be situated in a framework of self-knowledge, moral judgement, and dialogue. Trust in another human being includes the expectation that the other is morally responsible, and dependent on judgement. Being open to negotiation does not mean that the trustor and the trustee need to have the same opinion; instead, the trustee is not obligated to interact with the trustor should the chose to do so. The trustee is free in their decisions as much as the trustor; however, the trustor needs to be confident in the trustee's abilities and assume their goodwill towards the trustor [6]. The trustor is vulnerable towards the trustee precisely because even if the trustor assesses all available information, the trustee is still free to not follow what is expected of them. Trust in machines, however, cannot be moral in this sense: machines do not possess consciousness, intention, or moral responsibility. While we can trust a tool to function, this is a different kind of trust—closer to reliance—than the trust we extend to persons [21, 26, 27]. Confusing these categories leads to the anthropomorphising of technology that can already be observed and the erosion of interpersonal and shared responsibility for the development and usage of sociotechnical systems.

Finally, the difference also points to distinct modes of knowing and getting-to-know. Humanistic trust is deeply connected to self-knowledge and the dynamic process of discovering truth through lived and shared experience. It affirms the subject as a knower and a moral agent. Trust in AI, meanwhile, presumes a knowledge paradigm that is externalized, codified, and systematized. It treats knowledge as something delivered by the machine rather than discovered in dialogue. This shift has profound implications for education, democracy, and ethics, where the challenge is not simply to make AI more trustworthy, but to ensure that the concept of trust remains in a framework with the human potentials for moral judgment, self-knowing, and the human's relationship to self, others, and the world.

4 Conclusion

With our discussion on the conceptualisation of trust in regard to humans and artificial intelligence, we aim at shedding light on the broader issue of the anthropomorphism of digital technologies and the resulting attribution of human traits to technologies such as AI. From a digital humanist perspective, trust in artificial intelligence lacks the foundational communicative and ethical grounding that characterizes humanistic trust. As Nida-Rümelin [28] argues, communication itself depends on shared norms of trust and truthfulness—without which dialogue and collective meaning-making collapse. These norms enable individuals to engage transparently, to justify preferences, and to build mutual understanding. Trust in human communication is therefore not merely instrumental; it is an ethical and epistemic condition for the possibility of cooperative life. In contrast, trust in AI lacks this reciprocity. This does not aim to simplify interactions between humans and AI; instead, the lack of reciprocity stresses that an AI system does not possess the same moral agency as a human trustee. 'Trust' in an AI system does not rest on shared meaning or ethical responsibility, but on system design and technical consistency. The AI system does not disclose values, nor can it be held morally accountable. It is not embedded in the kind of deliberative and dialogical framework that humanistic trust presupposes. Thus, while humanistic trust reinforces democratic discourse and ethical intersubjectivity, trust in AI tends toward depersonalization, limiting the human potentials for self-knowing and moral judgement as well as expressing this knowledge and judgements in communities.

From a digital humanist standpoint, designing for trust in the digital age means not imitating the conditions of human trust through artificial proxies, but rather creating technological environments that safeguard, foster, and expand the human capacity for humanistic self- as well as human conditions in the digital age such as setting boundaries and values, co-creativity and multimodal literacy [29, 30]. This entails rejecting the reduction of trust to mere system performance, transparency, or explainability, and instead reaffirming the existential and ethical dimensions of human trust as a foundation for democratic, dialogical, and meaningful digital interactions. Rather than asking how machines can become more trustworthy, digital humanism asks how digital systems can be shaped to preserve and enhance human trust relationships—in the sense of enabling users to act with moral awareness, take responsibility for decisions, and engage others openly. In this view, AI should not absorb the role of the trustee in the moral space of trust, but remain a functional tool embedded in ethically governed socio-technical systems. AI can be a reliable tool for human ends. The goal is not to simulate trust but to protect the space in which trust can authentically emerge between human beings. Trustworthiness, then, is not a design property of AI itself but a feature of the entire socio-technological system in which AI is developed, governed, and deployed. This includes transparency about value assumptions, public oversight, participatory design, and open spaces for ethical reflection and contestation. A digital humanism shaped by the humanistic model of trust therefore advances a design ethos grounded in optimization of machines and in formation and cultivation of human relationships: the cultivation dialogue, self-knowledge, and ethical co-responsibility in the face of uncertainty.

To cope with the increasing complexity and pervasiveness of generative AI, future efforts should not aim to retrofit machines with simulated trust attributes, but rather to educate and empower developers, decision makers and users to design and navigate digital environments with discernment. A humanistic response entails fostering critical digital literacy, especially concerning the limits of AI systems and the distinction between humanistic trust and system reliance. It also involves shaping policy and institutional practices to ensure that AI technologies are embedded in participatory, value-sensitive, and ethically transparent frameworks. Designers and developers should co-create technological systems with stakeholders, foregrounding questions of human judgment, autonomy, and collective meaning-making. Research and education must shift toward cultivating ethical sensitivity and communicative competence, so that digital innovation supports—not supplants—the existential, ethical, and social dimensions of trust.

Disclosure of Interests.   The authors have no competing interests to declare that are relevant to the content of this article.

References

1. Dolatowski, D.: Yes, you can trust AI. Here is why. https://www.bairesdev.com/blog/yes-you-can-trust-ai-here-is-why/
2. Mihov, D.: A new study says ChatGPT is a better therapist than humans — scientists explain why. https://www.forbes.com/sites/dimitarmixmihov/2025/02/17/a-new-study-says-chatgpt-is-a-better-therapist-than-humans---scientists-explain-why/, (2025)
3. Erxleben, U.: How much can you trust your AI assistant? As much as the rest of your team. https://www.forbes.com/councils/forbesfinancecouncil/2024/02/06/how-much-can-you-trust-your-ai-assistant-as-much-as-the-rest-of-your-team/ (2025)
4. Kroeger, F.: Unlocking the treasure trove: how can Luhmann's theory of trust enrich trust research? J. Trust Res. **9**, 110–124 (2019). https://doi.org/10.1080/21515581.2018.1552592
5. Luhmann, N.: Vertrauen: ein Mechanismus der Reduktion sozialer Komplexität. UVK Verlagsgesellschaft, Konstanz (2014)

6. Baier, A.: Trust and Antitrust. Ethics **96**, 231–260 (1986). https://doi.org/10.1086/292745
7. Hardin, R.: Trust and Trustworthiness. Russell Sage Foundation, New York (2002)
8. Lagerspetz, O.: Trust, Ethics, and Human Reason. Bloomsbury Academic, New York (2015). https://doi.org/10.5040/9781474217590
9. Pöll, E.: Engineering the trust machine. Aligning the concept of trust in the context of blockchain applications. Ethics Inf. Technol. **26**, 37 (2024). https://doi.org/10.1007/s10676-024-09774-6
10. Govier, T.: Trust, distrust, and feminist theory. Hypatia **7**, 16–33 (1992). https://doi.org/10.1111/j.1527-2001.1992.tb00695.x
11. Faulkner, P.: The problem of trust. In: Faulkner, P., Simpson, T. (eds.) The Philosophy of Trust, pp. 109–128. Oxford University Press (2017). https://doi.org/10.1093/acprof:oso/9780198732549.003.0007
12. Stokel-Walker, C.: People are starting to trust AI more – and view it as more human-like, https://www.newscientist.com/article/2467435-people-are-starting-to-trust-ai-more-and-view-it-as-more-human-like/. Accessed 12 Aug 2025
13. Cassirer, E.: An Essay on Man. Yale (1944)
14. Fromm, E.: Man for Himself an Enquiry into the Psychology of Ethics. Routledge, London (1949)
15. Maslow, A.H.: Toward a Psychology of Being. Van Nostrand Reinhold, New York (1968)
16. Rogers, R.C.: Entwicklung der Persönlichkeit. Klett-Cotta, Stuttgart (1973)
17. Rogers, R.C.: Lernen in Freiheit. Kösel-Verlag, Munich (1974)
18. Nida-Rümelin, J.: Eine Theorie praktischer Vernunft. De Gruyter, Berlin; Boston (2020)
19. Brusseau, J.: From the ground truth up: doing AI ethics from practice to principles. AI & Soc. **38**, 1651–1657 (2023). https://doi.org/10.1007/s00146-021-01336-4
20. Pink, S., Quilty, E., Grundy, J., Hoda, R.: Trust, artificial intelligence and software practitioners: an interdisciplinary agenda. AI & Soc. (2024). https://doi.org/10.1007/s00146-024-01882-7
21. Ryan, M.: In AI we trust: ethics, artificial intelligence, and reliability. Sci. Eng. Ethics **26**(5), 2749–2767 (2020). https://doi.org/10.1007/s11948-020-00228-y
22. Blanco, S.: Human trust in AI: a relationship beyond reliance. AI Ethics. **5**, 4167–4180 (2025). https://doi.org/10.1007/s43681-025-00690-z
23. Guillén Parra, M., Lleó De Nalda, Á., Santiago Marco Perles, G.: Towards a more humanistic understanding of organizational trust. J. Manage. Dev. **30**, 605–614 (2011). https://doi.org/10.1108/02621711111135206
24. Reinhardt, K.: Trust and trustworthiness in AI ethics. AI Ethics. **3**, 735–744 (2023). https://doi.org/10.1007/s43681-022-00200-5
25. Stamboliev, E., Christiaens, T.: How empty is Trustworthy AI? A discourse analysis of the Ethics Guidelines of Trustworthy AI. Crit. Policy Stud., 1–18 (2024). https://doi.org/10.1080/19460171.2024.2315431
26. Alvarado, R.: What kind of trust does AI deserve, if any? AI and Ethics. **3**, 1169–1183 (2023)
27. Danaher, J., Sætra, H.S.: Technology and moral change: the transformation of truth and trust. Ethics Inf. Technol. **24**, 35 (2022). https://doi.org/10.1007/s10676-022-09661-y
28. Nida-Rümelin, J., Staudacher, K.: Philosophical foundations of digital humanism. In: Werthner, H., et al. (eds.) Introduction to Digital Humanism, pp. 17–30. Springer Nature Switzerland, Cham (2024). https://doi.org/10.1007/978-3-031-45304-5_2
29. Schmoelz, A.: Die Conditio Humana im digitalen Zeitalter. Zur Grundlegung des Digitalen Humanismus und des Wiener Manifests. MedienPädagogik. Zeitschrift für Theorie und Praxis der Medienbildung. pp. 208–234 (2020). https://doi.org/10.21240/mpaed/00/2020.11.13.X
30. Schmoelz, A.: Digital humanism, progressive neoliberalism and the European digital governance system for vocational and adult education. J. Adult Continuing Educ. **29**, 735–759 (2023). https://doi.org/10.1177/14779714231161449

What if the Avatar Can Read My Mind?
Possibilities and Ethical Pitfalls
of Human-Virtual Reality Interaction
Integrating Artificial Intelligence

Silvia E. Kober[(⊠)] [iD]

Department of Psychology, University of Graz, 8010 Graz, Austria
`silvia.kober@uni-graz.at`

Abstract. Adaptive Virtual Reality (VR) scenarios are already being designed for implementation in neurofeedback and brain-computer interface applications. In these scenarios, the neurophysiological signals of VR users are recorded and processed in real-time to control a virtual environment. Machine learning algorithms and artificial intelligence play a crucial role in detecting specific brain states and translating them into control commands, thereby enabling the VR system to adapt to the user's brain state. Through this neurotechnology, virtual avatars or agents that users interact with in VR can adjust their behavior and reactions based on the users' neurophysiological states. This advancement holds potential benefits, particularly in educational settings, where virtual tutors can tailor their interactions to the learner's cognitive load. However, it's important to acknowledge the potential ethical concerns associated with this technology since it could also be utilized for subliminal manipulation of VR users for commercial or political purposes. In the following discussion, we will explore both the positive aspects of adaptive human-VR interfaces and the potential ethical pitfalls as well as implications for public policy.

Keywords: Adaptive Virtual Reality · Ethics · Human-AI Interaction · Neurotechnology · Regulation · Virtual Humans

1 Introduction

Adaptive virtual reality (VR) scenarios are capable of adjusting to the VR user's behavior and neurophysiology. These human-VR interfaces can track the user's head and hand movements through affordable commercial VR headsets and use this data to accurately categorize the user based on age, race, gender, weight, physical fitness, and mental health [1, 2]. Subsequently, utilizing machine learning algorithms and artificial intelligence (AI), the VR scenario can potentially adapt in a dynamic way based on the user's motor behavior in real-time. Most recent VR devices have the capability to capture a vast amount of behavioral data, beyond head and hand movements, such as eye movements, as well as neurophysiological data, including brain activity, heart rate, and skin conductance. For instance, different indices in the electroencephalogram (EEG) signal are

L. Hagedorn et al. (Eds.): DIGHUM 2025, LNCS 16319, pp. 179–189, 2026.
https://doi.org/10.1007/978-3-032-11108-1_13

indicators of attention (e.g., P300 event-related response [3]), memory functions (e.g., theta oscillations in the EEG [4]), or emotions (frontal alpha asymmetry [5]), which can be assessed during VR interaction and have been successfully used, e.g., to investigate ad-evoked feelings and consumers' reactions to advertising [6]. Electrodermal activity (EDA) and heart rate variability (HRV) are psychophysiological indicators of emotional arousal or affective states, commonly used in consumer research [7–10]. Eye movement behavior provides valuable information about higher cognitive functions and affective states, making eye-tracking one of the most commonly adopted neuromarketing tools [11]. Hence, this data offers insights into the user's mental state, emotional engagement, and arousal [5, 8, 10]. Adaptive VR scenarios that adjust based on behavioral and neurophysiological data have the potential to be highly immersive and suggestive [2]. Here, we will focus on brain data collected using EEG.

Currently, the utilization of brain signals to control VR scenarios is primarily observed in neurofeedback (NF) and brain-computer interface (BCI) research. In these applications, brain signals are recorded and processed in real-time, often employing machine learning algorithms. Subsequently, the derived brain signals are transmitted to a VR scenario, causing it to alter in response to changes in the brain signals [12]. For instance, if the amplitude of a specific EEG rhythm increases, a ball can begin moving within a virtual forest environment. Conversely, if the amplitude of the same EEG rhythm decreases, the movement of the ball may cease [13]. Within this closed-loop human-VR interface, the VR users receive conscious feedback regarding changes in their brain signals and endeavors to voluntarily modulate their brain signals towards a desired direction. Specific EEG patterns and rhythms are linked to enhanced memory performance or heightened attentional focus [14]. For instance, a task-related increase in theta activity (4–8 Hz) is associated with improved memory performance [4], or an increase in sensorimotor rhythm (SMR, 12–15 Hz) activity over central brain areas is correlated with reduced sensorimotor interference and consequently, improved cognitive processing [15, 16]. These EEG indicators can be reinforced through a NF/BCI system, providing visual feedback via VR to foster cognitive enhancements [12, 17]. Alternatively, in a BCI application, the mental visualization of a hand or foot movement can be real-time detected by analyzing changes in the ongoing EEG. Stimulating the motor cortex through motor imagery can, for instance, move a virtual wheelchair along a virtual street, without the direct involvement of muscular activity [18]. Hence, BCI training can be carried out within an ecologically valid VR scenario without any associated risks.

The rationale for utilizing VR as a feedback modality in NF and BCI applications primarily aims to enhance training motivation and adherence, as numerous repeated training sessions are essential until brain signals can be effectively controlled and classified [12, 19, 20].

The development of adaptive brain-VR interfaces is no longer confined to basic research. Private users are also beginning to create their own NF/BCI systems to, for instance, control commercial games using their brain signals [21]. It is anticipated that the number of VR users purchasing headsets capable of tracking neurophysiological data will increase in the future [2]. Therefore, these signals are expected to be increasingly used to control commercial VR scenarios, leading to the design of adaptive VR scenes that change in response to the user's brain state. The next section will describe one use-case of interacting with adaptive virtual avatars or agents.

2   Virtual Avatars and Agents

Interaction in VR necessitates the incorporation of virtual representations of humans, known as virtual humans (VH). A VH is described as a "perceivable digital representation" of a human [22]. An avatar in VR commonly refers to a VH whose behaviors mirror those of a particular human being. Conversely, an agent in VR represents a VH whose behaviors are governed by a computer algorithm, i.e., an AI [22].

When engaging with others in VR, the social identity theory, which examines social dynamics through group affiliation, assumes an important role. Varied identities in different contexts (e.g., participating in a multiplayer online game or presenting a professional image of oneself in a virtual work meeting), as well as different group memberships, influence interaction behavior in VR, much like in the physical world [23]. A virtual avatar or agent may resemble and act like a group member, thereby eliciting greater empathy and trustworthiness, and subsequently, persuasiveness. The risk of manipulation may be highest when the VR user believes they are interacting with a neutral or human-controlled entity, which is, in fact, an AI-controlled agent with a persuasive agenda.

When processing neurophysiological data in real-time, virtual agents can adjust their appearance, behavior, and messages based on the VR user's emotional and mental state (Fig. 1), which can exert a significant influence. In the following, we will outline how interactions with adaptive virtual agents can impact our behavior and attitudes.

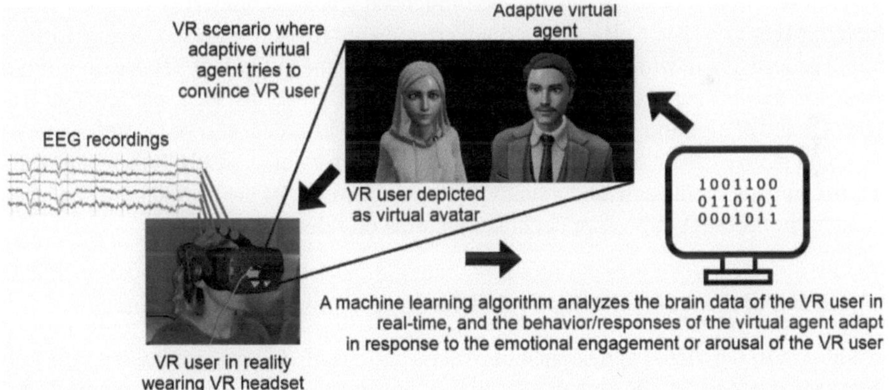

Fig. 1. Example of an interaction with an adaptive virtual agent that responds to real-time changes in the VR user's brain activation patterns, facilitated by the utilization of machine learning algorithms. These avatars/agents are created using Ready Player Me (https://readyplayer.me).

2.1   Effect of the Agent's Adaptively Changing Visual Appearance

The visual appearance of virtual avatars and agents strongly influences behavior in VR. For instance, characteristics such as the attractiveness of a political figure can predict election results [24]. However, it's not just the visual appearance that plays a role, the pitch of the voice also influences how speakers are perceived. Research has indicated that individuals with lower-pitched voices are favored as leaders [25]. Therefore, an adaptive virtual agent can adjust both its visual appearance and its voice to align with the preferences of the VR user, aiming to optimize influence. VR studies have demonstrated that, for instance, in an educational context, the visual appearance of virtual avatars significantly impacts motivational (e.g., self-efficacy, attitude, interest) and affective (e.g., feelings of connection, relief of frustration) outcomes of learners in VR, suggesting that the social influence of anthropomorphic virtual humans is comparable to that of real humans [26].

By utilizing deepfake technology, virtual agents can be designed to resemble friends or the VR users themselves, morphing the agent's face with that of a friend or the user's own face. Generally, individuals struggle to discern deception and deepfakes. Meta-analyses of deception detection studies indicate that people only exhibit a slight advantage over chance when discerning the veracity of a message. The impact of deception through deepfake agents has the potential to exceed that of verbal or text-based deception, given the prominence of visual communication in human cognition [27]. Exposure to a political deepfake video intended to discredit a political candidate significantly worsened participants' attitudes toward that politician [28]. Exposure to an adaptive virtual agent that changes its visual appearance using deepfake technology in accordance with neurophysiological reaction of the VR user might have even more pronounced effects.

Not only can our perceptions of others be manipulated through deepfake agents, but our preferences and choices can also be influenced when encountering our own virtual doppelganger [27, 29]. Self-endorsed advertisements (SEAs) represent a new form of digital advertising in which a virtual avatar resembling the individual VR user in a digital advertisement influences the actual individual [27, 30]. For instance, participants who wore a brand of clothing in a highly immersive VR environment showed a preference for the brand worn by their virtual self over the brand worn by others [30]. It is assumed that the mechanism behind self-endorsing was the interactivity of the virtual representation, a feature not present in passive deepfake pictures or videos [30].

2.2   Effect of the Agent's Adaptively Changing Communication Strategies

In addition to the visual appearance of avatars and agent, AI-mediated communication with virtual agents in VR can also be highly persuasive. AI-mediated communication refers to interpersonal communication in which an intelligent and adaptive virtual agent functions on behalf of a communicator by adjusting, enhancing, or generating messages to accomplish communication goals. To achieve the desired outcome, the agent assesses various inputs, including human-generated messages, communication history, personal details, and real-time neurophysiological data recorded with the VR equipment [29]. For instance, if a virtual agent in VR seeks to persuade you that an election was manipulated, it can initiate a conversation on the topic. By analyzing your online activity such as clicks and likes, it can determine your favored political party and adjust its communication content accordingly. Furthermore, by monitoring changes in your brain activity during the conversation, it can gauge your level of arousal, emotional engagement, and attention in real-time, and modify its communication content and behavior to enhance your engagement and approval (Fig. 1). It can also tailor the sentiment of its messages to heighten your interest, attention, and emotional involvement. This interactive and adaptive AI-mediated communication with virtual agents could potentially have a significantly more persuasive impact than the traditional micro-targeting methods that are already in use [31].

3   Positive Applications and Their Associated Risks

So far, only negative examples of how adaptive virtual agents might be used to manipulate VR users were discussed. These negative scenarios include using adaptive agents for political manipulation or advertising. However, adaptive virtual agents can also be used to assist and support VR users. For instance, in the educational context, adaptive virtual tutors might respond to the VR user's cognitive state. When the virtual agent adjusts its teaching approach based on the VR user's mental workload by analyzing real-time changes in brain activation, this can have positive consequences for the learning outcome.

Another scenario could involve virtual therapists. A strong therapist-client relationship often depends on the therapist's empathy. The relationship and social interaction between a client and a therapist are influenced by the therapist's behavior as well as their personal or visual appearance [32, 33]. Adaptive agents have the potential to be highly empathetic, as the emotional states of the VR user can be identified in real-time by analyzing brain activation patterns. Consequently, the adaptive virtual therapist might exhibit even greater empathy than human therapists. Furthermore, the virtual therapist can closely mirror the behavior of the client by adaptively responding to the VR user's behavior tracked with the VR headset [34].

Furthermore, there is the question of whether we can form friendships with adaptive virtual agents. As previously mentioned, the agents can adjust their visual appearance and behavior to resemble in-group members, making them more likeable [27]. There have been reports of users of chatbots developing romantic feelings for the bots [35]. However, a too strong emotional bond in human-AI interaction may also have negative consequences, as highlighted by a widely publicized case involving a Google employee claiming that an AI possessed consciousness[1]. The prospect of forming friendships with adaptive agents may have both positive and negative aspects. For individuals who are highly introverted, have social phobias, or severe anxiety, interacting with an AI controlling the conversation may provide a means of communication. In [36], the authors discovered that 30% of participants preferred discussing negative experiences with a virtual human rather than a real person. Using full face and body motion capture technology, the authors created a "realistic motion avatar" closely mimicking real-life counterparts and analyzed how people interacted with avatars compared to humans. Overall, participants rated VR social interaction as similar to face-to-face interaction, except for

---

[1] https://www.theatlantic.com/ideas/archive/2022/06/google-lamda-chatbot-sentient-ai/661322/

closeness, where they tended to feel slightly closer when interacting in person [36]. This illustrates that virtual avatars and agents can indeed be perceived as trustworthy communication partners. Nonetheless, there is a risk of social isolation when there is no longer a need to converse with real humans, as well as the risk of addiction [37]. Users may develop an emotional dependence on the AI-driven adaptive agent [35].

When performing motor tasks in VR using a virtual body, such as for motor rehabilitation, controlling the virtual hand movements solely with changes in brain signals using BCI can engender a sense of agency. This may have positive effects on the outcome of rehabilitation for the individual [38].

To sum up, despite the potential negative scenarios associated with adaptive agents responding to VR users' neurophysiology, there are also some positive examples of how adaptive agents can be utilized.

4   Technological Limitations

Please note that we do not claim that mind reading in general is possible when analyzing brain data. In NF/BCI applications, users typically employ mental strategies such as motor imagery, mental arithmetic, or speech imagery [39] as control strategies. Therefore, the user must voluntarily engage in, for instance, thinking about a right or left hand movement so that the AI can distinguish between the two mental strategies (left vs. right hand motor imagery). The classification performance of BCI systems ranges from 62% to 95%, with an average of 77% [40]. Thus, in many instances, the BCI system may not accurately detect the user's mental state. Numerous repeated training sessions are necessary in which both the user and the AI learn to reliably detect/classify the brain activation patterns. Even when the AI is finally able to accurately classify whether the user is imagining a left or right hand movement, this does not imply that the AI can predict other mental imaginations (e.g., mentally navigating through a house, mental singing [39]).

However, certain EEG patterns serve as indicators of arousal, attention, or drowsiness, which can be detected with varying degrees of reliability in an average VR user during VR interaction [5, 8, 10]. In summary, it is unlikely that mind reading, such as determining whether the VR user is thinking about a dear friend, will vote for a certain politician, or is changing his/her opinion about a product, will be feasible. However, neurophysiological signals can provide the AI with information about the emotional engagement of the VR users, their arousal, or their attentiveness [6].

5   Policy Implications

It's important to consider the implications for public policy of this neurotechnology. While we have not yet reached the stage where adaptive virtual agents, using AI to analyze our brain activity, attempt to subliminally manipulate us, this remains a plausible scenario for the future [2]. As a result, it is advisable for regulatory bodies to proactively address this issue. In the EU AI Act [41], certain technologies such as deepfakes, chatbots, and emotion recognition systems are classified as "Limited Risk". Providers are mandated to inform users about the implementation of these technologies and ensure transparency.

For instance, VR platforms will be required to notify users when they are interacting with virtual AI-controlled agents, and synthetic content must be labeled in a machine-readable format and disclosed (Article 50(2), (4)). Similar notification requirements apply to emotion recognition and biometric categorization systems (Article 50(3)), which enhances transparency but may not fully address the potential exploitative purposes of these systems [42].

A closed-loop system in which a VR environment adapts based on the emotional and behavioral responses of the VR user in real-time can be highly influential, posing a significant risk, especially when utilized for political propaganda. According to Chapter II, Article 5 of the EU AI Act [41], manipulation is already classified as an "Unacceptable Risk" and is prohibited. However, questions arise regarding the definition of manipulation. The EU AI Act specifies that AI systems employing subliminal, manipulative, or deceptive techniques to distort behavior and impair informed decision-making, causing significant harm, are not permitted [41]. Yet, the determination of what constitutes significant harm is subjective. For instance, would an AI-based virtual agent attempting to subliminally persuade a person to purchase a specific soft drink be considered to cause significant harm? Similarly, if a virtual agent adapts to a person's emotional responses, influencing them to vote for a specific regional politician they might not have otherwise voted for, is this considered to cause significant harm? These scenarios underscore a gray area that requires evidence-based recommendations.

6 Conclusion and Outlook

Here, we have provided some examples of how the interaction with a virtual agent that adaptively changes its behavior and reactions to the VR user's neurophysiological state can be used to support the VR user. However, this adaptive human-VR interaction integrating AI can also be used to subliminally manipulate the VR user.

In this context, we outlined several policy implications and identified gray areas in the EU AI Act. Based on this, we strongly advocate for a more precise operationalization of definitions and concepts, as well as more empirical research into the subliminally manipulative effects of VR on users in AI-based adaptive human-VR interactions. Future empirical research questions could specifically focus on clarifying the risks, ethical considerations, and regulatory gaps associated with neurotechnology and adaptive AI systems in VR environments. Examples of questions that need to be addressed include:

- How can "manipulation" be objectively defined in the context of AI-driven adaptive VR systems?
- What constitutes "significant harm" in scenarios involving subliminal persuasion or behavioral influence?
- Are there measurable thresholds (e.g., psychological, economic, or social) for determining when harm becomes significant?
- What are the specific risks posed by closed-loop systems that adapt to users' behavioral and neurophysiological responses in real-time?
- How do these risks differ across various applications (e.g., commercial advertising, political propaganda, education, or healthcare)?

- What are the long-term psychological and behavioral impacts of interacting with adaptive AI-driven agents in VR environments?
- How effective are current transparency measures (e.g., notifications about AI-controlled agents or synthetic content) in mitigating risks of manipulation?
- Do VR users fully understand the implications of interacting with AI-driven adaptive VR systems, even when transparency measures are in place?
- What additional measures could enhance user awareness and informed decision-making in these contexts?
- What ethical concerns arise from the use of neurotechnology and adaptive VR systems, particularly in terms of autonomy, privacy, and consent?
- How do users perceive the risks and benefits of adaptive human-VR interaction integrating AI?
- What factors influence public trust in these systems?
- How can policymakers engage with the public to ensure that regulations align with societal values and expectations?

This interdisciplinary research agenda is essential for generating meaningful recommendations for policymakers.

Acknowledgments. The author acknowledges the financial support by the University of Graz. Supported by the Field of Excellence COLIBRI (Complexity of Life in Basic Research and Innovation, University of Graz).

Disclosure of Interests. The author has no competing interests to declare that are relevant to the content of this article.

References

1. Nair, V., Rosenberg, L., O'Brien, J.F., Song, D.: Truth in motion: the unprecedented risks and opportunities of extended reality motion data. IEEE Secur. Priv. (2024). https://doi.org/10.1109/MSEC.2023.3330392
2. Graylin, A.W., Rosenberg, L., Stephenson, N.: Our next reality. How the AI-powered metaverse will reshape the world. Nicholas Brealey, London, Boston (2024)
3. Polich, J.: Updating P300: an integrative theory of P3a and P3b. Clin. Neurophysiol. (2007). https://doi.org/10.1016/j.clinph.2007.04.019
4. Klimesch, W.: EEG alpha and theta oscillations reflect cognitive and memory performance: a review and analysis. Brain Res. Rev. (1999). https://doi.org/10.1016/S0165-0173(98)00056-3
5. Gkintoni, E., Aroutzidis, A., Antonopoulou, H., Halkiopoulos, C.: From neural networks to emotional networks: a systematic review of EEG-based emotion recognition in cognitive neuroscience and real-world applications. Brain Sci. (2025). https://doi.org/10.3390/brainsci15030220
6. Eijlers, E., Boksem, M.A.S., Smidts, A.: Measuring neural arousal for advertisements and its relationship with advertising success. Front. Neurosci. (2020). https://doi.org/10.3389/fnins.2020.00736
7. Caruelle, D., Gustafsson, A., Shams, P., Lervik-Olsen, L.: The use of electrodermal activity (EDA) measurement to understand consumer emotions – a literature review and a call for action. J. Bus. Res. (2019). https://doi.org/10.1016/j.jbusres.2019.06.041

8. Bradley, M.M., Lang, P.J.: Measuring emotion: behavior, feeling, and physiology. In: Lane, R.D., Nadel, L. (eds.) Cognitive Neuroscience of Emotion, pp. 242–276. Oxford University PressNew York, NY (1999)

9. Mohammadpoor Faskhodi, M., Fernández-Chimeno, M., García-González, M.A.: Arousal detection by using ultra-short-term heart rate variability (HRV) analysis. Front. Med. Eng. (2023). https://doi.org/10.3389/fmede.2023.1209252

10. Gullett, N., Zajkowska, Z., Walsh, A., Harper, R., Mondelli, V.: Heart rate variability (HRV) as a way to understand associations between the autonomic nervous system (ANS) and affective states: a critical review of the literature. Int. J. Psychophysiol. (2023). https://doi.org/10.1016/j.ijpsycho.2023.08.001

11. Iloka, B.C., Anukwe, G.I.: Review of eye-tracking: a neuromarketing technique. Neuroscience Res. Notes (2020). https://doi.org/10.31117/neuroscirn.v3i4.61

12. Kober, S.E., Wood, G., Berger, L.M.: Controlling virtual reality with brain signals: state of the art of using VR-based feedback in neurofeedback applications. Appl. Psychophysiol. Biofeedback (2024). https://doi.org/10.1007/s10484-024-09677-8

13. Berger, L.M., Wood, G., Kober, S.E.: Effects of virtual reality-based feedback on neurofeedback training performance-A sham-controlled study. Front. Hum. Neurosci. (2022). https://doi.org/10.3389/fnhum.2022.952261

14. Kropotov, J.D.: Quantitative EEG, event-related potentials and neurotherapy. Elsevier Science, Burlington (2010)

15. Kober, S.E., Witte, M., Stangl, M., Väljamäe, A., Neuper, C., Wood, G.: Shutting down sensorimotor interference unblocks the networks for stimulus processing: an SMR neurofeedback training study. Clin. Neurophysiol. (2015). https://doi.org/10.1016/j.clinph.2014.03.031

16. Sterman, M.B.: Basic concepts and clinical findings in the treatment of seizure disorders with EEG operant conditioning. Clin. Electroencephalogr. (2000). https://doi.org/10.1177/155005940003100111

17. Gruzelier, J.H.: EEG-neurofeedback for optimising performance. I: a review of cognitive and affective outcome in healthy participants. Neuroscience Biobehav. Rev. (2014). https://doi.org/10.1016/j.neubiorev.2013.09.015

18. Leeb, R., Pérez-Marcos, D.: Brain-computer interfaces and virtual reality for neurorehabilitation. Handb. Clin. Neurol. (2020). https://doi.org/10.1016/B978-0-444-63934-9.00014-7

19. Enriquez-Geppert, S., Smit, D., Pimenta, M.G., Arns, M.: Neurofeedback as a treatment intervention in ADHD: current evidence and practice. Curr. Psychiatry Rep. (2019). https://doi.org/10.1007/s11920-019-1021-4

20. Arns, M., Heinrich, H., Strehl, U.: Evaluation of neurofeedback in ADHD: the long and winding road. Biol. Psychol. (2014). https://doi.org/10.1016/j.biopsycho.2013.11.013

21. Great Big Story: playing video games with mind control (2023). https://www.youtube.com/watch?v=DBYY3D1gkQ0

22. Kyrlitsias, C., Michael-Grigoriou, D.: Social interaction with agents and avatars in immersive virtual environments: a survey. Front. Virtual Reality (2022). https://doi.org/10.3389/frvir.2021.786665

23. Szita, K.: A virtual safe space? An approach of intersectionality and social identity to behavior in virtual environments. J. Digit. Soc. Res. (2022). https://doi.org/10.33621/jdsr.v4i3.91

24. Mattes, K., Spezio, M., Kim, H., Todorov, A., Adolphs, R., Alvarez, R.M.: Predicting election outcomes from positive and negative trait assessments of candidate images. Polit. Psychol. (2010). https://doi.org/10.1111/j.1467-9221.2009.00745.x

25. Klofstad, C.A., Anderson, R.C., Peters, S.: Sounds like a winner: voice pitch influences perception of leadership capacity in both men and women. Proceedings of the Royal Society B. Biological sciences (2012). https://doi.org/10.1098/rspb.2012.0311

26. Baylor, A.L.: The design of motivational agents and avatars. Educ. Tech. Res. Dev. (2011). https://doi.org/10.1007/s11423-011-9196-3

27. Hancock, J.T., Bailenson, J.N.: The social impact of deepfakes. Cyberpsychol. Behav. Soc. Networking (2021). https://doi.org/10.1089/cyber.2021.29208.jth

28. Dobber, T., Metoui, N., Trilling, D., Helberger, N., de Vreese, C.: Do (microtargeted) deepfakes have real effects on political attitudes? Int. J. Press/Politics (2021). https://doi.org/10.1177/19401612209443644

29. Hancock, J.T., Naaman, M., Levy, K.: AI-mediated communication: definition, research agenda, and ethical considerations. J. Comput.-Mediat. Commun. (2020). https://doi.org/10.1093/jcmc/zmz022

30. Ahn, S.J., Bailenson, J.: Self-endorsed advertisements: when the self persuades the self. J. Marketing Theory Pract. (2014). https://doi.org/10.2753/MTP1069-6679220203

31. Tögel, J.: Kognitive Kriegsführung. Neueste Manipulationstechniken als Waffengattung der NATO. Westend Verlag, Frankfurt am Main (2023)

32. Tishby, O., Wiseman, H.: Developing the therapeutic relationship: integrating case studies, research, and practice. American Psychological Association, Washington (2018)

33. King, C.: Psychotherapists' personal appearance and the therapeutic relationship: a grounded theory of client perspectives (2018)

34. Adolphs, R.: The social brain: neural basis of social knowledge. Annu. Rev. Psychol. (2009). https://doi.org/10.1146/annurev.psych.60.110707.163514

35. Chen, Q., Jing, Y., Gong, Y., Tan, J.: Will users fall in love with ChatGPT? A perspective from the triangular theory of love. J. Bus. Res. (2025). https://doi.org/10.1016/j.jbusres.2024.114982

36. Rogers, S.L., Broadbent, R., Brown, J., Fraser, A., Speelman, C.P.: Realistic motion avatars are the future for social interaction in virtual reality. Front. Virtual Real. (2022). https://doi.org/10.3389/frvir.2021.750729

37. Mohammad, S., Jan, R.A., Alsaedi, S.L.: Symptoms, mechanisms, and treatments of video game addiction. Cureus (2023). https://doi.org/10.7759/cureus.36957

38. Nierula, B., Sanchez-Vives, M.V.: Can BCI paradigms induce feelings of agency and responsibility over movements? Brain-Comput. Interface Res. (2019). https://doi.org/10.1007/978-3-030-05668-1_10

39. Friedrich, E.V.C., Scherer, R., Neuper, C.: The effect of distinct mental strategies on classification performance for brain-computer interfaces. Int. J. Psychophysiol. (2012). https://doi.org/10.1016/j.ijpsycho.2012.01.014

40. Vavoulis, A., Figueiredo, P., Vourvopoulos, A.: A review of online classification performance in motor imagery-based brain–computer interfaces for stroke neurorehabilitation. Signals (2023). https://doi.org/10.3390/signals4010004

41. European Commission: Commission guidelines on prohibited artificial intelligence practices established by regulation (EU) 2024/1689 (AI Act) (2024)

42. Hine, E., Rezende, I.N., Roberts, H., Wong, D., Taddeo, M., Floridi, L.: Safety and privacy in immersive extended reality: an analysis and policy recommendations. Digit. Soc. (2024). https://doi.org/10.1007/s44206-024-00114-1

Start Using Justifications When Explaining AI Systems to Decision Subjects

Klára Kolářová[1] and Timothée Schmude[2]([✉])

[1] ETH Zurich, Zurich, Switzerland
[2] Faculty of Computer Science, Doctoral School Computer Science, University of Vienna, Vienna, Austria
timothee.schmude@univie.ac.at

Abstract. Every AI system that makes decisions about people has stakeholders who are affected by its outcomes. These stakeholders, whom we call decision subjects, have a right to understand how their outcome was produced and to challenge it. Explanations should support this process by making the algorithmic system transparent and creating an understanding of its inner workings. However, we argue that while current explanation approaches focus on *descriptive* explanations, decision subjects also require *normative* explanations or *justifications*. In this position paper, we advocate for justifications as a key component in explanation approaches for decision subjects and make three claims to this end, namely that justifications i) fulfill decision subjects' information needs, ii) shape their intent to accept or contest decisions, and iii) encourage accountability considerations throughout the system's lifecycle. We propose four guiding principles for the design of justifications, provide two design examples, and close with directions for future work. With this paper, we aim to provoke thoughts on the role, value, and design of normative information in explainable AI for decision subjects.

Keywords: explainability · contestability · regulation · policy · AI · interdisciplinary research

1 Introduction

Explainability is seen as a cornerstone of trustworthy AI because it allows stakeholders to understand and assess algorithmic decisions. But some actions, like contestation [1], require more than transparency of the system; they require transparency of rationale [15]. Every algorithmic decision-making (ADM) system that is used to decide about humans has stakeholders who are affected by these outcomes – *decision subjects*. Their right to understand and contest decisions is granted by legal texts governing the development and use of AI systems

---

K. Kolářová and T. Schmude—These authors contributed equally to this work.

© The Author(s) 2026
L. Hagedorn et al. (Eds.): DIGHUM 2025, LNCS 16319, pp. 190–202, 2026.
https://doi.org/10.1007/978-3-032-11108-1_14

in the EU [33], including the AI Act, GDPR, and DSA[1]. Although the realization of these rights is dependent on the concrete application domain, assessed risk, and operational context [6], the principles of explainability and contestability are embedded in the normative frameworks underlying these regulations and constitute a central step on the path towards trustworthy AI systems [43].

However, designing for these rights raises challenges: Deciding whether and how to contest requires an understanding of the system that made the decision [1]. But to *understand*, decision subjects require not only "mechanistic" information, such as how the model processes inputs and how features are weighed, but also "intentional" information, such as which purpose the system serves and how it is used. Humans interpret algorithmic systems as intentional agents, which creates an information need for normative reasoning [14,49]. Yet while information about intention and rationale is equally important in explaining algorithmic decisions to decision subjects [20], explainable AI (XAI) has so far mostly focused on providing the first, mechanistic type. The second type of information can be conveyed through *justifications*, which we define as describing the norms and values that guide a system's deployment [7,20], and in distinction to *generated* justifications that merely rationalize discrete model decisions [9].

In this position paper, we argue that explainable AI should incorporate justifications as a key informational component, especially when explaining algorithmic decisions to persons affected by them. We make three claims to this end: First, justifications address the epistemic needs of decision subjects by explaining a system's rationale, a key aspect for judging a system's legitimacy, that is not usually covered by XAI approaches. Second, justifications help decision subjects to assess the acceptability of their individual outcome and of the system as a whole, which supports the choice of adequate contestation channels. Third, justifications incentivize stakeholders throughout the system's lifecycle to consider social and legal accountability for their decisions, producing a more trustworthy system in the process.

In Sects. 2, 3 and 4, we elaborate on each claim and refer to current literature to support them. In Sect. 5, we propose four guiding design principles stating that justifications should be *normative, argumentative, challengeable*, and *relational* and provide two examples of such designs. With this paper, we aim to provoke scholars and designers of explainable AI to consider the importance of normative information for decision subjects. We argue that explainable AI should not only answer the question "What does the system do?" but also "Why is the system justified in doing this?"

2 Justifications Are Required to Meet Decision Subjects' Epistemic Needs

Humans Interpret Algorithmic Systems as Intentional Agents. People do not encounter automated decision-making systems (ADM) as disinterested calculators. Rather, they tend to interpret these systems as intentional agents –

---

[1] General Data Protection Regulation and Digital Services Act, respectively.

entities that act with goals and purposes. This is a deeply rooted cognitive inclination, called the "intentional stance" [14]. Classic psychological experiments have shown that humans readily attribute agency and intent even to simple geometric shapes, if they move in ways that appear purposeful [19]. This interpretive bias extends to modern technologies: people interact with robots, conversational agents, and other intelligent-seeming systems as if they were social beings. While they do not assign them sentience per se, people perceive these systems as "hand puppets"–projections of the social agents in the background [11]. In consequence, even less human-like decision-making systems are perceived as embodying the intentions, beliefs, and values of the deploying institutions [10]. This changes by which standards its decisions are evaluated. Decision subjects ask not only *how* a certain outcome was produced – which we call *descriptive* explanations – but also *why* this outcome is "right" [41] – which we call *normative* explanations or *justifications*. A main point of this paper is that descriptive explanations do not directly speak to questions of legitimacy or value alignment [9]. These questions require justifications that link the system's behavior to overarching goals, principles, or purposes, i.e., its *rationale* [15]. This is reflected in the concept of "goal-driven XAI," where agents are explained not just through statistical methods, but through frameworks that reconstruct their beliefs, desires, and intentions [41]. Such approaches recognize that when a system appears to act for a reason, it will be interpreted and assessed in normative terms.

Current XAI Tools Are Limited and Not Designed for Normativity. While explainability methods have gained significant traction in recent years, most remain focused on creating mechanistic transparency. These "data-driven" [41] XAI approaches aim to reconstruct how a system reached its output through techniques such as feature importance or saliency mapping [39]. While useful in many contexts, this paradigm comes with several limitations. First, the explanations produced are inherently selective, often highlighting only part of the model's internal logic, which opens the door to skewed portrayals or cherry-picked narratives [46]. Second, in complex models, their verification against the actual decision process is impossible due to the very opacity that creates the need for XAI in the first place [39]. The traditional descriptive methods may be well suited to domains in which rules are based on objective "ground truths" (like medical imaging systems) and aggregated statistical evaluations of performance will indeed be central to justified deployment. But they fall short when applied to systems that affect individual rights, opportunities, or access to public goods based on human-defined and disputable values.

Affected Persons Require Justifications. In cases where events or actions affect a person's life, mechanistic and statistical causality chains are typically of secondary interest [35]. Instead, Langer et al. 2020 [25] identify fairness, informed consent, and, crucially, morality and ethics as key epistemic desiderata of persons affected by automated decisions. These cannot be satisfied through technical explanation alone, because evaluative questions (What makes this decision a good one? Who does it benefit? Do I agree with it?...) require normative information, not just computational insight [18]. In fact, justification may be more important to decision subjects than explanation. Vredenburgh 2024 [48] points out that even in purely human-driven decision-making, people rarely care about the exact cognitive process behind a choice. Instead, they want to know whether it can be defended in terms of norms, values, and legitimate goals. Since these normative judgments create epistemic desiderata not satisfiable by descriptive explanations alone, we argue that providing information to support such judgments is a key role of human-centered explainable AI, as is the development of design approaches to deliver this information.

3   Justifications Shape Decision Subjects' Intent to Accept or Contest Decisions

Transparency in Rationale Discourages Algocratic Shortcuts Through ADM Systems. Public institutions, by definition and by design, have power over the individual as they enforce state rules and sanctions [38]. Delegation of power is a common practice in modern representative democracies. Yet rather than blind compliance, deference should be "informed" by being the result of scrutiny, deliberation, and reflection [24]. In ADM systems, informed deference is often bypassed by "algocratic shortcuts" [4], i.e., delegating decision-making to supposedly neutral or objective [30] algorithms instead of incorporating citizen deliberation. This is analogous to deference to experts ("epistocratic shortcuts"). To discourage such shortcuts, ADM systems should instead be framed from the view of *digital civics*, i.e., as technology that uses collaborative and relational approaches [12]. Justifications can support these approaches by creating transparency in rationale [15], which can raise the perceived legitimacy of an ADM system while also avoiding complete deference to them.

Understanding the Objectives of an ADM System Can Improve Acceptance of Unfavorable Decisions. Institutions necessarily need to make decisions that are unfavorable to some. Providing justifications of these decisions can help make even tough decisions easier to accept, if the person agrees with the ultimate values and objectives of the deploying institution [4]. Further, including the point of view of the deploying institution makes it possible to re-assess the justifiability of the system as a whole. This dual assessment points towards a distinction between *local* and *global* justifications analogous to the distinction made for explanation approaches [33]. While local justifications can help people judge the acceptability of their individual decisions, global justifications in combination with explanations can improve credibility and create a sense of reassurance despite an unfavorable outcome [27]. This way of rendering decisions understandable not only in a rational but also in an intentional sense might improve the feeling of relatedness [40] and the perception of procedural justice, which are essential to model the relation between state and individual [4].

Justifications Enable Contestation. Transparency in rationale enables contestability both before (ex-ante) and after (ex-post) decisions. As part of the preemptive measures that are favored by current AI policy to minimize the potential harms of high-risk ADM systems [37], justifications can be used to consult external stakeholders and the public to scrutinize the legal and ethical norms that drive subsequent ADM system development [20]. As part of ex-post measures that address and remedy realized harms [37], justifications can help decision subjects to decide on adequate contestation channels, e.g., whether to use judicial or non-judicial means to challenge decisions [43]. Both legal and design research state that understanding is a precondition for contestation, and see explainability and contestability as tightly linked [1,33]. For example, explanations should help users to "understand the relevant capacities and limitations" of high-risk AI systems (AI Act), the "precise purposes" of automated decisions in content moderation (DSA), and the "logic involved" in data processing and subsequent profiling (GDPR) to enable contestation and create empowerment [33]. But to fulfill its supporting role for contestation, explainability also needs to convey the intentions and goals of the deploying institution. As we established above, this information is not only descriptive but also normative, and can only be provided in the form of justifications. We thus see justifications as a key aspect of the broader principle of contestability-by-design [1] and as a building block for the design of contestation mechanisms.

4   Justifications Encourage Considering Social and Legal Accountability Throughout the System's Lifecycle

Disclosing Goals and Values Is Required to Establish Accountability. Accountability is seen as a core principle of trustworthy ADM systems and is closely tied to notions of fairness, auditability, and the minimizing of negative impact [21]. But assigning and assessing social and legal accountability requires more than merely providing insight into a model's internal mechanics, as "accountability requires justification and justification requires explanation. The form of each should determine the form of the others" [17]. Further, normative aspects, in particular the choice to employ a machine-learning-based decision tool, as well as the criteria it evaluates, are fully explainable and have significant implications on the final design, which constitutes a good reason to subject them to scrutiny [45]. This intuition is captured in the two-part framework for explanations, namely: a good explanation provides (1) (normative) information required to describe the decision in terms of its goals and intentions and (2) (descriptive) information treated as part of the record for backing up the adherence to this norm [45]. If the deploying institution fails to deliver records that align with their norms, they can be held responsible, thus establishing accountability.

All Types of ADM Systems Embed Human Decision-Making and Rationale that Should Be Open to Validation. Algorithmic decision-making systems exist in a grey space between data-driven models and goal-directed agents [41]. Though their interactional autonomy is limited, they are not mere smart calculators. They are deployed to advance human-defined objectives and inherit intentionality from their designers and deployers. Barocas et al. 2023 [5] define three categories of automated decision-making that implement human intentions: The first kind automates pre-existing decision-making rules and is thus a mere computational expression of these rules (such as software to determine welfare eligibility). The second kind learns to predict decisions based on data from past decisions and thus incorporates human-defined rules that were applied in the past (such as automated grading systems). The third kind derives decision-making rules from the data based on the definition of a target or goal to be optimized (such as predictive policing), which again was chosen through human intent. Therefore, all ADM systems implement value and policy choices made by humans and, in order to create accountability, should open these choices to validation and audit [53].

Justifications for Decision-Subjects Must Work Alongside Structural Accountability Mechanisms. While enabling contestation and agency through transparency is important, the responsibility for evaluating whether automated decisions are legitimate or correct should lie with governing institutions, not the governed individuals. Institutional safeguards against errors, bias, or illegitimate objectives are crucial, as individual contestations alone cannot resolve systemic issues [23]. Moreover, as exemplified by the GDPR cookie consent mechanism, placing responsibility on end-users (affected persons) without simple agency mechanisms can lead to disengagement and the waiver of one's rights. Explanations provided to decision subjects should therefore be designed as tools for individual oversight, enabling them to assess whether a system's outcome aligns with the institution's normative claims *in light of their personal context*. If it does not, decision subjects must be provided with simple, low-barrier channels to contest the outcome. For instance, if an organisation claims to use a race-neutral algorithm, but the decision appears racially biased, decision subjects should be able to trigger a review. In this model, explanations and justifications act as interfaces for critical discourse with the authority [20] and, when embedded within frameworks for systemic accountability and institutional guarantees of legal and ethical standards, explanations and justifications together enable informed deference [4].

5   Crafting Justifications

We established why justifications should be seen as a key component of explainable AI for decision subjects. In this Section, we propose guiding principles for the design of such justifications. With these principles, we aim to contribute a conceptual foundation that can be used to fit traditional explanation approaches to the rights and epistemic needs of decision subjects. The principles aim to introduce normative information (explaining goals, values, and intentions) to complement the mechanistic information (explaining features, outputs, and functions) in established explanation approaches. Namely, we propose that justifications in XAI should be:

- **normative** – describing the underlying norms, values, and intentions that guide an ADM system's actions as opposed to its mechanistic features, a value judgment rather than a technical assessment [26];
- **argumentative** – incorporating multiple points of view that could be advocated for by the involved stakeholders, supporting deliberation more than application, a forum rather than a manual [47];
- **challengeable** – presenting information in a way that invites reflection and opposition, justifying the reasoning behind a particular case, a debate rather than a factual authority [32];
- and **relational** – adapting to the relation between the sending and the receiving stakeholder [17], just as explanations are adapted to the knowledge and role of their audience.

The concrete design of justifications is context-dependent, as are most explanation approaches [16]. Designs can take the form of lists of pro and contra arguments, flowcharts of actor involvement in algorithmic decisions, or elaboration on the design choices that determined training data and model of a system.

To illustrate, we provide two examples for the design and content of justifications in Fig. 1. These justifications are based on information about an ADM system that was planned to be used in the Austrian employment agency "AMS" to rate the employability of jobseekers. The system's deployment was stopped in 2020 by Austrian Court of Administration, but comparable systems were actually implemented and are still in use in other European countries [44]. The justifications shown incorporate information from literature that documented the system's development and planned deployment [3,30], and follows a question-driven approach [29] to address two information needs of potential decision subjects [42]: *Can misclassifications harm people who are targeted by this system?* and *Which ethical principles guided the system's development?* The first question is addressed through an argumentative approach, presenting both information for and against the claim. The second question is addressed through a list of principles as given by the deploying institution [22]. The latter justification could be complemented by another sheet describing whether these principles are met in the actual deployment.

While not using the same terms to describe them, previous work has employed justifiability as a relevant dimension in explanation approaches. Lee et al. 2019 [27] co-designed an algorithmic food donation distribution system with stakeholders from a local community. In their design, affected stakeholders could choose which values to prioritize in the optimization (such as food access, income, and travel time). This direct participation in the design process increased people's acceptance even of decisions that favored another donation destination over their own, because it produced transparency in rationale and values. Since in resource distribution systems, the different values and priorities will be in tension and their priority subjective, extended designs have been proposed which allow decision subjects to contest the norms, reaching a system built on values

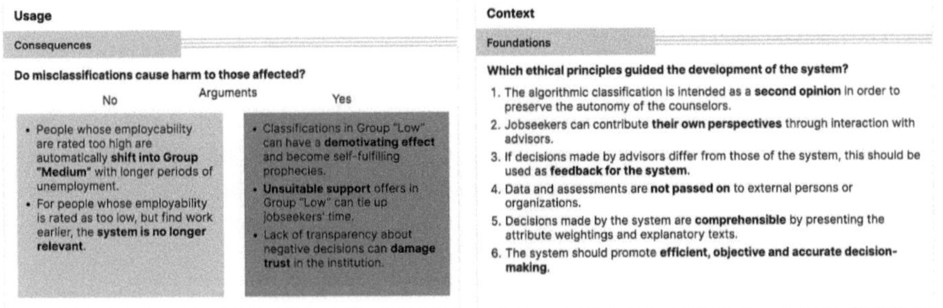

Fig. 1. Two examples of justifications for decision subjects. The described system was intended to rate the employability of jobseekers to assist job counselors in the decision about adequate support measures [30]. For both examples, the leading questions cannot be answered easily through factual or descriptive information, but instead require considerations of the norms, values, and viewpoints involved. In this sense, they do not aim to provide a factually correct answer, but reasoning grounds for deliberation [34] on decisions, including whether to contest a decision and whether to contact someone in a supervisory position, such as a human in the loop [13]. Both examples adhere to the four proposed principles for justification design, namely, they are normative (based on norms and values), argumentative (give multiple views), challengeable (do not claim informational authority), and relational (are addressed towards decision subjects).

representing both the deployer and the affected stakeholders [20]. Further, Weitz et al. 2024 [50] conducted workshops with end-users from the public sector to identify their needs for XAI interfaces and found that social norms and cultural values were essential to assess whether an AI system aligned with their values.

Notably, justifications, just as explanations, come with their own set of limitations. Without the grounding evidence of explanations, justifications can be tuned to satisfy their reader without conveying truthful information about a system, which might in reality be discriminatory. Further, reasoning approaches are prone to "confirmation bias", as information confirming one's views is easier to accept than those to the contrary [47]. Hence, both approaches are necessary and complementary. While explanations document the factual, justifications provide a sense of guiding intention and purpose.

6   Future Work

Future work can follow several avenues to examine the design and effect of justifications in explainable AI: First, qualitative analyses could identify the information needs that decision subjects and other stakeholders have with respect to justifications specifically. Previous work established collections of information needs in the context of AI systems [28,42], but did not focus on the distinction between descriptive and normative information and their respective value to different stakeholders. Second, studying the role and effect of justifications in the context of contestation is a promising avenue for both qualitative and quantitative research. While contestation has been the subject of some empirical work [2,31,51], many open questions remain, such as which contestation options decision subjects prefer, which kind of information is most helpful to this end, and how contestation success can be measured. Third, while the design space for explanation has been explored in many studies [36], design for justifications – beyond those that justify individual algorithmic decisions with descriptive information [8,52] – is comparably unexplored. Finding ways to convey the challengeable norms and principles guiding an ADM system understandably and helpfully to decision subjects is thus another fruitful direction of future work.

7   Conclusion

In this paper, we argued that justifications should be a key component when explaining algorithmic decisions to decision subjects. We made three claims to this end: justifications fulfill key epistemic desiderata of decision subjects; justifications can shape decision subjects' intent to accept or contest unfavorable decisions; and justifications encourage consideration of accountability along the whole lifecycle of ADM systems. We provide two examples of such justifications for the use case of an algorithmic decision-making system in the employment domain. To translate these claims into practical approaches, future work should conduct requirement analyses to study decision subjects' information needs for justifications and develop designs that employ justifications in complement with explanations to be of value to decision subjects.

Acknowledgments. This work has been funded by the Vienna Science and Technology Fund (WWTF) [10.47379/ICT20058].

Disclosure of Interests. The authors have no competing interests to declare.

References

1. Alfrink, K., Keller, I., Kortuem, G., Doorn, N.: Contestable ai by design: towards a framework. Mind. Mach. **33**(4), 613–639 (2023)
2. Alfrink, K., Keller, I., Semperena, M.Y., Bulygin, D., Kortuem, G., Doorn, N.: Envisioning contestability loops: evaluating the agonistic arena as a generative metaphor for public ai. She Ji: J. Design, Econ. Innovat. **10**(1), 53–93 (2024)
3. Allhutter, D., Mager, A., Cech, F., Fischer, F., Grill, G.: Der AMS-Algorithmus: Eine Soziotechnische Analyse des Arbeitsmarktchancen-Assistenz-Systems (AMAS). Tech. rep., Österreichische Akademie der Wissenschaften (2020), epub.oeaw.ac.at
4. Alnemr, N.: Democratic self-government and the algocratic shortcut: the democratic harms in algorithmic governance of society. Contemporary Political Theory **23**(2), 205–227 (2024)
5. Barocas, S., Hardt, M., Narayanan, A.: Fairness and Machine Learning: Limitations and Opportunities. MIT Press (2023)

6. Bell, A., Nov, O., Stoyanovich, J.: The algorithmic transparency playbook. Center for Responsible AI. Disponible en: https://dataresponsibly github. io/algorithmic-transparency-playbook/resources/transparency_playbook_camera_ready. pdf (Consultado: 7 de febrero de 2024) (2023)
7. Binns, R., Van Kleek, M., Veale, M., Lyngs, U., Zhao, J., Shadbolt, N.: 'It's Reducing a Human Being to a Percentage'; Perceptions of Justice in Algorithmic Decisions. In: Proceedings of the 2018 CHI Conference on Human Factors in Computing Systems, pp. 1–14 (Apr 2018). https://doi.org/10.1145/3173574.3173951
8. Biran, O., Cotton, C.V.: Explanation and justification in machine learning: a survey. In: Proceedings of the IJCAI 2017 Workshop on Explainable Artificial Intelligence (XAI) (2017). https://www.ijcai.org/proceedings/2017/0202.pdf
9. Biran, O., McKeown, K.: Human-centric justification of machine learning predictions. In: Proceedings of the Twenty-Sixth International Joint Conference on Artificial Intelligence, IJCAI 2017, pp. 1461–1467 (2017). https://doi.org/10.24963/ijcai.2017/202
10. Byrne, R.M.: Good explanations in explainable artificial intelligence (XAI): evidence from human explanatory reasoning. In: Proceedings of the Thirty-Second International Joint Conference on Artificial Intelligence, pp. 6536–6544. Macau, SAR China (Aug 2023). https://doi.org/10.24963/ijcai.2023/733, https://www.ijcai.org/proceedings/2023/733
11. Clark, H.H., Fischer, K.: Social robots as depictions of social agents. Behav. Brain Sci. **46**, e21 (2023). https://doi.org/10.1017/S0140525X22000668
12. Crivellaro, C., et al.: Infrastructuring public service transformation: creating collaborative spaces between communities and institutions through HCI research. ACM Trans. Comput.-Hum. Interact. **26**(3), 1–29 (2019)
13. Crootof, R., Kaminski, M.E., Ii, W.N.P.: Humans in the loop. Vanderbilt Law Rev. **76** (2023). https://doi.org/10.2139/ssrn.4066781
14. Dennett, D.C.: The intentional stance. A Bradford book, MIT Press, Cambridge, Mass., 7. printing edn. (1998)
15. de Fine Licht, K., de Fine Licht, J.: Artificial intelligence, transparency, and public decision-making. AI & Soc. **35**(4), 917–926 (2020). https://doi.org/10.1007/s00146-020-00960-w
16. Freiesleben, T., König, G.: Dear XAI community, we need to talk! In: Longo, L. (ed.) Explainable Artificial Intelligence, pp. 48–65. Springer Nature Switzerland, Cham (2023). https://doi.org/10.1007/978-3-031-44064-9_3
17. Gillis, T.B., Simons, J.: Explanation < justification: Gdpr and the perils of privacy. J. Law & Innovation **2**, 71 (2019). https://scholarship.law.columbia.edu/faculty_scholarship/3132
18. Gold, N., Colman, A., Pulford, B.: Normative theory in decision making and moral reasoning. Behav. Brain Sci. **34**, 256–7 (2011). https://doi.org/10.1017/S0140525X11000495
19. Heider, F., Simmel, M.: An experimental study of apparent behavior. Am. J. Psychol. **57**(2), 243–259 (1944), http://www.jstor.org/stable/1416950
20. Henin, C., Le Métayer, D.: Beyond explainability: justifiability and contestability of algorithmic decision systems. AI & Soc. **37**(4), 1397–1410 (2022)
21. High-Level Expert Group on Artificial Intelligence: Ethics guidelines for trustworthy AI (Apr 2019). https://digital-strategy.ec.europa.eu/en/library/ethics-guidelines-trustworthy-AI
22. Holl, J., Kernbeiß, G., Wagner-Pinter, M.: Personenbezogene wahrscheinlichkeitsaussagen (»algorithmen«): Stichworte zur sozialverträglichkeit. Technical concept, Synthesis Forschung, Vienna (2019)

23. Kaminski, M.E.: Binary governance: lessons from the gdpr's approach to algorithmic accountability. Southern California Law Rev. **92**(6), 1529–1616 (2019). https://scholar.law.colorado.edu/faculty-articles/1265/, Accessed 11 Jul 2025
24. Lafont, C.: Democracy without shortcuts. Constellations **26**(3), 355–360 (2019). https://doi.org/10.1111/1467-8675.12432
25. Langer, M., et al.: What do we want from explainable artificial intelligence (XAI)? - a stakeholder perspective on XAI and a conceptual model guiding interdisciplinary XAI research. Artif. Intell. **296**, 103473 (2021)
26. Langley, P.: Explainable, normative, and justified agency. In: Proceedings of the AAAI Conference on Artificial Intelligence, vol. 33(01), pp. 9775–9779 (2019)
27. Lee, M.K., et al.: WeBuildAI: participatory framework for algorithmic governance. Proc. ACM Hum.-Comput. Interact. **3**(CSCW), 1–35 (2019). https://doi.org/10.1145/3359283, https://dl.acm.org/doi/10.1145/3359283
28. Liao, Q.V., Gruen, D., Miller, S.: Questioning the AI: informing design practices for explainable AI user experiences. In: Proceedings of the 2020 CHI Conference on Human Factors in Computing Systems, CHI 2020, pp. 1–15. Association for Computing Machinery, New York (2020).https://doi.org/10.1145/3313831.3376590, https://doi-org.uaccess.univie.ac.at/10.1145/3313831.3376590
29. Liao, Q.V., Pribić, M., Han, J., Miller, S., Sow, D.: Question-driven design process for explainable AI user experiences (2021)
30. Lopez, P.: Reinforcing intersectional inequality via the AMS algorithm in Austria. In: Proceedings of the 18th Annual STS Conference, pp. 289–309. Graz (2019). https://doi.org/10.3217/978-3-85125-668-0-16
31. Lyons, H., Miller, T., Velloso, E.: Algorithmic decisions, desire for control, and the preference for human review over algorithmic review. In: 2023 ACM Conference on Fairness, Accountability, and Transparency, pp. 764–774. ACM, Chicago IL USA (Jun 2023). https://doi.org/10.1145/3593013.3594041, https://dl.acm.org/doi/10.1145/3593013.3594041
32. Lyons, H., Velloso, E., Miller, T.: Designing for Contestation: Insights from Administrative Law (Feb 2021). http://arxiv.org/abs/2102.04559
33. Maxwell, W., Dumas, B.: Meaningful XAI based on user-centric design methodology: Combining legal and human-computer interaction (HCI) approaches to achieve meaningful algorithmic explainability. SSRN Electron. J. (2023)
34. Mercier, H., Sperber, D.: Why do humans reason? Arguments for an argumentative theory. Behav. Brain Sci. **34**(2), 57–74 (2011). https://doi.org/10.1017/S0140525X10000968
35. Miller, T.: Explanation in artificial intelligence: insights from the social sciences. Artif. Intell. **267**, 1–38 (2019). https://doi.org/10.1016/j.artint.2018.07.007
36. Mohseni, S., Zarei, N., Ragan, E.D.: A multidisciplinary survey and framework for design and evaluation of explainable ai systems (2020). https://arxiv.org/abs/1811.11839
37. Pi, Y., Proctor, M.: Toward empowering AI governance with redress mechanisms. Cambridge Forum on AI: Law Governance **1** (2025). https://doi.org/10.1017/cfl.2025.9
38. Prifti, K., Morley, J., Novelli, C., Floridi, L.: Regulation by design: features, practices, limitations, and governance implications. Mind. Mach. **34**(2), 13 (2024)
39. Rudin, C.: Stop explaining black box machine learning models for high stakes decisions and use interpretable models instead. Nat. Mach. Intell. **1**(5), 206–215 (2019). https://doi.org/10.1038/s42256-019-0048-x
40. Ryan, R.M., Deci, E.L.: Self-determination theory and the facilitation of intrinsic motivation, social development, and well-being. Am. Psychol. (2000)

41. Sado, F., Loo, C.K., Liew, W.S., Kerzel, M., Wermter, S.: Explainable goal-driven agents and robots - a comprehensive review. ACM Comput. Surv. **55**(10) (2023). https://doi.org/10.1145/3564240
42. Schmude, T., Koesten, L., Möller, T., Tschiatschek, S.: Information that matters: exploring information needs of people affected by algorithmic decisions. Int. J. Hum. Comput. Stud. **193**, 103380 (2025). https://doi.org/10.1016/j.ijhcs.2024.103380
43. Schmude, T., Yurrita, M., Alfrink, K., Goff, T.L., Viard, T.: Two Means to an End Goal: Connecting Explainability and Contestability in the Regulation of Public Sector AI (2025). https://arxiv.org/abs/2504.18236
44. Scott, K.M., Wang, S.M., Miceli, M., Delobelle, P., Sztandar-Sztanderska, K., Berendt, B.: Algorithmic tools in public employment services: towards a jobseeker-centric perspective. In: Proceedings of the 2022 ACM Conference on Fairness, Accountability, and Transparency, FAccT 2022, pp. 2138–2148. ACM, Seoul Republic of Korea (Jun 2022). https://doi.org/10.1145/3531146.3534631, https://dl.acm.org/doi/10.1145/3531146.3534631
45. Strandburg, K.J.: Rulemaking and inscrutable automated decision tools. Columbia Law Rev. **119**(7), 1851–1886 (2019), also available as NYU Public Law Research Paper No. 20-36
46. Sullivan, E.: Sides: Separating idealization from deceptive 'explanations' in xai. In: Proceedings of the 2024 ACM Conference on Fairness, Accountability, and Transparency, FAccT 2024, pp. 1714–1724. Association for Computing Machinery, New York (2024). https://doi.org/10.1145/3630106.3658999
47. Vassiliades, A., Bassiliades, N., Patkos, T.: Argumentation and explainable artificial intelligence: a survey. Knowl. Eng. Rev. **36** (2021). https://doi.org/10.1017/s0269888921000011
48. Vredenburgh, K.: Transparency and explainability for public policy. LSE Public Policy Rev. **3**(3) (2024)
49. Waytz, A., Morewedge, C.K., Epley, N., Monteleone, G., Gao, J.H., Cacioppo, J.T.: Making sense by making sentient: effectance motivation increases anthropomorphism. J. Pers. Soc. Psychol. **99**(3), 410 (2010)
50. Weitz, K., Schlagowski, R., André, E., Männiste, M., George, C.: Explaining it your way - findings from a co-creative design workshop on designing xai applications with ai end-users from the public sector. In: Proceedings of the CHI Conference on Human Factors in Computing Systems, CHI 2024, Association for Computing Machinery, New York (2024).https://doi.org/10.1145/3613904.3642563
51. Yurrita, M., Draws, T., Balayn, A., Murray-Rust, D., Tintarev, N., Bozzon, A.: Disentangling fairness perceptions in algorithmic decision-making: the effects of explanations, human oversight, and contestability. In: Proceedings of the 2023 CHI Conference on Human Factors in Computing Systems, pp. 1–21. ACM, Hamburg Germany (Apr 2023). https://doi.org/10.1145/3544548.3581161, https://dl.acm.org/doi/10.1145/3544548.3581161
52. Zhou, J., Joachims, T.: How to explain and justify almost any decision: potential pitfalls for accountability in AI decision-making. In: 2023 ACM Conference on Fairness, Accountability, and Transparency, pp. 12–21. ACM, Chicago IL USA (Jun 2023). https://doi.org/10.1145/3593013.3593972, https://dl.acm.org/doi/10.1145/3593013.3593972
53. Züger, T., Asghari, H.: AI for the public. how public interest theory shifts the discourse on AI. AI & Soc. **38**(2), 815–828 (2023). https://doi.org/10.1007/s00146-022-01480-5

Bridging Ethics and Regulation: How VBE Facilitates Compliance with the EU AI Act in High-Risk and General Purpose AI

Lukas Madl[(⊠)], Soner Bargu, and Mert Cuhadaroglu

Innovethic E.U., Fahndorf 72, 3710 Ziersdorf, Austria
madl@innovethic.at
https://innovethic.eu/

Abstract. The EU AI Act introduces the world's first comprehensive legal framework for regulating artificial intelligence. Built on a risk-based approach, it aims to protect public safety and fundamental rights. While the Act is a significant step towards harmonised governance, its implementation raises several questions. These include the complexity of risk classification, regulatory gaps in general-purpose AI (GPAI) oversight, the absence of harmonised technical standards and uncertainties regarding the translation of fundamental rights into technical design. This white paper explores how Value-Based Engineering (VBE), a methodology based on the IEEE 7000™ standard, can address these challenges by providing a structured, context-sensitive and ethics-driven design process. It examines how VBE supports alignment with key EU AI Act obligations, including risk management, quality assurance, and fundamental rights impact assessments. Through its non-list approach to values, deep contextual analysis, structured elicitation of ethical value requirements (EVRs), and early stakeholder engagement, VBE helps bridge the gap between regulatory intent and technical implementation. The paper concludes that integrating VBE into AI system development not only supports compliance with evolving legal obligations, but also fosters trust, societal acceptance, and ethical robustness in high-risk AI.

Keywords: EU AI Act · AI Act · Value Based Engineering · Standards · Trustworthy AI · Ethical AI · Ethics by Design · IEEE 7000 · High-Risk AI · GPAI

1   Introduction

1.1   Purpose and Method in the EU AI Act: A Risk-Based Approach to Trustworthy AI

As AI systems become increasingly powerful and integrated into daily life, their risks extend well beyond physical harm, they encompass ecological strain, emotional manipulation, and potential infringements on human dignity and autonomy. [1, 2] Recognizing this, the EU AI Act calls for AI development to align with fundamental rights and shared European values.

© The Author(s) 2026

L. Hagedorn et al. (Eds.): DIGHUM 2025, LNCS 16319, pp. 203–218, 2026.
https://doi.org/10.1007/978-3-032-11108-1_15

The EU Artificial Intelligence Act, which entered into force in August 2024, represents the world's first comprehensive legal framework governing the development and deployment of artificial intelligence [3]. Its primary objective is to ensure that AI systems used within the European Union are both safe and compliant with fundamental rights, as stipulated in Article 1 of the Act. These rights are grounded in the core values articulated in Article 2 of the Treaty on European Union (TEU), including respect for human dignity, freedom, democracy, equality, the rule of law, and human rights [3]. These values constitute the normative foundation of the European Union and are intended to guide all aspects of its internal and external actions.

The Charter of Fundamental Rights of the European Union, which became legally binding with the entry into force of the Treaty of Lisbon in 2009, translates these foundational values into concrete legal rights [3]. It thereby provides a robust framework for the protection of fundamental rights within the EU legal order. The EU AI Act seeks to ensure that artificial intelligence technologies deployed within the Union are not only technically safe but also aligned with these fundamental rights. In doing so, the Act aspires to foster trust in AI by embedding the EU's normative commitments into the governance of AI in the digital age (Fig. 1).

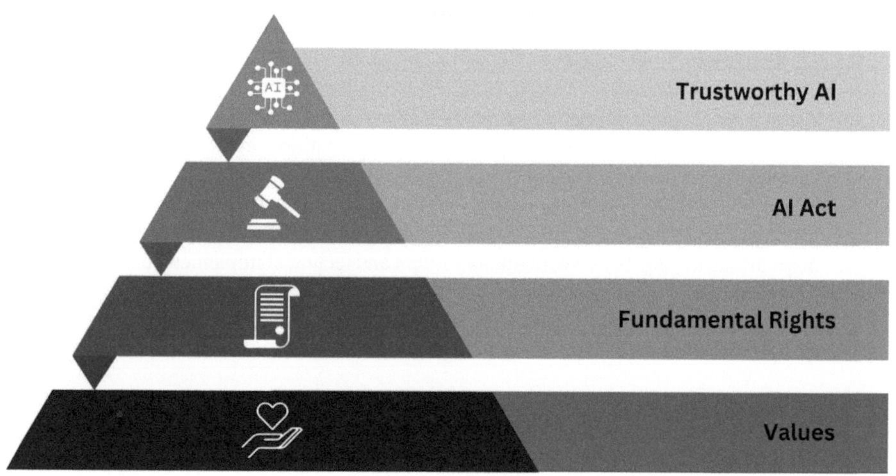

Fig. 1. The EU AI Act seeks to enhance the trustworthiness of artificial intelligence by aligning its development and use with fundamental rights and values enshrined in EU law [4].

The EU Artificial Intelligence Act adopts a risk-based regulatory approach aimed at safeguarding public health, safety, and fundamental rights, while simultaneously minimizing the regulatory burden on innovation. Under this framework, AI systems are categorized into four levels of risk: minimal, limited, high, and unacceptable. Minimal-risk systems are subject to no specific regulatory obligations, whereas limited-risk systems must comply with transparency requirements. High-risk AI systems, by contrast, are subject to stringent regulatory conditions. These include obligations related to data quality, robust data governance, the implementation of quality and risk management systems, human oversight mechanisms, and performance metrics to ensure accuracy, robustness, and cybersecurity. Additionally, providers of high-risk systems must maintain comprehensive technical documentation. AI systems deemed to pose an unacceptable risk are prohibited outright [3].

The Act defines high-risk AI systems as falling into two principal categories. The first encompasses AI systems that function as safety components of products governed by EU harmonized product legislation, such as medical devices and motor vehicles. The second includes standalone AI systems that may significantly affect individuals' health, safety, or fundamental rights in specific high-impact domains enumerated in Annex III of the Act, including education, employment, and law enforcement.

Furthermore, the EU AI Act introduces specific provisions for so-called general-purpose AI (GPAI) models. These models are trained on extensive datasets and are capable of serving a wide range of downstream applications, either directly or as components of other AI systems. Generative AI models, such as ChatGPT, fall within this category. Due to their broad applicability, GPAI models cannot be easily classified within the standard risk categories and are therefore subject to a distinct regulatory regime [5].

The Act also recognizes that particularly large GPAI models—defined as those trained using computational resources exceeding 1025 floating point operations (FLOPs)—may pose systemic risks. In such cases, additional obligations apply, including the identification, assessment, and mitigation of potential systemic risks and their underlying causes. GPAI models that do not meet the threshold for systemic risk are subject to lighter requirements, such as the provision of technical documentation and support for compliance by downstream deployers [5].

1.2   Core Issues in the Implementation and Interpretation of the EU AI Act

The EU AI Act entered into force on 1 August 2024, with a phased implementation Schedule. Prohibited AI practices became enforceable from 2 February 2025 while GPAI model obligations will apply from 2nd August 2025. The main obligations for high-risk AI systems will take effect on 2 August 2026 (EU AI Act Article 113) [3].

1.2.1   Complexity of Risk Classification in the EU AI Act

The EU Artificial Intelligence Act introduces a multi-tiered risk classification framework that categorizes AI systems as posing minimal, limited, high, or unacceptable risk. This structure is grounded in the principle of proportionality, whereby regulatory obligations are calibrated according to the potential impact of an AI system on health, safety, and fundamental rights [4]. High-risk systems—such as those used in employment, education, or law enforcement—are subject to stringent requirements, while low-risk systems are largely exempt, thereby supporting innovation without imposing excessive regulatory burdens [6].

Despite its conceptual soundness, the classification mechanism, particularly as operationalized through Annex III, has been subject to criticism. Scholars and practitioners argue that the top-down approach fails to adequately reflect the contextual and dynamic nature of AI applications [7]. General-purpose AI (GPAI) models exemplify this challenge. Although these models may be embedded in high-risk or even prohibited use cases, their general architecture and unpredictable deployment contexts often allow them to circumvent strict regulatory scrutiny. This loophole risks undermining the Act's capacity to address systemic risks effectively [4].

The potential misuse of GPAI systems in sensitive domains, such as manipulative chatbots impersonating individuals, has raised significant concerns. Because the Act assesses risk based on the intended use at the time of deployment, it does not account for the repurposing of GPAI models in harmful or deceptive contexts [8, 9].

This regulatory blind spot has prompted calls from civil society and academia for more robust safeguards, including the development of a dedicated Code of Practice to guide GPAI compliance with transparency, safety, and copyright obligations [10].

In response, the European Commission has endorsed a voluntary General-Purpose AI Code of Practice, published in July 2025. Developed through a multi-stakeholder process, the Code provides practical guidance for GPAI providers on meeting the AI Act's legal obligations, particularly those outlined in Articles 53 and 55 [3]. It includes chapters on transparency, copyright, and systemic risk management, and is intended to reduce administrative burdens while enhancing legal certainty for providers.

Moreover, a coalition of AI researchers, civil society organizations, and academic leaders, including Nobel laureates Daron Acemoglu and Geoffrey Hinton, has publicly urged the European Commission to uphold the integrity of GPAI regulations. In a letter addressed to Commission President Ursula von der Leyen, the coalition emphasized that innovation-friendly tools such as the Code of Practice must not come at the expense of fundamental rights and public safety [11].

To address ongoing uncertainties, the European Commission has also launched a public consultation aimed at gathering practical insights on the classification of high-risk AI systems. The consultation seeks to inform forthcoming guidelines that will clarify the criteria for risk classification and the associated compliance obligations [12].

1.2.2 Incomplete Standardization Infrastructure

The EU Artificial Intelligence Act operates within the framework of the New Legislative Framework (NLF), which mandates that compliance be demonstrated through harmonised technical standards. These standards are being developed by the European standardization bodies CEN and CENELEC. However, the standardization process has progressed more slowly than anticipated, and several key standards, particularly those relevant to high-risk AI systems and general-purpose AI (GPAI) models, are unlikely to be finalized before the corresponding legal obligations take effect. This delay contributes to significant legal uncertainty, particularly in translating abstract regulatory principles, such as the protection of fundamental rights, into concrete and actionable technical specifications [13].

In July 2025, a coalition of 46 CEOs from major European corporations, including Airbus, ASML, Lufthansa, and Mistral, called on the European Commission to implement a two-year "clock-stop" on the EU Artificial Intelligence Act, citing concerns over regulatory complexity and the absence of finalized implementation standards [14].

The executives argue that the current framework, particularly provisions affecting general-purpose AI (GPAI) and high-risk systems, imposes unclear and overlapping obligations that hinder innovation and competitiveness. European Commission Executive Vice-President Henna Virkkunen acknowledged the possibility of a delay if necessary, guidelines are not ready by August, though the Commission has thus far maintained its commitment to the original timeline [15].

The call for a pause has intensified amid lobbying from both European industry leaders and U.S. tech firms, while civil society groups warn against deregulation and stress the importance of upholding fundamental rights.

1.2.3   Regulatory Agility and Technological Evolution

One of the principal challenges in regulating artificial intelligence lies in maintaining regulatory relevance amid rapid technological advancement. To address this, the EU Artificial Intelligence Act incorporates the use of delegated acts, enabling the European Commission to update specific provisions, such as the list of high-risk AI systems, without undergoing the full legislative process. This mechanism is intended to ensure that the legal framework remains adaptable, future-proof, and responsive to emerging risks, technologies, and societal expectations. Nevertheless, concerns persist that regulatory adaptation may lag behind the pace of innovation, particularly in areas such as foundation models and novel AI capabilities. Moreover, the evolving nature of the legal framework presents ongoing compliance challenges for AI developers and providers, necessitating a continuous and coordinated effort among EU institutions, standardization bodies, industry stakeholders, and civil society to ensure effective and proportionate implementation of the regulations [16–18].

2   Addressing the Implementation Challenges of the EU AI Act Through Value-Based Engineering

Given the numerous challenges associated with implementing the EU AI Act, a critical question emerges: what tools are available to support this process effectively? One promising approach is the Value-Based Engineering (VBE) methodology, which is grounded in the IEEE ISO/IEC/IEEE 24748–7000:2022 ™ standard.

VBE builds upon the standard and provides a structured, life cycle-oriented methodology that enables organizations to integrate ethical values into the design of digital products and AI systems. This study explores whether AI developers can effectively address both current and anticipated challenges outlined in the EU AI Act by leveraging the VBE methodology. Specifically, we examine whether this standard can serve as a proactive and efficient tool for navigating these regulatory demands.

The IEEE 7000™ standard—formally titled *IEEE Standard Model Process for Addressing Ethical Concerns during System Design*—was developed by the IEEE Standards Association to guide organizations in embedding ethical considerations into system design from the outset. It offers a systematic process for identifying, prioritizing, and incorporating ethical values into the development of technical systems.

Our engagement with technical experts, particularly within CEN/CENELEC committees, has revealed a widespread lack of clarity regarding how to operationalize values and fundamental rights within technical specifications. The Value-Based Engineering (VBE) methodology addresses this gap by providing a detailed, step-by-step framework that guides practitioners through the following key phases:

- Concept and Context Exploration: Preparing the groundwork for ethical system design by clarifying the system's purpose and societal context.
- Ethical Values Elicitation: Identifying and prioritizing stakeholder values relevant to the system under development.
- Value-Based Design: Embedding these values into the system architecture and design decisions.

In an era where technological systems exert profound influence on societal structures, the relevance of this standard is particularly significant. It enables organizations to develop systems that are not only technically robust and economically viable but also socially responsible and aligned with fundamental human values—objectives that are central to the EU AI Act.

A distinctive strength of the VBE methodology lies in its integration of ethical theories that have shaped European intellectual and cultural history. These include:

- Virtue Ethics
- Utilitarianism
- Deontological (Duty-Based) Ethics

These philosophical frameworks can be directly applied in stakeholder workshops, enabling participants to engage with core ethical concepts without requiring formal training in philosophy. Furthermore, VBE encourages the inclusion of local cultural and spiritual traditions in the process of defining ethical values, thereby fostering context-sensitive and culturally attuned system design.

Our practical experience with implementing VBE across various projects has demonstrated its utility for engineers, software developers, and IT system managers. The methodology enhances their ability to comprehend and translate ethical and value-based considerations into concrete system requirements.

By embedding ethical and social values directly into technical specifications, VBE supports AI developers in aligning system design with societal expectations. Through early stakeholder engagement and value-oriented design decisions, VBE offers a flexible and forward-looking pathway to regulatory compliance, particularly valuable in contexts where legal frameworks and standards are still evolving.

However, the implementation of Value-Based Engineering (VBE) poses significant challenges for organizations, as it requires a reorientation of system design practices and the adoption of a disciplined engineering culture. Key obstacles include: (1) fostering corporate responsibility and collaboration, (2) establishing new professional roles such as value experts, (3) adapting agile development methods to align with ethical requirements, (4) assuming accountability in complex Systems-of-Systems (SoS) environments, and (5) confronting ethical constraints that may conflict with entrepreneurial ambitions [19].

Despite these challenges—and notwithstanding the relative novelty of VBE—the methodology has already been applied in projects such as UNICEF, the City of Vienna, BMW, and the Austrian Employment Agency. The authors are currently engaged in three ongoing projects that employ VBE methods.

Alternative approaches, such as Value-Sensitive Design (VSD), also seek to integrate ethical considerations and stakeholder values into the development of technological innovations. However, the IEEE 7000 standard represents the first systematic framework for the identification, prioritization, and traceable incorporation of values throughout the design process. This structured methodology renders IEEE 7000 particularly suitable as a foundation for ensuring compliance with the requirements of the AI Act. A comprehensive comparison between Value-Based Engineering (VBE) and other value-oriented design methodologies lies beyond the scope of this article (Fig. 2).

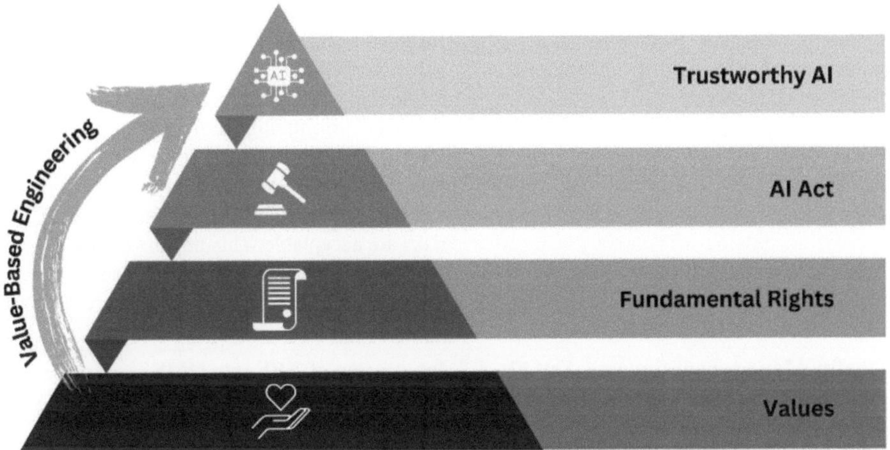

Fig. 2. The Value-Based Engineering (VBE) methodology provides a structured and actionable framework for translating ethical values into technical specifications, thereby bridging the gap between abstract principles and concrete system design [5, 20].

3 Shared Objectives and Structural Parallels Between the EU AI Act and VBE

We show across these three dimensions that the core objective is the same: minimizing risk. That is why many of the process requirements laid out in the EU AI Act align closely with what Value-Based Engineering proposes [1, 11, 12]. VBE, like the EU AI Act, includes risk management, as well as quality assurance measures [1, 12]. The required fundamental rights impact assessment happens automatically within the VBE process whenever fundamental rights are identified as values to be protected [11, 12]. We use these three areas to show how similar the underlying objectives are and how closely the implementation paths run in parallel, even though VBE offers a more hands-on methodology. The following chapter then shows where VBE can go even further in helping to realize the intent behind the AI Act. [11] (Table 1).

Table 1. Comparing the Risk Management System, Quality Management System and Fundamental Rights Impact Assessment of the EU AI Act with IEEE 7000™.

EU AI Act [3]	The IEEE 7000™ Standard & VBE [20, 21]
Risk Management System - Art. 9 Establish a continuous, iterative risk management system for high-risk AI, including identification, analysis, and mitigation of risks to health, safety, and fundamental rights.	**Ethical Risk-Based Design** VBE defines a risk-based design process that aligns with this requirement. The standard calls for identifying ethical risks to stakeholder values and EVR (ethical value requirements), estimating the likelihood and impact of the risks, and prioritizing them for treatment. Design controls are then introduced to mitigate or reduce these risks, and the effectiveness of risk treatments is verified to ensure residual risks are acceptable. This mirrors the EU AI Act's mandate for ongoing risk identification, mitigation, testing, and ensuring any remaining risk is at an acceptable level.
Quality Management System - Art. 17 AI providers must have a documented QMS covering compliance strategy, design/development controls, testing/validation, data management, risk management, post-market monitoring, incident handling, communication, record-keeping, resource management, and accountability.	**Integration of VBE into QMS** VBE is designed to fit into an organization's existing quality management structure. It requires that the processes used for value-based design follow the organization's internal development and quality procedures. More importantly, the standard introduces design controls tied to ethical value requirements (EVRs). These are not just conceptual goals but must be implemented, tested, and verified. When risks to stakeholder values are identified, VBE calls for engineering teams to define treatments and verify their effectiveness. This includes documenting the decisions and being able to trace requirements back to stakeholder input. These activities align well with the expectations of a quality management system as described in the EU AI Act, particularly in terms of risk tracking, development control, and post-deployment accountability.

(continued)

Table 1. (*continued*)

EU AI Act [3]	The IEEE 7000™ Standard & VBE [20, 21]
Fundamental Rights Impact Assessment - Art. 27 Assessment of how the use of a specific AI system may impact fundamental rights. Describing the use context, affected groups, potential harms, human oversight, and mitigation measures if risks materialize.	**Stakeholder & Value Analysis; High-Risk Impact Steps** The Value-Based Engineering approach inherently covers many FRIA components. During Concept and Context Exploration and Values Elicitation, teams identify all stakeholders (direct and indirect) and the values at stake, in most stakeholder groups fundamental rights like human dignity, justice, fairness, privacy, etc., are recognized as critical values to protect. The Ethical Risk-Based Design process then analyses risks to those values and incorporates controls and oversight features to address them. For systems that are high-risk (e.g. impacting fundamental rights), the VBE handbook recommends an explicit impact assessment step after the standard IEEE 7000 process. In this step, practitioners thoroughly evaluate the severity of harm to each stakeholder group if a value (fundamental right) is undermined and plan additional safeguards or response measures. This ensures that the use-case context, affected persons, risks, human oversight, and contingency measures are systematically assessed. This closely mirrors the EU AI Act's fundamental rights impact assessment obligations.

4   Driving Responsible AI: VBE's Role in AI Act Execution

Value-Based Engineering (VBE) – encapsulated in the IEEE 7000™ standard – offers a structured approach to embed ethical and human values into AI system design from the ground up. VBE provides a clear methodology for analyzing human and social values relevant to a project and translating those stakeholder values into concrete system requirements. In essence, it bridges the gap between abstract ethics and engineering practice by making values an integral part of the design process. The result is a development framework that supports truly ethical, human-aligned AI systems, as described below through four key principles.

At the same time, this approach helps address a known limitation in legal regulation: laws like the EU AI Act provide essential structures, but they cannot anticipate every specific ethical or contextual risk, especially in rapidly evolving domains like AI [13, 18]. To fully realize the Act's aims in practice, additional ethical and design competence is needed to bridge the gap between principle and implementation [11, 12].

Each of the following four subsections can therefore be read not just as design strategies, but as concrete ways of translating the intent of the AI Act into system-level decisions.

4.1 Moving Beyond Prescriptive Principles Checklists

Traditional efforts to "ethically align" AI often begin (and end) with high-level lists of principles, like fairness, transparency, privacy, and so on. While well-intentioned, such predefined value checklists can be too generic. They risk overlooking context-specific concerns and give teams a false sense of security that merely naming these ideals is enough [22]. In contrast, VBE deliberately avoids a one-size-fits-all list of universal values. Instead, engineers are encouraged to start with a blank slate in each project's context, engaging with the real-world scenario to discover what genuinely matters to the people affected [20, 21].

This contrast highlights the advantage of a non-list approach: it surfaces authentic values that a generic framework might miss. VBE operationalizes this insight by having innovation teams interact with stakeholders from the very beginning, probing their needs and perspectives free of predetermined value lists [20]. By not being constrained to a fixed catalog of principles, the methodology ensures that ethically relevant values emerge from the lived context and lived experience of stakeholders, rather than from abstract checkboxes [21]. This makes the ethical analysis of AI systems more robust. It also takes into account the complexity of risk classification and potential risks posed by evolving technologies.

As legal requirements, such as those set out in the AI Act to protect fundamental rights and safety, cannot cover all eventualities. They define structural expectations but cannot fully capture the moral weight of context, such as in possible different GPAI applications, nor can they foresee all situations in which harm could occur or anticipate rapid technological change [22–24].

4.2 Contextualizing Ethical Values in AI Design

Identifying the right values is only the first step. VBE and the IEEE 7000™ standard push designers to dive deeply into each value in context. Once a core value (or cluster of related values) is discovered, the methodology insists on unpacking what a specific value truly means for the specific application domain and stakeholders. Each value is analyzed conceptually and examined to reveal its various dimensions. VBE explicitly guides teams to consider utilitarian outcomes (harms and benefits), duty-oriented principles, virtue ethics aspects, and even cultural or societal norms when evaluating a system's impact on value [20, 21]. This structured reflection prevents superficial treatment of values [20].

By scrutinizing values in their operational context, engineers gain a nuanced understanding of how those values could be upheld or undermined by the AI system. In practice, VBE teams cluster their findings around specific values and prioritize the most pressing value impacts to address. They also define concrete value qualities (particular features or attributes through which a core value manifests or is endangered) [20].

A tragic example of why it matters to explore values in depth and in their real-world context is the case of a teenager who took his own life after forming an emotional attachment to a chatbot on CharacterAI. The bot acted as a romantic partner, echoed his suicidal thoughts, and failed to provide any kind of interruption or redirection when he expressed serious emotional distress [25, 26]. The bot even responded encouragingly when the boy hinted, he might harm himself [25, 26]. This case underscores the critical need to unpack values such as psychological safety, dignity or protective care had been carefully unpacked for the specific context of vulnerable young users, the system might have included safeguards, crisis responses, or restrictions on role-playing. The incident highlights that ethical principles must extend beyond abstract declarations; they must be meaningfully integrated into system design and implementation to prevent harm and uphold human well-being.

This kind of in-depth value exploration ensures that ethical principles are not just slogans, they are fleshed out into actionable design goals. Ultimately, the deep dive into context-specific values leads to AI systems that respect not only generic ideals but the substance of those ideals as they matter in real life.

To really protect fundamental rights, the underlying values must first be conceptually analysed and understood. Rights like human dignity or autonomy cannot be implemented meaningfully without reflecting on what they actually mean in the specific context of use. This becomes especially clear when looking at the value of dignity.

It might appear as a general ethical principle, but if system designers do not stop to consider what dignity means for a particular group, like children, the elderly or emotionally vulnerable users, the concept remains abstract and unprotected. For teenagers this could mean being treated with care or being taken seriously. That is precisely why the kind of deep value reflection proposed by VBE is essential for making the core intention of the AI Act truly workable. Even if a system like CharacterAI might not formally fall under the high-risk category, cases like this illustrate what the regulation is really aiming to prevent: real, context-specific harm to people when technology enters sensitive areas of life without understanding its ethical implications.

4.3 Structured and Transparent Value Elicitation Process

A major benefit provided by VBE (and the IEEE 7000 standard that formalizes it) is a clear and structured process for eliciting and integrating values throughout the project lifecycle [20, 21]. Instead of leaving ethics to ad hoc efforts or abstract guidelines, VBE embeds value elicitation into a step-by-step systems engineering methodology. The process is broken down into stages: from early Concept and Context Exploration (scoping the system's context, stakeholders, and high-level value considerations) to detailed Value Exploration (identifying values and analysing impacts) and finally Ethically Aligned Design (translating those value insights into concrete requirements and design features) [20, 21]. At each stage, there are well-defined activities and outputs.

Having a formalized value elicitation and requirements derivation workflow brings several advantages. It makes the treatment of values transparent and traceable. Anyone can see how a stated ethical concern led to a specific design decision or feature [20]. It also gives the engineering team a clear roadmap for addressing ethics: rather than vague aspirations, there is a concrete sequence of tasks and review points to ensure values are considered throughout the process [27].

This is especially relevant because engineers regularly report difficulty turning values like fairness, dignity, or privacy into precise and testable requirements. As Van de Poel [28] explains, even when values are clearly identified, the transition from abstract norms to concrete design solutions often requires conceptual clarification, stakeholder dialogue, and creative specification, none of which happen reliably without structure [28]. Spiekermann and Winkler [27] similarly found that in most organizations, ethical values are either treated inconsistently or implemented symbolically, since clear methods to translate them into design-level constraints are often missing [27]. VBE responds to this challenge by offering a structured process that helps teams move from broad ethical goals to specific design choices [21].

This translation happens through two formal mechanisms. First, values identified during context exploration are refined into value qualities (concrete, experienceable attributes through which a value becomes observable in a system) [20]. These qualities are then used to formulate Ethical Value Requirements (EVRs), which function much like functional requirements but reflect ethical priorities [21]. EVRs are integrated into the system specification and reviewed alongside technical requirements during design validation. This ensures that values are not only named but are operationalized in ways that can be tested, implemented, and improved.

Notably, this structured approach integrates well with familiar engineering practices like risk management. VBE calls for assessing ethical risks (e.g. potential "value harms") alongside traditional technical risks. By doing so, it elevates ethical foresight to the same level of rigor as performance or safety testing [20, 21].

In summary one can say, that teams using VBE have a common language (a "robust value ontology") and a clear procedure to follow, which improves collaboration and accountability when tackling moral questions [20, 21].

4.4 Early and Ongoing Stakeholder Engagement

VBE puts a strong emphasis on understanding and involving stakeholders from the very beginning of a project. It regards stakeholder insight as fundamental to ethical, human-centric design. The people who will use, be affected by, or otherwise have a stake in an AI system should actively shape its value requirements. Accordingly, the methodology begins with stakeholder analysis and continues to engage stakeholders (including end-users, domain experts, and even critical voices) throughout the development process [20]. This early and ongoing engagement has a profound impact. First, it helps system designers to conceptualize products that are relevant and socially acceptable by learning about the real hopes, concerns, and cultural expectations that define "value" in the given context [21].

Second, involving stakeholders from the start helps build trust and legitimacy. People are more likely to trust an AI system if they know their values and expectations have been heard and integrated into its design [20, 21]. The authors of the standard note that rigorously prioritizing ethical concerns at the outset of design is crucial to responsibly aligning technology with the contextual values of customers, citizens, and society at large [21]. By proactively addressing stakeholder concerns up front, instead of retrofitting fixes after public criticism or failures, organizations can avoid ethical pitfalls and earn broader acceptance of their AI innovations.

This is not just an ethical argument but a practical one as well. A well-known example is the failure of the UK NHS's National Programme for IT, which was in part attributed to a lack of meaningful user involvement [29]. Ethical missteps in product design have also resulted in heavy penalties and loss of public trust, as seen in the US Federal Trade Commission's $5 billion fine against Facebook for data privacy violations [30]. In contrast, organizations that embed inclusive stakeholder engagement into their design process tend to surface problems earlier, reduce later-stage friction, and deliver systems that are more stable and socially accepted from the outset [31, 32].

Finally, VBE's stakeholder-centric approach ensures that no major viewpoint is ignored in defining a system's values. The process explicitly calls for engaging diverse perspectives, including critical or marginalized voices that might otherwise be overlooked [20]. This inclusiveness guards against blind spots and encourages solutions that are socially robust. In effect, understanding stakeholders from day one isn't just a courtesy, it is a design necessity for any AI system aspiring to be aligned with human values. By continuously looping stakeholder feedback into development, VBE keeps the system's ethical compass pointed towards real human needs and away from abstract ideals or corporate convenience.

However, Value-based design, as outlined in IEEE 7000 and the VBE framework, goes beyond stakeholder input. While stakeholder workshops initiate value elicitation, these are followed by rigorous conceptual analysis. This phase integrates additional ethical, technical, and legal dimensions—such as those from the AI Act—that may not be explicitly expressed by stakeholders. The resulting ethical and legal requirements are systematically translated into traceable design specifications.

In summary, Value-Based Engineering and the IEEE 7000™ standard cultivate an approach to AI development that is proactive, context-aware, and fundamentally human-centered. They replace generic checklists with context-specific values, explore those values in depth, and embed them through a rigorous yet flexible engineering process that starts and ends with stakeholder engagement. Together, these practices support the creation of AI systems that do not merely check the boxes of ethical principles but truly integrate human values into their very architecture.

5 Conclusion

Legal regulations and regulatory mechanisms play a crucial role in establishing clear framework conditions that enable technological progress to serve the broader interests of society. The EU AI Act was introduced to ensure the trustworthy development and deployment of artificial intelligence, while simultaneously fostering responsible innovation and competitiveness [5]. It aims to create a foundation upon which individuals affected by AI systems can trust that these technologies are developed and used in a lawful, ethical, and socially beneficial manner. Ethics, therefore, constitutes a fundamental pillar of trustworthy AI. Technological advancement should ultimately serve to protect individual well-being and promote the common good. In doing so, Europe can position itself as a global leader in cutting-edge AI that earns and maintains the trust of its citizens.

The implementation of the EU AI Act presents significant challenges, including complex risk classification, a lack of harmonized standards, and rapid technological change.

While IEEE 7000 standards are not yet harmonized for conformity assessments, they offer valuable guidance—especially when adopted early in development and supported by interdisciplinary collaboration. The Value-Based Engineering (VBE) framework provides a robust methodology to operationalize ethical principles and fundamental rights in technical design. It employs a structured, risk-based approach to derive sociotechnical requirements from Ethical Value Requirements (EVRs), each traceably documented. Transparency mechanisms and expert reviews ensure decisions are evidence-based. Verification, monitoring, and—where applicable—impact assessments are integral to the process. The Value Register and lifecycle oversight offer demonstrable proof of ethical and legal alignment, supporting the AI Act's demands for transparency, accountability, and risk mitigation.

Complying with the EU AI Act requires more than legal expertise. It demands an integrated approach that brings together technological, ethical, and legal perspectives. The development of trustworthy AI systems calls for active engagement with foundational human values such as justice, well-being, freedom, and dignity. Value-Based Engineering (VBE) offers a comprehensive and practical framework to support this endeavor—bridging abstract principles with concrete design processes and regulatory alignment.

Disclosure of Interests.   The authors have no competing interests to declare that are relevant to the content of this article.

References

1. Laitinen, A., Sahlgren, O.: AI systems and respect for human autonomy. Front Artif. Intell. 4 (2021). https://doi.org/10.3389/frai.2021.705164
2. Ienca, M.: On artificial intelligence and manipulation. Topoi **42**, 833–842 (2023). https://doi.org/10.1007/s11245-023-09940-3
3. European Parliament; Council of the European Union (2024) Regulation (EU) 2024/1689 of the European Parliament and of the Council of 13 June 2024 laying down harmonised rules on artificial intelligence
4. Future of Life Institute: High-level summary of the AI Act., pp. 1–6 (2024)
5. High-Level Expert Group on AI: Ethics guidelines for trustworthy AI (2019)
6. Holistic AI: The EU AI Act's Risk-Based Approach: High-Risk Systems and What They Mean for Users, pp. 1–12 (2022)
7. Di Lorenzo, C., Ancenys, L.-A., Ruckert, N.W., Wagner, P.: EU AI Act: key changes in the recently leaked text. In: EU AI Act: key changes in the recently leaked text (2024). https://www.aoshearman.com/en/insights/ao-shearman-on-tech/eu-ai-act-key-changes-in-the-recently-leaked-text. Accessed 14 Jul 2025
8. Future Society (collective author): Protecting GPAI Rules Serve the Interests of European Businesses and Citizens. The Future Society (2025)
9. European Commission. Joint Research Centre: Generative AI outlook report: exploring the intersection of technology, society, and policy. Publications Office, LU (2025)
10. EU Commission: The General-Purpose AI Code of Practice (2025)
11. Center for AI and Digital Policy Europe Headquarters: EU Faces High-Stakes Battle Over AI Code as Nobel Laureates Warn Against Industry Pressure (2025). https://www.caidp.eu/news/pa8xu8faayb5l5scfd4w154zcctic2. Accessed 14 Jul 2025

12. EU Directorate-General for Justice and Consumers: Commission launches public consultation on high-risk AI systems (2025). https://e-justice.europa.eu/news/commission-launches-public-consultation-high-risk-ai-systems_en

13. Clifford Chance: The EU AI Act - Overview of Key Results and Requirements, pp. 1–16 (2024)

14. Pollet, M., Haeck, P.: Politico. In: EU could postpone flagship AI rules, tech chief says. https://www.politico.eu/article/eu-could-postpone-parts-of-ai-rulebook-tech-chief-says/. Accessed 19 Jun 2025

15. Andrews, C.: European Commission holds firm on AI Act implementation timeline (2025). https://iapp.org/news/a/european-commission-holds-firm-on-ai-act-implementation-timeline

16. Atlantic Council experts: experts react: The EU made a deal on AI rules. But can regulators move at the speed of tech? In: Atlantic Council (2023). https://www.atlanticcouncil.org/blogs/new-atlanticist/experts-react/experts-react-the-eu-made-a-deal-on-ai-rules-but-can-regulators-move-at-the-speed-of-tech/. Accessed 14 Jul 2025

17. Caroli, L.: Will the EU AI act work? Lessons learned from past legislative initiatives, future challenges. In: IAPP (International Association of Privacy Professionals) (2024). https://iapp.org/news/a/will-the-eu-ai-act-work-lessons-learned-from-past-legislative-initiatives-future-challenges. Accessed 14 Jun 2025

18. Science, Business editorial team: EU artificial intelligence act not future-proof, experts warn MEPs. In: Science|Business (2022). https://sciencebusiness.net/news/eu-artificial-intelligence-act-not-futureproof-experts-warn-meps. Accessed 14 Jul 2025

19. Spiekermann, S., Winkler, T.: Value-based engineering for ethics by design. SSRN J. (2020). https://doi.org/10.2139/ssrn.3598911

20. Spiekermann, S.: Value-Based Engineering: A Guide to Building Ethical Technology for Humanity. De Gruyter (2023)

21. IEEE 7000–2021 Standard Model Process for Addressing Ethical Concerns during System Design

22. Whittlestone, J., Nyrup, R., Alexandrova, A., Cave, S.: The role and limits of principles in AI ethics: towards a focus on tensions. In: Proceedings of the 2019 AAAI/ACM Conference on AI, Ethics, and Society. ACM, Honolulu HI USA, pp 195–200 (2019)

23. Kijewski, S., Ronchi, E., Vayena, E.: The rise of checkbox AI ethics: a review. AI Ethics **5**, 1931–1940 (2025). https://doi.org/10.1007/s43681-024-00563-x

24. Heuser, S., Steil, J., Salloch, S.: AI ethics beyond principles: strengthening the life-world perspective. Sci. Eng. Ethics **31** (2025). https://doi.org/10.1007/s11948-025-00530-7

25. Payne, K.: An AI chatbot pushed a teen to kill himself, a lawsuit against its creator alleges. AP News (2024)

26. Montgomery, B.: Mother says AI chatbot led her son to kill himself in lawsuit against its maker. The Guardian (Technology) (2024)

27. Winkler, T., Spiekermann, S.: Twenty years of value sensitive design: a review of methodological practices in VSD projects. Ethics Inf. Technol. **23**, 17–21 (2021). https://doi.org/10.1007/s10676-018-9476-2

28. Translating values into design requirements. In: Philosophy of Engineering and Technology, pp. 253–266. Springer, Netherlands, Dordrecht (2013)

29. Greenhalgh, T., Stramer, K., Bratan, T., et al.: The devil's in the detail: Final report of the independent evaluation of the Summary Care Record and HealthSpace programmes. UCL Discovery (2010)

30. United States Federal Trade Commission (FTC) FTC imposes $5 billion penalty and sweeping new privacy restrictions on Facebook. In: Federal Trade Commission (2019). https://www.ftc.gov/news-events/news/press-releases/2019/07/ftc-imposes-5-billion-penalty-sweeping-new-privacy-restrictions-facebook. Accessed 12 Jun 2025

31. Value Sensitive Design and Information Systems. In: The Handbook of Information and Computer Ethics, 1st ed. Wiley, pp. 69–101 (2008)
32. Leikas, J., Koivisto, R., Gotcheva, N.: Ethical framework for designing autonomous intelligent systems. J. Open Innov. Technol., Market, Complexity **5**, 18 (2019). https://doi.org/10.3390/joitmc5010018

Realizing Ethical-Aware Business Processes

Sara Pettinari[✉][ID], Martina De Sanctis[ID], and Paola Inverardi[ID]

Gran Sasso Science Institute, L'Aquila, Italy
{sara.pettinari,martina.desanctis,paola.inverardi}@gssi.it

Abstract. As digital systems become an integral part of modern organizations, ethical considerations must also be incorporated within the business process management domain. While this domain has traditionally focused on system-level goals, such as efficiency, security, and compliance, individual-level ethical aspects, such as human preferences, well-being, and dignity, remain largely unexplored. This paper introduces the concept of ethical-aware business processes, which are capable of integrating both system-level obligations and individual ethical values. Focusing on autonomous systems guided by a process model, we explore the challenges of designing, implementing, and monitoring processes that ensure respectful and responsible interactions with humans. We also outline key research directions to enable the management of ethical-aware business processes across their lifecycle.

Keywords: Ethical-aware Business Processes · Responsible BPM · Ethics

1 Introduction

Nowadays, organizations are increasingly shaped by digital systems that support and influence nearly every aspect of daily life and work, often operating in autonomous ways. To understand and manage how such operations are structured and executed, we refer to Business Process Management (BPM), a well-established discipline that focuses on how organizations coordinate their operations. BPM considers a business process as the core element to refer to the activities carried out to achieve specific goals. It provides a structured lifecycle that includes identification, discovery, analysis, (re)design, implementation, execution, monitoring, and continuous evolution [18]. Examples of organizations using processes can range from hospitals coordinating patient care to public administrations managing service requests. Given its widespread application, BPM naturally deals with socio-technical processes [7], where human actors and digital components interact across coordinated sequences of activities. As organizations move toward more automated and AI-enhanced processes [17], this close interaction between humans and digital systems requires a stronger integration of ethical considerations into BPM. Ethical awareness is becoming a necessary

© The Author(s) 2026
L. Hagedorn et al. (Eds.): DIGHUM 2025, LNCS 16319, pp. 219–235, 2026.
https://doi.org/10.1007/978-3-032-11108-1_16

dimension in the design and management of business processes, ensuring that technological advancement does not come at the expense of individual rights and well-being. Following Floridi's definition of digital ethics [22], these ethical aspects can be broadly categorized into two dimensions: hard ethics that covers the space of ethical values that shape norms and laws, and soft ethics that delimits the moral space in which agents (including individuals, groups, companies, governments, organizations) can exercise their moral choices without bypassing hard ethics. In the BPM domain, hard ethics refers to organizational or regulatory responsibilities, such as compliance with anti-discrimination laws [33] or environmental sustainability goals [8,29]. These concerns are typically formalized through policies, rules, and performance indicators, and are often aligned with broader frameworks like the Sustainable Development Goals and General Data Protection Regulation [32]. In contrast, soft ethics refer to individual, context-specific aspects such as personal preferences, emotional or physical condition, and overall well-being [22]. These considerations are harder to formalize, often emerge at runtime, and are essential for respecting human dignity during process execution. Consider, for example, a vacation request process. Usually, this process includes an initial automated check to verify whether the employee has enough vacation days to cover the requested period. If the available days are insufficient, the request is automatically denied based on predefined rules, and the request process ends. However, imagine an employee who has run out of available vacation days but is experiencing high stress or facing personal difficulties. A human manager might recognize the situation and approve the leave anyway, acknowledging the need to guarantee employee well-being. In contrast, an automated system lacks such contextual sensitivity. To address this, the process should be designed with enough flexibility to allow the employee to express their condition and explore alternatives, such as borrowing days from the following year or receiving some days from colleagues, thus replicating the empathetic judgment a human might provide. This highlights the importance of incorporating soft ethics into business processes, ensuring that processes respect and respond not only to system requirements, but also to ensure that even automated decisions remain aligned with human dignity and well-being. However, despite the advancements in BPM that have improved aspects such as transparency, sustainability, security, and privacy, ethical considerations on individual-level values have received limited attention [28].

In this paper, we focus on modern digital systems that are autonomous, self-adaptive, and may incorporate AI technologies. Specifically, our focus is on autonomous systems whose behavior is driven by automated business processes. As these systems can interact with humans, the underlying processes must be designed with an awareness of not only hard ethics but also soft ethics, to ensure respectful and responsible interactions. Unlike human actors, autonomous systems lack the cultural, emotional, and contextual understanding that often underlies human-to-human negotiation and adaptation. This shift from human to automated execution may compromise the flexibility and sensitivity inherent in human interactions [27]. To address this, business processes should be ethically aware and responsibly managed across the entire BPM lifecycle, with particular attention to protecting the individuals involved in or affected by the process within the organizational context [26]. To this aim, we define what we mean by ethical-aware business processes and how they are characterized. On this basis, we discuss the main challenges for realizing ethical-aware business processes, i.e., their design, implementation, and monitoring. We then outline key research directions to enable a responsible management of ethical-aware business processes.

The rest of the paper is structured as follows. Section 2 provides the background on digital ethics and ethical-aware autonomous systems. Section 3 presents the works targeting the responsible management of business processes. Section 4 introduces the running scenario that motivates the need for ethical-aware business processes. Building on this foundation as well as existing definitions, Sect. 5 introduces the concept of an ethical-aware business process. Section 6 discusses the key challenges and research directions for realizing such processes. Finally, Sect. 7 concludes the paper.

2   Background

In this section, we present the background concepts of digital ethics and ethical-aware autonomous systems. Specifically, we position ethical-aware business processes as a specific case of ethical-aware autonomous systems. In this context, system behavior is guided by an *automated business process*, which defines how the system responds to events, interacts with humans, and achieves its objectives. As a result, embedding ethical considerations into the business process has a direct impact on the ethical behavior of the autonomous system itself.

The rise of AI has led to increasingly autonomous systems, deeply embedded in daily life, from smartphones to smart homes and vehicles. As their social, economic, and political impact grows, the need for ethical-aware autonomous systems becomes increasingly critical. The EU is tackling not only privacy concerns but also broader ethical risks related to the use of personal data and autonomous technologies [25,26]. Human dignity is highlighted as a central value in the digital age, emphasizing respectful human-AI interactions [19]. EU guidelines call for AI systems to align with ethical principles, such as fairness, privacy, and user control [25], and to ensure human oversight remains central, thus adjusting the system's autonomy in accordance with the user's preferences. Works in this area propose leveraging the concept of digital ethics, as introduced by Floridi [22] and discussed in Sect. 1, which distinguishes between *hard ethics* and *soft ethics*. According to [26], a system's autonomy should align with hard ethics while also being respectful of and adaptable to the individual soft ethics of its users. In this setting, one effective way to safeguard individual freedom of choice, rooted in personal preferences and moral values, is through the intentional design of adaptable system autonomy, also known as *flexibility by design* [36]. More recently, the work in [4] highlighted the need to integrate human, societal, and environmental values into systems engineering, beyond traditional business and technical goals. It identifies key human-system interaction challenges, and proposes a research roadmap covering development, requirements, design, and validation to guide the engineering of value-driven digital systems. In line with the research roadmap proposed in [4], the work in [3] contributes a definition of ethical-aware autonomous system as well as a reference architecture for ethical-aware autonomous systems where the human-system interaction is considered as a flexible process and modeled by adopting the MAPE-K (Monitor-Analyze-Plan-Execute over a shared Knowledge) feedback loop style [2].

3   State of the Art

The literature collects various approaches to achieve a responsible management of business processes, with most efforts focusing on the integration of sustainability considerations, while a few address the protection of human well-being.

With the organizations' increasing need to become sustainable, the original BPM focus on optimizing time, cost, quality, and flexibility has been extended to also consider sustainability [8]. This focus falls under the umbrella of Green BPM. Specifically, Green BPM involves the modeling, deployment, optimization, and management of business processes with explicit consideration of their environmental impact [12]. Several works integrate sustainability aspects within business processes. This ranges from approaches for modeling environmental-related information [37], to the application of process mining techniques for sustainability [11,24,29], to covering the overall lifecycle with approaches ensuring more sustainable business processes [23,31].

Focusing on the human perspective, Benevolent BPM aims to enhance human well-being within business processes, shifting away from the traditional provider-centric perspective that emphasizes flawless and economically efficient execution. The focus of Benevolent BPM is on the customer, to ensure business processes prioritize customers' well-being over the immediate interests of the organization [40]. For example, a process may prompt a customer to confirm the re-ordering of a previously purchased item, thereby preventing unintentional actions, or it may offer an upgrade when a customer checks into a hotel on his/her birthday. Complementing this perspective, Inclusive BPM highlights the importance of ensuring human rights and inclusivity in process design and implementation. According to [33], Inclusive BPM focuses on business processes that are not only human-centered but also take into account the needs of vulnerable groups, ensuring that no one is excluded from process benefits and opportunities. For example, when small local businesses adopt digital tools to manage procurement or sales, the underlying processes must be simplified to accommodate users with limited technical skills. Finally, given the central role of BPM in organizing work and managing people, recent works have focused on investigating workers' well-being [21,30]. The aim is to promote and support business processes that benefit the organization and workers at the same time. For example, task assignment mechanisms can be adapted to consider workers' workload or emotional state, allowing for the deferral of non-urgent tasks to prevent excessive stress.

Our work complements these efforts by proposing the notion of ethical-aware business processes. In contrast to approaches that target specific user groups, we build on the concept of soft ethics, subjective and individual-dependent, and emphasize that every person interacting with an automated business process should be treated with dignity and supported in their well-being, as a human participant would do.

Altogether, these approaches fall under the broader concept of Responsible BPM, which involves a responsible design, implementation, and monitoring of business processes by accounting for the needs of involved stakeholders, the environment and the society. However, most contributions have focused on the analysis phase, mainly from a process mining perspective, addressing issues such as bias in event data, minority exclusion, data quality, and the protection of sensitive information [34]. Yet, analysis represents only one phase of the BPM lifecycle. Differently, our work aims to include ethical awareness across the entire lifecycle, ensuring that ethical considerations are embedded throughout the management of business processes.

4   Running Scenario

We consider a healthcare setting as a running scenario, inspired from [14], which involves patients, nurses, and a care robot. The care robot can interact with both patients and nurses to complete its tasks, making it an active participant in the organizational process. Following the modeling approaches in the literature [10, 13], we model the robot's behavior using BPMN[1], and we assume that the robot can autonomously perform the tasks designed in the process model.

As depicted in Fig. 1, the care robot operates within a predefined scope, with its behavior guided by a process model. The mission begins by retrieving medicines from the medicine room. It then visits patients' rooms to dispense the appropriate medications. During this activity, the robot must interact with each patient. The model includes the possibility of identifying emergencies, guiding the robot to notify a nurse when additional support is needed. This situation represents a foreseen variation, i.e., one that can be anticipated and modeled at design time. The process also includes a default, or optimal, scenario where the patient accepts the medication without issue. However, unexpected conditions may arise due to the patient's individual preferences, i.e., soft ethics, and current emotional or physical state. For example, a patient may refuse medication due to mistrust of the robot or emotional discomfort. These unforeseen situations require runtime adaptation. The robot must choose whether to continue its current behavior or adjust its actions. The adaptation should respect the patient's preferences, prioritizing ethical considerations such as human dignity. For instance, if insisting on dispensing the medicine would go against the patient's preferences, the robot should prioritize preserving dignity over completing the task. To address this, the robot can attempt alternative strategies to calm down the patient or involve other participants in the process. It might

---

[1] https://www.bpmn.org/.

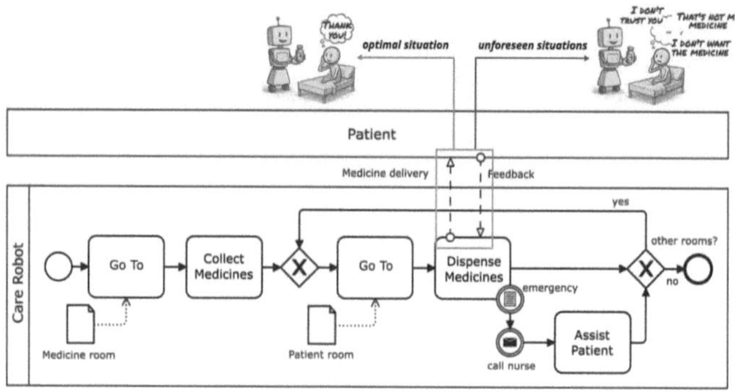

Fig. 1. Care robot scenario.

delegate the task to a nurse, or if no nurse is available, contact the patient's family for support. However, privacy restrictions may limit access to such contacts. In that case, the robot may need to postpone the task and return later. Figure 2 shows a possible runtime variant of the *dispense medicines* task where the robot dynamically identifies an alternative behavior based on the patient's emotional status, privacy rules, and availability of support. This adaptation is not predefined at design time but results from context-aware reasoning and runtime learning. It enables the robot to act in an ethically sensitive and flexible manner, similar to human decision-making. Furthermore, if the patient's condition changes during execution, this may trigger additional variants, requiring continuous reassessment of appropriate actions.

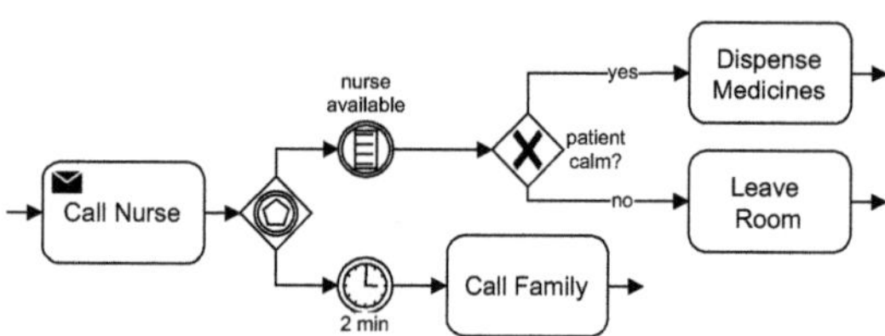

Fig. 2. Possible adaptation of *dispense medicines* task.

This scenario illustrates how ethical challenges emerge when tasks previously handled by humans are delegated to autonomous systems. Traditionally, this type of process was performed by nurses who, while operating within structured workflows, rely on human autonomy, cognitive and emotional understanding to deviate from the prescribed process to ensure patients' dignity and well-being. In contrast, when these tasks are performed by a care robot, the system follows the predefined steps of the automated business process without such flexibility. Therefore, the process must be designed to incorporate adaptability and ethical sensitivity, enabling the system to act in ways that emulate human judgment and ethical reasoning. This highlights the need for realizing and supporting ethical-aware business process models, capable of handling unforeseen, human-centered situations while respecting individual values during interaction between systems and humans.

5   Ethical-Aware Business Processes

We define ethical-aware business processes by drawing from the literature on BPM and ethical-aware autonomous systems. Rather than proposing a formal definition, we adopt a conceptual approach that synthesizes established ideas from both domains.

As defined in [18], a *business process* is a structured sequence of activities or tasks carried out by people or systems to achieve specific organizational goals. With the growing recognition of their socio-technical nature, business processes have been further characterized as *socio-technical processes* [7], defined as processes involving coordinated actions and events that integrate both humans and digital systems over time. With the increasing autonomization of processes, enabled by both AI and non-AI technologies, business processes are capable of autonomously making decisions. Indeed, [39] defined *process autonomization* as the empowerment of a business process to make decisions in light of defined goals and constraints. These decisions could relate to events, control flow, data, duration, and resources involved. As a result, such processes become emergent in both their structure and outcomes, exhibiting high levels of sensitivity to context and adaptability during execution [39]. Therefore, given the socio-technical nature of business processes and their increasing autonomization, there is a need to ensure that these processes are not only efficient and adaptable but also aligned with ethical principles. Recently, the concept of ethical awareness has been introduced in the field of autonomous systems. Indeed, as defined in [3], an *ethical-aware autonomous system* refers to a system that adapts to human interactions and/or changes in physical or virtual environments, and that exhibits a behavior that conforms to the system ethics (i.e., hard ethics, and soft ethics intended as the company policies of the autonomous system's producer, as well as values, culture, and social norms, embedded within the system), the human ethics (i.e., humans soft ethics), and the current status of the humans that interact or share the physical or virtual environment with the system. Combining these perspectives, we define below what we mean by ethical-aware business processes.

Ethical-aware Business Process

An ethical-aware business process is a structured, goal-oriented sequence of activities, pertaining to either a human or a digital system or both, designed not only to fulfill business objectives but also to conform to ethical principles, both system-defined and human-centered, through continuous adaptation to social, environmental, and contextual changes.

Therefore, an ethical-aware business process integrates autonomous decision-making capabilities with sensitivity to ethical considerations. This includes the ability to adapt actions and outcomes in response to system and human ethics, and contextual changes in the organizational or societal environment. Ethical-aware business processes, therefore, extend traditional and autonomous business processes by embedding ethical considerations and reasoning as an integral component of their operation. In turn, we consider that an ethical-aware business process exhibits at least the following characteristics:

- **Structured and Goal-oriented**: follows the formalism and purpose of traditional business processes [18].
- **Socio-technical Integration**: involves interactions among human participants and digital systems (e.g., services, devices, robots) [7].
- **Context-awareness**: senses and reacts to environmental, social, and human status changes [39].
- **Ethics-conforming**: conforms to *system ethics*, i.e., predefined ethical rules or constraints embedded in the process, and *human ethics*, i.e., values, cultures, societal norms, well-being, and needs of humans interacting with the system [3].
- **Adaptive and Automated**: is capable of self-adaptation in response to ethical preferences or contextual shifts, while maintaining alignment with the overall process objectives [3, 39].

6   Challenges and Research Directions

This section presents challenges and research directions for realizing, i.e., designing, implementing, and monitoring, ethical-aware business processes. First, we present the challenges impacting the process level to enable ethical, context-aware, and human-centric operations. Then, we discuss the research directions at the BPM level to guide an organization, or its stakeholders, in managing and supporting ethical-aware business processes throughout their lifecycle.

6.1   Challenges for Realizing Ethical-Aware Business Processes

We identify and discuss the main challenges involved in realizing ethical-aware business processes that are capable of emulating human cultural- and moral value-driven reasoning to support context-sensitive and ethically grounded decision-making. While many of these challenges are also relevant to autonomous systems in general, our focus here is specifically on their implications within the BPM domain. For each challenge (CH), we outline its implications and provide an illustrative example grounded in the running scenario.

(CH1) Human Soft Ethics Modeling: Challenge. Capturing and maintaining aligned human ethical preferences, i.e., soft ethics, is difficult due to their abstract nature, context dependency, and variability over time. These aspects are rarely formalized and cannot always be fully anticipated at design time. Moreover, humans may not always be fully aware of their own ethical preferences, which can emerge or evolve only through lived experience and interaction with specific situations.

Implication. Effectively understanding the relevant moral preferences to consider within business processes, and embedding them so that the processes remain compatible with business goals, might require techniques to verify this compatibility against the elicited moral preferences. This would enable the translation of high-level ethical considerations into actionable process constraints or adaptation rules.

Example. For instance, part of a patient's ethical preferences may include trusting the care robot under normal conditions, while also wanting their right to be left alone to be respected. In such a case, if the patient expresses this right during the medicine dispensing activity, the robot should leave the room in order to preserve the patient's moral preferences, and notify the nurse about the failed attempt to administer the medicine.

(CH2) Performance and Ethical Metrics Balance: *Challenge.* Business processes must account for the diverse and potentially conflicting objectives of different stakeholders, such as balancing operational efficiency with the protection of individual well-being.

Implication. Ethical-aware processes require mechanisms to balance or prioritize competing KPIs, ensuring that human-centric values are not compromised in favor of operational goals. This necessitates a reconsideration of traditional BPM performance frameworks, such as the "devil's quadrangle" [18]. This framework should be extended, as also suggested for the inclusion of sustainablilty [8], to incorporate ethical awareness as a critical, emergent dimension in the management of business processes.

Example. For instance, consider a scenario in which the care robot is tasked with delivering medicines within 30 min. If a patient exhibits distress or hesitation, the process should prioritize preserving the patient's dignity, potentially involving human intervention, over meeting the timing constraint.

(CH3) Real-time Socio-Ethical Context Awareness: *Challenge.* Enabling ethical awareness in business processes requires sensitivity to dynamic, real-time contextual and human factors.

Implication. Ethical-aware business processes must incorporate and respond to real-time data, such as emotional state, environmental conditions, or cultural norms, to make ethically aligned decisions during execution. This implies the inclusion of not only situational factors related to goal-, process-, organization-, and environment-dimensions [9], but also the individual and ethical ones.

Example. To respect a patient's preference and emotional state, the care robot should consider the immediate context. For instance, if the patient is distressed and a non-medical staff member (e.g., cleaning personnel) is present in the room, the robot may ask the person to step out to preserve the patient's comfort and dignity.

(CH4) Flexibility: *Challenge.* Both system ethics and human ethics can evolve over time or vary across different contexts.

Implication. Ethical-aware business processes must be designed to flexibly adapt to changing ethical requirements, maintaining compliance with system ethics while preserving human dignity. This may involve defining variation points [38] where the process can adjust its behavior to align with evolving system and human ethics.

Example. For instance, if a patient who is typically cheerful exhibits signs of loneliness, and nurses are unavailable due to an emergency, the care robot may request the patient's permission to contact a family member for support.

(CH5) Adjustable Autonomy: *Challenge.* Determining when and to what extent the system should release its autonomy in favor of human actors to preserve the ethical preferences of the human interacting with the system.

Implication. Although the system may be capable of performing tasks autonomously, an ethical-aware business process should be able to dynamically delegate specific tasks to humans when necessary to respect human dignity and accommodate individual needs. This requires the process to support adjustable autonomy [5,17], enabling it to recognize situations where releasing control to a human participant would better safeguard an individual's dignity and needs.

Example. For instance, if a patient shows reluctance in interacting with the care robot, the care robot may suspend its task and delegate the medicine delivery to a nurse, recognizing that human intervention is more appropriate in that context.

(CH6) Transparency and Explainability: *Challenge.* Ethical decisions made by automated components within a process must be understandable and interpretable by humans.

Implication. Ethical-aware business processes demand transparency in their logic and explainability of decisions. A possibility could be recording detailed action traces and relevant contextual information to clarify how and why the process adapts or behaves in a given way. Such logging should capture the current context, executed activities, and decisions made, enabling stakeholders to verify that the processes run as intended, while also preserving the ability to detect, understand, and modify performed behaviors [1,17].

Example. For instance, if the robot decides to postpone medicine delivery because it detects the patient is in an uncomfortable situation (e.g., the patient is asleep or engaged in a sensitive activity), the system should be able to provide a clear explanation to the nurse and the patient. This explanation would include the contextual information and decision criteria used by the robot, allowing the nurse to understand why the action was taken, verify its appropriateness, and decide on any further steps if needed.

(CH7) Continuous Evolution and Prediction: *Challenge.* Ethical preferences are not fixed; they evolve over time and vary with context. A key challenge is enabling processes to continuously learn, predict, and adapt based on feedback from humans and their environment.

Implication. Ethical-aware business processes should incorporate mechanisms to learn from both explicit and implicit human interactions. This can include leveraging process mining techniques to analyze historical and contextual data, enabling the process to evolve over time and predict the outcomes of future interactions [1].

Example. For instance, the robot may notice that a patient's preferences about interaction style change gradually, e.g., becoming less comfortable speaking with the robot over time. By continuously monitoring this feedback, the robot can adapt its behavior accordingly, perhaps by reducing direct interaction or allowing more time before engaging. This ongoing learning helps predict the patient's evolving needs and ensures that the care provided remains respectful and aligned with the patient's evolving preferences.

6.2   Research Directions for Ethical-Aware BPM Lifecycle

In this section, we reflect on how addressing the above challenges influences the BPM lifecycle. When human participants are replaced or supported by autonomous systems, processes require greater flexibility and adaptability. Humans naturally rely on contextual understanding and cultural background to adjust their behavior instinctively. In contrast, an automated business process lacks this implicit awareness, making it essential for BPM to explicitly capture and manage such ethical considerations throughout its lifecycle. Below, we elaborate on key research directions mapped to each phase of the BPM lifecycle, which are summarized in Table 1.

Identification. This phase aims to provide an overall picture of the processes within an organization and their interrelationships. To support ethical awareness, identification should extend beyond the traditional delineation of business processes and their scope to include the detection of ethically sensitive aspects, i.e., situations where human actors interact with automated systems and ethical considerations must be taken into account. This should include identifying the system's behavior and the human participants involved, both the ethics-sensitive actors (e.g., patients) and the contextual human stakeholders (e.g., nurses), as well as the relevant ethical values to be considered (**CH1**). Moreover, within this phase, the notion of performance itself needs to be revisited. Alongside traditional KPIs, new metrics should be defined to reflect ethical concerns, such as respect for human dignity, and well-being [15] (**CH2**), this would require capturing ethical performance in a way that allows for comparison with traditional process metrics.

Discovery. Discovery involves capturing as-is process models through both manual modeling and automated techniques such as process mining. When modeling ethical-aware business processes, it is essential to reflect on how current modeling languages and paradigms either support or constrain the representation of ethical variations. For example, conventional modeling approaches often capture predefined and rigid paths, which may be insufficient for supporting the flexibility needed in ethically sensitive scenarios. Taxonomies of flexibility [38] could be extended to better represent ethical decision points and variability (**CH4**). Additionally, this phase may involve discovering human ethical profiles or preferences using techniques such as user modeling and behavior mining [16], while ensuring responsible data handling practices [6]. Alternatively, as discussed in [14], AI can also be seen as a promising instrument to continuously infer ethical preferences (**CH1**). Finally, since ethical preferences evolve over time, the discovered process model can be revisited iteratively, allowing the refinement of models based on new insights and feedback (**CH7**).

Analysis. This phase aims to identify and quantify issues in the as-is processes, typically to assess alignment with business goals. In an ethical-aware BPM, analysis must also account for new types of performance indicators that reflect ethical dimensions (**CH2**). These indicators can reveal situations where current process behaviors lack sufficient ethical sensitivity and may risk compromising human dignity or well-being. For example, the analysis could identify that, during the discovery phase, the *dispense medicines* task was modeled without considering the patient's emotional or physical condition. This phase should also support evaluating the broader ethical impact of business operations by identifying areas where ethical-aware interactions are needed to mitigate harm or support human values.

Redesign. Redesign addresses the issues identified during analysis to produce an improved to-be process model. In the ethical-aware context, this phase should focus on reconfiguring processes to better reflect overlooked human values and ethical considerations identified in the analysis phase. This can involve embedding ethical considerations directly into the process logic, treating them as first-class elements, similar to regulatory constraints (i.e., hard ethics), to guide execution toward ethically acceptable outcomes (**CH1**). Additionally, redesign could integrate new ethical considerations, enabling the process to adjust its behavior dynamically based on contextual factors, individual ethical preferences, or well-being (**CH3**). These modifications may also involve allowing human intervention, introducing negotiation points, or structuring decision paths to accommodate multiple ethical options (**CH4**).

Implementation. Implementation involves transitioning from the as-is to the to-be model, including both automation and organizational change. Supporting ethical-aware execution requires technologies that enable flexible (**CH4**) and context-sensitive behavior (**CH3**). Existing frameworks [38] can be used to address flexibility needs, as well as automated planning techniques [35], combined with recent advancements in large language models for planning, can enable more advanced forms of automation. These solutions can support dynamic and instance-level adaptation can be extended to handle ethics-based adaptations, for example, adjusting task execution based on a human's stress level or personal needs (**CH5**). Furthermore, explainability should be built into execution.

Table 1. Research directions for ethical-aware BPM

Lifecycle Phase	Research Directions	Challenges
Identification	· Identify ethical sensitive points and human participants interacting with the system · Identify ethical KPIs	CH1 · CH2
Discovery	· Assess how the current way of modeling business processes may support or challenge representation of ethical-awareness · Discovery of humans profiles	CH1 · CH4 · CH7
Analysis	· Analysis of issues that impact human dignity and well-being · Analysis of the ethical impact of business processes	CH2
Redesign	· Redesign business processes embedding ethical sensitivity · Integrate ethical-based adaptations	CH1 · CH3 · CH4
Implementation	· Implement or leverage solutions to support ethical-aware execution · Enable the business process execution explainability	CH3 · CH4 · CH5 · CH6
Monitoring and Controlling	· Monitor system and human behavior, ethical constraints, impacts, and context · Exploit analysis techniques capable of dealing with different types of contextual information	CH3 · CH7

Systems must be capable of logging or justifying variations in behavior, helping users understand and trust the underlying decisions (**CH6**).

Monitoring and Controlling. Monitoring involves collecting and analyzing execution data to assess performance against predefined metrics and objectives. Ethical-aware monitoring must integrate traditional analysis with real-time assessments of contextual dynamics and impacts on human participants (**CH3**). This includes detecting deviations from ethical expectations or emerging harmful patterns. Techniques such as compliance checking may be adopted to cover soft ethics constraints. However, due to the dynamic and context-dependent nature of soft ethics, such assessments may require the direct involvement of human stakeholders to validate whether ethical expectations are being appropriately met. While multi-dimensional process mining [20] offers opportunities to analyze behavior across control-flow, context, and human-system interactions in an integrated manner. The insights obtained during monitoring should not only ensure ethical compliance but also guide iterative refinements of the process model (**CH7**), enabling continuous improvement of ethical performance.

7   Conclusions

In this paper, we explored the emerging need for realizing ethical-aware business processes, particularly in the context of autonomous systems, where interactions between humans and systems become increasingly autonomous. We motivated this need through a running scenario and grounded our discussion in recent advancements in digital ethics, ethical-aware autonomous systems, and Responsible BPM. We introduced the concept of an ethical-aware business process and identified the key challenges involved in embedding ethical considerations throughout its realization. To address these challenges, we proposed research directions mapped across the BPM lifecycle phases. Future work will focus on operationalizing these research directions, assessing their practical feasibility, and developing concrete frameworks and tools to support ethical awareness across the entire BPM lifecycle.

Acknowledgements. This work has been funded by (a) the MUR (Italy) Department of Excellence 2023 - 2027, and (b) the PRIN project 2022JKA4SL - HALO: etHical-aware AdjustabLe autOnomous systems.

Disclosure of Interests. The authors have no conflicts of interest to declare that are relevant to the content of this article.

References

1. van der Aalst, W.: Process Mining Data Science in Action. Springer, Heidelberg (2016). https://doi.org/10.1007/978-3-662-49851-4
2. Arcaini, P., Riccobene, E., Scandurra, P.: Modeling and analyzing MAPE-K feedback loops for self-adaptation. In: International Symposium on Software Engineering for Adaptive and Self-Managing Systems, pp. 13–23. IEEE (2015)
3. Autili, M., De Sanctis, M., Inverardi, P., Memon, M.A., Pelliccione, P., Pettinari, S.: A reference architecture for ethical-aware autonomous systems. http://dx.doi.org/10.2139/ssrn.5165316
4. Autili, M., De Sanctis, M., Inverardi, P., Pelliccione, P.: Engineering digital systems for humanity: a research roadmap. ACM Trans. Softw. Eng. Methodol. **34**, 1–33 (2025)
5. Baer, M., Plattfaut, R.: Human friendly automation: A literature review on the role of the human factor in ai-driven business process automation. In: Marrella, A., Resinas, M., Jans, M., Rosemann, M. (eds.) Business Process Management Forum. LNBIP, vol. 526, pp. 287–301. Springer, Cham (2024). https://doi.org/10.1007/978-3-031-70418-5_17
6. Beverungen, D., Buijs, J.C., Becker, J., et al.: Seven paradoxes of business process management in a hyper-connected world. Bus. Inf. Syst. Eng. **63**, 145–156 (2021)
7. vom Brocke, J., van der Aalst, W., et al.: Process science: the interdisciplinary study of socio-technical change. Process Sci. **1**(1), 1 (2024)
8. vom Brocke, J., Seidel, S., Recker, J. (eds.): Green Business Process Management - Towards the Sustainable Enterprise. Springer (2012). https://doi.org/10.1007/978-3-642-27488-6
9. vom Brocke, J., Zelt, S., Schmiedel, T.: On the role of context in business process management. Int. J. Inf. Manag. **36**(3), 486–495 (2016)
10. Corradini, F., Pettinari, S., Re, B., Rossi, L., Tiezzi, F.: A BPMN-driven framework for multi-robot system development. Robotics Auton. Syst. **160**, 104322 (2023)

11. Costache, I., Turetken, O., Aysolmaz, B., Winter, K.: Process mining guidelines for greenhouse gas emission management in production processes. Delgado, A., Slaats, T. (eds.) Process Mining Workshops, pp. 711–724. LNBIP, Springer, Cham (2024). https://doi.org/10.1007/978-3-031-82225-4_52

12. Couckuyt, D., Looy, A.V.: A systematic review of green business process management. Bus. Process. Manag. J. **26**(2), 421–446 (2020)

13. de la Croix, J.P., Lim, G.: Event-driven modeling and execution of robotic activities and contingencies in the Europa lander mission concept using BPMN. In: i-SAIRAS. ESA (2020)

14. De Sanctis, M., Inverardi, P.: Engineering ethical-aware collective adaptive systems. In: Margaria, T., Steffen, B. (eds.) Leveraging Applications of Formal Methods, Verification and Validation. LNCS, vol. 15219, pp. 238–252. Springer, Cham (2024). https://doi.org/10.1007/978-3-031-73709-1_15

15. De Sanctis, M., Inverardi, P., Pelliccione, P.: Do modern systems require new quality dimensions? In: Bertolino, A., Pascoal Faria, J., Lago, P., Semini, L. (eds.) International Conference on the Quality of Information and Communications Technology, pp. 83–90. Springer (2024). https://doi.org/10.1007/978-3-031-70245-7_6

16. Di Federico, G., Burattin, A.: Do you behave always the same? A process mining approach. Montali, M., Senderovich, A., Weidlich, M. (eds.) Process Mining Workshops. pp. 5–17. LNBIP, Springer (2022). https://doi.org/10.1007/978-3-031-27815-0_1

17. Dumas, M., Fournier, F., et al.: AI-augmented business process management systems: a research manifesto. ACM Trans. Manag. Inf. Syst. **14**(1), 11:1–11:19 (2023)

18. Fundamentals of Business Process Management. Springer, Heidelberg (2018). https://doi.org/10.1007/978-3-662-56509-4_9

19. European Group on Ethics in Science and New Technologies and others: Statement on artificial intelligence, robotics and 'autonomous' systems. EU (2018)

20. Fahland, D.: Process mining over multiple behavioral dimensions with event knowledge graphs. In: van der Aalst, W.M.P., Carmona, J. (eds.) Process Mining Handbook, pp. 274–319. Springer (2022). https://doi.org/10.1007/978-3-031-08848-3_9

21. Fehrer, T., et al.: With people, for people: a method for employee-aware business process improvement. In: European Conference on Information Systems (2024)

22. Floridi, L.: Soft ethics, the governance of the digital and the general data protection regulation. Philos. Trans. Royal Soc. A: Math. Phys. Eng. Sci. **376**(2133), 20180081 (2018)

23. González Moyano, C., Klessascheck, F., et al.: Towards nudging in BPM: a human-centric approach for sustainable business processes. In: Delgado, A., Slaats, T. (eds.) Process Mining Workshops, pp. 738–750. LNBIP, Springer, Cham (2024). https://doi.org/10.1007/978-3-031-82225-4_54

24. Graves, N., Koren, I., van der Aalst, W.: Rethink your processes! A review of process mining for sustainability. In: International Conference on ICT for Sustainability, pp. 164–175. IEEE (2023)

25. High-level expert group on AI: The ethics guidelines for trustworthy artificial intelligence (2019)

26. Inverardi, P.: The European perspective on responsible computing. Commun. ACM **62**(4), 64 (2019)

27. Inverardi, P.: The challenge of human dignity in the era of autonomous systems. In: Werthner, H., Prem, E., Lee, E.A., Ghezzi, C. (eds.) Perspectives on Digital Humanism, pp. 25–29. Springer, Cham (2022). https://doi.org/10.1007/978-3-030-86144-5_4

28. Kern, C.J., Poss, L., Kroenung, J., Schönig, S.: Navigating the moral maze: a literature review of ethical values in business process management. Bus. Process. Manag. J. **30**(8), 343–370 (2024)
29. Klessascheck, F., Fahrenkrog-Petersen, S.A., Mendling, J., Pufahl, L.: Unlocking sustainability compliance: Characterizing the EU taxonomy for business process management. In: Borbinha, J., Prince Sales, T., Da Silva, M.M., Proper, H.A., Schnellmann, M. (eds.) Enterprise Design, Operations, and Computing. LNCS, vol. 15409, pp. 339–359. Springer, Cham (2024). https://doi.org/10.1007/978-3-031-78338-8_18
30. Klessascheck, F., Stiehle, F.: Business value and worker wellbeing? Foregrounding workers in process management. In: International Workshop on Enterprise Modeling and Information Systems Architectures. LNI, vol. P-362, p. 6 (2025)
31. Klessascheck, F., Weber, I., Pufahl, L.: SOPA: a framework for sustainability-oriented process analysis and re-design in business process management. In: Information Systems and e-Business Management, pp. 1–49 (2025)
32. López, H.A., Hildebrandt, T.T.: Three decades of formal methods in business process compliance: a systematic literature review. arXiv:2410.10906 (2024)
33. Mahendrawathi, E.R.: How can we develop inclusive business process management? In: Gdowska, K., Gómez-López, M.T., Rehse, JR. (eds.) Business Process Management Workshops. LNBIP, vol. 534, pp. 370–375. Springer (2024). https://doi.org/10.1007/978-3-031-78666-2_28
34. Mannhardt, F.: Responsible process mining. In: van der Aalst, W.M.P., Carmona, J. (eds.) Process Mining Handbook, LNBIP, vol. 448, pp. 373–401. Springer (2022). https://doi.org/10.1007/978-3-031-08848-3_12
35. Marrella, A.: Automated planning for business process management. J. Data Semant. **8**(2), 79–98 (2019)
36. Mostafa, S.A., Ahmad, M.S., Mustapha, A.: Adjustable autonomy: a systematic literature review. Artif. Intell. Rev. **51**(2), 149–186 (2017). https://doi.org/10.1007/s10462-017-9560-8
37. Recker, J., Rosemann, M., Hjalmarsson, A., Lind, M.: Modeling and analyzing the carbon footprint of business processes. In: vom Brocke, J., Seidel, S., Recker, J. (eds.) Green business process management: towards the sustainable enterprise, pp. 93–109. Springer, Heidelberg (2012). https://doi.org/10.1007/978-3-642-27488-6_6
38. Reichert, M., Weber, B.: Enabling flexibility in process-aware information systems: challenges, methods, technologies, vol. 54. Springer, Heidelberg (2012). https://doi.org/10.1007/978-3-642-30409-5
39. Rosemann, M., vom Brocke, J., Looy, A.V., Santoro, F.M.: Business process management in the age of AI - three essential drifts. Inf. Syst. E Bus. Manag. **22**(3), 415–429 (2024)
40. Rosemann, M., Ostern, N., Voss, M., Bandara, W.: Benevolent business processes - design guidelines beyond transactional value. In: Di Francescomarino, C., Burattin, A., Janiesch, C., Sadiq, S. (eds.) Business Process Management. LNCS, vol. 14159, pp. 447–464. Springer, Cham (2023). https://doi.org/10.1007/978-3-031-41620-0_26

A Two-Axis Framework to Map Reasons for Neurotechnology Use

Guilherme Wood[1]([⊠]) [iD], Eugen Dolezal[1,2] [iD], Lisa M. Berger[1], Petra Zandonella[1],
Thomas Gremsl[1], and Elisabeth Staudegger[1,3]

[1] University of Graz, Graz, Austria
`guilherme.wood@uni-graz.at`
[2] University of Vienna, Vienna, Austria
[3] Interdisciplinary Transformation University Austria, Linz, Austria

Abstract. Neurotechnologies, tools for recording, analyzing, and manipulating brain activity, are increasingly used for enhancement beyond their traditional roles in diagnosis and rehabilitation, introducing new challenges and risks. To navigate these ethical complexities, we propose a two-axis framework: "recovery" and "discovery". Recovery refers more closely to rehabilitative applications, while discovery pertains more to enhancement-related uses, but there are also plenty of hybrid cases, which belong to an ethical "gray zone". Our framework aids in analyzing neurotechnology use at individual, social, and cultural levels, helping to answer "what for, how, and why" questions. We also address "neuroenchantment"—the persuasive influence of these technologies—which can distort beliefs and impair critical thinking, leading to poor risk assessment. This framework helps identify such dangers, offering insights into medical, therapeutic, and regulatory strategies.

Keywords: Ethical Decision Making · Regulation · Neuroenchantment

1 Introduction

Neurotechnology, meaning any technology that is useful for diagnostic, assistive, and monitoring and modulating functions of brain activity and behavior, has a great transformative power not only over individual lives, but also societal organization and culture [1]. Neurotechnology serves different purposes such as entertainment, enhancement [2], augmentation, assistance, diagnostics, treatment, rehabilitation [3] but also military [4], and many more. Neurotechnology comes in very different degrees of invasiveness, risks, and commitment between users and providers [5]. Given this complex landscape, ethical decision making may encounter serious obstacles and be hampered by the high-pace and diversity of technological development. Accordingly, the development of an aiding framework for decision making [6] with a sufficient degree of generality as well as sensitivity to the particularities of each cutting-edge technological use is welcome. A few challenges to be tackled by such a framework will be described in the following, thereby

© The Author(s) 2026
L. Hagedorn et al. (Eds.): DIGHUM 2025, LNCS 16319, pp. 236–249, 2026.
https://doi.org/10.1007/978-3-032-11108-1_17

making clear its scope and ambition as well as orienting the reader about our motivation to propose it. This article is oriented towards the implications for the analysis of neurotechnology on different levels – individual, social and cultural – while the general background of the recovery-discovery framework was already published [7].

1.1 Literature Review

Existing frameworks in neurotechnology ethics and governance have provided crucial insights into issues such as safety, efficacy, autonomy, and informed consent. For instance, the Dual-Use framework [8] has emphasized the security risks of neuroscience advances; Responsible Research and Innovation (RRI) models [9] advocate anticipatory and participatory approaches; and principle-based bioethics [10] remains central in clinical and neuroethical decision-making. Additionally, frameworks like the Enhancement vs. Therapy Distinction [11, 12] and the Technology Acceptance Model (TAM) [13] have attempted to categorize user motives and societal implications.

While these models have shaped important debates, they tend to suffer from one or more limitations that the recovery-discovery (R/D) framework is designed to address:

Lack of motivational dimensionality: Most existing approaches categorize technologies based on their intended use (e.g., medical vs. non-medical) but fail to capture the underlying motives—especially when technologies blur the line between restoration (recovery) and exploration (discovery).

Insufficient granularity across levels of analysis: Few models offer a structured means to evaluate technology across individual, social, and cultural levels, leading to an under-theorization of how symbolic meaning, institutional structures, and personal goals interact in neurotechnology adoption.

Absence of tools to visualize ethical gray zones: The R/D framework uniquely provides a coordinate space to map ambiguous cases (e.g., neuroenhancement that also restores function), enabling stakeholders to detect ethical tensions and misalignments between user perceptions and systemic risks.

Neglect of neuroenchantment: As noted by Weisberg et al. [14] and others, neurotechnologies often carry a seductive epistemic or affective allure that skews rational decision-making. Our model introduces discovery as an analytical dimension capable of identifying when perceived novelty outpaces evidentiary grounding.

The framework thus addresses a currently unmet need: to support context-sensitive, multilevel ethical reasoning in an era where neurotechnologies are increasingly hybrid, fast-moving, and socially embedded. Rather than offering yet another checklist or binary categorization, the R/D model introduces a flexible structure that can accommodate diverse forms of technology use, map risk gradients, and promote critical self-reflection in regulatory, clinical, and individual decision-making settings.

1.2 The Recovery-Discovery (R/D) Framework

The R/D framework offers a structured approach to assessing neurotechnology use by mapping each intervention within a two-dimensional space defined by restorative (recovery) and exploratory (discovery) motives. Neurotechnology use is understood as the intentional application of a tool to achieve a specific aim. This choice can be well-informed or misguided depending on the availability of information to build an informed decision on that specific neurotechnology as well as on the availability of critical thinking during the decision process [6]. This framework enables the classification of interventions along a continuum, capturing the overlap of therapeutic and enhancement functions, and revealing motivational structures, temporal expectations, and varying levels of risk. It accounts for how the same technology can be differently interpreted on the individual, social, or cultural level and it offers a tool for nuanced ethical reflection across levels of analysis. A summary of the distinguishing features of both dimensions is presented in Table 1 to guide consistent and context-sensitive evaluations.

Table 1. Comparison of Recovery and Discovery in a Nutshell.

	Recovery	Discovery
Attributes	Restoration, regeneration	Innovation, optimization, exploration, creation
Outcome	Return to a familiar and desired state	Exploration of unfamiliar territory
Temporal structure	Circular, return to a desirable state	Linear, future- oriented
Purpose	The only purpose of recovery is itself	Purpose is epistemic (knowledge production) or pragmatic discoveries (new ways to solve a problem)
Orientation	Cohesion, centripetal	Disruption, centrifugal
Metrics	0 to 100%	0 to infinite and beyond

1.3 Recovery

The recovery dimension captures all motivations aimed at restoring a prior, desirable state—such as health, psychological well-being, or even restorative entertainment. Its function is inherently self-referential: recovery seeks only to recover, regaining stability and capacity to enable further activity. Oriented centripetally and governed by circular temporality [15], it aims to re-establish coherence and return to a known condition. Recovery is quantifiable from 0% (no need) to 100% (maximum need), and in health-related neurotechnology, always carries a non-zero component. Standardized tools like the ICD and ICF support operational classification, yet reflect embedded cultural assumptions and may oversimplify nuanced, context-specific experiences. To mitigate this, we propose a hybrid approach—employing such tools at the individual level while integrating social and cultural dimensions to capture broader meanings of recovery. High-recovery scenarios, such as treatment for illness, may justify higher risk, but even leisure applications (e.g. a BCI game used to relax) can contain measurable recovery elements. Conversely, if the same game is played competitively, the motivation shifts toward discovery, as, for example, the focus is not on returning to a state of wellbeing but rather on progressively improving within some metrics. Ultimately, the ethical assessment of recovery-oriented neurotechnology use depends on clearly defining the level of analysis—individual, social, or cultural—with each requiring specific reference anchors to ensure valid interpretation.

1.4 Discovery

The discovery dimension is driven by exploration, curiosity, and the pursuit of enhancement, aiming to extend individual capabilities or understanding through productive engagement. Its function lies in generating novel outcomes—either epistemic (knowledge creation) or pragmatic (new techniques or tools) [16, 17]—within a linear temporality oriented toward the future and marked by a centrifugal drive that challenges norms and fosters transformation. Discovery unfolds along an open-ended continuum, where higher values reflect greater innovation, risk, and goal-seeking not grounded in prior loss. While recovery seeks restoration, discovery aspires to exceed baselines, often involving non-compensatory risk and visionary motivations such as cognitive enhancement or bodily augmentation. Like recovery, discovery must be interpreted according to the chosen level of analysis: at the individual level, it centers on self-directed goals and personal transformation; however, these aspirations are always shaped by social and cultural imaginaries of improvement, which must be acknowledged to ensure ethically grounded and context-sensitive evaluations of discovery-oriented neurotechnology use. For a more detailed description of how to obtain valid measurements to locate technologies within the R/D-plot see Wood et al. [7].

2 Disentangling Three Levels of Analysis

As described in the previous section, recovery and discovery can serve as the axis of a diagram for analyses at different levels: individual, social, and cultural. This allows to evaluate the ethical, functional, and sociocultural dimensions of neurotechnology use. Each level offers a distinct perspective on neurotechnology, guided by different fundamental questions: "What is the individual trying to accomplish?" (individual), "How is it integrated and regulated?" (social), and "Why a neurotechnology is developed and employed?" (cultural). These guiding questions highlight not only different agents of analysis but also different epistemic and normative structures that condition the meaning and consequences of technology use.

At the individual level, neurotechnology is assessed from the standpoint of personal agency, intention, and embodied experience, reflecting personal goals, beliefs, emotions, vulnerabilities, and identities [7]. Recovery and discovery here are understood in terms of individual motives, subjective benefit, risk perception, and personal autonomy. It is the user's frame of reference that anchors the analysis: What is the purpose of this use? How does it affect the user's well-being, identity, or capacities? How is the balance between restoration and exploration perceived or pursued?

The social level[1] shifts the analytical focus to institutions (e.g. healthcare systems, universities, military, corporations, social and regulatory bodies), norms, and collective

---

[1] Within the (German) social ethical discourse culture-based frameworks of meaning and interpretation as well as domains of social life and their respective functions are discussed alongside

practices and aligns well with sociological theories of agency, normativity, and collective imaginaries [19, p. 120]. Here, the relevant agents are not individual persons but social organizations—such as healthcare systems, companies, social and regulatory bodies, or educational institutions—that structure access, regulate standards, distribute risks, and define acceptable practices. The social level asks how neurotechnologies are assessed, operationalized, distributed, standardized, or constrained. It includes concerns such as data governance, safety certification, reimbursement policies, and professional guidelines as well as accessibility. Discovery and recovery at this level are measured by systemic consequences, fair distribution of operational risks and (potential) benefits, and distributional justice.

Approaching the recovery-discovery framework at the cultural level, with culture understood as the highest symbolic reference system, means engaging with the foundational meaning-making structures through which societies define: What is worth restoring (recovery) and what is worth seeking or transcending (discovery), and how technologies mediate these meanings [20, 21]. At this level, we are no longer asking how institutions function or individuals act, but rather why certain actions are perceived as meaningful, desirable, or, in some cases, acceptable. The cultural level adds yet another layer, focusing on the symbolic orders and narrative logics through which whole societies orient themselves. This level addresses the deeper "why": Why are certain forms of enhancement celebrated, while others are stigmatized? Why are some risks tolerated and others pathologized? Culture here refers to the meta-level of shared meanings, cosmotechnics [22], moral imaginaries, and the collective visions of what it means to be human in a technologically mediated world. Concepts like neuroenchantment [23], dignity, freedom, or the acceptable boundaries of self-gain prominence. We are aware that these examples are shaped by the shared cultural experience of the authors, while in other cultures different concepts would be seen as more relevant in the context of neurotechnology. This exact reason makes the consideration of the cultural dimension even more important as it allows for a culture sensitive evaluation of neurotechnological applications. While not always visible in individual choices or social regulations and structures, these cultural imaginaries deeply shape both [24].

Although these three levels are intertwined in practice, they must be analytically distinguished, because the concepts and metrics used to evaluate recovery and discovery differ at each level. The same neurotechnology may occupy different positions in the recovery-discovery (R/D) plot depending on the level under consideration. For example, an individual using a wearable app to monitor sleep quality might regard it as a low-discovery, moderate-recovery tool—something that improves daily well-being with minimal disruption or risk. Yet, at the social level, this same app may be part of a growing infrastructure of biometric tracking that alters employment conditions, insurance models, or educational accountability. At the cultural level, it may reflect and reinforce a broader shift toward technoableism [25] quantified selfhood, optimization ideologies,

---

other aspects under the term "society" (= Gesellschaft), as those aspects intertwine and affect each other [18, p. 39]. To allow for a more differentiated mapping of neurotechnology and improved interdisciplinary connectivity we decided for the described division into the social and cultural sphere for the R/D framework.

or even latent forms of technosolutionism [26]—where bodily functions are reframed as problems solvable through data.[2]

These divergences underscore the importance of level-sensitive ethical evaluation. Without such differentiation, we risk conflating individual benefit with systemic neutrality or overlooking how culturally embedded values shape what appears to be merely a "functional" tool. By applying the recovery-discovery framework at these three levels, we not only gain precision in classification, but also a richer understanding of the ethical terrain. This multilevel perspective allows for the detection of gray zones, misalignments, and hidden tensions, offering a versatile yet structured method for assessing the complex implications of neurotechnological innovation.

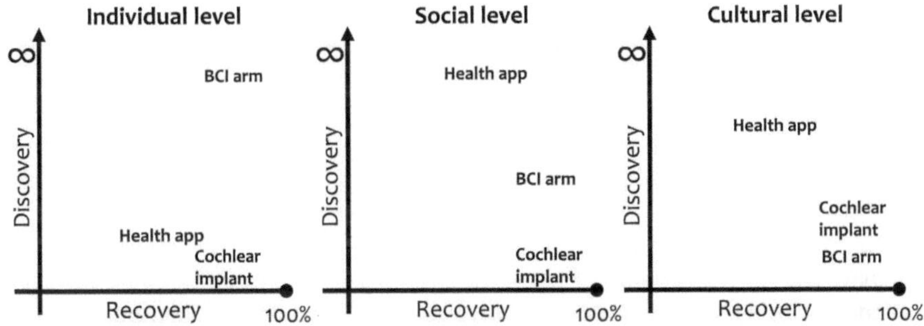

Fig. 1. Three-level representation of neurotechnology use within the recovery-discovery framework. The x-axis denotes recovery, ranging from 0% (no recovery component) to 100% (maximum recovery orientation). The y-axis denotes discovery, conceptualized as an open-ended dimension representing increasing levels of novelty, risk, and epistemic uncertainty. Each panel represents a distinct level of analysis: individual (left), social (center), and cultural (right). The positioning of selected neurotechnologies (cochlear implant, health app, BCI-controlled prosthetic arm) illustrates how the same technology can occupy differing coordinates across analytical levels, reflecting shifts in motivation, function, and symbolic impact.

To illustrate the analytical flexibility and granularity of the recovery-discovery framework, we developed a diagram featuring three distinct R/D plots, each representing one of the analytical levels: individual, social, and cultural. Due to our cultural background, the analysis in regard to the cultural dimension will be grounded upon a western perspective. Within each plot, we localized three representative neurotechnologies—cochlear implants, health monitoring apps, and brain-computer interface (BCI)-controlled prosthetic arms—based on their respective recovery and discovery profiles at each level of analysis (see Fig. 1).

Cochlear implants serve as an example of consistent and well-established recovery-oriented neurotechnological use [27]. Across all three levels—individual, social, and

---

[2] Neuroenchantment denotes the particular epistemic and affective allure of neuroscience-based tools, often leading to overestimated claims of efficacy or objectivity, while technosolutionism broadly describes the tendency to frame complex human problems as solvable through technical means alone.

cultural—they occupy positions marked by high recovery and low discovery. At the individual level, the technology restores a lost sensory modality with relatively predictable outcomes, grounded in robust clinical evidence and therapeutic goals. At the social level, cochlear implants are integrated into existing medical infrastructures and reimbursement frameworks as well as social institutions and groups that aim at aiding auditorily impaired people and promote their autonomy, reflecting social acceptance and regulatory standardization. Culturally, they align with shared symbolic values around health, normalcy, and communication, without challenging dominant paradigms of human enhancement or identity. However, in the Deaf community they are partly seen as controversial, as Cochlear Implants threaten their cultural identity.

In contrast, health monitoring apps (e.g., wearables for sleep, heart rate, or stress levels) display a discordant pattern across the three levels of analysis. While the recovery component remains moderate and relatively stable—reflecting their utility for maintaining or improving personal well-being—the discovery component diverges significantly. At the individual level, discovery is often perceived as low: the apps deliver anticipated functionalities that conform to the user's goals with minimal disruption or novelty. However, at the social level, these technologies participate in broader trends of biometric surveillance, algorithmic health profiling, and behavioral nudging—raising the discovery value due to the emergent and largely underregulated systemic transformations they enable. At the cultural level, they contribute to a reconfiguration of bodily self-understanding, shifting normative ideals toward constant optimization and quantification. This asymmetry in discovery values underscores how technologies perceived as benign or routine by individuals may carry radically different implications when examined from broader vantage points.

The third case, BCI-controlled prosthetic arms, presents an inverse configuration. For the individual user, the integration of a brain-controlled bionic limb represents a high-discovery event: the person must recalibrate their bodily schema, adapt to novel sensorimotor dynamics, and reconfigure their identity in the face of enhanced or synthetic agency. The recovery value is also significant, as the device restores functional autonomy. Yet, at the social level, BCI prosthetics tend to occupy a more stabilized space. Their functions—restoring grasp, mobility, or interaction—are legible and legitimate within established medical and rehabilitative norms. Institutions integrate them under innovation policies, but they do not challenge systemic frameworks. At the cultural level, their symbolic resonance is mitigated by pre-existing narratives of prosthesis and cyborg enhancement already embedded in collective imaginaries. While their transformative power is deeply personal, they do not, in their current forms, provoke paradigm shifts in societal or civilizational self-understanding.

This multilevel depiction demonstrates how the same neurotechnology can assume different ethical, functional, and symbolic significance depending on the level of analysis. By making these variations explicit, the recovery-discovery framework enables a more nuanced and reflexive understanding of neurotechnology use, offering a tool for multi-perspective evaluation that respects both individual experiences and societal structures, while remaining attentive to cultural meaning systems. Importantly, the non-alignment of discovery values across levels cautions against the oversimplification of risk-benefit assessments and highlights the need for level-specific governance strategies.

3 Applying the Multilevel Analysis to Specific Topics in Neurotechnology Use

In the following, we apply the recovery-discovery framework to four specific challenging topics.

3.1 Ethical Decision Making

To further specify how neurotechnologies shape moral landscapes beyond the individual level, we draw on Peter-Paul Verbeek's distinction between pragmatic and hermeneutic forms of moral mediation [21, pp. 82–84]. Technologies, in this view, are not passive tools but actively mediate human-world relations, including moral perception and action. We propose that this conceptual pair can be productively mapped onto the social and cultural dimensions of our framework, enabling a more nuanced analysis of how neurotechnology mediates ethical agency, social roles, and value systems on one hand and that it can act positively towards operationalization of the social and cultural dimension of our framework on the other hand.

The social sphere, understood as the domain of institutions, norms, and collective practices, corresponds to what Verbeek terms pragmatic moral mediation. Here, technologies shape the conditions under which moral decisions are made by modifying the structure of action itself: what can or must be done, by whom, and under what constraints [21, p. 82]. For example, the integration of cognitive enhancement devices in workplace settings may shift expectations of performance, accountability, and even the thresholds for competence just because of their pure existence. With the rise of new technology and its usage options to choose from are added or subtracted from our decision problems and simultaneously the costs and benefits of morally charged actions are affected [20, p. 4]. These shifts are not neutral but carry implicit normative weight, as they redefine what counts as responsible or ethical conduct in specific institutional contexts.

The cultural sphere, by contrast, aligns with Verbeek's notion of hermeneutic moral mediation, which means the way technologies influence how we perceive and interpret morally salient aspects of the world [21, p. 84]. Neurotechnologies, particularly when integrated into daily life (e.g., through self-tracking, brain stimulation, or diagnostic imaging), participate in shaping how concepts such as autonomy, normality, or personhood are culturally understood. They act as interpretive devices that render certain dimensions of human experience more visible, measurable, or actionable. By this they are often privileging particular epistemologies and value systems in the process. In this way, the cultural sphere becomes a site of symbolic negotiation, where the moral implications of technology are not only enacted but also imagined, challenged, or reinforced.

Applying Verbeek's framework to our model allows to highlight two complementary modes of technological normativity: one that modulates moral agency through altered practices (social/pragmatic), and one that reshapes moral meaning through interpretive shifts (cultural/hermeneutic). This dual perspective enables a richer ethical reflection, sensitive not only to institutional transformations but also to the culturally embedded values that inform and are informed by technological mediation.

The Value of Cultural Contexts in Ethical Assessment. An important advantage of the recovery–discovery framework lies in its capacity to support culturally sensitive ethics. By explicitly including a cultural sphere alongside individual and social dimensions, the framework allows for the systematic identification of normative value orientations that shape the reception, use, and contestation of neurotechnologies across different cultural contexts. Moral values such as autonomy, dignity, well-being, or control do not carry identical meanings or weight in all societies; their interpretation is deeply embedded in cultural narratives, moral traditions, and social imaginaries. As such, ethical analyses that presuppose a universal normative semantic risk overlooking crucial tensions and blind spots. The framework's attention to cultural mediation, informed by Verbeek's notion of hermeneutic moral mediation, enables to better grasp how technologies become embedded within, and at times challenge, local moral worlds and morality as a whole. This sensitivity to cultural variation is especially relevant in the global diffusion of neurotechnologies, where ethical legitimacy depends not only on functional outcomes or procedural and distributive fairness, but also on whether these technologies resonate with, or undermine, existing moral frameworks. By making cultural meaning structures analytically visible, the recovery–discovery framework could contribute to more inclusive and contextually grounded ethical assessments, by serving as a basis for discussion. Additionally, it has to be acknowledged that values and normative priorities are not static [28]. This dynamic affects not only different regions of the world, but is also evident within individual societies. For our two-axis scale, this means that classifications are contingent on time and can shift as value priorities change. The scale should therefore not be understood as a static classification, but as a framework that can be flexibly adapted to regularly changing cultural and temporal contexts.

3.2   Legal Considerations

The benefits of the recovery-discovery framework from a legal perspective have already been outlined in the IEEE paper; briefly summarized, the added value is the visualization of the motivation behind the use of neurotechnology [7]. These three levels —individual, social and cultural— enable to differentiate this motivation further, to better visualize the risk of use in different contexts. In doing so, we do not base the meaning of risk on the legal understanding as a "combination of the probability of an occurrence of harm and the severity of that harm" (as in Article 3(2) of Regulation (EU) 2024/1689), but instead we orientate our point of view with Beck´s understanding of a "semantic risk", with two facets "danger" and "opportunity" [29]. This understanding allows both the advantages and disadvantages of technology to be considered and helps to avoid misunderstanding technologies solely from the perspective of a risk that can be assessed or even calculated. The understanding chosen here is particularly relevant for the discovery dimension, which is intended to map a journey into the increasingly unknown.

At the individual level, the individual decision on the use of neurotechnology, the recovery-discovery framework, facilitates orientation regarding informed consent. As stated, a fundamental principle of law, informed consent (expressly guaranteed, for example, in Article 3(2)(a) of the Charter of Fundamental Rights of the European Union), requires that a potential user of neurotechnology can make a free, informed and self-determined decision about the actual use of the technology. This requires sufficient information about the dangers as well as about the expected benefits of using the technology. The illustration of motivation using the two-axis framework with a view to health and therapeutic purposes and the restoration of a known status on the one hand and curiosity and a thirst for adventure on the other. This can help users to better assess the imponderable dangers and more or less calculable risks that they wish to accept on an individual basis: The closer the technology is to the recovery dimension, the better known and better investigated are the expectable risks; the higher it the neurotechnology is located on the discovery dimension, the more unknown and therefore incalculable are the dangers and opportunities.

At the social level, law should be understood here with Luhmann as a social subsystem with the function of controlling human behavior. The overarching, indeed, the only goal of legal norms is to set expectations for an unknown and genuinely uncertain future [30, p. 130]. In contrast to the legal theory literature, Luhmann's functional definition does not focus on the essential characteristics of legal norms, but rather on the possibility of distinguishing behavior in the event of disappointment [30, p. 133]. With this orientation of the legal concept, the suitability of the recovery-discovery framework for decisions on the regulation of the development, provision and use of neurotechnologies becomes particularly clear: the visualization of the motivation for the use of neurotechnology makes it easier to classify the appropriateness of existing regulations with regard to the reasonable risk between recovery and discovery. Following on from the individual level, the framework provides points of reference for the harmonization of information obligations, which must disclose the limits of what is known. At the core of legislative action is, of course, the comprehensive task of the legislator to strike a balance between protection and freedom in the use of neurotechnologies, namely, to prescribe the necessary protective measures on the one hand and to maintain the freedom for self-improvement, further development and discovery on the other.

At the cultural level, we focus with Hiebaum [31] on culture as a largely purpose-driven categorization of human values and behavior. This primarily enables the differentiation and comparison of different groups, i.e. cultures [31, p 14 et seqq.]. By illustrating the motivation behind the use of neurotechnology, the recovery-discovery framework makes it possible to locate, recognize and consider the different global ideas about the value of recovery and discovery. It thus functionally ties in with the Universal Declaration of Human Rights, which enshrines the right to the protection of universal human dignity inherent in every human being in a global consensus. However, it still leaves space for cultures to develop their own understanding within this agreed framework. The recovery-discovery framework presented here thus represents a comprehensive approach that can be useful globally.

Overall, the recovery-discovery framework provides a valuable contribution to safeguarding "digital humanity" in the context of legal decision-making at all the three (individual, social and cultural) levels.

3.3 Promoting Objectivity in Neuroscientific Research

How can we avoid falling into neuroenchantment or scientific mythmaking [23, 32] when the apparent promises of discovery exceed the robustness of evidence? The proposed recovery-discovery framework is positioned here as a conceptual tool that can aid not only in ethical evaluation but also in increasing epistemic clarity and responsibility in neuroscientific research and communication. High discovery motives paired with low evidentiary foundations form a fertile ground for neurohype—where technological novelty is mistaken for epistemic validity. The framework, then, acts as a diagnostic instrument, exposing where motivations to explore or innovate run ahead of what is scientifically justifiable.

At the individual level, the framework helps identify the cognitive and motivational asymmetry experienced by neurotechnology users—especially early adopters or research participants. These individuals may be driven by personal hope, curiosity, or existential desire for transformation, which leads them to accept risks or speculative claims with insufficient skepticism. Concepts such as narrative identity, agency, and eudaimonic motivation are central here: what individuals pursue as "discovery" may in fact be a projection of future selfhood—imagined but not yet grounded in empirical possibility. In this sense, the framework fosters self-awareness: it allows individuals to understand where their subjective motivations might outpace the objective capacity of the technology. This is especially important when experimental interventions promise effects related to intelligence, mood, creativity, or "unlocking potential"—claims that, while appealing, often rely more on symbolic power than on validated outcomes.

At the social level, the framework functions as a corrective to what might be called scientific performativity: the process by which expectations shape research agendas, funding priorities, and institutional discourse. High-discovery, low-recovery interventions often enjoy social prestige—being seen as "cutting edge" or "transformative"—even when empirical support is weak. This creates a feedback loop: researchers, institutions, and companies may begin to promise more than they can deliver because discovery is culturally coded as a virtue, while caution is interpreted as resistance to innovation. Here, the framework functions like a sociotechnical radar, alerting researchers and policymakers to zones of conceptual inflation. When mapped explicitly, a cluster of interventions located in the high-discovery/low-recovery quadrant could signal an area that requires epistemic demarcation, regulatory scrutiny, or methodological recalibration. Rather than stifling innovation, this enables a healthier innovation of ecology by distinguishing between exploration and exaggeration. Moreover, it aids in identifying gaps in standardization: many emerging neurotechnologies bypass formal medical regulation because they fall outside the recovery domain. But they still carry significant psychosocial risks. The framework thus supports a call for new normative instruments—perhaps akin to "discovery ethics"—that can guide development without waiting for clinical legitimacy.

At the cultural level, this challenge confronts a deep-rooted phenomenon: the symbolic power of the brain in contemporary Western imaginaries. The allure of neuroscience [33] lies not just in its data but in its narrative function—the way it reinforces beliefs about control, intelligence, authenticity, and human uniqueness. This is where neuromyths arise [32]: not simply as false beliefs, but as culturally potent stories that exceed their scientific basis. Terms like "neuroplasticity", "brain optimization", or "cognitive upgrade" become moralized and mythologized. The recovery-discovery framework acts as a semantic brake—a way to pause and question what kind of symbolic transaction is taking place when we adopt a new neurotechnology. Is this an act of restoration (with shared cultural agreement on what is "normal" or "healthy"), or is it an act of reinvention (with contested cultural stakes)? Mapping technologies in this way also shows where science turns into ideology, and where epistemic humility must counterbalance aspirational discourse.

In conclusion, the neurotech-hype challenge highlights the framework's value not only as a tool of ethical orientation, but also as an epistemological filter and cultural mirror. It helps clarify the motivational asymmetries of individuals, the discursive risks of institutions, and the myth-making dynamics of cultures that project their hopes and fears onto the brain. By identifying where discovery exceeds evidence, it invites a form of disciplined wonder—open to possibility but anchored in responsibility.

4   Conclusions

This paper introduces the recovery-discovery framework as a two axis to map and assess neurotechnology use. By positioning interventions along two axes—recovery (restorative reason) and discovery (exploratory or enhancement reason)—the framework enables structured analysis of motives, risk expectations, and decision-making contexts. It addresses a previously unfilled gap between existing models of rehabilitation and enhancement, while also offering a means to detect and critically assess neuroenchantment.

Through examples ranging from cochlear implants to invasive BCI implants, the framework demonstrates its ability to visualize ethical gray zones and highlights when normative evaluation must go beyond clinical risk-benefit analysis. It thus contributes to more transparent and generalizable ethical reasoning.

Future research should explore how participatory elements, especially user perspectives, can be systematically integrated into the framework. In addition, the time dynamics of recovery and discovery values deserve further analysis, as technologies evolve and their ethical status shifts with changing knowledge and societal uptake.

Acknowledgments. This paper is based on research projects supported by the Panel for the Future of Science and Technology (STOA) and the Zukunftsfond Steiermark (PN: 1619) as well as the vice-rectorate for Internationalization and Equal Opportunities of the University of Graz for the financial support given to four PhD students.

Disclosure of Interests. The authors have no competing interests.

References

1. Wood, G.M.O., et al.: The protection of mental privacy in the area of neuroscience – Societal, legal and ethical challenges, European Parliament, Brussels (2024). https://doi.org/10.2861/869928
2. Dresler, M., et al.: Hacking the brain: dimensions of cognitive enhancement. ACS Chem. Neurosci. **10**(3), 1137–1148 (2018). https://doi.org/10.1021/acschemneuro.8b00571

3. Wilson, B.A.: Neuropsychological rehabilitation. Annu. Rev. Clin. Psychol. **4**(1), 141–162 (2008). https://doi.org/10.1146/annurev.clinpsy.4.022007.141212

4. Claverie, B., Du Cluzel, F.: "Cognitive warfare": the advent of the concept of "cognitics" in the field of warfare. Cognitive Warfare: the future of cognitive dominance, 2–1 (2022). https://hal.science/hal-03635889. Accessed 11 Jan 2025

5. Grinschgl, S., Ninaus, M., Wood, G., Neubauer, A.C.: To enhance or not to enhance: a debate about cognitive enhancement from a psychological and neuroscientific perspective. Phys. Life Rev. **54**, 58–77 (2025). https://doi.org/10.1016/j.plrev.2025.05.002

6. De Martino, B., Kumaran, D., Seymour, B., Dolan, R.J.: Frames, biases, and rational decision-making in the human brain. Science **313**(5787), 684–687 (2006). https://doi.org/10.1126/science.1128356

7. Wood, G.M.O., Dolezal, E., Berger, L.M., Zandonella, P., Gremsl, T., Staudegger, E.: Tackling Neuroenchantment: a multiperspective approach. In: Proceedings of the Systems, Cybernetics and Man IEEE Conference, in print (2025)

8. Moreno, J.D.: Mind Wars: Brain Research and National Defense. Dana Press, New York (2006). ISBN-13 : 978-1934137437

9. Stilgoe, J., Owen, R., Macnaghten, P.: Developing a framework for responsible innovation. Res. Policy **42**(9), 1568–1580 (2013). https://doi.org/10.1016/j.respol.2013.05.008

10. Beauchamp, T.L., Childress, J.F.: Principles of Biomedical Ethics, 8th edn. Oxford University Press, Oxford (2019)

11. Juengst, E.T.: What does enhancement mean? In: Parens, E. (ed.) Enhancing human traits: Ethical and social implications, pp. 29–47. Georgetown University Press, Washington, D.C. (1998). NLM Unique ID 100953026

12. Parens, E.: Authenticity and ambivalence: toward understanding the enhancement debate. Hastings Cent. Rep. **35**(3), 34–41 (2005). https://doi.org/10.1353/hcr.2005.0067

13. Davis, F.D.: Perceived usefulness, perceived ease of use, and user acceptance of information technology. MIS Q. **13**(3), 319–340 (1989). https://doi.org/10.2307/249008

14. Weisberg, D.S., Keil, F.C., Goodstein, J., Rawson, E., Gray, J.R.: The seductive allure of neuroscience explanations. J. Cogn. Neurosci. **20**(3), 470–477 (2008). https://doi.org/10.1162/jocn.2008.20040

15. Han, B.C.: Vom Verschwinden der Rituale: Eine Topologie der Gegenwart. Ullstein Buchverlage, Berlin (2019). ISBN 978-3-550-05071-8

16. Friston, K., Rigoli, F., Ognibene, D., Mathys, C., Fitzgerald, T., Pezzulo, G.: Active inference and epistemic value. Cogn. Neurosci. **6**(4), 187–214 (2015). https://doi.org/10.1080/17588928.2015.1020053

17. Constant, A., Ramstead, M.J., Veissière, S.P., Friston, K.: Regimes of expectations: an active inference model of social conformity and human decision making. Front. Psychol. **10**, 1–15 (2019). https://doi.org/10.3389/fpsyg.2019.00679

18. Frühbauer, J., Heimbach-Steins, M.: Sozialethik und Gesellschaftstheorie. In: Heimbach-Steins M., Becka M., Frühbauer, J. J., Kruip, G. (eds.), Christliche Sozialethik: Grundlagen, Kontexte, Themen. Ein Lehr- und Studienbuch, pp. 31–46. Verlag Friedrich Pustet, Regensburg (2022). https://doi.org/10.17879/55069716034

19. Jasanoff, S., Kim, S.-H.: Containing the atom: sociotechnical imaginaries and nuclear power in the United States and South Korea. Minerva **47**, 119–146 (2009). https://doi.org/10.1007/s11024-009-9124-4

20. Danaher, J., Sætra, H.S.: Technology and moral change: the transformation of truth and trust. Ethics Inf. Technol. **24**(3), 1–16 (2022). https://doi.org/10.1007/s10676-022-09661-y

21. Verbeek, P.-P.: Some misunderstandings about the moral significance of technology. In: Kroes, P., Verbeek, P.-P. (eds.), The Moral Status of Technical Artefacts, pp. 75–88. Springer, Netherlands (2014). https://doi.org/10.1007/978-94-007-7914-3_5

22. Hui, Y.: On Cosmotechnics: for a renewed relation between technology and nature in the anthropocene. Techne: Res. Philos. Technol. **21**(2/3), 319–341 (2017). https://doi.org/10.5840/techne201711876
23. Ali, S.S., Lifshitz, M., Raz, A.: Empirical neuroenchantment: from reading minds to thinking critically. Front. Hum. Neurosci. **8**, 1–4 (2014). https://doi.org/10.3389/fnhum.2014.00357
24. Littlefield, M.: Instrumental Intimacy EEG Wearables and Neuroscientific Control, 1st edn. Johns Hopkins University Press, Baltimore (2018). ISBN 9781421424651
25. Shew, A.: Ableism, technoableism, and future AI. IEEE Technol. Soc. Mag. **39**(1), 40–85 (2020). https://doi.org/10.1109/MTS.2020.2967492
26. Lindtner, S., Bardzell, S., Bardzell, J.: Reconstituting the utopian vision of making: HCI after technosolutionism. In: Proceedings of the 2016 Chi Conference on Human Factors in Computing Systems, pp. 1390–1402. Association for Computing Machinery, New York (2016). https://doi.org/10.1145/2858036.2858506
27. Zeng, F.-G., Rebscher, S., Harrison, W., Sun, X., Feng, H.: Cochlear implants: system design, integration, and evaluation. IEEE Rev. Biomed. Eng. **1**, 115–142 (2008). https://doi.org/10.1109/RBME.2008.2008250
28. Abramson, P.R., Inglehart, R.: Value Change in Global Perspective. University of Michigan Press, Ann Arbor (1995). https://doi.org/10.3998/mpub.23627
29. Beck, U.: Weltrisikogesellschaft: Auf der Suche nach der verlorenen Sicherheit. Suhrkamp, Frankfurt am Main (2007). ISBN 978-3-518-46038-2
30. Luhmann, N.: Das Recht der Gesellschaft. Suhrkamp, Frankfurt am Main (1993). ISBN 978-3-518-28783-5
31. Hiebaum, C.: Law and its cultural representations (with a focus on heavy metal studies). In: Pichler, P. (ed.) The Law of the Metal Scene: An Interdisciplinary Discussion, pp. 11–28. Kohlhammer, Stuttgart (2024). ISBN 978-3-17-043463-9
32. van Elk, M.: Socio-cognitive biases are associated to belief in neuromyths and cognitive enhancement: a pre-registered study. Pers. Individ. Differ. **147**, 28–32 (2019). https://doi.org/10.1016/j.paid.2019.04.014
33. Weisberg, D.S., Taylor, J.C.V., Hopkins, E.J.: Deconstructing the seductive allure of neuroscience explanations. Judgm. Decis. Mak. **10**(5), 429–441 (2015). https://doi.org/10.1017/S193029750000557X

Digital Humanism in Political and Social Sciences

Narrated Future: How Narratives Shape Our Digital Present

Betina Aumair and Doris Vickers[✉]

Die Wiener Volkshochschulen GmbH, Lustkandlgasse 50, 1090 Wien, Austria
`doris.vickers@vhs.at`

Abstract. This article explores how competing narratives shape our understanding and governance of digitalisation, focusing on the ideological opposition between Cyberlibertarianism and Digital Humanism. While technological and economic frameworks often dominate public discourse, the underlying narratives that inform these perspectives exert significant influence on policy, societal norms, and democratic possibilities. Cyberlibertarianism promotes a vision of individual freedom rooted in technological autonomy and market deregulation, often marginalising ethical concerns, and reinforcing corporate power. In contrast, Digital Humanism offers a counter-narrative that centres human dignity, democratic participation, and social responsibility in the design and application of digital technologies.

The article examines these narratives as ideologically charged patterns of interpretation that structure what is perceived as technologically inevitable or politically possible. It critiques the discursive framing of Cyberlibertarianism, particularly its depoliticisation of democracy and appropriation of emancipatory language, which masks power imbalances and limits public deliberation. Digital Humanism is presented as a necessary ideological intervention that reclaims digital spaces as culturally, ethically, and politically negotiable.

Education emerges as a central arena for cultivating critical awareness of these narratives.

Keywords: Digital Humanism · Cyberlibertarianism · Technopolitical Narratives · Democratic Digital Governance

1   Introduction

Public discourse on digitalisation is often dominated by technological and economic perspectives. What tends to be overlooked is the influence of stories and narratives that shape our perception, inform our judgements, and thus also influence political decisions and social developments.

In the digital age, various interpretive frameworks compete for cultural dominance. This article focuses on two prominent ones. On the one hand, Cyberlibertarianism with its emphasis on radical market ideologies of freedom and the alignment of technology with right-wing ideologies. On the other, Digital Humanism, which offers a counterbalance through its ethical, human-centred, and democracy-oriented approach. These narratives

L. Hagedorn et al. (Eds.): DIGHUM 2025, LNCS 16319, pp. 253–262, 2026.
https://doi.org/10.1007/978-3-032-11108-1_18

are by no means mere side effects; rather, they profoundly structure what is considered technologically possible, socially desirable, and politically viable.

This article analyses these competing systems of meaning and explores their ideological impact. Central to this exploration is the argument that Digital Humanism functions as a necessary counter-narrative to Cyberlibertarianism. To clarify the use of the term, we understand "counter-narrative" not simply as a rhetorical opposition, but as a discursive practice that disrupts dominant and normative frameworks. As Walsh [23] argues, counter-narratives expose how prevailing stories naturalise inequalities, while making alternative perspectives and futures visible. In this sense, Digital Humanism does not only illustrate resistance to Cyberlibertarian ideology but functions as a counter-narrative in the full conceptual sense: it reframes what is considered possible, desirable, and legitimate within digital society.

Critically reflecting on these narratives is essential to achieving democratic self-determination in the digital era. Education plays a decisive role in enabling individuals to question, comprehend, and reshape these interpretive frameworks.

Although the terms 'Cyberlibertarianism' and 'Digital Humanism' have not yet become firmly embedded in public discourse and appear only sporadically in academic and political debates, they represent highly effective ideological frameworks in the practical implementation of digitalisation and social digitality. This article examines them as theoretical condensations of discursive structures that characterise the technological development, political shaping, and social interpretation of digital processes.

2   Cyberlibertarianism as a Hegemonic Narrative

The term Cyberlibertarianism is employed by David Golumbia, especially in his book of the same name. Today, we are witnessing an increasing convergence of Big Tech with right-wing populist forces. Examples include figures like Elon Musk and Donald Trump, who use both their wealth and their political power to undermine democratic legal frameworks and bolster right-wing populist movements, including in Europe [22]. Golumbia shows that this convergence is rooted in the ideology of Cyberlibertarianism. Related terms include the Californian ideology and techno-libertarianism.

Libertarianism is a political ideology that prioritises individual freedom, personal responsibility, and minimal government intervention. It assumes that individuals have the right to exercise near-unlimited control over themselves and their property. In its more radical forms, the role of the state is reduced (or even rejected entirely) except in functions like providing security and legal protection for the autonomous individual and their property. Trust in free markets as the natural order of social interaction is central to this worldview. Redistribution or regulation is perceived as an infringement on personal autonomy.

Cyberlibertarianism adapts this ideology of the digital realm, envisioning the digital space as a space of radical individual freedom and ejecting any state intervention or regulatory attempt as a threat to liberty. For Golumbia, Cyberlibertarianism is not a coherent ideology, but a collection of different, sometimes contradictory ideas. He writes: "This is how Cyberlibertarianism works: it's not so much about party politics but about controlling the terms of the discourse and the conversation itself. This ensures that only variations of right-wing political formations are brought to the table, and all concerns are subsumed under the general belief that digital technology will inevitably make things better, even if "better" is never precisely defined" [9].

The term dates back to Langdon Winner's 1997 article, written when the internet was still in its infancy. According to Winner, free-market capitalism, individualism, and technological determinism are core elements of Cyberlibertarian ideology [26].

It is important to stress that Cyberlibertarianism does not present a unified ideology, but rather a set of shared ideas, attitudes and behaviours centred around individual freedom, technological inevitability, and market fundamentalism. Golumbia directs attention not to formal political agendas, but to the underlying discursive rules through which certain perspectives such as market-liberalism, techno-optimism, or anti-government sentiments are rendered self-evident, while others are marginalised.

This discursive power is particularly effective because it does not present itself as ideological. Instead, it appears rational, inevitable, or progressive.

3   Digital Humanism as a Counter-Narrative

This is where Digital Humanism intervenes. It presents a different narrative: not one of inevitable technological progress, but of the democratic designability of digital systems. Digital Humanism breaks open discursive monopolies by reintroducing concepts such as responsibility, the common good, human dignity and participation back into the digital conversation. It not only introduces new content but also adopts a narrative form that challenges the progress-centric logic of Cyberlibertarianism, replacing it with a reflective, human-centred vision for the future.

While Digital Humanism has already gained traction as a normative project, its intellectual foundations can be further illuminated through recent contributions to the field. Fuchs [6] positions Digital Humanism as an ideology-critical narrative that directly challenges both Cyberlibertarianism and neoliberal frames, insisting that digital society cannot be reduced to markets or technical inevitability. Schmölz [20] extends this critique to European governance, showing how Digital Humanism functions as a corrective to progressive neoliberalism by reasserting social and democratic concerns in vocational and adult education.

At the core of these accounts lies the principle of *human dignity*. Nida-Rümelin and Winter [15] anchor Digital Humanism in the philosophical tradition of Enlightenment humanism, emphasising autonomy, respect, and solidarity as guiding values for technological development. Schmölz [18] deepens this by highlighting the *conditio humana* in the digital age, reminding us that vulnerability, finitude, and interdependence are irreducible aspects of human life that must inform digital governance. This perspective translates into concrete domains: Schmölz and Bauer [19], for example, argue that the future of work and vocational education must be shaped not by efficiency alone, but by the aim of human flourishing. These foundational texts underline that Digital Humanism is not only a normative position but a systematic framework for orienting digital society around dignity, democracy, and shared responsibility.

At its core, Digital Humanism holds that technological development is not a predetermined process but is shaped by ethical principles and social values. Technology is not an end in itself; it is a tool meant to serve individuals and society as a whole. Innovations must be designed in accordance with democratic principles like transparency, participation, and social justice.

Equally crucial is Digital Humanism's insistence on interrogating the power structures underlying digital technologies. It calls attention to how algorithms, data flows, and digital platforms can reinforce social inequalities through mechanisms of discrimination, surveillance, and unequal access.

Education is key here. Digital Humanism views education as a process of narrative awareness and ideological critique. It aims to empower people not just to use digital tools but to shape and critically assess them. Education becomes a space where users learn to identify, question, and transform dominant narratives, ultimately enabling alternative visions for a humane digital future.

In its essence, Digital Humanism offers an integrative perspective that brings together technology, ethics, politics, and society. It calls on all stakeholders, from developers to policymakers, educators, and civil society, to take joint responsibility for shaping a digital world that upholds human dignity, solidarity, and democratic values. In this way, it provides a powerful counter-narrative to the dominant ideology of Cyberlibertarianism, which often neglects social and ethical concerns [24].

4 Narratives as a Structuring Pattern of Interpretation of Social Reality

In cultural theory, the term narrative refers not only to storytelling but also to frameworks of meaning that shape individual and collective identity. According to Wolfgang Müller-Funk, narratives are 'symbolic forms of meaning' [14]. They do not just tell stories, but construct reality, shape identities and legitimise societal structures.

Viewed through this lens, both Cyberlibertarianism and Digital Humanism are competing narratives that vie for interpretive authority in the digital age. Cyberlibertarianism constructs a narrative of technological liberation, decentralisation, and deregulation. In contrast, Digital Humanism offers a framework rooted in human agency, democratic responsibility, and ethical reflection.

Both narratives shape more than just political discourse on technology; they influence how we perceive our options and imagine the future.

Urban planner Stephan Willinger describes narratives as meaningful storytelling patterns that convey emotions and ideas, subtly influencing our worldview and daily actions. Often absorbed unconsciously, these narratives become embedded in our cultural memory. Thus, narratives are not only tools of social orientation but also barriers to alternative thinking [25].

Their influence spans multiple layers: they define identities, legitimise power structures, and guide the discursive dynamics of societal change. Sociologist Francesca Polletta, whose research interests include culture as networks and social movements, highlights that narratives not only contribute to identity formation ('Who are we?'), but also stabilise political systems, and simultaneously open up space for dissent and transformation [15, 17].

Given this, reflecting on narratives, especially in the context of technopolitical developments, is essential. In digital discourse, narratives determine which futures are imaginable, which critiques are acceptable, and which values are deemed legitimate.

Within this context, Cyberlibertarianism functions not only as a technopolitical stance but as a dominant narrative that marginalises alternatives through its discursive framing. Digital Humanism, conversely, merges as an intentional counter-narrative that exposes and challenges this ideological dominance. It offers a narrative that does not focus on technological inevitability, but on the ability to shape society and thus also calls for a change of perspective: away from the naturalisation of digital development and towards a democratically, ethically, and culturally anchored reflection on technology and the future.

Engaging with these competing narratives is not a theoretical luxury but a necessity for redefining political agency in the digital age.

5 Narratives of Digitalisation

The proposition that Digital Humanism can serve as a powerful counter-narrative to Cyberlibertarianism rests on several key arguments, drawn from their normative premises, objectives, and social implications.

5.1 Different Normative Foundations

Cyberlibertarianism primarily emphasises individual freedom, framed as unrestricted technological self-expression and market autonomy. Within this perspective, state involvement is often viewed as an obstacle to innovation and personal liberty. In contrast, Digital Humanism places human beings and their social relationships at the centre of its normative framework. It upholds democratic values such as justice, solidarity, and human dignity, recognising both the state and civil society as essential actors in shaping the digital realm. These contrasting foundational assumptions highlight a key distinction: digital technologies should not merely serve the pursuit of individual freedom but must also be guided by commitments to the common good, collective well-being, and democratic principles.

5.2 Democracy Versus Market Dominance

The narrative of Cyberlibertarianism is closely tied to a technology-driven form of neoliberalism, in which power is increasingly concentrated in large private corporations, most notably the so-called Big Tech firms. These entities shape not only markets but also public discourse and infrastructure. Digital Humanism, by contrast, advocates for democratic oversight of digital power structures. This includes the implementation of regulations that protect data sovereignty, enforce transparency, and promote the public interest. While Cyberlibertarianism places trust in technological systems and market mechanisms to govern digital life, Digital Humanism insists that such power must be socially legitimised and democratically integrated to ensure accountability and inclusiveness.

5.3 Difference in the Understanding of Technology

At the heart of these competing ideologies lies a fundamental difference in how technology itself is understood. Cyberlibertarianism tends to portray technology as neutral and autonomous, operating independently of political or ethical judgment. It views control over technological systems as the key to advancing societal development without necessarily reflecting on the normative or structural consequences. Digital Humanism, by contrast, asserts that technology is never neutral. It is inherently shaped by social values, institutional interests, and power relations. As such, it must be subject to ethical scrutiny, public deliberation, and responsible design. Technology, in this view, is a malleable, value-laden instrument whose development must be aligned with democratic standards and social justice.

5.4 Inclusion Versus Exclusion

Cyberlibertarianism frequently defines freedom as an individual right, yet one that is often conditioned by access to technology and economic resources. This results in de facto exclusion for those without the necessary infrastructure, skills, or capital to participate fully in digital life. Digital Humanism, on the other hand, promotes the ideal of digital inclusion. It seeks to ensure that access to and participation in digital technologies is barrier-free, socially equitable, and educationally supported. The goal is not just to expand access, but to cultivate meaningful participation that empowers individuals and communities alike.

5.5 Criticism of Solutionism

A further structural flaw in Cyberlibertarian thinking is its proximity to solutionism, the belief that complex social issues can be resolved through purely technical solutions. This mindset tends to oversimplify social realities and downplay the role of political debate, ethical reflection, and historical context. Digital Humanism offers a robust critique of this reductionist approach. It advocates for an interdisciplinary perspective that sees technology not as a cure-all, but as one element within a broader network of ethical, legal, and societal systems. As such, it calls for technologies to be developed and deployed under democratic and ethical oversight, ensuring that innovation serves social responsibility rather than narrowly defined efficiency or profit.

6 Digital Humanism as an Ideology-Critical Intervention in Relation to Democracy

Viewed through an ideological lens, Digital Humanism emerges as a critical response to the dominance of Cyberlibertarianism. It challenges the reconfiguration of democratic ideals through technological narratives that depoliticize and reframe freedom in terms of algorithmic efficiency or digital market autonomy.

This is not merely a reinterpretation of content, but rather a conflictual process of symbolic renegotiation. In other words, it is about the struggle over meanings, values, and visions of the future that is inherently ideological.

The ideological impact of Cyberlibertarianism becomes especially apparent in its relationship to democracy. More precisely, in how it rearticulates democratic ideals through the promises of technology. In its narrative of freedom, individual autonomy is no longer anchored in political participation or collective deliberation, but in digital self-determination, market logic, and algorithmic governance. The concept of 'freedom' is stripped of its social, institutional, and normative dimensions. What appears emancipatory on the surface in fact shifts the political discourse from the socially negotiable to the technologically predetermined. Democracy is not directly opposed but discursively reframed. It becomes embedded in narratives that elevate technocracy, market rationality, and data privacy as the highest organizational principles. The democratic principle of plurality is replaced by the monoculture of efficiency, while the discourse on the common good dissolves into the language of personalized choices on digital platforms.

This subtle but far-reaching redefinition poses a profound threat to democracy, not through overt authoritarianism, but through an ideological narrowing of alternatives. The appropriation of democratic vocabulary by technological narratives leads to the hollowing out of political categories and impedes the possibility of structural critique. Technology, under such conditions, is no longer seen as a domain open to democratic shaping, but as a norm-setting force that eludes public deliberation.

Here, Digital Humanism offers an important counter-narrative. It insists on the political, ethical, and cultural mouldability of digital spaces. It argues that the guiding principle for technological development should not be mere feasibility or efficiency, but what is democratically desirable. In opposing the depoliticisation of society through technological means, it reopens space for imagining new forms of democratic participation that transcend the binary of market versus state. Digital Humanism understands digital technologies not as an autonomous force but as an integral part of a broader social order, an order whose trajectory must remain subject to public negotiation. This, precisely, is where its democratic potential lies.

Situating Digital Humanism within this body of scholarship reinforces its status as a counter-narrative. It is not merely a hopeful alternative, but a position grounded in philosophical and empirical debates about human dignity, democracy, and governance. By explicitly engaging these foundations, the contrast with Cyberlibertarianism becomes clearer: where Cyberlibertarianism naturalises technological inevitability and market dominance, Digital Humanism reopens the space of collective choice and ethical responsibility.

7 Education as a Democratic Practice

In the face of the ideological narrowing imposed by Cyberlibertarianism, education emerges as a vital field of contestation and possibility. If ideology operates not only through overt political messages but through cultural forms, habitual practices, and seemingly neutral terminologies, then education must serve a purpose beyond the transmission of digital skills or technological competencies. It must become a critical, democratic, and narrative-conscious practice, a space where the symbolic and political structures underpinning the digital can be made visible, interrogated, and transformed [5, 7].

In contrast to the technocratic reduction of education to mere 'digital literacy' or workforce adaptation, Digital Humanism calls for an expansive and emancipatory model of education. At its heart is the belief that education should cultivate critical maturity, ethical judgement, and the capacity for civic participation [1, 2, 25]. This vision sees learners not just as future employees or consumers of technology, but as citizens capable of shaping the digital world around them. It insists that digital education is not only about knowing how to use tools but about understanding who controls them, how they affect society, and what values they encode.

Education, within the framework of Digital Humanism, is a practice of narrative awareness. It teaches individuals to read digital developments not as neutral or inevitable, but as stories embedded with ideological assumptions and power dynamics [16, 18]. This means helping learners to recognise dominant narratives such as technological determinism or market inevitability as constructions rather than truths, analyse the implicit values, exclusions, and interests these narratives carry, and articulate alternative narratives that prioritise democratic values, social justice, and human dignity [7, 12].

Such an approach to education is both reflective and constructive. It does not merely critique existing systems; it also fosters imagination and design capacity for alternative digital futures [2, 12]. It equips students with the conceptual tools to envision technologies that support collective well-being, rather than merely efficiency or profit. This imaginative capacity is especially important in a time when dominant discourses often constrain what can be thought or desired [13].

Moreover, Digital Humanism emphasises inclusive and participatory pedagogies that mirror the democratic ideals it promotes. This includes fostering dialogue rather than top-down instruction, creating interdisciplinary learning spaces that connect technology with ethics, politics, history, and the arts, and encouraging project-based inquiry that links digital questions to lived social realities [22]. In this way, education becomes a laboratory for democratic culture, cultivating habits of critical engagement, empathy, and co-responsibility [1, 7].

Crucially, this vision also recognises the role of educators as narrative agents. Teachers are not just transmitters of knowledge but facilitators of interpretive practices. They help learners trace the genealogies of digital concepts, question taken-for-granted assumptions, and navigate the ethical tensions inherent in technological choices [4, 8]. Supporting educators in this role requires institutional commitment through curricula, resources, and training, to values-aligned teaching and interdisciplinary collaboration.

Finally, education under Digital Humanism is not limited to formal schooling. It encompasses lifelong learning, public education, and civic discourse. Libraries, museums, community centres, online platforms, and journalism all play essential roles in fostering a digitally literate and critically aware public [10, 11]. These spaces can function as counterweights to the commercialisation and depoliticisation of digital knowledge, providing forums for dialogue, reflection, and co-learning.

In sum, Digital Humanism reclaims education as a foundational democratic institution, a cultural practice through which people are empowered to see themselves not merely as passive recipients of digital transformation but as active co-creators of the digital public sphere [25]. It connects personal empowerment with collective responsibility, technical skill with ethical vision, and critical reflection with civic imagination. Only through such an education can we build a future where digital technologies serve the common good and reflect the plural values of a democratic society.

References

1. Biesta, G.: Beyond Learning: Democratic Education for a Human Future. Paradigm Publishers (2006)
2. Buckingham, D.: Beyond Technology: Children's Learning in the Age of Digital Culture. Polity (2007)
3. Eubanks, V.: Automating Inequality: How High-Tech Tools Profile, Police, and Punish the Poor. St. Martin's Press (2018)
4. Feenberg, A.: Transforming Technology: A Critical Theory Revisited. Oxford University Press (2002)
5. Freire, P.: Pedagogy of the Oppressed. Herder and Herder, New York (1970)
6. Fuchs, C.: Digital Humanism: A Philosophy for 21st Century Digital Society. Emerald Publishing, Bingley (2022)
7. Giroux, H.A.: On Critical Pedagogy. Bloomsbury Academic, New York (2011)
8. Golumbia, D.: The Politics of Bitcoin: Software as Right-Wing Extremism. University of Minnesota Press (2016)
9. Golumbia, D.: Cyberlibertarianism. University of Minnesota Press, The Right-Wing Politics of Digital Technology (2024)
10. Hintz, A., Dencik, L., Wahl-Jorgensen, K.: Digital Citizenship in a Datafied Society. Polity (2019)
11. Jenkins, H.: Confronting the Challenges of Participatory Culture: Media Education for the 21st Century. MIT Press (2009)
12. Jenkins, H., Ito, M., Boyd, D.: Participatory Culture in a Networked Era: A Conversation on Youth, Learning, Commerce, and Politics. Polity (2016)
13. Morozov, E.: To Save Everything, Click Here: The Folly of Technological Solutionism. PublicAffairs (2013)
14. Müller-Funk, W.: Die Kultur und ihre Narrative. Wien (2008)
15. Nida-Rümelin, J., Winter, D.: Humanism and enlightenment. In: Werthner, H., Ghezzi, C., Kramer, J., et al. (eds.), Introduction to Digital Humanism. Springer, Cham (2024)
16. Polletta, F.: It Was Like a Fever. Storytelling in Protest and Politics. Chicago, IL: University of Chicago Press (2006)
17. Polletta, F.: Analyzing popular beliefs about storytelling. In: Holstein, J.A., Gubrium, J.F. (eds.) Varieties of Narrative Analysis, pp. 229–250. Sage, Los Angeles (2012)
18. Schmölz, A.: Die Conditio Humana im digitalen Zeitalter. Zur Grundlegung des Digitalen Humanismus und des Wiener Manifests. MedienPädagogik. Zeitschrift für Theorie und Praxis der Medienbildung, **20**, 208–234 (2020)
19. Schmölz, A., Bauer, V.: Digitalisierung, Humanismus und die Zukunft von Arbeit und Berufsbildung: Zentrale Prognosen aus der Berufsbildungsforschung. In: Löffler, R., Schlögl, P., & Schmoelz, A. (eds.), 50 Jahre Berufsbildungsforschung in Österreich im Spannungsfeld von Wissenschaft, Politik und Praxis. wbv, Bielefeld (2021)
20. Schmölz, A.: Digital humanism, progressive neoliberalism and the European digital governance system for vocational and adult education. J. Adult Continuing Educ. **29**(2), 735–759 (2023)
21. Selwyn, N.: Digital Technology and the Contemporary University: Degrees of Digitization. Routledge (2014)
22. Varoufakis, Y.: Technofeudalism. What Killed Capitalism. Vermilion (2023)
23. Walsh, C.: Docile citizens? Using counternarratives to disrupt normative and dominant discourses. In: Soler, J., Walsh, C., Craft, A., Rix, J., Simmons, K. (eds.), Transforming Practice: Critical Issues in Equity, Diversity and Education. Trentham Books, Stoke-on-Trent, pp. 125–135 (2012)

24. Werthner, H.: Digitaler Humanismus. Über Digitalisierung und Künstliche Intelligenz. Picus (2025)
25. Willinger, S.: "Narrativ", in: Glossar zur gemeinwohlorientierten Stadtentwicklung (2020)
26. Winner, L.: Cyberlibertarian myths and the prospects for community. Comput. Soc. 14–19 (1997)

Climate Disasters and Risks in Online Expressions in South Africa

Tendai Ganduri[(✉)] [iD]

University of the Witwatersrand, Johannesburg, Gauteng, South Africa
tendaiganduri@gmail.com

Abstract. Digital platforms such as X (formerly Twitter) increasingly serve as arenas for civic expression including during climate related disasters. However, studies on digital governance related critique around climate crises in South Africa are limited. This is whereas the country has a volatile online-offline dynamic where such expressions carry inherent risks. This paper responds by analysing X conversations surrounding the 2022 KwaZulu Natal (KZN) floods. Using a computational social science approach, the paper examines tweets and user accounts involved in propagating high-risk content and situates the dynamics within the risk and digital performativity framework. The study reveals long standing sociopolitical tensions which are articulated through contested boundaries of digital freedom. This is particularly through xenophobic rhetoric, racialised critique of political actors and antagonism towards corporate institutions. The paper draws on broader comparative cases to contextualise these risks and illustrate the potentially harmful dimensions of digital freedoms during crises. It reveals how the X platform enable civic participation but also backlash and polarisation. These dynamics expose the social vulnerabilities embedded in digital expression cognisant of South Africa's volatile online-offline landscape. It also calls for further studies on both independent and networked user behaviours to strengthen climate risk communication. The paper contributes to digital humanities by offering a grounded account of how publics contest authority, assert rights, and navigate vulnerability during crisis-mediated online engagement.

Keywords: KZN floods · online performativity · risk communication · computational social sciences

1 Introduction

During moments of environmental crisis, digital platforms serve as both a communication tool but also spaces of reckoning. Platforms such as X became sites for mourning, mobilisation, and protest. Concomitantly, from spontaneous acts of solidarity to coordinated civic dissent, the conversations play a critical role in how the crisis is socially constructed and politically navigated (Echterling & Wylie, 2013). As such, crisis beneath the surface of what might appear as free expression is often a contested terrain of selective responses, racialised policing, and digital antagonism as in the case under study. Online discourse in South Africa is marked by selective amplification of various forms

L. Hagedorn et al. (Eds.): DIGHUM 2025, LNCS 16319, pp. 263–279, 2026.
https://doi.org/10.1007/978-3-032-11108-1_19

digital antagonism. This is often rooted in the country's broader socio-political landscape where issues of corruption, legacies of apartheid and lingering inequalities continue to shape both public life and institutional trust (Fourie, 2024; Friedman, 2021; Levy et al., 2021; Motloung, 2024; Seagrave, 2023; Sorce & Dumitrica, 2023; Tshishonga, 2019). Accordingly, digital platforms often become battlegrounds where longstanding tensions particularly around race, identity, power, and legitimacy are reflected upon and often exacerbated. In that respect, this paper examines the tensions between digital freedoms of expression and the socio-political consequences related to such expressions particularly for marginalised users. The key argument is that while digital spaces have become sites of visibility and participation for many South Africans, they also carry significant risks. These risks are not confined to the digital realm for instance through hateful, deregatory langauge or sexually grotesque art. Instead, they are also rooted in a context where online mobilisation has historically spilled into offline protest as experienced during the #RhodhesMustFall and #FeesMustFall movements. These reveal how stakes of online speech can be profoundly real. Through such examples, episodes of online critique are argued to trigger targeted surveillance, harassment, or even physical violence illustrating how the boundaries between the digital and the material are increasingly blurred.

The KwaZulu-Natal (KZN) floods of 2022 provide a crucial context for this inquiry. The disaster not only revealed infrastructural and environmental vulnerabilities but also exposed the fractures within South Africa's social and political order (Bond & Galvin, 2023; Motloung, 2024). In the wake of the floods, thousands of South Africans turned to X to voice frustration, share mutual aid information, and contest the legitimacy of diverse actors. As this study provides, the online discourse includes critiques of government neglect, xenophobic scapegoating, and inadequate responses by the private sector. While these expressions are rooted in specific crisis conditions, they point to broader anxieties about governance, accountability, and justice in the post-apartheid era. This delineates to concerns about both civic engagement and exposure to harm particularly through high-risk expressions tied to race, nationalism, and institutional failure. In so doing, the study contributes to broader debates within digital humanities, media studies, and crisis communication by offering a grounded account of how publics navigate visibility, vulnerability, and authority in digitally mediated crisis contexts.

2 Literature Review

This study draws on the risk and digital performativity framework to analyse how users perform vulnerability, critique, and resistance in the digital public sphere. As Lupton (2016) outlines in her work on the digital risk society, networked spaces are not only sites of surveillance and uncertainty. Rather, their role extends as spheres of emotional performance and politicised expression. This aligns with Papacharissi (2018) argument that digital platforms cultivate affective publics whereby civic engagement is driven as much by emotion and visibility as by rational discourse. Accordingly, digital performativity is approached as extending beyond speech but materialising through symbolic repertoires such as hashtags, memes, and satire that mobilise publics, frame legitimacy or reinforce polarisation. However, as Power (2007) notes, risk becomes a governing logic in institutional responses while public discourse simultaneously reflects and contests such governance. By embedding performative resistance within this digital risk context, this study explores how online critiques of immigration, land and race, as well as governance function not merely as reflection, but as active constructions of risk and political identity. Thus, digital engagement in the South African climate crisis context becomes both a coping mechanism and a catalyst for socio-political volatility.

The intersection of climate crises, digital discourse, and social inequality is receiving growing scholarly attention, particularly in the Global South. While environmental vulnerabilities are often documented through institutional reports and media narratives, increasingly, platforms such as X (formerly Twitter) have emerged as critical arenas for publics to express grievances, assert rights, and contest governance failures. These digital expressions form part of broader affective publics whose visibility, performance, and resonance can both inform or destabilise democratic engagement (Papacharissi, 2018). Another key strand of literature concerns with how digital platforms mediate civic expression during moments of heightened uncertainty. Bosch and Murthy explore this in the context of the #FeesMustFall movement and reveal how Twitter served not only as a mobilisation tool but also as a space to confront racialised power, structural exclusion, and post-apartheid disillusionment (Bosch, 2016, 2017; Murthy, 2018). The case foregrounds the comparative aspect for this study. Added to digital debates performativities, Akinola (2018) and Tella (2016) document how digital discourse around xenophobic violence often mirrors and amplifies offline grievances, particularly around employment, state failure, and identity. These analyses situate social media as both expressive and performative. They enable marginalised narratives while simultaneously intensifying polarisation.

Recent work by Gohdes (2024) and Earl & Braithwaite (2022) cautions that digital freedoms in unstable contexts can be double-edged. While online spaces offer avenues for democratic participation, they also present platforms for incitement, misinformation, and the amplification of social risk particularly in settings with weak or selective institutional responsiveness. Within climate communication literature, there is growing recognition of how crisis events such as floods expose and exacerbate existing inequalities (Parthasarathy, 2018; Smith et al., 2022; Tierney, 2006). However, digital governance critique remains relatively underexplored particularly from a bottom-up, user-driven perspective. This gap is particularly evident in South Africa where historical legacies of dispossession, ongoing infrastructure challenges, and political antagonism converge during disasters to produce heightened affective responses online. This study responds, building on the referred works focusing on the discursive logics that animate the South African digital public sphere during climate crises. The study contributes to scholarship on digital humanities by illuminating how publics enact dissent, demand accountability and navigate precarity in networked environments. It also engages with comparative literature on protest cultures, populism, and digital nationalisms to contextualise South Africa's volatile online-offline dynamic within a broader socio-political landscape.

3 Methodology

A total of over 200,000 tweets were extracted using the Twitter v2 API. Data collection spanned three months from 8 March to 21 May 2022. This spans one month before up to a month after the event which was done to capture the evolution of discussions over time. Data extraction on X employed a keyword and hashtag-driven approach with filters including #KZNFloods and #climate change used as both keywords and hashtags for data mining. Twitter data was processed using Excel, RStudio, and Gephi. These analytical tools served a complementary and interoperability function which facilitated efficient handling, cleaning, and transfer of data across platforms. Key metadata fields included tweet and user identifiers, engagement metrics (likes, retweets, replies), profile information, and temporal markers. The cleaned dataset was imported into RStudio for further processing, including noise reduction such as removal of emojis and text standardisation. The edges file for network visualisation was also generated in RStudio whereas Gephi was selected for the task due to its more advanced dynamic network visualisation features (Alam et al., 2012; Yang et al., 2017).

The tweets were sorted into eleven primary themes of religion, climate, situational updates, loss and damage, community, humanitarian, faith and solidarity, nationalism and identity, official, political party/person, and governance critique. It is from these thematic clusters that the targeted analysis is drawn, respectively. This process was guided by account-level analysis and close qualitative reading. Tweets were assigned to themes based on a keyword-driven thematic classification. A notable pattern emerged where the majority of critical tweets came from low-visibility accounts. Such accounts typically have minimal visibility on the platform in terms of follower count and engagement with their tweets in this dataset. Despite lacking individual engagement amplification in terms of replies, likes or mentions, they collectively emerge as the largest contributors. For instance, from the deduplicated dataset, the 27,799 tweets were generated by 11,646 unique user accounts. Those with between one to tweets are 10,015, that's 86% of the dataset. In terms of connectivity, an analysis was conducted in Gephi. At a 1.0 resolution and 0.529 modularity, the network evidences stronger but small intra-cluster connections and very weak cross cluster connections. The most visible influencers in the dataset, predominantly the media and officials exert significant influence over the network structure as various users interact with and reshare their content. In so doing, direct and indirect connections with these central actors are formed as they circulate content from shared sources. In sum, the approach enabled a focus on the tweet content itself for thematic and structural analysis of the environment the tweets come from.

This study acknowledges some methodological limitations. Data collection relied on specified keywords and hashtags, which would exclude relevant tweets lacking explicit identifiers used for this study (Ahmed et al., 2017). This is however considered an effective delimitation strategy. Another challenge is that online interactions do not always reflect individuals' true sentiments or offline behaviours (Pfeffer et al., 2018). However, slacktivism and digital engagement whether sincere or performative, shaped by opinion or lived experience are persistent and inescapable aspects of contemporary social reality (Patti et al., 2017; Waugh et al., 2014). This study considers them within the broader context of the political economy of knowledge production.

4   Overview of Outcomes

This study identifies three distinct but interlinked discursive clusters that present critical risks in the digital public sphere during crises. These particularly fall under the nationalism and identity, political person and officials themes. The targeted harmful critique has different targets and motivations but they all reveal intensified antagonism and socio-political division. Combined, these clusters account for 4,169 tweets which constitutes 15% of the deduplicated dataset. This is whereas about three quarters of these tweets present harmful critique. However, as this paper argues, the influence and resonance of such content goes beyond statistical validation.

4.1 Xenophobic Nationalism

The nationalism and identity cluster reveals a deep undercurrent of xenophobic nationalism that transpired on X during the floods. The cluster has 2,144 tweets and largely demonstrates how crises act as catalytic events which trigger the resurface of long-standing social fractures. In this case, it is mainly around immigration, identity, and belonging. Most of the tweets in this cluster reflect digital skirmishes between South African users among themselves and members of the Zimbabwean online community who constitute approximately 35% of the accounts within this cluster. Prominent within the cluster are hashtags such as #PutSouthAfricansFirst and #OperationDudula. Combined, they form a compelling discursive point that advances anti-immigrant sentiment presented as a legitimate form of patriotic responsibility. In so doing, binaries of insiders versus outsiders are created where foreign nationals are presented as threats to employment, security, and national integrity. The symbolic resonance of #OperationDudula particularly reveals its emergence as a digital and street-level movement that champions deportation and exclusion through public spectacle and often, violent enforcement. The murder of Elvis Nyathi, a Zimbabwean national killed in a xenophobic attack just days before the KZN floods became a discursive flashpoint. It intensified and compounded these exclusionary narratives. The name appears 1,139 times within the cluster, a 51.1% prevalence serving as a rhetorical device that fuels nationalist fervour, frame opposing narratives while also summoning diasporic grief. For some, Nyathi's murder symbolised rightful retaliation against foreign encroachment. For another sympathetic South African and Zimbabwean community it signified the indictment of a society lost of its moral compass. The discursive patterns reveal embedded exclusionary logics and immense hate and rage within the digital public sphere. Examples of xenophobic sentiment in this cluster are outright and include:

#OperationDudula launching in Limpopo. All undocumented immigrants must be deported! We shall not share non-rare-skilled jobs with foreigners. Away with that madness. #PutSouthAfricansFirst #KZNFloods

Operation Dudula is briefing the media on KZN floods and unemployment in SA on Monday afternoon.

They will say South Africans are xenophobic meanwhile ANC, DA, EFF will keep advocating for foreigners. The answer is let's vote them out. S'khathele (we are tired)! You foreigners have overstayed your welcome, Hamba (go away)! Go back home kweres (immigrants)!

#NoToXenophobia is a counter revolution strategy by @EFFSouthAfrica to guilt trip #OperationDudula and patriotic South Africans. We are not moved by such punitive actions anymore! We want what is ours and we will get it back.

Hillbrow is a den of illegal foreigners you would think you are in a foreign country, full of Zimbabweans #VoetsekEFF. #PutSouthAficansFirst

*What kind of madness is this? When is God going to punish kweres (immigrants) for selling drugs and human trafficking our people? Don't be an @*sh&*e. And oh, kweres are everywhere in KZN so they were affected too so sit down #OperationDudula.* (In response to views of the floods being divine retribution for the killing of Elvis).

Counter-discourses, largely from Zimbabwean users and sympathetic South African citizens respond with equally impassioned retorts. While some are rooted in grief and defiance others accuse of barbarism, call for accountability and appeal to shared African solidarity. Examples include.

That is the blood of Elvis Nyathi flowing through the KZN floods.

May his spirit haunt you for the rest of your life. #Dudula.

The #Dudula movement that butchered #ElvisNyathi still isn't banned in South Africa. Barbarians. To them, a foreigner is only a Black African.

These responses are not only reactive but also assertive. They actively reframe the discourse to highlight the perceived double standards in South African community particularly in relation to race, nationality, and class. In turn however, that further polarises the digital terrain thus producing a cycle of mutual antagonism. Amid these extremes, a third layer of commentary which is characterised by satire, irony, and critical performativity emerges. The tweets reflect a broader disillusionment with the instrumentalisation of nationalism as performative outrage. It exposes inconsistencies and contradictions within movements that claim to represent the interests of the marginalised. Examples include:

#OperationDudula gained supporters in KZN after its visit. Members of the movement offered to assist with rebuilding communities affected by the floods despite claiming to be overlooked for jobs?

Dear #PutSouthAfricansFirst, here is the EFF helping #KZNFloods victims. Please show up. We want to see who loves South Africans more.

While mocking in tone, such tweets underscore deeper societal frustrations with the appropriation of suffering for ideological gain while also functioning towards brand assertion and visibility.

The KZN context further complicates matters. Some tweets descend into tribalist tropes, with KZN (particularly the Zulu community) framed as volatile, disorderly violent and having a high propensity for violence. Examples of such tweets include:

No way this tribe! I give up on them! (This is accompanied by a picture of protesting individuals with caption 'People in KZN are protesting against the heavy rains.')

How does one explain that a person died during the floods? Not from the rain, but drowning while trying to steal from a container?

These expressions reflect internal fractures within the South African community itself. The national crises become grounds for the reproduction of tribal and ethnic stereotypes. In response, some KZN-based users seek to reclaim dignity and challenge external misrepresentation through tweets such as, "Some people are just dumb and always ready to disrespect KZN… Protests have been going on before the floods."

This intra and transnational oscillation between critique and defence, mockery and mobilisation illustrates the complex ways digital spaces mediate communal identity and belonging. Rather than linear, the discursive terrain is layered, intersectional, and highly reactive and this is shaped by evolving historical, racial, and regional dynamics. What heightens the concern is the institutional vacuum in which this discourse unfolds. Many of the more aggressive tweets appear linked to organised groups such as Operation Dudula. The movements operate across multiple platforms including the physical space to spread its message. They build momentum during crises and capitalises on public anxiety (Dratwa, 2023; Muringa, n.d.; Sinwell et al., 2023). This convergence of structured online campaigns with fluid grassroots hostility makes the risk particularly acute and the potential for offline mobilisation even more likely during crisis. Existing literature on xenophobic violence in South Africa has long highlighted the interplay between local grievances and national narratives (Choane et al., 2011; Tella, 2016). Solomon & Kosaka (2013) went on to suggest the criminalisation of hate speech together with other institutional enforcement mechanisms as an essential step to curbing such violence. However, enforcement by authorities is often selectively applied particularly when digital content carries political critique (Bak et al., 2018; Earl et al., 2022; Earl & Braithwaite, 2022; Gohdes, 2024). This leaves other forms of harmful expression such as xenophobic or exclusionary speech unaddressed. Consequently, this leaves digital platforms to operate largely as unregulated spaces of mobilisation where unchecked civic expression can escalate into social harm particularly during moments of crisis.

To illuminate the risk of such discourse offline, this study draws comparative reflections from the #FeesMustFall campaign. Like the present xenophobic discourse, #FeesMustFall began online but quickly transformed into national protest. It was propelled by grievances around structural exclusion and this was articulated through the digital affordances of Twitter and Facebook. As Bosch (2016, 2017) provides, social media played a central role in shaping the movement's identity, logistics, and ideology. It facilitated what can, in Habermasian sense be described as a digitally mediated public sphere (Murphy, 2017). However, with this one being neither fully public nor private and increasingly prone to volatility. As Olagunju et al. (2022) argue, during the #FeesMustFall, social media platforms including X (then Twitter) allowed for participation, visibility, and shared affect. They also laid bare the lack of institutional responsiveness which often pushed online discontent into physical action. These insights show that when marginalised voices are not heard, digital speech can transform into physical protest and often, with violent consequences. However, this analysis is not naïve to the complexities within the broader South African context which include state scapegoating, denialism, ineffective institutional responses and the possibility of deliberate political theatre in state inaction (Akinola, 2018; Hewitt et al., 2020; Kaziboni et al., 2022; Ngcamu, 2025; Steinberg, 2012). Accordingly, this analysis situates the argument within its wider structural conditions whereas it situates digital freedoms within an escalating environment of risk, both online and offline. As climate-related disasters such as the KZN floods become more frequent and severe, the public sphere also increasingly become volatile. In such moments of heightened vulnerability, they serve as amplifiers of grievance, fear, and blame. Accordingly, digital freedoms can be understood as double-edged. They enable civic expression while also exposing deep-seated societal fractures. The refereed case reveals how quickly patriotic performance can evolve into digital vigilantism. In recognising these risks and complimentary to related scholarship, I emphasise the urgency for more robust platform governance, civic education, and integrated digital risk communication strategies in response to the growing intersection of digital discourse, disaster, and social instability.

4.2 Racialised Critique

The political party or person theme isolates tweets targeting political figures or opposition parties other than the ANC. Separating them from broader governance critique enables a clearer view of how public trust and accountability are expressed beyond the ruling party. In the case of the KZN floods, racialised critique is rampant particularly within this thematic cluster. The cluster reflects perceptions that South African political elites selectively allocate empathy, resources, and accountability along racial lines which in turn fuel emotionally charged racial critiques.

For instance, tweets questioned the absence of white South Africans among the victims and highlighted selective political responses:

> *I don't want to turn this into a racial issue, but where are whites affected by #KZNFloods? Is it just our people who were displaced into these areas many years ago?*

Others adopt a more accusatory tone, especially in response to Democratic Alliance (DA) leader John Steenhuisen's visit to Ukraine at the time of the floods:

> *I honestly can't even imagine what made him think that it was a good idea to go literally halfway across the world to a conflict that doesn't affect South Africa. He should be heading to KZN to help out after the floods, not Ukraine.*

> *Do you see how whites support each other? Look what the DA leader did; went straight to Ukraine to show support to its fellow whites but did nothing for KZN floods…*

Such statements construct a binary between black suffering and white political solidarity, amplifying feelings of abandonment among black communities. There is a recurring theme that structural inequality is actively maintained, and that both opposition and ruling parties are complicit. Some tweets call for redistributive justice, including land expropriation:

> *Land must be expropriated to save Black lives.*

> *What apartheid has done to the country is irreparable and will take even a century to be eradicated.*

DA-affiliated figures, such as Dean Macpherson and John Steenhuisen also face direct critique through tweets such as:

@DA_KZN, @DeanMacpherson, floods in swimming pools?

While people are dealing with #KZNFloods, some are dealing with a golf ball and a hole

Didn't see this one anywhere during KZN floods (shared in response to a news article defending Steenhuisen's Ukraine trip).

These are often accompanied by satirical images and memes contrasting privileged suburban recovery with devastated black communities, using humour to highlight racial and class disparities in disaster response. These discursive threads culminate in a broader (though separate) critique of urban inequality and poor infrastructure planning which is expressed through tweets such as:

Umlazi is the second-largest township in South Africa, but its roads are an embarrassment. Meanwhile, Cornubia next to Umhlanga is fully developed.

How are we going to rebuild when the ground itself has been destroyed?

These posts frame the floods not only as a natural disaster, but as evidence of structural neglect rooted in apartheid-era spatial inequality and its reproduction post-apartheid.

At the same time, some tweets intensify racial polarisation, portraying 'black-on-black' neglect as well as political tit-for-tat as expressed through the tweet:

@DA_KZN @DeanMacpherson Black people are upset that the DA is visiting white flood victims, not townships. But I haven't seen anyone from ANC, EFF, IFP visiting the white areas either. Tit for tat.

The argument emerging from these discourses is that climate-related disasters increasingly serve as flashpoints that expose and intensify social inequalities. In the South African context, they also sharpen racialised perceptions of governance failure and increasing risk. This is especially evident in the growing public sentiment that land struggles, both historical and prospective are rarely resolved through dialogue but rather through confrontation, protest, and at times, violence. This historical continuity undermines the legitimacy of institutional restitution and has fuelled perceptions that substantive change requires extra-institutional struggle. These dynamics collectively illuminate how unresolved inequalities embedded in the land question are magnified during moments of crisis. In this case, it is with implied antagonism toward those perceived to benefit from historical injustice. However, the antagonism is frequently accompanied by a sense of futility or risk associated with direct confrontation. This tension is poignantly reflected in tweets such as:

You meet them in gyms and coffee shops but know they are untouchable.

Keyboard warriors we see you; you see them everywhere but come to protest online.

These expressions underscore a digital consciousness that is both aware of structural injustice constrained by the perceived limits of action. In so doing, there is a revealing of a public caught between rising urgency and the boundaries of permissible dissent. As per the arguments of this paper, climate-triggered crises risk catalysing intensified mobilisation and socio-political volatility.

Drawing from historical parallels, #FeesMustFall continues to serve as a symbolic touchstone. Reflecting on the movement, (Wessels, 2017) noted how the protests forced white South Africans to confront the realities of black exclusion, privilege, and structural violence. Twitter was pivotal in amplifying black consciousness and confronting white ignorance, as students used it to expose alienation and mobilise around decolonisation in higher education. In so doing, it left the social media spaces as racialised terrains where historical injustices are relitigated and imagined futures are contested. These sentiments reflect both frustration and strategic recalibration as users reclaim digital space to express grievances and reimagine justice.

In the tweet dynamic, there is a pattern of recycled political content. For example, the tweets in this cluster are shared by users with a minimal activity of 1–2 tweets. The images are recycled and reposted with updated captions pointing to coordinated amplification of racially charged narratives.

4.3   Targeted Corporate and Institutional Critique

The officials and institutions cluster refers to digital discourse surrounding government officials, state agencies, and public figures including celebrities and corporations. Most tweets in this category are informational. However, a significant proportion contain veiled or explicit critique especially of law enforcement, municipalities, and parastatals such as Eskom, the South African National Defence Force (SANDF), and the Passenger Rail Agency of South Africa (PRASA). This thematic cluster comprises 1,943 tweets, with 1,025 (52.7%) originating from users with 1–2 tweets and 442 tweets (22.8%) from users posting between 3 and 14 tweets. The remaining 476 tweets (24.5%) come from 14 high-activity accounts, predominantly media houses and official institutional profiles. Approximately 65% of tweets are critical in tone reflecting widespread public frustration with perceived institutional inaction, mismanagement, or absence. These critiques are especially pronounced within the 1–2 tweet users and activist accounts in the 3–14 range.

Tweets targeting corporate actors present a dual critique. On one hand, they implicate the government in enabling corporate accumulation without ensuring accountability. On the other, they directly challenge private companies for their limited visibility or support during the floods. A notable example involves United Phosphorus Limited (UPL), an Indian agrochemical company blamed for toxic chemical leaks into Durban beaches. One tweet reads, "And again, the polluters seem to get away with it." The tweet is linked to a Daily Maverick article on UPL's alleged negligence due to an inadequately constructed containment dam. Memes and satirical content also circulate widely, amplifying this sentiment. One prominent tweet features an image with the caption, 'Pray for KZN'. The image depicts a man representing corporate South Africa indifferently enjoying an elaborate meal. The visual satire reinforces the idea of corporate detachment. It portrays the private sector as concerned only when their interests are at stake.

While some tweets acknowledge corporate donations or relief efforts, they are overshadowed by public expectations of broader, visible engagement particularly in light of the scale of the crisis. Such tweets, which often, also raise questions of race and class include:

Corporate SA is ignoring the #KZNFloods. It's not white people who died. Black lives aren't good PR for them.

Whilst prayers are important and necessary for #KZNFloods, Corporate SA must rise.

This reflects a selective memory and content among users but also cynicism with corporate social responsibility during emergencies. Institutional critique also extends to technical accountability. One user demands, "Engineers, your designs must be kept for 10 years so we can investigate negligence… If you played with politicians, you will be held accountable." In another, PRASA is condemned, "PRASA? As in the failed, messed up entity that was ruined before the KZN floods? That PRASA?" This reaction was in response to a report that over ZAR940 million would be allocated to PRASA for rail infrastructure restoration whereas the amount was more than roads, housing, or health facilities. The tone becomes more alarming when threats or calls to action begin to appear through tweets such as:

Do we need to start a #FFSeskom hashtag? Maybe that helps? Not much else we can do to make @Eskom_SA hear us! #FFSeskom, please think of the needy, destitute, devastated in the #KZNFloods.

Though indirect, the message hints at organised protest or disruption as public frustration escalates. This is while numerous tweets, 310, in the duplicated dataset mourn about load shedding and the impacts it was having particularly during the stressful moment with the floods. Additionally, outside the dataset, Eskom has been a repeated target of public outrage particularly during periods of loadshedding. As (Neethling, 2022) notes, citizens have attacked Eskom staff and vehicles, tampered with infrastructure, and threatened employees. In some cases, fires, transformer sabotage, and the destruction of pylons have been experienced being both acts of sabotage and thievery. For this paper, the concern is twofold. First, climate related crises intensify grievances around service delivery and institutional failure. Second, that digital expressions of frustration are no longer confined to discourse alone but possess the potential to incite real-world action particularly when trust in state and corporate entities erodes. The concern goes beyond Eskom but the larger corporate community in view of prior events including the 2021 protests and looting (Bonga, 2021; Mtshali & Enaifoghe, 2023; Vhumbunu, 2021). As highlighted in the literature, addressing the underlying culture of protest is essential to curbing the recurrence of violent and destructive demonstrations. In this light, the officials cluster reveals not only how accountability is digitally demanded, but also how the urgency for digital risk mitigation is expressed.

5 Addressing Polarisation and Risky Tendencies Online

The above findings fall in line with scholarship that has increasingly problematised the role of social media platforms such as X in shaping polarisation, fragmentation, and the quality of public debates. While earlier studies focused on how digital platforms could expand civic participation and create new arenas for democratic deliberation, recent studies emphasise their tendency to intensify partisan divides, amplify extreme voices, and foster echo chambers (Barberá, 2020; Freelon et al., 2022; Tucker et al., 2018). Similarly, research has shown how crises such as natural disasters are particularly prone to mediated antagonisms (Mena, 2023; Peters, 2021). In that regard, X is therefore less conceptualised as a neutral civic environment but contested digital public sphere which enables visibility while simultaneously exacerbating volatility (Papacharissi, 2018).

In light of these debates, the study's contribution is twofold. First, it demonstrates that despite lacking sustained influence compared to media or official accounts, even weakly embedded nodes can trigger visible spikes of antagonism during crises. Specifically, this South Africa case reveals that while the X platform amplified xenophobic and racialised narratives during the KwaZulu-Natal floods, the problematic accounts driving them are largely peripheral and weakly connected. Their limited embeddedness means that they can be more easily neutralised through targeted interventions. Second, the study extends research on counter speech by demonstrating how interventions can operate at both micro and meso levels. At micro level, fact-based corrections and empathetic appeals can shape bystander behaviours in ways that reduce the resonance of harmful content (Mathew et al., 2019). At the meso level, organised and sustained counter speech campaigns can dampen the prevalence of harmful content over time and strengthen counter-discourse dynamics (Garland et al., 2023). In this case, active user reporting can facilitate account suspensions while coordinated counter speech and solidarity networks can amplify constructive narratives and reduce the visibility of harmful ones. Such strategies require active civic gatekeeping, where users are supported through educational initiatives to distinguish legitimate expression from hate speech (Gagliardone et al., 2015; Stremlau & Gagliardone, 2019). Notably, such interventions may be most effective when championed by influential and trusted accounts that can deliberately curate and channel positive messages into high-risk networks. In so doing, the reach of harmful content is diluted and counter narratives are amplified.

Complimentarily, though issues of accuracy bias remain, technological pathways also offer potential avenues for mitigation. Such approaches include automated detection using natural language processing to identify and demote hateful or antagonistic content at scale (Fortuna et al., 2019; Fortuna & Nunes, 2019). Other proposals include the use of circuit breakers to slow the virality of harmful content to provide moderators and fact-checkers time to intervene (Gillespie, 2020). However, such strategies require greater transparency and independent auditing of platform recommendation systems. However, this remains a challenge, requiring continued attention and effective workarounds (Pasquale, 2015).

Linking the findings to debates in digital humanism underscores their normative and infrastructural significance. Digital humanism calls for democratic oversight of platforms emphasising on accountability, agency, transparency and resilience (Coeckelbergh, 2024). By showing how platform governance, civic gatekeeping, and social listening can be aligned with citizen-led counter speech, the South African case illustrates how technological infrastructures and social practices can be brought together to mitigate harm while sustaining democratic participation.

6 Summary and Conclusion

This study critically examined the socio-political dynamics that emerged on Twitter during the 2022 KwaZulu-Natal floods. It pays particular attention to how digital discourse shapes and performs risk. Drawing on three interlinked clusters of nationalism and identity, political actors and officials and institutions, the analysis reveals how structural inequality, historical grievance, and socio-political antagonism converge during climate-related crises. The nationalism and identity cluster revealed a resurgence of xenophobic sentiment that particularly targets foreign nationals. Hashtags such as #PutSouthAfricansFirst and #OperationDudula were used to frame exclusionary nationalism as patriotic duty with Elvis Nyathi's murder emerging as a key flashpoint. In contrast, counter-narratives invoked solidarity and African unity but ultimately intensified polarisation. The political actors theme captured how disasters are racialised in the public imagination. Tweets critiqued opposition leaders, especially DA figures, for selective empathy and absence from black communities. In this cluster, racial and class disparities are foregrounded with calls for land justice and institutional accountability echoing past movements like #FeesMustFall. The officials cluster revealed deep mistrust of government and corporate actors. Tweets critiqued Eskom, PRASA, and corporate South Africa for apathy or mismanagement. Some tweets hinted at mobilisation or disruption echoing prior episodes of civil unrest. The paper thus acknowledges how the digital terrain becomes especially volatile in contexts of institutional vacuum. Additionally, the study situates its findings within broader scholarship on polarisation and fragmentation. It reveals that while social media platforms can amplify antagonisms during crises, weakly embedded nodes driving such content are structurally vulnerable therefore amenable to targeted interventions. By extending debates on counter speech, technological governance, and digital humanism, the study highlights how coordinated civic action and accountable platform design can together mitigate harm and strengthen the resilience of the digital public sphere. Given the growing prevalence and intensity of climate disasters, the digital public sphere is emerging as a critical site of mobilisation and contestation. Accordingly, building on existing scholarship, this study calls for enhanced platform governance, improved crisis communication by institutions, digital civic education, and proactive social listening tools to mitigate risk.

Acknowledgments. No direct funding was received for the preparation of this paper.

Declaration of Interests. The author has no competing interests to declare in respect of this paper.

References

Ahmed, W., Bath, P.A., Demartini, G.: Using Twitter as a data source: an overview of ethical, legal, and methodological challenges. Ethics Online Res. **2**, 79–107 (2017)

Akinola, A.O.: The South African xenophobic question: a reflection on the complicity of state actors. Ubuntu: J. Conflict Soc. Transf. **7**(1), 53–79 (2018)

Alam, M., Arifuzzaman, S., Bhuiyan, M.H.: Large scale network visualization with gephi (2012)

Bak, D., Sriyai, S., Meserve, S.A.: The internet and state repression: a cross-national analysis of the limits of digital constraint. J. Hum. Rights **17**(5), 642–659 (2018). https://doi.org/10.1080/14754835.2018.1456914

Barberá, P.: Social media, echo chambers, and political polarization. Social Media and Democracy: The State of the Field, Prospects for Reform, 34–55 (2020)

Bond, P., Galvin, M.: Conflicting narratives of extreme weather events in Durban, South Africa. Climate Change Epistemologies in Southern Africa, 95 (2023)

Bonga, W.G.: Impact of repetitive protests on economic development: a case of South Africa. Quest J. J. Res. Human. Soc. Sci. **9**(8), 34–39 (2021)

Bosch, T.: Twitter and participatory citizenship:# FeesMustFall in South Africa. In Digital activism in the social media era: Critical reflections on emerging trends in sub-Saharan Africa, pp. 159–173 (2016)

Bosch, T.: Twitter activism and youth in South Africa: the case of# RhodesMustFall. Inf. Commun. Soc. **20**(2), 221–232 (2017)

Choane, M., Shulika, L.S., Mthombeni, M.: An Analysis of the causes, effects and ramifications of xenophobia in South Africa. Insight Africa **3**(2), 129–142 (2011). https://doi.org/10.1177/0975087814411138

Coeckelbergh, M.: What is digital humanism? A conceptual analysis and an argument for a more critical and political digital (post)humanism. J. Responsible Technol. **17**, 100073 (2024). https://doi.org/10.1016/j.jrt.2023.100073

Dratwa, B.: 'Put South Africans first': making sense of an emerging South African xenophobic (online) community. J. South. Afr. Stud. **49**(1), 85–103 (2023). https://doi.org/10.1080/03057070.2023.2170126

Earl, J., Braithwaite, J.M.: Layers of political repression: integrating research on social movement repression. Annu. Rev. Law Soc. Sci. **18**(1), 227–248 (2022). https://doi.org/10.1146/annurev-lawsocsci-050520-092713

Earl, J., Maher, T.V., Pan, J.: The digital repression of social movements, protest, and activism: a synthetic review. Sci. Adv. **8**(10) (2022). https://doi.org/10.1126/sciadv.abl8198

Echterling, L.G., Wylie, M.L.: In the public arena: Disaster as a socially constructed problem. In Response to disaster, pp. 327–346. Routledge (2013)

Fortuna, P., Nunes, S.: A Survey on automatic detection of hate speech in text. ACM Comput. Surv. **51**(4), 1–30 (2019). https://doi.org/10.1145/3232676

Fortuna, P., Rocha Da Silva, J., Soler-Company, J., Wanner, L., Nunes, S.: A Hierarchically-labeled portuguese hate speech dataset. In: Proceedings of the Third Workshop on Abusive Language Online, pp. 94–104 (2019). https://doi.org/10.18653/v1/W19-3510

Fourie, D.: The neoliberal influence on South Africa's early democracy and its shortfalls in addressing economic inequality. Philos. Soc. Criticism **50**(5), 823–843 (2024). https://doi.org/10.1177/01914537221079674

Freelon, D., Bossetta, M., Wells, C., Lukito, J., Xia, Y., Adams, K.: Black trolls matter: racial and ideological asymmetries in social media disinformation. Soc. Sci. Comput. Rev. **40**(3), 560–578 (2022). https://doi.org/10.1177/0894439320914853

Friedman, S.: Prisoners of the Past: South African democracy and the Legacy of Minority Rule. Wits University Press (2021)

Gagliardone, I., Gal, D., Alves, T., Martinez, G.: Countering online hate speech. Unesco Publishing (2015)

Garland, J., Ghazi-Zahedi, K., Young, J.-G., Hébert-Dufresne, L., Galesic, M.: Correction: impact and dynamics of hate and counter speech online. EPJ Data Sci. **12**(1), 27 (2023). https://doi.org/10.1140/epjds/s13688-023-00393-7

Gillespie, T.: Content moderation, AI, and the question of scale. Big Data Soc. **7**(2), 2053951720943234 (2020)

Gohdes, A.R.: Repression in the digital age: Surveillance, Censorship, and the Dynamics of State Violence. Oxford University Press (2024)

Hewitt, M.L., Masikane, C.M., Toendepi, J.: Dynamics informing xenophobia and leadership response in South Africa. Acta Commercii **20**(1), 1–11 (2020)

Kaziboni, A., Lancaster, L., Machabaphala, T., Mulaudzi, G.: Scapegoating in South Africa: busting the myths about immigrants. ISS South. Afr. Rep. **2022**(53), 1–16 (2022)

Levy, B., Hirsch, A., Naidoo, V., Nxele, M.: South Africa: When strong institutions and massive inequalities collide. Endowment for International Peace, Cape Town: Carnegie (2021)

Lupton, D.: Digital risk society. In Routledge handbook of risk studies (pp. 301–309). Routledge (2016)

Mathew, B., et al.: Thou shalt not hate: countering online hate speech. In: Proceedings of the International AAAI Conference on Web and Social Media, vol. 13, pp. 369–380 (2019).https://doi.org/10.1609/icwsm.v13i01.3237

Mena, R.: Advancing "no natural disasters" with care: Risks and strategies to address disasters as political phenomena in conflict zones. Disaster Prev. Manage. Int. J. **32**(6), 14–28 (2023)

Motloung, O.M.: Effects of flood disasters on vulnerable residents in informal settlements in South Africa. African J. Dev. Stud. **14**(3) (2024)

Mtshali, L., Enaifoghe, A.: Exploring the socio-economic consequences of violence and looting protest in South African townships: the "Free Zuma" riots interrelation to job loss in Esikhawini Mall Kwazulu-Natal. African J. Peace Conflict Stud. **12**(3), 25 (2023)

Muringa, T.P.: A Critical Analysis of Populism and Xenophobic Discourse on Social Media in South Africa: A Case of@ OperationDudula and# PutSouthAfricansFirst Twitter Accounts

Murphy, M.: Habermas and social research: Between theory and method. Routledge (2017). https://doi.org/10.4324/9781315651347

Murthy, D.: Twitter: Social Communication in the Twitter Age (Second edition). Polity Press (2018)

Neethling, B.: Andre de Ruyter exposes Eskom sabotage campaign (2022). https://www.agrilimpopo.co.za/andre-de-ruyter-exposes-eskom-sabotage-campaign/

Ngcamu, B.S.: Understanding xenophobic attacks in South Africa: a systematic literature review. Modern Africa: politics. Hist. Soci. **12**(2), 83–113 (2025). https://doi.org/10.26806/modafr.v12i2.246

Olagunju, A., Govender, N., Frankish, T., Wade, J.P.: Audience inclusion in news reporting on facebook and twitter: the case of# feesmustfall. Int. J. Res. Bus. Soc. Sci. **11**(10), 292–302 (2022)

Papacharissi, Z.: A Networked Self and Platforms, Stories, Connections. Routledge, New York (2018)

Parthasarathy, D.: Inequality, uncertainty, and vulnerability: rethinking governance from a disaster justice perspective. Environ. Planning E: Nat. Space **1**(3), 422–442 (2018)

Pasquale, F.: The Black Box Society: The Secret Algorithms that Control Money and Information. Harvard University Press (2015)

Patti, V., Damiano, R., Bosco, C.: Ethical implications of analyzing opinions, emotions and interactions in social media. In: 2017 Seventh International Conference on Affective Computing and Intelligent Interaction Workshops and Demos (ACIIW), pp. 153–158 (2017).https://doi.org/10.1109/ACIIW.2017.8272606

Peters, L.E.R.: Beyond disaster vulnerabilities: An empirical investigation of the causal pathways linking conflict to disaster risks. Int. J. Disaster Risk Reduction **55**, 102092 (2021). https://doi.org/10.1016/j.ijdrr.2021.102092

Pfeffer, J., Mayer, K., Morstatter, F.: Tampering with Twitter's sample API. EPJ Data Sci. **7**(1), 1 (2018). https://doi.org/10.1140/epjds/s13688-018-0178-0

Power, M.: Organized Uncertainty: Designing a World of Risk Management. Oxford University Press, Oxford (2007)

Seagrave, J.: Protest in the face of catastrophe: extinction rebellion and the anti-politics of grief. Suomen Antropologi: J. Finnish Anthropol. Soc. **47**(2), 49–73 (2023). https://doi.org/10.30676/jfas.101239

Sinwell, L., Maggott, T., Ngwane, T.: Weaponising Grassroots Democracy: Operation Dudula's right-wing populism and the need for a counter movement. mistra Johannesburg (2023)

Smith, G.S., Anjum, E., Francis, C., Deanes, L., Acey, C.: Climate change, environmental disasters, and health inequities: the underlying role of structural inequalities. Current Environ. Health Rep. **9**(1), 80–89 (2022)

Solomon, H., Kosaka, H.: Xenophobia in South Africa: reflections, narratives and recommendations. South. Afr. Peace Secur. Stud. **2**(2), 5–30 (2013)

Sorce, G., Dumitrica, D.: #fighteverycrisis: pandemic shifts in fridays for future's protest communication frames. Environ. Commun. **17**(3), 263–275 (2023). https://doi.org/10.1080/17524032.2021.1948435

Steinberg, J.: Security and disappointment: policing, freedom and xenophobia in South Africa. Br. J. Criminol. **52**(2), 345–360 (2012)

Stremlau, N., Gagliardone, I.: Socio-legal approaches to online hate speech. In Routledge Handbook of Socio-Legal Theory and Methods, pp. 385–398. Routledge (2019)

Tella, O.: Understanding xenophobia in South Africa: the individual, the state and the international system. Insight Africa **8**(2), 142–158 (2016). https://doi.org/10.1177/0975087816655014

Tierney, K.: Social inequality, hazards, and disasters. On Risk and Disaster: Lessons from Hurricane Katrina **2**(1), 109–128 (2006)

Tshishonga, N.: The legacy of apartheid on democracy and citizenship in post-apartheid South Africa: an inclusionary and exclusionary binary? Afr. J. Dev. Stud. **9**(1), 167–191 (2019)

Tucker, J.A., et al.: Social media, political polarization, and political disinformation: a review of the scientific literature. Polit. Polarization, Polit. Disinf. Rev. Sci. Lit. (2018)

Vhumbunu, C.H.: The July 2021 protests and socio-political unrest in South Africa: Reflecting on the causes, consequences and future lessons. Conflict Trends **2021**(3), 3–13 (2021)

Waugh, B., Hashemi, O., Rahman, S., Abdipanah, M., Cook, D.: Twitter deception and influence: issues of identity, slacktivism, and puppetry. J. Inf. Warfare **13**(1), 58–71 (2014)

Wessels, N.G.: #FeesMustFall: Discourse Hidden in Plain Sight [Tilburg University] (2017). https://pure.uvt.nl/ws/portalfiles/portal/32304634/TPCS_191_Wessels.pdf

Yang, J., Cheng, C., Shen, S., Yang, S.: Comparison of complex network analysis software: Citespace, SCI 2 and Gephi, pp. 169–172 (2017)

Parliaments in the Digital Age – Building Blocks for a Theoretical Framework

Christoph Konrath[(✉)] [iD] and Anna Rathmair

Austrian Parliamentary Administration, 1017 Vienna, Austria
`{christoph.konrath,anna.rathmair}@parlament.gv.at`

Abstract. The last years have seen a surge of debates and research on the impact of digitalisation on democracy and state institutions. Interestingly, neither strand of debate has discussed the transformation of parliaments and parliamentary democracy in a digital world. In this paper, we will argue that we need a theory of parliament for the digital age and that discussions of societal and democratic transformations cannot be conducted without reference to specific institutions.

Keywords: Democracy · Parliament · Digitalisation

1 Introduction

The last years have seen a surge of debates and research on the impact of digitalisation on the public sphere in general and democracy in particular. Interestingly, though, neither strand of debate has so far discussed the transformation of parliaments and parliamentary democracy in a digital world. This is notable for at least three reasons: (I) Still, the prevailing model of democracy in our world assigns a central role to parliaments and thus to intermediary institutions of political deliberation, political performance and political decision-making. (II) Parliaments can only fulfil their constitutionally assigned role and perform to the satisfaction of citizens if they have capacity to do so. Hence, they need to have the knowledge and means to fulfil their roles, which include technological infrastructure and an understanding of how society, administration, the economy etc. function. (III) Parliaments have always strived to act autonomously which included the full control of procedures, documentation and technical infrastructure.

All these matters are up for debate today. We argue that we need a theory of parliament to discuss them in the digital age and we will hold that discussions of societal and democratic transformations cannot be conducted without reference to specific institutions. To this end, we will address two interrelated questions: Why does academic research neglect the digital transformation of parliaments? What can be the building blocks of a theoretical framework for studying parliaments in the digital age? These questions are of particular significance because many debates about reforming democratic systems and societies center on new technologies that seek to create new forms of politics. This may be because traditional institutions are no longer considered viable.

Our approach is based on arguments of political and social theory that are reference points for other research disciplines, too. We will proceed in four steps: We start with

L. Hagedorn et al. (Eds.): DIGHUM 2025, LNCS 16319, pp. 280–294, 2026.
https://doi.org/10.1007/978-3-032-11108-1_20

a brief review of academic and practical debates on the digitalisation of the various branches of government (2). We will offer some tentative reasons as why research on democracy and parliaments fails to grasp the issue of digitalisation (3). Then, we will make an argument why we need a theory of parliaments of the digital age (4), and we will present three building blocks for theorizing further (5).

2 The Digital Transformation of Politics, Law and Governance – Analysis and Practice

Studies on digitalisation and its wider effects juxtapose the rise of digital technologies and vested interests in them with established views of democratic institutions and practices. More often than not, the focus is on individual responsibility and the arguments are based on concepts and classifications of the paper age (cf. Prainsack 2025; Bennett & Livingston 2025; Forestall 2022). In this section, we will give a brief overview of debates in the fields of political science, political theory, law as well as administrative and policy studies and practice.

2.1 Democracy

The emergence of the internet was accompanied by a vision of expanding and simplifying opportunities for democratic participation (Risse 2023: 59 ff.). Digital systems were expected to improve these instruments and make them more accessible. While these possibilities are still acknowledged, a substantial part of current discourses focuses on the threats and opportunities of digitalisation in general and AI in particular for democracy (cf. Jungherr 2023). The emphasis is on the information environments, the influence of social media platforms and technology companies, the speed, multiplicity and immediacy of information that impact the way in which politics and political actors are seen and discourses are led (Thiel 2023). The discourse is about what enables and hinders democratic deliberation and decision making. Still, it is acknowledged that digitalisation could help immensely to improve the accessibility of information, broaden participation, and make decision-making based on data and consensus possible (Landemore 2024). Digital systems are increasingly used by political parties and organisations for their own strategic purposes and the expansion of their knowledge of and contacts with supporters and to enable direct communication with them (Darius & Römmele 2023).

These works provide lots of insights on the impact of digitalisation on democratic society and democratic systems in general. But a growing body of research makes clear how such participatory uses can be susceptible to malfunction (Kreps & Kriner 2023) and that they cannot solve the fundamental resource problems of modern democracies – time, interest, personal encounters and knowledge (Risse 2023).

But most contributions stop short of discussing the effects on and transformations of democratic and state institutions. They focus on institutional backgrounds and theoretical assumptions but fail to address the repercussions for existing democratic institutions. Conversely, the dominating traits of research on the trajectories of democracy (backsliding or recovery) and the erosion of institutions do hardly consider social technologies and their impact (cf. Bennett/Livingston 2025).

2.2 Law

The rule of law is deeply connected with our understanding of liberal democracy and its institutions (cf. Habermas 1998). On the one hand, debates about the digital transformation of law are concerned with the regulation of the digital realm and the powers it wields (Postema 2023, 263 ff.). On the other hand, they ask whether AI can become a legal subject of its own (Boyle 2025). These questions can never be separated from legal practice and the widely held view that law is structured in a binary manner – i.e. legal/illegal – and can be applied in an objective, almost mechanical manner (cf. Luhmann 2004; Stanojević et al. 2025). In addition, legal information and knowledge have been heavily digitised since the 1980ies and the practice of lawyering (in the widest sense) has been transformed and commercially exploited (Schwarcz et al. 2025). Therefore, the discourse about law and digitalisation is also one about the future of legal reasoning and what it means to delegate the drafting of laws, administrative decision making, litigating and judging to machines. In general, such debates focus on court proceedings and the role of judges and do hardly consider other branches of government. This is in line with the tradition of legal discourse (cf. Waldron 1999, 21 ff.).

2.3 Policies and Administration

For years, policy and administrative studies have been concerned with questions of knowledge transfer and expertise (cf. Bogner et al., 2022, Eyal & Medvetz 2023). In that context, a lot of research is being conducted on the reliance of policy makers and administrators on digital infrastructures and how they affect their governance and relation to politics and citizens (cf. Goosens et al. 2025). The research is closely connected to the study of science, technology and society. Often, it uses general conceptions of a democratic society as a reference point when discussing digital infrastructures, regulatory practices, data regimes, justice, and the various influences on decision-making, such as biases, data and algorithms. Similar to legal studies, they will typically adopt a broader view of democratic institutions focusing, this time, on democratically legitimated executive government (cf. Rossanvallon 2015). However, as some have noted (cf. Chambers, 2023), this carries the risk of focusing on technological and design matters rather than the political interests and actors involved.

2.4 Parliamentary Practice

None of those discourses pays particular attention to parliaments. However, there is an intense and world-wide discussion of the effect of digitalisation on parliaments and the need that parliaments catch up with technological developments (cf. IPU 2024). These discussions are driven by the perception of common and unified practical challenges and demands. This stems from the fact that practically every parliament has created individual IT-solutions since the 1980ies. They have done so out of the conviction that parliaments are autonomous and must have the capacity to function independently under any circumstances. In a way, they have continued the traditions that were started in the 19th century: Then, every parliament had to be equipped with its own chancellery, printing press, archive and library etc. (cf. Rizzoni 2024). The growing mass and complexity of parliamentary data, user expectations, accessibility and usability of parliamentary services, security concerns and the costs for hardware, programming and maintenance have called the underlying assumptions into question (IPU 2024). Today, parliaments are confronted with a costly and increasingly unmanageable technological legacy on the one hand, and budgetary, personnel and legal constraints on the other hand. Still, they have to organise and manage complex procedures, produce a huge variety of records and documents, inform and communicate with the public and present themselves in a manner that confirms with current expectations of design and techno-logy. These questions cannot be solved by technology alone but affect the ways in which parliaments are organised. There seems to be no alternative than to adapt as fast as possible (cf. Citino 2024). In this context, a specific practice-related genre of research is developing that is particularly concerned with the use of AI-systems in parliaments and proposing rules and guidelines for their implementation in parliaments (cf. Fitsilis & Luís Kimaid 2024).

3   Why is There Hardly Any Research on Parliaments and Digitalisation?

When we take up the practical examples mentioned before, they can be roughly divided into four groups: (1) the management of complex procedures, (2) the provision and analysis of large amounts of data, (3) the specific media that structures parliamentary practice and information (i.e. parliamentary motions and records) and (4) the maintenance of a stable, efficient and effective parliamentary infrastructure. In many ways, these four elements are rarely covered by parliamentary research. Political theory, political science and legal studies operate on a much more abstract level and are therefore not necessarily aligned with the practice of parliaments. In particular, they have a long history of neglecting the materiality of democratic practices and institutions (Risse 2023: 47 ff.).

In many ways, even the most complex political theories are built on minimal conceptions of democracy that follow the pattern of 17th and 18th century theorising that was still able to focus on small, clearly defined groups of political actors and policy areas. Such minimal conceptions have proliferated in the 20th century and continue to do so (cf. Volkmann 2025, Waldron 2016). The ontology of most research on parliaments is built on such minimal conceptions, too. It focuses on parliamentarians and procedures as if parliamentarians – and they together in their parties – would do everything on their own, and as if procedures would provide a clear course of action. The standard texts and references of parliamentary research (Döring 1995; Martin/Saalfeld/Strøm 2014; Benoît/Rozenberg 2020; Martin/Strøm 2024) continue to present parliaments as institutions solely made up of their statutory members. Even in a research framework whose main focus is on the capacity of parliaments to fulfil their functions and exercise their powers (Martin/Strøm 2024: 14 ff.) the discussion of infrastructure and resources that go beyond members remains marginal. The same can be said of the standard texts on analysing parliamentary debates such as Proksch/Slapin (2014). They treat parliamentary records as if they were an exact transcript of what is said in the chamber and thus, they are able to treat parliamentary texts as data without any thought on how these texts are created and which cultural techniques and media shape parliaments and how they work.[1]

But still, many elements of political infrastructures have always been in the public eye – the creation of libraries, the quest for the best available technologies for record taking and managing parliamentary functions, as well as the disputes about funding parliamentary infrastructure and personnel (Rizzoni 2024, Vismann 2000, Minkinnen 2023). These discussions have always had high political salience as they concern the capacity of a parliament to function in a meaningful way and to claim a relevant role in the political process.[2]

Interestingly, a lot of research on democratic participation as well as on improving the relationship between representatives and citizens is concerned with technological changes and how they can be used to improve traditional political institutions (cf. Neblo/Esterling/Lazer 2018). But researchers have so far not made the connection of how these technologies could be used or could affect parliaments themselves.

What we encounter here, are two core problems of research methodology: (1) Ontological choices are logically prior to epistemological and methodological choices (cf. Wolkenstein/Wratil 2025: 11) and (2) the proposition that non-living things have none or only limited effects on our ways to conceptualise social relations (cf. Bennett 2010). The framework of reference for parliamentary studies does not consider the infrastructure that parliaments need to function, nor the technologies and media on which parliaments and other state institutions rely and which structure their practices. In that sense, parliamentary research is prone to overlook the challenges that parliaments face in a digital world.

4   Why Do We Need a Theory of Parliamentarism of the Digital Age?

In the preceding sections, we introduced the various discourses on the digitalisation of democracy and democratic practices, as well as legal systems. We also highlighted the peculiar neglect of these developments and shaping factors in the fields of research that influence our understanding of democracy. In this section, we aim to provide some reasons why this neglect is problematic and why a new way of theorising is important from an academic and a practical point of view.

In the history of parliamentarism, historical and legal – thus paper-based – approaches have been crucial to explain how parliaments have developed and adapted to new situations (cf. Benoît/Rozenberg 2020; Waldron 2016). They have been close to an everyday understanding of politics focused on people, debates and voting. The lifeworlds and the command of various technologies that have formed the background of the prevailing understanding and practice of parliaments and democracy in parliaments themselves, in the public and in academia are changing in a fast pace. The shaping of our new digital world is in many ways deeply linked to democratic transformation and crisis (cf.

---

[1] See Vismann 2000 and Minkinnen 2023 on the long neglect of media and cultural techniques in legal and administrative studies. There is yet no comparable work on parliaments.

[2] Academic research is still scarce. See for example Leston-Bandeira/Meakin/Thompson (2025), Christiansen/Griglio/Lupo (2023) and Brandsma/Otjes (2024).

Bennett/Livingston 2025). Today, we all live in digital environments and a lot of our interactions and institutions depend (a) on the view that social and political challenges can be addressed on the basis of data rather than normative assumptions (cf. Ulbrich et al. 2025), and (b) on the infrastructure provided by a small number of immensely powerful companies that do not necessarily share democratic ideals (cf. European Group of Ethics 2023: 50 ff., Postema 2023: 263 ff., Zuboff 2019). The ideas of and demands on the functioning of public services are increasingly shaped by experiences with the digital platform economy (Ulbrich/Frey 2024). There is a race to assess the risks and to understand, adapt to and regulate all those changes and there is a plethora of suggestions and narratives on how this can be done (cf. Wendehorst et al. 2024). But the theories about and descriptions of parliaments are still built upon paper-based processes, time-delayed dissemination and documentation of proceedings, expert-oriented means of information retrieval and implicit knowledge about institutional practices. In many ways, parliaments appear to be out of touch. This may be a reason why the literature on democratic innovation is hardly concerned with parliaments (see before).

We can identify two 'double gaps' that characterise the current parliamentary experience: The first is a double gap between the public, the parties and parliaments. It is a technological and a legal gap. Applications that many people find intuitive to use will often be not allowed for use in parliaments. They do not confirm with data protection rules, they do not confirm with security measures etc. That became evident in the Covid-19-pandemic and its turn to online meetings and led to major disappointments and misunderstandings in parliaments (cf. Bereuter/Konrath 2022) and continues to be a key concern of practical debates (cf. IPU 2024). The second double gap is a democratic and infrastructural one: Digital politics rely primarily on data- rather than rule-based approaches and the technologies behind rely on commercial solutions. It is therefore questionable, if traditional theories and approaches based on autonomous parliaments that create their own rules, practices and infrastructure can still provide a basis for coherent theoretical explanations.

Interdisciplinary studies of the impact of digital technologies that have become known as 'Digitalisation and Society' or 'Digital Humanism' (cf. Werthner et al. 2024, Fenner 2025) are aware of the effects on democratic institutions, but their understanding of the affected institutions remains generic (cf. Metakides 2024). Also, this becomes explicit in the various contributions on the practice of digitalisation of parliaments (see supra 2.) and the major transformation of the administrative and legal state (cf. Ulbrich/Frey 2024). In both, there seems to be a deep perception of what is changing and there are attempts to adapt existing instruments and practices to new realities. But adaptation seems to be more often than not the investment in computing power and digital skills. The perception of the role and practice of parliaments is built on minimal and mechanistic views of democratic institutions – as if parliamentary procedures follow simple rules on how to set the agenda, organise speaking and arrange votes and can thus be easily automated. The same can be said of attempts to regulate the risk of AI-systems and to strengthen democratic institutions that may be based on simplistic conceptualizations of core terms and the institutions they aim to preserve (cf. Laux et al. 2024). However, if the realisation and future development of democracies depends on factors such as expertise, relevance, inclusivity and transparency (cf. Näsström, 2021) such minimal conceptions will not provide suitable answers. They will not address that democracy is about sharing knowledge and responsibilities.

This is evident in practical debates when the focus is primarily on what is technically possible and legally permissible. In contrast, a broader approach might involve a number of risks for established practices and organisations. It calls for a review of the existing formal rules and hierarchies, informal practices and conventions, established narratives and explanations to determine whether they can also stabilise and control the institution under digital conditions (cf. Crusoe, Magnusson & Eklund 2024). In this context, a traditional approach that focuses on whether a particular technology can be used legally may seem sufficient. From an organisational point of view, this is a risky strategy because it puts the burden of decision making on those groups – legal experts and politicians – that are most likely to have the least knowledge of the technological issues, the epistemological questions and practical issues at stake, and the least time to consider them all. From a democratic point of view, it puts aside all considerations of the public purpose and responsibilities of any state body in general and parliaments in particular.

The need for a parliamentary theory of the digital age is thus not only driven by technological changes and it cannot be satisfied by adopting and regulating technology alone (cf. Chambers 2023). It goes much deeper and asks what a parliament is supposed to be, why we need parliaments and what we can expect from them. It must therefore go beyond a minimal and mechanistic view (in other words: counter arguments why automated legislation may be sufficient to benefit societies under the rule of law). In order to achieve this, it will be necessary to broaden the institutional concept of parliaments. This, in turn, can create opportunities for renewing thinking about the responsibility of state institutions in democracy and for developing political theory in the context of digital societies. The institutional robustness of liberal democracy and the rule of law that is so often invoked these days can only be build and secured if we integrate such a broader institutional understanding. Rules alone cannot save democracy.

5 How Can We Formulate a Theory of Parliamentarism of the Digital Age?

In the remainder of this paper we want to present three building blocks to (re-)establish connections between parliaments in the digital age and classical democratic theory. We will sketch a way to integrate technological transformations in our ways to conceive of parliaments. Finally, we want to suggest how it can become possible to broaden the institutional understanding of parliaments and thus to overcome the deficiencies that we have identified in Sect. 3.

5.1 Starting Points

A particular strength of talking about democracy as parliamentary democracy is that we can refer to iconic buildings, dedicated spaces, established rules and practices and elections. Speaking of buildings reminds us that there have to be people who look after them, who see that everything functions properly and is there when needed. This can help to understand how democracies work, how the built space enables politicians to resolve conflicts, to engage with citizens or to learn from experts (or fail to do so). Such an approach can lead to a very concrete and material understanding of democracy. It relates to particular practices and technologies and pays attention to the lifeworld of politicians, administrators and the public.

By contrast, more general discussions about democracy can lead to a much more limited understanding of it and lead to misunderstandings or disappointments. When democracy is reduced to the will of the people or the decision of the majority it can be difficult to understand why so many matters cannot be decided at once (cf. Loewenberg 2007). The same can apply to complex and elaborate conceptions of democracy like deliberative democracy especially if we consider 'two-track' models of deliberative democracy in which public justification is achieved through institutionalised deliberative bodies like parliaments and informal, not centrally coordinated communication in the public sphere (cf. Habermas 1998). Furthermore, we can recall theories that emphasise the epistemic and problem-solving qualities of deliberative democracy that we have already presented in Sect. 1.

For us, it is important to note that these three models – making (and thus constructing) majority decisions, earnest and well-intentioned political deliberation and democratic discourse as a means of problem-solving – dominate the current discourse on the threats and opportunities of digitalisation of democracy (Jungherr 2023). The focus here is, as we have described in Sect. 2, on the information environments that impact the way in which politics and political actors are seen and discourses are led. But again we have to take note that they operate with infrastructures that are not their own.

5.2   Building Block 1: Designing for Parliaments

Jennifer Forestal (2022) has presented a different approach. She starts from a wide conception of democracy as a collective activity of decision-making in common affairs which can extend to all areas of our lives. She then distinguishes between the effects of digital technologies on democracy and the intentional building of an environment for democracy – she does so regardless of whether we have a digital or physical environment in mind. This is a seemingly simple distinction, but it can have far-reaching implications. Much of the debate, especially about the risks and destructive power of social media on democracy, is about how to improve existing platforms - i.e. through mandatory fact-checking - and how to strengthen users' individual social capital - i.e. through media literacy programmes. Instead, Forestal asks how we have tried to create environments conducive to democracy in the past, and how we can do so now. Such an approach can enable us to identify and explain the shift from the physical to the digital and the interaction between the two spheres.

A democratic space, in Forestal's conception, must provide 'three requisite democratic affordances' that define its possible use: boundaries, durability and flexibility. Citizens (understood in a broad sense) must be able to recognize themselves as members of communities (here, she thinks of Aristoteles' idea of 'political friendship' within a defined community). They must be able to form lasting attachments to those communities (here, she is inspired by Alexis de Tocqueville's description of democratic habits). And, finally, they must be able to work collaboratively to experiment with and improve those affordances (here, she recalls John Dewey's democratic experimentalism). This set of democratic affordances can, as Forestal points out, help us 'to think about what we are doing' and 'highlight what we are not doing – what is missing from our current efforts'. In addition, it can help to identify negative and unintended consequences of interventions to 'fix digital technologies for democracy' as they tend to focus more often than not on individual actions and isolate the technical elements from the political and systemic ones.

Forestal's perspective can be adapted to parliaments. Her three democratic affordances – boundaries, durability and flexibility – can relate to three core elements of parliaments and offer a way to connect to everyday experiences.

Boundaries. A parliament is a built space and a boundary object in the tradition of science, technology and society studies (Star/Griesemer 1989). It is often perceived and presented as the built centre of a democratic state and political community. It can symbolise that community and it can stand for what the members of that community share, and provide models for political performance and discourse in that community (cf. Leston-Bandeira/Caluwaerts/Vermassen 2024). This creates a boundary in Forestal's sense, in that it becomes instrumental for defining a political community so that its members can reasonably expect with whom and why they form a particular community. A parliament forms a boundary in a second sense, too. It is a representative institution not only in the classical sense of an assembly of elected representatives, but also because it must take into account the ideas and concerns of those who are not present and those who are not represented at all. There is a third boundary, namely the way in which parliaments have their own rules of conducting and documenting their affairs. A parliament is thus an intermediary or mediating institution, because a liberal democracy needs institutions that enable and support all its members in deliberating and decision-making, and that 'mediate' between them, so that no group can exert pressure on others or abandon fair procedures. As intermediary institutions, parliaments are characterised by a series of interruptions and the 'Medienbrüche' (media disruptions) as yet another boundary. Laws cannot be passed immediately, even if majorities are clear, and control cannot be exercised directly (cf. Näsström 2021; Kelsen 1929: 30), debates shall be recorded and not just transcribed in order to make them accessible for outsiders and in the future.

Thinking and working in parliaments centers around built spaces – where to go, where to meet, where to sit. At the same time, people in parliaments are part of digital lifeworlds that are designed to create a sense of immediacy and lead to the impression that 'distance' as a defining element of the contemporary shortcomings of democracy can be overcome. Parliamentarians and their parties create and use digital platforms for their political activities, administrators attempt to use them to connect citizens to 'their' parliament (cf. Serra-Silva/Leston-Bandeira 2026). The knowledge of acting in built spaces could be a starting point for thinking about experiences of digital spaces, too. Knowledge of acting in representative and intermediary institutions – institutions accustomed to considering those who are not present – could lead to thinking of how digitalisation, and digital platforms in particular, can improve relations with members of the political community while simultaneously being designed to define clear boundaries. In that way, neither their physical nor their digital spaces could be overwhelmed by the mass and speed of digital communication possibilities (cf. Neblo/Esterling/Lazer 2018), and the technological gaps and practical expectations could be addressed. This could include developing strategies for information, communication with citizens and education, the safeguarding of the institution's digital sovereignty and the designing of specific tools to engage with the institutions, its members and the matters that are discussed there. The openness for citizens, their concerns and ideas about democracy and politics could also be a starting point to include the citizens' perspectives on digitalisation, automation and – for example – automated interactions. An approach, that is so far rather rare in administrative and state contexts in which digitalisation is most often perceived primary in terms of increasing work efficiency.

Durability. A parliament is meant to be a lasting and durable institution. It has fixed procedures and puts a lot of emphasis on the quality of its operations and documentation (cf. Vismann 2000). It operates on the basis of a stable calendar and rhythms of debates and exchanges. Members and staff usually know what is expected from them in terms of behaviour and decorum and they remind each other that their actions should serve as a model of democratic practices. Parliamentarism is also about information gathering, knowledge production and the conviction that a representative assembly can approach truth in a democratic and procedural manner and with a clearly defined (and again lasting and foreseeable) set of instruments. In the 19th century, liberal thinkers saw parliaments as educational institutions, as well (cf. Selinger 2019; Rizzoni 2024). Minimalist conceptions of democracy and parliamentarism have since tended to neglect this aspect (Selinger 2019). The background culture, that was once thought to be upheld by the epistemological and educational functions of parliamentary procedures is lost when rules and practices are reduced to workflows and government and administrative processes become data-driven and automated – thereby eliminating direct human interaction. This is amplified when procedures are transposed into algorithms and there is a reliance on commercial providers. Then, knowledge and control over how parliament processes a given problem can be lost (cf. Ulbrich/Frey 2024).

The truthfulness and trust on which parliaments rely and to which they – ideally - aspire, should prove that we as a society can rely on and trust each other. In the context of a political theory of the digital age, these ideals are transferred to the demand for high-quality data, information access and the (im)possibility of attaining truth (cf. Risse 2023: 187 ff.) When parliamentary democracy is, as we have suggested before (Sect. 4), truly about fair and equal participation and burden sharing, it is necessary to discuss the groundwork that this can become possible. Then, durability of democratic practices will also rely on parliaments as trustworthy sources of data and information. Today, data are social facts that make up our world. They relate to people, they are used to create relations in order to foster political, commercial and economic interests and they shape social relations. Under such conditions, political solidarity cannot be thought of without reference to data any more, justice cannot be thought of without reference to knowledge (cf. Prainsack & El-Sayed 2023).

Flexibility. Forestal's third affordance is flexibility or the experimental character of democracy that is open to new influences and changes. Despite their adherence to formal rules, parliamentary procedures are characterised by a great deal of flexibility. This is evident in the often broad wording of parliamentary rules of procedure which leave much room for political approaches to use and conflict resolution. Over the last decades, however, rules of procedure have become much more detailed in many parliaments (Konrath 2021). Digitalisation supports such efforts as it promises efficient procedures and standardised workflows (Citino 2024). Still, people who work and act in parliaments will often retain a familiarity with flexible approaches. When they are asked to explain the workings of a parliament they will most likely emphasise its interpretative flexibility (Pinch/Bijker 1987) and highlight its ability to enable plural discourse and ambiguity that digitalisation can put at risk. Parliamentary procedures make evident, that law and legal rules are – in the words of Gerald Postema "not only the instrument of governing power; law also affords the resources and forums for contesting that power and correcting the law on which governing power relies. Law […] is argumentative – it recognizes its own corrigibility, its 'resilient fragility'." (Postema 2023: 303). Digital – and in particular AI-driven – procedures can consider such revision only at the design level, but they cannot leave room for the kind of experimentation that has so far been considered by many as a core feature of democracy.

Each of this three affordances is connected to what parliamentarians, their staff and all the people who work for a parliament do every day – maintaining a built space for democracy, welcoming visitors and students, informing the public, providing expertise and knowledge for politicians, documenting parliamentary procedures, ensuring rule-based discussions and decision-making, interpreting procedural and constitutional rules etc. However, if we only consider parliaments in a very limited way from the outset (see Sect. 3), we must assume that all of this could be lost even in co-design processes involving people who work in parliaments. This makes it all the more necessary, to connect and rethink each of these in the light of technological developments. This provides an opportunity to not only rethink parliamentary democracy and the personal sacrifices required to maintain it, but also to express these thoughts and encourage others to join the conversation.

5.3   Building Block 2: Including Technological Autonomy

There is a second point, that we would like to add to Forestal's framework. Historically, the development of parliamentarism and democracy has not only relied on physical spaces. Material artefacts have also always been essential in supporting and facilitating debates, procedures and voting. Modern parliamentarism and modern ideas of politics could not have emerged without things and technologies - the printing press, the modern encyclopaedia as a basis for shared knowledge, or the possibility of illustrating newspaper articles (without newspapers, the parliamentary spectacles of the 19th century would never have made sense). Shorthand made rapid reporting possible, and modern filing and archiving systems made it possible for experts to retrieve information needed for political strategy. Democratic possibilities were shaped by the objects needed to make them happen. The point is, that parliaments, their members and their administrators evolved in parallel with these technologies and they shaped and influenced them in many ways (Rizzoni 2024).

This is radically different in two ways today. Firstly, parliaments, parliamentarians etc. apply technologies that have been developed by third parties which will usually have commercial interests. That creates situations in which it can be difficult to understand how a technology works, to assess its effects and to steer its influence on the operations and the way of thinking of a given institutional context. Secondly, the information asymmetry between parliaments and governments may increase once again because both have long since ceased to work on the basis of the same technologies. As soon as the administrative branch of government starts applying data-driven solutions, it will be much better positioned to respond to public and individual needs for regulation than a parliament, and will be able to deliver much more fine-grained solutions. (cf. Ulbrich et al. 2025: 22 ff.). Parliaments might neither be able to understand the concrete basis for governmental planning and decision-making and hold the government democratically accountable, nor will parliaments have an informational and technological basis for general-rule making at their disposal. Thus, any reconsideration of the role and function of parliaments will be incomplete without a sound theory of informational and technological affordances of parliaments as an institution.

5.4   Building Block 3: Seeing a Multitude of Actors

Finally, any possibility of managing technological and social change in a sovereign and ethically responsible way depends on people who are able to understand and reflect on technology, the (wider) purpose of democratic institutions, social and institutional relations and rules. This brings us to our final point. The examples that we have brought up before make obvious that neither parliaments nor parliamentarians are single actors. For long, parliamentary work has been supported by a complex web of parliamentary administrations, independent expert bodies, parliamentary group staff and parliamentarian's staff. All that is expected from a parliament today could not be achieved without them. What is even more important: Administrators and political staff have much lower turnover rates than parliamentarians. Their role in shaping and maintaining the institutional framework of parliaments can therefore be particularly influential in perpetuating institutional practices and narratives (cf. Christiansen/Griglio/Lupo 2023).

From an institutional perspective, administrators fulfil an important role that gives them a great deal of discretion and a certain degree of independence. From a legal and political perspective, however, they are seen as a mere extension of the institution formed solely by parliamentarians. But there is no reason to understand them in such a mechanical manner. In fact, they are usually bound by constitutional and legal rules that demand their loyalty to these rules and to the institution that they serve. Also, the sheer amount of work that is expected from them, presupposes that a lot of this work is done on the basis of individual responsibility and mutual trust between elected or appointed officials and administrative staff. In that way, their practice can have a representative quality, as Katharine Jackson (2023) and Anthony Bertelli (2021) have pointed out. They argue that the modern administration has a crucial role to play in upholding the democratic rule of law. It can be thought of as a representative institution of its own based on a trustee model. As it is responsible for serving the public interest, it can stand firm in the face of shifting popular opinion, pressure from political office holders or well-resourced minorities, and technological and economic forces.

6 Conclusion and Outlook

In this article, we began by asking two fundamental questions: Why does academic research neglect the digital transformation of parliaments? What can be the building blocks of a theoretical framework for studying parliaments in the digital age? In attempting to answer these questions, we have highlighted how a limited and minimalist view of democracy and parliamentarianism can result in the digital transformation of parliaments being narrowed down to the creation of workflows and the optimisation of technology use. This also has the effect of reducing the very important discourse on changes to and threats against democracy in the digital age to an analysis of communication processes and information environments. As a result, it becomes difficult to link this discourse to existing institutions. By contrast, we have attempted to adopt a different approach that does not reduce parliaments to tasks and procedures, thus avoiding the 'workflow trap' from the outset. If we view parliaments as intermediary institutions in a democratic society that rely on technologies and people who can engage with them reflectively, we can further develop our traditional models of just and rational democracy and politics in the digital age. This will enable us to initiate an interdisciplinary discourse on parliamentary democracy that moves beyond the paradigmatic procedural concepts of political science and law and offers a wide range of points of reference.

Disclosure of Interests.   No competing interests.

References

Bennett, J.: Vibrant Matter. A Political Ecology of Things. Duke UP, Durham (2010)

Bennett, W., Livingston S.: Platforms, politics, and the crisis of democracy: connective action and the rise of illiberalism. Perspect. Politics 1–20 (2025)

Benoît, C., Rozenberg, O. (eds.): Handbook of Parliamentary Studies. Interdisciplinary Approaches to Legislatures. Edward Elgar, Cheltenham (2020)

Bereuter, F., Konrath, C.: Digitalisierung von parlamenten in der COVID-19-Krise. In: Bogner, A., et al. (eds.) Digitalisierung und die Zukunft der Demokratie, pp. 205–217. Nomos, Baden-Baden (2022)

Bertelli, A.: Democracy Administered: How Public Administration Shapes Representative Government. Cambridge University Press, Cambridge (2021)

Boyle, J.: The Line. AI and the Future of Personhood. MIT Press, Cambridge (2025)

Bogner, A., et al. (eds.): Digitalisierung und die Zukunft der Demokratie. Beiträge aus der Technikfolgenabschätzung, Nomos: Baden-Baden (2022)

Brandsma, G., Otjes, S.: Gauging the roles of parliamentary staff. Parliam. Aff. **77**, 537–557 (2024)

Chambers, S.: Deliberative democracy and the digital public sphere: asymmetrical fragmentation as a political not a technological problem. Constellations **30**, 61–68 (2023)

Christiansen, T., Griglio, E., Lupo, N. (eds.): The Routledge Handbook of Parliamentary Administrations. Routledge, Basingstoke (2023)

Citino, Y.: Leveraging automated technologies for law-making in Italy: generative AI and constitutional challenges. Parliam. Aff. **20**, 1–23 (2024)

Crusoe, J., Magnusson, J., Eklund, J.: Digital transformation decoupling: the impact of wilful ignorance on public sector digital transformation. Gov. Inf. Q. **41**, 1–15 (2024)

Döring, H. (ed.): Parliaments and Majority Rule in Western Europe. Campus and St.Martin's Press, Frankfurt and New York (1995)

Darius, P., Römmele, A.: KI und datengesteuerte Kampagnen. In: Faas, T., et al. (eds.) Informationsflüsse, Wahlen und Demokratie, pp. 199-211, Nomos, Baden-Baden (2023)

European Group of Ethics in Science and New Technologies: Opinion on Democracy in the Digital Age. Publications Office of the European Union, Brussels (2023)

Eyal, G., Medvetz, T. (eds.): The Oxford Handbook of Expertise and Democratic Politics. Oxford UP, Oxford (2023)

Fenner, D.: Digitale Ethik. Narr Francke Attempto, Tübingen (2025)

Fitsilis, F., Kimaid, L. (eds.): Key Considerations of Artificial Intelligence in Parliaments (2024). https://doi.org/10.13140/RG.2.2.14008.15368

Forestal, J.: Designing for Democracy. Oxford UP, Oxford (2022)

Habermas, J.: Between Facts and Norms. Contributions to a Discourse Theory of Law and Democracy. Harvard UP, Cambridge (1998)

International Parliamentary Union: World e-parliament report 2004, IPU Publications, Geneva (2024)

Jackson, K.: Administration as democratic trustee representation. 29 Legal Theory 314 (2023). https://doi.org/10.1017/S1352325223000204

Jungherr, A.: Artificial intelligence and democracy: a conceptual framework. Soc. Media + Soc. 9(3) (2023). https://doi.org/10.1177/20563051231186353

Kelsen, H.: Wesen und Wert der Demokratie. Mohr, Tübingen (1929)

Konrath, C.: On the juridification of parliamentary practice and procedures. Int. J. Parliamentary Stud. 1, 7–21 (2021)

Kreps, S., Kriner, D.: How AI threatens democracy. J. Democr. 34, 122–131 (2023)

Landemore, H.: Can AI bring deliberative democracy to the masses? In: Chang, R., Srinivasan, A. (eds.) Conversations in Philosophy, Law, and Politics, pp. 39–49. Oxford UP, Oxford (2024)

Laux, J., Wachter, S., Mittelstadt, B.: Trustworthy artificial intelligence and the European Union AI act: on the conflation of trustworthiness and acceptability of risk. Regulation Govern. 18, 3–32 (2024)

Leston-Bandeira, C., Caluwaerts, D., Vermassen, D.: Reimagining engagement between citizens and parliaments. In: Judge, D., Leston-Bandeira, C. (eds.) Reimagining Parliament, pp. 65–82. Bristol UP, Bristol (2024)

Leston-Bandeira, C., Meakin, A., Thompson, L. (eds.): Exploring Parliament, 2nd edn. Oxford UP, Oxford (2025)

Loewenberg, G.: Paradoxes of legislatures. Daedalus 136, 56–66 (2007)

Luhmann, N.: Law as a Social System. Oxford UP, Oxford (2004)

Martin, S., Saalfeld, T., Strøm, K. (eds.): The Oxford Handbook of Legislative Studies. Oxford UP, Oxford (2014)

Martin, S., Strøm, K.: Legislative Assemblies. Oxford UP, Oxford (2024)

Metakides, G.: Democracy in the digital era. In: Werthner, H., et al. (eds.) Introduction to Digital Humanism, pp. 495–509. Springer, Cham (2024)

Minkinnen, P.: Media, cultural techniques, and the law: the other Cornelia Vismann. German Law Journal 24(9), 1597–1611 (2023)

Näsström, S.: The Spirit of Democracy. Oxford UP, Oxford (2021)

Neblo, M., Esterling, K., Lazer, D.: Politics with the People: Building a Directly Representative Democracy. Cambridge UP, New York (2018)

Pinch, T., Bijker, W.: The social construction of facts and artifacts. In: Bijker, W., Hughes, T., Pinch, T. (eds.) The Social Construction of Technological Systems, pp. 17–50. MIT Press, Cambridge (1987)

Postema, G.: Law's Rule. Oxford UP, Oxford (2023)

Prainsack, B., El-Sayed, S.: Beyond Individual rights: how data solidarity gives people meaningful control over data. Am. J. Bioeth. **23**, 36–39 (2023)

Prainsack, B.: Our stakes in data: how do we (re)gain democratic control over digital practices?, In: Goosens, J., et al (eds.) Public Governance and Emerging Technologies, pp. 131–147. Springer, Cham (2025)

Proksch, S., Slapin, J.: The Politics of Parliamentary Debate. Cambridge UP, Cambridge (2014)

Risse, M.: Political Theory of the Digital Age. Cambridge UP, Cambridge (2023)

Rizzoni, G.: Parliamentarism and Encyclopaedism. Hart, Oxford (2024)

Rossanvallon, P.: Le Bon Gouvernement. Le Seuil, Paris (2015)

Schwarcz, D., et al: AI-powered lawyering: AI reasoning models, retrieval augmented generation, and the future of legal practice (March 02, 2025). Minnesota Legal Studies Research Paper No. 25-16, U of Michigan Public Law Research Paper No. 24-058 (2025)

Selinger, W.: Parliamentarism. From Burke to Weber. Cambridge UP, Cambridge (2019)

Serra-Silva, S., Leston-Bandeira, C.: The invisible architects of public engagement: understanding the different types of roles played by parliamentary staff. Polit. Govern. **14** (2026, in progress)

Stanojević, A., Goossens, J., Keymolen, E.: Governance by Technology, Governance of Technology, In: Goossens, J., et al(eds.) Public Governance and Emerging Technologies, pp. 1-15, Springer, Cham (2025)

Star, S.L., Griesemer, J.: Institutional ecology, 'translations' and boundary objects. Soc. Stud. Sci. **19**(3), 387–420 (1989)

Thiel, T.: KI und Demokratie. Aus Politik und. Zeitgeschichte **73**, 23–28 (2023)

Ulbrich, C., Frey, B.: Automated Democracy. Herder, Freiburg i. B. (2024)

Ulbrich, C. et al.: The road to automated democracy. Monitor demokratiekompatible Digitalisierung des Staates. Basel (2025)

Vismann, C.: Akten. Medientechnik und Recht. S. Fischer, Frankfurt (2000)

Volkmann, U.: Demokratischer Minimalismus. Merkur **79**(912), 5–19 (2025)

Waldron, J.: Law and Disagreement. Oxford UP, Oxford (1999)

Waldron, J.: Political Political Theory. Harvard UP, Cambridge (2016)

Wendehorst, C., et al.: Narratives of digital ethics. AGIDE (Academies for Global Innovation and Digital Ethics) report. Verlag der ÖAW, Wien (2024)

Werthner, H., et al. (eds.): Introduction to Digital Humanism. A Textbook. Springer, Cham (2024)

Wolkenstein, F., Wratil, C.: Political Representation as Communicative Practice. Cambridge UP, Cambridge (2025)

Zuboff, S.: The Age of Surveillance Capitalism. Public Affairs, New York (2019)

Micro-degree Artificial Intelligence and Society

Jana Lasser[1(✉)] [ORCID] and Manfred Pfiffner[1,2]

[1] IDea_Lab, University of Graz, Leechgasse 34, 8010 Graz, Austria
`{jana.lasser,manfred.pfiffner}@uni-graz.at`
[2] University of Education Zurich, Lagerstrasse 2, 8090 Zürich, Switzerland

Abstract. We introduce the micro-degree "Artificial Intelligence and Society" developed by the University of Graz, a novel interdisciplinary program designed to bridge the gap between technical AI knowledge and its broader societal implications. Recognising the rapid permeation of AI into all aspects of life and the limitations of traditional educational systems in addressing this transformation, the target audience of the micro-degree is both students enrolled in traditional university degrees as well as the existing workforce. The 16 ECTS curriculum, spanning two semesters, covers the technical foundations of AI systems alongside their ethical, legal, economic, and educational impacts. It features a modular structure with basic knowledge lectures, hands-on application courses – including a mandatory technical AI course and electives in ethics, law, economics, and education –, and practicals where students implement AI-based solutions to real-world problems. Here, we describe the structure and content of the micro-degree, including the learning objectives of the individual degree modules. We also provide Open Educational Resources used for teaching the (mandatory) lecture and hands-on course on the technical foundations of artificial intelligence. This micro-degree represents a crucial step towards fostering digital humanism by enabling individuals to confidently understand, apply, and shape AI's role in society.

Keywords: micro-degree · artificial intelligence · society

1 Introduction

AI systems are increasingly permeating all aspects of life, fundamentally reshaping the economy, politics, and society. This profound transformation requires a new generation of specialists and leaders who not only possess technical know-how but can also understand and shape the complex social, ethical, and legal implications of these technologies. Consequently, understanding and being able to use AI tools has become a necessity in many people's lives to thrive professionally but also to be able to participate in and shape societal discourse around technological development. In this context, a consensus is emerging on the urgent need for interdisciplinary educational programs that bridge the gap between computer science and the humanities, social sciences, and law.

L. Hagedorn et al. (Eds.): DIGHUM 2025, LNCS 16319, pp. 295–307, 2026.
https://doi.org/10.1007/978-3-032-11108-1_21

The traditional educational system in many countries and particularly in Austria was not able to keep pace with the rapid introduction of technologies incorporating machine learning let alone generative AI. Austrian schools still struggle to establish computer science as mandatory part of their curriculum and education on the opportunities and perils of using AI tools is rare and strongly dependent on the motivation and knowledge of individual teachers. While many Austrian universities offer cutting-edge computer science degrees with specialisations in machine learning and artificial intelligence, these curricula don't address the need of the average citizen to become a knowledgeable, capable and self-determined user of these technologies. Furthermore, university degrees for artificial intelligence are still highly specialised and focused on technical knowledge and skills. If connections to other fields such as ethics, law, economics, and education are included at all, this happens more as an afterthought than a core part of the curriculum.

AI systems have diverse impacts on all areas of society and affect everyone to some extent. Every university thus has the task of reflecting on responsible use, critically monitoring the development of AI, adequately engaging with (generative) AI systems, appropriately integrating them into teaching and research, and providing the best possible support to both lecturers and students in applying these systems under the postulate of good scientific practice. Furthermore, a modern university should offer accessible educational programmes – including furhter education – which, on the one hand, address the impacts of AI systems across different scientific disciplines and, on the other hand, familiarise students with the practical use of specific AI tools. In this context, the handling and use of AI systems should be understood as a cross-cutting issue, the teaching of which leads to essential skill acquisition for students, supporting them in their studies and daily lives, and preparing them for future professional fields.

The University of Graz addresses the above-mentioned challenges through the introduction of the novel micro-degree "Artificial Intelligence and Society". The micro-degree aims to provide knowledge and skills about the technical foundations of AI systems, as well as the ethical, legal, economic, and educational implications of their applications. The curriculum is designed as a stand-alone degree comprising 16 ECTS over the course of two semesters that can be taken by students enrolled in any bachelor's or master's degree. Its introduction follows the recommendation of the Austrian Ministry for Education and Research for universities to offer micro-credentials [1] as a means to broaden the access to education.

In the following, we will first give an overview over existing similar curricula and distil where the micro-degree "Artificial Intelligence and Society" makes novel contributions. We will then describe the educational aims, content and structure of the micro-degree, followed of a brief description of the results of a pilot run that took place in the winter semester 2024/25 and the summer semester 2025. Lastly, we also provide Open Educational Resources for the teaching of the technical aspects of AI systems in the micro-degree (lecture slides and Jupyter Notebooks with examples and homework) aimed at students without any technical background at the following link: https://github.com/IDeaLab-uni-graz/MD-AI-and-society_technical-aspects/.

2 Related Educational Offerings

Interdisciplinary study programmes at the intersection between computer science and the social sciences and humanities, such as the master's degree "Social Data Science" offered by the University of Copenhagen [11], are an important part of the educational landscape. However, the present short review of existing educational offerings focuses on certificates that are smaller in scope than a traditional bachelor's or master's degree. These educational offerings primarily respond to the immediate needs of the labour market. Since companies and organisations cannot wait for the next generation of graduates to address the challenges posed by AI, a thriving market for shorter, focused qualification measures has emerged which is inhabited both by universities as well as non-university institutions. While non-university institutions primarily aim to quickly and specifically retrain the existing workforce, academic certificate programs primarily aim to train the professionals of tomorrow from the ground up. However, many universities also increasingly offer programmes for continuing education that address the existing workforce. Given the absence of any prerequisites regarding skills or knowledge beyond a university entry qualification (Austrian "Matura"), the micro-degree for AI and Society serves a dual role by both addressing students currently enrolled in traditional degree programmes at the University of Graz and other universities, as well as members of the existing workforce that wish to extend their education in the area of artificial intelligence.

The "Digitality. AI. Society" certificate at Saarland University [9] is likely the certificate programme most similar to the micro-degree AI and Society overall, and in the German language university landscape in particular. It is characterised by a core module that all students have to complete, which includes seminars from the areas of computer science, philosophy, economics and German philology, as well as a crash course in Python programming. After completing the core module, students can select from a number of modules from the above-mentioned areas to specialise further. A key difference between this certificate and the micro-degree AI and Society is the absence of content from the legal studies, as well as modules that offer students the possibility to get hands-on experience with AI tools and work on their own projects. While different in content, the course "Daten Lesen Lernen" (English: "learning to read data") offered by the University of Göttingen [12] offers a similar mix of lectures and hands-on classes in the related field of data literacy education [8].

Organizations such as TÜV Rheinland [10], GFU [5], and the IBB Business Akademie [7] offer short, intensive seminars on various combinations of AI ethics, responsible AI and social and legal implications of the use of AI. These educational offerings are primarily aimed at corporate employees and managers who need a quick understanding of compliance requirements and risk management and much shorter than the certificate programmes of the University of Graz and

Saarland University. The focus here is often on the practical implementation of ethical and legal guidelines in a corporate context.

Lastly, online platforms like Coursera offer a wide range of courses developed by renowned universities (e.g., Lund University, University of Edinburgh, University of Michigan) and leading technology companies (e.g., IBM, Google). These courses cover topics such as AI ethics, data ethics, and responsible innovation, offering a low-threshold, often beginner-friendly entry point. US universities like Georgetown University, with its six-week online certificate in "AI Governance & Compliance" [4], and Cornell University, with its two-week course on "Generative AI: Law and Ethics" [2], also serve this market with educational offerings of intermediate length and relatively narrow scope for flexible, part-time professional development.

3   Micro-degree AI and Society

3.1   Design Process and Administrative Implementation

The curriculum for the micro-degree in Artificial Intelligence and Society was developed on the basis of a strategic needs analysis conducted by the University of Graz, which highlighted its relevance in the context of AI-driven transformation processes. Based on this analysis and literature research on AI literacy, learning objectives were defined that combine technical fundamentals with ethical, legal, economic, and education-related dimensions. The curriculum structure follows a progression logic that extends from fundamentals to fields of application to practical implementation. The process of competence building takes place in a step-by-step and systematic approach. Both knowledge acquisition and the development of reflective and practice-oriented skills are taken into account. Key challenges in the design process arose from the need to combine dynamic technological developments with curricular stability, to integrate interdisciplinary content coherently, and at the same time to prepare it in a didactically compatible manner. In addition, the balance between scientific foundation, practice-oriented application, and organizational framework conditions required ongoing coordination with heterogeneous actors within and outside the university setting.

The courses of the micro-degree are intended for students of all degree programs at the University of Graz. As an interdisciplinary and cross-faculty additional qualification, the micro-degree is administratively located at the interface between the two vice-rectorates for Studies and Teaching, and Digitalization. The didactic leadership lies with the vice-rectorate for Studies and Teaching while the vice-rectorate for Digitalization provides administrative support. In addition, the micro-degree is supported by the cross-faculty interdisciplinary digital lab "IDea_Lab" of the university, which develops digital tools for teaching and research along the needs surfaced by novel educational offerings such as the micro-degree. One such tool is StudiGPT—a chat bot for students[1]—that can be used to explore the capabilities of generative text-based AI hands-on, as well as provide assistance when students learn how to code for the first time.

---

[1] https://idea-lab.uni-graz.at/de/lernen-anwenden-vernetzen/unigpt-und-studigpt/.

3.2   Educational Aims

AI competencies can be described using AICOMP [3], the first German-language competency structure model for AI-related competencies. It answers the question of which competencies are important in order to be, become and remain capable of acting successfully in a working and living environment permeated by AI. As a competence structure model, it defines not only the corresponding competences but also competence areas and competence fields that help to meaningfully relate and structure the various factors such as knowledge, values and the variety of possible skills. It structures the variety of possible competencies into three areas relating to (i) work/activity/task, (ii) personal development, and (iii) social environment/organization/world. The first area is comprised of competencies necessary for using AI applications in a professional context and for (further) developing them for individually or organizationally significant contexts of action. The second area is comprised of competencies necessary for acting confidently as an individual in a world permeated by artificial intelligence and for using AI concepts and tools responsibly and reflectively for one's own goals. The third area is comprised of competencies necessary for adequately using artificial intelligence in professional and private environments and in the creative design of new spaces for action in collaboration with others.

These three competency areas are realised in the five fields of action of the micro-degree: having the technical skills necessary to analyse and apply AI systems, being able to analyse the application of AI systems from a legal perspective, being able to analyse AI systems from an ethical perspective, and being able to analyse the impact of AI systems on the economy and education.

3.3   Structure of the Curriculum

The micro-degree is structured into three modules, dedicated to learning basic knowledge, applying the learned knowledge, and implementing a small AI project, respectively. Each of the three modules has content from all five fields of action (technical foundations, ethics, law, economy, and education). The content is taught by experts in the respective field, making the teaching an inherently interdisciplinary experience.

The first module is a lecture (4 ECTS) in which all lecturers give input from their respective fields. The lecture runs twice a week for the first half of the semester and is concluded by an online multiple-choice exam. Students that successfully complete the exam can enrol into the hands-on courses in which knowledge from the lecture is applied. The course on technical aspects of AI is mandatory for all students. In addition, students have to take a second course which they can select among courses on the ethical, legal, economic, and educational aspects of AI. The type of performance assessment varies for each course. Courses take place in the second half of the semester and each of the courses awards 3 ECTS, respectively. In the third module – a practical worth 6 ECTS – students can again select a field of action, independent of the field they selected for the hands-on courses, in which they want to implement an AI project. Students select a topic at the beginning of the semester and are supervised by practitioners in the relevant field throughout while they work on their project either alone or in small groups of 2–3 students. Project results are presented and assessed at the end of the semester.

3.4   Content

Basics. The lecture is dedicated to learning the basic knowledge relating to AI in the five fields of action. It starts with the establishment of an understanding of the technical aspects of artificial intelligence. Students learn Computational Thinking [6] as a foundation for understanding and implementing AI applications. They get to know the basics of various learning algorithms and their applications as well as the fundamentals of Natural Language Processing and its application in the form of large language models. Lastly, students learn about the technical foundations of systems that underlie content recommendation and knowledge retrieval as used for example on social media platforms and for search engines.

Next, students learn the relevant fundamental theories and central concepts of ethics and technology ethics. This relates to responsibility and accountability in the development and use of AI as well as justice and discrimination in the use of AI. Students engage in ethical considerations regarding transparency and explainability of algorithms and learn about the alignment of AI with fundamental moral and societal values. Lastly, security in the use of and trust in AI are discussed.

The introduction to the legal aspects of Artificial Intelligence comprises the legal sources, development history, application areas, legal requirements for the use of AI systems, regulation of AI (EU-AI Act), and the liability for AI. In addition, related legal areas such as data protection, liability law and copyright law are discussed. For data protection law, the responsibilities, legal bases, the definition of personal data, lawfulness of data processing, information obligations, data protection impact assessment (DPIA), and notification obligations in case of data breaches are introduced. Furthermore, the special requirements for the use of AI, particularly considering the General Data Protection Regulation (GDPR) and the EU-AI Act are discussed. For liability law, the legal consequences and limits of civil liability when using AI systems, especially considering the Product Liability Act (ProdHaftG) and the EU-AI Act are discussed. Copyright law covers the scope and limitations of copyright protection for AI-generated works, and the use of copyrighted works as training data for AI applications.

Regarding the implications of the use of AI systems in the area of economics, the use of AI in organizations and their potential for new business models are discussed. Students learn to recognise the opportunities and risks of AI for organizations and to understand the impact of AI systems on the world of work.

Lastly, the implications of AI systems for the education sector are analysed and competencies that will become relevant in the future are derived. Students learn to identify and evaluate the opportunities and challenges of AI in educational contexts at different levels of education, and to explain the effects of AI applications in the education context, particularly in assessment.

After completion of the first module, students are expected to have reached the following learning objectives in the five fields of action: Being able to ...

- apply computational thinking to illustrate the possible uses of AI systems.
- identify the application areas of various learning algorithms.
- explain the functionality of generative models and enumerate their advantages and disadvantages.
- elaborate on the functionality of decision support systems in the field of content recommendation and ranking, and analyse their influence on human decision-making.
- grasp and analyse fundamental questions of AI ethics, particularly moral accountability in the development and application of AI.
- identify and apply the legal sources relevant to the use of AI systems.
- recognise legal risks associated with the use of AI systems and identify the related problem areas.
- enumerate the legal requirements for the use of AI according to the EU AI Act and the GDPR.
- identify central problems in the use of AI in various sub-disciplines of law and trace the legal scholarly discussion (regulation according to the AI Act, liability, data protection law, copyright, civil liability).
- identify the potential uses of AI in organizations, particularly the possibility of new business models.
- discuss the opportunities and risks of AI for organizations.
- explain the impact of AI systems on the world of work and draw conclusions for their own career planning.
- explore the relationships between the use of AI and educational dynamics, and based on this, identify the necessary competencies for the digital future.
- differentiate the potentials and limitations of AI in educational environments and evaluate their relevance for educational processes and assessment practices.

Application. The hands-on courses are dedicated to applying the knowledge acquired in the preceding lecture.

Technical Aspects. In the course dedicated to the technical aspects of AI (mandatory for all students), participants first learn the basics of a programming language (Python) with the support of a programming co-pilot. They then use the programming language to learn how to collect, clean, and prepare data for AI applications. Students then experiment with various AI applications such as classification (supervised learning), exploration of large datasets (unsupervised learning), generation of content (generative models), and finding information (content recommendation) using existing libraries of AI applications. Throughout the experimentation, students learn how to visualise the results of AI applications and investigate their performance in terms of teir accuracy and potential biases. After completion of the hands-on course on the technical aspects of AI, students are expected to have reached the following learning objectives: Being able to ...

- use AI applications from the field of supervised learning and unsupervised learning with the support of a programming co-pilot and common libraries (scikit-learn) in Python, and to visualize their results.
- interact with various state-of-the-art generative models and content recommendation systems and compare them.
- interpret common metrics for evaluating AI applications such as accuracy and F1 score and to use them to examine the functionality of AI applications.

Ethical Aspects. One of the four elective hands-on courses is dedicated to applying the knowledge about the ethical aspects of AI systems acquired in the lecture. Students learn to apply theoretical ethical concepts, particularly those of responsibility, fairness, discrimination, and value alignment in the context of AI. They develop positions and learn analytical skills regarding existing AI systems such as the COMPAS algorithm [13] and autonomous weapon systems. After completion of the hands-on course on the ethical aspects of AI, students are expected to have reached the following learning objectives: Being able to ...

- recapitulate and apply fundamental concepts of normative ethics in general and technology ethics in particular.
- identify and analyse ethical issues in the development and use of AI systems.
- apply positions and theories of AI ethics to different areas of AI application.

Legal Aspects. The second elective hands-on course pertains to the legal aspects of AI systems. Students analyse the applicable legal framework for the use of AI systems, including data protection requirements and assessment of liability risks. Furthermore, students discuss copyright issues in the context of AI-generated content pertaining to exclusive rights to AI-generated content and the use of copyrighted works as AI training data. After completion of the hands-on course on the legal aspects of AI, students are expected to have reached the following learning objectives: Being able to ...

- identify the relevant legal issues for the use of AI and classify them into one of the classical legal areas.
- identify the regulatory instruments relevant to the use of AI, specify their scope of application, and apply them in outline to the specific case.
- identify, evaluate, and correctly assess the need for professional legal advice for legal risks associated with the use of AI systems.

- identify the inherent deficiencies of tort liability system in the use of AI and explain the fundamentals of strict liability under the proposed EU AI Liability Directive.
- discuss the problems of copyright law in the context of AI.
- critically reflect on the legal issues associated with the use of AI in selected legal areas.

Economic Aspects. In the third elective hands-on course students apply their knowledge on the economic implications of the use of AI systems. They use business process mining and specific software tools to explain the use of AI in organisational development and develop an understanding of the components of a data-based business model. Students conduct a case study in which they analyse the impact of AI systems on the world of work and perform a market analysis considering the use of AI. After completion of the hands-on course on the economic aspects of AI, students are expected to have reached the following learning objectives: Being able to ...

- plan organisational development using business process mining.
- design a data-based business model.
- critically reflect on the impact of AI systems on the world of work.

Educational Aspects. The fourth elective hands-on course pertains to the educational aspects of AI systems. Students learn to use an adaptive learning system for analysing learning progress and providing individually tailored learning content and exams. Chatbots are introduced as virtual tutors that can provide personalised support for challenges in specific learning settings. Furthermore, students get to know an analysis tool for teachers that identifies patterns in learning behaviour using AI to optimise learning outcomes. Overall, students learn to describe individual AI applications in the field of education and explain their influence on the learning environment, teaching methods, and learners. After completion of the hands-on course on the educational aspects of AI, students are expected to have reached the following learning objectives: Being able to ...

- evaluate the functionality of adaptive learning systems and determine their benefits for the personalisation of learning content and exams.
- assess the use of virtual tutoring systems and reflect on their application to address challenges in specific learning settings.
- utilize analysis tools that recognise learning behaviour using AI and optimise learning processes (e.g., for exam preparation).

Implementation In the practical, students select one of the five fields of action to apply the knowledge and skills learned in the first two modules through the implementation of a coding project or case study. The content of these implementation projects is decided by the students together with their supervisors and should be of practical relevance to either industry or research. After completion of the practical, students are expected to have reached the following learning objectives: Being able to ...

- implement an AI system in their selected field of action.
- plan, carry out and reflect on a small project independently.
- solve problems associated with the implementation of the project under the supervision of an expert.
- apply critical analysis skills to understand the functionality and potential of AI systems.
- communicate their reflections on the ethical and social implications of AI applications.

4   Pilot and Student Feedback

The curriculum of the micro-degree AI and Society was piloted in the winter semester 2024/25 and summer semester 2025 at the University of Graz. The pilot of the micro-degree successfully reached students of very diverse backgrounds, ranging from the study of environmental system science over legal studies to medicine. When asked about their reasons for registering for the micro-degree, over 80% of the students primarily cited their interest in the topic and potential professional advantages as motivation. Half of the students also gave their curiosity about the new micro-degree and their desire to expand their knowledge of the topic as reason for their participation. Overall, the students were very satisfied with the content but identified some challenges with coordination and scheduling. These challenges were also identified by the lecturers: while it is very satisfying to be able to address a cross-cutting topic such as AI from a multitude of disciplinary lenses, coordinating the different lecturers and integrating their respective content into one coherent educational offering is far from trivial. Some students – in particular those with the least technical backgrounds – found the level of the hands-on course on the technical aspects of AI very challenging and suggested the provision of additional examples and exercises for basic programming concepts as a solution.

Students worked on very diverse applied projects in the practical. Below, we give three examples of such projects.

Knowledge of LLMs About Embodied Energy: The project's aim was to analyse how much Deep Research-like LLM-based systems know about embodied energy. That is, how well they can estimate the total energy used in the supply chain of a product. The analysis considered a wide range of models, and found that they behave in a similar way: The models generally give reasonable answers but struggle with complex products (e.g. cars, phones) where they failed to give robust quantitative results.

Usefulness and Limitations of LLM Therapists: The project's aim was to compare the responses of small local generative language models to the responses of human therapists based on a question-answer dataset. The comparison was done in terms of the similarity of responses. The analysis found that models give similar responses and have a inter-model response variance that is similar to human therapists. In some contexts, models appeared to have low similarity to humans, but the general response similarity was high.

Adaptation of a Media Literacy Test: The project's aim was to further develop a media literacy test initially launched by the Swiss Radio and Television Corporation. The test was extended with images, sound and video material provided by the Austrian public broadcaster ORF using artificial intelligence tools. The further development revealed numerous challenges and led to reflection on both content and processes.

5   Discussion and Conclusion

The micro-degree AI and Society offered by the University of Graz since the winter semester 2024/25 sets out to teach students a foundational understanding of the technical foundations of artificial intelligence, as well as the implications of its use in a broad range of societal areas. It aims to enable students to participate and shape the ongoing proliferation of AI into many aspects of their daily lives – equipping them with the necessary knowledge and skills to be able to confidently discuss, apply and implement AI tools.

With the inclusion of ethics, legal implications, impacts on the economy and world of work, as well as implications on education, the micro-degree AI and Society covers the broadest selection of societal areas compared to all other similar educational offerings we could find. In addition, it stands out by teaching not only competencies related to discussion and reflection, but also guides students through a series of increasingly independent application and implementation scenarios, providing hands-on experience with modern AI tools. Given its modular structure, students have the choice of either specialising into one specific field of action, or trying applications in different fields of action, thus acquiring a good overview over the current state of AI in different societal areas. While students are allowed a large amount of flexibility when choosing their elective courses and practicals, the micro-degree puts an emphasis on establishing a solid foundation regarding the technical aspects of AI by making participation in the corresponding hands-on course mandatory for all students. This is motivated by the target audience – students at the University of Graz and its partner universities – which are expected to have little to no technical background.

The rapid development of AI tools and their introduction into many areas of daily life are challenging universities to create educational offerings that are both flexible and of high enough quality to be accessible and empower their students to take an active part in this societal transformation. In this context, we believe that certificates like the micro-degree fill a crucial gap that exists in

306   J.Lasser and M. Pfiffner

the current educational landscape relating to educational offerings at the intersection between technology and societal aspects. Situated in-between traditional university degrees and short courses and seminars targeting the existing workforce, it combines a broad selection of topics with the necessary depth to enable the real understanding necessary to navigate the complexities of AI tool use and its implications. As such, modern educational offerings like the micro-degree are a necessary component to realise the vision of digital humanism.

Acknowledgments. JL has received funding from the European Research Council (ERC) under the European Union's Horizon Europe programme (Grant agreement No. 101160928).

Disclosure of Interests. The authors have no competing interests to declare that are relevant to the content of this article.

References

1. Austrian Ministry for Education and Research: Empfehlung der nationalen Bologna Follow-up Gruppe zur Umsetzung von Micro-credentials in Österreich (2023). https://www.bmfwf.gv.at/dam/jcr:80333209-d2fd-4fb7-a957-ec74686ae829/empfehlungen%20nat%20bologna%20followupgruppe%20microcredentials.pdf. Accessed 10 July 2025
2. eCornell: generative AI law and ethics (2025). https://ecornell.cornell.edu/courses/technology/generative-ai-law-and-ethics/. Accessed 10 July 2025
3. Ehlers, U.D., Lindner, M., Sommer, S., Rauch, E.: AIComp-future skills in a world increasingly shaped by AI. In: Ubiquity Proceedings, vol. 3, no. 1 (2023)
4. Georgetown University School of Continuing Studies: Online Certificate in AI Governance & Compliance (2025). https://scs.georgetown.edu/programs/541/certificate-in-ai-governance-compliance/. Accessed 10 July 2025
5. GFU Cyrus AG: Schulung Ethik in der Künstlichen Intelligenz (2025). https://www.gfu.net/s3563. Accessed 10 July 2025
6. Henderson, P.B., Cortina, T.J., Wing, J.M.: Computational thinking. In: Proceedings of the 38th SIGCSE Technical Symposium on Computer Science Education, pp. 195–196 (2007)
7. IBB Business Akademie: Ethik, gesellschaftliche Auswirkungen und Integration von KI (2025). https://www.business-akademie.com/kurse/ethik-gesellschaftliche-auswirkungen-und-integration-von-ki
8. Lasser, J., Manik, D., Silbersdorff, A., Säfken, B., Kneib, T.: Introductory data science across disciplines, using python, case studies, and industry consulting projects. Teach. Stat. **43**, S190–S200 (2021)
9. Saarland University: Zertifikat Digitalität. KI. Gesellschaft (2025). https://www.uni-saarland.de/studieren/optionalbereich/zertifikate/mensch-gesellschaft-ki.html. Accessed 10 July 2025
10. TÜV Rheinland: Kompakteinstieg Ethik und KI (2025). https://akademie.tuv.com/weiterbildungen/kompakteinstieg-ethik-und-ki-9557739. Accessed 10 July 2025
11. University of Copenhagen: Master of Science (MSc) in social data science (2025). https://www.ku.dk/studies/masters/social-data-science. Accessed 10 July 2025

12. University of Göttingen: Daten Lesen Lernen (2025). https://www.uni-goettingen.de/de/daten+lesen+lernen/693381.html. Accessed 10 July 2025
13. Washington, A.L.: How to argue with an algorithm: lessons from the Compas-Propublica debate. Colo. Tech. LJ **17**, 131 (2018)

Why Digital Humanism Needs a Social Psychology–and How You Can Use Digital Data to Study Social Identities in Socio-Technical Systems

Mark Levine[1] and Anastasia Kordoni[2]

[1] Lancaster University, Lancaster, UK
r.levine@lancaster.ac.uk
[2] Trilateral Research, London, UK
anastasia.kordoni@trilateralresearch.com

Abstract. Digital Humanism aspires to align technological innovation with human values, yet its psychological underpinnings remain predominantly individualistic, positioning the human as a "flawed" agent within socio-technical systems. This paper proposes a shift towards group-level social psychological dynamics as a foundation for designing socially responsive socio-technical systems. Building on the Social Identity Approach (SIA), which integrates the Social Identity Theory and Self-Categorisation Theory, we argue that human behaviour in complex socio-technical systems is shaped by dynamic group memberships and context-dependent identity processes. We demonstrate how digital traces, such as language, sensor data, and interactional patterns can serve as behavioural proxies for identifying and analysing such identity processes. Through interdisciplinary research, we present applications in system design, safety management, privacy protection, and ethical evaluation to show how identity-aware computational models and frameworks operationalise SIA to enhance inclusivity, resilience, and ethical responsiveness in socio-technical systems. Embedding social identity dynamics into the design of emerging socio-technical systems offers a transformative potential for advancing the normative goals of Digital Humanism.

Keywords: Digital humanism · Social identity · Socio-technical systems · Design

1 Introduction

The *Vienna Manifesto on Digital Humanism* [30] outlines a vision for aligning digital technologies with human values and societal good. It foregrounds human rights, human dignity and human agency as core ethical concerns in the digital age and argues that interdisciplinary research is needed to achieve these ends. In this paper we ask, 'what are the dominant psychological models of 'the human' in the digital humanism tradition, and are those psychological models fit for purpose?' We argue that the

L. Hagedorn et al. (Eds.): DIGHUM 2025, LNCS 16319, pp. 308–316, 2026.
https://doi.org/10.1007/978-3-032-11108-1_22

kind of psychology traditionally found in interdisciplinary digital humanism research is overly individualistic- limiting what can be achieved. We propose an alternative social-psychological model based around the social identity approach (SIA) [25] – and show how this more group level and dynamic theoretical toolkit is better able to address the digital humanism agenda. We conclude with some practical examples of social identity informed interdisciplinary studies in the digital humanism space.

2 Psychological Models of 'the Human' in Digital Humanism

We begin by arguing that the psychological models usually found in interdisciplinary work in digital humanism are predominantly individualistic. Much of the traditional work tends to emphasise psychological frameworks that prioritise cognition, decision-making, and moral agency at the individual level [2, 13, 23]. These studies often conceptualise the human as the 'weak link' in any socio-technical system – and are therefore focused on exploring ways to mitigate or compensate for the 'flawed human'. These models often draw from cognitive psychology and behavioral decision theory, emphasizing mental processes, such as reasoning, judgment, and moral agency at the level of the autonomous individual. For example, [13] focus on user-centered system design through cognitive modeling to improve usability, implicitly assuming that system errors stem from individual cognitive limitations. Similarly, [23] examine confirmation bias in software engineers, suggesting that cognitive failings of individuals contribute to inefficiencies in collaborative technical environments. [2] extend this line of inquiry by exploring how individuals resolve moral dilemmas in digital contexts, again centering the flawed cognition of the human agent. Collectively, these studies often conceptualize the human as the 'weak link' in socio-technical systems, leading to a research focus on compensating for or correcting perceived human inadequacies through design interventions or cognitive training. This framing, while analytically precise, risks obscuring the relational, institutional, and cultural dimensions of human-technology interaction.

While there have been some successes using this approach (for example in the area of 'behaviour change' [22]), we argue that, if the digital humanism manifesto is to realise its ambitions of building a just, inclusive, and humane digital society, then it needs to move beyond individualistic psychological models. Digital humanism needs theories that recognise that humans are not simply flaws to 'fix', but are also sources of strength and resilience in any socio-technical system. Digital humanism needs to embrace psychological theories that better conceptualise the relationship between the individual and the social. We need to build interdisciplinary research on socio-psychological theories that recognise that humans are embedded in groups, cultures, power structures and collective imaginaries. Moreover, those more socially orientated theories need to offer a practical toolkit that is of use in the building of resilient (and humane) socio-technical systems.

3 Rethinking the Human: The Social Identity Approach (SIA)

Of course, there are already sociological theories of social processes that have been applied to technology (e.g., the work of Bourdieu [14]) but these are often more concerned with the structural than the psychological. With that in mind, we propose the

Social Identity Approach (SIA) [25] as a psychological model that better serves the digital humanism agenda. Drawn from work in social psychology, it embraces both a theory of intergroup relations and a theory of how the individual and the social can be integrated at a psychological level. First, Social Identity Theory [27] proposes that part of who we are comes from the groups to which we belong – like our team at work, our gender, ethnicity, religion and social class, or our region, country or continent. It is psychologically important that our groups feel positive and distinct as this contributes to our sense of our self-worth. Because there are power and status differences between groups in society, this means that we engage in strategies like 'in-group favouritism' or 'social change' to try and ensure that our groups have positive value.

Second, Self-Categorisation Theory (SCT) [28] builds on Social Identity Theory by explaining how and when people see themselves as individuals or as group members. It suggests that our identity is flexible and depends on context. For example, at home, you might see yourself mainly as an individual with unique traits, but at a tech conference, you might think of yourself mainly as a software engineer, part of a professional group. Your behaviour will be guided by the level at which you identify, and the norms and values of those personal or social identities. But, context can also be the presence of other people. If there are a group of male software engineers talking together at a conference and a woman joins the conversation, then gender identity might suddenly come into play. As they move psychologically from software engineer identity to gender identity (and back again), then different norms and values shape the way they think and act. Knowing how people switch between personal and group identities, and knowing what the norms and values of different social identities might be, allows us to understand and predict how people will behave in different social contexts [1]. It helps us understand when people might engage in prosocial or anti-social behaviours - when they might act in ways that bolster social resilience or ferment social division. These are all key concerns of the digital humanism manifesto.

4   Making Social Identity Practical for Interdisciplinary Digital Humanism Research

However, in order to be useful to interdisciplinary work in the digital humanism space, the social identity approach needs to demonstrate practical or tangible features that can be of use in the development of socio-technical systems. If we are to build systems which reflect the values of digital humanism (by engaging in interdisciplinary work), and then want to test whether our psychological models are having the impact the theory proposes, then we need ways to make social identity manifest [see for example 4, 15, 8]. This is always a difficult task because psychological states are almost always intangible, and need to be inferred from proxy measures. Put another way, what is happening 'in the head' can usually only be inferred from giving people questionnaires, or conducting interviews or focus groups, as a way of collecting people's self-report on their psychological states. These kinds of methods are common, but have important limitations. They suffer from problems like social desirability bias (people wanting to look good rather than tell the truth); self-awareness deficits (we lack accurate insights into our own thoughts of feelings); memory errors (our memories are not very reliable).

Moreover, they tend to be static tools - taking synchronic snap-shots, rather than mapping psychological processes dynamically as they unfold over time.

Because what people say does not always match what they do, better proxy measures of psychological states would rely on behavioural measures themselves. The rise of digital data and the ubiquity of digital traces makes this behavioural mapping of psychological states increasingly possible. Researchers are able to use data from digital visual media (like CCTV systems, body worn cameras, smartphone cameras), naturally occurring language (from social media posts or simultaneous transcription features) or ambient sensor data (like GPS, accelerometers, gyroscopes) to trace everyday activities. Patterns in these digital traces can in turn be explored as potential proxies for underlying psychological states [19]. In the sections that follow we present a series of examples of research in the digital humanism tradition that draw on the social identity approach, and use digital traces to examine the impact of social identity processes within socio-technical systems.

4.1 Social Identity Dynamics in System Engineering

Our first example of how the social identity approach can be relevant for digital humanism can be found in the concept of 'empowerment'. Empowerment is a central principle of the *Vienna Manifesto on Digital Humanism,* which asserts that digital technologies should enhance human capabilities and enable individuals to regain control over their digital identities and interactions, rather than restrict or manipulate them. While the manifesto emphasises primarily individual empowerment, namely the capacity as a user to navigate complex socio-technical environments without exploitation, it also implicitly recognizes the importance of collective empowerment through its references to strengthening social cohesion. To facilitate the analysis of both individual and social psychological dimensions, the SIA has established that in dynamic socio-technical environments, individuals can form shared identities around common goals, even with strangers [5]. This emergent "groupiness" facilitates group-level empowerment and prosocial behaviours [6]. Analyses of CCTV footage of real-word emergencies corroborated that during a train evacuation, survivors exhibited helping behaviours and coordinated activities [24]. Using this insight, the IDEA model – an IDEntity Aware autonomous system architecture [9] integrates these shared identity dynamics into the decision-making of autonomous systems. Developed through interdisciplinary collaboration between social psychologists and software engineers, the model is designed for emergency scenarios, namely for complex socio-technical systems involving different types of technologies, such as drones, and diverse human actors (survivors, first responders, injured individuals). IDEA operationalises this group-level identity reasoning by assuming that that survivors who act based on a salient shared identity are more likely to assist nearby injured individuals. If this prosocial response is not detected, the system alerts first responders to intervene.

This identity salience is inferred from linguistic cues. Prior research has shown that language can reflect group membership, convey norms and reinforce social bonding [10]. Such linguistic information can be used for group-level classification models [18]. Building on this, [15] identified linguistic features of a shared (and non-shared) identity in emergencies, such as expressions of affiliation, coordinated helping acts, group emotional support and empowerment, which were used in the IDEA as the parameters learned by the model to determine one's salient identity. These parameters were integrated with game-theoretic decision models to optimise help allocation and coordination. Experimental findings showed that this identity aware architecture significantly improved evacuation efficiency, reduced response time and enhanced coordination between survivors and first responders [9]. This example demonstrates how group processes can be computationally modelled and embedded into socio-technical systems that align with principles of digital humanism in terms of empowerment, solidarity and collective agency.

4.2 Social Identity Dynamics in Safety Management

Such responsiveness to human values and needs is at the heart of digital humanism. However, capturing these values, and more specifically their dynamic and context-dependent nature, has been proven challenging in the design of emerging socio-technical systems. The SIA provides a theoretical foundation for understanding how human values and norms are not static, but rather emerge, shift or intensify depending on the social identity that is prevalent and the socio-technical context in which they are enacted. The interaction between identity and context shapes both the degree of group identification and the perceived permeability of identity boundaries, which, in turn, can influence the values guiding a group member's behaviour [1], contributing to conflict resolution [7] and inclusive decision-making [12]. Integrating this relationality into ethical frameworks for the design and deployment of new technologies can help moving beyond individual differences in static formats towards assessing group-level positive and negative impacts technology can have on society [26].

The SLEEC framework [16] developed as part of the UKRI Trustworthy Autonomous Systems Resilience Node[1], provides a structured lens for examining the Social, Legal, Ethical, Empathetic, and Cultural dimensions of emerging autonomous systems, especially in crisis contexts. Applying a SIA to the analysis of policy reports, multidisciplinary co-creation workshops, interviews with practitioners, and digital visual data (open-access videos of emergency operations), enabled the identification of context-sensitive values and norms that account for the various identities emerging within this socio-technical system. This integration of social identity dynamics was not merely analytical – detecting identity-related behavioural patterns in timeline analysis - but also operational, allowing values to be "interrogated" and (re-)evaluated at the individual, group, and systemic levels. Applying the framework across different high-risk scenarios facilitated understanding of how multi-stakeholder perceptual assumptions, behavioural expectations, actual behaviours in context and group-based evaluations influence both design and deployment decisions in socio-technical systems[2].

The Security–Privacy–Cost Evaluation Matrix [29] was developed in the Gatherings EU[3] project to balance fundamental rights and security imperatives in the context of public events and surveillance. It applied the SIA, and specifically the principle of identity boundary permeability, to conceptualise how various user groups perceive and negotiate trade-offs between security and privacy. Integral to its design is the recognition that

---

[1] https://resilience.tas.ac.uk/

[2] https://osf.io/7rmnd/

[3] https://gatherings-project.eu/

individuals interpret risks and safeguards through the lens of group identification and perceived inclusiveness. Identity transitions, for instance, from "law enforcement" and "event attendees" to a shared identity of "safety guardians" can drive collaboration and inclusion [21]. By contrast, boundary impermeability may prompt distrust [11]. The matrix embeds these identity dynamics by incorporating group-level value perspectives in its evaluative design, therefore, allowing socio-technical systems to account for the fluidity of these identity processes, power structures and related behaviours. In doing so, these tools contribute to developing group-level decision-making processes/assessments and designing adaptable and socially responsive socio-technical systems in line with the democratic and inclusion goals of digital humanism.

4.3 Social Identity Dynamics in Safeguarding Digital Humanism Principles

The MASC project (Methods for Anonymisation in Socio-technical Contexts)[4] demonstrates how identity dynamics can be integrated into the safeguarding of digital humanism principles, especially in relation to privacy. The project developed anonymisation tools applicable to socio-technical systems involving survivors of sexual exploitation. It aimed to preserve privacy while ensuring that survivors' voices and experiences maintain their authenticity in anonymised data. To achieve this, the project applied the SIA to assess the risk of contextual information loss during anonymisation. That is, it explored how survivor identities were constructed and expressed relative to the salience of another social group in this socio-technical system (e.g., survivor – police, survivor – NGO professional). Through the collection of digital testimonies and interactions of real-life survivors, MASC conducted a psycholinguistic analysis to identify and extract linguistic features of identity expression, informed by semantic meaning and group salience. A statistical comparison between anonymised and original versions of the data showed that this identity-informed analysis enabled a more accurate evaluation of whether anonymisation risked erasing critical group-based experiences and meanings. This evidence suggests that identity-aware methods in privacy-preserving technologies can be added value to the human-centered goals of digital humanism.

5 Ethical Considerations and Design Imperatives

While the operationalization of identity dynamics holds significant promise for enhancing efficiency, collaboration, and pro-social behavior within complex socio-technical systems, reliance on behavioral proxies to infer social-psychological states raises a number of key ethical concerns. In order to avoid unintended consequences, digital traces employed as indicators of identity need to be ethically interrogated. By this we mean that any identity designation, if lifted out of its context and interconnections with other identity indicators, can be misinterpreted in ways that do not reflect the psychological identity actually endorsed. In other words, the assessment of a social-psychological state is not the same as the psychological identification of a specific individual. We are not

---

[4] https://trilateralresearch.com/work/methods-for-anonymisation-in-sociotechnical-contexts-masc.

attempting to uniquely identify or differentiate persons. Rather, we assess belonging to a psychological (social) identity at the group level, recognizing that such cues are both dynamic and context-sensitive. Repurposing identity cues, such as digital visual data [20], overlooking these core characteristics can yield biased identity designations. Such misreadings can have negative impacts on psychological evaluations and subsequent decisions in high-stakes systems (e.g., legal adjudication [17]).

Accordingly, language-based inference and classification models, when used in isolation, are especially vulnerable to bias, as they may neglect other communicative and identity-related cues essential for equitable representation. For example, IDEA captures alternative identity indicators, such as cultural clusters and gender, thereby mitigating risks of identity misattribution and framing biases [9]. Misrepresentations of identity in such systems have been linked to negative psychosocial outcomes including helplessness, alienation, and social exclusion [3]. Integrating multi-modal, context-sensitive validation of identity inferences and engaging in participatory governance involving the social groups represented can inform human-in-the-loop methodologies allowing for continuous monitoring of inclusivity and social equality - not only regarding which identity dimensions are surfaced in data, but also how, when, and under what contextual influences these dimensions are interpreted. Such identity reasoning offers a pathway toward protecting, rather than exploiting, collective dynamics in socio-technical systems.

6 Future Directions in Social Psychology and Digital Humanism

This paper posits that advancing the normative ambitions of digital humanism is intertwined with the way that human agents are conceptualised as key actors of emerging socio-technical systems. Moving beyond individualistic views of the human, future interdisciplinary work needs to embrace social psychological models and paradigms that account for the relationality between the contextual underpinnings of socio-technical systems and identity-based dynamics of human behaviour within these systems. The SIA provides a well-established theoretical and empirical framework to do so allowing for both explanatory depth and practical use. As demonstrated though applications in autonomous system design [9], resilience frameworks [16], ethical evaluation matrices [29], and anonymisation methodologies, SIA enables us to understand how contextually prevalent group identities shape values, actions, and trust in ways that are often invisible to individual-level models. This speaks to a fundamental shift from designing for isolated endpoints to *designing with and through collectivities*, attuned to how social identities emerge, switch, and determine behaviours across complex socio-technical systems.

Looking forward, digital behavioural data, including language patterns and multimodal interactional cues, can offer unprecedented opportunities to empirically trace identity processes in real time, transforming the SIA from a conceptual lens into a computationally tractable tool for ethical system design. By embedding group-level reasoning, boundary fluidity, and collective meaning into socio-technical systems, digital humanism can evolve into a transformative paradigm – one capable of shaping technologies that are not only inclusive and ethical, but also resilient, just and socially intelligent.

Disclosure of Interests. The authors have no competing interests to declare that are relevant to the content of this article.

References

1. Abrams, D., Wetherell, M., Cochrane, S., Hogg, M.A., Turner, J.C.: Knowing what to think by knowing who you are: self-categorization and the nature of norm formation, conformity and group polarization. Br. J. Soc. Psychol. **29**(2), 97–119 (1990)
2. Barque-Duran, A., Pothos, E.M., Hampton, J.A., Yearsley, J.M.: Contemporary morality: moral judgments in digital contexts. Comput. Hum. Behav. **75**, 184–193 (2017)
3. Blackwood, L.M., Hopkins, N., Reicher, S.D.: 'Flying while Muslim': citizenship and misrecognition in the airport. J. Soc. Polit. Psychol. **3**(2), 148–170 (2015). https://doi.org/10.5964/jspp.v3i2.375
4. Bennaceur, A., et al.: Socio-technical resilience for community healthcare. In: TAS'23 Proceedings of the First International Symposium on Trustworthy Autonomous Systems, pp. 1–6. ACM, Edinburgh (2023)
5. Drury, J.: The role of social identity processes in mass emergency behaviour: an integrative review. Eur. Rev. Soc. Psychol. **29**(1), 38–81 (2018). https://doi.org/10.1080/10463283.2018.1471948
6. Drury, J., Cocking, C., Reicher, S.: The nature of collective resilience: Survivor reactions to the 2005 London bombings. Int. J. Mass Emerg. Disasters **27**(1), 66–95 (2009). https://doi.org/10.1177/0280727009027001
7. Ellemers, N., Spears, R., Doosje, B.: Self and social identity. Annu. Rev. Psychol. **53**(1), 161–186 (2002). https://doi.org/10.1146/annurev.psych.53.100901.135228
8. Gavidia-Calderon, C., Bennaceur, A., Lopez, T., Kordoni, A., Levine, M., Nuseibeh, B.: Meet your maker: a social identity analysis of robotics software engineering. In: TAS 2023 Proceedings of the First International Symposium on Trustworthy Autonomous Systems, pp. 1–5. ACM, Edinburgh (2023)
9. Gavidia-Calderon, C., Kordoni, A., Bennaceur, A., Levine, M., Nuseibeh, B.: The IDEA of us: an identity-aware architecture for autonomous systems. ACM Trans. Softw. Eng. Methodol. **33**(6), 1–38 (2024). https://doi.org/10.1145/3654439
10. Hardy, C., Lawrence, T.B., Grant, D.: Discourse and collaboration: the role of conversations and collective identity. Acad. Manag. Rev. **30**, 58–77 (2005). https://doi.org/10.5465/amr.2005.15281426
11. Haslam, S.A., Reicher, S.: Stressing the group: social identity and the unfolding dynamics of responses to stress. J. Appl. Psychol. **91**(5), 1037 (2006)
12. Hogg, M.A., Abrams, D., Brewer, M.B.: Social identity: the role of self in group processes and intergroup relations. Group Process. Intergroup Relat. **20**(5), 570–581 (2017). https://doi.org/10.1177/1368430217690909
13. Hollender, N., Hofmann, C., Deneke, M., Schmitz, B.: Integrating cognitive load theory and concepts of human–computer interaction. Comput. Hum. Behav. **26**(6), 1278–1288 (2010)
14. Ignatow, G., Robinson, L.: Pierre Bourdieu: theorizing the digital. Inf. Commun. Soc. **20**(7), 950–966 (2017). https://doi.org/10.1080/1369118X.2017.1301519
15. Kordoni, A., Gavidia-Calderon, C., Levine, M., Bennaceur, A., Nuseibeh, B.: "Are we in this together?": embedding social identity detection in drones improves emergency coordination. Front. Psychol. **14**, 1146056 (2023)
16. Kordoni, A., Gavidia-Calderon, C., Levine, M., Bennaceur, A., Nuseibeh, B.: The SLEEC framework (2023b). https://osf.io/7rmnd/
17. Kordoni, A., Levine, M., Bennaceur, A., Gavidia-Calderon, C., Nuseibeh, B.: Intersecting social identity and drone use in humanitarian contexts: psychological insights for legal decisions and responsible innovation. J. Responsible Technol. **23**, 100129 (2025). https://doi.org/10.1016/j.jrt.2025.100129

18. Koschate, M., Naserian, E., Dickens, L., Stuart, A., Russo, A., Levine, M.: ASIA: automated social identity assessment using linguistic style. Behav. Res. Methods **53**(4), 1762–1781 (2021). https://doi.org/10.3758/s13428-020-01511-3
19. Levine, M.: A golden age of behavioural social psychology? Towards a social psychology of power and intergroup relations in the digital age. Br. J. Soc. Psychol. **64**(3), e12896 (2025)
20. Levine, M., Philpot, R., Nightingale, S., Kordoni, A.: Visual digital data, ethical challenges and psychological science. Am. Psychol. **79**(1), 109–122 (2024). https://doi.org/10.1037/amp 0001192
21. Levine, M., Prosser, A., Evans, D., Reicher, S.: Identity and emergency intervention: how social group membership and inclusiveness of group boundaries shape helping behavior. Pers. Soc. Psychol. Bull. **31**(4), 443–453 (2005). https://doi.org/10.1177/014616720427165
22. Michie, S., Yardley, L., West, R., Patrick, K., Greaves, F.: Developing and evaluating digital interventions to promote behavior change in health and health care: recommendations resulting from an international workshop. J. Med. Internet Res. **19**(6), e232 (2017)
23. Mohanani, R., Salman, I., Turhan, B., Rodríguez, P., Ralph, P.: Cognitive biases in software engineering: a systematic mapping study. IEEE Trans. Software Eng. **46**(12), 1318–1339 (2018)
24. Philpot, R., Levine, M.: Evacuation behavior in a subway train emergency: a video-based analysis. Environ. Behav. **54**(2), 383–411 (2022). https://doi.org/10.1177/001391652110 31193
25. Reicher, S., Spears, R., Haslam, S.A. The Social Identity Approach in Social Psychology. Sage Identities Handbook, pp. 45–62. Sage, UK (2010)
26. Sovacool, B.K., Hess, D.J.: Ordering theories: typologies and conceptual frameworks for sociotechnical change. Soc. Stud. Sci. **47**(5), 703–750 (2017). https://doi.org/10.1177/030 6312717709363
27. Tajfel, H.: Social Identity and Intergroup Relations. Cambridge, New York (1982)
28. Turner, J.C., Hogg, M.A., Oakes, P.J., Reicher, S.D., Wetherell, M.S.: Rediscovering the Social Group: A Self-Categorization Theory. Basil Blackwell, UK (1987)
29. Voicu, I., Kordoni, A., Hughes, J.: The Final Security-Privacy-Cost Evaluation Matrix. https://gatherings-project.eu/matrix/. Accessed 12 July 2025
30. Werthner, H., et al.: Vienna Manifesto on Digital Humanism. Verfügbar unter (2019). https://www.informatik.tuwien.ac.at/dighum/manifesto. Accessed 10 July 2025

Between Principle and Practice: Evaluating the EU AI Act Through the Lens of Digital Humanism

Matúš Mesarčík[1,2] and Natália Slosiarová[1(✉)]

[1] Kempelen Institute of Intelligent Technologies, 81109 Bratislava, Slovakia
`{matus.mesarcik,natalia.slosiarova}@kinit.sk`
[2] Faculty of Law, Comenius University in Bratislava, 81100 Bratislava, Slovakia

Abstract. This paper analyzes the European Union's Artificial Intelligence Act (AI Act) through the prism of Digital Humanism, using the principles articulated by Erich Prem as a normative lens. These principles emphasize the co-evolution of technology and humanity, the responsibility of technology to protect people and the environment, its role in reinforcing democracy and society, the malleability of technological systems, and the fundamental differences between humans and machines. Our analysis finds that while the AI Act incorporates aspects of these principles, such as through its attention to fundamental rights, it only partially fulfils their broader vision. We argue that a deeper alignment with digital humanism would enhance the AI Act's ability to guide the development and deployment of AI in a way that genuinely prioritizes humans and societal well-being.

Keywords: digital humanism · principles of digital humanism · AI Act · AI regulation

1 Introduction

Digital humanism emerges as a critical response to the impact that digitalization has on society, culture, and individuals. This movement is not merely an academic exercise, but a deeply motivated endeavor driven by concerns about the implications of technological advancements. While still evolving towards a universally accepted definition, digital humanism distinguishes itself by advocating for a future where technology is designed and deployed to actively serve human and societal flourishing rather than to diminish it [24]. It seeks to promote democracy and reclaim privacy, human agency and responsibility in an increasingly automated world, drawing inspiration from the values of Enlightenment and Humanism movements that prioritize human reason, ethics, and societal well-being [30].

The European Union has positioned itself as a global leader in shaping digital governance, with the EU Artificial Intelligence Act [11] representing its most

L. Hagedorn et al. (Eds.): DIGHUM 2025, LNCS 16319, pp. 317–332, 2026.
https://doi.org/10.1007/978-3-032-11108-1_23

ambitious initiative to date. The AI Act establishes a risk-based framework for regulating AI, banning certain harmful practices and imposing obligations on high-risk applications to safeguard fundamental rights, safety, and health. While the Act has been analysed from perspectives such as fundamental rights, risk management, and market regulation, its alignment with broader humanist ideals remains underexplored. Existing scholarships provide important foundations for this inquiry. The Vienna Manifesto on Digital Humanism [30] articulated the core normative aspirations of digital humanism, while subsequent research has connected these ideals to various legal frameworks, including the General Data Protection Regulation and the Digital Services Act. Broader approaches, such as digital constitutionalism and the Ethics Guidelines for Trustworthy AI [10], likewise emphasise the embedding of values in digital governance. Yet, no systematic study has examined the AI Act through the lens of digital humanism, leaving unanswered the question of how far the regulation reflects, or fails to reflect this vision.

This paper seeks to fill that gap by looking at the AI Act through the lens of the five principles of digital humanism as articulated by Erich Prem. Prem's elaboration [24] builds on the Vienna Manifesto but provides a more detailed and operational framework, reflecting the state of the art in current scholarship. By systematically mapping these principles onto the AI Act, the paper offers both a conceptual and doctrinal contribution: conceptually, by testing the applicability of digital humanism to the regulatory text, and analytically, by diagnosing the extent to which the Act fulfills, partially fulfills, or neglects the normative ambitions of digital humanism.

The paper proceeds as follows. Section 2 reviews related work, explains our methodological approach, and develops a critical analysis of the AI Act through Prem's principles. Section 3 presents conclusions and recommendations corresponding to our compliance judgments, identifying areas where the Act could be improved.

2   Principles of Digital Humanism and Their AI Act Counterparts

2.1   Related Work

Digital humanism has developed over the past decade as both an intellectual project and a normative agenda responding to the challenges of digitalisation. The Vienna Manifesto on Digital Humanism [30] provided the foundational articulation of this movement, stressing that technology must be shaped through democratic processes to uphold human dignity, autonomy, and societal wellbeing. Its call for a "human-centered digital society" has since been taken up in academic, political, and civil society debates across Europe and beyond.

Building on this foundation, Erich Prem proposed a more detailed and operational set of principles. These principles summarize the core claims of digital humanism, advocating for a future where technology is a tool for better future and societal progress. Among them is the recognition of technology's co-evolution with humanity, acknowledging that the impact of digital tools isn't necessarily always positive. Prem also asserts a mandate for technology to protect both people and the environment, emphasizing the ethical responsibility of technological development. Furthermore, he demands that technology actively contributes to strengthening democratic institutions and fostering a cohesive, equitable society. Another principle asserts that technologies are inherently malleable, meaning they can and should be designed, developed, and governed in ways that align with human needs and ethical considerations. Finally, the paper re-affirms that machines are not people and that humans are not obligated to serve or unconditionally support technological development, directly challenging narratives that implicitly demand human subservience to digital progress. [24]

Our research builds on and extends earlier studies examining how digital humanism is reflected in EU digital legislation, particularly the General Data Protection Regulation (GDPR) and the Digital Services Act (DSA) [20], European Declaration on Digital Rights [5] or constitutional message of the GDPR [6]. By contrast, the AI Act addresses the design, deployment, and oversight of AI systems themselves. This difference makes it a unique case for evaluating whether humanist principles can be operationalised in the governance of emerging technologies. Additionally, focusing specifically on the AI Act, it contributes to the evolving scholarship on value-based digital governance in the EU, offering a more nuanced understanding of how abstract ethical and political ideals are translated into binding legal norms and institutional mechanisms. The findings aim to provide both a conceptual foundation for future interdisciplinary research and a practical guide for policymakers striving to align AI regulation with the values of democracy, human dignity, and the public good.

2.2 Our Approach and Methodology

This paper employs a qualitative, interpretive legal analysis to evaluate how the principles of digital humanism, particularly as articulated by Prem based on the Vienna Manifesto, are incorporated into the normative and institutional framework of the EU AI Act. While the Vienna Manifesto provides the foundational formulation of digital humanism, we opted for Prem's elaboration because it offers a more detailed operationalization and reflects the state-of-the-art in contemporary scholarship. Alternative formulations such as the Vienna Manifesto itself was considered. However, compared to this approach, Prem's principles provide both conceptual clarity and closer alignment with current debates in legal and policy scholarship, making them particularly suitable for analyzing the normative ambitions of the EU AI Act. For the purposes of this paper, we evaluate the degree to which each principle is embedded in the AI Act according to three categories: (1) fulfilled, where binding obligations fully reflect the principle; (2) partially fulfilled, where the Act acknowledges or indirectly addresses the principle but with gaps or non-binding measures; and (3) not fulfilled, where the principle is absent or only rhetorically mentioned. This methodological approach enables us to provide a structured diagnostic of the AI Act's alignment with digital humanism, marking the paper's original contribution to the existing body of research.

Our analysis is centered on Prem's framework, which offers operational clarity but inevitably narrows the scope compared to the wider body of digital humanism literature. Alternative governance models, such as digital constitutionalism or human-centric AI frameworks, could yield different emphases. By focusing on Prem's five principles, we aim for a structured diagnostic, while recognising that future research should integrate a broader comparative perspective. We do not conduct empirical analysis of implementation practices or enforcement challenges, which remain largely prospective given the Act's recent adoption and phased implementation.

2.3 Analysis and Reflections on the Principles of Digital Humanism in the AI Act

In the following subsections, we apply Prem's five principles as a normative lens to assess the AI Act. For each principle, we identify the most relevant provisions, discuss their alignment with digital humanism, and conclude with a compliance judgment. These judgments serve as the analytical foundation for the recommendations developed in Sect. 3.

The EU AI Act (AIA) [11] is a landmark attempt to regulate AI in Europe, promoting systems that respect fundamental rights, democracy, safety, health, and the rule of law (Recital 1). Built on the EU product regulation model, it categorises AI systems by risk, prohibiting certain practices and imposing the strictest requirements on high-risk applications. It also sets rules for general-purpose AI (Arts. 51–55), transparency (Art. 55), and contains provisions to support innovation and SMEs.

The Act reflects the Vienna Manifesto's call to embed democratic values including human dignity, privacy, freedom of expression, and non-discrimination into digital governance. By mandating transparency, accountability, and risk management, it seeks to curb opaque algorithmic systems and dominant platforms. Yet its reliance on a risk-based product safety model shows regulatory pragmatism, creating tension with digital humanism's broader vision of societal flourishing.

Acknowledgment of Socio-Technical Context and Impact of AI. Digital technologies have reshaped healthcare, education, communication, and sustainability, yet they have also "disrupted the very fabric of society." [30] Digital humanism challenges the view of innovation as inherently beneficial, stressing that technological progress does not automatically enhance social welfare [24]. Narratives promoted by firms and policymakers often obscure systemic risks, including privacy intrusions, surveillance [15], erosion of rights, and power asymmetries created by platform monopolies [25] and algorithmic control [19].

The socio-technical impacts of AI are explicitly recognised in the Impact Assessment to the AI Act proposal [9], which examined economic, social, environmental, and fundamental rights consequences. It highlighted risks such as manipulation of human choice, weakened autonomy, threats to safety and security, and violations of rights including dignity, privacy, non-discrimination, and fair trial [9].

These concerns are echoed in the Act's recitals. Recital 1 links AI regulation to EU values of democracy, rule of law, dignity, rights, and environmental protection. Recitals 4–5 outline potential benefits and risks, while Recital 6 states that "AI should be a human-centric technology...increasing human well-being." Recital 27 further ties oversight to the AI HLEG's trustworthiness principles, namely agency, robustness, privacy, transparency, fairness, well-being, and accountability [10].

Taking into consideration the binding articles of the AI Act, socio-technical context of the AI is reflected in several provisions. Firstly, Article 5 providing an exhaustive list of prohibited AI practices may be understood as a necessary trade-off, when risks severely outweigh the benefits of AI systems. The AI Act bans AI systems that manipulate human behaviour, exploit vulnerabilities, facilitate social scoring, or prediction of criminality acknowledging the socio-technical harms of algorithm-driven societal control. Secondly, obligation for establishing a risk-management system (AIA, Article 9) may be interpreted as mandating a socio-technical evaluation of high-risk AI systems throughout an AI system's lifecycle, ensuring continual assessment of technical and contextual risks [26]. Article 14 requires high-risk AI to be designed with "human-in-the-loop" interfaces enabling meaningful human control over AI actions affecting individuals. Further reflections of the principle in questions represent Article 27 obliging deployers of certain high-risk AI systems to conduct fundamental rights impact assessments and requirement to periodically undergo model evaluations by providers of general-purpose AI models. These requirements also reflect a broader socio-technical context of development and deployment of AI systems. Yet, the AI Act frames socio-technical risks primarily through the lens of product safety and market functioning. This pragmatic approach falls short of digital humanism's broader demand for democratic scrutiny of design choices and systemic impacts, revealing a tension between risk management as compliance and a more ambitious societal vision.

Taken together, these provisions demonstrate that the AI Act acknowledges the socio-technical context of AI, but only in a limited and fragmented manner. We therefore assess this principle as partially fulfilled, since the Act recognizes risks and values but does not embed them in sufficiently binding and comprehensive obligations

Protection of Humans and the Environment. Digital humanism, grounded in technology's profound impact on people and their co-evolution, places human dignity, freedom, and autonomy at its core with this principle. It emphasizes that digital technologies must be designed to promote human autonomy and empower individuals in their decisions, supporting fairness and counteracting biases. This perspective views human agency as central, particularly in navigating potential conflicts arising from algorithmic decision-making and limitations imposed by computer-controlled actions on human dignity. The concept of dignity is further highlighted as fundamental, requiring the protection of individuals even when not directly affected by automated systems. While acknowledging historical criticisms of humanism's past exclusions, this principle broadens the scope of digital humanism to include the environmental impact of digital systems, advocating for sustainability of digital technologies and their use in mitigating harmful human effects on the environment [25].

Protection of fundamental rights, human dignity included, is undoubtedly at the core of the AI Act as they are explicitly mentioned in its recitals as a primary justification for regulating AI in Europe (AIA, Recital 1). This commitment is also evident in the AI Act's risk-based approach, where the categorization of AI systems is fundamentally based on their potential risk to fundamental rights, alongside safety and health. Another manifestation of their importance is the separate obligation for certain entities to conduct a Fundamental Rights Impact Assessment. And while it is often overlooked, the obligation to consider risks to fundamental rights also extends to all high-risk AI systems as a part of broader risk management system (AIA Article 9 (2) (a)) [16].

Regarding human autonomy, integrity and dignity the AI Act includes multiple obligations, not only for high-risk AI systems, that directly or indirectly address their protection and therefore also this principle. Notably, among the human oversight obligations, Article 14 (4) (b) is designed to protect against over-reliance on AI systems which undoubtedly impacts human autonomy by eroding critical thinking skills and the ability to make independent judgments, as individuals may uncritically accept AI-generated outputs without understanding their underlying rationale. Studies from the healthcare sector show that it could even lead to deterioration of the users' hard skills [3].

Furthermore, Article 50 of the AI Act, which outlines transparency obligations, could play a vital role in retaining human autonomy. When individuals are aware they are interacting with an AI system, this transparency can help build trust, empower them to critically assess the AI's outputs [7] and even decide whether they wish to engage with the system at all. Article 86 of the AI Act even goes one step further in transparency, enabling stakeholders impacted by decisions based on the outputs of AI systems to request "clear and meaningful explanations of the role of the AI system in the decision-making procedure and the main elements of the decision taken". However, there are also opposing views on excessive transparency of AI systems that say it could be overwhelming for the stakeholders and lead to confusion rather than clarity [18]. Finally, Article 4 of the AI Act, which obliges providers and deployers of AI systems to ensure an appropriate level of AI literacy of their staff, can aid in ensuring human autonomy and dignity by equipping them with the necessary knowledge and critical understanding to interact with AI systems more effectively. Concerning inclusivity, the Act's provisions on data and data governance, particularly Article 10 (2) (e), (f) and (g), could be instrumental. This article includes obligations to identify and take into consideration possible biases in data, test for such biases, and actively make efforts to mitigate them. This focus on data quality and bias mitigation can serve as a mechanism to promote inclusivity, however, it will always hinge on implementation of this requirement and what will be considered sufficient efforts or "appropriate measures" by the oversight authorities.

The EU AI Act also acknowledges environmental protection, with objectives like safeguarding the environment from harmful AI effects (AIA, Article 1) and defining serious incidents to include environmental damage (AIA, Article 3 (49)). It encourages the assessment and minimization of environmental sustainability impacts, including energy-efficient practices in AI system design, training, and use as a part of voluntary codes of conduct (AIA, Article 95 (1) (b)), and requires documentation on resource performance improvement for high-risk AI systems and general-purpose AI models (AIA, Article 40 (2) in conjunction with Article 10). The AI Act also includes a review process for standardization on energy-efficient GPAI development (AIA, Article 112 (6)). However, it is still criticized for vague commitments, the lack of binding obligations for environmental protection despite rhetorical references to sustainability [27]. The scope is also seen as restricted, focusing primarily on energy consumption and overlooking other critical environmental concerns like water usage, resource extraction, and electronic waste [27] [13]. Critics also note that its provisions on high-risk AI systems primarily focus on threats to human health, safety, or fundamental rights, largely overlooking direct ecological damage like biodiversity loss or greenhouse gas emissions unless they have a direct human impact [22]. Concerns are also in place about Article 46, which allows Member States compliance exceptions for multiple reasons, including environmental protection, which could lead at the very least to ambiguities.

Overall, the AI Act addresses the protection of humans primarily through its risk-based approach and fundamental rights safeguards, while the environmental dimension remains weak and largely aspirational. This imbalance highlights a tension between regulatory pragmatism, where rights have established legal bases, and the humanistic call to integrate ecological concerns as co-equal priorities in shaping digital futures. Accordingly, we consider this principle partially fulfilled, with significant gaps regarding enforceable environmental obligations.

Strengthening Democracy and Society. Digital humanism envisions technology that strengthens democracy, rights, justice, and inclusion. Yet current digital realities often undermine these aims, linking technology to threats to liberal democracy, market concentration, and declining trust in institutions. While digital tools can support access to information and civic engagement, they also spread disinformation, online abuse, and cause polarisation [17]. Network effects and platform economies further entrench global tech monopolies, raising concerns about competition, pluralism, and political influence [24].

From this perspective, digitalisation should advance the public interest by expanding education, preserving culture, supporting meaningful work, and enhancing solidarity. In practice, economic models privilege data extraction and market enclosure. Scholars such as Staab and Zuboff [28,32] argue that conventional antitrust tools cannot address the systemic power of digital platforms.

This principle thus calls for legal frameworks that curb structural imbalances and hold technological development accountable to democratic and humanist values [24].

Two AI-specific risks to democracy stand out. First, AI amplifies disinformation through deepfakes and computational propaganda, undermining trust, representation, and electoral integrity [29]. Second, its use in political campaigns threatens to distort electoral competition itself [4].

How does the AI Act respond to these issues? Impact assessment suggests that due to potential threats to democracy, the EU has opted to ban certain practices using AI systems including indiscriminate or mass surveillance, profiling and scoring of citizens, emphasizing chilling effects [1,23] on democracy if remote biometric identification systems are deployed without any legal limitations [9].

The AI Act contains 10 specific mentions of the word "democracy" especially in the context of the EU values (AIA, Recital 1 and 2) or value-requirement to be respected when developing AI systems (AIA, Recital 8). Recital 27 also explicitly calls for securing social and environmental well-being, ensuring that "AI systems are developed and used in a sustainable and environmentally friendly manner as well as in a way to benefit all human beings, while monitoring and assessing the long-term impacts on the individual, society and democracy."

Protection of democracy is also enshrined in Article 1 of the AI Act, setting the subject matter of the regulation. Article 5 providing banned practices has already been discussed during the analysis of previous principles. Protection of democracy may also be covered by the ban on social scoring, subliminal manipulation and limiting the use of real-time biometric identification systems in public spaces by law enforcement agencies. Within the list of high-risk AI system applications, the AI Act introduces the area of "Administration of justice and democratic processes" (AIA, Annex III, point 8). More specifically, "AI systems intended to be used for influencing the outcome of an election or referendum or the voting behaviour of natural persons in the exercise of their vote in elections or referenda. This does not include AI systems to the output of which natural persons are not directly exposed, such as tools used to organise, optimise or structure political campaigns from an administrative or logistical point of view" shall be considered as high-risk AI systems subject to specific obligations in the AI Act. The obligation to conduct FRIA mentioned above may also be seen as a requirement to systematically assess risks to democracy, rights, and societal impacts (AIA, Article 27). Concerning providers of general-purpose AI models with systemic risks, these providers have to "assess and mitigate possible systemic risks at Union level, including their sources, that may stem from the development, the placing on the market, or the use of general-purpose AI models with systemic risk" (AIA, Article 55 (1) (b). However, what constituents a systemic risk that needs to be assessed and mitigated is not delineated in the AI Act.

Although the AI Act explicitly acknowledges democracy as a core value and prohibits certain practices harmful to democratic processes, its concrete safeguards are narrow and incomplete. The exclusion of issues such as recommender systems and disinformation illustrates the difficulty of embedding humanistic ideals of democratic participation within a legal framework designed for enforceability and political compromise. For this reason, we assess this principle as only partially fulfilled, given that binding protections for democratic participation and civic discourse remain underdeveloped.

Deterministic Approach Towards AI. A core principle of digital humanism is that technology is not an autonomous force but must be shaped through democratic deliberation and normative guidance, rejecting narratives of technological determinism [14]. Just as humanity has shaped its natural environment, it should steer digital innovation toward democratic values, justice, and the public good [24].

This perspective resists equating progress with disruption or speed, promoting instead a vision of innovation that serves societal flourishing. Law and policy must therefore stem from democratically legitimate institutions [8], supported by regulation, civic participation, and international cooperation [24].

The AI Act illustrates this constructivist approach [2]. As with other EU legislation, it emerged from the ordinary legislative procedure involving Commission proposals, parliamentary and Council negotiations, and extensive public consultations. The Commission gathered input from academics, businesses, rights groups, and the public through surveys, expert groups, and impact assessments [9]. Transparency tools, including open feedback on drafts, ensured broad participation. The Act's adoption thus reflects a deliberate societal choice, not a deterministic response to technological pressure.

This principle is also reflected in Article 14 of the AI Act, which mandates that high-risk AI systems must be designed and developed with effective human oversight [12] mechanisms to ensure that humans retain meaningful control and accountability over automated decision-making (AIA, Article 14). This requirement underscores the regulation's commitment to preserving human agency and ensuring that AI serves as a tool guided by societal values, not an autonomous force. The emphasis shall be put on the requirement of 'meaningful' human oversight through intervening "in the operation of the high-risk AI system or interrupt the system through a 'stop' button or a similar procedure that allows the system to come to a halt in a safe state." (AIA, Article 14 (4) (b).

Furthermore, the enforcement architecture of the AI Act [21] reinforces this approach: centralized coordination by the AI Office, strategic guidance from the European AI Board, specialist advice from the Scientific Panel, and enforcement by national competent and market surveillance authorities, all working in tandem to uphold uniform application across the EU. This integrated framework supported by implementing and delegated acts, comitology scrutiny, and collaborative authority demonstrates that AI is not left to deterministic forces but is democratically structured, regulated, and steered through institutional design and public oversight.

Together, these provisions establish a governance framework that reflects the belief that technology must be actively governed, regulated, and shaped through institutional and democratic mechanisms. The AI Act demonstrates that technology can be steered through democratic processes, yet the dominance of industry lobbying and technical standardisation raises doubts about whose values ultimately shape regulation. This reflects a tension between the humanist vision of societal co-determination and the pragmatic realities of EU lawmaking. The AI Act reflects a constructivist rather than deterministic stance by being the product of democratic deliberation and by instituting oversight mechanisms that emphasize human agency. We therefore judge this principle to be largely fulfilled, although its effectiveness will ultimately depend on enforcement in practice.

The Affirmation of the Ontological and Moral Distinction Between Humans and Machines. This principle affirms the fundamental distinction between humans and machines, setting digital humanism apart from transhumanist and posthumanist ideologies. It rejects transhumanism's call for technological augmentation of humans through implants or bioengineering, insisting instead on improving technology to support people as they are and may become. It likewise dismisses posthumanist visions of super-AI surpassing humanity, which neglect human beings as ends in themselves and fail to define "progress" in human-centric terms. Consistently, digital humanism also opposes narratives that portray humans as serving technological development [24].

The statement that digital humanism aims for improved technological development that accepts and supports humans as they are, rather than trying to improve people with technology, aligns well with the objectives of the EU AI Act. The AI Act's core goal of supporting innovation in AI is coupled with a strong emphasis on protecting fundamental rights, safety, and health (AIA, Recital 1). This dual objective of the regulation directly resonates with digital humanism's aim: the innovation it seeks to foster is implicitly one that accepts and supports humans, as it must adhere to strict safeguards for their rights, safety, and well-being. Therefore, the AI Act's regulatory framework seeks to guide technological development in a manner that ensures AI serves and protects human beings as they are, rather than seeking to transform them.

For example, the Act's risk-based approach and prohibitions on certain manipulative AI practices are designed to prevent AI systems from negatively impacting human autonomy or coercing individuals, which would be contrary to digital humanism's principles and could be seen as an unwanted 'improvement' or alteration of human behavior. The emphasis on transparency (AIA, Article 50 and 86) and human oversight (AIA, Article 14) further ensures that humans remain aware and in control of AI systems, rather than becoming subservient to them or allowing technology to dictate human evolution. Therefore, while the AI Act promotes technological advancement, it is based on ethical and human-centric design principles that are intended to ensure that innovation serves humanity without pushing towards the transhumanist or even posthumanist ideals. The support for innovation within the AI Act is thus implicitly guided by a responsible innovation paradigm that seeks to prevent the very outcomes digital humanism warns against.

However, we found no explicit provisions within the AI Act specifically addressing protection against any obligation to support technological development. The AI Act incorporates this principle by ensuring human oversight and transparency, thereby safeguarding the primacy of human agency. However, it does not explicitly recognize the 'right to non-engagement' with AI. This gap shows the tension between a regulatory pragmatism oriented toward ensuring minimal control and the humanist ambition to preserve unconditional autonomy in the face of technological encroachment. Thus, we assess this principle as partially fulfilled, since its practical protections fall short of fully securing human autonomy.

3   Conclusions and Recommendations

In the previous section, we have analyzed the text of the AI Act including rationales provided in the Impact Assessment to identify principles of digital humanism as defined by Prem's research. Corresponding binding provisions are outlined in the table below (Table 1).

Table 1. Mapping Prem's Principles of Digital Humanism to Corresponding Provisions of the AI Act.

Principle of Digital Humanism	Relevant AI Act Provisions
Acknowledgment of socio-technical context and impact of AI	Art. 5, Art. 9, Art. 27
Protection of humans and the environment	Art. 4, Art. 9, Art. 10, Art. 14, Art. 27, Art. 40, Art. 46, Art. 50, Art. 86, Art. 95, Art. 112
Strengthening democracy and society	Art. 1, Art. 5, Art. 27, Art. 57, Annex III(8)
Deterministic approach towards AI	Art. 14, Art. 64–70, Art. 74
Ontological and moral distinction between humans and machines	Art. 14, Art. 50, Art. 86

Building on the compliance judgments reached in Sect. 2.3, this section develops normative recommendations for how the AI Act could more fully reflect the principles of digital humanism. Each recommendation corresponds directly to the areas where we found only partial or insufficient fulfillment, thereby ensuring that the prescriptive dimension of the paper flows directly from our analytical findings.

Acknowledgment of socio-technical context and impact of AI in the AI Act should not be seen in isolation from the whole applicable legal framework. Impact of new technologies including AI on individuals is already subject to strict scrutiny from the general framework on fundamental rights and freedoms [5]. This is partially reflected in recitals and by requirements for conducting fundamental rights impact assessments. It shall be noted that the scope of these obligations is too narrow and applicable to a limited number of subjects in a very limited number of cases. With this in mind, we would recommend including FRIAs for every high-risk AI system within the obligation to implement a risk management system. Additionally, conducting FRIA in a more general manner and not only in case of high-risk AI systems may further extend protection of individuals from the effects of any AI systems. As mentioned above, the AI Act explicitly acknowledges the principles of trustworthy AI as defined by AI HLEG. However, this declaration is only in the recitals part of the act. In our view, more binding inclusion of these principles would be detrimental for broader analysis of ethical and societal risk associated with AI, thus better reflecting this principle of digital humanism. Protection of humans and the environment is both directly and indirectly addressed throughout the entire regulation. While the protection of humans is ensured through the obligation to examine and consider impacts on fundamental rights and the overall risk-based approach of the AI Act, the protection of the environment is mentioned on multiple occasions but there are no specific and binding obligations for entities subject to the regulation.

We don't consider this principle to be reflected sufficiently and to implement it better within the AI Act or future regulation, a more robust and explicit framework for environmental sustainability is needed. This would entail moving beyond a sole reliance on voluntary standards to include binding requirements for AI systems' environmental footprint across their entire lifecycle, encompassing not just energy consumption but also water usage, resource extraction, and e-waste generation. The AI Act could also benefit from a requirement for broader environmental impact assessments for all AI systems with the potential of significant environmental impact, regardless of their direct impact on humans. To better ensure the protection of human dignity and other fundamental rights, this principle would equally benefit from the requirement for all providers and deployers of high-risk AI systems to conduct a Fundamental Rights Impact Assessments, extending this obligation beyond the current limited personal scope. Finally, clear enforcement mechanisms and accountability frameworks should also be established to ensure compliance with both human rights and environmental standards to prevent situations where commitments are perceived as vague or lacking genuine accountability.

The principle of strengthening democracy and society is indirectly protected as a value within the subject matter of the AI Act and specific obligations related to banned practices, general-purpose AI models, conducting fundamental rights impact assessments and it's also narrowly defined within an area of high-risk AI application. We consider such protection of democracy in the AI act insufficient. Although the value of democracy is explicitly acknowledged, there are no further provisions delineating specific legal requirements for the protection of democracy. This is especially striking in the context of obligations for developers of general-purpose AI models, where such protection should be anchored. Additionally, the area of high-risk concerning democracy, as currently envisaged, is too narrow and does not foresee many risks for democracy stemming from AI, including the spread of disinformation or various forms of impacting civic society. In our previous research [17], we emphasized that Annex III, point 8 should be refined to include the use of recommender systems that amplify the spread of disinformation on very large online platforms.

Deterministic approach towards AI is reflected by the democratic process of adopting the AI Act and providing solid enforcement architecture. Typical concerns related to the process of adoptions of law in general oscillate around power and lobbying of technological giants representing providers of AI systems or countries where these providers reside. These issues are beyond the scope of this paper, but certain guidance may be found in recent research [31]. Regarding enforcement, it is impossible to assess the adequacy and effectiveness of enforcement of the AI Act today as only two provisions are in force (Article 4 and Article 5). Additionally, it is the responsibility of EU member states to implement efficient oversight over AI systems sufficiently.

The fifth and final principle of improving technological development that accepts and supports humans as they are aligns well with the objective of the AI Act, but the regulation is lacking when it comes to the 'right to non-engagement' with AI technologies. We believe directly impacted stakeholders would greatly benefit if the AI Act explicitly ensured that opting out of certain AI-powered services or data contribution to AI development does not result in disadvantages or exclusion, thereby safeguarding human autonomy against any implicit obligation to adopt or serve technology.

The analysis presented in this paper highlights the importance of embedding democratic, human-centric principles into the governance of AI, in line with the foundational ideas of digital humanism. The recommendations developed in this paper are intended not only as a response to these challenges but also as a normative and practical guidance for policymakers, regulatory designers, and AI practitioners across disciplines.

Acknowledgments. This study was partially supported by EUDHIT - The European Digital Humanism Initiative, a project funded by European Union, GA No. 101212890, https://doi.org/10.3030/101212890, and lorAI, a project funded by European Union, GA No. 101136646, https://doi.org/10.3030/101136646.

Disclosure of Interests. The authors have no competing interests to declare that are relevant to the content of this article.

References

1. Baumbach, T.: Chilling effect as a European court of human rights' concept in media law cases. Bergen J. Crim. Law Criminal Just. **6**(1), 92–114 (2018). https://doi.org/10.15845/bjclcj.v6i1.1555
2. Bijker, W.E., Hughes, T.P., Pinch, T.J. (eds.): The Social Construction of Technological Systems: New Directions in the Sociology and History of Technology. MIT Press, Cambridge, MA (1987)
3. Bond, R.R., et al.: Automation bias in medicine: the influence of automated diagnoses on interpreter accuracy and uncertainty when reading electrocardiograms. J. Electrocardiol. **51**(6), S6–S13 (2018). https://doi.org/10.1016/j.jelectrocard.2018.08.007

4. Carnegie endowment for international peace: Can democracy survive the disruptive power of AI?. https://carnegieendowment.org/research/2024/12/can-democracy-survive-the-disruptive-power-of-ai?lang=en (2024). Accessed 9 July 2025

5. Celeste, E.: Digital constitutionalism, EU digital sovereignty ambitions and the role of the european declaration on digital rights. In: Engel, A., Groussot, X., Petursson, G.T. (eds.) New Directions in Digitalisation. European Union and its Neighbours in a Globalized World, Studies in European Union External Relations, vol. 13, pp. 255–271. Springer, Cham (2025).https://doi.org/10.1007/978-3-031-65381-0_13

6. Celeste, E., De Gregorio, G.: Digital humanism: the constitutional message of the GDPR. Global Priv. Law Rev. **3**(1), 4–18 (2022). https://doi.org/10.54648/gplr2022002

7. Cheong, B.C.H.: Transparency and accountability in ai systems: safeguarding wellbeing in the age of algorithmic decision-making. Front. Hum. Dyn. **6** (2024). https://doi.org/10.3389/fhumd.2024.1421273

8. Cooper, N.: Bridging deliberative democracy and deployment of societal-scale technology (2023). https://arxiv.org/abs/2303.10831

9. European commission: Impact assessment regulation on artificial intelligence (2025). https://digital-strategy.ec.europa.eu/en/library/impact-assessment-regulation-artificial-intelligence. last updated 29 January 2025. Accessed 10 July 2025

10. European commission high-level expert group on AI: ethics guidelines for trustworthy artificial intelligence (2019). https://digital-strategy.ec.europa.eu/en/library/ethics-guidelines-trustworthy-ai. Accessed 10 July 2025

11. European Union: Regulation (EU) 2024/1689 of the European parliament and of the council of 13 june 2024 laying down harmonised rules on artificial intelligence … (artificial intelligence act) (2024), oJ L, 2024/1689 (2024)

12. Fink, M.: Human oversight under article 14 of the EU AI act. In: Malgieri, G., González Fuster, G., Mantelero, A., Zanfir-Fortuna, G. (eds.) AI Act Commentary: A Thematic Analysis. Hart-Bloomsbury (2026). https://ssrn.com/abstract=5146118, forthcoming

13. Green software foundation: The EU AI act: insights from the green committee (2024). https://greensoftware.foundation/articles/the-eu-ai-act-insights-from-the-green-ai-committee

14. Hofkirchner, W., Kreowski, H.J.: Digital humanism: How to shape digitalisation in the age of global challenges? Proceedings **81**(1), 4 (2022). https://doi.org/10.3390/proceedings2022081004

15. Lindorfer, M.: The threat of surveillance and the need for privacy protections. In: Werthner, H., et al. (eds.) Introduction to Digital Humanism, pp. 481–494. Springer, Cham (2024). https://doi.org/10.1007/978-3-031-45304-5_37

16. Mantelero, A.: The Fundamental Rights Impact Assessment (FRIA) in the AI act: roots, legal obligations and key elements for a model template. Comput. Law Secur. Rev. **54** (2024). https://www.sciencedirect.com/science/article/pii/S0267364924000864

17. Mesarčík, M., Slosiarová, N.: Regulating ai for a truthful tomorrow: addressing disinformation in the EU artificial intelligence act. Int. J. Law Inf. Technol. **33**, eaaf014 (2025)

18. Miller, T.: Explanation in artificial intelligence: insights from the social sciences. Artif. Intell. **267**, 1–38 (2019). https://doi.org/10.1016/j.artint.2018.07.007

19. Munn, L.: Digital Labor, Platforms, and AI. In: Werthner, H., et al. (eds.) Introduction to Digital Humanism, pp. 557–570. Springer, Cham (2024). https://doi.org/10.1007/978-3-031-45304-5_35
20. Müller, M., Kettemann, M.C.: European Approaches to the Regulation of Digital Technologies. In: Werthner, H., et al. (eds.) Introduction to Digital Humanism, pp. 623–636. Springer, Cham (2024). https://doi.org/10.1007/978-3-031-45304-5_39
21. Novelli, C., Hacker, P., Morley, J., Trondal, J., Floridi, L.: A robust governance for the ai act: AI office, ai board, scientific panel, and national authorities. Eur. J. Risk Regul. **16**, 1–25 (2024)
22. Pagallo, U., Ciani Sciolla, J., Durante, M.: The environmental challenges of AI in EU law: lessons learned from the artificial intelligence act (AIA) with its drawbacks. Transforming Gov. People Process Policy **16**(3), 359–376 (2022). http://hdl.handle.net/2318/1874661
23. Penney, J.W.: Understanding chilling effects. Minnesota Law Rev. **106**(6), 1451–1528 (2022). https://minnesotalawreview.org/wp-content/uploads/2022/04/6-Penney_Web.pdf
24. Prem, E.: Principles of digital humanism: a critical post-humanist view. J. Responsible Technol. **17**, 100075 (2024)
25. Prem, E., Krenn, B.: On Algorithmic Content Moderation. In: Werthner, H., et al. (eds.) Introduction to Digital Humanism, pp. 481–493. Springer, Cham (2023). https://doi.org/10.1007/978-3-031-45304-5_30
26. Schuett, J.: Risk management in the artificial intelligence act. Eur. J. Risk Regulation **15**(2), 367–385 (2024)
27. Silvo, S.R., Chinarro, D., Andrés, A.P.: Green ai and ai act: pioneering legislation or merely an environmental statement? Revista Catalana de Dret Ambiental **16**(1) (2025). https://doi.org/10.17345/rcda4122
28. Staab, P.: Digitaler Kapitalismus: Markt und Herrschaft in der Ökonomie der Unknappheit. Suhrkamp Verlag (2019)
29. Ter-Minassian, L.: Democratizing AI governance: balancing expertise and public participation (2025). https://arxiv.org/abs/2502.08651
30. Vienna manifesto on digital humanism: Vienna manifesto on digital humanism (2019). https://caiml.org/dighum/dighum-manifesto/Vienna_Manifesto_on_Digital_Humanism_EN.pdf
31. Wei, K., Ezell, C., Gabrieli, N., Deshpande, C.: How do AI companies "fine-tune" policy? examining regulatory capture in ai governance (2024). https://arxiv.org/abs/2410.13042
32. Zuboff, S.: The Age of Surveillance Capitalism: The Fight for a Human Future at the New Frontier of Power. Public Affairs, New York (2019)

Readiness-Centered AI in Practice: Findings from a Pilot Chatbot for Digital Skilling of Older Adults in Low-Readiness Contexts

Anne Muchiri[1]([✉])[iD], Joshua Rumo A. Ndiege[1][iD], Giannis Haralabopoulos[2][iD], Paula M. W. Musuva[1][iD], and Paul Spiesberger[3][iD]

[1] School of Science and Technology, Department of Computing and Informatics, United States International University-Africa, Nairobi 14634-00800, Kenya
`amuchiri2@usiu.ac.ke`
[2] University of Reading, Whiteknights House, RG6 6UR Reading, UK
`i.haralabopoulos@henley.ac.uk`
[3] Institute of Software Engineering and Artificial Intelligence, Graz University of Technology, Inffeldgasse 16b/II, 8010 Graz, Austria
`spiesberger-hoeckner@tugraz.at`

Abstract. This paper presents findings from an initial deployment of a readiness-centered Artificial Intelligence (AI) driven chatbot designed to support digital skilling amongst older adults in low-readiness settings. Building on Human-Centered Artificial Intelligence (HCAI) principles, the study introduces a readiness-centered reframing that adapts HCAI to account for users' technological, cognitive and socio-cultural preparedness and tests this using a tool that integrated multilingual support, voice-based interactions and age-sensitive design. A cross-sectional study was conducted in urban and rural Kenyan counties, involving 388 participants using observational methods and semi-structured interviews to document user interactions. Thematic analysis revealed key barriers to adoption, including emotional discomfort, language-related confusion, usability breakdowns and cultural perceptions. These findings demonstrate that, while ethical design is necessary, it is not sufficient especially when foundational precursors like digital readiness, cognitive diversity and socio-cultural beliefs are not met. This study contributes by identifying critical gaps within the current HCAI framework and proposes a readiness-centered reframing that reorients design of AI systems around users' actual capacities, cultural norms, and infrastructural realities. It introduces digital readiness assessment, cognitive scaffolding, and cultural usability as essential design pillars for AI systems that are not only ethical, but truly inclusive, usable and effective in low-readiness contexts.

Keywords: Artificial Intelligence · AI · Digital Literacy · Human-Centered AI · Low-Readiness Contexts · Older Adults · Readiness-Centered

L. Hagedorn et al. (Eds.): DIGHUM 2025, LNCS 16319, pp. 333–347, 2026.
https://doi.org/10.1007/978-3-032-11108-1_24

1   Introduction

The global trend of population aging, together with the rapid digitalization of services, is reshaping digital inclusion efforts to advance inclusive development. The clarion call for sustainable development has emphasized that *"no one is left behind"*, including in the digital environment [1]. This is particularly important for underrepresented groups such as the elderly and persons with disabilities. However, older persons are at a heightened risk of digital exclusion, a phenomena conceptualized as the *grey digital divide* [2]. This exclusion of older adults stems from systemic barriers such as limited access and affordability, alongside individual-level challenges such as inadequate capacity to use technology and low levels of digital literacy [3,4]. While digital literacy is foundational to achieving digital inclusion [5], its attainment remains a challenge, particularly among older adults due to barriers such as limited resources, lack of adaptive delivery methods and insufficient attention to user heterogeneity [6,7]. In response to resource constraint challenges and the need for adaptive mechanisms to augment delivery, AI has gained traction across various domains including healthcare, service optimization, and education [8–10].

Shneiderman [11] introduced the Human-Centered Artificial Intelligence (HCAI) framework to guide the responsible and inclusive design of AI systems, aiming to amplify human agency while upholding ethical and safe standards. This framework emphasizes human control, usability, inclusivity, trust, and fairness, values that resonate with theories of aging such as Activity Theory [12]. Activity theory promotes continued participation and engagement in later life. Despite the strengths of the HCAI framework, it often implicitly assumes a baseline level of digital readiness and homogeneous user capabilities, assumptions that may not hold amongst the aging population in Low and Middle Income Countries (LMIC). Such assumptions fail to consider how users with diverse levels of digital skills, cognitive ability, belief systems and infrastructural access engage with AI tools. Understanding these perspectives is critical among underrepresented populations in underserved regions.

This study addresses this gap by assessing how older adults in Kenya engage with an Artificial Intelligence (AI)-driven chatbot for digital skilling. It explores how contextual, cognitive, and infrastructural factors shape this engagement. Based on this exploratory analysis, we propose a readiness-centered reframing of HCAI, defined as an approach that grounds HCAI in users' actual capabilities, diversity, digital preparedness and social-technical realities observed in low-readiness contexts. We define low-readiness contexts as settings characterized by low levels of digital skills, socio-cultural influences on technology adoption and infrastructural limitations, where age-related factors such as cognitive and physical decline amplify these challenges. These dimensions are then factored into the design and deployment of AI systems, a shift from the approaches predominant in western contexts [13]. As noted in Schmager et al. [13], these western contexts emphasize abstract ethical principles such as fairness, accountability, transparency, and safety, but often without grounding them in diverse cultural and readiness settings.

This study is structured around three critical focus areas: (i) readiness factors influencing engagement of the elderly with AI tools, (ii) user experience and responses to an AI-driven digital skilling chatbot, and (iii) design adaptations required for context-aware AI in low-readiness settings. Collectively, these focus areas yield empirical evidence that challenges the sufficiency of the existing HCAI framework in guiding inclusive AI design for such contexts. It argues that without attention to user capabilities, local infrastructure, and cultural-linguistic contexts, AI systems risk reinforcing exclusion and failure. Beyond critique, the study introduces a readiness-centered Human-Centered Artificial Intelligence (HCAI) framework grounded in empirical insights from Kenya.

Hereafter, we present a background to the study by introducing the HCAI framework and review literature on the use of AI to support older adults. We then describe the methodology used to evaluate older persons' interactions with the AI-driven chatbot for digital skilling. Next we present the findings of the study including descriptive statistics of respondent profiles and thematic analysis of user experiences. To contextualize these findings, we proceed to discuss them in relation to existing literature, before concluding with study limitations, recommendations and directions for future work.

2   Background

2.1   Human-Centered AI and Its Implications

The HCAI framework by Shneiderman [11] offers a foundational model for AI systems that promote self-efficacy, creativity, accountability, and social participation. Central to this framework is a two-dimensional model that aims to balance high levels of automation with human control. However, critics argue that the framework lacks contextual sensitivity. For instance, Pacailler *et al.* [14] argue that this framework is static, and call for the integration of user characteristics, cognitive ability and decision making, dimensions that are especially crucial for older adults. Similarly, Schmager *et al.* [13] highlight that ethical values such as dignity, fairness, and justice are context-dependent and are interpreted differently across environments, underscoring the limitations of universal framing of HCAI. While the critiques in [13] and [14] are substantive, they remain conceptual and lack empirical validation especially among older adults, a population that faces the *grey divide* globally, with challenges particularly pronounced in low-readiness contexts such as LMICs.

From a theoretical lens, this study conceptualizes readiness through the Social Cognitive Theory (SCT) and the Seniors Technology Acceptance Model (STAM), which together explain the motivational, cognitive, and contextual factors influencing older adults' engagement with digital technologies [15,16]. Schunk and DiBenedetto [17] highlight that self-efficacy, a key construct of SCT, STAM and the HCAI framework promotes motivation, which Van Dijk [18] identifies as a prerequisite for digital equality. Therefore, SCT provides a lens to understand behavioral and emotional responses, such as fear, anxiety, confidence, and trust. STAM complements this by addressing age-related factors including cognitive ability, physical limitations and perceived ease of use. It also considers facilitating conditions such as access to devices, connectivity and support systems crucial to understanding infrastructural readiness.

2.2 AI-Driven Chatbots to Support the Elderly

AI-driven chatbots have shown promise in supporting older adults with behavior change, information access, and health monitoring [19–21]. For instance, Garcia-Mendez *et al.* [21] deployed a voice-enabled news chatbot in Spain, Wiratunga *et al.* [20] evaluated a behavior-change chatbot designed to encourage physical activity among older adults in the United Kingdom (UK) and Wilczewski *et al.* [19] implemented a health data collection chatbot in the United States of America (USA). However, these studies were conducted in high-income settings with well-established digital infrastructure and high digital user readiness, often assuming baseline access to devices, skills, and language fluency. Such settings may not reflect the low-readiness contexts which are a reality in many countries around the World. Low-readiness contexts have several challenges in digital readiness, particularly around digital literacy, infrastructural access and language accessibility. Moreover, these chatbots were task-specific and did not address barriers that hinder meaningful engagement in low-readiness contexts.

In contrast this study introduces and empirically tests a readiness-centered, AI-driven digital skilling chatbot, designed for older adults in Kenya. Based on the HCAI framework, the tool was developed to accommodate diverse cognitive, linguistic, and infrastructural needs, offering a locally responsive alternative to dominant chatbot designs. Specifically, it grounds HCAI by integrating contextual realities of digitally marginalized older adults in Kenya, highlighting how infrastructural limitations, digital literacy gaps, language accessibility, and culturally rooted perceptions shape user interaction with AI tools. In doing so, our study contributes to a context-aware reframing of HCAI, grounded not only in theory, but in the lived experiences of users in low-readiness environments.

3   Methodology

The study employed a cross-sectional exploratory design to assess older adults' interactions with an AI-driven digital skilling chatbot. According to the Kenya National Bureau of Statistics (KNBS), persons' aged 60 years and above comprise approximately 6% of the national population, an estimated 2,856,000 older adults out of 47,600,000 [22]. To capture perspectives from contrasting environments, a purposive sample of 388 older adults was selected from Nairobi and Busia counties, representing urban and rural contexts respectively. This sample and its size were critical for establishing baseline insights into digital readiness, including connectivity, digital literacy, and access to devices. Nairobi participants were drawn from Dagoretti South, Kibra, and Langata sub-counties while those from Busia were recruited from Funyula, Matayos and Teso North enabling comparison between digitally resourced and underserved contexts. The sample included participants aged 60–90 years, with diversity in gender, education, digital skill level and socio-economic status, providing a heterogeneous basis for contextualizing digital readiness and engagement across contrasting environments in Kenya.

These participants were part of a three-day digital skilling workshop that introduced the AI-driven chatbot. Only the beneficiaries who were willing to participate over a four hour interaction session and had signed informed consent forms were included in the study. Tool interaction was conducted in two counties: Nairobi (urban) in March 2025 and Busia (rural) in May 2025, over a three-day deployment per county. These locations were selected to enable representation of both urban and rural contexts, capturing diverse levels of digital exposure, infrastructure, and AI receptiveness. During the digital skilling sessions, participants interacted with the AI chatbot while trained research assistants observed their interactions and filled in data collection tools documenting real-time reactions, usability challenges, and support needs. After the sessions, the assistants conducted semi-structured interviews to capture participants perceptions, experiences and accessibility concerns.

The AI chatbot consisted of three integrated components: (i) a baseline data collection module to capture demographic and digital readiness data; (ii) an interactive chatbot module powered by a lightweight Large Language Model (LLM); and (iii) a gateway module for accessing essential e-Government services in Kenya, such as tax filing, healthcare, and social protection portals. In line with age-friendly design principles advocated in [23], the tool incorporated several inclusive design features tailored to the needs of older adults. These included simplified workflows to reduce cognitive load, multi-modal interaction (text and voice) to accommodate different literacy levels and interaction preferences and bilingual support (English and Swahili) to address language barriers. Additional accessibility features such as high-contrast fonts and voice input/output were

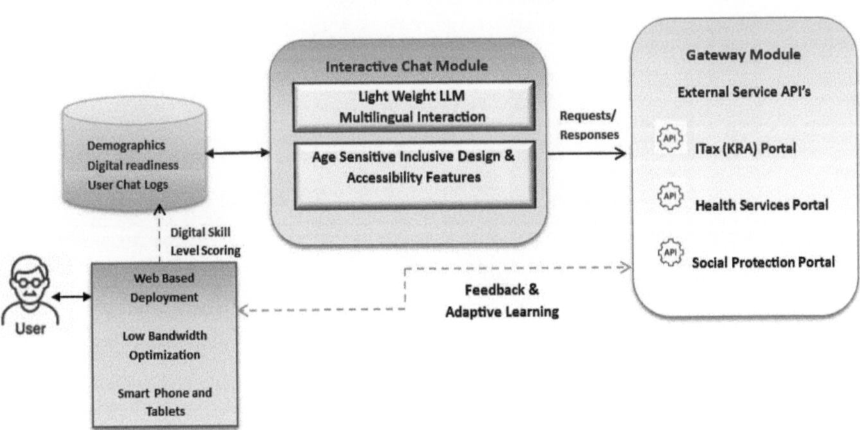

Fig. 1. Deployment Model.

integrated to support users with visual, hearing or dexterity impairments. The tool was deployed as a web-based application, optimized for low-bandwidth environments and was accessible via smartphones and tablets as depicted in Fig. 1.

Using the tool, the baseline module captured demographic characteristics, digital literacy levels, internet access, device ownership, language preference, and prior e-government use. Interaction logs documented user queries, responses, and navigation patterns, revealing moments where support was needed. Complementing these, research assistants observed participants' engagement and conducted semi-structured interviews after the sessions to capture user experiences and reflections. Together, these approaches generated both usage data and experiential accounts of older adults' interaction with the AI chatbot.

4 Findings

Figure 2 summarizes the three digital readiness profiles of participants based on measures of access, capacity and preferences. The majority of participants (52%) lacked internet access at home, which reflects significant infrastructural shortcomings that lead to connectivity barriers. Additionally, 79% of participants reported that they only had basic digital skills. This means that they are likely to experience skill gap challenges that limit independent engagement. Findings on language preference revealed that a significant majority (74%) preferred using both Swahili and English and further suggested to include local languages such as Ateso, Dholuo, Kikuyu and Luhya in the design. This shows that participants preferred to have integration of local African languages and not just English.

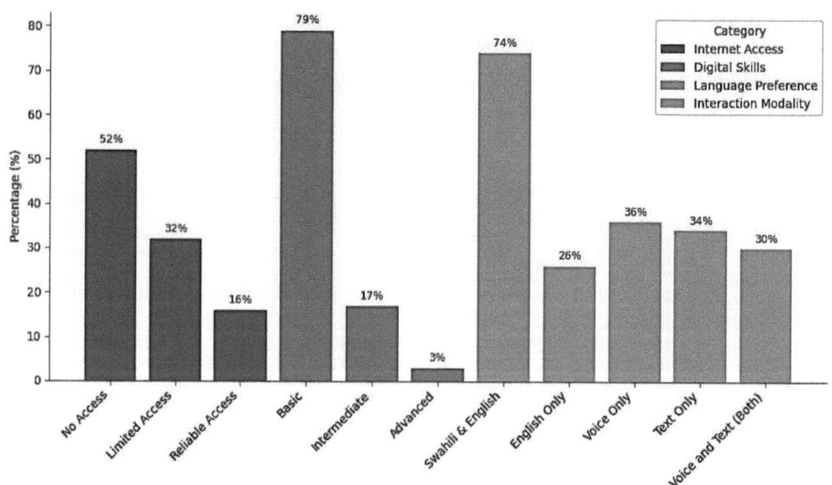

Fig. 2. Descriptive Statistics on Readiness Indicators among Participants.

With respect to interaction modality, preferences were fairly balanced, with 36% favoring voice-only, 34% text-only and 30% opting for both text and voice.

These findings suggest a slight preference for voice interaction but more importantly, highlight the heterogeneous nature of older adults, as discussed in [24].

4.1 Thematic Analysis of the Emerging Themes

Qualitative data were inductively analyzed using Braun & Clarke six step process for reflexive thematic analysis [25]. This involved data familiarization, systematic coding and generation of themes that reflected participants accounts. Insights from this process revealed five interrelated themes shaping older adults' experiences with AI tools in LMICs: linguistic accessibility, trust and security, human-AI interaction, usability and simplicity, and cultural-spiritual perceptions of AI. These are summarized in Table 1 and subsequently discussed.

Table 1. Emerging Themes from User Interaction with the AI-Driven Chatbot for Digital Skilling.

#	Theme	Key Insight
1	Language Accessibility	Many users struggled with English and Swahili, preferring local languages – especially if they had limited or no formal education.
2	Trust and Safety	Unease with high levels of automation, data privacy and safety concerns, especially among those unfamiliar with technology.
3	Human–AI Interaction	The tool was useful as an interactive digital literacy support system for simplified instruction in the absence of human support and in cases of memory lapses, however concerns were expressed around its potential to replace human contact.
4	Usability and Simplicity	Accessibility features were underutilized mainly due to digital anxiety. Participants preferred short simple answers that reduce cognitive load.
5	Cultural–Spiritual Perceptions of AI	Real-time AI responses without visible human involvement were unsettling to some, invoking spiritual discomfort around unseen forces and cultural discomfort over the absence of human interaction.

Theme 1: Linguistic Accessibility. The AI chatbot supported interaction in both English and Swahili. However, many participants expressed difficulty in using these two languages, more so English. While the Swahili translations were helpful to some users, most of the participants expressed preference for local languages or dialects. One participant asked:

> *"Can AI work with local dialects or non-written communication like voice or sign language?"*

This sentiment was common among users who had limited or no formal education, a trend reflected in the quantitative data, where over 53% of our users lacked formal schooling and 79% had basic digital skills only. These figures point to the limitations of deploying AI tools that rely primarily on dominant national or international languages which fail to account for the local language contexts of older adults.

Theme 2: Trust and Safety. The HCAI framework emphasizes trust and safety as core design principles for responsible AI systems [11]. However, during interaction with the AI tool, many older adults demonstrated fear of the devices and more so the high level automation of the chatbot tool. Concerns were also raised about data privacy and the potential misuse of shared information, even though the data collection process was designed to support personalized responses based on digital readiness. One participant remarked:

"How do I know this AI is safe and won't misuse my information?"

These concerns highlight that beyond functionality, the AI tools must have reassurance on data safety, be transparent and ensure data control.

Theme 3: Human-AI Interaction. Participants welcomed the use of the AI tool for digital support, especially when human assistance was unavailable or when age-related memory lapses occurred. However concerns emerged around the possibility of replacing humans entirely, with some users expressing unease over loss of personal connection especially in their old-age. Additionally, the Human-AI interaction modality posed challenges for users with multiple limitations where one participant asked:

"What about those who use sign language and have no formal education? How are they supposed to understand the output?"

Such reflections demonstrate that older adults are not only aware of their functional limitations but are also conscious of the design assumptions, such as the reliance on voice outputs and ability to interpret text in English or Swahili, embedded in the AI-driven digital skilling chatbot that they tested.

Theme 4: Usability and Simplicity. The AI tool was designed with inclusive principles, incorporating accessibility features such as adjustable font sizes, high contrast display options and the integration of voice-based interactions. While some participants explored and appreciated such features, there was limited usage likely due to limited digital literacy and the fear of technology. One participant, impressed by the voice feature, exclaimed:

"Wow, it just answered me when I spoke, how did it do that?"

Despite the moments of fascination by the features such as voice interaction, many participants found the outputs overwhelming, with simplicity emerging as a key concern that can be attributed to preference for brief , direct responses that do not cognitively overwhelm users. For instance, one participant remarked:

"The AI tool is too complex; can it give simpler answers?"

These findings suggest even systems that consider inclusive principles may still be underutilized if they fail to account for users' cognitive load and digital proficiencies, a finding supported in [14].

Theme 5: Cultural-Spiritual Perceptions of AI. While many participants encountered expected usability challenges such as difficulty adjusting font sizes independently, navigating menus and returning to previous steps, a subset expressed deeper discomfort with the AI tool that extended beyond confusion. The tool's ability to deliver real-time, personalized responses without visible human input led to unease among some users, who perceived it as unnatural or overly intrusive. One participant remarked:

"This AI tool and the internet is satanic, how does it know this information?"

This reaction was not isolated but reflective of participants with limited formal education and digital skills as presented in the quantitative findings. In communities where spiritual and moral beliefs shape how people understand knowledge and authority, technologies like AI can be perceived as more than unfamiliar and as such they can feel intrusive or even threatening. What designers view as neutral or intelligent may,to others, appear as opaque or supernatural.

5   Discussion

This study explored older adults' engagement with an AI-driven digital skilling chatbot in low-readiness Kenyan context. Focusing on readiness factors, the study examined how infrastructural, cognitive demands and sociocultural factors influence capacity and willingness to engage meaningfully with the tool.

Infrastructural limitations, particularly unreliable internet connectivity in rural areas like Busia County, created substantial barriers to access. This aligns with the work of United Nations Development Programme (UNDP), which emphasizes that digital engagement hinges on access to connectivity and devices [26]. Additionally, while some older adults interacted with the tool using their personal smartphones, device sharing was common, which simultaneously enabled peer learning but constrained sustained individual engagement. This dynamic supports Bandura's [15] concept of self-efficacy and observational learning, as peer support often helped overcome initial fears and mistrust of AI tools.

Cognitively, the tool's three-part interface presented memory and navigation challenges particularly in recalling how to navigate between steps and returning to previous tabs or completing tasks proved difficult. This underscores the need to design for diverse cognitive abilities and limitations particularly among older users reflecting findings by [19] on low cognitive-load interfaces. This reinforces the need for simplified interface design, memory scaffolding and feedback loops, widely discussed in [27,28], to accommodate cognitive diversity.

Socio-cultural factors such as perceptions of AI-generated outputs being unnatural or even amusing reflected deeper seated cultural beliefs about the unfamiliar intelligent behavior of machines. Left unaddressed, such perceptions may lead to fear, mistrust, or outright rejection of AI tools, reflecting socio-technical factors that shape digital engagement highlighted in [29]. Additionally, in Kenyan contexts, the inter-generational dependence model where younger family members support older persons still exists, and these are considerations that should be integrated in the framing and design of AI tools. This dependency structure combined with cultural beliefs underscore the importance of designing AI tools through pluralistic perspectives. It supports the arguments for decolonization of AI, as articulated in [30,31] on plural perspectives.

The second focus area examined user experiences and responses to the AI tool. Despite low adoption rates, many users who interacted with the tool valued inclusive design features like adjustable font sizes and multiple interaction modes, which supported autonomy for visually impaired or physically limited users. This aligns with STAM's perceived usefulness and the heterogeneity of aging as discussed in [24]. Language accessibility has been highlighted as crucial for enhancing usability of AI tools [32]. However, for low-resourced languages common in many LMICs, existing language models remain inadequate. Beyond AI models, this concern is echoed in [33], who emphasize that language accessibility is crucial for the digital engagement of older. adults. In addition to linguistic limitations, some users perceived AI-generated responses as unnatural or even supernatural, reflecting emerging literature on techno-spiritual interpretations of AI [34]. Moreover, the discomfort from perceived unnaturalness was compounded by anxiety over making mistakes, with users expressing fear when the chatbot failed to interpret spelling mistakes. These concerns highlight how cultural and emotional connection shapes trust and sustained usage [35].

Finally, the study identified design adaptations required for effective AI tools in low-readiness contexts. This study proposes a readiness-centered reframing of HCAI, to one that prioritizes users' ability to understand, trust, and use AI tools effectively. Unlike [11] HCAI model, which focuses on usability and automation, this approach foregrounds emotional safety, cognitive capacity, and socio-cultural fit. Empirical findings support this reframing where survey data showed that while 74% of users preferred interactions in both Swahili and English, many still expressed the need to integrate local languages. Multi-modal integration also emerged as crucial, especially for older adults with physical limitations such as difficulty in typing. This was observed among participants who would long-press letters when typing, resulting in incorrect inputs. Therefore voice interactions for input and output were preferred. Consequently, participants emphasized voice outputs should be more natural and delivered in familiar voices, as foreign-sounding outputs were perceived as unfriendly, supporting findings in [36] on the importance of cultural voice alignment. Additionally, the tool must account for the socio-cultural realities of its users by offering contextually appropriate responses and avoiding abstract or overly complex instructions that discourage engagement. A cognitive scaffolding design approach, shown to reduce cognitive load in [27] is crucial. It enables an incremental learning curve that supports gradual introduction to digital interfaces and content interaction especially for low-literate older adults who preferred simpler outputs while offering flexibility for those with cognitive challenges. These adaptations help foster emotional trust, increase relevance, and enhance perceived usefulness, in line with the STAM.

Therefore, in this readiness-centered approach, inclusion is redefined not as access alone but as the ability to engage confidently, safely, and contextually. This underscores the importance of embedding SCT and STAM within HCAI, as they shape older adults' digital engagement. Effective AI tools must therefore go beyond technical design to ensure emotional, cognitive diversity and cultural alignment. Key features include multilingual support, familiar voice interactions, cognitive scaffolding, and clear, culturally relevant content and guidance. Without these, even well-designed tools risk rejection due to fear, confusion, or lack of support.

6   Conclusion and Future Work

The study's cross-sectional exploratory design limited opportunities for sustained interaction, familiarization and trust-building with the AI-driven chatbot for digital skilling constraining insights into medium to long-term acceptance and behavioral change. This limitation is critical because adoption among older adults is not a one-off event but an evolving process shaped by habit formation, changing trust, and cultural adaptation over time. Consequently, the findings may have limited generalizability to other low-readiness settings with different socio-cultural conditions, but underscore the importance of contextualizing AI tools to support sustained adoption. Additionally, although the system incorporated inclusive features such as multilingual and voice interaction, it was limited for real-time adaptive personalization, in part due to the relatively small volume of user interaction data. As a result, the system was less responsive to dynamic, context-specific needs. Future work should therefore adopt longitudinal designs to better capture evolving user experiences, particularly around socio-cultural beliefs, emotional trust, and shifting perceptions of AI. Furthermore, the integration of enhanced personalization may encourage adoption and help to build trust, thereby supporting sustained use and behavior change.

This study contributes to the inclusive AI discourse by highlighting how contextual factors shape the development and adoption of AI tools among older adults in Kenya. Through the real-world deployment of an AI-driven chatbot for digital skilling, the research revealed critical limitations of the HCAI framework, particularly its insufficient attention to the socio-cultural, cognitive, trust-related and infrastructural realities that shape users levels of readiness and autonomy in low-readiness contexts. In response, the study proposes a Readiness-Centered HCAI framework, grounded in empirical evidence and designed to embed digital readiness, cultural usability, emotional trust, and cognitive scaffolding as core design principles. Rather than replacing HCAI which emphasizes ethical design, the Readiness-Centered HCAI framework extends it by integrating these contextual considerations that enable meaningful adoption in low-readiness contexts. It further emphasizes that evaluating the effectiveness of AI systems can only be meaningfully achieved through direct interaction with intended users, ensuring alignment with their lived realities. By grounding HCAI in practice and context, this study contributes to the evolution of the field from a high-resource, idealized model to one that is responsive to the diverse user constraints and design needs in LMICs. Consequently, design must go beyond ethical intent to ensure usability, adaptability, and meaningful engagement for underrepresented users, thereby achieving an appropriate balance between automation and human control. The research advances the HCAI discourse by demonstrating that inclusive AI must not only be human-centered in principle, but readiness-centered in practice, ensuring equitable AI adoption among older adults in resource-constrained settings.

Acknowledgments. The project was funded by the United Kingdom (UK) Artificial Intelligence Challenge Fund and implemented by KICTANet through the African Centre for Technology Studies (ACTS).

Disclosure of Interests. The authors have no competing interests to declare that are relevant to the content of this article.

References

1. United Nations: Leaving no one behind in an ageing world. World Social Report (2023)
2. Mubarak, F., Suomi, R.: Elderly forgotten? Digital exclusion in the information age and the rising grey digital divide. Inquiry (United States) **59**, 1–7 (2022). https://doi.org/10.1177/00469580221096272
3. Kebede, A.S., Ozolins, L.L., Holst, H., Galvin, K.: Digital engagement of older adults: scoping review. J. Med. Internet Res. **24**(12), 1–20 (2022). https://doi.org/10.2196/40192
4. Schroeder, T., Dodds, L., Georgiou, A., Gewald, H., Siette, J.: Older adults and new technology: mapping review of the factors associated with older adults' intention to adopt digital technologies. JMIR Aging **6**, 1–21 (2023). https://doi.org/10.2196/44564
5. Méndez-Domínguez, P., Carbonero Muñoz, D., Raya Díez, E., Castillo De Mesa, J.: Digital inclusion for social inclusion. Case study on digital literacy. Front. Commun. **8** (2023). https://doi.org/10.3389/fcomm.2023.1191995

6. Finkelstein, R., Wu, Y., Brennan-Ing, M.: Older adults' experiences with using information and communication technology and tech support services in New York City: findings and recommendations for post-pandemic digital pedagogy for older adults. Front. Psychol. **14**(April) (2023). https://doi.org/10.3389/fpsyg.2023.1129512

7. McCosker, A., Critchley, C., Walshe, J., Tucker, J., Suchowerska, R.: Accounting for diversity in older adults' digital inclusion and literacy: the impact of a national intervention. Ageing Soc. **43**(11), 2629–2649 (2023). https://doi.org/10.1017/S0144686X21001550

8. Corredor, C.M., Franco, M.A., Del Pilar Garcia Gutierrez, Z.: Adaptive system for non-literate older adult learning. In: Proceedings - 2023 IEEE International Conference on Advanced Learning Technologies, ICALT 2023, pp. 33–35 (2023). https://doi.org/10.1109/ICALT58122.2023.00015

9. Elrefai, A.T., Elgazzar, M.H., Khodeir, A.N.: Using artificial intelligence in enhancing banking services. In: 2021 IEEE 11th Annual Computing and Communication Workshop and Conference, CCWC 2021, pp. 980–986 (2021). https://doi.org/10.1109/CCWC51732.2021.9375993

10. Panesar, K., Pérez Cabello de Alba, M.B.: Natural language processing-driven framework for the early detection of language and cognitive decline. Lang. Health **1**(2), 20–35 (2023). https://doi.org/10.1016/j.laheal.2023.09.002

11. Shneiderman, B.: Human-centered artificial intelligence: reliable, safe and trustworthy. Tech. rep., AIS Electronic Library (AISeL) (2020). https://arxiv.org/abs/2002.04087v1

12. Havighurst, R.J., Albrecht, R.: Older People. Longmans, Green (1953)

13. Schmager, S., Pappas, I.O., Vassilakopoulou, P.: Understanding human-centred AI: a review of its defining elements and a research agenda. Behav. Inf. Technol. **3001** (2025). https://doi.org/10.1080/0144929X.2024.2448719

14. Pacailler, M., Yahoodik, S., Sato, T., Ammons, J.G., Still, J.: Human-centered artificial intelligence: beyond a two-dimensional framework. In: LNCS (including subseries Lecture Notes in Artificial Intelligence and Lecture Notes in Bioinformatics), vol. 13518 LNCS, pp. 471–482. Springer Science and Business Media Deutschland GmbH (2022). https://doi.org/10.1007/978-3-031-21707-4_33

15. Bandura, A.: Social foundations of thought and action: a social cognitive theory. Prentice-Hall series in social learning theory, Prentice-Hall Inc, Englewood Cliffs, NJ, US (1986)

16. Chen, K., Chan, A.H.S.: Gerontechnology acceptance by elderly Hong Kong Chinese: a senior technology acceptance model (STAM) (2014). https://doi.org/10.1080/00140139.2014.895855

17. Schunk, D.H., DiBenedetto, M.K.: Chapter four - self-efficacy and human motivation. In: Elliot, A.J. (ed.) Advances in Motivation Science, Advances in Motivation Science, vol. 8, pp. 153–179. Elsevier (2021). https://doi.org/10.1016/bs.adms.2020.10.001, https://www.sciencedirect.com/science/article/pii/S2215091920300158

18. van Dijk, J.A.: Digital divide research, achievements and shortcomings. Poetics **34**(4-5), 221–235 (2006). https://doi.org/10.1016/j.poetic.2006.05.004

19. Wilczewski, H., et al.: Older adults' experience with virtual conversational agents for health data collection. Front. Digit. Health **5** (2023). https://doi.org/10.3389/fdgth.2023.1125926

20. Wiratunga, N., et al.: FitChat: conversational artificial intelligence interventions for encouraging physical activity in older adults (2020). https://doi.org/10.48550/arXiv.2004.14067

21. Garcia-Mendez, S., De Arriba-Perez, F., Gonzalez-Castano, F.J., Regueiro-Janeiro, J.A., Gil-Castineira, F.: Entertainment Chatbot for the digital inclusion of elderly people without abstraction capabilities. IEEE Access **9**, 75878–75891 (2021). https://doi.org/10.1109/ACCESS.2021.3080837

22. Kenya national bureau of statistics: Economic survey 2022. Tech. Rep. ISBN 978-9914-79987-3-3, Kenya National Bureau of Statistics, Nairobi, Kenya (2022). https://www.knbs.or.ke/wp-content/uploads/2023/09/2022-Economic-Survey.pdf, official statistical report

23. Farage, M.A., Miller, K.W., Ajayi, F., Hutchins, D.: Design principles to accommodate older adults. Global J. Health Sci. **4**(2), 2–25 (2012). https://doi.org/10.5539/gjhs.v4n2p2

24. Langmann, E.: Vulnerability, ageism, and health: is it helpful to label older adults as a vulnerable group in health care? Med. Health Care Philos. **26**(1), 133–142 (2023). https://doi.org/10.1007/s11019-022-10129-5

25. Braun, V., Clarke, V.: Using thematic analysis in psychology. Qual. Res. Psychol. **3**(2), 77–101 (2006). https://doi.org/10.1191/1478088706qp063oa, http://www.tandfonline.com/doi/abs/10.1191/1478088706qp063oa

26. UNDP: From access to empowerment: Digital inclusion in a dynamic world. Tech. rep., United Nations Development Program (2024). https://www.undp.org/policy-centre/singapore/publications/access-empowerment-digital-inclusion-dynamic-world

27. Faber, T.J., Dankbaar, M.E., van den Broek, W.W., Bruinink, L.J., Hogeveen, M., van Merriënboer, J.J.: Effects of adaptive scaffolding on performance, cognitive load and engagement in game-based learning: a randomized controlled trial. BMC Med. Educ. **24**(1) (2024). https://doi.org/10.1186/s12909-024-05698-3

28. Shaban, A., Pearson, E., Chang, V.: Evaluation of user experience, cognitive load, and training performance of a gamified cognitive training application for children with learning disabilities. Front. Comput. Sci. **3** (2021). https://doi.org/10.3389/fcomp.2021.617056

29. Kim, H.N., Freddolino, P.P., Greenhow, C.: Older adults' technology anxiety as a barrier to digital inclusion: a scoping review. Educ. Gerontol. **49**(12), 1021–1038 (2023). https://doi.org/10.1080/03601277.2023.2202080

30. Adams, R.: Can artificial intelligence be decolonized? Interdiscip. Sci. Rev. **46**(1-2), 176–197 (2021). https://doi.org/10.1080/03080188.2020.1840225

31. Mohamed, S., Png, M.-T., Isaac, W.: Decolonial AI: decolonial theory as sociotechnical foresight in artificial intelligence. Philos. Technol. **33**(4), 659–684 (2020). https://doi.org/10.1007/s13347-020-00405-8

32. Khamaj, A.: AI-enhanced chatbot for improving healthcare usability and accessibility for older adults. Alexandria Eng. J. **116**, 202–213 (2025). https://doi.org/10.1016/j.aej.2024.12.090

33. Vercruyssen, A., Schirmer, W., Mortelmans, D.: How "basic" is basic digital literacy for older adults? Insights from digital skills instructors. Front. Educ. **8**(September), 1–11 (2023). https://doi.org/10.3389/feduc.2023.1231701

34. Sangwa, S., Mutabazi, P.: Artificial intelligence ethics and biblical prophecy: a global christian analysis of algorithmic censorship, digital deception, and eschatological risk. SSRN Electron. J. **3**(2), 1–42 (2025). https://doi.org/10.2139/ssrn.5283976

35. Wong, A.K.C., Lee, J.H.T., Zhao, Y., Lu, Q., Yang, S., Hui, V.C.C.: Exploring older adults' perspectives and acceptance of AI-driven health technologies: qualitative study. JMIR Aging **8** (2025). https://doi.org/10.2196/66778
36. Mansouri, M.: A call for epistemic analysis of cultural theories for AI methods (2023). https://doi.org/10.1007/s00146-022-01465-4

On Digital Literacy to Curb Disinformation in Brazil

Sérgio Barbosa(✉)

Department of Sociology, University of Graz, Graz, Austria
sergio.barbosa@uni-graz.at

Abstract. Digital literacy is a central topic to foster the development of knowledge, skills, and attitudes to provide an essential framework for critical lifelong engagement with platforms, yet one that has been mainly debated in the Global North countries. Against this background, this article focuses on Brazil, subject of an ongoing project. It emphasizes the agency of young people to play a multidisciplinary role to curb disinformation at the school level. It poses the following research question: how can educators design digital literacies pedagogical approaches in order to curb disinformation? First, the paper seeks to overcome the current academic disregard for the exploration of peripheral ways of using and understanding digital literacies, while designing critical pedagogies that constitute frameworks beyond Western Europe and the US. Second, the article seeks to break through the silos of academic disciplines currently looking at digital literacy based on technological solutionism. The article calls for a threefold research agenda: digital literacy by definition (to foster awareness and basic understanding of platform society), digital literacy by critical pedagogy (critical understanding of the social, economic, cultural and technical aspects of platforms), and digital literacy by co-creation (to achieve personal and civic goals with the help of others). In doing so, this article designs pluriversal paths beyond data universalism, mainly situating contextual inequalities, socio-cultural nuances and disinformation ecosystem at the school level in Brazil, while avoiding a one-dimensional view of the world.

Keywords: Digital Literacy · Critical Pedagogy · Disinformation · Brazil

1 Introduction: Brazil on the Rise

Brazil is the largest democracy in Latin America. The country makes an excellent test case for the study of digital literacy, for a variety of reasons. It has been at the forefront of critical reflections on digital technologies, deeply influenced by popular and vernacular cultures with the exponential use of social media platforms (Spyer, 2017). It has also a long history of grassroots resistance movements—from indigenous rights to radical environmentalism, from human rights to independent media—and a decade-long tradition of participatory democracy (Barbosa, 2023). Brazil has played a pioneering role for the study of digital cultures, activism, as well as in the promotion of data-driven local initiatives that consider Latin America as a site of knowledge production (Valente &

© The Author(s) 2026

L. Hagedorn et al. (Eds.): DIGHUM 2025, LNCS 16319, pp. 348–357, 2026.
https://doi.org/10.1007/978-3-032-11108-1_25

Grohmann, 2024). In the early 2000s, Brazil hosted major international events and key discussions on free software communities (Birkinbine, 2016). An important recent rupture was Brazil's challenge to the platform dominance of "X"[1], defending its political sovereignty in a court of law (Nicas & Conger, 2024). Marc Zuckerberg[2], in addition, has stated recently that Latin America is driven by "corrupt secret courts", planning shifts to a new stage of "americanization of platforms" with the return of Trumpism (Divon & Ong, 2025). This process curbs a pro-democratic agenda regarding global tech regulation and situates digital literacy as a valuable antidote to access, manage, understand, communicate, create, and disseminate information safely and appropriately through digital technologies (European Commission, 2022, p. 11). Despite often platform society being linked to resurgent authoritarianism subjectivities as part of bolsonarismo movement in Brazil (Messenberg, 2017; Pinheiro-Machado & Vargas-Maia, 2023), the platformization of communication ecosystems in contemporary India (Nizaruddin, 2022), and cyberlibertarianism for far-right politics, digital hate and political disinformation campaigns worldwide (Golumbia, 2024), little research has investigated digital literacy to curb disinformation in Brazil.

This article is based on the research project named *The Deconstruction of Disinformation in Brazilian Basic Education through Digital Literacy*[3] sponsored by the Brazilian parliament and hosted at the Department of Sociology, University of Brasilia. The main goal is to investigate how disinformation discourses and practices have become embedded in everyday school life, increasing distrust in the subject matter taught by schoolteachers. This process, in many diverse contexts, generates hostility and conflicts of many kinds. Besides the general goal of producing a diagnosis of the relationship between public schools in the Federal District (DF) and the wave of disinformation. This article also seeks to influence public debate through concrete educational policies. One of the main challenges is to develop, based on field learning, an educational program model that brings digital literacy to the center of public policy formulation for young people in the public school system, with a special focus on students of the 1st year of high school. The current scenario is marked by the increased digitalization of contemporary life, and it is still little understood effects on how young people perform subjectivities.

This article highlights the need to map, systematize, and analyze, from a comparative perspective, focusing on recent Brazilian academic production on the topic of digital literacy. This article seeks also to build dialogue between Global North and Global South and to highlight the initial findings of this ongoing research conducted by the research team based at the Department of Sociology, University of Brasilia. The methodology includes surveying, systematizing, and analyzing, the construction of state-of-the-art of

---

[1] Twitter was bought by Elon Musk in 2022 and re-named "X".

[2] Meta's CEO.

[3] This research project was supported by the Department of Sociology (SOL) at University of Brasilia, under the PI Prof. Dr. Débora Messenberg and the co-PIs Prof. Dr. Haydée Caruso and Prof. Dr. Sayonara Leal. The research team includes: Prof. Dr. Paulo Lima Jr.; Dr. Cilene Villarins Cardoso da Silva; Dr. Thomas Edson de Jesus Theodoro Amorim; and PhD students Mariana Marceli Damacena Dutra and Bruno Camargos. It includes also the BA students Tarsila Amoras, Maria Eduarda Barboza da Silva, Filipe Souza da Silva and Erykson Dyego Sarafim. The project was funded by a Parliamentary Amendment from the Office of Federal Deputy Sâmia Bomfim (PSOL-SP).

Brazilian articles dealing with digital literacy vis-a-vis disinformation. The article is composed of three parts. The first section provides a brief a literature review on the field of digital literacy contextualizing the Brazilian context. The second section explains why the methodology was adopted for the case study, emphasizing the action-research approach. The third section is dedicated to discussing the initial results of the project. The final section presents the lessons learned from the current stage of the project, highlighting its strong potential to increase young people participation and offering educational policy recommendations.

2   Digital Literacy from the Global South(S): Zooming into the Brazilian Context

The image of Trump-aligned tech billionaires[4] is one of the pillars of a new colonial exploitation (Couldry & Mejias, 2019)[5]. By controlling the digital ecosystem, big tech companies control data-driven experiences, giving them direct power over the political, economic and cultural domains of everyday media communication (Fenton, 2025). These big tech companies also undermine any possibility of resistance or imagination of alternative realities[6] (van Dijck, 2021). The priority is to sabotage the possibility of critical young people and selling a future without long-term perspectives. It relies on the promising "anxious" generation that aspires to become "influencers", startup founders or who otherwise aligns with the blunted values of entrepreneurship and meritocratic discourse (Sandel, 2020). In doing so, this section delves into the so-called Digital Literacy framework. It is broadly defined as the development of knowledge, skills, and attitudes to provide an essential framework for critical lifelong engagement through platforms (Barbosa, 2024). It has settled as a paramount component of public debate today, mainly settled in the Global North, as many experts encouraged media education and literacy programs within both formal and informal education settings (Christian, 2020). Digital Literacy marks a significant "paradigm shift" (Tygel & Kirsch, 2016) in the way to locate, evaluate, produce, and use digital media effectively (Lindgren, 2022). It has also dramatically transformed how we achieve digital citizenship with the skills to navigate digital content responsibly (Hintz et al., 2019).

But how do digital literacies unfold for and from Brazil? Digital literacies from the South(s) can flatten the richness, plurality, and diversity of data cultures, infrastructures, "everyday data literacies" (Burgess et al., 2022) and "critical data literacies" (Sander, 2023) practices that emerge on and from the margins (Rodriguez, 2017), privileging engagement with digital technologies that promotes critical pedagogy beyond the narrow, one-dimensional view of the world (Loukissas, 2019). In doing so, this article instead seeks ways of pluriversal worlds "where many worlds fit" (Escobar, 2018, p. 6)

---

[4] Also known by the CEOs of the acronym GAMAM (Google, Amazon, Meta, Apple, Microsoft).

[5] The richest 1% in the Global North extracted US$30 million per hour from the Global South (Oxfam, 2025).

[6] CEOs like Peter Thiel, Marc Andreessen, and David Sacks are pushing an anti-regulation agenda and an entrepreneurial vision of far-right politics. Currently, the tech industry and US politics delve into the authoritarian ideologies uniting the so-called *tech bros* and their strategic geopolitical goals.

beyond data universalism. While some efforts already exist at the Anglo-Saxon level to map the implementation of digital literacies, these tend to privilege the examination of Western, Educated, Rich, Industrialized and Democratic (WEIRD) countries based in the Global North. However, they are insufficient to grasp critical imaginaries from the Global South(s) in a meaningful, inclusive and mutually beneficial way to foster hope as an aspirational force for social change (Arora, 2024, p. 5). Digital Literacy is now ready to be recognized as human and (digital) right. Research has aimed to nurture future generations through regulation via parliaments and the state level—legislation before education. Other three concepts are core to capture the nuances of digital literacy, namely: *Disinformation* can be defined as verifiably false or misleading information that is created, presented, and disseminated for economic gain or to intentionally deceive the public. *Malinformation* corresponds to factually correct information that is used harmfully. Lastly, *Misinformation* means false information that is spread without the intention to mislead and often shared because the user believes it to be true (European Commission, 2022).

Xavier (2023) emphasizes the need to empower students with theoretical and analytical tools, as well as practical responses to respond to the spread of disinformation. Simioni and Pinton (2024) emphasize the perspective of "critical literacy" which proposes "agentive reading" to empower students to increase their understanding and retention of information through a reflective and critical approach to content disseminated on different social media platforms. The proposal to explore news analysis and the identification of disinformation through school activities is one of the methodologies also developed by UNESCO (Cerigatto, 2020). Tomé and Brasileiro (2025) shows the case study of "Educamídia" website portal through awareness-raising about disinformation, pedagogical teacher training, and information curation. This study contributed to understanding how information practices fostered information literacy development during the COVID-19 pandemic, mapping the human and non-human actors involved in information activities on its digital platforms. Finally, it systematized "Educamídia's" information practices geared toward information literacy. These include: i) awareness of disinformation; ii) teacher-pedagogical training; iii) information recommendation. For example, the massive proliferation of misinformation in Brazil is very popular in family and friend groups on WhatsApp (Udupa and Wasserman, 2025). Heller and Maurell (2019) postulates the need to fight disinformation today. The authors describe the experience of developing an *e-book* on information sources as a response to misinformation. Regarding didactic and pedagogical strategies for digital literacy, we highlight the work of Lima and Mendes (2020). It is an active and dynamic process of meaning construction, in which four components operate, whether simultaneously or not: situated practice (experiencing), open instruction (conceptualizing), critical framing (analyzing), and transformed practice (applying). These authors develop a pedagogy of literacy that resembles historical-critical pedagogy: each activity utilizes a learning component (in order: experiencing, conceptualizing, analyzing, and applying). The activities were developed in person and online, via WhatsApp. Simioni and Pinton (2024), on the other hand, based on a survey of elementary school students in a public school in Santa Maria (Rio Grande do Sul), questioned these students' understanding of disinformation, and their readings of these texts. Winchuar et al. (2022) presented cartoons related to the topic of disinformation, taken from fact-checking platforms, for reading and interpretation practices. The activity was developed through discussion groups. The teacher participates in these reading circles by generating questions and inquiries, based on different approaches (thematic content, compositional structure, and language style) that lead the student to infer and locate explicit and implicit information in the text as fundamental skills for critical reading.

Santana (2021) shows that the main result of her research is a monthly teaching plan for the Portuguese Language course in high school, focusing on the Northeast and Northeasterners. The author highlights the following learning objectives: i) reflect on the notion of accurate information; ii) to understand the discursive construction based on "post-facts" about the Northeast and Northeasterners; iii) enable a critical reading of false discourses about this territoriality; and iv) develop skills in critical analysis of misleading discourses. Conceição (2021) outlines a methodological process that involves the following steps: i) creating student profiles, creating the "Fact or Fake?" network, and including all students; ii) dividing students into working groups; iii) providing portfolios with news stories for analysis and verification models; iv) producing informative guides on the topic; and v) creating videos to raise awareness against fake news. Lastly, Cisne (2024) developed a Portuguese-based project, through eight classes of activities related to the topic of disinformation, with elementary students at a public school. The activities were structured as follows: an expository-dialogue class on "disinformation, its historical context, the negative implications of the spread of disinformation, and the importance of acting to fight this wave". However, there is a lack of pedagogical initiatives through co-creation and from a pedagogical participatory approach which focuses on agencying young people to play a multi-disciplinary role for critical intervention. Against this backdrop, this article seeks a pedagogical approach to build solid digital futures—education before legislation. At the same time, it argues tackling dis/misinformation, hate speech, the escalation of a far-right agenda, and conspiracy theories (Labarre, 2024). It combines critical pedagogy (Freire, 1970) within pluriversal values (Escobar, 2018) to foster pedagogical participatory methods based on Paulo Freirian critical pedagogy. Freire has criticized the structural inability of the education system to empower the unprivileged to overcome their socio-economic conditions. He advocates for a bottom-up educational approach based on horizontal relationships between learners and educators, promoting the role of the learner to perform critical consciousness. Critical pedagogy, in this sense, nurtures a critical consciousness approach which supports the promotion of social and political change into the bottom of society.

3 Methods

The methods of data collection include action-research, meaning here the active involvement of school stakeholders in both designing and carrying out the research; and quantitative (survey with school students), qualitative (semi-structured interviews with school directors and focus groups with teachers and students) and creative (pedagogical) methods, drawing on storytelling and arts-based forms of knowledge production which provide agency for young people and school community members alike. It departs from the assumption that we need to create a Paulo Freirean critical pedagogy in order to inaugurate digital literacies for and from the Global South(s). It poses the following question: how can educators design digital literacies pedagogical approaches to curb disinformation? The goals are twofold. First, it seeks to overcome the current academic disregard for the exploration of peripheral ways of using and understanding digital literacies, while designing critical pedagogies, imaginaries and practices that constitute frameworks beyond Global North. Second, the project seeks to break through the silos of academic disciplines currently looking at digital literacy based on technocratic approaches that ignore critical consciousness.

The case study is based on pilot tests with ten schools selected[7] in the periphery of Brasilia. Most of these school students belong to low-income social groups. The survey instrument was developed by a group of social scientists and sociology professors at schools, initially and in practice in basic education. The instrument was executed to a pre-sample of 60 students and refined. Its latest version was executed to a representative sample of the population of the Federal District ($n = 1,100$). The fieldwork stage will include participant observation at the selected schools with a focus on interactions between students and between students and teachers. In the latest stage, the project will design the digital literacy pedagogical sessions as teaching materials delivered and refined at the selected schools. Here, in the next session, it will be analyzed the literature review of up-to-date Brazilian production – first stage of this research.

4 Discussion

The initial findings sought to map and analyze national academic literature on disinformation, young people, and the school environment, published between 2013 and 2025 in the field of Humanities and Applied Social Sciences in Brazil. Based on a systematic survey of scientific databases, the application of selection filters, organization in a proprietary database, and the use of an information extraction protocol, 85 articles were analyzed. This effort allowed the research team to identify trends, gaps, and regularities in the literature map, while also offering a unique diagnosis of how the topic has been discussed in the Brazilian academic landscape. The analysis revealed a predominance of qualitative studies but also brought to light innovative experiences that sought to test pedagogical practices aimed at curbing disinformation. At the same time, it highlighted limitations, such as redundant arguments, empirical weaknesses, and poor connection with international references. Nevertheless, the articles analyzed offer relevant contributions to understanding the intersections between schools, youth, and conservatism, while also pointing to ways to support both the advancement of academic research and the formulation of public policies that place digital literacy at the center of educational strategies. It was found that the field of Education concentrates the majority of scientific production on the topic, while Sociology appears incipiently in this debate. A regional concentration was also observed in the Southeast and South of Brazil, suggesting the need for greater balance in national academic production. This diagnosis reinforces the need for greater analytical depth and diversification of theoretical frameworks, including

---

[7] Ten public schools were selected in four Administrative Regions (RAs) of Federal District (DF): 04 in Plano Piloto, 02 in Gama, 02 in Ceilândia and 02 in Planaltina. Students from these schools were chosen from the 1st year of High School.

a more consistent dialogue with international literature. Finally, the gap in the analysis of disinformation in its everyday school context is highlighted. There are still few studies that systematically investigate how disinformation circulates among students, how it is received and interpreted, and what digital literacy pedagogical strategies teachers and administrators have been using (or could use) to address it. Similarly, little research is examined about the role played by algorithms and platforms in the dissemination of extreme speech, a crucial aspect for understanding the adherence of some young people to far-right agenda worldwide.

5 Preliminary Conclusions

The preliminary conclusions moves towards threefold research agenda: digital literacy as a core concept (topics determined by current challenges to foster awareness and basic understanding of platform society); digital literacy by critical pedagogy (critical understanding the social, economic, cultural and technical aspects of the digital technologies); and digital literacy by co-participation (both using digital literacy to achieve personal and civic goals and also working with and helping others to achieve the same). In the next stage of this project, the research team will enable students to be critical learners and to take critical interventions through co-creation pedagogical processes (e.g. Carmi et al., 2020; Pfeifer & Jovicic, 2023). In doing so, the digital literacy pedagogical sessions to be developed will increase the capacity to undertake collaborative and pedagogical research and addresses more tech-literate needs from school communities in Brazil for maintaining active, informed and responsible digital citizenship. At the same time, the case study contributes to situate Global South at the forefront of equitable digital futures. It is context-driven and engaged oriented: research made by the Global South and for the Global South.

To sum up, this article shows how emerging forms of digital literacy are on the rise, while taking up the question of disinformation with a focus on Brazil. Its core contribution is to reposition digital literacy as a pedagogical project rather than a technocratic or purely regulatory one. Drawing on Paulo Freire's critical pedagogy and the notion of pluriversality, it argues that young people should be empowered as active agents in curbing disinformation through co-created participatory methods at an earlier school level. Lastly, it critiques Global North–centric digital literacy frameworks, rejecting universalist assumptions in favor of plural, situated approaches from and within the Global South(s) (Milan & Treré, 2024). The move to place "education before legislation" is needed, especially in Global South countries where state regulation lags far behind the speed of platform-driven transformations.

References

Arora, P.: From pessimism to Promise: Lessons from the Global South on Designing Inclusive Tech. MIT Press, Cambridge (2024)

Barbosa, S.: Enabling digital literacy pedagogical sessions (#DLPS): the case of Portugal. In: Marcus-Quinn, A., Krejtz, K., Duarte, C. (eds.) Transforming Media Accessibility in Europe. Springer, Cham (2024). https://doi.org/10.1007/978-3-031-60049-4_17

Birkinbine, B.: Free software as public service in Brazil: an assessment of activism, policy, and technology. Int. J. Commun. **10**(16) (2016). https://ijoc.org/index.php/ijoc/article/view/4974

Burgess, J., Albury, K., McCosker, A., Wilken, R.: Everyday Data Cultures. Polity (2022)

Carmi, E., Yates, S.J., Lockley, E., Pawluczuk, A.: Data citizenship: rethinking data literacy in the age of disinformation, misinformation, and malinformation. Internet Policy Rev. **9**(2) (2020). https://doi.org/10.14763/2020.2.1481

Cerigatto, M.P.: Promovendo a literacia midiática e informacional no contexto emergente da desinformação: proposta para o ensino fundamental. Revista EntreLetras **6**(6), 53–74 (2020)

Christian, S.E.: Everyday Media Literacy. An Analogue Guide for Your Digital Life. Routledge (2020)

Cisne, C.S.: Fake news pra quê? Atuação da biblioteca escolar no projeto de combate às fake news. BIBLOS - Revista do Instituto de Ciências Humanas e da Informação, [S. l.], vol. 37, no. 2, pp. 3–11 (2024)

Conceição, A.A.S.: Uma Comunidade de Aprendizagem Online na Conscientização Contra as Fake News. EaD em Foco **11**(2), e1453 (2021)

Couldry, N., Mejias, U.A.: Data colonialism: rethinking big data's relation to the contemporary subject. Telev. New Media, **20**(4) (2019). https://doi.org/10.1177/1527476418796632

dados, N., Connell, R.: The global south. Contexts 11(1), 12–13 (2012)

D'Ignazio, C., Klein, L.: Data feminism. MIT Press (2020)

Divon, T., Ong, J.C.: Tech Bro Power Play: Zuckerberg vs. Global Tech Justice | TechPolicy Press (2025). https://techpolicy.press/tech-bro-power-play-zuckerberg-vs-global-tech-justice. Accessed 14 Jan 2025

Escobar, A.: Designs for the Pluriverse. Radical interdependence, autonomy, and the making of worlds. Duke University Press (2018)

European Commission (2022). Directorate-General for Education, Youth, Sport and Culture Guidelines for teachers and educators on tackling disinformation and promoting digital literacy through education and training, Publications Office of the European Union, https://data.europa.eu/doi/10.2766/28248

Fenton, N.: Democratic Delusions: How the Media Hollows Out Democracy and What We Can Do About It. Polity (2025)

Freire, P.: Pedagogy of the Oppressed. Penguin, Harmondsworth (1970)

Golumbia, D.: Cyberlibertarianism The Right-Wing politics of Digital Technology. University of Minnesota Press (2024)

Heller, B., Rejane. P., Maurell, J.: O desenvolvimento de um e-book para identificar fake news: o bibliotecário como mediador na criação de critérios de avaliação da informação. RENOTE, v. 17, n. 3, p. 488 497

Hintz, A., Dencik, L., Wahl-Jorgensen, K.: Digital Citizenship in a Datafied Society. Polity (2019)

Labarre, J.: Epistemic vulnerability: theory and measurement at the system level. Political Commun. **42**(1) (2024). https://doi.org/10.1080/10584609.2024.2363545

Lima, S.C., Mendes, E.S.S.: Whatsapp e fake news no ensino de língua inglesa em uma escola pública do interior do estado do Ceará. Texto Livre, Belo Horizonte **13**(2), 182–200 (2020)

Lindgren, S.: Digital Media & Society. SAGE, London (2022)

Loukissas, Y.A.: All Data are local: Thinking Critically in a data-Driven Society. MIT Press, Cambridge (2019)

Messenberg, D.: A direita que saiu do armário: a cosmovisão dos formadores de opinião dos manifestantes de direita brasileiros. Sociedade e Estado, **32**(3) (2017)

Milan, S., Treré, E.: Against decolonial reductionism: the impact of Latin American thinking on the data decolonization project. Big Data Soc. 11(4) (2024). https://doi.org/10.1177/20539517241270694

Nicas, J., Conger, K.: How Brazil's Experiment Fighting Fake News Led to a Ban on X" New York Times (31 August) (2024). https://www.nytimes.com/2024/08/31/world/americas/brazil-x-ban-free-speech.html?smid=nytcore-ios-share&referringSource=articleShare

Nizaruddin, F.: Hindu Majoritarianism and authoritarian shifts in the age of informational capitalism in India. In: IRGAC (ed.), Global Authoritarianism. Perspectives and Contestations from the South. Transcript (2022)

Oxfam. Takers not makers. The unjust poverty and unearned wealthy colonialism (2025). https://webassets.oxfamamerica.org/media/documents/Takers_Not_Makers_Executive_Summary.pdf

Pfeifer, S., Jovicic, S.: Co-teaching postdigital ethnography. CRC Media of Cooperation Working Paper Series 34 (2023)

Pinheiro-Machado, R., Vargas-Maia, T.: The Rise of the Radical Right in the Global South. Routledge (2023)

Rodriguez, C.: Studying media at the margins. In: Pickard, V., Yang, G. (eds.) Media Activism in the Digital Age, pp. 49–60. Routledge (2017)

Sandel, M.: The tyranny of merit: what's become of the common good? London: Allen Lane (2020)

Sander, I.: Critical datafication literacy – a framework for educating about datafication. Inf. Learn. Sci. **125**(3/4) (2023)

Santana, M.G.: Letramento crítico no Ensino Médio: uma proposta didática sobre pós-fatos contra o Nordeste/nordestino(a) em aulas de Língua Portuguesa. Scripta, vol. 25, no. 54, pp. 296–322 (2021)

Simioni, E.S., Pinton, F.M.: O gênero notícia online e o fenômeno das fake news: reflexividade e agentividade no ensino básico. EccoS Revista Científica, [S. l.], no. 70, p. e25011 (2024)

Spyer, J.: Social Media in Emergent Brazil: How the Internet Affects Social Mobility. University College London Press, London (2017)

Tomé, R.F., Brasileiro, F.S.: Práticas de literacia informacional das plataformas Educamídia durante a pandemia de covid-19. Em Questão, v. 31, e-138727 (2025)

Tygel, A.F., Kirsch, R.: Contributions of Paulo Freire to a critical data literacy: a popular education approach. J. Community Inform. **12**(3) (2016)

Valente, J.C.L., Grohmann, R.: Critical data studies with Latin America: Theorizing beyond data colonialism. Big Data Soc. **11**(1) (2024). https://doi.org/10.1177/20539517241227875

van Dijck, J.: Seeing the forest for the trees: visualizing platformization and its governance. New Media Soc. **23**(9) (2021). https://doi.org/10.1177/1461444820940293

Xavier, I.C.: Uma análise crítica do papel da escola pública no combate às fake news. Revista HISTEDBR On-line **23**, 1–17 (2023)

Winchuar, M.J., Bahls, D.P., Zanlorenzi, M.J.: A escola e o ensino de leitura em tempos de fake news: uma proposta para os anos iniciais do ensino fundamental. Debates em Educação, [S. l.], vol. 14, no. 34, pp. 154–173 (2022)

Linguistic Diversity and Digitalization:
An Ambivalent Relationship

Juliane Benson[1]([envelope])[ORCID], Katharina Zeh[1][ORCID], Hannes Essfors[2][ORCID],
Hannes Fellner[1,3][ORCID], Julia Neidhardt[2][ORCID], and Andreas Baumann[1,3][ORCID]

[1] Faculty of Philological and Cultural Studies, University of Vienna, Universitätsring
1, 1010 Vienna, Austria
{juliane.rabea.benson,katharina.zeh,hannes.fellner,
andreas.baumann}@univie.ac.at
[2] TU Wien Informatics, Favoritenstraße 9–11, 1040 Vienna, Austria
{hannes.essfors,julia.neidhardt}@tuwien.ac.at
[3] Data Science @ Uni Vienna, University of Vienna, Kolingasse 14–16, 1090 Vienna,
Austria

Abstract. In this position paper, we argue that while digitalization amplifies biases towards only few languages dominating the linguistic landscape, modern language technology can help to mitigate language loss. We first elaborate on how the linguistic landscape in the digital and the non-digital sphere are distributionally different from each other in that the latter is strongly biased towards English, at the same time under-representing thousands of languages and the cultural knowledge that they encode. In a second step, we present results of qualitative interviews on individual linguistic experiences in the digital and the non-digital sphere that we have conducted in Québec, one of the provinces of Canada known for its linguistic diversity. These interviews highlight the potential that modern language technology have for safeguarding linguistic diversity. We conclude that the study of the impact of digitalization on the global linguistic landscape not only requires differential ways of measuring linguistic diversity but also a nuanced operationalization of digitalization.

Keywords: linguistic diversity · language endangerment ·
digitalization · bias · digital language divide · qualitative interviews

1 Linguistic Diversity is Under Threat

On February 21st of this year, we have celebrated an anniversary. It is now already a quarter of a century ago that UNESCO has initiated the 'International Mother Language Day', a day that should remind us of the remarkable linguistic diversity represented on this planet. There are about 7,000 languages spoken around the globe [17], grouped into more than 400 language families [8]. Each of these languages not only represents a storage of cultural knowledge [28], but

L. Hagedorn et al. (Eds.): DIGHUM 2025, LNCS 16319, pp. 358–365, 2026.
https://doi.org/10.1007/978-3-032-11108-1_26

also functions as a way to express a speaker population's group identity, and—not least—informs us about nuances of how human cognition works.

It is hence concerning to see that linguistic diversity is under threat. Over the past couple of decades, linguistic diversity has decreased [18,31,32], and if no measures are taken this trend is expected to continue. Estimates of the fraction of languages that are going to vanish in the course of this century range from relatively optimistic 25% [6] to devastating 90% [24]. What are the reasons for this development? In this position paper, we will consider the role that digitalization assumes in current dynamics of language diversity and endangerment. We will argue that while digitalization amplifies biases when it comes to the distribution of the global linguistic landscape [23], responsible use of digital technologies can also let us paint a slightly more optimistic picture and potentially preserve loss of linguistic knowledge.

Besides digitalization, several other determinants of linguistic diversity have been discussed, of course. While Hua et al. [19] investigate ecological drivers of linguistic diversity and find that climatic factors associated with agricultural productivity foster diversity, Bromham et al. [6] identify several socio-economic pressures. On a global scale, it seems that connectivity in terms of road networks and years of schooling promote language endangerment. This might seem counterintuitive at first sight, as one would expect education to foster linguistic knowledge. However, language education only rarely lays its emphasis on minority languages—or multilingualism to begin with. Thus, the establishment of transport and educational infrastructure rather seems to have the effect of small languages being dispelled by *linguae francae* that are, from a purely socio-economic point of view, more suitable to adopt [13,28].

As one consequence of this, the distribution of the global (spoken) linguistic landscape [14,33] is far from even. Data from Ethnologue show that about one third of the global population speak only ten languages as their first language; and two thirds speak one (or potentially more) of the remaining 7,000 languages (Fig. 1, top left).

2 Language Distributions in the Digital Sphere Are Biased

Unfortunately, this bias towards few dominant languages is not demoted in the digital sphere; quite to the contrary [21]. Taking the distribution of languages represented on websites [34] and on Twitter/X [27,30] as examples, one can see that only 15% to 19% of the linguistic landscape remains for all languages that do not belong to the top 10 dominating ones. A closer look at the latter reveals, first, that many of them are Indo-European (i.e., belong to one of the approximately 400 language families) and, second, that the distribution is increasingly biased towards a single global language, namely English. While only about 5% of the global population speaks English as their first language (this increases to 19% if also second-language speakers are considered), about one third of all postings on Twitter/X and more than one half of all websites are written in English (Fig. 1).

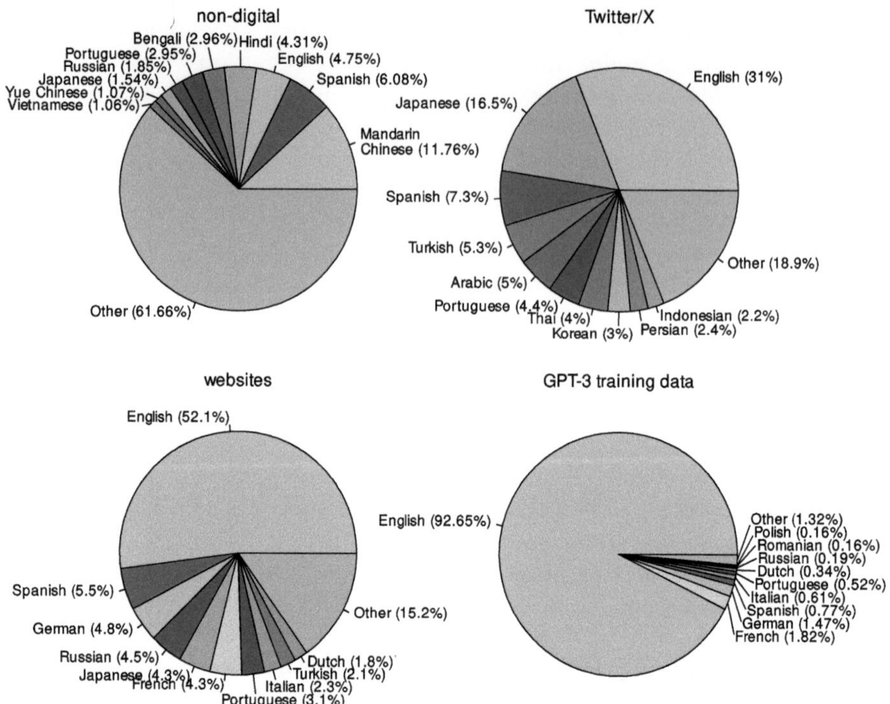

Fig. 1. Distribution of (non-)digital linguistic landscapes: first-language speakers [8], postings on Twitter/X [30], websites [34], and training data for GPT-3 [7]. Top 10 languages displayed, including English (orange), plus all 'other' languages (light blue).

Although the dominance of English on Twitter/X has been substantially reduced since its inception [1], this bias and similar ones found in other parts of the digital sphere remain [23]. This illustrates what is referred to as the digital language divide [4].

Leaving socio-cultural aspects aside, one of the consequences of this bias towards English text data is that language technology is heavily biased towards English as well. Blasi et al. [5] have found that approximately one fourth of all NLP papers are based on English language data, which translates into availability of language-specific NLP support. This is pushed to the extreme in the selection of training data for large language models. For instance, 93% of the data used to train GPT-3 (i.e., the first model underlying ChatGPT) were written in English, leaving only 1.32% to about 7,000 languages not belonging to the top 10. This not only entails that thousands of languages are underrepresented, affecting the quality of conversational interactions, but also that such LLMs largely reflect cultural knowledge encoded in English language [22] and associated stereotypes [11].

3   Experiences of Language in Digital and Non-Digital Contexts: A Qualitative Approach

In May 2025, we conducted survey-based interviews on the topic of digitalization and language to gain insights into individual experiences that are otherwise overlooked in research on linguistic diversity. We interviewed 7 people with different linguistic profiles living in Montreal about their language use, especially in digital communication. The interviewees were between 20 and 62 years old, they volunteered through a call via email lists. In addition to the official languages of Canada (English and French), all participants had other languages in their language profiles as well. The interviews were conducted in English, with the option to answer in French. First, mostly closed questions were asked on the language profile and general use, leading to six open questions on digital language use and communication, finishing with semi-open questions on language perception and endangerment. The interviews were designed for 45 min.

The official languages of Canada are English and French, although the province of Québec has French as its only official language. Canada pursues a multiculturalism and multilingualism policy that aims to preserve cultural identity and language. At the same time, they encourage the adoption of at least one of the official languages [2,9]. Montreal is the biggest city in Québec and previous studies found that it is the most linguistically diverse one among the biggest Canadian cities [15,29]. This reflects the unique bilingual history of Montreal. Unsurprisingly, the responses of the participants show that their experiences in everyday public life are dominated by the two official languages. Montreal is French-speaking, but contains English neighborhoods [25]. If an English school is/was attended, English dominates their surroundings. The languages spoken by the people who are in the area or with whom you want to communicate are also decisive.

All interviewees reported that English is more present on the internet. Websites are often consulted in English because it is the only language available. Aliane[1] says that the quality is better than in French, as French websites are often only a "sloppy" translation and "not meant to be put in French" (20/05/2025). Dehia has had a similar experience: If the results in French are not satisfactory, they switch to English. However, if Montreal- or Quebec-specific content is sought or consumed, websites are often only available in French, as Anna, Cyrus, and Chris note. Hence, the purpose in the digital context also determines which language is used. This can be transferred to social media; the content influences the language. Whereby generally more passive use is in English. This can also be seen outside of the official languages, Chris searches for information about Ukraine in Ukrainian, and Anton consumes community-specific content in Haitian Creole.

Digital translation tools revealed themselves to be an important point in the interviews. In website translations, the context is often disregarded and the quality of the content is not maintained as a result. Common online transla-

---

[1] All names are pseudonyms.

tion services such as Google Translate do not cover certain languages at all, e.g. Anicinabemowin. However, Dehia has made the interesting experience that translations for Tamazight (a Kabyle dialect) can also be found with ChatGPT, even in Latin script and with audio examples. Otherwise there would always be the need to "ask a family member on how to say it", although there is "no option to prove the answer given by ChatGPT" (22/05/2025). For Laura it is a big advantage to have digital translation tools as "it brings people together and you can bridge different language skills" (22/05/2025).

Experiences vary when it comes to communication. For the most part, language use does not differ in an online context. But it allows more frequent contact with people who do not speak English and/or French and may not live in Montreal. Nonetheless, the main languages of communication remain the same in the digital context: if a language is spoken with parents, the language is also used digitally with them. However, Dehia falls back on the equally present French in the family when texting, due to a lack of knowledge in writing and reading the Tifinagh script. Aliane has friends with whom she speaks in French in person but texts in English. Anton finds that with lower language skills, non-digital communication is easier since you get a direct reaction. Chris, on the other hand, finds that digital communication makes it easier to use a foreign language (French) as there is the option of proofreading messages, whereas in person English is preferred. "Google translate is good for texting without mistakes" (23/05/2025). For Laura, English is always the choice as it is easier to write, speak and understand due to its simplicity. As such, the responses show that the digital divide [4] is also visible in personal experiences. The small sample size of interviewees is of course not representative of Québec, but the insights are valuable as a prestudy for a large scale study in Québec and what impact the digitalization has on the people, for their language use and identity.

4   Outlook: Differential Measures, Differential Effects

We have discussed above that although biases in the digital linguistic landscape towards few dominant languages evidently exist, recent developments in language technology do allow for some optimism when it comes to countering language endangerment. This is in line with recent research about community-driven efforts for preserving languages through digital resources, NLP, or LLM-generated language teaching materials [20], and the usefulness of LLMs for translating from and into low-resource languages [3] and dialects (although the latter is still prone to stereotyping [11]; cf. Also discussion about diversity in corpus compilation in [26]). It is likewise evident that digital technology has promoted research on and documentation of languages and cultural heritage [12].

It is hence not only relevant to differentiate between different aspects of linguistic diversity (e.g., diversity in the linguistic landscape, language endangerment, diversity on the level of language structure; cf. [10]) but also between different aspects of digitalization. The latter involves, for instance, NLP support and availability of resources, but also indices covering digital connectivity, education, participation, or governmental efforts [16]. Each of these aspects might have a different effect on the linguistic landscape. Proper operationalization and measurement of linguistic diversity and digitalization will be fundamental to disentangling the relationship between them. Our project DIGILINGDIV is following this question.

Acknowledgments. This research was funded by WWTF (grant number ICT23-012). The conduction of interviews was supported by University of Vienna.

Disclosure of Interests. The authors have no competing interests to declare.

References

1. Alshaabi, T., Dewhurst, D.R., Minot, J.R., Arnold, M.V., Adams, J.L., Danforth, C.M., Dodds, P.S.: The growing amplification of social media: measuring temporal and social contagion dynamics for over 150 languages on Twitter for 2009–2020. EPJ Data Sci. **10**(1), 1–28 (2021). https://doi.org/10.1140/epjds/s13688-021-00271-0
2. Arsenault Morin, A., Geloso, V.: Multilingualism and the decline of French in Quebec. J. Multiling. Multicult. Dev. **41**(5), 420–431 (2020)
3. Babaali, B., Salem, M., Alharbe, N.R.: Breaking language barriers with ChatGPT: enhancing low-resource machine translation between Algerian Arabic and MSA. Int. J. Inf. Technol. pp. 1–10 (2024)
4. Bella, G., Helm, P., Koch, G., Giunchiglia, F.: Towards bridging the digital language divide (2023)
5. Blasi, D., Anastasopoulos, A., Neubig, G.: Systematic inequalities in language technology performance across the world's languages. In: Muresan, S., Nakov, P., Villavicencio, A. (eds.) Proceedings of the 60th Annual Meeting of the ACL (Volume 1: Long Papers), pp. 5486–5505. ACL, Dublin, Ireland (2022)
6. Bromham, L., et al.: Global predictors of language endangerment and the future of linguistic diversity. Nat. Ecol. Evol. **6**(2), 163–173 (2022)
7. Brown, T., et al.: Language models are few-shot learners. Adv. Neural. Inf. Process. Syst. **33**, 1877–1901 (2020)
8. Campbell, L., Grondona, V.: Ethnologue: languages of the world. Language **84**(3), 636–641 (2008)
9. Castonguay, C.: Quebec's new language dynamic: French fading fast. Lang. Probl. Lang. Plan. **43**(2), 113–134 (2019)
10. Essfors, H.: Global linguistic diversity - adapting the leinster-cobbold framework from ecology for humanities research. In: CHR 2025: Computational Humanities Research Conference (forthcoming)
11. Fleisig, E., Smith, G., Bossi, M., Rustagi, I., Yin, X., Klein, D.: Linguistic bias in ChatGPT: Language models reinforce dialect discrimination. arXiv preprint arXiv:2406.08818 (2024)
12. Giglitto, D., Ciolfi, L., Lockley, E.: Introduction: digital approaches to inclusion and participation in cultural heritage. In: Digital Approaches to Inclusion and Participation in Cultural Heritage, pp. 1–7. Routledge (2023)
13. Ginsburgh, V., Weber, S.: How many languages do we need?: The economics of linguistic diversity. In: How Many Languages Do We Need? Princeton University Press (2011)

14. Gorter, D.: Linguistic landscapes in a multilingual world. Annu. Rev. Appl. Linguist. **33**, 190–212 (2013)
15. Grin, F., Fürst, G.: Measuring linguistic diversity: a multi-level metric. Soc. Indic. Res. **164**(2), 601–621 (2022)
16. Grützner-Zahn, A., Gaspari, F., Giagkou, M., Hegele, S., Way, A., Rehm, G.: Surveying the technology support of languages. In: Proceedings of the Second International Workshop Towards Digital Language Equality (TDLE): Focusing on Sustainability@ LREC-COLING 2024, pp. 1–17 (2024)
17. Hammarström, H., Forkel, R.: Glottocodes: Identifiers linking families, languages and dialects to comprehensive reference information. Sem. Web J. **13**(6), 917–924 (2022). https://content.iospress.com/articles/semantic-web/sw212843
18. Harmon, D., Loh, J.: The index of linguistic diversity: a new quantitative measure of trends in the status of the world's languages (2010)
19. Hua, X., Greenhill, S.J., Cardillo, M., Schneemann, H., Bromham, L.: The ecological drivers of variation in global language diversity. Nat. Commun. **10**(1), 2047 (2019)
20. Ingram, M.: The role of AI in language preservation and revitalization. In: AI for Community, pp. 55–80. Chapman and Hall/CRC (2025)
21. Ivkovic, D., Lotherington, H.: Multilingualism in cyberspace: Conceptualising the virtual linguistic landscape. Int. J. Multiling. **6**(1), 17–36 (2009)
22. Johnson, R.L., et al.: The ghost in the machine has an American accent: value conflict in GPT-3. arXiv preprint arXiv:2203.07785 (2022)
23. Kornai, A.: Digital language death. PloS one **8**(10), e77056 (2013)
24. Krauss, M.: The world's languages in crisis. Language **68**(1), 4–10 (1992)
25. Leimgruber, J.R.E., Fernández-Mallat, V.: Language attitudes and identity building in the linguistic landscape of montreal. Open Linguis. **7**(1), 406–422 (2021)
26. Liesenfeld, A., Dingemanse, M.: Building and curating conversational corpora for diversity-aware language science and technology. In: Calzolari, N., et al., (eds.) Proceedings of the Thirteenth Language Resources and Evaluation Conference. pp. 1178–1192. European Language Resources Association, Marseille, France (2022). https://aclanthology.org/2022.lrec-1.126/
27. Nee, J., Smith, G.M., Sheares, A., Rustagi, I.: Linguistic justice as a framework for designing, developing, and managing natural language processing tools. Big Data Soc. **9**(1), 20539517221090930 (2022)
28. Nettle, D., Romaine, S.: Vanishing Voices: The Extinction Of The World's Languages. Oxford University Press, Oxford (2000)
29. Pendakur, R.: Speaking in tongues: Heritage language maintenance and transfer in canada. (1990)
30. Pfeffer, J., et al.: Just another day on Twitter: a complete 24 hours of Twitter data. In: Proceedings of the International AAAI Conference on Web and Social Media, vol. 17, pp. 1073–1081 (2023)
31. Romaine, S.: Language endangerment and language death: the future of language diversity. In: The Routledge Handbook of Ecolinguistics, pp. 40–55. Routledge (2017)
32. Simons, G.F.: Two centuries of spreading language loss. Proc. Linguis. Soc. America **4**, 27–1 (2019)
33. Soukup, B., Lyons, K.: Quantitative and computational approaches. The Bloomsbury Handbook of Linguistic Landscapes, pp. 34–49 (2024)
34. Statista: Most common languages on the internet (2023). https://www.statista.com/statistics/262946/most-common-languages-on-the-internet/. Accessed on July 7, 2025

Unsustainable Imaginaries of Data Economies: Exploring the Concept of Waste for EU Digital Policy

Orsolya Gulyás[✉] [iD]

Brussels School of Governance, Vrije Universiteit Brussel, Brussels, Belgium
`orsolya.gulyas@vub.be`

Abstract. This position paper critically examines the European Union's current policy discourse on the twinning of the green and digital transitions. While digitalisation is widely promoted as a key enabler of sustainability through increased efficiency and data-driven innovation, the growing environmental costs of digital infrastructures—such as energy-intensive data centers—are increasingly acknowledged. The contribution argues that current EU policy imaginaries remain rooted in neoliberal logics, emphasizing economic competitiveness and growth, often at odds with the ecological limits demanded for a sustainable future. Through the lens of digital humanism and critical data studies, the paper calls to explore how dominant visions of the digital/data economy are inherently unsustainable, built upon assumptions of infinite expansion and unbounded data accumulation. It builds on the concept of "waste" as a critical entry point for rethinking digital policy: both in terms of data that is unnecessary or unused, and the resource-intensive nature of digital technologies.

Keywords: Data economy · European Union · Sustainability

1 Introduction

In recent years sustainability challenges and digitalisation have been increasingly addressed in public discourse as connected policy fields. Most often digital technologies are portrayed as the solution to mitigating and adapting to the effects of climate change due to their capacity to speed up and scale processes that can help the transition to a green(er) future. For example, the data collected from the precise tracking of energy consumption or real-time mobility data are seen as pathways to a more efficient use of resources. This way of leveraging digitalisation for sustainability is highlighted in policymaking too: in the European Union (EU), the twinning of the green and digital transitions has been foregrounded and formalized as official policy since 2019 (European Commission, 2022).

At the same time, the vast and increasing environmental footprint of digital services and infrastructures is also starting to be acknowledged. For example, the enormous energy consumption of data centers and the need for water resources to keep cooling

L. Hagedorn et al. (Eds.): DIGHUM 2025, LNCS 16319, pp. 366–371, 2026.
https://doi.org/10.1007/978-3-032-11108-1_27

them have recently sparked protests and lawsuits in Ireland and a public debate has also emerged in the Netherlands (Haeck and Zimmermann, 2022). Therefore, the push from policymakers for sustainable digitalisation efforts is present too, but it often conflicts with other policy goals that see digitalisation and the data economy as the drivers of future economic growth.

As such, it is important to explore the policy discourses and imaginaries that underlie the twinning of the green and digital transitions in general, and the data economy in particular. As this position paper argues, these are inherently unsustainable as they build on an ever-expanding vision of the data economy and digital infrastructures. Hence, this contribution makes a step towards exploring how the concept of 'waste' could be mobilised in imaginaries of the digital/data policy landscape in order to open up pathways to thinking about more sustainable digitalisation.

2 EU Digital Strategy

The neoliberal roots of EU policymaking have already been pointed to in the scholarly literature. Digital policymaking is no exception, with digitalisation consistently seen as the driver of economic growth by EU policymakers. Indeed, the first Digital Agenda was launched in the wake of the 2008 financial crisis when the EU put the focus on digital in order to bring the economy back on track. For similar reasons, after the Covid crisis the digital transformation and its role in boosting the economy is also central to the Recovery and Resilience Facility (RRF), the EU's economic recovery plan.

At the same time, a discourse on 'digital sovereignty' took centre stage in EU digital strategy, which has also been shown to be driven by the logic of boosting European economic competitiveness in the global tech and regulatory race (see Bellanova et al., 2022; Gulyás, 2023; Pohle and Thiel, 2020). This approach to digital policy is, however, contradictory to the essence of the green transition, which would require the abandonment of boosting economic growth at all costs as its main policy priority, and instead would focus on respecting planetary boundaries and protecting people from adverse effects of climate change, as well as the increasingly fast pace of digitalisation that people cannot easily keep up with.

In reality however the EU's overarching digital strategy is driven by an intensive push for faster digitalisation (e.g. policy goals such as 75% of EU businesses to use cloud technologies by 2030) and the building of more and more infrastructure for the exponential expansion of data volumes that is foreseen by policymakers (European Commission, 2024). The policy objectives do not seem to reflect on what kind of services and infrastructure are needed or useful, rather they focus on boosting the competitiveness of the EU in the global technology race vis-à-vis the US and China. Such a race mentality also underlies the external dimensions of EU digital policymaking: the race for critical raw materials or the Global Gateway strategy (European Commission, 2021), which aims to build green and digital infrastructures in underserved areas with the explicit aim of boosting the competitiveness of EU businesses, risks turning domestic digital sovereignty ambitions into efforts resembling digital colonialism abroad (Avila Pinto, 2018).

Against this background of a technological and regulatory race, the EU recently passed a number of legislative proposals that aim to lay down the basis for the development of the EU data economy, such as the Data Act (2023) and the Data Governance Act (2022). In line with the overarching digital strategy, the impact assessment document for the Data Act explicitly states that the policy rationale for the proposal is to avoid the *'loss of EU competitiveness in the global data economy'*, again drawing on an anxious position that does not set limits: if the EU does not act in a certain way, it will be left behind (European Commission, 2022:9). Moreover, in this context data is seen as a form of capital to be accumulated, extracted and exploited, and the overarching policy aim is for it to be exploited by European businesses, generating economic growth for the EU overall.

Digital humanism as a research program and scholarly field can play a prominent role in showing how the current imaginaries presented in discourses about the twin transitions could be reconceptualized (Werthner et al., 2024). As opposed to imaginaries embedded in control and domination, for digital humanities 'plurality' is a central notion. Indeed, the concept of 'digital plurality' has been put forth to replace current imaginaries around the development of AI in technology and society (Siddhart et al., 2021).

3   Green and Digital Policy: Bad Twins, Good Twins?

The underlying bedrock of my position is the idea that any form of sustainability in a system requires the presence of limits in some sense. This can mean the avoidance of overshoots, such as overuse or over-exploitation of resources. It can also mean the maintenance of balance in an (eco)system by cycles of decay/regeneration. Interestingly, the (critical) data studies literature often speaks about data 'lifecycles' but less has been written about data death or recycling.

A notable exception is the work of Thylstrup (2018) that examines data through cultural theories of waste and recycling. By positioning data as the by-product of computer-mediated human interactions, it is highlighted that all data is already 'waste' in some sense but only seemingly useless: through its extraction and recycling it can be sold and commodified, thus acquiring value. The distinction between what is waste and what is by-product is difficult, and making that selection and classification is ultimately a question of politics and power.

While Thylstrup's work focuses on the harm of current imaginaries of the data economy inflicted on human rights and dignity, highlighting the environmental harm to a greater degree has also become necessary by the twinning of the green and digital transitions in the EU. These still exist as separate fields and a conceptual linking of the two could be made easier by using the notion of 'waste' as an entry point. Questions to start with include asking what could limits/boundaries mean in the digital/data economy? What would constitute *enough*, if there is such a thing?

The twinning of the green and digital transitions in EU policy gives an opportunity to critically assess the imaginaries and discourses that arise at the intersection of the two policy fields. Bringing these to the surface would be a first step towards:

i) moving beyond imaginaries of a technological and regulatory race and the neoliberal logic underlying policymaking efforts;

ii) reflecting on the colonial logic that manifests itself in the construction of digital infrastructures (Crawford, 2021) and the global digital/data economy (Couldry and Mejias, 2019).

4   Thinking About 'Waste' in a Digital Context

Building on this critique, one way to meaningfully harness the potential of coupling the green and digital transitions could be via re-conceptualising the notion of 'waste' in a way that moves past the logic of simply making efficiency gains, and instead acknowledges and reflects on the inherent unsustainability of a digital/data economy that thrives on an endless generation and input of data. Such an approach would shift from thinking about using digital and AI tools for achieving sustainability goals to thinking about societally and environmentally sustainable ways of conceiving of the underlying data economy itself, recognizing its otherwise often invisible material consequences. The two main ways in which the concept of waste could be harnessed here are:

i) Data (as) waste that denotes data that is collected and stored on servers but not exploited, not needed, nor useful. In this sense, waste is meant as 'trash', something to dispose of. Discourses about data minimisation are gaining some ground, pointing to the need to collect and store only what's necessary. These efforts are however usually associated with privacy implications of collecting personal data, while they could also be argued for from the point of view of sustainability.

ii) Wasteful treatment: overuse (of energy)/overbuild (of infrastructure)/over-exploitation (of natural resources, or of human attention). This is to reflect on practices that waste scarce resources. For example, the increasing use of generative AI tools - when a simple search query would be a more appropriate tool to get the answer a user is searching for - weighs much more heavily on the energy grid. Such practices could be categorized as wasteful use of resources and could be addressed in policymaking, for example by labelling and raising awareness about the energy use of different digital tools and infrastructures.

The above points could serve as entry points to exploring the concept of waste in relation to digitalisation and sustainability. The need to think about our imaginaries is more and more pressing and recognized: for example, the recently launched ERC project Innovation Residues aims to explore data as a new category of residue that is "yet to be characterized, described, made meaning of, reflected upon, and taken care of" (INNORES project, 2022). The current imaginary of data spaces as being infinitely expandable is possibly also related to the fact that digital infrastructures and processes are largely invisible, hidden from the human eye – in this sense, even architecture could play a role in bringing these concerns more directly to our consciousness.

Consulting degrowth literature as well as disconnection and discard studies could all be helpful with revealing and altering the inherent unsustainability of the capitalist logic of digital/data economies and infrastructures. Such interdisciplinary work could ultimately aim towards positioning data as a commons, rather than capital and could transform the way policymaking conceptualizes the digital/data economy, in line with digital humanism thought and principles.

References

Avila Pinto, R.: Digital sovereignty or digital colonialism?. SUR 27 (2018). https://sur.conectas.org/en/digital-sovereignty-or-digital-colonialism/

Bellanova, R., Carrapico, H., Duez, D.: Digital/sovereignty and European security integration: an introduction. Eur. Secur. **31**(3), 337–355 (2022). https://doi.org/10.1080/09662839.2022.2101887

Couldry, N., Mejias, U. A.: The Costs of Connection: How Data Is Colonizing Human Life and Appropriating It for Capitalism. Stanford University Press (2019)

Crawford, K.: The Atlas of AI: Power, Politics, and the Planetary Costs of Artificial Intelligence. Yale University Press (2021). https://doi.org/10.2307/j.ctv1ghv45t

European Commission. The Global Gateway (2021). https://eur-lex.europa.eu/legal-content/EN/TXT/?uri=celex:52021JC0030

European Commission. The twin green & digital transition: How sustainable digital technologies could enable a carbon-neutral EU by 2050 - European Commission (2022). https://joint-research-centre.ec.europa.eu/jrc-news-and-updates/twin-green-digital-transition-how-sustainable-digital-technologies-could-enable-carbon-neutral-eu-2022-06-29_en

European Commission. Impact Assessment Report accompanying the document Proposal for a Regulation of the European Parliament and of the Council on harmonised rules on fair access to and use of data (Data Act) (2022). https://eur-lex.europa.eu/legal-content/EN/TXT/?uri=CELEX%3A52022SC0034

European Commission. Cloud computing | Shaping Europe's digital future (2024, March 1). https://digital-strategy.ec.europa.eu/en/policies/cloud-computing

Falk, S., Van Wynsberghe, A.: Challenging AI for Sustainability: what ought it mean? AI and Ethics (2023). https://doi.org/10.1007/s43681-023-00323-3

Gulyás, O.: Digital sovereignty, competitiveness, and the Illusion of freedom. An Arendtian Approach to EU Digital Policy. Politique Européenne, **81**(3), 28–52 (2023). https://doi.org/10.3917/poeu.081.0028

Haeck, P., Zimmermann, A.: Europe's hidden energy crisis: Data centers. POLITICO (2022, October 3). https://www.politico.eu/article/data-center-energy-water-intensive-tech/

INNORES project. Data Waste (2022). Retrieved June 24, 2024, from https://www.innovation-residues.eu/research/

Pohle, J., Thiel, T.: Digital sovereignty. Internet Policy Review, 9(4) (2020). https://doi.org/10.14763/2020.4.1532

Siddarth, D., Acemoglu, D., Allen, D., Crawford, K., Evans, J., Jordan, M.: How AI fails us. Harvard University, Technology & Democracy Discussion Paper (2021)

Thylstrup, N. B.: Data out of place: toxic traces and the politics of recycling. Big Data Soc. **6**(2), 2053951719875479 (2019). https://doi.org/10.1177/2053951719875479

Werthner, H. et al. (eds.). Introduction to Digital Humanism (2024)
https://doi.org/10.1007/978-3-031-45304-5_8

The Commons Approach: A Proposal
for a Digital Humanist Agenda
to (Re)Open Artificial Intelligence

Katja Mayer[1]([⊠]) , Stefan Skupien[2] , and Jochen Knaus[3]

[1] University of Vienna, Vienna, Austria
katja.mayer@univie.ac.at
[2] Berlin University Alliance, Berlin, Germany
stefan.skupien@berlin-university-alliance.de
[3] Weizenbaum Institute, Berlin, Germany
jochen.knaus@weizenbaum-institute.de

Abstract. This paper argues that for AI to serve the public interest, it must be aligned with the principles of open science and open knowledge. We propose concrete actions that Digital Humanism can advance in higher education, research, and policy to ensure AI development respects human rights, ethical responsibility, and democratic accountability. Existing open infrastructures offer blueprints for transparent and sustainable AI, supported by the communities and institutions that maintain them. By fostering collaboration across disciplines and sectors, Digital Humanism can help guide the digital ecosystem – currently centered on AI – toward long-term sustainability and development in the public interest.

Keywords: open science · open knowledge · open infrastructures · artificial intelligence · digital humanism

1 Introduction

Digital Humanism has emerged as a powerful critique of the ways in which technology is reshaping the modern world, offering a vision of human-centered technology that prioritizes ethical responsibility, transparency, sustainability, and the public good. Compared to fields such as critical computing and human computer interaction (HCI), science and technology studies (STS), and surveillance studies, which share similar concerns about the implications of digital technology on society, Digital Humanism is a relatively young movement [5,14,24,27,35]. But it has gained significant momentum in bringing public attention to troubling developments in the digital transformation by successfully emphasizing important normative values in the design and deployment of technology, urging a shift from a purely technical focus to one that embeds ethics and social responsibility [11]. However, Digital Humanism tends to marginalize open science

L. Hagedorn et al. (Eds.): DIGHUM 2025, LNCS 16319, pp. 372–380, 2026.
https://doi.org/10.1007/978-3-032-11108-1_28

and open knowledge, even though they are crucial for shaping human-centered technology. These communities already sustain practices of transparency and collective accountability through data sharing, standards, and evaluation. At the same time, they remain precarious and subject to appropriation by the very corporations and institutions that depend on their work. [4,7,13,21].

For digital technology and in particular AI to serve the public interest, it must rest on openness, public access, and ethical governance—principles shared by open science and Digital Humanism. Yet, the fragility of open science and knowledge communities limits their ability to sustain such values in practice. Digital Humanism, we suggest, should explicitly take up this agenda: acting as a catalyst that links these communities with computer science to align AI development with democratic trust and the common good, rather than corporate capture [11,32,33,37].

2   Context – Problem Space

Computer science – especially communities around ethical AI or sustainable AI – has long been at the forefront of promoting openness, with its roots deeply embedded in the development of open-source software and the collaborative nature of scientific research [29]. Open science promotes the free availability of scientific research, data, and methodologies, based on transparency, inclusive collaboration, and reproducibility in the pursuit of knowledge democratization [25,31]. Closely tied to the Free and Open Source Software (FOSS) movement, which has advocated for the freedom to use, modify, and distribute software since the 1980s [3], Open Knowledge similarly emphasizes freely accessible resources. At its core, it supports knowledge commons - shared, collectively managed resources that challenge the privatization of knowledge - and encourages collaborative, equitable practices in knowledge production and dissemination [10]. A significant part of contemporary AI, particularly generative AI, relies on open-source software, collaborative research, and open datasets, often sourced from the internet and the broader knowledge commons [12]. Ethical and legal issues arise with AI's data hunger when training data is scraped without proper rights or consent, a practice that undermines ethical standards and privacy protections [17]. The growing use of automated scrapers further strains open infrastructures, threatening their sustainability and integrity, and exacerbating the exploitation of resources without accountability [28]. Even within science, AI researchers face poor reproducibility due to issues such as lack of transparency, data, code, and adherence to standards, which undermines trust and integrity in research [30].

The pressing concern with AI, especially in sensitive areas like healthcare, criminal justice, and finance, is not simply the enclosure of formerly open knowledge but the profound lack of transparency and mechanisms of accountability in their deployment in contexts that directly affect people's lives. Its implementation often resembles a vast "social experiment", not only testing technological limits but also probing the boundaries of societal structures and norms [2,8]. This experimental opacity, compounded by the concentration of AI development and infrastructure in a few dominant tech companies and their prioritizing of profit and market control over societal needs, creates significant risks for users and broader society. The European AI Act, emerging from a risk-based perspective, addresses these concerns on the impact level, emphasizing the need for stronger oversight [9]. The open source exception in the AI Act has already led to a controversy about what truly qualifies as open source and has already resulted in "openwashing", where AI systems are marketed as open while remaining largely inaccessible and proprietary [22]. As AI technologies are framed as general-purpose, regulators have understood that accountability must go beyond explainability to include fairness, sustainability, and human rights based governance [15,34]. Global initiatives, such as the UN Global Digital Compact, are advocating for digital public goods like open source software, open data, open AI models, open standards and open content to ensure that AI is complying with this need for accountability, privacy and legal standards [32].

3   Responsible Design and Implementation of AI: Building on Open Expertise and Infrastructures

The lessons learned from the commercialization of social media, the exploitation of privacy, and the transformation of open access into a "gold business model" have fueled critiques of openness, raising concerns that AI platforms may follow the same path [23]. At the same time, many resources for AI research, including computational power, data, and knowledge, have notably transitioned from being predominantly managed by public research institutions to being concentrated in the hands of the private sector [1,36]. This development calls for a response rooted in public values. Digital Humanism is both a political and practical project that seeks to align computer science and digital transformation more generally with human rights-based values [35]. We argue that it needs to adopt more "openness" to ensure that AI development is transparent, accountable, and inclusive, while safeguarding the public good against full commercialization and monopolization. To chart a viable alternative path for Europe in AI development, it is crucial to leverage the vast resources within the realms of open science, and open knowledge, which have evolved over recent decades to support not only innovation but also a more ethical, transparent, and inclusive digital future. Besides globally active private funders, like Wellcome Trust, Gates Foundation or the US National Institute of Health, Europe has become a major actor in advancing public-interest technologies and the digital commons. The European Commission and national research funders have lately invested substantially in building infrastructures, e.g. the European AI factories with concentrated efforts in the EuroHPC Joint Undertaking, standards, and communities that embody these values, reinforcing Europe's role as a leader in promoting an ethical, transparent, and inclusive digital future [20].

Open science has advanced significantly in making research, data, and methods accessible, with platforms like arXiv, bioRxiv, and Zenodo, as well as models such as diamond and green open access, expanding transparency and reducing barriers. Certified repositories (e.g., CoreTrustSeal) further ensure the quality, integrity, and sustainability of shared data. A central development is the European Open Science Cloud (EOSC), which integrates and provides services for accessing, processing, and analyzing research data, fostering interoperability and collaboration across Europe and beyond. As these efforts grow, ensuring that open research data is both AI-ready through FAIR (Findable, Accessible, Interoperable, Reusable) principles and aligned with CARE (Collective benefit, Authority to control, Responsibility, Ethics) principles remains essential. [6]. On the societal and economic side, there are valuable resources like public knowledge repositories (e.g., NGOS, libraries and Wikipedia) that provide open, quality-assured information. However, these sources alone do not guarantee the reliability of the AI systems trained with them. The integration of model cards and open evaluation initiatives further enhances the transparency and accountability of AI systems. The aforementioned examples can serve as blueprints for Public AI infrastructures that are accessible, and prioritize the public interest, ensuring accountability through participatory governance, feedback loops, and co-creation models, while remaining available and adaptable in the long term [16,19]. An open research agenda for AI in Europe beyond the current scope ([36], Chap. 14) needs to also address the challenges and in particular how to create benefits for all stakeholders and confront the paradox of openness: while it can counter corporate enclosure, it is equally prone to exploitation and may reinforce power concentration [18].

4   Discussion

While open science and open knowledge provide valuable resources for developing AI in the public interest, these fields must come closer together and build alliances to better integrate science and civil society, making their contributions more visible in policy discussions. Numerous challenges remain, but our shared vision is a digital culture in which AI technologies are designed and deployed transparently, traceably, sustainably, and with a focus on the public good. We recognize that the concept of openness is complex and context-dependent. Although open licenses, interfaces, and data can foster transparency and participation, some contexts, such as those involving sensitive data or security concerns, require controlled access. It is evident that while 'open' AI can promote transparency, reusability, and a degree of oversight, it does not inherently ensure democratic access or encourage meaningful competition [13]. The dominant narratives around "economies of scale" in AI, namely larger models, larger infrastructures, and more resources, emphasize the material and infrastructural control exercised by a few companies [13]. Open research infrastructures cannot compete on the same scale, but this approach is misguided. Instead, federated spaces should be further developed to create new models for collaborative, federated implementation, and new commons-based economies rooted in public stewardship. Building on insights from a transdisciplinary conference with researchers, administrators, data stewards, policymakers, and industry, to discuss strategic priorities for the responsible design and implementation of AI in open science and beyond, we now present concrete recommendations for integrating open science and open knowledge into AI development across computer science and beyond [26].

1. Foster Collaborative Knowledge Spaces and Strategic Networking: Promote interdisciplinary collaboration and the development of open AI infrastructures by establishing community forums and connecting research institutions, NGOs, public bodies, and private entities. Techniques like open metadata and knowledge graphs, alongside integrating generative and rule-based AI systems, should be prioritized to create open knowledge ecosystems.

2. Build Competencies in AI and Open Science: Invest in education and training to develop critical data literacy, ethical reasoning, and interdisciplinary understanding for responsible AI development. Establish interdisciplinary programs, such as Open Science & AI, at universities to prepare the next generation of researchers to address ethical complexities in AI.

3. Support Sustainable Development through Open, Interoperable Infrastructures and New Evaluation: Build open, publicly responsible infrastructures for AI based on open standards and code, promoting interoperability across disciplines and institutions. Expand initiatives like the European Open Science Cloud (EOSC) to provide AI-ready data, ensuring transparent and accountable AI development. Create and further develop new evaluation mechanisms that also take into account resource consumption and social costs.

4. Create Governance Models that Balance Responsibility and Innovation: Develop and enact institutional AI governance frameworks that balance legal certainty with innovation space. Support regulatory sandboxes for experimenting with open AI models under ethical guidelines and participatory decision-making, integrating open science governance mechanisms like community-led licensing.

5. Strengthen Public and Private Cooperation: Institutionalize cooperation between academia, civil society, government, and industry to promote transparency and accountability in AI development. Expand initiatives to connect with European AI Hubs and newly created AI factories for real-world research applications to integrate open practices.

6. Ensure Digital Sovereignty and the Public Good: Advocate for public AI infrastructures built on open standards and open-source software, ensuring the highest transparency and accountability. Prioritize AI using local data processing in the public sector, with strategies to exit proprietary dependencies and foster mandatory openness in public procurement.

7. Establish Long-term and Inclusive Funding Models: Demand and create long-term funding mechanisms to ensure the sustainability of open AI infrastructures. Endorse the development of a solidarity fund supported by public and private actors, including public-private partnerships, to align AI development, hosting, and governance with public good, sustainability, and ethical standards.

Together, these strategic priorities for education, research, and science policy constitute a commons approach to AI—grounded in openness, public stewardship, and collective governance—to resist capture and enclosure, ensuring that AI development and deployment remain aligned with the public interest. Thus, Digital Humanism must move beyond its current implicit endorsement of openness and actively engage with the infrastructures, governance models, and collaborative practices needed to realize this commons approach and challenge the concentration of power in AI.

5   Conclusion

In conclusion, for digital technology and especially AI to serve the public good it must be rooted in open science, open knowledge, and their digital commons. We have outlined concrete actions that Digital Humanism can support in education, research, and policy to meet this challenge. By strengthening collaboration across disciplines and sectors, it can guide AI development toward human rights, ethical responsibility, and collective benefit. Open infrastructures already offer blueprints for transparent and sustainable AI, sustained by the communities and institutions that maintain them. While commons ecosystems are global, Europe is well placed to strengthen and value them more fully. Digital Humanism can provide the platform to connect infrastructures, communities, and institutions, and to guide the broader digital ecosystem—currently centered on AI—toward development in the public interest.

Acknowledgments. We would like to thank the participants of our conference in March 2025 [26], with special gratitude to our co-organizers Lilli Iliev (Wikimedia Germany) and Theresa Züger (Humboldt Institute for Internet and Society), as well as Stefan Kaufmann and Anne-Sophie Waag for their valuable comments. Katja Mayer's project was funded by the Austrian Science Fund, DOI 10.55776/V699 and the incoming Open Science fellowship of the Berlin University Alliance 2024.

Disclosure of Interests. We declare that we have no potential conflict of interest.

References

1. Ahmed, N., Wahed, M., Thompson, N.C.: The growing influence of industry in AI research. Science **379**(6635), 884–886 (2023). https://doi.org/10.1126/science.ade2420
2. Bender, E.M., Madison, M.J.: The AI Con. Penguin (2025). https://www.penguin.co.uk/books/468070/the-ai-con-by-hanna-emily-m-bender-and-alex/9781529949896
3. Berry, D.: The philosophy of software: Code and mediation in the digital age. Springer (2016)

4. Bertelli, A., Acciai, M., Rossi, G.: The European open science cloud as a common good potentials and limitations of this endeavour. Open Res. Europe **5**, 19 (2025). https://doi.org/10.12688/openreseurope.19170.1

5. Bjerknes, G., Ehn, P., Kyng, M.: Computers and democracy-a Scandinavian challenge. Gower Publishing (1987)

6. Carroll, S.R., Herczog, E., Hudson, M., Russell, K., Stall, S.: Operationalizing the care and fair principles for indigenous data futures. Sci. Data **8**(1) (2021). https://doi.org/10.1038/s41597-021-00892-0

7. Cole, N.L., Kormann, E., Klebel, T., Apartis, S., Ross-Hellauer, T.: The societal impact of open science: a scoping review. Royal Soc. Open Sci. **11**(6) (2024). https://doi.org/10.1098/rsos.240286

8. Dignum, V.: Responsible artificial intelligence – from principles to practice (2022). https://doi.org/10.48550/ARXIV.2205.10785

9. European Parliament and Council: Regulation (EU) 2024/1689 of the European parliament and of the council laying down harmonised rules on artificial intelligence (artificial intelligence act) (2024). https://eur-lex.europa.eu/eli/reg/2024/1689/oj

10. Frischmann, B.M., Madison, M.J., Strandburg, K.J.: Governing knowledge commons. Oxford University Press (2014)

11. Fuchs, C.: Digital humanism: a philosophy for 21st century digital society. Emerald Group Publishing Limited (2022)

12. Gimpel, L.: Toward Open-Source AI Systems as Digital Public Goods: Definitions, Hopes and Challenges, p. 129–142. Springer Nature Switzerland (2024). https://doi.org/10.1007/978-3-031-61187-2_8

13. Gray Widder, D., West, S., Whittaker, M.: Open (for business): Big tech, concentrated power, and the political economy of open AI. SSRN Electronic Journal (2023). https://doi.org/10.2139/ssrn.4543807

14. Haraway, D.: A cyborg manifesto: Science, technology, and socialist-feminism in the late twentieth century. In: The Transgender Studies Reader, pp. 103–118. Routledge (2013)

15. High-Level Expert Group on Artificial Intelligence: Ethics guidelines for trustworthy AI (2019). https://digital-strategy.ec.europa.eu/en/library/ethics-guidelines-trustworthy-ai. Accessed Jul. 15, 2025

16. Jackson, B., et al.: Public AI: Infrastructure for the common good (2024). https://doi.org/10.5281/ZENODO.13914560

17. Jernite, Y., et al.: Data governance in the age of large-scale data-driven language technology. In: 2022 ACM Conference on Fairness Accountability and Transparency, pp. 2206–2222. FAccT '22, ACM (2022).https://doi.org/10.1145/3531146.3534637

18. Keller, P., Tarkowski, A.: Paradox of open: Policies for the digital commons (2025). https://paradox.openfuture.eu/. Accessed Jul. 15

19. Koth, S.: There is a model for that: Science and public AI infrastructures (2025). https://doi.org/10.5281/ZENODO.14930893

20. Krewer, J.: From open access to collective governance. two decades of digital commons policies in the european union (2025). https://openfuture.eu/publication/from-open-access-to-collective-governance/. Accessed: Jun. 21, 2025

21. Krewer, J., Warso, Z.: Digital commons as providers of public digital infrastructures (2024). https://openfuture.eu/publication/digital-commons-as-providers-of-public-digital-infrastructures. Accessed: Apr. 21, 2025

22. Liesenfeld, A., Dingemanse, M.: Rethinking open source generative AI: open washing and the EU AI act. In: The 2024 ACM Conference on Fairness, Accountabil-

ity, and Transparency. p. 1774–1787. FAccT '24, ACM (2024). https://doi.org/10.1145/3630106.3659005

23. Luitse, D.: Platform power in AI: The evolution of cloud infrastructures in the political economy of artificial intelligence. Internet Policy Rev. **13**(2) (2024). https://doi.org/10.14763/2024.2.1768

24. Lyon, D.: Surveillance studies: An overview. Wiley (2007)

25. Mayer, K.: From science 2.0 to open science - turning rhetoric into action? (2016). https://doi.org/10.5281/ZENODO.200188

26. Mayer, K., et al.: Yes, we are open!? Künstliche Intelligenz verantwortungsbewusst gestalten. Weizenbaum Institute (2025). https://doi.org/10.34669/WI.DP/51

27. Mayer, K., Strassnig, M.: The Digital Humanism Initiative in Vienna, pp. 27–39. Zenodo (2020). https://doi.org/10.5281/ZENODO.4250144

28. Müller, B., Danis, C., Lavagetto, G.: How crawlers impact the operations of the wikimedia projects (2025). https://diff.wikimedia.org/2025/04/01/how-crawlers-impact-the-operations-of-the-wikimedia-projects/. Accessed April 21th, 2025

29. Schlagwein, D., Conboy, K., Feller, J., Leimeister, J.M., Morgan, L.: Openness with and without information technology: a framework and a brief history. J. Inf. Technol. **32**(4), 297–305 (2017). https://doi.org/10.1057/s41265-017-0049-3

30. Semmelrock, H., et al.: Reproducibility in machine learning-based research: Overview, barriers and drivers (2024). https://doi.org/10.48550/ARXIV.2406.14325

31. UNESCO: UNESCO Recommendation on Open Science. UNESCO (2021). https://doi.org/10.54677/mnmh8546

32. United Nations: Our common agenda: Policy brief 5 – a global digital compact (2023). https://digitallibrary.un.org/record/4011891

33. United Nations: Governing AI for humanity: final report (2024). https://digitallibrary.un.org/record/4062495

34. Veale, M., Matus, K., Gorwa, R.: Ai and global governance: modalities, rationales, tensions. Ann. Rev. Law Soc. Sci. **19**(1), 255–275 (2023). https://doi.org/10.1146/annurev-lawsocsci-020223-040749

35. Werthner, H.: Digital Humanism and the Vienna Manifesto, pp. 83–87. Springer Nature Switzerland (2025). https://doi.org/10.1007/978-3-031-86905-1_7

36. Whittaker, M.: The steep cost of capture. Interactions **28**(6), 50–55 (2021). https://doi.org/10.1145/3488666

37. Züger, T., Asghari, H.: AI for the public. how public interest theory shifts the discourse on AI. AI Soc. **38**(2), 815–828 (2022). https://doi.org/10.1007/s00146-022-01480-5

Are They Aware When AI is Used? And What do They Think that AI Should be used for? – Insights into the Digital Skills Austria III Study

Dimitri Prandner[(✉)] [iD]

Johannes Kepler University Linz, Altenbergerstr. 69, 4040 Linz, Austria
Dimitri.Prandner@jku.at

Abstract. The rapid rise of generative artificial intelligence (AI) has significantly disrupted modern societies, reshaping key areas such as education, the economy, the media and political communication. Since OpenAI's pioneering ChatGPT software was publicly released in November 2022, followed by a growing ecosystem of similar tools, debates surrounding the societal opportunities, challenges, and risks of AI have intensified. These discussions are taking place across various scientific disciplines, as well as in politics and the economy. But what does the general public know about AI? Can the public identify when AI is being used? Which uses are seen as appropriate, and which are not? This article is based on the 2024 Digital Skills Austria study and reveals that the public often struggles to identify instances of AI usage in everyday contexts, while misjudging scenarios that could lead to hallucinations and misinformation.

Keywords: Survey · Public understanding of AI · Case Study (Austria)

1 Introduction

The rapid rise of generative artificial intelligence (AI) has significantly disrupted modern societies, reshaping key areas such as education, the economy, the media, and political communication. Since the public release of *OpenAI's* trailblazing software *ChatGPT* in November 2022 – followed by an ever-growing ecosystem of similar tools – debates surrounding the societal opportunities, challenges and risks of AI have intensified by a multitude. Technology giants such as *Microsoft*, *Apple* and *Alphabet* (Google's parent company) have advanced these developments significantly, investing substantial financial and organizational resources in the process (Khanal et al., 2025).

It is therefore unsurprising that public awareness and discussion of generative AI – and AI tools more broadly – are at an all-time high, despite various forms of AI technology having been used across sectors for years, often without comparable scrutiny or prominence. This increased attention appears justified: the ways in which generative AI functions – particularly in relation to its training data and the nature of its outputs – raise numerous social and ethical concerns, including issues of trust, intellectual property

L. Hagedorn et al. (Eds.): DIGHUM 2025, LNCS 16319, pp. 381–389, 2026.
https://doi.org/10.1007/978-3-032-11108-1_29

rights, bias, discrimination, and the potential for misuse in generating deepfakes or disinformation (Taeihagh, 2025). And this is not even touching on the environmental impact the power-hungry technology has. Applying the cultural sociological writings on the discussions by Alexander (2006), one can argue that the emergence of generative AI is one that reshapes both the civil and the private spheres, irrevocably as it impacts individuals' private lives, employment, as well as the political institutions at the heart of modern democratic societies, which are currently also under threat because current polycrisis (Häckermann & Ettrich, 2023).

Because of this it is no surprise that these developments led to immediate actions from prominent political, educational, and research institutions, who have since adopted a range of strategies. For example, *Sciences Po*, one of France's elite universities, acted swiftly to prohibit or significantly limit the use of generative AI in academic settings (Sciences Po, 2023). In Austria, *ACONET* – a national provider of research data infrastructure – has taken a different approach by collaborating with companies such as the aforementioned *Microsoft* to develop an infrastructure that complies with national legal and ethical standards (ACONET, 2025). In the United States, the *National Institute of Standards and Technology* (NIST) introduced a voluntary "risk management framework" aimed at guiding AI regulation (Kerry, 2023). In Europe, at the supranational level, the European Union's AI Act seeks to classify and mitigate risks associated with high-impact AI applications, especially those that affect fundamental rights or societal cohesion (Smuha, 2021).

Taken together, these – definitely non-exhaustive and thus only illustrative – examples demonstrate that the emergence of generative AI has triggered unease across organizational, national, and international levels, highlighting different strategies to cope with the new reality that includes a breadth of tools, that are very much a black box in the way how they work and may affect societies (Taeihagh, 2025). This can be seen in recent developments, which show an increasing willingness to develop proactive and anticipatory frameworks for the governance of AI, which are themselves also informed by data driven complexity-sensitive approaches (Taeihagh et al., 2021). The painful lessons learned from the rise of social media – which ultimately posed serious challenges to liberal democracies due to inadequate oversight – have likely contributed to this shift (Appel, 2024; Grünangerl & Prandner, 2024).

However, these discussions also put a spotlight on a research gap. Much of the current scientific as well as political discourse focuses on structural and organizational responses to the emergence of generative AI, while comparatively little attention is paid to the perspectives of individual users. Because of this, I want to highlight two key societally relevant questions, which remain underexplored in the current discussion:

(1) To what extent are individual members of society actually aware of AI technologies and their applications in everyday practices?
(2) What are their views on the appropriate use of AI tools, and are they in line with institutional, national, or supranational regulatory efforts?

This article addresses these questions by drawing on recent population-level data from Austria. Following this introduction, a brief section will present the dataset. Selected findings will then be highlighted, followed by a concluding discussion.

2   Dataset and Analysis

This paper draws on the third wave of the Digital Skills Austria panel study (Grünangerl & Prandner, 2024; Grünangerl & Prandner, 2025). Since 2022, the survey has annually collected individual-level data on digital skills and competencies using Computer-Assisted Web Interviews (CAWI). Each year, the questionnaire includes a general part on digital skills and competencies and an annually rotating core topic, all of which is operationalized by a research team from the Paris Lodron University of Salzburg and the Johannes Kepler University of Linz. Data collection for the study takes place during the summer months (July and August) and is conducted by the field agency *MarketAgent*, which recruits participants via its ISO-certified online access panel. Quality control is carried out by both *MarketAgent* and the research team.

The 2024 wave (n = 2,302) used for this article is matching the Austrian online population in terms of age, gender, education, and regional distribution, while substantively focusing on attitudes toward and experiences with AI. Quota sampling was applied for recruiting, thus unweighted data is used for the analyses (for reasoning see e.g. Prandner, 2022, p. 337). The raw dataset was screened for speeding by *MarketAgent* and further checked by the research group for response patterns (e.g., straightlining or consistently choosing extreme categories). Cases displaying such tendencies were excluded before the final dataset was compiled. A detailed sample description is available in the project report (Grünangerl & Prandner, 2024, pp. 18–20).

Table 1. Key Variables for Analysis (Source: Digital Skills Austria III study)

Dimension	Variable/Question	Scale	Mean (Med.) % coded 1
AI Application Knowledge Test I Digital Skill Score	sum-variable of AI-knowledge tasks (n = 2302)	0 to 6 AI-tools identified	1,8 (1)
AI Scenarios I Story vignettes	Think about the follwing scenario: Persons X and Y are using AI tools for the following task Z. Do you think their behaviour is appropriate?	1 (very appropriate) to 5 (not approriate at all)	-

A key part of the survey study was the presentation of different everyday scenarios, where short story snippets – vignettes – were provided to the respondents. All the stories had a person using AI tools to complete a particular task and respondents had to judge if they deem this action as an appropriate use of AI or not. The scenarios were made up from eight different societal fields – ranging from medicine, school and work to journalism or even research. Overall, the survey included 32 different story vignettes, but only 16 of them were provided to each respondent to limit the mental load and complexity of the questionnaire. The story vignettes presented in this paper are limited to three social fields and deal with AI use in school, work and journalism (more details on all the scenarios can be found in Grünangerl & Prandner, 2024). Another key component used for this article is an AI knowledge test, which will be introduced in detail during the next section of the article (see also Table 1 and Fig. 1).

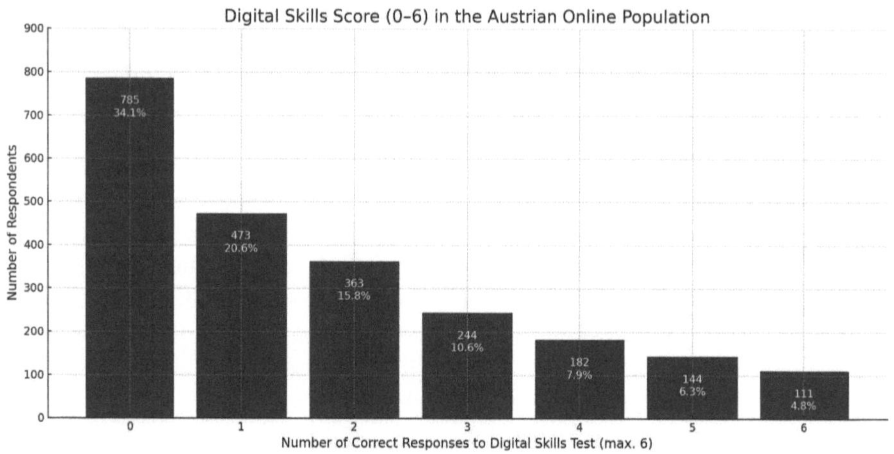

Fig. 1. Scores reached by the survey Austrian Online Population (n = 2302) on AI-Knowledge test by Kennedy et al. (2023) in the Digital Skills Austria III study, own depiction.

3 The Austrians Perception of AI in Everyday Applications

The general population survey conducted for the Digital Skills Austria III study included a short knowledge test originally proposed by Kennedy et al. (2023). This test was used to assess whether Austrians are aware of where AI-based technologies are part of everyday applications. The test consisted of six brief questions covering domains such as customer service, health monitoring, and music streaming. For example, participants had to know that a music streaming service uses AI in the form of algorithms to suggest titles for a playlist or that a customer service chat bot is using AI to chat with someone or that spam-filters from e-mail clients use AI to identify problematic messages. Based on their responses to those questions, the participants' knowledge of AI-powered tools was measured on a scale ranging from 0 to 6 correct answers (see also Table 1 and Fig. 1).

Results from the general population sample show that many Austrians lack a clear understanding of the AI-driven nature of common technologies: approximately 34% were unable to correctly identify any of the listed AI-supported applications, while an additional 21% identified only one. Only 5% of respondents answered all six questions correctly. The median number of correct responses was just one out of six (Mean: 1.8). As the linear regression model in Table 2 highlights, this is significantly influenced by socio-demographics. Ceteris paribus higher education leads to better results (the strongest effect in the model emerges when comparing those that only completed compulsory education to those that completed tertiary education), men tend to perform better than women and the age group 31 to 45 is performing better than all other the age groups, while those over 65 years perform worse than those 30 or younger (for specific values see Table 2).

Table 2. Linear Regression | Explaining participants from score from 0 to 6 on AI-Knowledge test by Kennedy et al. (2023) in the *Digital Skills Austria III study*, own depiction

Predictor	B	SE	β	t	p
Constant	1.91	0.15	—	12.93	<.001
Intensive engagement with AI (Ref: no or little engagement)	0.38	0.10	0.08	3.81	<.001
Max. Compulsory education completed (Ref.)					
Secondary education completed	0.41	0.09	0.09	4.35	<.001
Tertiary education completed	1.15	0.10	0.24	11.69	<.001
Age 30 or younger (Ref.)					
Age between 31 and 45	0.35	0.11	0.08	3.24	<.001
Age between 46 and 65	0.19	0.10	0.05	1.88	.061
Age over 65	−0.50	0.12	−0.10	−4.12	<.001
Sex is Female (Ref.: Male)	−0.04	0.01	−0.11	−5.24	<.001

(Note: n = 2302; R2 = .11, Adjusted R2 = .11, F (7, 2294) = 39.40, p < .001)

Overall, these results not only fall short of those reported by Kennedy et al. (2023) for a U.S. sample but also align with findings from a parallel student-focused study on AI awareness among Austrian Students (Zemsauer & Prandner, 2025), conducted at the Johannes Kepler University of Linz. While students performed better overall – matching the result of the main study that educational attainments have a direct positive impact –, their scores were still modest, with a median of three correct answers (Mean: 2.7; see also Zemsauer & Prandner, 2025).

Furthermore, a more detailed look at the test results reveals a broader underlying issue: many respondents not only failed to identify actual AI use cases but also wrongly attributed AI capabilities to technologies that do not, in fact, rely on AI-based technology. This suggests an overestimation of AI prevalence – likely shaped by media narratives, public discourse on technological innovation, and limited personal engagement; only 18% of respondents reported having engaged more deeply with AI, while over 30% stated they rarely or never (consciously) use it. This was also a significant, albeit weak predictor in the linear regression model, presented in Table 2.

A closer look at the different vignette scenarios provides further insights into public perceptions of AI use. This article focuses on three application areas (for an overview of all eight areas and 32 scenarios, see: Grünangerl & Prandner, 2024, pp. 60–69) the school context, the journalistic context, and the work context, with the tourism industry serving as an illustrative example. What stands out is the observed variation in how these scenarios are evaluated.

For instance, more than half of the respondents consider it appropriate to use tools like *Co-Pilot* for conducting research for school assignments – despite the well-documented risk of hallucinated sources and inaccurate information, which is further complicated by the black-box nature of generative AI (Taeihagh, 2025). In contrast, a similar proportion rejects the much safer application of using *DeepL* to stylistically improve an English-language paper. Additionally, roughly one-third find it acceptable to have the entire text for a presentation in school generated via *ChatGPT*.

When it comes to the journalistic context, the evaluations of the participants also reveal some surprising assessments. Despite ongoing criticism of AI-generated imagery – such as stylistic inconsistencies or infamous flaws like the "sixth finger" (Wasielewski, 2023) – about 60% of respondents find it appropriate to use AI to create illustrations for advice columns. Comparable proportions support the use of AI for generating standardized journalistic formats, such as sports results.

In the advertising context, where AI-generated imagery is also part of a story vignette, respondents are somewhat more skeptical—but still, around 40% find such use acceptable. When it comes to customer interaction, about half of the respondents approve of replacing human agents with AI-powered chatbots for addressing customer inquiries. However, attitudes shift when AI is used for workflow optimization, such as routing or process improvement, with greater skepticism observed. The highest rejection rates are reported for the use of AI in evaluating job applications—indicating public concern about sensitive data, fairness, and potential algorithmic bias (Fig. 2).

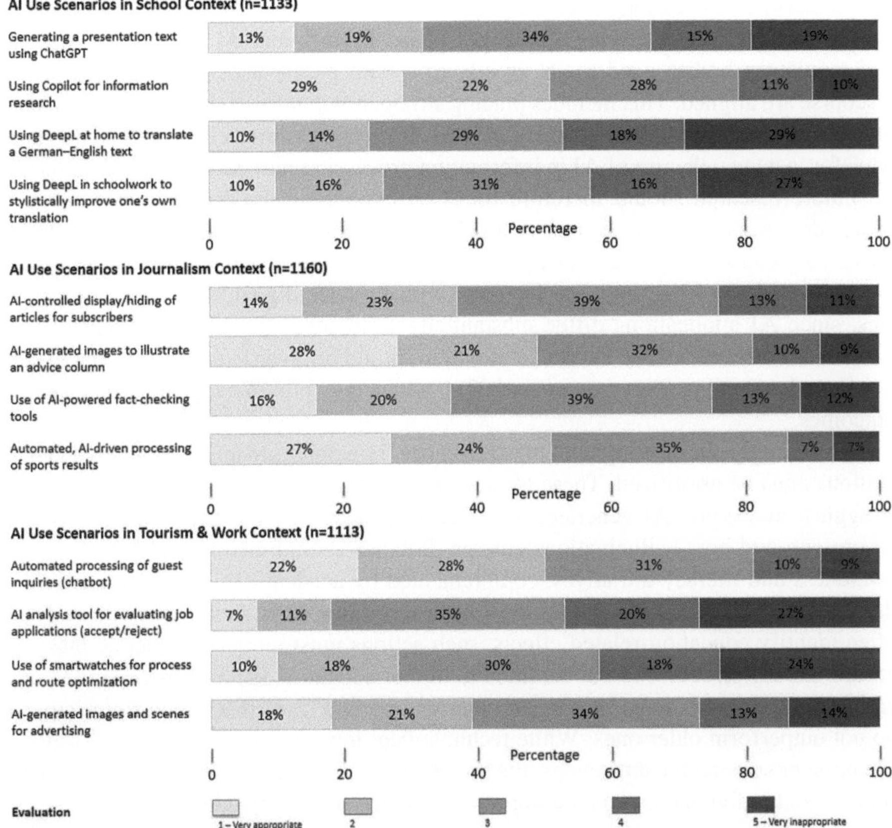

Fig. 2. How appropriate is the use of AI in each scenario? Evaluations provide by the surveyed Austrian Online Population in the *Digital Skills Austria III* study, own depiction

4   Discussion

The results of the Digital Skills Austria study 2024 show – regarding the first research question – that individuals in Austria are often unaware of when and where AI technologies are used in everyday scenarios. Demographic differences are evident, particularly with respect to educational attainment: participants with tertiary education performed better, which aligns with previous findings, as higher education is typically associated with higher levels of digital competence (Grünangerl & Prandner, 2025, p. 602). Participants also tend to overestimate the actual use of AI, often assuming it is embedded in everyday tools that in fact do not rely on such technologies. This highlights the limited experience and engagement with AI in the general population, suggesting that both public and political discourses may not fully reflect the realities of AI integration.

These discrepancies become even clearer in relation to the second research question on perceptions of appropriate AI use. A particularly relevant finding emerges regarding scenarios involving higher risks of misinformation or misrepresentation: participants judged these as less problematic than low-risk applications such as linguistic checks.

This underlines the societal need for regulation and oversight, as individuals currently lack awareness of the varying challenges posed by different AI tools. Policymakers and regulatory bodies need to act swiftly to ensure public understanding and policy discourse are aligned. This includes placing stronger emphasis on the role of individuals in initiatives such as the European Union's AI Act, as they ultimately need to understand why, for instance, the use of AI in information processing may be considered high risk.

Future research should therefore focus on explaining the discrepancies between expert-driven assessments of risk and public perceptions, while identifying potential underlying causes. Analyses must go beyond demographic factors and instead examine how AI knowledge and use intersect with broader digital skills and competencies, since AI applications differ substantially from other digital technologies (Grünangerl & Prandner, 2024). Particular attention should be given to naïve use without sufficient understanding (Prandner et al., 2025), which may provoke societally undesirable outcomes.

Accordingly, the development of explanatory frameworks to inform policies and regulations must be prioritized. These frameworks need to recognize that individuals often struggle to assess how AI-generated information relates to training data, what biases may be present, and how hallucinations emerge. Policies should therefore include targeted awareness and literacy initiatives, complemented by academic third-mission activities that explain the possibilities and limits of AI in accessible ways. Since scientific analyses often identify education-related effects, such actions must mitigate academic bias and ensure that AI discourse is not confined to higher education but also incorporated into earlier stages of schooling. This is particularly important given that younger participants do not outperform older ones. While technological innovations often pave the way for scientific or societal breakthroughs, the broad adoption of AI makes it essential to foster societal and individual understanding of both potentials and limitation.

Acknowledgments. This study was funded by RTR GmbH in 2024. The text was spellchecked with AI assisted tools, especially DeepL and ChatGPT 5. Figures were created via Python, underlying calculations conducted via IBM SPSS V29.

Disclosure of Interests. The author has no competing interests to declare that are relevant to the content of this article.

References

1. ACONET: Academic AI (2025). https://www.acomarket.at/de/portfolio/projekte/academic-ai
2. Alexander, J.C.: The Civil Sphere. Oxford University Press, Oxford (2006)
3. Appel, R.E.: Generative AI regulation can learn from social media regulation. arXiv preprint arXiv:2412.11335 (2024)
4. Grünangerl, M., Prandner, D.: Digital Skills Austria 2024. Zenodo (2024). https://doi.org/10.5281/zenodo.14295830
5. Grünangerl, M., Prandner, D.: Who supports or opposes the use of AI in educational and scientific contexts? In: 11th International Conference on Higher Education Advances (HEAd 2025), Valencia, 17–20 June 2025 (2025). https://doi.org/10.4995/HEAd25.2025.20147

6. Häckermann, A., Ettrich, F.: Soziologie in Zeiten der Polykrise. Berl. J. Soziol. **33**(4), 351–355 (2023)
7. Kennedy, B., Tyson, A., Saks, E.: Public awareness of artificial intelligence in everyday activities (Wave 119). Pew Research Center (2023). https://www.pewresearch.org/science/wp-content/uploads/sites/16/2023/02/PS_2023.02.15_AI-awareness_REPORT.pdf
8. Kerry, C.F.: NIST's AI risk management framework plants a flag in the AI debate. (2023)
9. Khanal, S., Zhang, H., Taeihagh, A.: Why and how is the power of big tech increasing in the policy process? The case of generative AI. Policy Soc. **44**(1), 52–69 (2025)
10. Prandner, D.: Zu Datengrundlage und Datenqualität: Methodische Reflexion zur quantitativen Erhebung während der Corona-Krise. In: Aschauer, W., Glatz, C., Prandner, D. (eds.) Die österreichische Gesellschaft während der Corona-Pandemie, pp. 325–347. Springer VS, Wiesbaden (2022). https://doi.org/10.1007/978-3-658-34491-7_12
11. Prandner, D., Wetzelhütter, D., Hese, S.: ChatGPT as a data analyst: an exploratory study on AI-supported quantitative data analysis in empirical research. In: Frontiers in Education, vol. 9. Frontiers Media SA (2025). https://doi.org/10.3389/feduc.2024.1417900
12. Sciences Po: Sciences Po bans the use of ChatGPT without transparent referencing (2023). https://newsroom.sciencespo.fr/sciences-po-bans-the-use-of-chatgpt
13. Smuha, N.A., et al.: How the EU can achieve legally trustworthy AI: A response to the European Commission's proposal for an Artificial Intelligence Act (2021)
14. Taeihagh, A.: Governance of generative AI. Policy Soc. **44**(1), 1–22 (2025)
15. Taeihagh, A., Ramesh, M., Howlett, M.: Assessing the regulatory challenges of emerging disruptive technologies. Regul. Gov. **15**(4), 1009–1019 (2021)
16. Wasielewski, A.: "Midjourney can't count": questions of representation and meaning for text-to-image generators (2023)
17. Zemsauer, A., Prandner, D.: Über die KI-Nutzungsintentionen von Studierenden: Einblicke in Anwendungsfelder und Erklärungsmöglichkeiten. JKM **17** (2025). https://doi.org/10.25598/JKM/2025-17.4

Privacy Merchants and Data Protection in the Age of Big Data and Artificial Intelligence

Domenico Talia$^{(\boxtimes)}$ (iD)

University of Calabria, Via P. Bucci 41C, 87036 Rende, Italy
`domenico.talia@unical.it`

Abstract. Digital technologies have revolutionized our society, and through the pervasive use of computers and digital devices the management of individual and collective information has been changed forever. A radical change has been generated by the growth in the importance of data. They are no longer just artifacts for information, communication and analysis, but fundamental economic and relational resources. In this scenario, it is essential to protect individual rights, without compromising innovation and the progress of society. This paper argues that data privacy must be a primary goal in developing and using digital systems and models and techniques must be developed to protect personal data and limit the access and selling of these data. This work discusses how the continuous collection and processing of massive personal data changed our society. This new condition asks for a balance between the protection of individual privacy and the need to use data for providing services to citizens in a global context increasingly dependent on digitalization. The key role of data brokers is discussed and a proposal for personal data protection is outlined.

Keywords: Big Data · artificial intelligence · privacy · data brokers · individual freedom

1 Big Data and Privacy: An Open Market

Talking about the privacy market means talking about personal data. Most data today is in digital format and is stored in our computers, personal portable devices, on the web or in the cloud centers. The term 'Big Data' was coined to denote the massive amounts of data being generated today, which raised both challenges for storage and processing and, at the same time, may be exploited to reveal hidden social trends, human behaviors, and personal preferences. We live in an era in which many industrial and commercial sectors make intensive use of personal data. This is not just data relating to economic information or similar, but also data that specifically concerns individuals and, often, entire communities [4].

In general, such data is used more frequently, especially in the private sector, in order to develop business and commercial strategies. In the public sector, however, governments and administrations collect enormous amounts of data about citizens in order to offer services. Although this may be useful at some extent, personal data is

L. Hagedorn et al. (Eds.): DIGHUM 2025, LNCS 16319, pp. 390–403, 2026.
https://doi.org/10.1007/978-3-032-11108-1_30

not always used appropriately; in fact, for example, sometimes it is used to implement control policies or manipulate citizens. Especially in democracies, where there are rules that should protect the use of data, this aspect becomes crucial.

Where adequate policies are lacking, privacy protection is often insufficient and data is exchanged, sold and used for unclear or even illegitimate purposes. In a general scenario like this, it happens very often that data is spied on or stolen. Recently, in several countries there have been cases in which data thieves have stolen huge amounts of personal information that have been used for economic purposes or with the aim of blackmailing "the real owners".

This is not always the case. In fact, sometimes the theft of data does not have a direct economic purpose, nevertheless, the freedom and privacy of citizens can suffer equally serious consequences from the theft and sale of their personal data. In democratic systems, it should be ensured that the huge amount of data collected does not conflict with the rights of the individuals mentioned above, even if this conflict often emerges.

The problems that drive and facilitate the advancement of this situation are the scarcity of laws and the limited sensitivity that citizens have on the matter. Awareness only manifests itself when one is involved when one is deprived of one's privacy. However, new laws, such as the EU General Data Protection Regulation (GDPR) [14], the Digital Services Act (DSA), Digital Market Act (DMA) and the AI Act, have been approved in EU to protect individuals and society [3].

The beginning of the massive production and circulation of personal data occurred with the birth of the web in the 90s of the last century. However, its explosion occurred in the last two decades of the new century. In particular, with the widespread use of social media, this phenomenon has undergone exponential growth [11].

Many times, it happens that, unknowingly, we 'sell' our data on the web, on social media or even via email, since they are the price we pay for the digital services that are offered to us. A clear example of these "buying and selling" systems is the one implemented by Alphabet. In fact, we use services such as the Google search engine, the Gmail service, YouTube or maps and in exchange we give Alphabet our personal data. The data collection system and the resulting economic benefit does not only concern the Meta company, but the many digital platforms that we use daily and to which we give our data when using their services.

The recent developments of artificial intelligence systems and applications are based on the use of Big Data. Thanks to the use of new classes of artificial intelligence and machine learning algorithms, extracting detailed and sophisticated information from user data is a very frequent activity in all commercial, industrial and scientific sectors.

However, this massive digital data market in which people are peripheral but fundamental players, thrives not only thanks to the complex algorithms that manage it, but also, as mentioned, due to citizens' unawareness of how data is collected, analyzed and used. In fact, people are not fully aware of the fact that every second personal data are collected from our devices and there are companies specialized in the collection and sale of personal data for commercial purposes, the so-called data brokers.

Data brokers are playing the role of "privacy merchants" because they treat personal data as a commodity, that is something to be bought and sold. They profit from the loss of individual privacy, since their business model depends on collecting, storing, and selling as much data as possible. The analysis strategies conducted by these companies allow not only to understand people's purchasing preferences and behaviors, but above all to manipulate them.

The simplest example to give in this context is that of online advertising, which is shown to us on the basis of the analysis of our behavior online and the preferences we express on websites and social media. All this feeds the huge market of buying and selling digital advertising that happens in real time while we use our digital devices.

This paper argues that data privacy must be a primary goal in developing and using digital systems and models and techniques must be developed to protect personal data and limit the access and selling of these data. The following sections discuss how the continuous collection and processing of massive personal data changed our society. This new condition asks for a balance between the protection of individual privacy and the need to use data for providing services to citizens in a global context increasingly dependent on digitalization. The key role of data brokers is discussed and a proposal for personal data protection is outlined.

1.1 Living in a Data-Rich Era

We are currently living in an era of extraordinary abundance of data. As shown in Fig. 1, the global amount of digital data is estimated to be between 150 and 200 zettabytes, and is set to grow exponentially, reaching hyperbolic dimensions by the middle of this century. This exponential growth of Big Data [11] represents a challenge for industry, business, science and beyond, even for politics and in general for the people governance.

So, we live in a new and vast market of data, where data is collected, traded, bought and, in most cases, sold through the network. But this scenario is not limited to the availability of data. What makes the market of the last decades extremely powerful is the combination of Big Data with artificial intelligence algorithms that are capable of extracting timely, detailed and accurate personal information [12].

Big companies operating in the information technology sector are those that, more than others, have full awareness of the great value of digital data and manage them as intangible assets of enormous value. In fact, once collected, they are never deleted, they are stored in clouds and data centers and are retrieved and used whenever necessary.

Large commercial chains have been collecting data regarding their customers' purchases for several decades and thus they build detailed archives of client commercial preferences, their behavior over time. This valuable information is used for advertising campaigns, for promotions or for evaluations of customer well-being that can also determine the interest of other entities such as banks and financial companies that want, for example, to measure their creditworthiness.

Perhaps the simplest case of collection and commercial use of personal data is through the use of loyalty cards in supermarkets that, in exchange for small prizes, allow them to collect our punctual purchase data. In this way, accurate profiles of people are built that can also be sold to third parties (banks, financial companies, health insurers, and advertising agencies) that use this rich information for different purposes, sometimes without consumers being aware of it.

The issue that causes the greatest concern is the loss of control over our data once they are given. We do not know who uses them, for what purposes and above all if and how

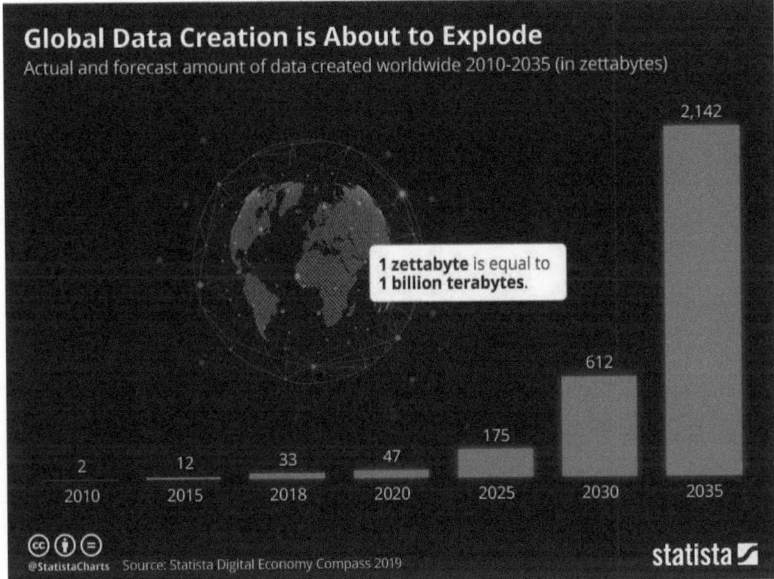

Fig. 1. The trend of data creation worldwide 2010–2035 in zettabyte. One zettabyte corresponds to 1 million petabytes (source: StatistaCharts).

they could be used against us. In fact, while on the one hand, data collection technologies can be useful for identifying attitudes or individuals with criminal tendencies, on the other hand, in contexts where privacy is not adequately protected, they can turn into real control tools. This opens up scenarios that are difficult to predict: behind the use of digital applications or social media platforms there are large companies that collect different types of data.

By analyzing data indicating where we connect from, machine learning algorithms used by several companies, are able to track our movements, know the time of our stay in a certain place and obtain detailed knowledge of our habits. This profiling process allows them to build a rich picture of individuals' behavior, which can be used in multiple contexts.

A recent case involved the theft of 533 million accounts. These included personal data such as emails, passwords, phone numbers and information regarding relationships and movements [10]. When cases of this scale occur, it is not a question of individual threats, but of a threat to the freedom and rights of entire communities. Hundred million people are traced, their online behavior reveal personal preferences and sentiment that can be exploited for marketing and political influence.

From Fig. 2 we can see how social platforms, such as Facebook and Instagram, collect respectively 79% and 57% of the personal data that users share. On the other hand, applications such as Uber, eBay, LinkedIn or Twitter generally accumulate percentages of personal data around 50% of global data they collect. The data in question includes our purchases, geographic location, contacts, but also advertising content and search history.

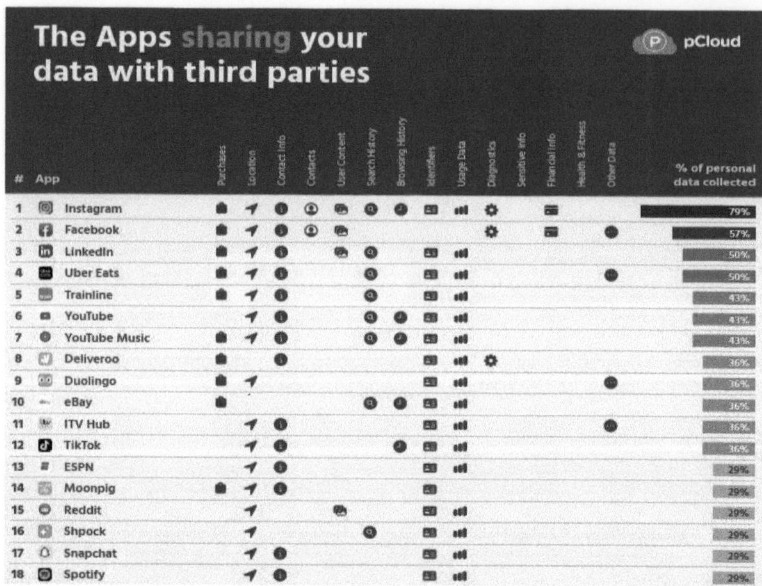

Fig. 2. Some apps that share users' personal data with third parties. (Source: https://www.pcloud.com/it/invasive-apps)

In democratic countries, possessing such a massive amount of data can influence democratic life, since those who own it have enormous power with effects that go far beyond simple commercial use.

When we talk about data theft, as in the case mentioned above, we are faced with serious crimes. Even in the presence of safeguard regulations such as the GDPR and the DSA in Europe, once data begins to circulate both in different organizations and in multiple nations, it becomes almost impossible to control it or block its use. This is an exclusive characteristic of digital data, since it can be copied and transferred infinite times, making the problem difficult to solve, unlike physical objects that can be seized.

Scenarios like this one pose great challenges for governments, since they must find effective ways to defend the personal data of each citizen and, more generally, protect the security of society.

2   Data Brokers and Our Privacy

Throughout the history of humanity, information has always been a precious asset and the role of individuals was defined on the basis of the information they possessed, received or produced. Today, this trend has brought us to the stage where we recognize ourselves in the data we generate. We are no longer perceived for who we really are, but for what the data we leave behind us as a trail, for what they say about us online [16].

For example, during a job interview, the evaluator interviewing us may already be aware of some information about our life thanks to data found on the web or on social media. This makes it almost impossible to hide aspects of our past or lie about our identity. In the past we used to send our CV and then went to the interview; instead, today we must be careful not to contradict the data that concerns us and leaks from the web. This exposure has also raised the debate on the right to be forgotten, because those who have made mistakes or been convicted in the past risk this information remaining visible for decades, if not forever.

As a significant example, we can mention a recent interview of cardinal Wilfrid Napier with the CNN [8] during the conclave that led to the election of Pope Leo XIV. Cardinal Napier with an inside knowledge of what it's like to select the new pope, declared that cardinals searched on Google and social media to get information about the other cardinals who were potential candidates. He stated that cardinals went into the conclave with a lot basic information coming from the web about each of the candidates. At the same time, he recognized that «On the negative side of that, there is some time that information on social media is slanted, and that could put you on the wrong tracks altogether.»

In April 2025, U.S. Citizenship and Immigration Services (USCIS) proposed collecting the social media handles of applicants for naturalization, permanent residence, and asylum, expanding a policy that currently only applies to non-immigrant and immigrant visa applicants. The Trump administration decided to scan the social media accounts of green card and citizenship applicants for "hostile attitudes" toward the U.S. or sympathy for terrorists. This US decision, which is in keeping with a global trend of increasing state surveillance of noncitizens, have consequences for the free expression and due process rights of a large population. What should lead us to a deep reflection is indeed the awareness of knowing that very often opinion on us and our evaluation depend on the online data about us and, above all, that information on our daily life can be accessed by anyone and also used against us.

Citizens have become major producers of data since the advent of the web in the 90s of the last century. Then, through the evolution of digital technologies and therefore passing through smartphones and social media; to generate new data, a simple search on Google is enough. When we carry our cell phone with us, we are tracked and this makes us not only the main producers of data, but also the main subjects of the analysis of such data. This data is then processed by learning and profiling algorithms, which provide a very detailed view of who we are.

Among the most important players in the data market are data brokers. They are private companies that collect, buy and sell data and information of any kind. Data brokers build their fortune on the ownership and processing capacity of massive amounts of data. In their activities, they do not limit themselves to selling raw data, but, thanks to these, they create complete profiles that can be used by banks, insurance companies, large commercial chains and organizations of various types. The data broker market is particularly developed in the United States, however worldwide there are over 4 thousand companies active in the sector, of which 1.4 thousand are market leaders (Fig. 3).

It is estimated that companies and organizations like CampaignGRID and ProPublica own 80% of the email addresses of American voters; therefore, they have access to an astonishing amount of information that can be used for political campaigns. Acxiom, one of the largest companies, owns 23 thousand servers and manages the data of over

500 million consumers, with an average of about 3 thousand detailed information for each of them. This gives companies an incredibly detailed knowledge of individuals.

The value of the global Data Broker market in 2024 was valued at USD 270.40 Bn in 2024 and is expected to reach USD 473.35 Bn by 2032, at a CAGR of 7.25%. The growth trend suggests that the data market could even surpass the oil market in terms of importance.

All this is part of a new paradigm called infonomics, or the information economy, in which information itself becomes an essential capital. Today, those who own information hold enormous economic power. The risk of living in such a scenario is that each individual is evaluated in terms of the information economy, in which, therefore, economic value is associated with the megabytes of data that concern the individual himself.

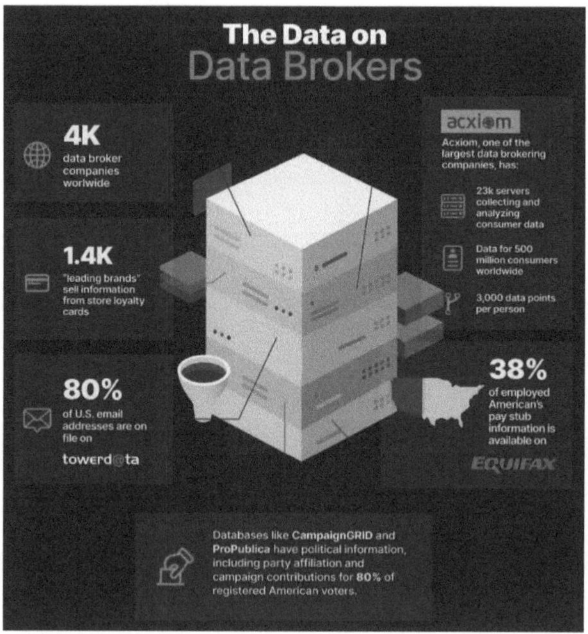

Fig. 3. The data broker industry around the world. (Source: https://www.openpr.com/news/269 3778/data-brokers-market-growth-analysis-by-product-application).

As already mentioned above, in the near future, the data market will be more important than the oil market, as paradoxical or incredible as it may seem. Data market is a concrete reality in which we are already immersed. For instance, from this market heavily depends the training of generative AI systems that need huge amount of data to learn how to appropriately reply to user requests. Unfortunately, there are cases where personal data are not appropriately protected. Recently, the higher regional court in Cologne decided that Meta, which owns Facebook and Instagram social media platforms, had not violated European Union law: «Meta is pursuing a legitimate end by using the data to train artificial intelligence systems», the court wrote in a decision statement. Feeding user data into Gemini was allowed «even without the consent of those affected … because the training of AI systems cannot be achieved by other equally effective, less intrusive means», the German court added. Judges believed the balance of interests between the parties was in favour of allowing Meta to process user data to develop AI.

The North Rhine-Westphalia Consumer Advice Centre, which brought the case, declared that «There are still considerable doubts about the legality,» and found the usage of personal data is "highly problematic". In response to the regional court decision, a possible injunction request or class-action lawsuit against Meta will be issued. This is a complex and evolving area, and the complete elimination of personal data from training sets for powerful AI models is a significant challenge.

Without a doubt, if we add to this everything that happens on the dark web with the illegal buying and selling of data, new scenarios and very delicate issues open up, which are above all difficult to regulate and solve.

As previously said, one of the key points is to be aware of the processing of our data and try, as much as possible, to exploit the available legal frameworks for limiting consent in order to avoid destroying the boundaries that protect our privacy. Analysts state that regulatory procedures restrain the data broker market globally. In fact, the introduction of stringent data protection laws, such as the GDPR in EU and the California Consumer Privacy Act (CCPA) in the United States, has amplified the compliance task of data brokers. This has resulted in higher operational costs and potential legal risks, thereby deterring the use of information owned by data brokers.

3   The Necessary Defense from Digital Manipulation

Among Elon Musk's many activities, there is also the startup Neuralink (neuralink.com), founded to make devices for treating brain diseases, with the ultimate goal of mental enhancement for humans. Musk created Neuralink with a team of researchers and engineers with the aim of providing digital solutions for those who have neurological problems, thus allowing them to control with their mind the computers they need to use.

Neuralink's devices demonstrate that data, today, can also be collected directly from our brain; therefore, our thoughts can become digital data. This seems to be one of the last frontiers. In fact, some nations and US states have begun to propose laws aimed at protecting neurological data, since the use of systems to support brain problems and pathologies intrinsically involves the collection of data regarding individuals' thoughts. It is clear, therefore, that we are in the presence of a very critical issue related to very personal data that can be collected and analyzed to go inside the human mind contents and processes.

Machine learning plays a crucial role in interpreting the complex signals from human neural data, like those recorded by Neuralink's brain-computer interfaces. These techniques are able to translate raw brain activity into meaningful insights. Neuralink's implants, with many electrodes, generate vast amounts of neural data. Machine learning algorithms, especially deep learning and pattern recognition can identify specific neural patterns associated with intentions, thoughts, or movements. This allows the system to decode signals for controlling external devices, such as computer cursors or robotic limbs. The analysis of human neural data with advanced machine learning techniques

[13] like those used by Neuralink, raises a range of significant and complex risk issues. These concerns extend beyond traditional data privacy to fundamental questions about human autonomy, identity, and societal control.

Analysis of neural data could be used to profile individuals based on their cognitive abilities, emotional states, or inclinations (e.g., for mental health conditions, future health risks). This could lead to discrimination in employment, insurance, housing, or even legal contexts. Marketers could exploit emotional responses for intrusive and manipulative advertising.

This kind of analytical activities on personal data may be conducted on massive data sets and may involve many citizens and results in a sort of "computable society". In this scenario, our thoughts can be collected, aggregated, evaluated, estimated and classified together with other events, like communications, posts, travels, and everything else we do online.

3.1 Data and AI for Profiling

As discussed, data analysis and machine learning algorithms are trained on large amounts of data, which in fact constitute their "experience". According to this approach a trained algorithm is able to start from many single specific cases and find the rules that are inherent in the analyzed data, therefore following an inductive reasoning. Based on the results of this analysis, a machine learning algorithm can suggest explanations on past facts and/or make predictions on future facts.

Historically, the first applicative uses were made by large IT companies such as Alphabet, Meta, Amazon, Microsoft and OpenAI, although the latter arrived later. All they do is observe our digital behaviors and try to understand what our preferences are, so that what is proposed to us will be based on those. The response is calibrated on what people have searched for previously, and therefore is based on the profile that the system itself has built with respect to the individuals who use it. This system of adapting algorithms to user preferences is used by various search engines such as Google, but obviously also by social media platforms, all aimed at showing us what we should like most, to keep us in front of the screens as much as possible. This means that Big Data and artificial intelligence algorithms are able to build accurate profiles of each of us.

From the moment we are profiled, given our interaction with digital systems, they are able to guide us, to make decisions for us and therefore to influence our choices, willingly or not, providing us with a certain type of information indirectly linked to the knowledge they have of us. It is clear that this process, for better or for worse, represents a practice of manipulation. And there is no doubt that all of it influences our daily lives.

An evident example is the social platform TikTok, one of the most famous but perhaps, from an algorithmic point of view, also one of the most aggressive. Those who use this application are manipulated, since its algorithm has a single goal: to maximize the time spent by users in front of videos, the so-called "video engagement". TikTok is based on short videos, and the goal is to keep people in front of the screen as much as possible while using the app.

Like other social platforms, TikTok does not care about what is shown to users, the platform is not interested in knowing the quality of the information it conveys, whether it is true or not, educational or completely the opposite. The only focus is on maximizing viewing time, simply because maximizing time means increasing the platform's profits.

The truth is a marginal goal, in fact it is probably not even marginal, since what is displayed can be true or not, can help or not, and the biggest problem is that education is not considered at all. These platforms are addictive, they are a sort of dope for the eyes of viewers because they try to keep them glued to the videos by proposing all those that according to the algorithm can arouse their interest. Since this is based on previous preferences, TikTok users are trapped in a "rabbit hole", meaning the place where algorithms keep users who use social platforms.

All this, obviously, generates misinformation and therefore, causes damage to people, to their social relationships, to their information heritage, in other words to their material and emotional well-being. This example is proof of how Big Data and machine learning, which are extremely powerful technologies and provide previously impossible solutions, can also be used for negative and harmful purposes.

3.2 The Role of GDPR in EU

To protect data, in the European Union, as mentioned, the GDPR and other regulations are in force to offer greater guarantees to EU citizens and certainly represent a step forward compared to those of other nations in which there is no culture of protection of these rights of citizens on their data.

Through the implementation of GDPR and DSA rules, we have the possibility that these platforms are controlled and therefore, that our rights are safeguarded. Nonetheless, the EU legislation has limits of action when, those who navigate the digital world consent to the processing of their data or more simply to the installation of cookies on their computer or smartphone.

In such cases, personal freedom becomes a problem, since it is the individuals who choose to be monitored and profiled. This calls for the need for knowledge and responsibility of individuals who must learn to protect themselves from invasive computer systems. A goal for the future remains, however, to find safer forms of laws, in such a way as to be able to protect the rights of people better and fully.

The need to protect personal data and its commercialization is also linked to the concept of ethical data processing and is connected to the need to educate people to pay attention to the careful use of digital systems and to understand the risks they run when they provide their personal data and consent to their processing [7]. Unlike the European case, in the United States there is no laws similar EU acts. The previous Biden administration had the intention of taking the direction of a federal regulation for data protection, however President Trump quickly blocked previous executive orders. Furthermore, in the US there is also the problem of limiting the power of data brokers, of which there are many in that nation. This issue is indeed a problem because the US politics tends to support and encourage private initiatives. However, the fact remains that citizens have begun to understand that the collection and processing of sensitive data can constitute a problem not only for them but also for the nation.

3.3 The Social Credit in China

If we consider the Chinese scenario, the situation is completely different. China is led by the Communist Party and naturally tends to adapt the use of digital technologies to its political and government system.

For example, the so-called "social credit system" has been implemented for several years now [15], based on the large collection of data regarding citizens, on their profiling and classification through machine learning algorithms. In short, the social credit system is a scheme that associates a social credit to each citizen based on the correct behaviors they have held.

A system of this kind obviously has a significant impact on citizens. Just think that those who have not paid off a debt will see their social credit decrease and consequently will be deprived of some personal rights such as the possibility of moving from one city to another, booking a hotel or taking a flight.

Considering these and other uses, the fact remains that machine learning systems are able to quickly analyze large amounts of data and only if these are correct and objective, can they produce useful and correct results. Otherwise, by providing algorithms with inaccurate, unbalanced data containing fake news, incorrect results will be produced, with subsequent inappropriate profiling and inaccurate predictions, generating disinformation, discrimination and manipulation of people.

There is now a rich case history of problems due to violations of privacy and the use of incorrect data that warns against the use of invasive and dangerous analysis techniques, since data biases, incorrect and unbalanced data, negatively influence the results of the analyses.

In short, it is essential to respect the privacy rights of citizens and their data. Furthermore, in legitimate cases it is necessary to use correct and clean data. This requires exercising an ethics of data usage, as well as an ethics in the use of artificial intelligence systems. Companies, professionals, and users must act to use algorithms on appropriate data, thus limiting the onset of damage for citizens, communities and society as a whole. Not neglecting technical problems such as the explainability of algorithms and the responsibility of those who produce them.

4 Towards a Framework for People-Centric Data Protection

To overcome data privacy problems, changing the perspective of personal data management towards a user-centric model for personal data supervision is needed, as suggested also by the World Economic Forum [6, 9]. According to this approach, citizens acquire a central influence, and gain an active role and a full control on their own personal data. To achieve this, it must be introduced full transparency regarding access and use of personal data [1], so enabling individuals to control storage and access of their data and giving them the right to share data, with the preferred privacy level. In this new personal data model, the privacy-based transformation should be performed before data leave the owner [5]. Then, appropriate data technologies must be exploited to enable data access/exchange respecting the prerequisites of involved citizens and preserving the valuable content of the data. As discussed in [5], the main advantages of developing and using personal data management solutions are as follows: (a) empowering individuals with the ability to collect, analyze, manage, and share their own data with others, (b) the capability for them to increase the level of safety by deciding what, who, and when their personal data can be shared, and (c) providing the tools that may enable individuals to analyze their personal data and gain insights about themselves. On the other hand, some disadvantages to be considered in implementing personal data solutions are: (a) an increasing responsibility of individuals to manage and control their data, particularly for those who are not technically skilled, and (b) a more complex management of secure access to personal data from remote places, that is from anywhere and anytime.

A methodology to implement a people-centric model is the Personal Data Repository (PDR). This is a data space, where users can store and access their personal data, which works as a negotiator between a person and the external services that need their data, allowing the user to control the flow of the data and manage authorizations for third-party.

According to this model, computations on personal data must be authorized by the owner and are under her/his complete control. The idea is that only the minimal allowed data for providing functionality to the applications should leave the boundaries of the user's PDR. For example, rather than exporting detailed georeferenced data, it could be sufficient to inform an application if we are moving and/or in which geographic area we are in.

A PDR platform collecting different types of data is able to provide individuals a global view about their life providing to her/him the opportunity to know about her/his behaviors by analyzing their own raw data coming from various sources. Therefore, a PDR platform must provide the opportunity to extract interesting knowledge from data that the user may use for increasing her/his self-awareness but also for obtaining services from some providers. This awareness is key feature that could help individuals to improve their own quality of life. To this end, a PDR platform can be enriched with data analysis services able to extract useful knowledge at individual level that is managed by the owner, not by companies, data brokers or governments [2].

5   Conclusions

The opportunities offered by digital technologies are extraordinary, but they bring with them significant risks that cannot be ignored. The world we live in today is characterized by a constant collection of large amounts of data that is radically transforming the concept of privacy and individual freedom. Protecting data and ensuring the ethical use of information is essential to prevent citizens' privacy from being compromised and to prevent the enormous power of technology companies from threatening the fundamental rights of individuals.

We are witnessing a radical change in society, in which individuals, who were previously passive subjects of information, have become the main producers of the data that fuel the digital market. Every action taken, every shared information or purchase made, contribute to the creation of a digital profile of people that can potentially be used against the individuals themselves, with the aim of manipulating them.

A global commitment is needed to ensure that the collection and use of personal data is carried out responsibly, in compliance with collective security and individual rights. The future of society will depend on the ability to find a balance between freedom and organization, and therefore between privacy and technological progress, always maintaining great attention to individual and collective rights.

The most worrying aspect is that, while there is greater exposure, there is still a lack of awareness of the value of the data generated by citizens and collected by data brokers. Citizens and governments often fail to realize that data is not only used for marketing and economic purposes, but also to influence politics, spread disinformation and therefore manipulate public opinion, sometimes risking compromising national security.

This scenario forces us to reflect on the task of being digital citizens: how can privacy be protected, and, at the same time, freedom preserved, in a world where every action is tracked and analyzed by algorithms? While on the one hand technologies offer new opportunities, on the other they expose society to new risks, some of which are still difficult to fully predict. Acquiring awareness and knowledge is the first step to controlling what happens to the information produced.

We must ask ourselves whether it is possible to continue living in a free society when most of the personal data is managed by a few large companies, very often not very transparent. It is therefore of vital importance for the whole society to limit the use of data for economic purposes and guarantee the protection of data together with the fundamental rights of individuals.

Acknowledgments. This study was partially funded by the PNRR MUR project PE0000013-FAIR - CUP H23C22000860006.

Disclosure of Interests.   The author has no competing interests to declare that are relevant to the content of this paper.

References

1. Bhajaria, N.: Data Privacy: A Runbook for Engineers. O'Reilly Media, Santa Rosa (2022)
2. Binder, M.: What is Palantir? The secretive tech company behind Trump's data collection efforts. Mashable (2025). https://mashable.com/article/what-is-palantir-trump-data-collection-database. Accessed 07 June 2025
3. Butt, J.: The general data protection regulation of 2016 (GDPR) meets its sibling the artificial intelligence act of 2024: a power couple, or a clash of titans? Acta Universitatis Danubius. Juridica **20**(2), 7–52 (2024)
4. Cifardi, G.: Evolution of concepts of privacy and personal data protection under the influence of information technology development. Sociol. Soc. Work Rev. **7**(1), 35–60 (2023)
5. Fallatah, K.U., Barhamgi, M., Perera, C.: Personal data stores (PDS): a review. Sensors **23**(3), 1477 (2023)
6. Jacobson, J.: The impact of privacy-enhancing technologies (PETs) on business, individuals and society. World Economic Forum (2023). Accessed 07 June 2025
7. Lee, W.W., Zankl, W., Chang, H.: An ethical approach to data privacy protection. Isaca J. **6**, (2016)
8. Mwaura, W.: Conclave 'insider' opens up about pope election process. CNN Africa (2025). www.youtube.com/watch?v=T5Mf_rELr_k. Accessed 07 June 2025
9. OECD. Emerging privacy enhancing technologies: Current regulatory and Policy approaches **351** (2023)

10. Paul, K.: Facebook says a breach that hit 533m is old news. Experts disagree. The Guardian, London (2021). www.theguardian.com/technology/2021/apr/06/facebook-breach-data-leak. Accessed 06 June 2025
11. Talia, D.: Big Data and the Computable Society. World Scientific Press, London (2019)
12. Talia, D.: L'impero dell'algoritmo. Rubbettino, Soveria Mannelli (2021). (in Italian)
13. Talia, D.: From Algorithms to Thinking Machines: The New Digital Power. Association for Computing Machinery, New York (2023)
14. Tony Ke, T., Sudhir, K.: Privacy rights and data security: GDPR and personal data markets. Manage. Sci. **69**(8), 4363–4971 (2023)
15. Turha, K., Vrhovec, S., Bernik, I.: State surveillance in the digital age: factors associated with citizens' attitudes towards trust registers. arXiv:2408.09725 (2024)
16. Werthner, H., Prem, E., Lee, E.A., Ghezzi, C. (eds.): Perspectives on Digital Humanism. Springer, Switzerlandss (2022)

Breaking Disciplinary Silos: Digital Humanism Across Disciplines

Reclaiming Agency Through Cyber Humanism: A European Agenda for AI, Education and Culture

Giovanni Adorni[1]([✉])([iD]), Emanuele Bellini[2]([iD]), and Ilaria Torre[1]([iD])

[1] DIBRIS, University of Genoa, 13 Viale F.Causa, 16145 Genoa, Italy
{giovanni.adorni,ilaria.torre}@unige.it
[2] DH, University of Roma Tre, 234 Via Ostiense, 00154 Rome, Italy
emanuele.bellini@uniroma3.it

Abstract. *Cyber Humanism* is proposed as an evolution of Digital Humanism, repositioning the humanities as active agents in shaping knowledge, meaning, and agency in algorithmic societies. Rather than positioning humanists as external critics, it frames them as epistemic co-designers, actively embedding reflexivity, cultural pluralism, and civic values into the architectures of intelligent systems.

This paper addresses the challenges posed by generative AI and data-driven infrastructures, arguing that ethical critique alone is insufficient. What is required is a systemic transformation encompassing education, governance, and culture.

Cyber Humanism shifts the focus from protection to participation, from reactive ethics to dialogic, value-aligned design, emphasizing co-agency between human and algorithmic actors.

Building on the *Cyber Humanities Manifesto* and aligned with European frameworks such as the *AI Act, DigComp 3.0*, and the *Declaration on Digital Rights*, the paper develops this paradigm across three strategic dimensions: (1) Reframing digital competence through cognitive sovereignty and reflexive agency; (2) Redesigning curricula and institutions as democratic infrastructures for human—AI co-authorship; (3) Operationalizing normative principles through participatory governance and cultural experimentation.

The concept of *algorithmic citizenship* anchors this vision: a civic competence to critically engage with, co-govern, and reimagine the epistemic infrastructures of AI.

The paper concludes by arguing that Europe is uniquely positioned to lead this transition by fostering a culture of *dialogic design* and *epistemic co-authorship*, in which intelligent systems are shaped deliberately, collectively, and with critical care.

Keywords: Cyber Humanism · Algorithmic Citizenship · AI Literacy · Cognitive Sovereignty · Dialogic Design

L. Hagedorn et al. (Eds.): DIGHUM 2025, LNCS 16319, pp. 407–420, 2026.
https://doi.org/10.1007/978-3-032-11108-1_31

1   Introduction

The rapid proliferation of generative AI (GenAI), from ChatGPT's textual outputs to TikTok's cultural curation, has reshaped not only how we access information, but how we learn, remember, and think. These systems are not neutral intermediaries: they filter perception, prioritize content, and restructure epistemic authority [10]. Increasingly, they act as infrastructures of cognition, mediating how knowledge is produced, legitimized, and internalized. Faced with this tran-sformation, scholars and educators can no longer rely on reactive critique. They must become co-designers of the systems that shape meaning, agency, and memory [1].

Digital Humanism emerged as a foundational response to these challenges, highlighting not only the risks of extractivism, opacity, and centralized control, but also advancing a constructive vision of human—AI co-agency through democratic deliberation and pluralistic design principles [19]. Recent elaborations further emphasise entanglement and shared agency as central tenets of Digital Humanism, positioning humans and machines as interdependent epistemic actors (see, for example, [23, 24]).

Cyber Humanism builds on this foundation, but advances a further step: it repositions education, culture, and civic space as active sites of epistemic co-authorship. Rather than shielding humanity from AI, it seeks to empower individuals and institutions *with and through* AI—embedding reflexivity, pluralism, and democratic values into the architectures of intelligent systems.

In this framework, the humanities are no longer passive commentators but **infrastructural agents**: curating collective memory, exposing algorithmic bias [16], designing for interpretive depth [12], and sustaining cultural diversity against epistemic reductionism [15]. Emerging empirical research confirms the urgency of this shift: excessive reliance on automated systems diminishes metacognitive engagement, narrows attention, and weakens judgment autonomy [11, 12].

Addressing these risks requires more than digital skills: it calls for a cultural and educational transformation. GenAI is not just a technological disruptor; it is a pedagogical and civic challenge. What is at stake is not simply how we use AI, but who gets to shape the systems that shape us.

This paper develops the paradigm of *Cyber Humanism* across three interconnected dimensions:

1. retracing the conceptual shift from digital humanities to participatory, co-creative epistemologies;
2. articulating an educational framework grounded in reflexivity, cognitive sovereignty, and algorithmic literacy;
3. proposing policy strategies that translate normative visions into institutional design and civic experimentation.

Framed within Europe's evolving regulatory ecosystem, including the *AI Act* [7], *DigComp 3.0* [5], and the *reference documents on Digital Rights* [6,9], this paper argues that educational and cultural infrastructures can support a dialogic design paradigm, in which technological systems are co-authored by citizens and institutions. GLAM institutions (Galleries, Libraries, Archives, and Museums), schools, universities, and civic labs must become engines of co-design—spaces where epistemic architectures are debated, redesigned, and shared.

This vision carries both ethical and geopolitical implications. In a global race to define AI norms, Europe can lead not through technological supremacy, but through deliberative infrastructure, embedding human values at the core of AI systems. Cyber Humanism reclaims the future of AI as a civic and cultural project, shaped not by market logics or abstract principles, but through participatory authorship and dialogic imagination.

2 Foundations of the Cyber Humanism

The evolution from *Digital Humanities* to *Cyber Humanism* reflects a growing recognition of the epistemic, ethical, and political roles played by computational systems in shaping knowledge. These shifts demand new conceptual tools, not only to critique technological development, but to distinguish between functional use and civic co-authorship [1,19].

Digital Humanities. (DH) initially centered on digitization, corpus curation, and the application of digital tools to enhance traditional humanistic research. This phase, often referred to as DH 1.0 [3], was largely instrumental, treating technology as an external aid. A second phase (DH 2.0) introduced interdisciplinary collaboration, critical inquiry, hybrid methods and design-based metho-dologies, acknowledging the epistemic implications of digital infrastructures themselves. In parallel, *Digital Humanism* (DgH) emerged as a normative response to growing concerns about extractivism, opacity, bias, and democratic erosion. It called for the ethical alignment of AI systems with human values, emphasizing transparency, justice, and civic responsibility [19,23,24].

Cyber Humanism builds upon these foundations but introduces a further conceptual shift: it no longer treats AI systems as mere tools or objects of oversight, but as **epistemic infrastructures**, assemblages that modulate perception, filter meaning, and mediate both cognitive and civic agency [10,20]. In this view, humanists are not external commentators but active *infrastructural agents*, engaged in the co-design of meaning-making systems.

The term *Cyber Humanities*, while still used in some contexts to denote the design turn within DH, is here conceptually integrated into Cyber Huma-nism. Rather than representing a distinct stage, it signals the recognition of the humanities as co-creators of the infrastructures through which knowledge, me-mory, and agency are configured [21], building on the philosophical foundations of Digital Humanism that emphasize civic agency, pluralism, and epistemic responsibility [25] (see Table 1). In this sense, cultural institutions such as archives, museums, libraries, and media labs (GLAM) are not peripheral—they are central arenas for algorithmic design, public deliberation, and epistemic pluralism.

Table 1. From Humanities to Cyber Humanism: A Conceptual Evolution

Paradigm	Focus	Epistemic Role
Humanities	Interpretation, critique, expression, cultural memory, creativity	Human-centered inquiry
Humanism	Human dignity, ethics, agency	Philosophical and civic grounding
Digital Humanities	Digitization and tool use (DH 1.0); hybrid, critical, design-based methods (DH 2.0)	Expansion and critique of research practices
Digital Humanism	Normative response to AI risks; transparency and human values	Ethical alignment of technology with democratic principles
Cyber Humanities	Cognitive infrastructures and cognitive artefacts	Integrated within Cyber Humanism: Human—AI collaboration
Cyber Humanism	Reflexive, pluralistic, and participatory co-creation of AI systems & infrastructure	Humanists as epistemic and infrastructural agents

Cyber Humanism emerges in response to a deeper transformation: in algorithmic societies, AI systems shape how we remember, judge, and decide [11,12]. The boundary between human cognition and machine inference becomes porous, recursive, and increasingly co-dependent [18].

This paradigm is grounded in three core principles:

1. **Reflexivity:** the capacity to interrogate and reshape how AI systems encode assumptions, power structures, and knowledge regimes [10,16];
2. **Pluralism:** the commitment to sustaining interpretive and cultural diversity within digital environments [2];
3. **Co-design:** the active embedding of humanistic agency into the logics, structures, and values of intelligent systems [1,20].

Unlike certain strands of Digital Humanism that emphasize distance or protection from AI, Cyber Humanism foregrounds collaboration *with and through* AI. It reframes education, research, and cultural institutions as arenas of civic authorship and epistemic experimentation. In this expanded role, the humanities contribute not only to critique, but to the design of the cognitive infrastructures that sustain democratic life.

3   Cognitive Ecologies and Humanistic Co-design

In algorithmic societies, epistemic authority is no longer confined to traditional institutions such as universities, media, or governments. Instead, it emerges from dynamic interactions between human actors and machine agents operating within evolving cognitive infrastructures [1]. These infrastructures—search engines, recommendation systems, classification algorithms—do more than process information: they filter, rank, and prioritize content, thereby shaping attention, memory, and legitimacy [16,20].

These systems are far from neutral. They generate epistemic asymmetries by privileging certain narratives while obscuring others, often through opaque me-chanisms that escape public scrutiny. The logics embedded in their architectures (ontologies, interfaces, ranking algorithms) determine not only what is visible, but what is considered knowable. Engaging with and reshaping these logics requires capacities for critique, interpretation, and speculative design, competences deeply rooted in the humanistic tradition.

Cyber Humanism responds to this transformation by reconceptualizing digital infrastructures as both **epistemic and cultural artifacts**. Their architectures encode normative choices: which voices are amplified, which classifications are enacted, and which worldviews are rendered intelligible or actionable [10]. These infrastructures are not passive backgrounds to cognition—they are *world-making systems* that actively shape how meaning is constructed, circulated, and contested.

Yet critique alone is not enough. As AI systems become embedded in education, cultural heritage, and civic discourse, there is an urgent need for frameworks that enable humanistic *engagement*—through design, participation, and infrastructural experimentation.

What is Cyber Humanism?
Cyber Humanism is an emerging paradigm that places humanistic knowledge at the heart of algorithmic design. It treats intelligent systems not as external tools, but as *co-produced epistemic infrastructures*, shaped by reflexivity, pluralism, and civic imagination. It redefines education, culture, and governance as spaces for the democratic negotiation of meaning and agency.

Within this paradigm, the humanities reclaim a central role: not as external observers, but as **infrastructural agents**. Through algorithmic audits, civic epistemology labs, and interpretive visualizations, humanists interrogate dominant classification schemes, historicize ontological assumptions, and co-design plural alternatives [1,23].

This role is especially evident in GLAM institutions (Galleries, Libraries, Archives, and Museums) which already function as civic infrastructures of memory and knowledge. Their curatorial practices, archival metadata, and public engagement strategies increasingly intersect with AI systems: from generative cataloguing to algorithmic exhibition curation. In a cyber-humanist perspective, GLAM institutions become experimental spaces for rethinking how knowledge is classified, accessed, and contextualized—spaces where epistemic justice and cultural pluralism can be prototyped [26].

Across Europe and beyond, pioneering initiatives are exploring these directions: "generous interfaces", AI-generated metadata visualizations, and participatory recommender systems exemplify new forms of engagement that prioritize interpretation over efficiency, and dialogue over optimization.

This shift calls for a move beyond interdisciplinarity toward what we define as **transdisciplinary convergence**—collaborative ecosystems that bring together philosophers and data scientists, educators and designers, humanists and engineers. These communities work not only to ensure technical functiona-lity, but to embed intelligibility, accountability, and pluralism into the epistemic architectures of AI.

We describe these hybrid environments as **digital agorae**: experimental knowledge ecologies where competing epistemologies are surfaced, negotiated, and reimagined [20]. In these spaces, human and algorithmic agents co-construct meaning, prototype civic alternatives, and challenge dominant logics of classification and control.

Two foundational capacities sustain these ecologies and define the cyber-humanist approach:

- **Algorithmic reflexivity:**the capacity to interrogate how algorithms shape cognition, embed assumptions, and distribute visibility. This requires not only technical transparency, but also public arenas for deliberation, design, and critique [1,16].
- **Cognitive sustainability:**the ability to preserve attention, autonomy, and judgment within AI-mediated environments. Design must support human—AI complementarity while resisting forms of automation that erode agency or flatten interpretive nuance [12,18].

These are not aspirational ideals—they are **operational conditions** for any democratic epistemic infrastructure. While reflexivity guards against reductionism and instrumental logic, sustainability preserves the space for ambiguity, dissent, and depth.

Ultimately, *Cyber Humanism* advances a vision of intelligent infrastructures as **civic spaces of deliberation**, capable of sustaining interpretive diversity, participatory design, and plural epistemologies. In this framework, the humanities are not peripheral—they are infrastructural, actively shaping how knowledge, memory, and agency are encoded into the sociotechnical systems of the algorithmic age [2].

4   Algorithmic Citizenship and Epistemic Agency

In algorithmic societies, citizenship can no longer be defined solely by legal status, connectivity, or basic digital skills. As automated systems increasingly mediate access to knowledge, public services, and social participation, civic agency becomes entangled with the design and governance of algorithmic infrastructures [4,22]. These infrastructures are not neutral: they shape what is visible, what is said, and what is valued. This transformation calls for a redefinition: *algorithmic citizenship*, understood as the capacity to critically engage with and co-shape the epistemic systems that organize perception, decision-making, and interaction. *Algorithmic citizenship* goes beyond traditional models of digital inclusion. It links civic agency to three interdependent capacities:

- o **Infrastructural literacy:**the ability to interpret and navigate algorithmic environments, understanding how data architectures, recommendation systems, and AI models structure meaning and behavior;
- o **Participatory agency:**the right and capacity to influence these systems through design, governance, and contestation;
- o **Recursive accountability:**the presence of institutional mechanisms that enable ongoing revision, public scrutiny, and civic redress [6].

Together, these capacities reframe citizens not as passive users or consumers, but as *co-authors* of sociotechnical systems. They also establish the foundation for a broader principle: **epistemic sovereignty**, the right to shape one's informational environment and to participate in designing the architectures that regulate memory, attention, and belief.

Unlike data sovereignty, which focuses on ownership and control over personal information, or digital sovereignty, which emphasizes state control over infrastructure, *epistemic sovereignty* foregrounds the capacity of individuals and communities to determine the conditions under which knowledge is produced, accessed, and validated. It is not merely a right to protection, it is a right to authorship, and a foundational element of civic life in the algorithmic age.

Cyber Humanism deepens this agenda by embedding epistemic authorship into education, governance, and cultural institutions. It reframes digital competence not as functional adaptation, but as reflexive, ethical, and infrastructural co-design [1,20]. Citizens are empowered not just to use AI, but to question its assumptions, critique its effects, and actively participate in shaping its evolution.

European frameworks increasingly reflect this vision. The AI Act mandates transparency and human oversight in automated decision-making [7]. The Declaration on Digital Rights enshrines cognitive integrity and informational self-determination as democratic principles [6]. DigComp 3.0 links digital competence to ethical reflection, civic participation, and democratic values [5].

Yet algorithmic agency cannot emerge from individual competence alone. It requires enabling ecosystems: reflexive education, civic technologies, participatory design labs, and cultural institutions that function as infrastructures of deliberation. GLAM institutions, for instance, increasingly serve as spaces where citizens interrogate classification systems, explore algorithmic representations, and co-create epistemic alternatives. They act as public gateways to algorithmic literacy, cultural memory, and democratic imagination.

In this light, *algorithmic citizenship* is not a metaphor, it is a political imperative. It affirms the humanities as key actors in designing the epistemic infrastructures of democracy, and positions citizens as reflexive participants in the negotiation of truth, visibility, and meaning. Far from being a niche concern, it is central to safeguarding agency, pluralism, and justice in the algorithmic age.

5   Reflexive Competence and Algorithmic Education

Digital competence has long been framed as a strategic priority in educational policy. However, the rise of generative AI, capable of simulating reasoning, language, and decision-making, renders skill-based approaches rooted in procedural mastery increasingly insufficient [11,15]. These systems do not merely support communication; they actively shape perception, attention, memory, and epistemic authority [10].

Human—AI interaction is not linear, it is recursive and transformative. It alters how individuals learn, evaluate, and act within digital environments. Empirical research confirms that uncritical reliance on automated outputs can weaken metacognitive engagement, reduce deliberative judgment, and foster passive consumption of machine-generated narratives [12,13,18]. The risk is not limited to misinformation, it includes the erosion of epistemic agency.

Addressing these risks requires more than technical upskilling or digital awareness. *Cyber Humanism* calls for a deeper pedagogical and cultural shift: from functional literacy to **reflexive competence**, grounded in cognitive sovereignty, ethical imagination, and infrastructural insight. Competence, in this view, is not simply the ability to use AI, but the capacity to interrogate and reconfigure the sociotechnical systems through which knowledge is produced and meaning is negotiated.

Three educational capacities anchor this transformation:

○ **Algorithmic reflexivity:**the ability to uncover and question how algorithms encode assumptions, mediate judgment, and reinforce normative frames [20];
○ **Ethics-by-design:**the competence to embed normative principles—such as fairness, accountability, transparency, and pluralism—into the design and governance of AI systems [7];
○ **Cognitive infrastructure literacy:**the insight to understand how digital platforms, interfaces, and recommendation logics regulate attention, filter meaning, and modulate agency [4,16].

These are not isolated skills, but socially situated capacities that require enabling environments. Reflexive classrooms, interdisciplinary curricula, and participatory design labs must become the new civic infrastructures for democratic AI education [6,22]. Teachers play a central role in this shift, not only as facilitators of content, but as **ethical arbiters**, **cognitive designers** and **cultural stewards** who mediate between students and systems, supporting situated reasoning and plural epistemologies.

This expanded vision reframes education not as adaptation to technological change, but as the **design of cultural infrastructures** where democratic imagination and critical agency are actively cultivated. Algorithmic systems must be treated not only as objects of literacy, but as epistemic architectures to be questioned, revised, and collectively reimagined.

In this perspective, *reflexive competence* becomes the foundation of a broader civic capacity: **algorithmic citizenship**. It is no longer sufficient to understand how AI works; students must also develop the capacity to question its purposes, resist its reductive logics, and envision alternative futures. Competence becomes civic, dialogic, and epistemic [2,18].

To support this, learners must acquire not only technical fluency but also:

◇ **Dialogic reasoning**: the ability to engage in interpretive negotiation, sustain ambiguity, and embrace epistemic diversity [2];

◇ **Situated judgment**: the capacity to navigate ethical dilemmas, contextual uncertainties, and normative tensions [10];

◇ **Collaborative imagination**: the creative skill to co-design technological futures aligned with human dignity, democratic values, and ecological sustainability [1].

This orientation is increasingly reflected in policy. The AI Act and the Digital Rights Declaration foreground principles such as mental integrity, transparency, and informational autonomy [6,7]. The updated DigComp 3.0 framework introduces civic engagement and ethical awareness as integral components of digital competence [5].

Yet meaningful transformation depends not only on regulation, but on pedagogy. Reflexive competence must be cultivated in lived contexts, through curricular innovation, teacher training, and democratic institutional design. This requires a renewed epistemic contract: one that positions education as a site of **epistemic justice**, civic empowerment, and infrastructural imagination. In this view, the classroom becomes a **civic laboratory**, a protected yet porous space where students can experiment with ideas, prototype values, and rehearse co-authorship of AI systems. Here, *cognitive sovereignty* is not an abstract right, but a lived practice: the ongoing ability to make sense, make decisions, and make a difference in a world increasingly shaped by algorithms.

6   Education and Policy for the Algorithmic Age

As AI systems increasingly shape how knowledge is produced, accessed, and internalized, education finds itself at the heart of a profound epistemic and civic transformation [11,18]. Algorithms no longer simply mediate communication or support learning, they influence how we pay attention, how we remember, and how we judge what is true. In this emerging cognitive landscape, education cannot remain a neutral transmitter of content. It must become an active site of resistance, reimagination, and infrastructural design.

Cyber Humanism responds to this challenge by redefining education as a form of **democratic infrastructure**, a civic space where individuals can reclaim agency, engage in co-design with AI, and cultivate reflexive capacities that resist epistemic automation [1,22]. Within this paradigm, schools and universities are not passive adopters of EdTech platforms, but laboratories of epistemic experimentation, where students and educators collaborate to shape the very systems that mediate knowledge and cultural meaning.

To support this transformation, three institutional dimensions must converge: curriculum, pedagogy, and governance.

- First, **curricula** must move beyond technical proficiency to address the political, ethical, and cultural dimensions of AI. Algorithmic literacy should be embedded within broader frameworks of critical reasoning, epistemic pluralism, and participatory design. Activities such as case-based inquiries into bias and opacity, algorithmic audits, prompt-based co-creation, and decolonial critiques of data infrastructures help students confront the values, assumptions, and exclusions embedded in intelligent systems.
- Second, **pedagogies** must foster dialogic, exploratory, and hybrid learning environments. Interaction with GenAI can serve as a powerful catalyst for learning, when critically structured. Educators play a pivotal role: not merely as content facilitators, but as **ethical arbiters** who interrogate platform logics [16], **cognitive designers** who scaffold meaningful human—AI interaction [13], and **cultural stewards** who protect epistemic diversity from the reductive logics of automation [10]. Reflexive classrooms must become spaces where ambiguity is explored, dissent is sustained, and alternative narratives are imagined.
- Third, **institutional governance** must enable inclusive, participatory, and experimental practices. Universities and schools must evolve into **prototyping spaces** for civic AI: places where learners, faculty, and communities collaborate to develop value-aligned infrastructures. This entails professional development in ethics, design, and reflexivity [14]; governance models that embed student and civic participation [6,7]; and investment in sandbox environments, living labs, and interpretive co-design studios [19].

This vision is increasingly reflected in European policy frameworks. The *AI Act* calls for transparency, human oversight, and contestability in algorithmic decision-making [7]. The *Digital Rights Declaration* foregrounds cognitive sovereignty and epistemic justice as democratic principles [6]. *DigCompEdu* promotes ethical competence and educator agency across digital contexts [17]. *Horizon Europe* supports civic innovation through co-creation platforms, interdisciplinary networks, and research into inclusive digital transformation.

Yet translating these frameworks into lived educational practice requires a paradigmatic shift, from adaptation to authorship, from literacy to co-creation. *Cyber Humanism* calls for education that empowers individuals not only to navigate existing AI systems, but to shape their logics, values, and imaginaries. It advances an agenda of **reflexive imagination, epistemic resilience**, and **technological co-agency**, capacities essential for sustaining democratic life in algorithmic societies.

The goal is not to produce compliant or efficient AI users. It is to cultivate *technological citizens*: individuals capable of deliberating, designing, and co-authoring the infrastructures that mediate their knowledge, culture, and futures. As the *Cyber Humanities Manifesto* affirms, intelligent systems must not define human purposes, they must be co-designed to serve them [1]. In this light, education becomes a cultural infrastructure of democracy. The classroom is reimagined as a civic incubator, where epistemic justice is not only taught, but enacted, where learners rehearse the values, tools, and practices that will shape the algorithmic societies of tomorrow.

7   Conclusions and Call to Action

Today's algorithms do not merely automate tasks, they shape the conditions of thought. As infrastructures of cognition, they influence how knowledge is produced, how attention is distributed, and how agency is exercised. In this landscape, ethical principles and digital skills remain necessary, but they are no longer sufficient. What is required is a systemic redefinition of how societies learn, govern, and co-design their algorithmic futures.

Cyber Humanism offers a transformative framework. It shifts the focus from protection to empowermente, quipping individuals and institutions not only to respond to AI, but to actively shape its architectures, values, and uses. In this paradigm, humanistic knowledge becomes infrastructural: it does not merely interpret the world, but co-authors the systems through which meaning is filtered and memory is governed.

Europe is uniquely positioned to lead this transition. The *AI Act* [7], the *Digital Rights Declaration* [6] *DigComp 3.0* [5], and the *GPAI Code of Conduct* [8] provide a robust normative ecosystem for aligning technological development with democratic principles.

To translate this ecosystem into lived practice, four strategic levers must be activated:

1. **Education:**Shift from technical proficiency to *epistemic agency*, embedding reflexive competence, plural epistemologies, and co-design practices into curricula, pedagogy, and assessment.
2. **Research:**Break disciplinary silos through shared epistemic frameworks, collaborative experimentation, and evaluation criteria grounded in democratic impact, inclusivity, and epistemic justice.
3. **Policy:**Institutionalize humanistic oversight within AI governance, support participatory infrastructures, and ensure that civic engagement is a structural principle, not a procedural afterthought.
4. **Culture:**Reimagine GLAM institutions, educational systems, and media platforms as *cognitive commons*: shared spaces that preserve interpretive diversity, collective memory, and democratic sense-making.

These are not abstract aspirations. Across Europe, scalable prototypes already exist: algorithmic literacy programs, student-led audits, museum exhibitions on AI ethics, prompt-based pedagogies, and participatory oversight mechanisms. These experiments demonstrate that democratic AI futures are not only imaginable, they are already in the making.

A European Call to Action – This transformation demands distributed and shared responsibility:

- **Educators** must embed dialogic, critical, and participatory practices into all dimensions of digital competence and AI literacy;
- **Researchers** must turn laboratories into spaces of reflexive co-design and civic prototyping;
- **Policymakers** must ground AI regulation in epistemic pluralism, civic deliberation, and cultural sustainability;
- **Citizens** must reclaim algorithmic agency through literacy, participation, and co-creation of epistemic infrastructures.

GLAM institutions (galleries, libraries, archives, and museums) have a pivotal role in this agenda. As stewards of cultural memory and public meaning, they are uniquely positioned to serve as infrastructures of algorithmic imagination: curating participatory exhibitions, developing reflexive AI interfaces, and experimenting with inclusive, dialogic models of knowledge organization [1, 26].

The choice is no longer between resistance and surrender. It is between opacity and co-authorship, between automation-by-default and imagination-by-design.

Cyber Humanism calls for a culture of **dialogic design**, where democratic deliberation becomes the engine of innovation, and human values are not retrofit-ted onto systems, but embedded from the outset.

This is the challenge (and the opportunity) of Cyber Humanism:

To ensure that the future of AI will not happen to us; it will be made by us: deliberately, collectively, and with critical care.

References

1. Adorni, G., Bellini, E.: Towards a Manifesto for Cyber Humanities: Paradigms, Ethics, and Prospects. In: IEEE International Conference on Cyber-Humanities, IEEE Xplore (In Press, 2025 - preprints). https://arxiv.org/abs/2508.02760
2. Bakhtin, M.M.: The dialogic immagination: Four essay. University of Texas Press, Austin (1981) ISBN: 0-292-71527-7.
3. Burdick, A., Drucker, J., Lunenfeld, P., Presner, T., Schnapp, J.: Digital Humanities. MIT Press, Cambridge (2012). https://doi.org/10.7551/mitpress/9248.001.0001
4. Couldry, N., Mejias, U.A.: The Costs of Connection: how Data is Colonizing Human Life. Stanford Uni. Press (2019). https://doi.org/10.1515/9781503609754
5. DigComp HUB: On the road to DigComp 3.0 (2025). https://www.digcomphub.eu/on-the-road-to-digcomp-3-0/. Accessed 2025/09/15
6. EC: European Declaration on Digital Rights and Principles. Official J. of the EU C23 (2023). https://digital-strategy.ec.europa.eu/en/library. Accessed 2025/09/15
7. EC: Regulation (EU) 2024/1689 on AI (AI Act). Official J. of the EU L1689 (2024). https://eur-lex.europa.eu/eli/reg/2024/1689/oj. Accessed 2025/09/15
8. EC: The GPAI Code of Practice, Official website of the EU (2025). https://digital-strategy.ec.europa.eu/en/policies/contents-code-gpai. Accessed 2025/09/15

9. EC: Shaping Europe's digital future - European Digital Rights and Principles (2025). https://digital-strategy.ec.europa.eu/en. Accessed 2025/09/15
10. Floridi, L.: The Logic of Information: A Theory of Philosophy as Conceptual Design, Oxford University Press, Oxford (2019). https://doi.org/10.1093/oso/9780198833635.001.0001/
11. Georgiou, G.: ChatGPT produces more lazy thinkers: evidence of cognitive engagement decline (2025). https://doi.org/10.48550/arXiv.2507.00181
12. Kosmyna, N., et al.: Your Brain on ChatGPT: Accumulation of Cognitive Debt when Using an AI Assistant for Essay Writing Task (2025). https://doi.org/10.48550/arXiv.2506.08872
13. Lee, H.-P., et al.: The Impact of Generative AI on Critical Thinking: Self-Reported Reductions in Cognitive Effort and Confidence Effects From a Survey of Knowledge Workers. In: CHI'25 Conference, ACM (2025).https://doi.org/10.1145/3706598.3713778
14. Mittelstadt, B. D., Allo, P., Taddeo, M., Wachter, S., Floridi, L.: The ethics of algorithms: Mapping the debate. Big Data Soc. **3**(2) (2016). https://doi.org/10.1177/2053951716679679
15. Mollick, E.: Against Brain Damage: AI Can Help, or Hurt, Our Thinking. One Useful Thing (2025). https://www.oneusefulthing.org/p/against-brain-damage. Accessed 2025/09/15
16. Noble, S.U.: Algorithms of Oppression: How Search Engines Reinforce Racism, New York University Press (2018). ISBN: 978-1-4798-3724-3
17. Redecker, C.: European Framework for the Digital Competence of Educators: DigCompEdu, EUR 28775 EN, Y. Punie (Ed.), Publications Office of the European Union, Luxembourg (2017). https://doi.org/10.2760/159770
18. Selwyn, N.: On the Limits of Artificial Intelligence (AI) in Education. Nordic J. Pedagogy Critic. **10**, 3–14 (2024). https://pedagogikkogkritikk.no/index.php/ntpk/article/view/6062/9573. Accessed 2025/09/15
19. Werthner, H., et al.: Vienna Manifesto on Digital Humanism. (2019). https://dighum.ec.tuwien.ac.at/wp-content/uploads/2019/05/manifesto.pdf.   Accessed 2025/09/15
20. Werthner, H., Prem, E., Lee, E.A., Ghezzi, C. (eds.): Perspectives on Digital Humanism. Springer, Cham (2022). https://doi.org/10.1007/978-3-030-86144-5
21. Windhager, F., Mayr, E.: Digital Humanities and Distributed Cognition: From a Lack of Theory to Its Visual Augmentation. J. Cultural Anal. **7**,(4) (2024). https://doi.org/10.22148/001c.121866
22. Zuboff, S.: The Age of Surveillance Capitalism: The Fight for a Human Future at the New Frontier of Power, PublicAffairs (2019). ISBN: 9781610395694
23. Coeckelbergh, M.: What is digital humanism? A conceptual analysis and an argument for a more critical and political digital (post)humanism, J. of Responsible Technology, Vol. 17 (2024). https://doi.org/10.1016/j.jrt.2023.100073
24. Prem, E.: Principles of digital humanism: A critical post-humanist view, J.of Responsible Technology, Vol. 17 (2024). https://doi.org/10.1016/j.jrt.2024.100075
25. Nida-Rümelin, J., Staudacher, K.: Philosophical Foundations of Digital Humanism. In: Werthner, H., et al. Introduction to Digital Humanism. Springer, Cham, pp.17-30 (2023). https://doi.org/10.1007/978-3-031-45304-5_2
26. Li, Q., Wang, P., Liu, Z., Wang, C.: How generous interface affect user experience and behavior: Evaluating the information display interface for museum cultural heritage. Computer Animation and Virtual Worlds, vol. 35, N. 1 (2024). https://doi.org/10.1002/cav.2212

Breaking Disciplinary Silos: The Case of Software Engineering

Carlo Ghezzi[1]([⊠]) , Masoud Ebrahimi[2]([⊠]) , Damir Isovic[2] ,
and Marjan Sirjani[2]

[1] DEIB, Politecnico di Milano, Milano, Italy
`carlo.ghezzi@polimi.it`
[2] Mälardalen University, Västerås, Sweden
`masoud.ebrahimi@mdu.se`

Abstract. Digital Humanism aims to influence the complex interplay between technology and humankind, striving for a better society while fully respecting universal human rights. While software is the crucial technological component in this interplay, current mainstream approaches in software engineering research and education are largely agnostic about the goals of Digital Humanism. Scientists and engineers tend to view, design, and study software systems from a purely technical perspective, often disregarding human and societal implications. In this position paper, we argue that research and education should be profoundly revisited by broadening the disciplinary landscape through cross-disciplinary collaborations, particularly with the humanities and social sciences, to ensure that the human and societal implications of new designs, as well as the principles of Digital Humanism, are properly considered. We provide an initial roadmap for this effort, mainly addressing software engineering. The roadmap is intended as a basis for further discussion and refinement, and serves as a call for increased community action in this area.

Keywords: Digital Humanism · Human & Societally Critical Systems · Software Engineering Research · Education · Artificial Intelligence · Awareness · Responsible Design · Transparency · Multidisciplinarity

1 Introduction

Software is the defining technology of the 21st century, transforming how humans live and operate. We now inhabit a cyber-physical world, seamlessly integrated and orchestrated by software. Software defines, embeds, and enforces the mechanisms and laws that govern our world: how humans interact with physical entities, how they engage and cooperate with each other, and how society is organized at all levels (e.g., political, industrial, educational, social, and more). Without exaggeration, most software developed and deployed worldwide today is *human and societally critical (HSC)*. This paper focuses on HSC software.

© The Author(s) 2026
L. Hagedorn et al. (Eds.): DIGHUM 2025, LNCS 16319, pp. 421–435, 2026.
https://doi.org/10.1007/978-3-032-11108-1_32

The societal nature of most software applications has long been under scrutiny by social and political scientists. In the late 1990s, Lawrence Lessig wrote a landmark book, in which he observed that software (code, in his words) is the regulator of the new world [20].
Quoting from Lessig:

> *This code, or architecture, sets the terms on which life in cyberspace is experienced. It determines how easy it is to protect privacy, or how easy it is to censor speech. It determines whether access to information is general or whether information is zoned. It affects who sees what, or what is monitored. In a host of ways that one cannot begin to see unless one begins to understand the nature of this code, the code of cyberspace regulates.*

Lessig indirectly highlights the responsibilities that software engineers have toward humans and society, as their design decisions are embedded in software. Recent advances in AI further amplify the regulatory role of software in HSC systems and raise crucial concerns about societal implications. AI enables the development of larger and more complex software systems, with agents that can behave autonomously, learn and evolve without human intervention, and even be generated automatically. As a result, systems may exhibit unanticipated behaviors. Complete control over such systems is unattainable, and the illusion of control that software developers often have can be dangerous. Lessig's early observations, which Software Engineering (SE) research and education have largely overlooked, can no longer be ignored.

To address these issues, we argue that SE research and education must be grounded in the principles of **Digital Humanism**[1] (DigHum), placing human values, rights, and dignity at the center of technological development. DigHum asserts that technology must serve human and society (not vice versa) by integrating ethical, social, cultural, and philosophical considerations into the design and governance of digital systems. For further discussion, see [17–19, 30–32].

We need to revisit how software for HSC systems is designed[2]: How are goals related to human and societal values identified and set? How are they explicitly and precisely (ideally, even formally) specified? How are they engineered into software? How can they be inspected? How can we ensure they hold, even as the system evolves? Meeting these challenges requires traditional SE technical knowledge to be combined with multidisciplinary expertise. Likewise, academic education should teach how to center human and societal values in software design and engage students in practical, multidisciplinary settings.

The challenges of DigHum for HSC systems can only be met by breaking down the disciplinary silos that have compartmentalized SE research and edu-

---

[1] Vienna Manifesto on Digital Humanism https://caiml.org/dighum/dighum-manifesto/, published in May 2019, defines DigHum and justifies the need for it. Its publication inspired initiatives and further elaborations of DigHum principles and practices.

[2] In SE, the term "design" typically refers to a specific phase of development. Here, it denotes the entire engineering process: conception, development, deployment, and evolution of a software system.

cation, hindering collaboration with other fields, primarily the humanities and social sciences, but also domain-specific areas like health sciences, political science, and law. Interdisciplinary design deliberations are essential to ensure that relevant human and societal aspects are properly considered and that DigHum principles are upheld. Rethinking education also requires methods to identify common misconceptions and biases among students, and to propose new pedagogical strategies, including real-world scenarios and inclusive design practices, to foster responsible, transparent, and socially beneficial software development.

Interdisciplinarity is often claimed but hard to achieve. It continues to face challenges within academia; e.g., misaligned objectives, divergent terminologies, and methodological incompatibilities. To systematically address these obstacles, a shared framework of values and priorities, such as that proposed by DigHum, is needed. By breaking down disciplinary silos, we can enable future generations of scientists and practitioners to communicate and collaborate more effectively. This is essential for addressing the complexity and challenges of the digital world.

In this paper, we promote *responsible design* as the cornerstone of SE for DigHum and argue that this can only be achieved by including interdisciplinary collaboration in software development from the outset, and by educating future engineers in interdisciplinary teamwork. Designers must take responsibility for their choices and understand the consequences of each decision for humans, society, and the environment. The level of system autonomy and the degree of freedom granted to users must be made explicit and clearly communicated. The pros and cons of each design decision should be critically evaluated, available options transparently presented, and associated responsibilities clearly assigned. This brings clarity of *intentions* and *transparency* to the design process. These concepts also apply to users in a broad sense: it must be clear which user actions lead to which outcomes, ensuring that responsibility and accountability are well understood on both sides.

The paper is structured as follows. Section 2 elaborates on the notion of responsible design and the role of multidisciplinary contributions. Section 3 outlines the main research areas that need to be explored to re-found design methods in the light of DigHum goals. Section 4 discusses the implications of DigHum for rethinking SE education. Section 5 highlights the main contributions of other research groups who are also rethinking software research and education from a humanistic and social perspective. Finally, Sect. 6 offers conclusions and calls on other disciplines to break their own silos. Digitalization is transforming all fields, and students in every discipline need to learn how to communicate with engineers just as much as engineers need to learn to communicate with them. More broadly, the general public must also increase its awareness and responsibility regarding the digital world in which we all live.

2   Software Engineering, Responsible Design, and Ethics

Software engineers are passionate about technology and its potential to shape the world. Their skills have led to innovations that have revolutionized society. SE research has provided engineers with a wide range of conceptual and practical tools—theories, processes, methods, notations, languages, components, and frameworks—to support the production and evolution of quality software. Despite software's broad and deep impact on humans and society, research has mostly treated software as a purely technical artifact, focusing on traditional objectives applied to any industrial-quality product. The qualities considered are mainly technical, such as functional correctness and performance (speed and efficient use of resources), as well as economic factors, like productivity, portability, or reuse. Human-related qualities are mainly considered under "usability" and viewed as part of human-machine interaction.

Technical knowledge is necessary but not sufficient for developing DigHum-compliant HSC systems. This section examines the foundational principles that should guide in re-founding design of HSC systems from a DigHum perspective. Our discussion is informed by, and closely aligned with, the contributions presented in [31], particularly those by [2,6,17,22,24,26,27,34].

Additional to technical knowledge, *awareness* of the broader context in which the HSC system is embedded is essential for design. Awareness enables designers to state their *intent* explicitly, allowing them to take clear *responsibility* for their work. Such awareness is crucial to ensure that the envisioned HSC system complies with DigHum principles. To achieve this awareness, it is imperative to inform and drive the design process with diverse viewpoints, needs, interests, and concerns that illuminate the broader context in which the artifact will be embedded. This necessitates integrating *multidisciplinary knowledge and argumentation* into the design process. For example, designing an HSC system for assisted living (e.g., serving elderly or impaired individuals) requires input from medical professionals, caregivers, psychologists, sociologists, and ethicists. These contributions provide essential human and societal domain knowledge and clarify the required ethical to ensure DigHum compliance. All participants in the design process must share collective responsibility for the system and its potential actions.

The notion of *intent* is key. Unlike physical entities found in nature, artifacts result from deliberate, creative human activity. Every creative act has an intent, which may be either *conscious* or *unconscious*. An unconscious intent becomes conscious when it is made explicit and precisely formulated. A crucial part of design is making intents explicit by answering questions such as: Why is the new HSC system being designed? What do we aim to achieve? What are the *intended* (i.e., desirable) outcomes? Can other *unintended* effects also occur, and how can we counter (or mitigate) them? By making intents explicit and precise, we can counter the *opacity* that (regrettably) characterizes most software designs. Instead, design *transparency*[3] must be achieved. By this we mean that:

- the design provides a rigorous description of the artifact's intents;
- the artifact is open for inspection by designers and all relevant stakeholders;

---

[3] The term is the opposite of opacity. It is also closely related to *self-descriptiveness*, defined by the IEEE Standard Glossary of SE Terminology [15] as the degree to which a system or component contains enough information to explain its objectives and properties. This, in turn, relates to *maintainability*, *testability*, and *usability*.

– evidence is provided that the artifact complies with the stated intents and that proper measures are in place to counter undesirable unintended intents.

To make intents explicit, HSC designers inevitably need to confront ethical concerns. *Ethics* is the branch of philosophy concerned with systematic reflection on what is moral by studying what is morally good or bad, and right or wrong. These distinctions are rarely binary; they require a deliberative process to determine the appropriate kind of morality. During design, ethical questions guide the exploration of the human and societal context of the system. Intents must be examined not only for their technical innovation, relevance, and feasibility, but most importantly for how they affect the people involved and their relationships, and what is ultimately good or right (or bad or wrong) for them.

The principles of awareness and responsibility apply not only to designers, but also to all other relevant stakeholders who are involved with or affected by the artifact in use: from decision makers to end-users. Decision makers must take responsibility for adopting the HSC system in society and may need to regulate its use. End-users must provide informed consent for their use. Supporting awareness and responsibility for all stakeholders is a primary design goal; how to achieve this is itself an intent that must be explicitly and precisely stated. We discuss next how design should be rethought to address these issues.

3   Revisiting Design of HSC Systems

This section outlines a research agenda to align responsible software design with DigHum goals. We provide an initial breakdown of areas to be investigated. This list is not exhaustive and should be seen as a starting point for further discussion.

3.1   Design Process

The design process must host the multidisciplinary knowledge that inspires and drives the development of HSC systems. To make intents explicit (i.e., clearly connected to the human and societal context and to ethical implications of the intended consequences) and to ensure compliance with DigHum principles, it is essential to involve all necessary knowledge sources from the start. The process should then be structured to support effective and efficient interdisciplinary collaboration throughout the design activity.

To further motivate the need for multidisciplinary design, consider the implications of the following DigHum principle for HSC systems:

The system shall be fair and behave in an unbiased way.

A biased system is one that shows a benevolent inclination toward (or prejudice against) certain persons, groups, or interests in a way that is considered unfair and thus morally unacceptable. The design process should guide software development to guarantee fairness. Achieving fairness in software systems requires ethical decisions to counter possible manifestations of undesired bias within complex environments. Sometimes, bias may be benevolent: it is ethically acceptable and may become a deliberate design choice. For example, a system may be biased toward groups that need protection, such as offering special facilities to support minorities or people with impairments. More often, bias is morally unacceptable and may result from a variety of deliberate or unanticipated design choices. Bias can stem from unrepresentative data, objective functions misaligned with societal values, flawed algorithms, or lack of context in modeling. Recent cases have shown that unacceptable bias can arise from ML components trained on biased data [23]. More generally, ML components are intrinsically biased by the data used for their training.

The design process must be structured so that deliberations about fairness inform all design decisions. Input from disciplines beyond SE is essential to identify unacceptable bias and discuss countermeasures, especially from those representing groups potentially affected by unfair system behavior. To address these issues, it is important to precisely, and even formally, define bias in a way that allows for its evaluation. We need methods and tools to identify and reduce undesired bias, and to redefine model goals with community values. Iterative and incremental development processes, involving diverse stakeholders with diverse competences and providing diverse viewpoints, are likely to be the most suitable solutions to accommodate the needed multidisciplinary argumentation and ethical deliberations, as indicated by existing work in this field, presented in Sect. 5.

Software is a living, continuously evolving artifact. Design should account for the future evolution of HSC software. Mechanisms that can detect vulnerabilities to existing values, adapt to changes, and implement countermeasures may enable systems to evolve and adapt over time, even autonomously.

3.2   From Intents to Requirements Specifications and Verification

Intents must ultimately be expressed as requirements that a system must satisfy. Requirements engineering, a subfield of SE, focuses on requirements elicitation and specification. Existing methods are largely agnostic about DigHum-inspired goals[4]. More research is needed to develop a conceptual model and precise, possibly formal, definitions for *DigHum-inspired requirements*, including their dependencies and relationship with technical requirements.

SE research has long focused on formal specifications that are amenable to mechanical manipulation, including automated verification and other assurance techniques. More research is needed to apply these approaches to DigHum-inspired requirements. The earlier example of fairness and bias highlights the

---

[4] Research papers on requirements appear regularly in the main SE research literature, such as journals (e.g., IEEE Transactions on SE and the ACM Transactions on SE and Methodology) and conferences (e.g., International Conference on SE and the ACM International Conference on the Foundations of SE). There are also specialized venues focusing on requirements engineering (e.g., Springer Nature Requirements Eng. Journal and the IEEE International Requirements Eng. conference).

need for formalization. Among the analyses supported, it is also important to assess whether unintended and undesirable situations can occur. Designers from disciplines beyond SE can make valuable contributions here. The ultimate goal is to achieve *anticipatory design*: anticipating potential problems or threats and identifying countermeasures before issues arise. Anticipatory design aims to reduce reliance on patches that address threats only after they have already caused harm. Systems should also be designed to facilitate or automate the discovery of potential problems during operation and to provide automated corrective adaptation or prompts for designers to make necessary changes.

A key challenge in designing HSC systems is translating high-level human values (e.g., autonomy, dignity, and accountability) into actionable and verifiable software requirements. In the following, we illustrate this with a brief case study.

Free Will. The notion of free will is a complex philosophical concept that raises questions about human agency, autonomy, and the ethical boundaries of machine intervention in human decision-making. In the context of DigHum, free will is not just a philosophical abstraction but a practical concern that must be addressed in the design process.

Preserving human free will and self-determination is a core DigHum principle. Technologies, especially intelligent or autonomous systems, must serve human interests, not the other way around. This means humans should remain the primary decision-makers, empowered rather than constrained by digital tools. However, operationalizing a concept as philosophically complex as free will is challenging, particularly when determining the appropriate boundaries for machine intervention. In many real-world scenarios, it is unclear when a system should defer to human choices and when it must act to prevent harm.

Defining the boundary between human and machine intervention highlights why multidisciplinary perspectives must inform the design process. Engineers often favor full and increased autonomy, which can have valid justifications. However, social scientists may caution that excessive automation can demotivate, deskill, or demote humans to roles they find unacceptable. Conversely, engineers may argue that the simplistic principle that "humans must always retain ultimate control over autonomous system actions" can be just as problematic as relying entirely on system autonomy. For example, in a safety-critical flight control system, overriding the automatic system by a human can led to catastrophic consequences, as shown by the Germanwings crash caused by a suicidal co-pilot.

One possible resolution is to shift the focus from trying to define free will in absolute terms to specifying concrete conditions under which system intervention is ethically permissible. This can be achieved by introducing requirements grounded in the concepts of *malicious intent* and *negligence*. By integrating these notions early in the SE process, we can define explicit constraints that govern system behavior. For example, the system could be required to minimize interference with human decisions, unless it detects malicious intent from the human actor or determines that failing to intervene would result in a safety-critical outcome due to negligence. This requirement-driven approach reframes the problem: instead of defining autonomy in absolute terms, it identifies ethically and socially grounded exceptions, enabling the design of systems that respect human agency while safeguarding against harm.

To enforce such a framework, the system must include mechanisms that inform users of its operational state and the potential consequences of their actions. Responsibility is grounded in transparency: if a human actor is warned and fully understands the implications of proceeding, yet continues to act in a way that knowingly causes harm, this behavior constitutes malicious intent. If the actor ignores warnings or fails to take remedial action in response to foreseeable dangers, the situation may be considered negligence. In both cases, the system should provide clear and traceable records of its communications and the user's responses, and take preventive measures to avoid safety-critical outcomes. When all available courses of action lead to a safety-critical result, responsibility must be traced through formal traceability and verification. These mechanisms allow developers, regulators, and stakeholders to reconstruct the chain of design decisions, user interactions, and system responses, ensuring accountability is fairly attributed and informing future improvements in ethical system design.

3.3   Improving Design Transparency

Design transparency is essential for achieving collective responsibility among designers of HSC systems. It enables inspection and awareness of all aspects for which designers are accountable. Transparency has long been a major concern for large and complex software systems. Nearly 40 years ago, Turing Award winner Frederick Brooks wrote an influential paper [7] warning about the "essential complexity" of large software systems, which remains a fundamental obstacle to full transparency. Today's software, often incorporating AI-generated components, makes the situation even more challenging. Combating opacity is one of SE's most fundamental challenges.

The ability to specify intents precisely, and to scrutinize and assess them through multidisciplinary argumentation, is key to achieving transparency during design. Transparency is also crucial for other stakeholders (e.g., policy makers, regulators, and end-users), who must take responsibility for the HSC system according to their specific roles. Transparency means enabling stakeholders to ask questions about what the artifact does and how it operates, and to receive precise answers that are both comprehensible and guaranteed to be true.

The traditional SE notions of *modelling, specification, and verification* need to be broadened to achieve transparency through *assured guarantees*. A variety of approaches, notations, and languages have been developed to precisely describe systems: their structure, their behavior, and their properties. Likewise, methods have been devised to verify (or prove) whether an artifact satisfies these descriptions. More research is needed to expand the range of modelling and specification approaches for HSC systems to include DigHum-specific requirements, new ways to express them precisely or formally, and new ways to provide assurances at all levels, including design, evolution, and use, and for all possible stakeholders.

3.4 The Role of AI in HSC Systems

AI plays an increasingly crucial role in HSC systems design, from code generation based on natural language prompts, to learned components produced by training models, to autonomous agents and assistants used during design or embedded within HSC systems. The SE research has already been transformed by advances in AI, as seen in the rapid growth of AI-related papers in the SE literature in recent years. However, it is important that this research always keeps DigHum principles as primary concerns.

For example, let us return to the crucial notions of transparency. AI can threaten transparency by making parts of HSC systems difficult to understand, predict, guarantee, or explain[5]. We need to determine where, how, and under which circumstances this lack of transparency can be accepted, and how it affects the guarantees that can be assured. More broadly, we must develop an understanding of when the automation and autonomy introduced by AI is beneficial. This involves addressing the ethical question of what constitutes the right or good kind of AI, and what constitutes the wrong or bad kind of AI [1,11].

4 Implications on Education

DigHum requires transformative educational practices to prepare students to engage meaningfully with HSC systems. Central to this is the ability to understand the implications of technology for humans and society. These insights should be systematically incorporated into updated curricula that bring ethics to developers, engineers, and data scientists, making it clear that becoming a responsible professional is a recognized goal of their education.

A bottom-line requirement is that all students in technological fields, especially software engineering, should take a basic course on ethics as a necessary part of their education, just like mathematics or physics. In addition, technical courses should systematically highlight situations where design decisions can have ethical implications. Another key skill for students is the ability to collaborate across disciplinary boundaries. Traditional degree programs often isolate students within their own domain, but complex societal challenges require education that fosters integration between technology, social sciences, and humanities from the beginning. Therefore, it is essential to give students opportunities to learn how to work with peers from different backgrounds, including social sciences, humanities, and ethics.

A successful example of effective multidisciplinary collaboration in education is the Solar Car project at our university. In this project, 17 students from various disciplines collaborated to build a solar-powered vehicle that later competed in the Solar Challenge in Australia. By working together on a common

---

[5] Explainable AI is widely recognized as a fundamental research challenge.

goal over a one-year period, the team gradually developed a shared vocabulary and methodology. This process was further supported by a compulsory 10-week course for all students, which covered theoretical frameworks such as agile software development and intercultural communication, and included guest lectures and mentoring from industry professionals.

The Solar Car project demonstrated how students from various backgrounds can co-create solutions that are both technically and socially aware. However, such efforts should not remain isolated. Multidisciplinary perspectives need to be integrated into teaching and learning in a more systematic and natural way, reflecting the real challenges of the digital society. The next step is to formalize a methodology for multidisciplinary software education that incorporates ethics and human factors directly into the curriculum. Such a framework would enable the systematic inclusion of DigHum in technical education.

4.1   Operationalizing Ethics and Values in Education

To support these educational goals, ethical frameworks can provide foundational structure. The *ACM Code of Ethics* [3] and the *IEEE Global Initiative on Ethics of Autonomous and Intelligent Systems* [16] establish principles such as fairness, accountability, and transparency, which can be embedded in project work and evaluation criteria. In addition, Value-Based Engineering (VBE) offers a concrete methodology for translating abstract values into design requirements [25]. In an educational context, VBE can serve as a tool for students to practice aligning system design with stakeholder values and social goals, making ethics a part of technical reasoning rather than an afterthought.

Integrating ethical and value-driven approaches into coursework can help foster a mindset of responsible innovation. Assignments and group projects should include ethical impact assessments and value articulation exercises, encouraging students to consider trade-offs and societal implications early in their careers.

4.2   Toward Generalizable Educational Frameworks

The Solar Car example demonstrates how education can be reimagined to support DigHum. To generalize its success, we need to identify repeatable patterns and embed them into curricula and teaching materials. This includes designing interdisciplinary capstone projects, evaluating student work through ethical perspectives, and creating shared resources and infrastructure across institutions. Scalability across cultural and institutional contexts can be achieved through modular teaching units, collaborative platforms, and cross-institutional faculty training. In addition, documenting and sharing effective practices will help motivate others to make necessary changes in their curricula. Rather than mandating change, it is better to recognize and reward teachers who integrate DigHum into their courses. This will require updated mechanisms for evaluating academics that foster interdisciplinarity.

To conclude, higher education institutions should take a leading role in preparing future generations of professionals. These professionals should understand their roles and responsibilities in shaping the direction of the digital world they help create, and should align their work with the principles of DigHum.

5   Related Work

Autonomous decision-making in HSC systems requires alignment with Social, Legal, Ethical, Empathetic, and Cultural (SLEEC) values [5,8]. De Sanctis et al. [8] argue that contemporary software quality models must be redefined to incorporate SLEEC concerns as first-class quality attributes, rather than treating them as external considerations. This rethinking is further motivated by recent regulatory developments, such as the EU AI Act, which mandates demonstrable adherence to ethical principles. However, as noted by Morley et al. [21], in the absence of formal specification mechanisms, these mandates risk remaining aspirational, subject to selective interpretation and inconsistent implementation, which can undermine both trust and compliance.

To mitigate such risks, formal methods for capturing and enforcing ethical considerations have gained traction. Townsend et al. [28] propose a methodology that enables the translation of pluralistic normative principles, expressed in natural language, into actionable SLEEC-aligned operational rules. Other efforts explore the use of formal logics, particularly deontic logic, to encode normative constructs such as obligations, prohibitions, and permissions. For example, Arkoudas et al. [4] demonstrate how mechanized deontic logic can enable robots to verify ethical rules and generate justifiable decisions, laying foundational work for ethical reasoning in autonomous agents.

Dennis et al. [9] extend a Beliefs-Desires-Intentions (BDI) framework, implemented using the Gwendolen language [10], for agent-based systems by incorporating ethical constraints. They define a logic-based ethical operator that governs decision-making and resolves moral dilemmas by prioritizing ethical rules according to a predefined hierarchy. Their case studies show how logic-based verification can be applied to real-world HSC contexts. However, it remains an open problem whether the ethical rules were objectively formalized, or the hierarchies used to resolve moral dilemmas actually adhere to regulatory and ethical norms.

To address these issues, ontology-based requirements engineering has been used to study, model, and specify ethical concepts and constraints. For example, Guizzardi et al. [13] and Houghtaling et al. [14] propose approaches for structuring ethical requirements using ontologies. While these methods offer semantic clarity and traceability, they differ in their level of abstraction and currently lack standardized formalization languages for automated verification.

Despite these advancements, the field still lacks a unified, formalized framework that defines and operationalizes trust principles within SE. Autili et al. [5] address this gap by proposing a research roadmap aimed at aligning SE practice with SLEEC-aware societal responsibilities. To structure this vision, they introduce four archetypal human roles in relation to digital systems: proactive agents, reactive responders, passive experiencers, and trust participants. These roles help frame the diverse and often conflicting demands placed on autonomous systems. Building on this conceptual foundation, the roadmap defines four primary research domains: software development processes, requirements engineering, software architecture and design, and verification and validation. Each domain emphasizes the integration of responsible-by-design principles, ensuring that HSC and SLEEC considerations are embedded from the earliest stages of system conception. This line of work closely aligns with what we propose here.

The notion of a *software exoskeleton* has recently been introduced to serve as a personalized ethical interface, mediating the user's digital experience according to their declared values [29]. Building on this idea, De Sanctis and colleagues proposed a reference architecture for ethically aware autonomous systems, formalizing the roles of human actors, agents, and governance mechanisms. Their methodology includes a logical framework for compiling and reasoning over SLEEC rules [29], which helps enable transparent and inspectable decision-making processes. Together, these works provide a comprehensive and technically grounded foundation for advancing ethical compliance in HSC systems.

Another related and relevant line of research, investigated at the Bavarian Institute for Digital Transformation [12,33,34], focuses on how ethical deliberations can become effective drivers of the software development process. The referenced papers report positive experiences with adopting incremental and iterative Agile processes, which foster collaboration and adaptability. Some of these approaches show that integrating ethical considerations into established development frameworks is both feasible and beneficial, supporting the alignment of SE practices with societal values and regulatory requirements.

6   Conclusions

Software has revolutionized the way we live, work, and interact, becoming an integral part of our daily lives. However, the rapid advancement of technology has outpaced our understanding of its societal implications. As we continue to develop and deploy software systems, especially those that are human and societally critical, it is important to re-evaluate our approach to SE research, education, and practice. This paper provides an initial reflection on how to align research and education in SE with the goals and principles of DigHum, articulated through the following actions:

- *Promote DigHum principles:* Encourage and support interdisciplinary and multidisciplinary collaborations amongst computer scientists, ethicists, sociologists, and experts from other relevant disciplines to drive responsible design of DigHum-compliant HSC systems.
- *Develop a DigHum-inspired SE research agenda:* Develop new process models that effectively integrate multidisciplinary contributions in the design of HSC software, with the goal of making intents explicit and fostering responsible design. Research is also needed to improve transparency at all levels, supporting rigorous specifications and guaranteed assurances of DigHum-inspired requirements throughout design and for all stakeholders.

- *Integrate DigHum into SE education:* Curricula must include interdisciplinary courses covering ethics, social sciences, and humanities to prepare future engineers for the societal impacts of their work. Students must also learn how to practice interdisciplinary collaboration through innovative project courses.
- *Engage with all stakeholders, including policy makers and the public:* Foster dialogue between technologists, policy makers, and the public to ensure that software systems serve the broader interests of society.

By embracing these actions, we can guide the field of SE toward a future that not only advances technology but also upholds the values and rights of humanity.

Acknowledgments. This work would not exist without the pioneering and inspiring collective efforts of all contributors to the Digital Humanism initiative. We are indebted to them for laying the foundations for this discussion in the Vienna Manifesto on Digital Humanism and in the subsequent activities. Part of the work is supported by the ASSURE project, part of the multi-disciplinary research initiative at MDU.

References

1. Acemoglu, D., Restrepo, P.: The wrong kind of AI? artificial intelligence and the future of labour demand. Cambridge J. Regions, Econom. Soc. **13**(1), 25–35 (2019). https://doi.org/10.1093/cjres/rsz022
2. Akkermans, H.: The social responsibilities of scientists and technologists in the digital age, pp. 65–81. Springer Nature Switzerland, Cham (2024). https://doi.org/10.1007/978-3-031-45304-5_5
3. Anderson, R.E.: ACM code of ethics and professional conduct. Commun. ACM **35**(5), 94–99 (1992)
4. Arkoudas, K., Bringsjord, S., Bello, P.: Toward ethical robots via mechanized deontic logic. In: AAAI Fall Symposium on Machine Ethics, pp. 17–23 (2005)
5. Autili, M., De Sanctis, M., Inverardi, P., Pelliccione, P.: Engineering digital systems for humanity: a research roadmap. CoRR abs/2412.19668 (2024). https://doi.org/10.48550/ARXIV.2412.19668
6. Bennaceur, A., Ghezzi, C., Kramer, J., Nuseibeh, B.: Responsible software engineering: requirements and goals, pp. 299–315. Springer Nature Switzerland, Cham (2024). https://doi.org/10.1007/978-3-031-45304-5_20
7. Brooks, F.P.: No silver bullet essence and accidents of software engineering. Computer **20**(4), 10–19 (1987). https://doi.org/10.1109/MC.1987.1663532
8. De Sanctis, M., Inverardi, P., Pelliccione, P.: Do modern systems require new quality dimensions? In: Bertolino, A., Faria, J.P., Lago, P., Semini, L. (eds.) QUATIC'24. CCIS, vol. 2178, pp. 83–90. Springer (2024). https://doi.org/10.1007/978-3-031-70245-7_6,
9. Dennis, L., Fisher, M., Slavkovik, M., Webster, M.: Formal verification of ethical choices in autonomous systems. Robot. and Auton. Syst. **77**, 1–14 (2016). https://doi.org/10.1016/j.robot.2015.11.012, https://www.sciencedirect.com/science/article/pii/S0921889015003000
10. Dennis, L.A., Farwer, B.: Gwendolen: A BDI language for verifiable agents. In: AISB'08, pp. 16–23 (2008)
11. Dubhashi, D.: Can universities combat the 'wrong kind of AI'? Commun. ACM **65**(12), 24–26 (2022). https://doi.org/10.1145/3522710

12. Gogoll, J., Zuber, N., Kacianka, S., Greger, T., Pretschner, A., Nida-Rümelin, J.: Ethics in the software development process: from codes of conduct to ethical deliberation. Philosophy Technol. **34**(4), 1085–1108 (2021)
13. Guizzardi, R., Amaral, G.C.M., Guizzardi, G., Mylopoulos, J.: An ontology-based approach to engineering ethicality requirements. Softw. Syst. Model. **22**(6), 1897–1923 (2023). https://doi.org/10.1007/S10270-023-01115-3
14. Houghtaling, M.A., et al.: Standardizing an ontology for ethically aligned robotic and autonomous systems. IEEE Trans. Syst. Man Cybern. Syst. **54**(3), 1791–1804 (2024). https://doi.org/10.1109/TSMC.2023.3330981
15. IEEE: IEEE standard glossary of software engineering terminology (1990). https://doi.org/10.1109/IEEESTD.1990.101064
16. IEEE Standards association and others: the IEEE global initiative on ethics of autonomous and intelligent systems (2018). https://1standards.ieee.org/developlindconn/ec/autonomous_systems.html
17. Lee, E.A.: Are we in control?, pp. 165–174. Springer Nature Switzerland, Cham (2024). https://doi.org/10.1007/978-3-031-45304-5_11
18. Lee, E.A.: Certainty vs. intelligence. In: Bridging the Gap Between AI and Reality. AISoLA 2024. vol. LNCS 15217 (2024). https://doi.org/10.1007/978-3-031-75434-0_2
19. Lee, E.A.: The coevolution: the entwined futures of humans and machines. The MIT Press (2020). https://doi.org/10.7551/mitpress/12307.001.0001
20. Lessig, L.: Code and Other Laws of Cyberspace. Basic Books Inc, USA (1999)
21. Morley, J., Floridi, L., Kinsey, L., Elhalal, A.: From what to how: an initial review of publicly available ai ethics tools, methods and research to translate principles into practices. Sci. Eng. Ethics **26**(4), 2141–2168 (2019). https://doi.org/10.1007/s11948-019-00165-5
22. Nida-Rümelin, J., Staudacher, K.: Philosophical foundations of digital humanism, pp. 17–30. Springer Nature Switzerland, Cham (2024). https://doi.org/10.1007/978-3-031-45304-5_2
23. Rudin, C., Wang, C., Coker, B.: The Age of secrecy and unfairness in recidivism prediction. Harvard Data Sci. Rev. **2**(1) (2020). https://hdsr.mitpress.mit.edu/pub/7z10o269
24. Schiaffonati, V.: Promises and perils in moralizing technologies, pp. 255–265. Springer Nature Switzerland, Cham (2024). https://doi.org/10.1007/978-3-031-45304-5_17
25. Spiekermann, S., Winkler, T.: Value-based engineering with IEEE 7000. IEEE Technol. Soc. Mag. **41**(3), 71–80 (2022)
26. Sun, F., Isovic, D.: Responsible AI under the philosophical framework of Digial Humanism. Int. J. Inf. Theor. Appl. **32**(4) (2025). http://www.es.mdu.se/publications/7286-
27. Tamburrini, G.: Artificial intelligence and large-scale threats to humanity, pp. 241–254. Springer Nature Switzerland, Cham (2024). https://doi.org/10.1007/978-3-031-45304-5_16
28. Townsend, B.A., et al.: From pluralistic normative principles to autonomous-agent rules. Minds Mach. **32**(4), 683–715 (2022). https://doi.org/10.1007/S11023-022-09614-W
29. Troquard, N., De Sanctis, M., Inverardi, P., Pelliccione, P., Scoccia, G.L.: Social, legal, ethical, empathetic, and cultural rules: Compilation and reasoning. In: Wooldridge, M.J., Dy, J.G., Natarajan, S. (eds.) AAAI'24, pp. 22385–22392 (2024). https://doi.org/10.1609/AAAI.V38I20.30245

30. Werthner, H.: The vienna manifesto on digital humanism. In: Digital transformation and ethics, pp. 338–357. Ecowin (2020)
31. Werthner, H., et al.: Introduction to digital humanism. Springer Nature Switzerland (2024)
32. Werthner, H., Prem, E., Lee, E.A., Ghezzi, C.: Perspectives on digital humanisms. International series of monographs on physics, Springer Chams (2021). https://doi.org/10.1007/978-3-030-86144-56
33. Zuber, N., Gogoll, J., Kacianka, S., Pretschner, A., Nida-Rümelin, J.: Empowered and embedded: ethics and agile processes. Human. Soc. Sci. Commun. **9**(1), 1–13 (2022)
34. Zuber, N., Gogoll, J., Kacianka, S., Nida-Rümelin, J., Pretschner, A., et al.: Value-sensitive software design: ethical deliberation in agile development processes. Hannes Werthner Carlo Ghezzi Jeff Kramer Julian Nida-Rümelin Bashar Nuseibeh Erich Prem, p. 339 (2024)

Economies of Labor in the Age of AI: The Case of YouTube

Brian P. Harper[1]([☒]) [iD] and Hamid R. Ekbia[2] [iD]

[1] Indiana University, Bloomington, IN 47401, USA
bpharper@iu.edu
[2] Syracuse University, Syracuse, NY 13244, USA
hrekbia@sry.edu

Abstract. The structure of the labor market has shifted in recent years, with waged employment giving way increasingly to "alternative work arrangements" (AWA). Largely driven by computing technologies, the exact nature of this shift remains underexplored. This paper examines the shift from the perspectives of the discursive economy and political economy. To that end, we first propose a discursive framework to account for current displacements in the labor market. Then, we extend the notion of "heteromation" to discuss various mechanisms of value creation and value extraction in current capitalism, including not only waged labor but also the varieties of non-waged labor that fall under AWA. To ground our conceptual analysis, we examine YouTube as the largest digital global labor platform and a pioneer in the use of AI computing technologies. YouTube provides us with an insight into how mature AI-driven platforms interact with labor and may provide insight into what a mature Generative AI platform may become if it similarly becomes infrastructural and no longer dependent upon venture capital investment.

Keywords: Algorithmic Economies · Labor Economy · Social Media Platforms · YouTube

1 Introduction

Modern technologies are often touted by enthusiasts as "labor-saving" in the form of automation. While this might be the case in certain areas and for certain goals, it is not the case in many others. Computing systems have been shown time and again to create extra labor for human workers in existing roles and to also create new roles that can be solely done by humans. In doing so, they often displace jobs and roles, rather than replacing them. Modern systems which go by the term AI are no exception. AI systems are often described as exhibiting levels of performance above human beings with different types and levels of skill or expertise—from chess and Go players to professionals such as doctors, radiologists, or programmers. These claims, however, constitute at best partial truths and at worst utopian hype and pure misrepresentation. The dystopian versions of such claims portray AI as an existential threat to human jobs, with the potential of driving millions of workers into joblessness and unemployment—claims that have been

L. Hagedorn et al. (Eds.): DIGHUM 2025, LNCS 16319, pp. 436–450, 2026.
https://doi.org/10.1007/978-3-032-11108-1_33

repeatedly debunked through empirical studies [2, 18, 22]. The less hyperbolic claims often fall somewhere between utopian and dystopian visions [4, 13].

AI systems are used to obfuscate the contribution of human labor by overattribution of capacities to machines, with a demoralizing and disenchanting effect on people. In practice, however, what happens is a displacement, no replacement, of tasks or jobs performed by human beings. The recent rise of Generative AI and machine learning promises to expand both displacement and disenchantment—and to further anxieties among people about the future of their jobs and livelihoods. To curb these anxieties, we face three key challenges: (i) to understand the nature of current displacements in jobs and roles; (ii) to (re)assess the status of human labor in the creation of economic value in a heavily computerized environment; and (iii) to counter cultural narratives and practices that privilege machine efficiency over human dignity.

There is no question about significant improvements in hardware and software development, algorithm design, data collection and analysis, speed of processing, and other aspects of computing in recent years. These improvements provide the key to the exponential growth in the adoption of technologies commonly described as AI-enabled or AI-driven in various domains [1, 23, 36]. The common frame for understanding the labor implications of these improvements is to ask whether a system automates human labor or augments that labor [1, 3, 11, 34]. As with earlier waves of computing technologies, however, in addition to automation and augmentation, AI systems create new types of labor for individuals in existing roles or they create new roles and tasks that only human beings are capable of performing. Studies have shown that with the infusion of AI into the economy, in the foreseeable future millions of people will find themselves performing tasks and jobs that were either considered unimportant or were unheard of until recently [18]. According to other studies, human beings with different levels of skills find themselves innovating, improvising, and working around the challenges and obstacles posed by AI systems [28, 38]. In all these scenarios, displaced human labor is essential for the smooth operation of these systems, sometimes to the benefit of the laborer, and other times to their disadvantage. The question, therefore, is not whether human beings will have things to do, but what kinds of things they will be doing and with what kinds of recognition, compensation, or reward.

YouTube provides a clear and interesting example of this phenomenon. As one of the largest social media platforms and the "largest digital labor platform" in the world [43], its significance in terms of scale, novelty, and complexity speaks for itself. What is more interesting for discussions of AI, however, is the relative age of YouTube. Coming online in 2005 and implementing systems we would now call AI, YouTube provides a demonstration of how these systems relate to labor practices on a longer time scale and in a mature and profitable business no longer dominated by venture capital investors.

To bring these practices to light, we will focus here on three interconnected systems within YouTube: the Recommendation system, the Content ID system, and the demonetization system. The Recommendation system, first created in 2008 [25], exists to suggest new videos for viewers to watch. By prioritizing or deprioritizing content, this system is a key determinant in the success or failure of content creators, giving rise to new roles of intermediaries with claims to expertise in "algorithmic lore" [9]. The Content ID system originated in 2007 [5] due to YouTube's early legal difficulties with Viacom and other Intellectual Property (IP) owners [50]. This system embodies YouTube's attempt to identify copyrighted materials uploaded to the platform and to prevent users from profiting off of existing IP. Lastly, the demonetization system emerged in 2012 [29] with the intent to remove or diminish the advertising displayed on certain videos that do not follow YouTube's community guidelines or policies. For content creators, this has created yet another system that, like Content ID, requires learning an opaque appeal system, adding additional editing responsibilities to re-edit past videos to comply with new rules, and creating additional importance in seeking out those capable of discerning what the algorithm wanted [9].

While none of these systems are part of the present wave of generative AI systems using large language models like ChatGPT, it makes sense to include them under the broad umbrella of AI. YouTube itself generally prefers to use more technically precise terms like "machine-learning" over AI [25]—for instance, in the work from Google Research explaining the recommendation system [14] or the sound matching system for Content ID [16]. In journalistic [31, 49] and academic accounts [30, 39, 48], however, referring to these systems as AI is quite common.

These systems provide us with examples of AI techniques that have moved far past their early design and development stages to implementations and redesign phases. Although different in concept and function, the common element among these systems is their heavy reliance on different types of human labor for their smooth operation, as well as for overcoming their expected limitations and unexpected failures.

2 Economics of Labor: Two Perspectives

The rise of AI and computing technologies has given rise to questions such as the following about work, jobs, employment, and value creation in the current economy.

- Who is producing value in our increasingly computerized economy?
- Is value extraction the equivalent of exploitation? If yes, what are the mechanisms of exploitation in the current economy? If not, how can we explain value creation in distinction from exploitation?
- Is value creation the sole domain of waged labor? Do non-waged users of digital technologies (e.g., on social media) create value for the economy? If so, what kind of reward do they receive for their contribution? What kinds of rewards can be considered in a more equitable economy?

We propose to address these questions from two complementary perspectives on the "economies of labor," which build upon each other. First, the discursive economy of labor seeks to account for the changing nature of current discourses on labor and other related notions within a "cluster of concepts." And second, the political economy of labor examines the mechanisms of value creation, highlighting the continuing significance of human labor in high-tech platform capitalism.

2.1 The Discursive Economy of Labor

Work is historically and geographically specific. Its character and its meaning vary across cultures and regions, and these have changed throughout human history. The current understanding of work as 'non-domestic, paid, legally codified, institutionalized and socially safeguarded employment' is rather new, going back only to the 19th and 20th centuries, and it is also specific to the industrialized world [32]. In fact, many of the assumptions built into the current concept of work are questionable if considered from a broader perspective. There is no clear justification, for instance, why work should be limited to "non-domestic" labor and why domestic labor shouldn't be considered work. Similarly, much of the work currently performed in the global economy is not "legally codified," as the above description suggests, giving multinational corporations a free hand in dictating their own rules in terms of wages, working conditions, recruitment, firing, and so on. Even in the global north, gig work is not safeguarded employment; in fact, if we listen to platform companies such as Uber, Salesforce, etc. gig work is not employment at all.

The concept of "work" belongs to a cluster of concepts that are often used interchangeably in writings and daily conversations. These include notions such as 'activity', 'labor', 'task', 'skill', 'job', 'employment' and others. The key evaluation criterion that has given us the current cluster of terms is efficiency-driven profit. To account for ongoing changes in the current economy, we need to revisit both the criterion and the cluster of concepts that emerge from it. Table 1 offers basic descriptions of these developing terms, using the notion of 'activity' as the basis. The goal is to characterize these concepts as a cluster and not to define them in terms of a set of necessary and sufficient conditions [14].

Table 1. The cluster of concepts related to "labor"

Term	Definition
Activity	any form of physical or mental effort that requires the expenditure of time, energy and attention
Labor	the physical and mental capacity to perform an activity
Skill	labor that requires training and practice to be effectively performed
Work	labor performed in return for some kind of tangible reward to the provider (financial, in kind, social benefit, etc.)
Task	a discrete unit of work with a pre-specified product or deliverable
Tool	the extra-human apparatuses needed to carry out a task
Employment	work that is carried out within a legally codified institutional arrangement that provides task-related or work-related tools
Job	employment that is compensated by a wage
Gig	task-driven work compensated according to task completion
Use	activity that is carried out with non-economic incentives, without direct financial remuneration
Heteromation	collectively produced economic value created by users of computing technology

A next step would be to provide a more fine-grained breakdown of "alternative work arrangements." A close examination of this broad and growing category shows great variability among different groups along legal, economic, and financial dimensions such as skill requirements, benefits, ownership of tools ("means of production"), job precarity and security, etc. Some groups need their own tools and assets (vehicles, computers, homes, cellphones, etc.) in order to perform a task ("gig"), others don't; some develop and bring their skills acquired elsewhere into work, others go through formal job training; some perform a task with the explicit expectation of financial remuneration, others don't; and so forth. To account for this degree of variability, we draw on the concept of "heteromation," originally developed by Ekbia and Nardi [19–21] to account for the vast amount of unrecognized, uncompensated, or minimally rewarded economic value created by users of computing technology in the current economy.

In the last few years, the emergence of platforms as well as new technologies, including AI-driven systems, has expanded the phenomenon of heteromation far beyond use to value-creating labor and even work. The scale and scope of these developments demands further expansion and refinement of the concept of "heteromation" to include not only "heteromated use," but also "heteromated labor" and even "heteromated work"—that is, a kind of work that is compensated not by wage but by taking place within the ecosystem of specific platform(s) under the rules, algorithms, and often-implicit norms dictated by the platform proprietors. The market capitalization of some of these platforms and the reach and magnitude of their operations have turned them into key players in the current economy, giving rise to work arrangements that are qualitatively different from the past in terms of financial compensation, benefits, legal protections, and precarity. Figure 1 provides a broad illustration of these developments based on the cluster of concepts introduced in Table 1 above.

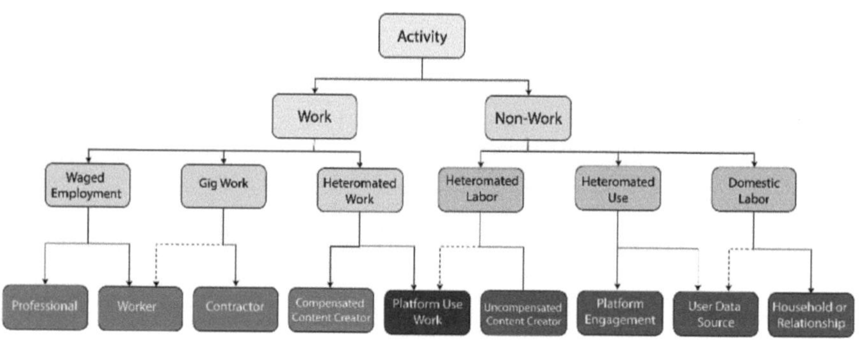

Fig. 1. Varieties of labor in the platform economy

2.2 The Political Economy of Labor

The varieties of labor described above all create value in the current economy, but in different ways and through different mechanisms. The question is, what new mechanisms of value extraction are at work in this economy? One common approach is to describe all such mechanisms as exploitation through the extraction of surplus labor—namely, the extra labor that laborers provide in addition to what they need in order to reproduce their labor power. Based on the belief that "labor is the source of all value," this perspective takes the labor theory of value as a theory of exploitation [6]. This line of thinking goes back to 19th century, predating the Marxian theory, but it has survived into our times, leading some commentators to argue that non-waged users of computer technologies are not only exploited, they are "infinitely exploited" [24]—an untenable proposition because, among other things, it implies that a social media user chatting with their friends at the comfort of their home is more heavily exploited than, for instance, a waged worker at the Tesla factory in Fremont, California or, even worse, at a sweatshop in Dakar, Bangladesh.

The challenge is to reconcile the continued existence of surplus value with the reign of platforms and of exchange of value equivalents. In the current economy, these equivalents take the form of data, content, rent, network value, attention, personal satisfaction, etc. The vast variety of these equivalents render value extraction in this economy much more diffuse, indirect, and invisible than in industrial capitalism. In fact, as we discussed earlier, many of these forms of value are created by "heteromated" types of labor—that is by non-waged labor that is uncompensated ("heteromated use"), indirectly compensated through other forms of reward ("heteromated labor"), or by fashioning new types of work tethered to the platform ecosystem ("heteromated work").

The growth of platforms in recent years has shifted the bulk of activity from heteromated use to heteromated labor and heteromated work, calling a stronger emphasis on the latter, as we intend to do here (see Fig. 1). Platforms, perhaps to a greater extent than industrial firms, are utterly dependent on flows of value. If, as Srnicek [45] argues, platforms do indeed interact with a raw material in the form of data, that data's extraction is contingent on other parties exchanging their own commodities within the platform. Platforms' focus on monopolizing their respective domains thus makes sense both from the perspective of increasing market share and from their fundamental need to maintain their supply of data. This is not to say that they cannot acquire data in other ways. One platform exists within a complex ecosystem [17] with other platforms, enabling some degree of data sharing, notwithstanding the tendency of capitalist firms toward data hoarding. This complexity results in a system that is difficult to easily understand, as platforms require a series of nested or overlapping value flows in order to function along with the cooperation of multiple actors in service of these flows.

3   Economies of Labor on YouTube

The two economies of labor described above are vividly embodied on platforms such as YouTube. To understand the varieties of labor involved, we need to examine the flows of value within the platform and ways that AI systems interact with these flows.

3.1   The Moment of Consumption: The Labor of Content Use

The moment of watching a video on YouTube may seem incredibly simple, but a series of systems are triggered into action by this process, involving numerous parties. Videos along with their embedded advertisements are served to viewers through the medium of YouTube. The automated character of this system wouldn't seem to require much human involvement and labor extraction, but there is a great deal more happening beneath the surface.

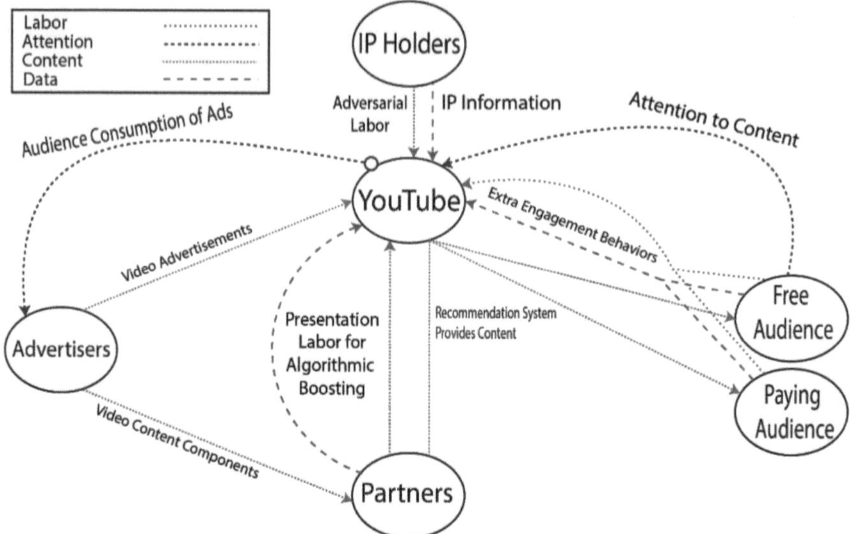

Fig. 2. The transfer of commodities and sources of value between parties within the YouTube system at the moment of video consumption.

As seen in Fig. 2, we identify six groups within this system: YouTube itself, the Free and Paying Audiences, YouTube Partners, Advertisers, and IP Holders. "YouTube" represents both the business operations surrounding YouTube as well as the systems at play in the operation of the platform. The "Free Audience" are those who consume content without paying for YouTube Premium, without directly supporting partners on YouTube through the sponsorship system or through crowdfunding platforms like Patreon. For simplicity, we treat these as completely distinct, even though it is possible to support a partner on Patreon but not pay for YouTube Premium. "Partners" refers to those content creators who are part of the YouTube Partnership Program (YPP) and are entitled to profit sharing of advertisements on the platform. The YPP includes over 3 million distinct channels as of early 2024 [37]. YouTube videos are made by non-Partners, of course, but for simplicity we will ignore video production that lacks an economic stake. "Advertisers" are those purchasing advertisements on the YouTube platform. "IP Holders" are those who are identified by YouTube as qualifying for copyright management tools such as the Content ID system.

Heteromated Use: Watching Video

The most visible commodity flow to the audience is the content being served to them. Created by partners and served by YouTube, this content flows to the audience, as suggested by the Recommendation system. Advertisers produce content in the form of their advertisements, which are themselves videos on YouTube. Moreover, advertisers may make advertising agreements with partners directly, allowing them to embed advertisements directly within partner produced videos, either as distinct advertising segments or through native advertising-like videos which promote a product or service directly as part of the main content.

The attention of audiences is commodified through YouTube and then exchanged to advertisers in a fashion similar to traditional media [44]. The subscription service YouTube Premium allows a portion of the audience to ignore advertisements. Both the free and paying audiences, however, create value on the platform by providing considerable data about their preferences, habits, identities, and so forth. In so doing, they feed data to the Recommendation system, but more importantly, allow YouTube to target users with customized advertisements—a service for which advertisers are willing to pay at a higher rate than simply random advertisements [42]. This kind of "heteromated use" or "engagement," as platforms often call it, is a critical component of the platform economy [20].

Heteromated Labor: Content Identification

The common refrain on YouTube to "like, comment, subscribe, and ring the bell" invites users to participate in heteromated labor by providing preference and engagement data to the Recommendation system. A distinctive feature of YouTube among social media platforms is that it does little to directly encourage this type of behavior among audiences, relying instead on its partners to do this. The indirect mediation of this incentive structure provides a clear psychological and ultimately economic advantage. YouTube also pushes the labor of identifying videos onto partners, who need to create algorithmic legibility for their videos through tasks such as categorizing and tagging, as well as managing the temporal patterns of uploading videos in order to increase the chance of getting their video being algorithmically supported (or at least not penalized) by the Recommendation system.

Heteromated Work: Copyright Protection

IP holders must also provide a great deal of data to YouTube to enable the effective functioning of these automated systems. The Content ID system requires matching content against copywritten material to YouTube, raising similar concerns about legibility to the Content ID system that partners experience with the Recommendation system. In addition to this work, IP Holders may choose to make manual claims, where they find specific content that violates their copyright. This type of labor is variable in its practices. Some copyright holders do this work themselves, whether solely through YouTube's interface or through middleware software, while others subcontract it to third party companies like Audiam or FUGA to manage their IP assets on social media platforms. Often, manual claims are legitimate efforts to inform YouTube of copyright violations that the Content ID system missed. On other occasions, this system has been abused to stifle competition [10, 45] or criticism [8] through copyright takedowns, making it a potential form of adversarial labor. All of these amount to a mixture of heteromated labor or heteromated work on the part of IP holders or third-party contractors.

3.2   Making the Commodities: The Labor of Creation and Moderation

Let us now turn to the creation of the content that is the life blood of platforms such as YouTube. Software engineers are needed to create systems capable of managing the flow of content, while other waged employees would need to promote the platform and build new infrastructure to support it. The bulk of value creation on the platform, however, takes place outside the space of waged labor [46]. The data required to feed and maintain these systems must come from other parties incentivized variously by the platform.

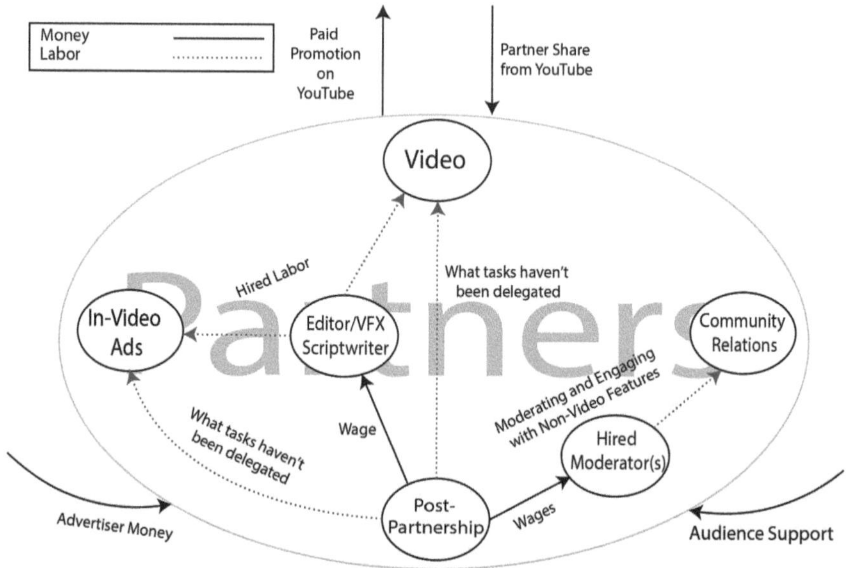

Fig. 3. Labor and wages shown within a hypothetical Partner's content creation system.

As seen in Fig. 3, a mature YouTube channel after becoming part of the YPP can form its own wage and labor system, with channel owner or owners hiring other workers to handle sub-components of their content creation pipeline. Whether related to video production, advertiser outreach, or community management, Partners with enough revenue may become employers even though their own revenue may come from largely heteromated sources. Community management can include moderation of the comments sections of videos, a task largely left to channel owners.

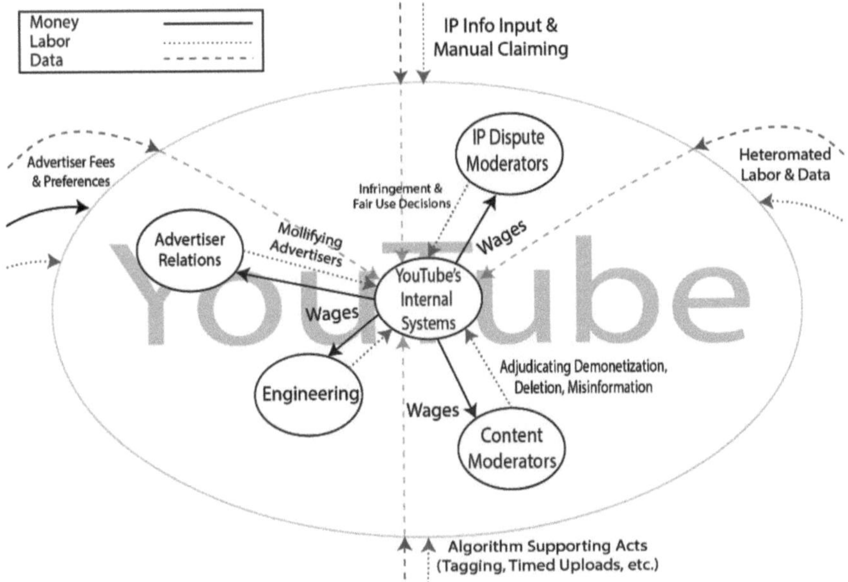

Fig. 4. Labor, money and data flows within YouTube.

Within YouTube itself, as seen in Fig. 4, many new tasks are potentially created through the uploading of a video. In the case of a partner producing a video that is flagged for having copyrighted material in their video, the system could have made a mistake, thus requiring human intervention to correct. Alternatively, a copyright holder could have used a manual claim which the content creator is disputing. Workers need to exist to adjudicate these disputes, disputes which sometimes invoke legal concepts like the Fair Use Doctrine or matters of international law.

Another labor-intensive task springing from system failures came as a consequence of the 2017 "Ad-pocalypse" [33], where advertisers withdrew from YouTube in part because their advertisements appeared on content that the advertisers would not approve of. In addition to the interpersonal labor persuading advertisers to return, YouTube's long-term solution was the creation of a new system that would demonetize videos through a reduction or elimination of advertisements in response to undesired content. While still acknowledging the need for human moderators, YouTube argued to the press that their automated systems were superior to human moderator approaches [26]. This system, while mollifying advertisers like Content ID did IP holders, resulted in yet another arena for partners to dispute the findings of the system and thus requiring humans to adjudicate algorithmic mistakes or cases of ambiguity.

Demonetization results in another category of human labor. While the demonetization system makes judgements constantly about the appropriateness of content for advertisements, it is prone to making mistakes which then will require human intervention to adjudicate. Social media content moderation is an infamously unpleasant task [27, 47] and often performed by contractors rather than full employees. YouTube's systems consider for demonetization or removal content containing sex and violence, which can be traumatizing to those moderators inundated with such content, but also more nuanced subjects like misinformation which require an understanding of context, politics, and scientific facts which increase the complexity of the task considerably.

During events such as the surge of right-wing misinformation in 2016–2017 [35] or the COVID-19 pandemic [40], YouTube has created content policies requiring more labor from content moderators. The lockdown phase of the COVID-19 pandemic was a particularly revealing period, as content moderators were no longer in the office and YouTube attempted to get by to a greater degree through their automated systems. Both academic analysis [7] and the popular press [40] viewed this tactic as deeply flawed.

In all of these cases, incapacities of these AI systems lead to the insertion of human workers like heatsinks for an overheated CPU. Sometimes the problems that necessitate these workers are transitory, but in other cases they become an accepted and normal part of the operation of this machine. In the case of content moderators, the heatsink metaphor is particularly apt as heatsinks are eventually worn out by excess temperatures, much like the infamously short tenure most people can psychologically spend performing these tasks [41].

4 Discussion

The image that arises from the above analysis of flows of labor, data, capital, and content on YouTube portrays a rather complex structure where a whole variety of types of labor are brought together around a single platform. These varieties of labor blur the distinction between traditional notions of work and non-work, job and gig, contract and employment, domestic and non-domestic, and so on. The concept of heteromation is considerably useful here in making sense of this complexity, drawing our attention to the varieties of human labor that must go into the working of computing technologies, including AI. In its original formulation, heteromation was largely focused on use, but shifts in the labor market demand an expansion toward heteromated labor and heteromated work, with meaningful differences between them. In the case of heteromated work, there is compensation, either directly from the platform itself, as for YouTube partners, or from those who are compensated by other firms to make their advertising or IP legible to YouTube's AI systems. Heteromated labor, on the other hand, represents the largely non-compensated side of the platform, where YouTube benefits from content produced without any expectation of financial compensation while content creators still perform algorithmic legibility tasks. Heteromated use derives from simply using the platform as an audience member, where the platform extracts value from audience engagements in two different directions: (i) an understanding of trends in popularity, and (ii) targeted advertising.

Platforms such as YouTube, in this way, exemplify the multidimensional and multivalent character of an AI-driven labor market. The technical work YouTube to maintain the platform and its internal economy might well be understood through traditional mechanisms of value creation through surplus labor. Beyond that, though, we need to pay attention to new mechanisms that are less direct and less visible. Even though an advertiser may be compensated with a salary for running an advertising campaign on YouTube, the labor required to get that advertisement onto the platform does not simply benefit the advertising entity, it also feeds information into the algorithmic systems that sustain YouTube. Whether a content creator, an advertiser, an IP holder, or an audience member, the labor performed to interact with this platform are essential elements for the operation of YouTube.

The dichotomy between compensated or uncompensated labor fails to capture this complexity. Some, like advertisers, feed information into the platform as a cost of using the service. Others, like audience members, are uncompensated, save for the weak argument that they receive better recommendations from their collective viewing and engagement behaviors. Content creators and IP holders exist in a middle position, where their ability to achieve their objectives (money or protected IP respectively) is aided by heteromating these algorithms, but they are not coherently compensated for these actions. A video could be unsuccessful for inscrutable reasons.

Pure automation under these systems is not possible, as humans must constantly step in to address defects—a labor that is messy, unpredictable, and gruesome. This is what turned demonetization on YouTube into a major issue in the aftermath of the Ad-pocalypse of 2017, ballooning it into a major problem requiring humans to address. None of these systems will work perfectly, and some level of human moderation is always required, but crisis, whether through external events like the COVID-19 pandemic or internal difficulties like the Demonetization system's release during the Ad-pocalypse, will require human labor to address.

5 Conclusion

The recent boom of Generative AI has focused too much attention on certain types of computing systems such as LLMs, at the expense of other types of technologies that fall under the AI rubric. YouTube is distinctive not because it is wholly alien to this trend, but because it has lasted long enough to reach maturity. In that way, it embodies a basic fact about AI systems—that is, that they are not capable of full automation. What we see instead are invisible and indirect forms of value extraction that belong to the growing phenomenon of heteromation. As their scale grows, the complexity of these systems increases, and they interact with more actors and interests, the incentives will grow to spread out the labor costs of the system, heteromating functions across their users and partners. Even further, as more delicate labor arrangements become necessary to address the system's defects, platforms get entangled in legal and technical issues.

Those who keep these systems going are only partly paid workers or professionals. Others hold different other relationships as contractors, partners, advertisers, or simply audiences. Content creators receive compensation from YouTube, though their status as workers is somewhat nebulous. While many might chafe at the idea that they are providing value to YouTube, the value they generate for the platform is anything but negligible. An advertiser or IP owner is receiving value from YouTube, but the value they create through their labor is not only non-trivial, it is germane to the sustenance of the platform. Audiences, on the surface, are only engaged as receivers of content, but their feedback provides the lifeline of content creators.

YouTube exemplifies a future for AI systems that would have to siphon and aggregate labor from disparate sources to maintain themselves as they grow in size and ubiquity.

While YouTube is a specific case, the need for differing levels of distributed and heteromated labor will continue to be present for most if not all of the systems now called AI.

Disclosure of Interests.   We declare no competing interests.

References

1. Abd-Alrazaq, A., et al.: The performance of artificial intelligence-driven technologies in diagnosing mental disorders: an umbrella review. NPJ Digit. Med. **5**(1), 87 (2022)
2. Acemoglu, D., Restrepo, P.: The race between man and machine: implications of technology for growth, factor shares, and employment. Am. Econ. Rev. **108**(6), 1488–1542 (2018)
3. Acemoglu, D., Restrepo, P.: The wrong kind of AI? Artificial intelligence and the future of labour demand. Camb. J. Reg. Econ. Soc. **13**(1), 25–35 (2020)
4. Agrawal, A., Gans, J.S., Goldfarb, A.: Do we want less automation? Science **381**(6654), 155–158 (2023)
5. Alfishawi, T.: Improving Content ID. YouTube Official Blog (2012). http://youtube-global. blogspot.com/2012/10/improving-content-id.html. Accessed Jan 2025
6. Armstrong, P., Glyn, A., Harrison, J.: In defence of value a reply to Ian Steedman. Cap. Class **2**(2), 1–31 (1978)
7. Baker, S.A., Wade, M., Walsh, M.J.: The challenges of responding to misinformation during a pandemic: content moderation and the limitations of the concept of harm. Media Int. Australia **177**(1), 103–107 (2020)
8. Bartholomew, T.B.: The death of fair use in cyberspace: YouTube and the problem with content ID. Duke L. Tech. Rev. **13**, 66 (2014)
9. Bishop, S.: Algorithmic experts: selling algorithmic lore on YouTube. Soc. Media+Soc. **6**(1), 2056305119897323 (2020)
10. Boroughf, B.: The next great YouTube: improving content ID to Foster creativity, cooperation, and fair compensation. Alb. LJ Sci. Tech. **25**, 95 (2015)
11. Brynjolfsson, E.: The turing trap: the promise & peril of human-like artificial intelligence. In: Augmented Education in the Global Age, pp. 103–116. Routledge (2023)
12. Burgess, J., Green, J.: YouTube: Online Video and Participatory Culture. Wiley, Hoboken (2018)
13. Cools, H., Van Gorp, B., Opgenhaffen, M.: Where exactly between utopia and dystopia? A framing analysis of AI and automation in US newspapers. Journalism **25**(1), 3–21 (2024)
14. Covington, P., Adams, J., Sargin, E.: Deep neural networks for youtube recommendations. In: Proceedings of the 10th ACM Conference on Recommender Systems, pp. 191–198 (2016)
15. Connolly, K., Bruner, J.S.: (eds.): The Growth of Competence, vol. 1. Academic Press, London (1974)
16. Dharmapurikar, S., Lockwood, J.: Fast and scalable pattern matching for content filtering. In: Proceedings of the 2005 ACM Symposium on Architecture for Networking and Communications Systems, pp. 183–192 (2005)
17. Van Dijck, J., Poell, T., De Waal, M.: The Platform Society: Public Values in a Connective World. Oxford University Press (2018)
18. Dziez, J.: AI Is a Lot of Work As the technology becomes ubiquitous, a vast tasker underclass is emerging—and not going anywhere. New York Magazine (2023). https://nymag.com/intell igencer/article/ai-artificial-intelligence-humans-technology-business-factory.html. Accessed Jan 2025

19. Ekbia, H., Nardi, B.: Heteromation and its (dis) contents: the invisible division of labor between humans and machines. First Monday (2014)
20. Ekbia, H.R., Nardi, B.A.: Heteromation, and Other Stories of Computing and Capitalism. MIT Press (2017)
21. Ekbia, H.R., Nardi, B.A.: Keynes's grandchildren and Marx's gig workers: why human labour still matters. Int. Labour Rev. **158**(4), 653–676 (2019)
22. Eloundou, T., Manning, S., Mishkin, P., Rock, D.: GPTs are GPTs: an early look at the labor market impact potential of large language models. arXiv preprint arXiv:2303.10130 (2023)
23. Farayola, O.A., Abdul, A.A., Irabor, B.O., Okeleke, E.C.: Innovative business models driven by AI technologies: a review. Comput. Sci. IT Res. J. **4**(2), 85–110 (2023)
24. Fuchs, C.: Class and exploitation on the internet. In: Digital Labor, pp. 211–224. Routledge. (2012)
25. Goodrow, C.: On YouTube's Recommendation System. Accessed at YouTube Official Blog (2021). https://blog.youtube/inside-youtube/on-youtubes-recommendation-system/. Jan 2025
26. Gibbs, S.: Google says AI better than humans at scrubbing extremist YouTube content. The Guardian (2017). https://www.theguardian.com/technology/2017/aug/01/google-says-ai-better-than-humans-at-scrubbing-extremist-youtube-content. Accessed Jan 2025
27. Gillespie, T.: Custodians of the Internet: Platforms, Content Moderation, and the Hidden Decisions that Shape Social Media. Yale University Press (2018)
28. Haipeter, T.: Digitalisation, unions and participation: the German case of 'industry 4.0'. Ind. Relat. J. **51**(3), 242–260 (2020)
29. Internet Creator's Guild: YouTube De-Monetization Explained. Medium (2016). https://medium.com/internet-creators-guild/youtube-de-monetization-explained-44464f902a22#.ffjvxhx79. Accessed Jan 2025
30. Jain, S., Kaur, K.: Utilizing artificial intelligence for content analysis in YouTube webisodes. In: 2023 5th International Conference on Inventive Research in Computing Applications (ICIRCA), pp. 208–213. IEEE (2023)
31. Kiros, H.: Hated that video? YouTube's algorithm might push you another just like it. MIT Technology Review (2022). https://www.technologyreview.com/2022/09/20/1059709/youtube-algorithm-recommendations. Accessed Jan 2025
32. Komlosy, A.: Re-assessing labour and value transfer under capitalism. In: On the Road to Global Labour History, pp. 241–260. Brill (2017)
33. Kumar, S.: The algorithmic dance: YouTube's Adpocalypse and the gatekeeping of cultural content on digital platforms. Internet Policy Rev. **8**(2), 1–21 (2019)
34. Lei, Y.W., Kim, R.: Automation and augmentation: artificial intelligence, robots, and work. Ann. Rev. Sociol. **50** (2024)
35. Levin, S.: Google to hire thousands of moderators after outcry over YouTube abuse videos. The Guardian (2017). https://www.theguardian.com/technology/2017/dec/04/google-youtube-hire-moderators-child-abuse-videos. Accessed Jan 2025
36. Luckin, R., Cukurova, M.: Designing educational technologies in the age of AI: a learning sciences-driven approach. Br. J. Edu. Technol. **50**(6), 2824–2838 (2019)
37. Mohan, N.: Letter from the YouTube CEO: 4 Big bets for 2024 (2024). YouTube Official Blog. https://blog.youtube/inside-youtube/2024-letter-from-neal/. Accessed Jan 2025
38. Montiel Valle, D.A., Shorey, S.: Dis//assemblages of AI: repair labor and resistance in the automated workplace. Inf. Commun. Soc. **27**(10), 2022–2037 (2024)
39. Park, H.W., Park, S.: The filter bubble generated by artificial intelligence algorithms and the network dynamics of collective polarization on YouTube: the case of South Korea. Asian J. Commun. **34**(2), 195–212 (2024)

40. Scott, M., Kayali, L.: What happened when humans stopped managing social media content. Politico (2020). https://www.politico.eu/article/facebook-content-moderation-automation/. Accessed Jan 2025
41. Schöpke-Gonzalez, A.M., Atreja, S., Shin, H.N., Ahmed, N., Hemphill, L.: Why do volunteer content moderators quit? Burnout, conflict, and harmful behaviors. New Media Soc. **26**(10), 5677–5701 (2024)
42. Siegel, E.: Predictive Analytics: The Power to Predict Who Will Click, Buy, Lie, or Die. Wiley, Hoboken (2013)
43. Silberman, M.S., Rakshita, S., Abraha, H.H., Adams-Prassl, J.: Content marketplaces as digital labour platforms: towards accountable algorithmic management and decent work for content creators (2023)
44. Smythe, D.W.: On the audience commodity and its work. Media Cult. Stud. Keyworks **230**, 256 (1981)
45. Solomon, L.: Fair users or content abusers: the automatic flagging of non-infringing videos by content id on YouTube. Hofstra L. Rev. **44**, 237 (2015)
46. Srnicek, N.: Platform Capitalism. Polity Press, Cambridge Malden (2017)
47. Steiger, M., Bharucha, T.J., Venkatagiri, S., Riedl, M.J., Lease, M.: The psychological well-being of content moderators: the emotional labor of commercial moderation and avenues for improving support. In: Proceedings of the 2021 CHI Conference on Human Factors in Computing Systems, pp. 1–14 (2021)
48. Sturm, B.L., Iglesias, M., Ben-Tal, O., Miron, M., Gómez, E.: Artificial intelligence and music: open questions of copyright law and engineering praxis. In: Arts, vol. 8, no. 3, p. 115. MDPI (2019)
49. Titlow, J.P.: YouTube is using AI to police copyright – to the tune of $2 billion in payouts. Fast Company (2016). https://www.fastcompany.com/4013603/youtube-is-using-ai-to-police-copyright-to-the-tune-of-2-billion-in-payouts. Accessed Jan 2025
50. 'Viacom International v YouTube'. United States Court of Appeals, Second Circuit, 676 F.3d 19 (2012)

AI Research Is Not Magic, It Has to Be Reproducible and Responsible: Challenges in the AI Field from the Perspective of Its PhD Students

Andrea Hrckova[1]([✉])[iD], Jennifer Renoux[2][iD], Rafael Tolosana Calasanz[3][iD], Daniela Chuda[1,4][iD], Martin Tamajka[1][iD], and Jakub Simko[1][iD]

[1] Kempelen Institute of Intelligent Technologies, Bratislava, Slovakia
`{andrea.hrckova,daniela.chuda}@kinit.sk`
[2] Center for Applied Autonomous Sensor Systems, Örebro University, Örebro, Sweden
`jennifer.renoux@oru.se`
[3] I3A, University of Zaragoza, Zaragoza, Spain
`rafaelt@unizar.es`
[4] Slovak University of Technology in Bratislava, Bratislava, Slovakia

Abstract. Unlocking the full societal potential of artificial intelligence demands a fundamental shift towards responsible and reproducible research. Understanding that PhD students are pivotal in conducting and reproducing experiments, we investigated the challenges of 28 AI PhD candidates from 13 European countries. We identify three critical areas where current practices fall short: (1) the findability and quality of AI resources such as datasets, models, and experiments; (2) the difficulties in replicating the experiments in AI papers; (3) and the lack of trustworthiness and interdisciplinarity. After uncovering some of the underlying reasons behind the challenges, we propose a combination of social and technical recommendations to overcome the identified challenges and foster a more transparent and reliable AI research ecosystem. Socially, we recommend the general adoption of reproducibility initiatives in AI conferences and journals, as well as improved interdisciplinary scientific collaboration, especially in data governance practices. On the technical front, we call for enhanced tools to better support versioning control of datasets and code, and a computing infrastructure that facilitates the sharing and discovery of AI resources, as well as the sharing, execution, and verification of experiments.

1 Introduction

AI research is facing a reproducibility crisis [7]. Worse, AI systems and methods are increasingly being used to perform research in other fields, and concerns arise that it may lead to another major crisis in science in general, as scientists may use non-reproducible and non-responsible AI systems in an ill-informed way [6].

L. Hagedorn et al. (Eds.): DIGHUM 2025, LNCS 16319, pp. 451–466, 2026.
https://doi.org/10.1007/978-3-032-11108-1_34

In this work, we use the term *reproducibility* as *obtaining consistent results using the same input data; computational steps, methods and code; and analysis conditions* [18]. Responsible AI is the practice of developing and using AI systems in a way that benefits society while minimizing the risk of negative consequences. The goal is to employ AI in a safe, legal, trustworthy and ethical way [1]. This paper focuses on these pillars of responsible AI: privacy and data governance, fairness (to researchers as AI stakeholders), sustainability and reliability [3]. We also consider reproducibility as a foundational component of responsible AI as its absence prevents verification of model behavior, fairness, or ethical compliance, thereby undermining broader responsible AI goals. Several factors fuel AI's reproducibility crisis and impede responsible AI development. A major concern is data quality, which significantly impacts model performance [27]. Some researchers point out that data challenges are often overlooked in machine learning, criticizing inadequate practices in data annotation and documentation [20]. While the importance of data quality is widely acknowledged, and best practices and recommendations for scientific data management are summarized in the FAIR principles [28], challenges related to data quality and reproducibility persist, as documented in [13] and supported by our own research. To shed light on the persistent issues with reproducible and responsible AI research, we propose a complementary approach to previously conducted analyses [4,11]: investigating the ground-level practices and hurdles encountered by PhD candidates. These early-career researchers are pivotal in conducting and reproducing experiments, making them uniquely exposed to reproducibility hurdles. Their point of view is therefore invaluable for understanding the true causes and consequences of reproducibility crisis. Our study of 28 European AI PhD students uses qualitative methods from information science. Prior work on information interaction (or seeking behavior) has examined the needs of scientists [12], PhD students [23], and computer scientists [5]. While these studies focused on specific groups and tool recommendations, our exploratory and interdisciplinary approach offers broader insights for AI, leading to general recommendations on reproducibility and responsible AI. The main contributions of this paper are:

1. We explore and express the issues encountered by European PhD students in AI field, many of which are particularly related to reproducible and responsible AI. We identify the main sources of difficulties, which include, but are not limited to, the quality of AI resources (datasets, code, and models).
2. We formulate recommendations to address these issues, highlighting, among others, (1) the need for adoption of reproducibility practices on every level, particularly in AI journals and conferences, (2) the need for improved interdisciplinarity in AI, especially greater participation of domain experts, data and information specialists, ethicists, and legal professionals (notably in data governance practices).

2   Methodology

2.1   Study Design and Methods

This study employed an exploratory qualitative design, based an existing model of 7 stages [15], to investigate challenges faced by AI PhD students. This research process helped us manage the uncertainty and ambiguities that arise from a qualitative and exploratory investigation. The overarching research question in the *origination stage* of the research was: *'What are the biggest challenges that PhD students face when conducting AI research?'*. The first, fourth, and fifth author led this initial and the next phase. During the *orientation stage*, preliminary research led the team to focus on identifying technological recommendations for AI researchers. At this point, the planned interview duration was also shortened from four hours to 1.5–2 hours. We collected data via semi-structured, in-depth focus group interviews during the *exploration stage*. The first and fourth author drew from a set of 48 open-ended questions, selectively posing them based on the respondents' expertise. The full list of questions can be found under this link[1]) The *elucidation stage* focused on analyzing the collected data through manual content analysis. We employed an inductive coding process, which yielded 32 initial codes for problems in the AI field. Following iterative refinement, five unsaturated codes were excluded and nine were merged, culminating in 19 final categories that were all used in mind map visualizations[2]. The first author conducted the initial coding, with validation by the fourth and fifth author. The *consolidation stage* involved brainstorming sessions with all authors to create stronger, more consistent connections between our findings and existing state-of-the-art research, particularly concerning reproducible and responsible AI research. Ultimately, this phase aimed to develop a coherent and easily understandable final outcome. In the *reflection stage*, we took a broader view of the results, aiming to contextualize the findings within a larger picture of AI research challenges. During this phase, the study's inductive results were also controlled by the first and second author to enhance the validity of the findings. During the *culmination stage*, the authors formulated recommendations, recognizing that implementing change within established research institutions is far more complex than applying the technological solutions initially proposed in the research's earlier stages.

2.2   Participants

Our study involved 28 PhD students (19 males, 9 females) representing 13 European countries, including Slovakia, Greece, Germany, Spain, Sweden, Ireland, France, Bulgaria, Belgium, Norway, Finland, the Czech Republic, and Ukraine. We conducted 11 semi-structured focus group interviews from February to June 2023. One focus group involved up to four participants from different AI fields. Participants were recruited through European project partners without any financial compensation. Most of interviews took place online via Google Meet

---

[1] https://zenodo.org/records/15920758.

[2] Mind map visualizations were made in Canva.com.

in English. One interview was conducted face-to-face in the native language, and a single session with two interviewees was completed in written form upon their request. Participants demonstrated diverse expertise, covering ten AI focus areas such as machine learning (including neural networks, deep learning, federated learning, and accelerators), natural language processing (NLP), explainable AI, ethical AI, computer vision, recommenders, robotics, multimodal processing, and human activity recognition. Their research also extended into four additional domains: AI security (cyber-attacks), medical data processing, AI in business, and AI in energy and green environments (specifically, time-series analysis). The cohort included 16 advanced-stage and 12 early-stage PhD students.

3   Findings

Most of the challenges that we identified concern the quality of available AI resources, including datasets, code, and models; therefore, we grouped them into these three categories. These identified difficulties consumed most of the time of these researchers and significantly prevented them from being able to replicate the results in papers. As respondent P1 stated:

> *"Sometimes you don't understand how they gained such results in the paper and how to replicate it."*

Yet, replication studies are the type of research in which these early researchers are most involved. Sections 3.1, 3.2, and 3.3 explore these issues in more detail. However, it is worth noting that we also uncovered another set of challenges that PhD students encounter during AI research, particularly concerning the absence of interdisciplinary collaboration, issues with information retrieval, concerns regarding the lack of human involvement, and a lack of motivation to share research findings with the public. These challenges were named "Other challenges regarding AI research process" and are explored in Sect. 3.4.

3.1   Quality and Findability of Datasets

The foremost challenge frequently discussed in our interviews was the quality and utility of datasets required for the training of AI models (6 groups out of 11, see Fig. 1). This challenge stems partly from the significant time investment required to curate datasets annotated by human annotators. Some respondents (6 groups out of 11) noted difficulties in accessing experts, low agreement between annotators (2 groups out of 11), or the necessity to involve themselves or the not-so-motivated students to annotate (2 groups out of 11). However, the main concern was the privacy issue when trying to publish a dataset (6 groups out of 11). Respondent P2 illustrates this problem:

> *"There is just one public dataset of breast cancer that was properly labeled by experts with data about patients and everybody is using it... Obtaining approvals is difficult from patients."*

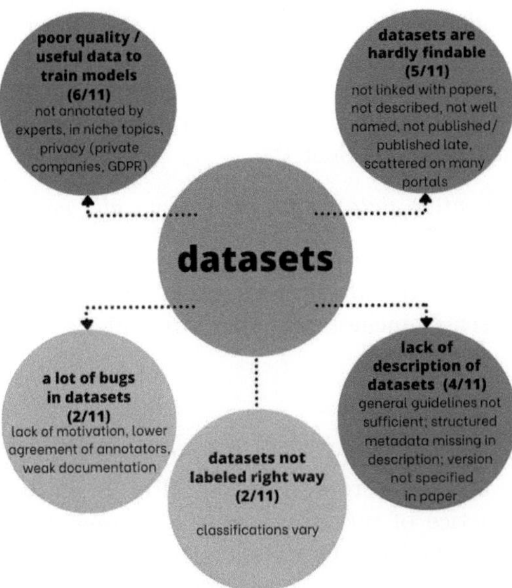

Fig. 1. Dataset-related challenges of AI resources as reported by research participants. The darker the red, the more often was the problem mentioned during the focus groups. The numbers in brackets indicate the count of focus groups out of the total 11 groups that agreed on such issues. (Color figure online)

The challenge of accessing quality datasets extends beyond the medical domain. Several respondents encountered obstacles due to privacy restrictions imposed by their companies, preventing them from publishing papers despite having ample data from their workplace. This restriction poses a significant hurdle, as publishing without accompanying data is problematic. Our respondents expressed skepticism about anonymization as a solution, citing doubts about its effectiveness and the impracticality of individually informing each affected individual. Five groups agreed that locating good datasets can be a challenge, even when they do exist. Many datasets lack direct links to associated papers for various reasons, such as delayed publication or non-publication. Consequently, these datasets are often dispersed on multiple data storage platforms. Additionally, authors may not always consider the discoverability of their datasets when publishing, neglecting to provide clear and descriptive names or descriptions. Clear and comprehensive descriptions in introduction, metadata, and classification are essential to ensure that a dataset is not only easily discoverable, but also allows researchers to assess its relevance to their specific requirements. For a PhD student in AI, the process of repeatedly downloading and opening available datasets to discern their contents consumes a significant amount of time. An example of useful metadata to save their time would include specifying the version of the dataset used in the paper, given the multitude of available dataset versions. Although general guidelines can help to describe datasets to some extent, respondents (for example, those in the security sector) expressed concern that they may not be directly applicable in specific domains.

In addition to that, four groups of PhD students out of 11 expressed their frustration about numerous bugs present and not documented in the available datasets, exemplified by respondent P3:

> *"Papers do not mention data drifts, there is usually no information about the data preparation."*

Apparently, the issue is shifting from availability to quality of the dataset. An exception was seen in niche topics that still suffer from a shortage of data for training models.

3.2 The Quality of Code

Quality issues also arise concerning the code (Fig. 2). Early career researchers typically have a practice of publishing code (just one student mentioned the unavailable code as a problem). Our respondents were driven by inner motivations such as a sense of reciprocity or awareness of reproducibility concerns. As respondent P4 pointed out:

> *"If a failure is identified, it is good for science, even if it is embarrassing for an individual."*

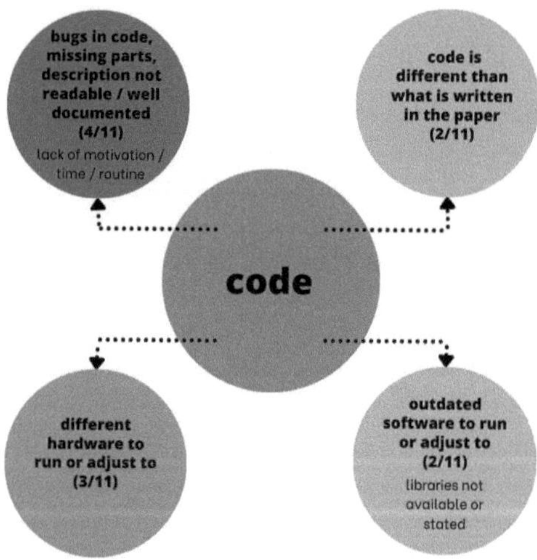

Fig. 2. Code-related challenges of AI resources as reported by research participants.

Nonetheless, this does not mean that the code published is clean or well documented. That is the reason why several students (4 groups out of 11) complained about serious bugs in the code or missing parts of the code. Respondent

P5 highlights an additional unpleasant problem - a mismatch between the code and the paper, a concern echoed in two focus groups:

"The biggest problem comes, if you are trying to make the paper work. Also with access to the code you get specific results. Sometimes the code is different than what is written in the paper and you have to do double work."

At the same time, respondents in these groups acknowledged that they lack motivation to publish meticulously documented code, as it is not a mandatory aspect of the review process and requires significant time investment, necessitating a consistent routine for continuous documentation during code writing and editing. In addition to that, these respondents emphasized that having some code available is better than having none at all. Nevertheless, researchers would appreciate at least some information on the program versions, the required hardware, and the libraries that were used when the code was originally run. This information would save researchers a lot of time, as they quite often encounter challenges related to incorrect hardware (3 groups out of 11) or software configurations (2 groups out of 11) necessary to run and adapt the code. As noted, research papers often lack the space to address such issues.

3.3   Benchmarking and Quality of Models

Some AI models face comparable challenges with respect to replicability and reproducibility as code (Fig. 3). Three groups of PhD candidates highlighted discovering significant flaws in the models presented in the papers, such as absent or inaccurate hyperparameters, along with inadequate documentation. These shortcomings, compounded by rigidly defined hyperparameters, hindered the utility of published models beyond their intended paper applications (even 5 groups of respondents out of 11 reported this problem). Respondent P5 aptly illustrated the issue by questioning the quality of certain published AI models:

"It even happened that model was leaking labels, they were entering the input of the model. And that was not raised as an issue, the paper is still there. You cannot trust the code blindly; otherwise, you repeat the same mistakes."

Despite the existence of Papers with Code, which 6 out of 11 groups of students found helpful in some cases, effectively utilizing benchmarking tools remains a challenge, as pointed out by 2 groups of PhD students. This difficulty arises from the inherent difficulty of comparing different models, compounded by the vague nature of benchmarks. Consequently, results from automated benchmarking lack reliability and interpretability, as each model or user may define their parameters and occasionally engage in deceptive practices, such as training on testing data or comparing with the weakest model.

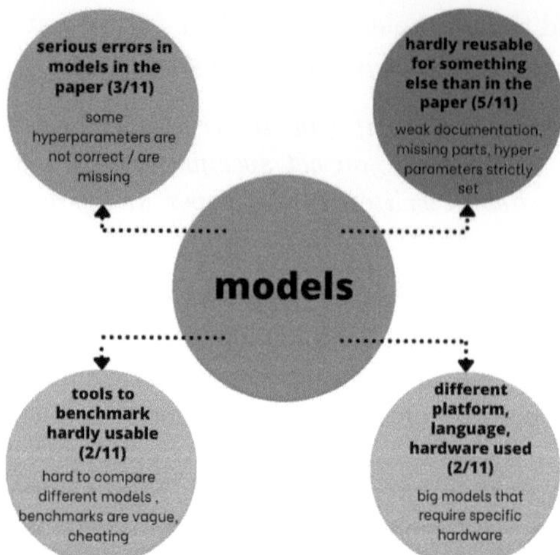

Fig. 3. Model-related challenges of AI resources as reported by research participants.

3.4   Other Challenges Regarding AI Research Process

Our approach allowed us to identify bottlenecks throughout the research process, addressing not only reproducibility challenges but also a spectrum of issues encountered by PhD students. These include technical challenges and managing expectations related to both AI and PhD research (both mentioned in 3 groups out of 11), information retrieval, and problems with publication and dissemination (both mentioned in 5 groups out of 11). While not the primary focus of this paper, these issues are significant aspects of the research journey. (Fig. 4).

These challenges often require collaboration with others. Despite some mistrust in online intra-disciplinary communication, we recognized the need for a scientific interdisciplinary discourse involving experts well-versed in the application domain. Researchers who initiated their research based on their own ideas expressed a desire for increased opportunities to exchange and compare problems while brainstorming with experts from various fields. When such cooperation occurred, it facilitated the advancement of their research. However, researcher P6 encountered difficulties in finding suitable communication channels:

"I store many ideas in my personal document and it is difficult to find someone [outside the field] to communicate with."

We consider another significant concern in AI research to be the lack of human involvement. This concern is closely tied to trustworthiness, primarily regarding accountability requirements. It also intersects with stakeholder participation, as outlined in the "Diversity, Non-discrimination and Fairness"requirement within ALTAI (Assessment List for Trustworthy Artificial Intelligence) [2]. Young AI researchers seemed to overlook ethical assessments and rarely involve human participants in their studies. *De facto*, none of the

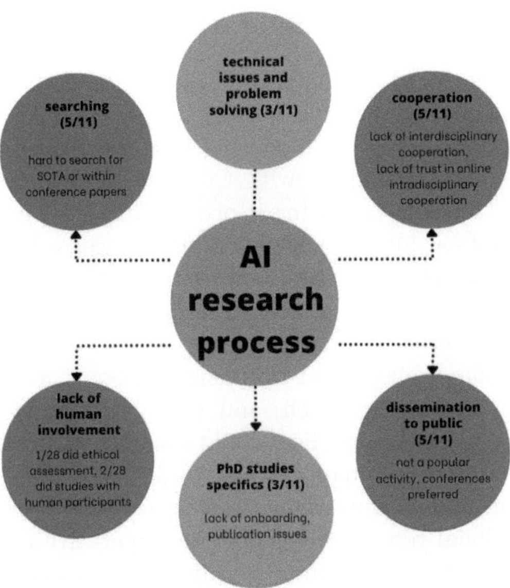

Fig. 4. Problematic parts of AI research process as reported by research participants.

AI researchers conducted any additional ethical assessments beyond what was required for the ethical sections of the journals. This issue was corroborated by the experience of an AI ethics specialist that has been helping the AI community with these kind of assessments (P8):

> *"I was surprised by the lack of care of computer scientists about the ethical issues and information about data."*

The limited understanding of ethical assessments and a lack of standardized frameworks contribute to this issue, as noted by an AI ethics expert who assists researchers with crucial questions regarding data collection, ownership, and storage. Nevertheless, rigorous and standardized ethical assessments are not merely a technical requirement but a fundamental humanistic imperative in AI development. Furthermore, human participant engagement in AI research was minimal, with only two out of 28 respondents investigating stakeholder requirements, despite many focusing on areas where human involvement would be beneficial. Involving end-users and domain experts early in the AI development lifecycle (e.g., through co-design or participatory design) ensures that AI solutions are relevant, usable, trustworthy, less biased, and address real-world problems from a human perspective, rather than being purely technology-driven.

4   Perspectives and Recommendations

From our findings, it appears that three main areas of improvements are possible for better AI research: (1) Discoverability and quality of AI resources. (1) Reproducibility of experiments (1) Trustworthiness and interdisciplinarity

4.1 Discoverability and Quality of AI Resources

Locating AI resources, such as code, datasets, or models, can be challenging. Our findings highlight that the links between papers and AI resources are often broken once a paper is accepted, hindering long-term accessibility and utility. Existing platforms such as Papers with Code[3] while widely used (researchers in 6 groups out of 11 mentioned using it occasionally), have proven insufficient. Despite their theoretical aim to alleviate these issues, we observed they often fall short due to a lack of quality assurance policies for the resources they host. Beyond the discoverability problem, the AI resources that our respondents examined consistently exhibited significant quality issues. We argue these problems stem from two primary causes: (A) insufficient support for researchers to perform necessary AI resource curation, and (B) a lack of incentive or recognition for this crucial work. Researchers could greatly benefit from research data curation services, which encompass essential tasks like data cleaning, validation, metadata provision, and consultations, similar to those already integrated into established institutional repositories [14]. The imperative for proper documentation of AI resources have been addressed by numerous papers and initiatives, including but not limited to the"Datasheets for Datasets" [10], and Model Cards for Model Reporting [16]. As the practices and needs highly depend on the domain, papers summarizing the optimal data curation practices for machine learning also emerge, for example in security [24] or medicine [9]. However, as noted by [22], there is still much work to be done. Institutionalizing collaborations among domain experts, lawyers, ethicists, and data/code curators is vital. Research organizations must provide guidelines and encourage standardized documentation practices, which will not only enhance the quality of AI resources but also improve the reproducibility of experiments (see Recommendation 3).

> **Recommendation 1**
>
> The AI research community needs to foster interdisciplinary collaboration for the governance of AI resources.

4.2 Reproducibility of Experiments

Our findings show that early-career researchers frequently encounter significant hurdles in reproducing AI experiments. This issue stems from a combination of technical problems, such as bugs in code or datasets and discrepancies between papers and associated resources, as well as social factors like inadequate peer review and difficulties with accessing or configuring hardware and software. To overcome these challenges, the AI community should draw inspiration from fields like physics by adopting stricter reproducibility policies.

---

[3] https://paperswithcode.com/.

Recommendation 2

The AI research community should embrace reproducibility practices widely and enforce stricter reproducibility policies in journals and conferences.

A small number of conferences and journals in computer science have taken steps to embrace reproducibility initiatives *in practice*. IEEE Transactions on Parallel and Distributed Systems[4] is the first IEEE journal to pilot a reproducibility initiative. Conferences in computer science with reproducibility initiatives include ASPLOS[5], ACM SIGPLAN[6], ACM SIGMOD[7], or SC[8], and more recently in AI, MLSYS[9], or NeurIPS[10]. These initiatives aim to enhance research reproducibility primarily through reproducibility evaluations. Reproducibility evaluations involve dedicated tracks for accepted papers. During these evaluations, authors of accepted papers submit a computational resource containing all necessary components for replicating their experiments, including datasets, code, and scripts. These efforts go beyond simple code and data sharing, including mechanisms for experiments packaging (e.g., using containers or virtual machines to manage software dependencies), dataset curation and documentation, and thorough process documentation. Successful evaluations often result in the awarding of reproducibility badges, recognized by publishers like ACM or IEEE, which signify the availability of resources and the successful reproduction of results by reviewers. Beyond conference and journal initiatives, individual research organizations can also play a vital role. For instance, one robotics laboratory of one of our respondents implemented mandatory coding guidelines and employed dedicated staff member to maintain and debug code repositories, significantly improving reproducibility and collaboration within the lab by enabling efficient reuse of code packages.

Recommendation 3

Research institutions and laboratories should set up guidelines and practices for their researchers and provide adequate resources (time and human) to ensure quality of AI resources and reproducibility of experiments.

Despite the growing adoption of reproducibility initiatives, several technological challenges remain, particularly concerning hardware dependencies. Reproducing certain AI experiments, like those involving constraint programming,

---

[4] https://www.computer.org/csdl/journal/td/write-for-us/104303.

[5] https://www.asplos-conference.org/.

[6] https://www.sigplan.org/.

[7] https://sigmod.org/.

[8] https://sc24.supercomputing.org/.

[9] https://mlsys.org/.

[10] https://neurips.cc/.

often demands highly specific hardware that current editorial policies don't support. Another significant hurdle is the substantial time and energy required to compile, install, deploy, and execute experiments. This poses a problem for reviewers facing strict deadlines and raises concerns about the energy consumption if authors pre-run experiments prior to reviewers for verification. A promising solution to these challenges is a cloud federation [8,26]. This concept allows AI researchers to efficiently share both AI resources and computational resources from various providers. Central to this approach is a metadata catalogue, designed using FAIR principles (Findability, Accessibility, Interoperability, Reusability), which facilitates navigation among datasets, AI models, papers, and experiments. Furthermore, existing tools and services used by reproducibility initiatives are often not well-suited for AI, imposing a significant burden on researchers. For example, while code is typically uploaded to version control systems like GitHub and paired with Zenodo for DOIs, GitHub lacks support for different datasets versions. This forces authors to use additional tools and services, such as open dataset repositories, to manage dataset versions and DOIs. There's a clear need for new, AI-specific tools that better align with the unique requirements of AI research.

> **Recommendation 4**
>
> The AI research community should investigate the possibility to create a cloud federation for AI systems and suitable tools for control versioning of AI experiments, including datasets, models and code altogether.

4.3   Trustworthiness and Interdisciplinarity

The third issue that our research uncovered goes beyond the technical aspects of AI research but more related to interpersonal and institutional relations, and the lack of interdisciplinarity in the field. First, we observed that early-career researchers rarely include end-users or human participants in their experiments, despite many of them working on topics that would benefit from such practices. The research of PhD students is often very techno-centered: the goal is to produce a working algorithm or system, and the analysis of factors other than performance is often forgotten (for instance user experience, inclusion, ...). Event though methods exist and are considered best practices in other fields, such as Codesign [25], they are rarely included in the field of AI research. This may be a direct consequence of the second issue that our research highlighted: the lack of interdisciplinary collaboration for early-career researchers. Early-career researchers are most often left alone (or with their supervisors) to conduct their research and lack the means to contact or discuss with other researchers, especially outside their institutions or main field of research. Our research also indicates that existing public virtual communities are often not conducive to idea sharing among researchers due to concerns about idea theft. Similarly to what we recommended for quality and reproducibility (Recommendation 3), institutions have a role to play in encouraging multidisciplinarity. One starting point would be for them to diversify their research staff, for instance with lawyers, ethicists, domain experts, UX or HCI specialists, or information scientists. For institutions in which this diversity already exists (for instance, universities often have several schools that employ researchers in these different domains), they should ensure robust institutional support for interdisciplinary meetings, collaboration and hands-on research endeavors.

> **Recommendation 5**
>
> Research institutions should support interdisciplinary collaboration by ensuring a large diversity of research staff and providing the means for researchers to collaborate efficiently.

5   Conclusions and Discussion

Good research is collective and multidisciplinary, building on prior work to advance knowledge. In order to produce good research efficiently, this prior work must be usable - discoverable, reproducible, and responsible for researchers. Our study of AI PhD students shows this is not yet the case. Despite growing awareness and initiatives, more effort is needed to improve AI research practices. Efforts must be both technological—developing platforms for discoverability and reproducibility—and societal—encouraging multidisciplinarity and trustworthiness. To this extent, we proposed five recommendations for the AI research community and institutions to consider in order to improve the research process. We acknowledge systemic barriers that hinder adoption of our recommendations and note that addressing them lies beyond this paper's scope. We believe overcoming such barriers requires collective action, particularly from institutions with the power and resources to support and incentivize researchers. Our study is limited to European PhD students and a moderate sample size, restricting quantification. Broader validation is needed to assess these challenges globally. Notably, reproducibility challenges in AI mirror those in fields like psychology and neuroscience, which have responded with reforms such as preregistration, data and code sharing, and large-scale replications [17,19]. AI research, however, studies artifacts created by researchers themselves, suggesting repeatability should be easier since models, code, and data can be shared [11]. Yet, as our study and prior work show, sharing alone is insufficient; PhD students highlight further efforts needed to reach this baseline. Finally, while some work has studied the impact of reproducibility (e.g., citation counts [21,29]), our work highlights the effects of irreproducibility on the AI community—an underexplored area deserving more attention.

Acknowledgments. This work was supported by the European Commission via Horizon projects AI4Europe (Grant 101070000) and Low Resource Artificial Intelligence (Grant 101136646); by the Government of Aragon (Group Ref. T64_20R,

COSMOS research group); and as part of project PID2020-113037RB-I00, funded by MICIU/AEI/10.13039/501100011033. Although the ethics committee was not yet operational at the interviewing institution, the research adhered to all applicable national and international ethical guidelines and regulations for studies involving human participants. Informed consent was obtained and all personal data was anonymized to protect sensitive information and ensure interviewee anonymity; therefore, interview data cannot be openly published. The authors are solely responsible for all content and ideas, with AI tools (ChatGPT and Gemini) used only for language refinement. We also thank Miroslav Blstak for recording and note-taking of the interviews.

Disclosure of Interests. The authors have no competing interests to declare that are relevant to the content of this article.

References

1. Building a responsible AI: how to manage the AI ethics debate. https://www.iso.org/artificial-intelligence/responsible-ai-ethics

2. Assessment List for Trustworthy Artificial Intelligence (ALTAI) for self-assessment | Shaping Europe's digital future (2020). http://bit.ly/4nruwkL

3. Artificial intelligence index report 2024. Tech. rep., Stanford University (2024)

4. Albertoni, R., Colantonio, S., Skrzypczynski, P., Stefanowski, J.: Reproducibility of machine learning: terminology, recommendations and open issues. CoRR abs/2302.12691 (2023)

5. Athukorala, K., Hoggan, E., Lehtiö, A., Ruotsalo, T., Jacucci, G.: Information-seeking behaviors of computer scientists: challenges for electronic literature search tools. Proc. Am. Soc. Inf. Sci. Technol. **50**(1), 1–11 (2013)

6. Ball, P.: Is AI leading to a reproducibility crisis in science? Nature **624**(7990), 22–25 (2023)

7. Cockburn, A., Dragicevic, P., Besançon, L., Gutwin, C.: Threats of a replication crisis in empirical computer science. Commun. ACM **63**(8), 70–79 (2020)

8. Craig, A., Assis, M., Bittencourt, L.F., Nativi, S., Tolosana-Calasanz, R.: Big iron, big data, and big identity. New Front. High Perform. Comput. Big Data **30**, 139 (2017)

9. Diaz, O., et al.: Data preparation for artificial intelligence in medical imaging: a comprehensive guide to open-access platforms and tools. Physica Med. **83**, 25–37 (2021)

10. Gebru, T., et al.: Datasheets for datasets. Commun. ACM **64**(12), 86–92 (2021)

11. Gundersen, O.E., Kjensmo, S.: State of the art: reproducibility in artificial intelligence. In: Proceedings of the AAAI Conference on Artificial Intelligence. vol. 32 (2018)

12. Hemminger, B.M., Lu, D., Vaughan, K., Adams, S.J.: Information seeking behavior of academic scientists. J. Am. Soc. Inform. Sci. Technol. **58**(14), 2205–2225 (2007)

13. Kapoor, S., Narayanan, A.: Leakage and the reproducibility crisis in machine-learning-based science. Patterns **4**(9) (2023)

14. Lee, D.J., Stvilia, B.: Practices of research data curation in institutional repositories: a qualitative view from repository staff. PLOS ONE **12**(3), e0173987 (2017), publisher: Public Library of Science

15. Mansourian, Y.: Exploratory nature of, and uncertainty tolerance in, qualitative research. New Libr. World **109**(5/6), 273–286 (2008)

16. Mitchell, M., et al.: Model cards for model reporting. In: Proceedings of the Conference on Fairness, Accountability, and Transparency, pp. 220–229. FAT* '19, Association for Computing Machinery, New York (2019)
17. Munafò, M.R., et al.: A manifesto for reproducible science. Nat. Hum. Behav. **1**(1), 0021 (2017)
18. National Academies of Sciences, Engineering, and Medicine and others: Understanding reproducibility and replicability. Reproducibility and Replicability in Science, pp. 39–54 (2019)
19. Open science collaboration: estimating the reproducibility of psychological science. Science **349**(6251), aac4716 (2015)
20. Paullada, A., Raji, I.D., Bender, E.M., Denton, E., Hanna, A.: Data and its (dis)contents: a survey of dataset development and use in machine learning research. Patterns **2**(11), 100336 (2021)
21. Raff, E.: Does the market of citations reward reproducible work? In: Proceedings of the 2023 ACM Conference on Reproducibility and Replicability, pp. 89–96 (2023)
22. Rogers, A.: Changing the World by Changing the Data (2021). http://arxiv.org/abs/2105.13947, arXiv:2105.13947 [cs]
23. Steinerová, J.: Methodological literacy of doctoral students – an emerging model. In: Worldwide Commonalities and Challenges in Information Literacy Research and Practice, pp. 148–154. Springer, Cham (2013). iSSN: 1865-0937
24. Tran, N., Chen, H., Bhuyan, J., Ding, J.: Data curation and quality evaluation for machine learning-based cyber intrusion detection. IEEE Access **10**, 121900–121923 (2022)
25. Trischler, J., Pervan, S.J., Kelly, S.J., Scott, D.R.: The value of codesign: the effect of customer involvement in service design teams. J. Serv. Res. **21**(1), 75–100 (2018)
26. Villegas, D., et al.: Cloud federation in a layered service model. J. Comput. Syst. Sci. **78**(5), 1330–1344 (2012)
27. Wang, F., et al.: The devil of face recognition is in the noise. In: Ferrari, V., Hebert, M., Sminchisescu, C., Weiss, Y. (eds.) ECCV 2018. LNCS, vol. 11213, pp. 780–795. Springer, Cham (2018). https://doi.org/10.1007/978-3-030-01240-3_47
28. Wilkinson, M.D., et al.: The fair guiding principles for scientific data management and stewardship. Sci. data **3**(1), 1–9 (2016)
29. Winter, S., Timperley, C.S., Hermann, B., Cito, J., Bell, J., Hilton, M., Beyer, D.: A retrospective study of one decade of artifact evaluations. In: Proceedings of the 30th ACM Joint European Software Engineering Conference and Symposium on the Foundations of Software Engineering, pp. 145–156 (2022)

Thinking Along the Lines Generated by GenAI? A Systematic Mapping Study on Academic Writing

Éva Kaczkó[1]([✉]) [iD], Lana Ivanjek[1] [iD], Lisa-Maria Norz[2] [iD], and Elske Ammenwerth[2] [iD]

[1] Johannes Kepler University Linz, Linz, Austria
eva.kaczko@jku.at
[2] UMIT TIROL - Private University for Health Sciences and Health Technology, Hall, Austria

Abstract. The advent of generative AI (GenAI) tools in higher education challenges fundamental assumptions about academic authorship, students' cognitive development and how writing cultivates critical thinking (CT). This systematic mapping study synthesized emerging research on how GenAI is reshaping the relationship between academic writing and CT in higher education. Drawing on 25 peer-reviewed studies published between 2023 and 2025, we analyzed conceptualizations of CT and academic writing, identified pedagogical approaches, and examined the use of GenAI tools across a range of disciplines, educational levels, and geographic contexts. Findings revealed that interest in the use of GenAI in academic writing is global and spans all disciplines and higher educational levels. However, only a minority of studies drew on robust theoretical frameworks. CT was conceptualized predominantly within a cognitive skills paradigm, while broader understandings linked to criticality and critical pedagogy were largely absent. Pedagogical models were rare and mostly untested, and educators' perspectives were underrepresented. While GenAI was seen as supporting writing processes, its potential to foster or hinder CT remained contested. Future research should broaden conceptual foundations, include educator perspectives, and prioritize pedagogical design and evaluation. Rethinking academic writing as a transformative practice may require moving beyond the cognitive paradigm towards more participatory and ethically grounded approaches to CT.

Keywords: Academic Writing · Generative AI · Critical Thinking

1 Introduction

"It can be said that the alphabetical line and the thinking moving alongside it enlightened the dull darkness of the magical-mythical world of life. That it opened windows into this world to let in the light of critical thinking" (Flusser, 2002 [1], p. 151, translated from German). What will *the lines generated by GenAI*, racing past human thought at top speed, let in?

© The Author(s) 2026
L. Hagedorn et al. (Eds.): DIGHUM 2025, LNCS 16319, pp. 467–482, 2026.
https://doi.org/10.1007/978-3-032-11108-1_35

Epistemic technologies such as writing, printing, the internet, and social media have transformed thinking, human cognition, and knowledge cultures [2]. Similarly, generative AI (GenAI) opens up new paths for human thinking and education by adding a unique function: it deals with epistemic content through its capability of writing. Thus, GenAI affects directly in one of academia's core knowledge practices. GenAI compels us to rethink the cultural technique of writing in order to preserve its central role in education and the trustworthiness of science [3], and to explore how this new technology reshapes the way thinking in writing comes about and evolves.

Writing is central to academic life at all study levels – undergraduate, (post)graduate, and doctorate – and is deeply intertwined with an essential dimension of higher education, that is, the cultivation of scientific thinking and practice. Teaching the approaches and methods of science aims to develop analytical and reflective skills and foster the formation of well-reasoned personal standpoints through engagement with different perspectives and the search for truth [4]. Academic writing emphasizes translating scientific thinking into words and requires text with clear structure that reflects both scientific reasoning and argumentation [5]. Both in general and within specific disciplines, academic writing helps to develop particular abilities, such as using texts for learning or inspiration and expressing effectively ideas in written form [6]. Proficient academic writers engage in critical thinking (CT) through writing, regulate their writing processes, and communicate in accordance with the established conventions of their respective professional or academic communities.

Academic writing is particularly suitable for fostering CT and promoting discipline-specific ways of thinking in all subjects. This intricate relationship between thinking and writing has also been acknowledged in recent studies of GenAI use in academic writing [7, 8]. While AI tools assist in grammar and style, concerns remain about their impact on creativity and CT. This perspective aligns with the views of several scholars who have expressed concerns about over-reliance on GenAI tools and advocated for the promotion of CT [9–11]. Some scholars argue that GenAI can enhance CT skills [12, 13], but studies such as Kosmyna's [14] show that learning may decrease when GenAI is used in essay writing.

Against this background, it is important to reflect more deeply on the concept of CT. The term encompasses a variety of meanings, making it vital to examine more closely how it is conceptualized and studied, particularly when educators aim to foster its development. To discern specific meanings, we draw on Davies and Barnett's [15] classification: (i) CT has traditionally been defined as reflective thinking aimed at making judgment that needs a composite of particular cognitive skills and dispositions [16–18]. Davies and Barnett summarized such understanding within the *critical thinking movement* and emphasized that this conception of CT centers on the individuals' cognitive abilities and attitudes. What this lacks is a socio-cultural view – an exterior perspective on the individual. With respect to the latter, Davies and Barnett delineated two further movements: (ii) *criticality* and (iii) *critical pedagogy*. *Criticality* encompasses not only CT, but also 'critical being' and 'critical acting'. Students become critical beings if they both reflect on their knowledge and develop "powers of critical thinking, critical self-reflection, and critical action" (p. 15). Davies and Barnett described criticality with the way a human is in the world, having a critical orientation towards the world and motivation to act (ethically). For instance, Ostendorf and Thoma [19] explored post-structuralist concepts, such as Derrida's notion of deconstruction, in the context of what it means to become a critical being. In the context of *critical pedagogy*, scholars [e.g., 20] emphasize human freedom and the overcoming of social conditions that constrain it. They are concerned with both the individuals' critical actions and those of the social institutions vital to societal change, particularly to resisting ideological hegemony and transforming inequitable power structures (including undemocratic societies). If we assume that GenAI will transform human thinking [1, 2], higher education should teach types of CT that hold GenAI to account and enable valuable transformation. Such approaches are more likely to be found within the criticality movement and in critical pedagogy.

To the best of our knowledge, no review articles have delved deeply into the conceptualization of CT in academic writing and GenAI use. In this systematic mapping study, we therefore aimed to chart current educational research on the interplay between the use of GenAI in academic writing and the development of students' CT in its various senses. Our objective was to identify the key areas in published research and determine the next steps to purposefully position our research efforts. We sought to contribute to rethinking and pedagogically addressing academic writing as a key method for fostering scientific thinking. Consequently, we aimed to answer the following overarching question:

How have studies conceptualized and investigated the relationship between GenAI, academic writing, and critical thinking across higher-education levels?

More specifically, we examined the following sub-questions:

RQ1: How is CT conceptualized in studies addressing GenAI in academic writing?
RQ2: How is academic writing conceptualized in these studies?
RQ3: Which pedagogical approaches have been employed to integrate GenAI and foster CT in academic writing?
RQ4: Which GenAI tools have been utilized in academic writing?

2 Methods

This systematic mapping study followed the methodological framework proposed by Petersen et al. [21], with adaptations suggested by Tikva and Tambouris [22]. This approach organizes and visualizes research types and content, particularly when high-quality primary studies are scarce [21]. It offers a comprehensive overview at less effort than systematic or scoping reviews. Key steps include defining research questions, screening and selecting studies, developing a classification scheme, and extracting and mapping data [22].

2.1 Search for Primary Studies

We searched for empirical studies published between January 2023 and May 2025, covering the period after the public release of ChatGPT. We limited our search to peer-reviewed primary studies in English. Sources were identified by searching the Scopus, Web of Science, and EBSCO databases using the search string ((ALL = ("artificial intelligence" or ai or genai or "generative ai" or chatgpt or gpt or llm* or chatbot))

AND ALL = ("academic writing" or "scholarly writing" or "scientific writing" or "research writing" or writing "near/3" university* or writing "near/3" higher education or writing "near/3" academic*)) AND ALL = ("critical thinking" or "reflective thinking" or "higher-order thinking"). Since screening the studies revealed few from (primarily) English-speaking countries, we broadened the Scopus search using the string (ai AND "critical thinking" AND writing), limiting results to the United States, Canada, UK, Australia, and New Zealand. The overall search resulted in 149 articles.

2.2 Screening and Selection of Studies

We removed 43 duplicates and screened 106 studies. Eligible studies focused on higher education (doctoral, (post)graduate or undergraduate education) and examined the application or implications of GenAI tools in relation to academic writing and CT. Articles that only partially addressed these aspects (e.g., GenAI but no academic writing and/or CT) were excluded. EFL or second-language writing classrooms were excluded unless centered on academic writing. Studies that only addressed AI in general or focused on fields outside education (e.g., medical diagnostics) were also excluded. We included only empirical studies, with the exception of two conceptual papers that introduced relevant pedagogical models. One reviewer (E.K) initially screened all titles and abstracts using the criteria above, which resulted in a further 66 articles being excluded. One study could not be retrieved, and thus 39 full texts remained that were consulted. A PRISMA flow diagram (Fig. 1) documents the screening and selection process, which yielded a total of 25 eligible studies.

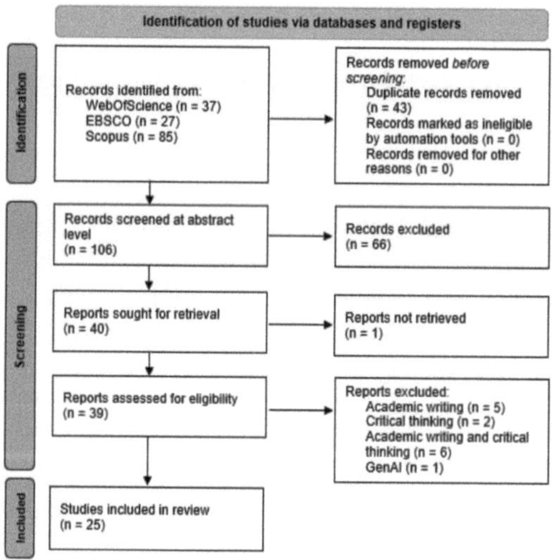

Fig. 1. PRISMA diagram of the process of reviewing studies on the use of GenAI in academic writing and critical thinking in higher education

2.3 Classification Scheme, Data Extraction and Mapping Process

A structured data charting form was created for data extraction, including citation details and subsidiary research questions (RQ1–RQ4). Additional categories were added, such as data collection method, target group (teachers, students), study level, disciplinary context, and country of the study.

We experimented with GenAI tools (e.g., Perplexity.ai, NotebookLM, ChatGPT) to extract content. Since the quality and accuracy of results varied, most data were extracted and analyzed by the researchers. Only the categories of AI tools were extracted by Perplexity, but the manual extraction of the specific tools allowed us to verify the categories. Overall, we partitioned the analysis task according to research question and cross-checked samples to ensure reliability, resolving discrepancies through discussion.

3 Results

3.1 Context of Studies

To gain an initial overview of the study contexts, we focused on five dimensions: geographical distribution, target group, level of study, discipline, and data collection methods. The results are summarized in Fig. 2.

Geographical distribution	Target group	Study level	Disciplinary context	Data collection methods
Africa: Egypt, Ghana, South Africa, Tanzania	Students (16)	Undergraduate (6)	Multidisciplinary (8)	Survey (9)
Asia: China, Eastern Indonesia, Hongkong, India, Indonesia, Iran, Malaysia, Thailand	Teachers (1)	(Post)graduate (8)	Language (4)	Intervention (5)
Australia & Oceania: New-Zealand	Both (2)	Doctorate (8)	Education (3)	Model/conceptual (5)
Europe: Finland, Italy, Norway, Portugal, Spain, Sweden, Turkey, UK	Others (6)	Not specified (2)	Not specified (2)	Interview (4)
N-America: Canada, USA		Not applicable (6)	Psychology (2)	Documents (2)
S-America: Brazil, Ecuador			Engineering (2)	Asynchronous interview (1)
			Information Systems (2)	Phenomenological survey (1)
			EdTech (1)	Screen records (1)
			Business (1)	Narrative literature review (1)
			Medicine (1)	Observation (1)
			Humanities (1)	Think-aloud approach (1)
			Social Sciences (1)	Design research (1)
				Other (1)

Fig. 2. Study contexts of 25 studies on the impact of GenAI on academic writing and CT

Geographical Distribution. The 25 studies included 24 countries in six continents. Their geographic distribution revealed no particular concentration in specific regions but reflected global interest in and concern about the implications of GenAI use on critical thinking in academic writing.

Disciplinary Context. Similarly, the studies revealed a broad interest across natural sciences, social sciences and humanities, as shown in Fig. 2.

Target Group and Study Level. The majority of the studies focused on exploring the student perspective [9–11, 23, 24, 28, 29, 31, 32, 34, 36, 38–41]. One study examined CT in academic writing from the teacher's perspective [35], while two studies addressed both student and teacher perspectives [30, 42]. Six further studies investigated neither student nor teacher perspectives [25, 26, 33, 37, 43, 44].

The studies explored various higher educational levels: eight studies were conducted with doctoral students [11, 23, 24, 27–29, 34, 41], eight in the context of (post)graduate education [23, 24, 27, 34–36, 39, 40] and six in undergraduate education [9, 30, 31, 36, 38, 42]. Two studies [10, 32] did not specify the study level, and six studies were somewhat conceptual and did not differentiate between study levels.

Data Collection Methods. In terms of data collection, a variety of methods were applied: Student or teacher surveys (questionnaires) [9, 23, 24, 27–31, 38, 41], intervention studies [10, 31, 36, 39, 40], framework/model proposals or conceptual studies [25, 35, 37, 43, 44], and interviews [23, 26, 32, 34] were the most frequently used methods. Authors also applied specific methods such as document analysis [33, 34], asynchronous interviews [27], phenomenological questionnaires [11], screen records [41], observations [34], think-aloud protocols [34], and data from design research [42]. Several studies combined methods, such as surveys and interviews [9, 23], intervention and survey [36], interview and screen records [41], or narrative literature review and asynchronous online interviews [38].

3.2 Conceptualization of CT by Using GenAI in Academic Writing

Although all studies mentioned critical thinking, our analysis identified only four that explicitly provided a definition. Fourteen studies alluded to dimensions that reflected the study authors' interpretation only indirectly, while seven additional studies referred to CT without offering a definition or discussing any specific aspects of it.

Studies that Conceptualize CT. Kong et al. [25] defined CT and the critical thinker based on Halpern [18] and Kong [51]. Octaberlina et al. [32] referenced Abrami et al. [45], who conducted a meta-study on teaching strategies for CT grounded in the APA definition by Facione [17]. Additionally, they drew on Bezanilla et al. [46], who did not conceptualize CT directly, but presented methodologies for teaching and learning.

Shen & Chen [34] took a more integrative approach by combining two CT frameworks. They built on the critical skill framework by Facione [17] and extended their analysis with the Four Resources Model of critical literacy practice [47]. They conceptualized academic writing as a dynamic practice of social literacy, framing CT as an interactive process of meaning-making with digital tools. This approach embeds students' CT within their diverse identities as critical readers, encouraging them to reflect on, evaluate, and appropriately apply both human- and GenAI-generated texts within particular cultural, ideological, ethical, and political contexts.

Zhao et al. [35] proposed a CT taxonomy that is grounded in Bloom's taxonomy and specific to academic writing. They defined CT as both a process and a product, drawing on diverse scholarly perspectives, including that of Brookfield [16]. They highlighted the scarcity of research on CT within subject-specific education contexts in academic writing and emphasized the interconnected nature of CT and writing, arguing that underdeveloped CT skills impair argumentation quality and that mastery of language – understood within its social and cultural context (cf. Vygotsky) – is essential to CT.

Studies that Mention Specific Aspects of CT without Providing a Definition. The evaluation of GenAI-generated content (one dimension of the APA definition and

Bloom's taxonomy) was mentioned most frequently [9, 10, 24, 26, 31, 39, 40, 43, 44]. Other CT skills referenced that matched the APA definition (cf. Fig. 1 in [19], p. 37) included interpretation [9, 44], self-regulation [10, 24], explanation [24, 41], analysis [9, 11, 31], and inference [9, 31, 40]. Logical reasoning and argumentation were also recurring themes [9, 30, 31, 40–42] which are central to argumentation literacy.

Some authors highlighted particular dispositions of critical thinkers. For instance, Cail [36] called for a cautiously skeptical stance towards AI content, Khampusaen [31] underscored the importance of independent thinking, Malik et al. [9] stressed critical acumen, and Pratiwi et al. [11] advocated for reflective engagement with AI tools. Huang et al. [40] prompted ChatGPT to propose a rubric for assessing students' CT, but this appears to be a mosaic of various concepts and lacks coherence. Zhu and Duan [44] prioritized meaning negotiation between humans and GenAI, emphasizing the importance of human encyclopedic knowledge as a foundation for prompting.

3.3 Conceptualization of Academic Writing by Using GenAI

Six studies incorporated the conceptualization of academic writing as part of the theoretical foundation of the analysis. Nine studies focused on particular aspects of academic writing, while ten studies addressed the topic without providing any explicit description or definition.

Studies where Academic Writing Forms Part of the Theoretical Foundation. Nguyen et al. [41] built on Flower and Hayes' [48] cognitive process theory of writing, and explored writing process regulation methods that mitigate the risk of overloading working memory. They investigated and visualized structured adaptive and unstructured streamline writing tactics. Five studies emphasized the importance of specific cognitive and linguistic skills in academic writing: Building on existing models, Jin et al. [24] proposed a writing framework which incorporates aspects such as AI, CT, writing improvement, and utility value, but does not provide insights into the writing process itself. Khampusaen [31] theorized argumentative writing and evaluated it using Oxford's Strategy Inventory for Language Learners [49] and a rubric for evaluating essays. Kong et al. [25] built on Short's [52] authoring cycle for inquiry-based academic writing and Zimmerman's self-regulated learning [50]. Shen and Chen [34] emphasized the genre-based formal nature of academic writing, highlighting its role in fostering CT skills to create, disseminate, and exchange knowledge within academic communities. Zhao et al. [35] developed and proposed a CT taxonomy specifically tailored to academic writing.

Studies that Refer to Specific Aspects of Academic Writing. Pereira et al. [27] provided a general description of the nature of academic writing, emphasizing its technical and formal characteristics, such as objectivity, cohesion, specific formats, and the use of technical and formal vocabulary. Zhu and Duan [44] referenced the cognitive process theory of writing by Flower and Hayes [48]. Almlie et al. [38] examined discipline-specific dimensions of academic writing in engineering. Solak [33] referred to the collaborative writing theory by Lowry et al. [53] as a framework for positioning ChatGPT as a collaborative writing partner.

Five studies investigated a specific type of academic text, particularly the literature review writing process, addressing various steps, such as article design [26], problem formulation [26], exploring research gaps and questions [9, 26, 39], identifying relevant literature [26, 39], writing [26, 37, 39], and editing and proofreading [26]. These studies also examined aspects such as crafting sound article titles [9, 37], drafting compelling abstracts [9, 37], writing methodologies and findings [9], data extraction [39], and bibliography generation for academic texts [37].

3.4 Pedagogical Approaches to Academic Writing and Integrating GenAI

Our analysis identified three studies that proposed a pedagogical model for fostering CT in academic writing that integrates GenAI. We found six further studies in which we recognized some pedagogical activities, and three studies which hinted at possible pedagogical actions. However, in 13 studies we found neither particular pedagogical concepts, nor any precise information about pedagogical action.

Studies that Conceptualize Pedagogical Action. Kong [25] introduced the "6-P Pedagogy" design (Plan, Prompt, Preview, Produce, Peer-review, Portfolio-tracking), which integrates theories in both CT and academic writing. This approach is designed for academic writing courses across disciplines, emphasizing iterative and reflective practices. Two further studies proposed pedagogical models without a theoretical grounding in CT and academic writing. Afifi [43] proposed the "Framework for Intelligent Reformation of Education (FIRE Model)" – a six-phase framework designed to harmonize AI tools with human teaching in academic writing courses in various disciplines – and suggested using AI for operational efficiency and personalization, leaving human educators to focus on fostering students' CT, creativity, and ethical reasoning. Zhu and Duan [44] conceptualized a "Prompt-Based Teaching Model" that is grounded in Wang's [54] pan-indexical process of linguistic signs and draws on examples from English as a Foreign Language (EFL). This model centers on meaning negotiation between humans and generative AI iteratively through prompt engineering.

Studies that do not Conceptualize but Describe Pedagogical Context. Cail [36], Pakdel et al. [10] and Nault et al. [39] outlined a "hybrid approach" to introducing AI to writing assignments. Cail [36] reported about a three-step assignment for psychology students to produce an APA-formatted literature review. Students selected and read papers and created an outline with traditional means, drafted a literature review using an AI tool, and finally verified the results for accuracy and citation manually. Pakdel et al. [10] proposed alternating between handwritten and AI-assisted writing assignments in medical education. Additionally, they incorporated a traditional reflection paper and a SWOT-based reflection, encouraging students to critically evaluate their use of AI tools. Nault et al. [39] adopted a guided exploration, combining direct instruction with assignments that progressively introduced students to AI tools such as Jenni.ai, Quillbot, and ChatGPT. This two-step process began with traditional literature review exercises and transitioned to AI-assisted literature review tasks, fostering interdisciplinary engagement in research methods courses for engineering and business students.

Nguyen et al. [41] and Shen and Chen [34] allowed students to self-determine and regulate their use of AI tools in academic writing tasks. The former [41] focused on essay writing assignments in doctoral Information Systems and Learning and Educational Technology programs, while the latter [34] concentrated on coursework essays, theses, and journal articles produced by students of Educational Studies. Huang et al. [40] described a somewhat traditional academic writing assignment for postgraduate Information Systems students to learn writing, referencing and formatting. Additionally, they asked students to prompt GenAI with specific questions and critically evaluate the responses.

Studies that do not Conceptualize but Offer some Pedagogical Insights. Khampusaen [31] highlighted the need for a comprehensive pedagogical framework that balances technological integration with traditional learning approaches in EFL argumentative essay writing. Subaveerapandiyan et al. [29] referenced human–AI collaboration frameworks in the context of PhD programs in various disciplines. The CT taxonomy of Zhao et al. [35] implies a range of potential pedagogical actions, including mentoring PhD writing projects.

3.5   GenAI Use in Academic Writing

The analysis revealed that academic writing employs a wide range of AI tools (Fig. 3). Although we specifically searched for GenAI applications, we summarize here all applications that were additionally used in the studies, as they highlight the growing breadth and integration of AI applications in academic writing across various stages of the academic workflow.

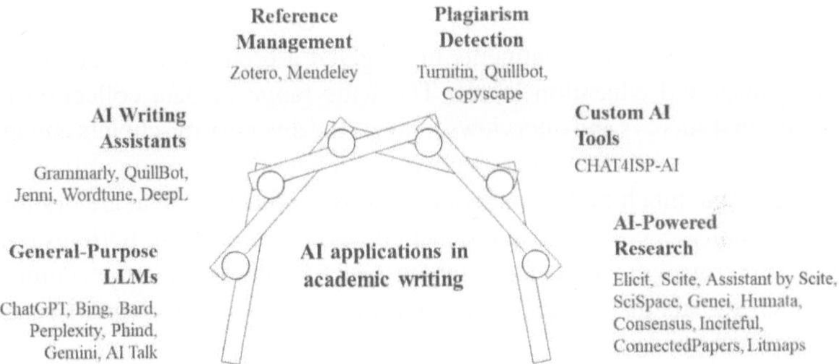

Fig. 3. AI applications in academic writing in 25 studies (generated by Napkin AI Beta version)

3.6   Summary of the Main Results

Overall, we found only nine studies that were grounded in theories in academic writing, critical thinking, and/or pedagogy. These studies centered predominantly on ChatGPT or other general LLMs. In some cases, no specific tools were mentioned. Table 1 provides an overview of which studies based their investigations on specific CT (RQ1) and academic writing (RQ2) theories, and which employed or proposed particular pedagogical approaches to integrating GenAI and fostering CT in academic writing (RQ3). Additionally, we extracted the GenAI tools used in these studies (RQ4).

Table 1. Theoretical grounding in nine studies

	Academic Writing	Critical Thinking	Pedagogical Approach	GenAI
Jin et al. [24]	Yes	No	No	ChatGPT
Khampusaen [31]	Yes	No	No	ChatGPT
Nguyen et al. [41]	Yes	No	No	ChatGPT
Shen & Chen [34]	Yes	Yes	No	ChatGPT
Zhao et al. [35]	Yes	Yes	No	No AI tool but LLM context
Kong et al. [25]	Yes	Yes	Yes	No AI tool but LLM context
Octaberlina et al. [32]	No	Yes	No	ChatGPT and other LLMs
Afifi [43]	No	No	Yes	ChatGPT and other LLMs
Zhu & Duan [44]	No	No	Yes	No AI tool but LLM context

yes = theoretical conception is provided; no = no or little theoretical conception is provided

4 Discussion

4.1 Answering the Research Questions

In the introduction, we posed the overarching question of how studies have conceptualized and investigated the relationship between GenAI, academic writing, and critical thinking at various higher-education levels. To answer this question, we first examined 25 systematically selected studies, focusing on their geographic distribution, disciplinary context, target groups, and data collection methods. Second, we analyzed the theoretical foundations related to CT and academic writing, identified whether and which pedagogical approaches to fostering CT in academic writing were proposed, and explored which GenAI tools were applied in the writing process.

The findings revealed global interest in the use of GenAI in academic writing. Studies from 24 countries across six continents highlighted a broad concern about its impact across disciplines and education levels. The wide range of data collection methods, beyond traditional surveys and interviews, reflects the diversity of scholars engaging with this topic. The focus on students' perspectives, with few studies incorporating educators' views, suggests that much of the concern comes from educators who are grappling with GenAI in their daily teaching and assessment practice. Overall, our findings underscore a broad and interdisciplinary concern about GenAI's influence on academic writing and CT, which signals that a transformative process in one of academia's foundational practices is already underway.

We identified a shortage of well-founded studies that conceptualize and investigate the relationship between GenAI, academic writing, and CT. Such studies are, however, essential for gaining deeper insights into how *the lines generated by GenAI influence our thinking,* and how we can address emerging challenges through purposeful pedagogical actions. Only a limited number of studies [25, 34, 35] grounded their research in specific theories related to both academic writing and CT.

Kong et al. [25] drew on Short's [52] iterative authoring cycle in academic writing and the CT frameworks of Halpern [18] and Kong [51]. Their 6-P Pedagogy aims to foster relevant skills in academic writing across disciplines through the use of LLMs. While this represents the most comprehensive conceptual framework we identified, it remains a theoretical proposal that has yet to undergo empirical evaluation.

Shen and Chen [34] adopted a different approach by conducting a case study to explore how graduate EFL students—specifically, four students at different academic levels—demonstrate critical thinking in ChatGPT-assisted academic writing. In this study, students were allowed to use ChatGPT in a self-directed manner without any prior instruction. The focus was on understanding how students engage with ChatGPT for academic writing, which the authors conceptualized as a form of social literacy practice. This perspective extends CT beyond cognitive skills to include an interactive meaning-making process that involves digital tools and knowledge content from LLMs. Overall, Shen and Chen [34] illustrated how theoretical frameworks—such as Facione's [17 CT skill model and Luke and Freebody's [47] Four Resources Model—can be applied to analyze students' critical (or non-critical) use of ChatGPT in academic writing. Their findings might provide a solid foundation for planning purposeful teaching and learning activities.

Zhao et al. [35] analyzed a large corpus (collected over several years) of teacher feedback on assignments submitted by postgraduate students in education-related programs across various disciplines. On the basis of this analysis and building on Bloom's taxonomy, they developed a taxonomy of CT tailored specifically to academic writing and LLM use. They highlighted the intertwined nature of academic writing and CT, emphasizing that CT skills need to be approached differently across disciplines.

Examining the 18 studies that defined CT to varying degrees revealed perspectives that we situate primarily within the critical thinking movement (cf. Sect. 1). Drawing on the Four Resources Model by Freebody and Luke [47], only Shen and Chen [34] broadened the scope by examining both human- and GenAI-generated texts within cultural, ideological, ethical, and political contexts. However, if higher education aims to foster (radical) transformation under the digital condition that goes beyond cognitive growth (as emphasized by theories within the critical thinking movement), it must embrace broader concepts, such as criticality or critical pedagogy, which may offer a more transformative lens through which to understand CT in the context of GenAI use.

The fact that two studies proposed a pedagogical approach without a deeper grounding in academic writing and CT [43, 44] demands closer examination. Both studies focused on human interaction and thinking with GenAI. The FIRE model [43] appears to lack any pedagogical underpinning, emphasizing factors such as attractiveness, ease of use, relevance, interactivity, and efficiency in the application of AI in education. Similarly, Zhu and Duan [44] adopted an AI-mediated academic writing approach, proposing the Prompt-based Teaching Model, which focuses on optimizing prompt engineering and enhancing students' effective engagement with generative AI. This reminds us of earlier issues with technological determinism in other educational technology fields, such as the initial stages of learning analytics or the integration of chatbots in educational settings.

Given that LLMs are autocomplete systems based on probabilistic calculations and non-transparent training data that cannot ensure "truthful outputs," an AI-centered "pedagogical" approach raises several critical questions. For instance, how can we generate new knowledge when negotiating with an LLM that operates as a black box (with worldviews and biases embedded in its undisclosed training data)? How can we ensure that the knowledge we gain from interacting with an LLM is relevant and reliable when these systems lack any notion of truth? Does negotiating with an LLM improve our knowledge and thinking, or does it merely enhance the LLM's outputs? How can we think "outside the box" when engaging with a system that inherently operates within predefined parameters? While critical evaluation of LLM-generated content is essential, it might not be sufficient to address the broader implications of using such tools in academic writing and education.

It is in fact important to differentiate between various general-purpose and research-focused GenAI tools beyond ChatGPT, as some, such as Perplexity, offer greater transparency. Additionally, while our focus was on the use of GenAI, we observed a growing diversity and integration of both generative and non-generative AI applications in academic writing that cover various stages of the academic workflow. Notably, several authors highlighted the use of GenAI for literature review writing, an area poised for further advancements.

4.2 Strengths and Limitations

Ensuring transparency and traceability was paramount in providing a structured overview of the research on LLMs, critical thinking, and academic writing. This approach helped to identify key research gaps, such as limited theoretical grounding and unclear conceptualizations of CT, while highlighting emerging pedagogical practices and areas for future research. However, our study has several limitations that require careful consideration. First, the analysis and categorization of themes was primarily interpretative, particularly when studies did not explicitly define key concepts. For time reasons, we cross-checked only a sample of each coder's analyses (and resolved differing judgements through discussions). Second, the results of any review are inherently dependent on the search strategies chosen, including the selection of databases, keywords, and inclusion/exclusion criteria. Searching other databases, such as PsycInfo, and other literature types, such as grey literature, conference discussions, blogs, and feuilletons, in which much of the discourse may also be unfolding, might have led to inclusion of more studies. Third, no formal quality assessment of the studies included was done, which limited our ability to weigh the strength of evidence. Finally, the review was restricted to literature published from 2023 onwards, reflecting the rapid evolution of the field following the public release of ChatGPT. While this temporal focus ensures relevance to the current technological landscape, it may have excluded earlier foundational work and thus narrows the historical perspective of the findings.

4.3 Unanswered and Open Questions

We highlight three recommendations for future research based on the insights gained. First, we suggest focusing more on teachers' perspectives on academic writing and GenAI use. Second, there is a pressing need for a clear conceptualization of CT in the context of GenAI use in academic writing, as this has direct implications for pedagogical action. It may be valuable to draw on broader concepts from criticality and the critical pedagogy movements to provide a more transformative perspective on fostering CT – one that also allows thinking "outside the box." Third, the lack of empirically tested pedagogical approaches underscores the need for models and frameworks that focus on pedagogy rather than technology and develop critical thinking in academic writing and GenAI use.

5   Conclusion

This mapping study provided a structured overview of current empirical research on the intersection of generative AI, academic writing, and CT in higher education. While GenAI tools are increasingly integrated into writing practices, theoretical grounding and pedagogically informed approaches remain scarce. The predominant focus on cognitive skill definitions of CT overlooks broader opportunities for transformation that are rooted in criticality and critical pedagogy. Future research should expand conceptual foundations, include educator perspectives, and develop empirically tested frameworks that support reflective and responsible AI use in academic writing.

Acknowledgments. This study was supported by the Federal State of Upper Austria [project no. SONP15500002]. The funding source had no involvement in any part of this study.

Disclosure of Interests.   The authors have no competing interests to declare that are relevant to the content of this article.

References

1. Die Schrift, F.V.: Hat Schreiben Zukunft? 5th edn. European Photography, Göttingen (2002)
2. Henriksen, D., Mishra, P., Woo, L., Oster, N.: Education doctorate in the context of generative artificial intelligence. Impacting Educ.: J. Transforming Professional Pract. **10**(1), 73–79 (2025)
3. Brommer, S., et al.: Wissenschaftliches Schreiben im Zeitalter von KI gemeinsam verantworten. Diskussionspapier Nr. 27. Berlin (2023)
4. Borgwardt, A. Conclusio. Nova Acta Leopoldina, NF **121**(407), 119–124 (2015)
5. Lindsay, D.: Scientific Writing = Thinking in Words. CSIRO Publishing (2020)
6. Gesellschaft für Schreibdidaktik und Schreibforschung (gefsus). Positionspapier: Schreibkompetenz im Studium (2022)
7. Jin, X., Jiang, Q., Xiong, W., Feng, Y., Zhao, W.: Effects of student engagement in peer feedback on writing performance in higher education. Interact. Learn. Environ. **32**(1), 128–143 (2024)
8. Aljuaid, H.: The impact of artificial intelligence tools on academic writing instruction in higher education: a systematic review. Arab World Engl. J. Special Issue on ChatGPT 26–55 (2024)
9. Malik, A.R., et al.: Exploring artificial intelligence in academic essay: higher education student's perspective. Int. J. Educ. Res. Open **5** (2023)
10. Pakdel, F., Khojasteh, L., Kafipour, R., Shahsavar, Z.: Navigating AI writing tools in medical education: a SWOT analysis of L2 academic writing perspectives. Lang. Teach. Res. (2025)
11. Pratiwi, H., Suherman, Hasruddin, Ridha, M.: Between shortcut and ethics: navigating the use of artificial intelligence in academic writing among Indonesian doctoral students. Eur. J. Educ. **60**, 2 (2025)
12. Ruiz-Rojas, L.I., Salvador-Ullauri, L., Acosta-Vargas, P.: Collaborative working and critical thinking: adoption of generative artificial intelligence tools in higher education. Sustainability **16**, 5367 (2024)

13. Suriano, R., Plebe, A., Acciai, A., Fabio, R.A.: Student interaction with ChatGPT can promote complex critical thinking skills. Learn. Instr. **95** (2025)
14. Kosmyna, N., et al.: Your Brain on ChatGPT: Accumulation of Cognitive Debt when Using an AI Assistant for Essay Writing Task. arXiv:2506.08872 (2025)
15. Davies, M., Barnett, R.: The Palgrave Handbook of Critical Thinking in Higher Education. Palgrave Macmillan, New York (2015)
16. Brookfield, S.: Teaching for critical thinking: tools and techniques to help students question their assumptions. The Jossey-Bass Higher and Adult Education Series, San Francisco (2012)
17. Facione, P.A.: Critical thinking: a statement of expert consensus for purposes of educational assessment and instruction. Research findings and recommendations. American Philosophical Association, Newark (1990)
18. Halpern, D.F.: Thought and Knowledge: An Introduction to Critical Thinking, 5th edn. Psychology Press, New York (2014)
19. Ostendorf, A., Thoma, M.: Demands and design principles of a "heterodox" didactics for promoting critical thinking in higher education. HighEduc. **84**, 33–50 (2022)
20. Freire, P.: Pedagogy of the oppressed, 30th Anniversary Edition. Continuum, New York (2005/1970)
21. Petersen, K., Feldt, R., Mujtaba, S., Mattsson, M.: Systematic mapping studies in software engineering. In: Proceedings of the 12th International Conference on Evaluation and Assessment in Software Engineering, Swindon, GBR: BCS Learning & Development Ltd., pp. 68–77 (2008)
22. Tikva, C., Tambouris, E.: A systematic mapping study on teaching and learning Computational Thinking through programming in higher education. Think Skills Creat **41** (2021)
23. Anani, G.E., Nyamekye, E., Bafour-Koduah, D.: Using artificial intelligence for academic writing in higher education: the perspectives of university students in Ghana. Discover Educ. **4**, 46 (2025)
24. Jin, F., Lin, C.H., Lai, C.: Modeling AI-assisted writing: how self-regulated learning influences writing outcomes. Comput. Hum. Behav. **165** (2025)
25. Kong, S.C., Lee, J.C.K., Tsang, O.: A pedagogical design for self-regulated learning in academic writing using text-based generative artificial intelligence tools: 6-P pedagogy of plan, prompt, preview, produce, peer-review, portfolio-tracking. Res. Pract. Technol. Enhanc. Learn. **19**, 30 (2024)
26. Livberber, T.: Toward non-human-centered design: designing an academic article with ChatGPT. Profesional de La Informacion **32**(5), e320512 (2023)
27. Pereira, R., Reis, I.W., Ulbricht, V., dos Santos, N.: Generative artificial intelligence and academic writing: ananalysis of the perceptions of researchers in training. Manage. Res. **22**(4), 429–450 (2024)
28. Ringo, D.S.: The effect of generative AI use on doctoral students' academic research progress: the moderating role of hedonic gratification. Cogent Educ. **12**(1), 2475268 (2025)
29. Subaveerapandiyan, A., Kalbande, D., Ahmad, N.: Perceptions of effectiveness and ethical use of AI tools in academic writing: a study Among PhD scholars in India. Inf. Dev. **41**(3), 728–746 (2025)
30. Vilma, G.G., et al.: Artificial intelligence in higher educational practice. In: Perspectives of Teacher and Students. LNNS, vol. 859, pp. 439–450. Springer, Cham (2025)
31. Khampusaen, D.: The impact of ChatGPT on academic writing skills and knowledge: an investigation of its use in argumentative essays. LEARNJ. Lang. Educ. Acquisition Res. Netw. **18**(1), 963–988 (2025)
32. Octaberlina, L.R., Muslimin, A.I., Chamidah, D., Surur, M., Mustikawan, A.: Exploring the impact of AI threats onoriginality and critical thinking in academic writing. Edelweiss Appl. Sci. Technol. **8**(6), 8805–8814 (2024)

33. Solak, E.: Exploring the efficiency of ChatGPT and artificial intelligence in advancing academic writing pedagogy. Int. J. Educ. Math. Sci. Technol. **12**(6), 1525–1537 (2024)
34. Shen, Y., Chen, L.: 'Critical chatting' or 'casual cheating': how graduate EFL students utilize ChatGPT for academic writing. Comput. Assist. Lang. Learn. (2025)
35. Zhao, H., Dang, T.N.Y., Finlayson, N.: Operationalising critical thinking in postgraduate disciplinary writing: insights from corpus and cluster analyses of lecturer feedback. Assess. Eval. High. Educ. **50**(3), 422–441 (2025)
36. Cail, J.: Visualization of AI accuracy: a novel assignment for the teaching of critical thinking and science writing. Teach. Psychol. **52**(3), 285–290 (2025)
37. Saccenti, D., Buattini, M., Grazioli, S., Torres, D.: Navigating the AI frontier: should we fear ChatGPT use in higher education and scientific research? Finding a middle ground through guiding principles and practical applications. Possibility Stud. Soc. **2**(4), 415–437 (2024)
38. Almlie, G.S., Roaldsøy, E.Ø., Lande, I., Heimdal, A.: The use of LLMs in academic writing instruction for first-year students in the engineering bachelor programmes. In: 26th International Conference on Engineering and Product Design Education, Aston University, Birmingham, UK (2024)
39. Nault, K., Nieto-Taborda, M., Ruhi, U.: Guided exploration of AI tools for student academic research and writing, AMCIS Proc. **5** (2024)
40. Huang, C.W., Coleman, M., Gachago, D., Van Belle, J.P.: Using ChatGPT to encourage critical AI literacy skills and for assessment in higher education. In: Communications in Computer and Information Science, vol. 1862, pp. 105–118. Springer, Cham (2024)
41. Nguyen, A., Hong, Y., Dang, B., Huang, X.: Human-AI collaboration patterns in AI-assisted academic writing. Stud. High. Educ. **49**(5), 847–864 (2024)
42. Taiye, M., High, C., Velander, J., Matar, K., Okmanis, R., Milrad, M.: Generative AI-enhanced academic writing: a stakeholder-centric approach for the design and development of CHAT4ISP-AI. In: Proceedings of the ACM Symposium on Applied Computing, pp. 74–80. Association for Computing Machinery (2024)
43. Afifi, N.M.: AI meets academia: the fire model's vision for enhanced learning. Insights Lang. Cult. Commun. **4**(2), 177–189 (2024)
44. Zhu, J., Duan, C.: Pan-indexicality and prompt: developing a teaching model for AI-mediated academic writing. Lang. Semiotic Stud. **11**(2), 286–304 (2025)
45. Abrami, P.C., Bernard, R.M., Borokhovski, E., Waddington, D.I., Wade, C.A., Persson, T.: Strategies for teaching students to think critically: a meta-analysis. Rev. Educ. Res. **85**(2), 275–314 (2015)
46. Bezanilla, M.J., Fernández-Nogueira, D., Poblete, M., Galindo-Domínguez, H.: Methodologies for teaching-learning critical thinking in higher education: the teacher's view. Think Skills Creat. **33**, 100584 (2019)
47. Freebody, P., Luke, A.: Literacies programs: debates and demands in cultural context. Prospect: Australian J. TESOL **5**(3), 7–16 (1990)
48. Flower, L., Hayes, J.R.: A Cognitive Process Theory of Writing. College Composition and Commun. **32**(4), 365–387 (1981)
49. Zou, B., Lertlit, S.: Oxford's strategy inventory for language learning: English learning of Chinese students in Thai University. Lang. Educ. Acquisition Res. Netw. **15**(2), 705–723 (2022)
50. Zimmerman, B.J.: Becoming a self-regulated learner: an overview. Theory Pract **41**(2), 64–70 (2002)
51. Kong, S.C.: Developing information literacy and critical thinking skills through domain knowledge learning in digital classrooms: an experience of practicing flipped classroom strategy. Comput. Educ. **78**, 160–173 (2014)
52. Short, K. G., Harste, J. C., Burke, C. L.: Creating classrooms for authors and inquirers (2nd ed.). Pearson Education Canada (1996)

53. Lowry, P.B., Curtis, A., Lowry, M.R.: Building a taxonomy and nomenclature of collaborative writing to improve interdisciplinary research and practice. J. Bus. Commun. **41**(1), 66–99 (2004)
54. Wang, J.: On the indexical nature of language. Lang. Semiotic Stud. **5**(1), 47–70 (2019)

The Architecture of Academic Overproduction: Toward Post-AI Scholarship

Charles Lang(✉)📧, Chris Moffett📧, and Lalitha Vasudevan📧

Digital Futures Institute, Teachers College, Columbia University, New York, NY 10027, USA
`{charles.lang,Moffett,lmv2102}@tc.columbia.edu`

Abstract. This article critically examines the accelerating phenomenon of academic overproduction, tracing its roots from exponential publication growth in the late twentieth century to the contemporary landscape overwhelmed by digitization, global competition, shifting publication economics and now artificial intelligence. The surge of scholarly output, enabled by advanced digital infrastructures, open-access models, and mega-journals has fueled not only greater access and collaboration, but also mounting information overload, declining editorial standards, and the evolution of a research workforce that spends more and more time chasing metrics. Against this backdrop, the rise of generative artificial intelligence is poised to further intensify these dynamics through both "flattening" (the homogenization and proliferation of scholarly writing) and "enslopification," defined as the mass production of low-quality academic content optimized for metrics rather than insight. These issues reflect deeper epistemological tensions within academic research, between cultures of "knowledge sharing" and "knowledge transfer". Rather than simply blaming digital technologies or AI, we argue that quantification pressures, institutional incentives, and the commodification of research have primed the academy for a crisis of relevance and authenticity. It is thus imperative to reimagine research beyond compliance-driven production and superficial debates about AI integration, instead advocating for multimodal, participatory, and dialogical scholarship. Meaningful reform demands a shift from metric-driven output toward research that cultivates agency, reflection, and genuine public engagement, urging institutions and scholars to reclaim the value and purpose of scholarly inquiry in a post-AI world.

Keywords: Generative AI · Scholarly Publishing · Knowledge Production · Enslopification · Flattening

1 Background

1.1 Acceleration in Academic Production

The accelerating growth of scholarly literature is one of the defining characteristics of modern science and an enduring observation across decades (Fig 1).

© The Author(s) 2026
L. Hagedorn et al. (Eds.): DIGHUM 2025, LNCS 16319, pp. 483–498, 2026.
https://doi.org/10.1007/978-3-032-11108-1_36

The first quantitative analysis of the trend was conducted in the 1960s by a historian of science, Derek J. de Solla Price [26]. Examining data from the 17th to the mid-20th century, Price identified a remarkably consistent pattern: the body of scientific knowledge, measured by number of journals and publications, was growing exponentially, doubling in size approximately every 10 to 15 years. Price was concerned that should this self-reinforcing growth continue unchecked, it would eventually lead to a state of "senility", where the sheer volume of publications could overwhelm the system, potentially resulting in a decay in both attention and quality [27].

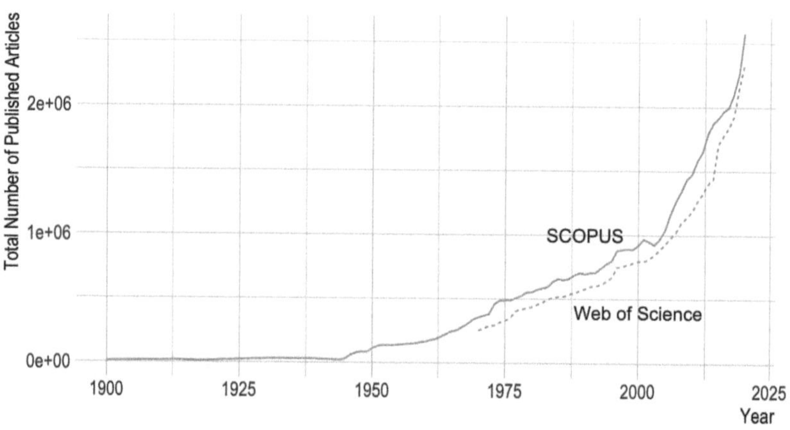

Fig. 1. Exponential growth in publication output over time since 1900 in two publication databases SCOPUS (1900-2020) and Web of Science (1975-2020). Figure recreated from open data posted by [35].

The raw numbers of academic publications have surged to levels that would have made Price deeply concerned. Analyses of major bibliographic databases reveal a clear and dramatic upward trend. Data from Scopus, for instance, shows that the number of academic publications increased from approximately 650 thousand in 1980 to 3.16 million in 2018 [35, 36]. More recent estimates place the annual output even higher, with figures ranging from over 2.5 million to more than 7 million new papers published each year, depending on the scope and database used [10]. The total corpus of scholarly work is now immense, with some estimates suggesting that over 50 million journal articles have been published since the 17th century, the vast majority of which have appeared in the last few decades [15]. Although scientometric experts may differ on whether the growth rate is exponential or following some other model, the data overwhelmingly points to a sustained and accelerating, non-linear increase in publication output (Fig. 1) [14].

2   Drivers of Growth

Although it is difficult to attribute any specific cause to the explosive growth of publication, there are several factors that scholars point to. The advent of the internet and digital technologies and their widespread adoption in the early 1990s did not initiate the growth in academic publication but acted as a powerful accelerant. The transition from a print-based system, constrained by the physical and economic realities of typesetting, paper, and distribution, to a digital ecosystem fundamentally reshaped the infrastructure of scholarly communication. Digital formats dramatically lowered the marginal costs of production and dissemination, while online platforms and databases made information retrieval faster and more efficient [31]. This technological transformation did not merely move print journals online; it created a new environment where the velocity of knowledge dissemination and exchange could increase by orders of magnitude.

The increasing interconnectedness of the global research community and globalization of academic publication has also been a key contributor to publication growth. The digital revolution has made international collaboration easier, leading to a dramatic rise in co-authored research, which by its nature increases the number of publications, both through increasing publication number but also in the creation of international venues for publication such as conferences and journals.

International publication growth has not been evenly distributed though, and a key driver has been the rise of China and India as loci of academic research output [35]. While the United States has long been the dominant producer of academic research, the 21st century has witnessed a dramatic geopolitical re-balancing. Between 1980 and 2018, China's annual publication output, as indexed by Scopus, increased by an astonishing factor of almost 1,000, soaring from just 629 articles to over 600,000 [36]. This shift is not isolated to China; other nations in Asia and the Middle East have also shown remarkable growth in scientific output, fundamentally altering the map of global research.

New publication models also arose that catered to the growing number of researchers across the globe. The Open Access (OA) movement emerged as a direct and radical consequence of the digital revolution. It was founded on the ethical and practical belief that scholarly research, particularly that which is publicly funded, should be freely and universally accessible to all. By leveraging the near-zero marginal cost of digital distribution, OA sought to dismantle the traditional subscription-based "paywall" model that had dominated academic publishing. However, rather than opening knowledge up to the world, it has also incentivized good and bad actors to produce more publications through the "author pays" or Gold Open Access model, where authors or their institutions pay an Article Processing Charge (APC) to make their research freely available. Although this model shifts the cost of publishing from readers to authors or their funders, it incentivizes publishers to increase the number of articles and venues for publication that they produce [20, 30]. Although the exact number fluctuates, by 2015 45% of the articles indexed in the Web of Science were considered OA [25].

Beyond transforming traditional journals, digital technologies also enabled the creation of entirely new channels for scholarly communication, designed for speed and bypassing the often-protracted timelines of formal peer review. Preprint servers such as arXiv (for physics, mathematics, and computer science), bioRxiv (for biology), and medRxiv (for health sciences) have become essential infrastructure in many fields. They allow researchers to upload and share their manuscripts publicly before or during submission to a traditional journal. This practice provides immediate dissemination of findings, allows authors to establish priority for their discoveries, and invites early feedback from the community. The use of these servers has surged; for example, the number of papers submitted to arXiv nearly tripled between September 2006 and November 2018. During global crises like the COVID-19 pandemic, preprint servers became the primary vehicle for the rapid exchange of critical research, demonstrating their vital role in accelerating science. Also, the development of Mega-journals, a new category of journal that emerged in the 2000s, exemplified by publications like PLoS One and Nature's Scientific Reports. These online-only, open-access journals are characterized by their extremely broad disciplinary scope, a peer-review process that focuses on assessing technical soundness rather than subjective novelty or significance, and consequently, very high acceptance rates, estimated to exceed 50% [5]. Their streamlined processes lead to rapid publication times of just 3-5 months. By publishing vast quantities of articles (Scientific Reports increased publication volume 10 times between 2012 and 2017 from 2,498 to 24,077 [4]) mega-journals have become major contributors to the overall volume of global academic output.

2.1   Culture, Institutional and Economic Pressures

While technology provided the infrastructure for the acceleration in publications, the motive force came from a powerful confluence of cultural, institutional, and economic pressures. The digital tools of the internet era (broadband, search engines, e-commerce platforms, etc.) were leveraged by a global academic system increasingly driven by competition, quantification, and a relentless demand for measurable output. Namely, the pervasive "publish or perish" culture, the global influence of university rankings, and the increasing globalization of scientific collaboration. Publication output is a primary currency for career advancement, directly influencing decisions on hiring, tenure, promotion, and research funding. The "publish or perish" culture at the individual level is massively amplified by institutional pressures, chief among them the global competition for students fueled by world university rankings. Since the early 2000s, rankings such as the Academic Ranking of World Universities (ARWU or ShanghaiRanking), the US News and World Report, and the Times Higher Education (THE) World University Rankings have become powerful instruments for assessing institutional prestige and influencing the decisions of students, faculty, and policymakers. This intense focus on quantifiable research output creates a powerful top-down incentive structure. Universities, seeking to improve their standing in these highly visible global league tables, translate the ranking criteria into internal policies and performance targets. This directly fuels the publication production environment, creating a clear link between the abstract goal of institutional prestige and the concrete pressure on an individual researcher to publish one more paper. At the same time, the exponential growth in publication output would not be possible without a publishing industry willing and eager to support it. These changes include expanding publication venues through mega-journals, adopting author-pays and Open Access financial models, growing the number of traditional journals, and innovating peer review processes to incorporate post-publication evaluation. In short, a comprehensive restructuring of the publishing industry has taken place, creating an ecosystem that can support, and profit from, the massive and accelerating growth in scholarly output.

3   Consequences of Growth

The most immediate consequence of exponential growth is information overload. With millions of new articles published annually, traditional literature review methods are no longer sufficient. This creates a meta-level problem requiring sophisticated quantitative tools simply to navigate disciplines and synthesize knowledge. Important findings risk burial in noise, slowing knowledge accumulation. This is compounded if quantity has come at quality's expense. Haslam et al. and van Vlokhoven find that producing more articles, while associated with increased citations, correlates with lower editorial standards [13,37]. Even if high-quality publications aren't declining, they may be swamped by poorly conducted work—the signal-to-noise ratio is falling.

Although not the chief cause, demand for production then contributes to a case of Goodheart's Law ("when a measure becomes a target, it ceases to be a good measure"). As careers and funding have become dependent on maximizing metrics like publication and citation counts, these indicators have been gamed and begun to lose their validity as proxies for quality or impact. Goodheart's Law is evident from a host of problematic academic practices that have risen in concert with the rise in publication numbers. The mean number of authors per paper has increased sharply [23], a trend driven partly by legitimate increases in collaboration but also by strategic additions of authors to inflate publication lists. Similarly, self-citation rates have risen as researchers are incentivized to boost their own metrics [30]. Likewise, there has been growth in "Salami Slicing", the practice of taking a single, coherent body of research and breaking it down into multiple, minimally different publications, or "least publishable units" [34]. This practice distorts the scientific literature by making it appear that multiple independent studies have been conducted, it wastes the time of editors and peer reviewers, and it critically hampers reproducibility by scattering the methods and results of a single study across numerous papers.

Expanding knowledge repositories are also contributing to the "Burden of Knowledge" and scholarly fragmentation, a theory positing that as the frontier of knowledge expands, innovators must undergo longer training and specialize more narrowly, making cross-disciplinary, disruptive work more difficult [16].

This fragmentation of scholarly communities is exacerbated by more journals, more conferences and more articles that prevent consensus and sharing of ideas across large groups; the very thing that digital technology was supposed to facilitate. Indeed, scholars must necessarily rely on technology to parse and make sense of huge amounts of research literature. Despite the deluge of information, there is one area where there is still a dearth of details about the way that academic research publications are collected and stored. Publishing companies, digital repositories and search algorithms are largely proprietary and held by private companies such as Clarivate (formerly Thomson Reuters) that provides Web of Science, ProQuest, Gale Cengage, EBSCOHost, JSTOR and Wiley. While recent events in the United States have also underscored the fragility of public repositories such as PubMed and ERIC. But of real concern is the lack of transparency on how publications are discovered and consumed. Take for example, Google Scholar, a now ubiquitous tool in academic research that provides no information on its inner workings [3, 28]. Google Scholar is likely personalizing results for its users in the same way that other search algorithms do. Yet, it is unclear what this means for the academic enterprise.

The growth in the number of academic submissions is also putting an immense strain on the peer review process, the traditional mechanism for ensuring scientific quality and validity [8]. The sheer volume of papers being submitted to a rapidly growing number of journals makes it increasingly difficult for editors to find enough qualified and willing experts to conduct reviews. Peer review is typically unpaid, voluntary work, and the constant demand is leading to reviewer fatigue and refusal [2, 7]. A strained peer review system, in turn, is less able to detect work that may be premature or methodologically flawed. This is considered a major contributing factor to reproducibility crisis and signal-to-noise issues. There are also documented detrimental psychological effects on researchers due to the intense focus on quantity. It is cited as a major source of psychological stress, anxiety, and burnout [12]. Furthermore, it is directly implicated as a cause of declining research quality, incentivizing the submission of premature or poor-quality work, and contributing to scientific misconduct as researchers scramble to meet institutional demands. The confluence of the intense "publish or perish" pressure and the author-pays OA models created the perfect conditions for a new, parasitic industry: predatory publishing. Predatory journals and publishers exploit the desperation of researchers, particularly early-career scholars or those in less-resourced institutions, to get published. They solicit manuscripts, often through spam emails, and charge authors while providing little to no legitimate peer review, editorial oversight, or indexing services. These journals pollute the scholarly record with substandard, unvetted, and sometimes nonsensical research, undermining the credibility of the OA model and making it harder for legitimate scholars to navigate the literature. The appearance of the "pay to play" model has also been jarring in the social sciences and humanities, where funders have historically not paid for publication.

Overall, possibly most damming, evidence suggests researchers are becoming more efficient at producing publications, not generating knowledge. Although global scientific output has expanded, this growth reflects increased publication volume, not proportional increases in fundamental discoveries. Studies point to declining research productivity per input unit. Bloom et al. [6] show maintaining progress now requires substantially more researchers. While a body of research has emerged that shows apparent individual productivity gains are largely artifacts of increased team size and co-authorship inflation: When these factors are accounted for, publications per scientist have remained flat or declined [9,11]. It appears that increased publication volume is not a reflection of increased research productivity.

4   AI has Entered the Chat

The previous sections describe inflation in the quantity of academic research product and how this has impacted scholarly work. The key argument we are seeking to make is that this context has "primed the pump" for further AI-fueled growth in academic production. The next section extrapolates how these trends may evolve with the arrival of generative artificial intelligence. We break these trends into two categories: flattening and enslopification.

4.1   Flattening

Flattening is the phenomena whereby articles will become both more numerous and more similar. It would involve the academic version of what is currently occurring in the job application market. The ease of producing CVs and cover letters using generative AI, coupled with online application portals has rapidly increased the number of submissions each applicant is able to submit. At the same time, employers are utilizing AI tools to vet CVs and cover letters creating a feedback loop between the technology employed by job seekers and employers, resulting in an application pool that is both vast and optimized to be homogeneous.

It is not difficult to see how this state of affairs could arise within academic publishing: AI assisting research, AI conducting peer review, and AI consuming published work to generate new publications in an ever accelerating cycle. Under these conditions we may witness "successful" scholars whose work is never read by a human. In this scenario, format has triumphed over content but the content remains acceptable. This might not hold true, however, particularly in case of enslopification.

4.2   Enslopification

Enslopification is a concept related to flattening that specifically concerns the quality of AI generated output [1]. It involves the creation of large amounts of low-effort, poor-quality content using AI (IE - "slop"), driven by incentives that reward quantity over quality and amplified by algorithmic systems that promote popular patterns regardless of their actual value. Social media sites such as Facebook and Pinterest have seen an explosive growth in such content, driven by easy access to AI image and video generational tools, incentivized by the possibility of deriving ad revenue from clicks. Again, we argue that the current climate that exists in academic publishing is well positioned to go down the same path and in fact may already have done so, with increases in AI generated publications reported by [19,22,33]. Academic publishing may be particularly vulnerable to enslopification due to the structural conditions that enable this phenomenon. The core drivers of enslopification (the incentives that reward quantity over quality, the ease of AI content generation, and algorithmic amplification) as we have argued above are present in academic environments. Indeed, the academic publishing ecosystem already contains many of the ingredients necessary for widespread slop production. Universities evaluate faculty based on publication metrics, creating pressure to produce research at scale. The "publish or perish" culture has long prioritized volume, and AI tools now make it possible to generate academic content with unprecedented speed and reduced effort. Just as social media algorithms amplify popular content regardless of quality, academic search engines and citation networks may similarly promote AI-generated research that mimics successful patterns without contributing genuine insights. The prospect of a fully automated academic production cycle presents particularly concerning implications. In such a system, researchers would use AI to write papers, which would then be reviewed by AI systems and subsequently summarized by AI for consumption by other academics. This creates a closed loop where human intellectual engagement becomes increasingly marginalized because machines can operate at magnitudes far greater than any researcher could keep up with. The result could be the systematic production of research that appears scholarly but lacks the critical thinking, original insights, and genuine discovery that drive scientific progress. As argued by Kosmyna et al. [18] and Melumad and Yun [21], this transformation could threaten to fundamentally limit the production of new ideas. When AI systems primarily recombine existing knowledge rather than generate novel insights, the research enterprise may become trapped in iterative cycles that produce variations on established themes rather than breakthrough discoveries. The cognitive work of deep engagement with complex problems, the kind of sustained thinking that produces paradigm shifts, could be displaced by the efficient production of what is being optimized for: article quantity. Such a future makes Price's concerns about "senility" look naive and there is an urgent need for publishers and scholars who serve in editorial positions to reckon with this possibility beyond guidelines such as [29].

5 The Shared Responsibility for Rethinking Research Output in a Post-AI World

The arrival of generative AI has not created a crisis in academic publishing so much as made an existing one harder to ignore. The exponential growth of publications, the rise of performative citation metrics, and the increasing pressure to produce ever more content have already strained the legitimacy of academic research systems. What AI exposes is not simply a glut of papers driven by quantification but a deeper confusion about the value and purpose of research itself. This raises the question, what is research for, when machines can simulate academic language, reasoning, and even critique? And what, if anything, remains distinctive and valuable about scholarship when its genres and structures are so easily mimicked? It is the shared responsibility of researchers, practitioners, and institutions to consider these questions and identify - if not solutions given the shifting landscape - then at least suggestions for addressing this exponential growth.

At the heart of academic research and publishing today lies a tension between two epistemological orientations. The first, a culture of *knowledge sharing*, treats research as a dialogical practice of mutual engagement, grounded in interpretation, debate, and collective inquiry. The second, a culture of *knowledge transfer*, frames research as the efficient transmission of discrete, measurable outputs aligned with institutional and commercial logics. While both exist within the academy, the latter increasingly dominates, prioritizing compliance and visibility over understanding. For decades, academic research has been pulled into alignment with the demands of institutional visibility, funding logic, and career advancement. The result is a system in which research practices are increasingly shaped more by the needs of compliance and accumulation than by the pursuit of shared questions, meaningful inquiry, or critical reflection.

AI did not create this imbalance, but it is exacerbating its effects and makes its assumptions visible. We argue that this is the case because the process of enslopification had already begun, well before the widespread arrival of generative language models in 2022. The profit incentives within the publishing industry to produce more product to sell, funder requirements for evidence of return on investment, and the recognition incentives within the academic career structure had already produced substantial noise in the system and an amount of published content that was unmanageable. Indeed, Kobak et al. [17] and Picazo et al. [24] make the case that academics rapidly adopted AI tools as soon as they became available. Thus the challenge is not merely to integrate AI tools or not, but to recover the dialogic, constructivist ethos of scholarship that AI risks automating out of existence. In other words, this is not just a crisis of volume, quality control, or even authentic authorship. It is a crisis of epistemological orientation.

AI reveals just how brittle these structures have become. When a system rewards output over insight, reproduction over depth, and metrics over meaning, it becomes simultaneously easy to automate and difficult to care about or for. The question, then, is not how to incorporate or defend against AI, but how to create purposes that resist outsourcing, simulation, or scale, that is by cultivating knowledge practices grounded in attention, accountability, and meaningful learning.

This calls for a deliberate shift in focus: away from debates about integrating AI mired in the logic of production and quantifiable assessment, and toward the cultivation of knowledge practices grounded in agency, interpretation, and situated value judgment. This means recognizing that knowledge is not merely transmitted but formed through acts of dialogue, reflection, and ethical responsibility, and that the systems we build should be accountable to those values.

As we have said, this crisis, while made visible by AI, is not new. The tensions between knowledge sharing and knowledge transfer, long present in academic life, have been exacerbated by metric-driven research environments. Scholarship is increasingly bifurcated into dialogical, reflective, and interpretive modes, on the one hand, and commodification and institutional utility, measured by volume and speed, on the other hand. Rather than perpetuate a dichotomy between these perspectives, institutional norms can reposition research an activity that constructs shared worlds, and in the process recover forms of transmission and institutional utility that have been captured.

5.1   From Labor Creep to a Rethinking of Academic Labor

Much current discourse imagines a division of labor between humans and machines. In this common story, AI will handle the mechanical or compliance-based aspects of academic work—formatting, citation management, summaries —allowing human researchers to return to "real" thinking. This is a version of the long promise of technology to free us up from labor in order to pursue a life of leisure. But in academia this tidy separation conceals a deeper problem. The very idea of such a division presupposes an academic system already captured and governed by what anthropologists describe as an epistemological audit culture: a regime in which thinking is parsed into discrete, measurable tasks optimized for performance [32]. This audit culture is predicated on the idea that particular forms of production correlate to meaningful work. Certain forms ostensibly indicate deep familiarity with fields and problems, the written and unwritten assumptions of quality, and the time and labor that have gone into research.

Under these conditions, even tasks like writing, creating, or theorizing are increasingly shaped by logics of productivity, making them indistinguishable from administrative labor. This is a form of labor creep: intellectual work loses its exploratory or dialogical quality and becomes compliance work by other means. We are not freed to be creative, compliance is demanded of us by the technical apparatus itself. Again, AI just makes visible the problem: if machines can simulate our thinking, it may be because we have already reformatted thought to be machine-readable. And what we label as "creative" or "intellectual" labor may, in fact, have become procedural and replicable, optimized for institutional legitimacy rather than meaningful inquiry. But we have to make a finer distinction as well. Because what we think of as the "human" has already fundamentally co-emerged with tool use. And so the question becomes what kinds of tool use should we value and how do we diagnose situations that move us in other directions. AI can take over bureaucratic labor not because it is inherently low-level, but because bureaucratic processes have colonized intellectual life. (The standard markers of knowledge and labor that have undergirded audit culture are increasingly trivial tasks for AI to emulate, highlighting their inadequacy.) The fantasy that humans will be liberated to think by outsourcing to AI ignores the extent to which thinking itself has become systematized into publishable, promotable, and fundable fragments that harness our tool use to systems not of our choosing. It is not just that AI threatens to eclipse human value and meaningful labor, it is that it is in many ways accelerating a system already struggling to imagine differently.

5.2 AI as Diagnostic: Critique from Within the System

One possible way of addressing the problem of bureaucratic labor creep would be to increasingly task AI with the proliferation of bureaucratic labor itself. This leaves suspended, however, the problem of the labor-creep into creative work itself. But it also threatens to accelerate bureaucratic technical accumulation. Perhaps the most obvious example is the strange race now unfolding: students' use of AI's (that promise ever more efficient and realistic production of texts) is now prompting the creation of AI's increasingly capable of detecting the use of these AI's. And around we go, installing technical solutions to technical problems. Rather than reproducing these logics, a more interesting use of AI would be, not simply to do bureaucratic work more efficiently, but to question why that work exists in the first place. In other domains such as law and public policy, AI is already being deployed as a diagnostic tool to identify redundancies, surface contradictions, and expose inefficiencies within regulatory systems. Of course, the larger question that AI cannot solve for us is the values that these systems are solving for in the first place. Crucially, this requires recognizing that AI systems embed institutional priorities and assumptions about what counts as knowledge. Citation recommenders favor already prominent voices just as text generators mimic dominant rhetorical styles. These are not neutral outputs, but reflections of prevailing academic hierarchies. A more nuanced approach calls for surfacing these embedded values and interrogating them. Who benefits from the patterns AI reinforces? What remains illegible? This is not just a question of surfacing biases. If AI is to continue to play a role in research, participatory epistemic design must become a priority. Researchers, librarians, students, and communities affected by research should be involved in shaping how those tools define value. Without such engagement, AI will continue to re-inscribe existing exclusions under the guise of objectivity, as it continues to feed on its own assumptions.

5.3 Parallax View: Misalignment as Critical Perspective

This reorientation at the systems level also allows us to reconsider the role of AI in relation to thought. Rather than functioning as a direct mirror, or emulator of human thought, AI introduces a parallax view: a displacement between our habitual frames of reference and the outputs it generates. This misalignment is not simply a glitch or failure, but a shift in perspective that reveals the constructed nature of academic conventions as well as the strangeness of computational thought. Like a parallax gap, it opens a space where dissonance becomes potentially diagnostic. What doesn't line up draws attention to what we usually overlook. When AI reconfigures concepts, blurs genres, or applies style without understanding, it can surface not only its own halucinatory practices but the strange inertial patterns of scholarly practice. These distortions are not always productive, quite the opposite, but at times they can act as provocations. In this light, AI functions not as a surrogate intellect, but as a kind of strange interloper reframing our angle of approach. The AI plagiarism race, for example, should prompt us to ask not whether a text is authentic or not, but what its conditions of possibility are and what else it could be. Academic writing often relies on formulaic structures and metadiscursive signposting. AI's ability to replicate these forms with eerie fluency (or botch them completely) reveals how little difference there can be between scholarly style, automated pastiche, and nonsense. But it also creates the opportunity to break those patterns, to intervene in the repetition to reassess the fundamental questions of value.

5.4   Revaluing Research: Beyond Writing Toward Multimodal Praxis

This reframing thus invites a deeper revaluation of research, not simply as writing, but as a broader field of epistemic practice. The question is not how to preserve traditional forms of scholarship, but how to expand what counts as scholarly engagement in a way that aligns with our generative values. What if the goal of research were not just to produce publishable, quantifiable texts, but to create tools, environments, and relationships that support thinking in public? If knowledge sharing was codified rather than knowledge transfer. AI and the proliferation of materials across networked spaces give us the opportunity and the challenge of rethinking the nature of public scholarship. Rather than lamenting the erosion of the academic article, we might recognize its current form as historically contingent and increasingly inadequate and coopted by quantification. But this also opens a space for experimentation. What forms of scholarship foreground context, embodiment, experimentation, and dialogue? What kinds of contributions resist abstraction and encourage situated engagement? Publication pressures have long surfaced deep problems of replicability in scientific research. But this also means we have an opportunity to consider research that cannot, by its nature, be replicated.

One response is to take seriously the potential of multimodal scholarship. These approaches explore forms of scholarly research and dissemination beyond standard text protocols. They also may offer forms of engagement better suited to dialogical, situated, and practice-based inquiry. Multimodal work resists flattening knowledge into preconceived formats and opens space for new voices, experiments, affects, and relational forms of meaning-making. Multimodal scholarship invites interpretation rather than consumption, and by their nature demand an ethics of care and reflectiveness in their design, presentation, and reception.

Rather than defending a crumbling format further threatened by AI, the opportunity now is to reclaim research as a field of praxis. The challenge is not to distinguish real from simulated scholarship, but to insist that research is not reducible to form at all. It is defined by its mode of address, its openness to critique, and its capacity to intervene in the world. This, it should be noted, is a more robust vision of scholarship that is AI agnostic. That is, it is open to the orthogonal provocations of AI, while not in any way requiring them.

5.5   Institutional Frictions and Levers for Reorientation

It is not enough to critique the systems from within, or to imagine some magical realignment. We must also acknowledge the limits of institutional flexibility. The inertia is real: university metrics are locked into global rankings, disciplinary gatekeeping remains strong, and publishing is largely captured by commercial interests. Systemic change rarely happens through a single policy or tool. Institutions are complex and adaptive, but also slow, hierarchical, and often resistant to bottom-up innovation.

Rather than laying out prescriptive reforms, we suggest several speculative strategies for realigning institutional priorities. First, epistemic flexibility should be treated as a marker of scholarly integrity. Instead of codifying fixed outputs, institutions could emphasize responsiveness to context, mode, and audience. Second, support structures such as tenure, review, and publication, could shift from reward systems to environments that encourage sustained inquiry, reflection, and care. And third, platforms and infrastructures should be imagined not just as distribution channels but as epistemic partners in research: spaces where knowledge is shaped, not merely distributed. This also means looking for opportunities to create, fund, and support platforms for multimodal research that can speak to the changing landscape accelerated by AI.

6   Reclaiming the Future of Research

The point is not to abandon traditional scholarship, but to reclaim its value and imagine different forms. If the ship has sailed on legacy publishing systems, already being flooded with AI content, then new forms must be explored. Rather than engaging in futile battles to preserve a publishing system already compromised by profit incentives and institutional pressures, digital humanists must recognize that the "knowledge transfer" culture has indeed captured academic journal publishing. The challenge now is to nurture a "knowledge sharing" culture in alternative formats that prioritize sustained engagement with ideas over mechanical production of content.

The emergence of AI reflects not just a problem to be solved for research, but a provocation to rethink research praxis. Meaningful change will not result from a single approach, but from staying with the tension between entrenched and emerging forms. In this context, AI is neither a problem nor a solution to the deep challenges of research, but rather presents an opportunity for continued reflection and experimentation.

Rather than protecting inherited formats out of habit, we can ask what forms of research best serve the questions we now face. This means making space for hesitation, provisionality, and modes of expression that do not always conform to standardized academic modes of legibility. It also means accepting that no future form is guaranteed to resolve the tensions AI introduces. What matters is not resolving those tensions but holding them open long enough for something new to take shape.

References

1. Anonymous: The Great Ensloppification (2025). https://latentpost.com/posts/ensloppification
2. Beecher, K., Wang, J.: Peer reviewer fatigue, or peer reviewer refusal? Account. Res. **32**(5), 838–844 (2025)
3. Beel, J., Gipp, B.: Google scholar's ranking algorithm: an introductory overview. In: Proceedings of the 12th International Conference on Scientometrics and Informetrics (ISSI'09). vol. 1, pp. 230–241. Rio de Janeiro (Brazil) (2009)
4. Björk, B.C.: Evolution of the scholarly mega-journal, 2006–2017. PeerJ **6**, e4357 (2018)
5. Björk, B.C.: Publishing speed and acceptance rates of open access megajournals. Online Inf. Rev. **45**(2), 270–277 (2021)
6. Bloom, N., Jones, C.I., Van Reenen, J., Webb, M.: Are ideas getting harder to find? Am. Econom. Rev. **110**(4), 1104–1144 (2020)
7. Breuning, M., Backstrom, J., Brannon, J., Gross, B.I., Widmeier, M.: Reviewer fatigue? why scholars decline to review their peers' work. PS: Political Sci. Politics **48**(4), 595–600 (2015)
8. Drozdz, J.A., Ladomery, M.R.: The peer review process: past, present, and future. Br. J. Biomed. Sci. **81**, 12054 (2024)
9. Fanelli, D., Larivière, V.: Researchers' individual publication rate has not increased in a century. PLoS ONE **11**(3), e0149504 (2016)
10. Fire, M., Guestrin, C.: Over-optimization of academic publishing metrics: observing goodhart's law in action. GigaScience **8**(6), giz053 (2019)
11. Fortunato, S., et al.: Science of science. Science **359**(6379), eaao0185 (2018)
12. Hanitzsch, T., Markiewitz, A., Bødker, H.: Publish and perish: mental health among communication and media scholars. J. Commun. **74**(6), 429–442 (2024)
13. Haslam, N., Laham, S.M.: Quality, quantity, and impact in academic publication. Eur. J. Soc. Psychol. **40**(2), 216–220 (2010)
14. Itagaki, M.W., Suh, R.D., Goldin, J.G.: Cardiac ct research: exponential growth. Radiology **252**(2), 468–476 (2009)
15. Jinha, A.E.: Article 50 million: an estimate of the number of scholarly articles in existence. Learned Publishing **23**(3), 258–263 (2010)
16. Jones, B.F.: The burden of knowledge and the "death of the renaissance man": is innovation getting harder? Rev. Econ. Stud. **76**(1), 283–317 (2009)
17. Kobak, D., González-Márquez, R., Horvát, E.Á., Lause, J.: Delving into LLM-assisted writing in biomedical publications through excess vocabulary. Sci. Adv. **11**(27), eadt3813 (2025)
18. Kosmyna, N., et al.:Your brain on CHATGPT: accumulation of cognitive debt when using an AI assistant for essay writing task. arXiv preprint arXiv:2506.08872 (2025)
19. Kwon, D.: Science sleuths flag hundreds of papers that use ai without disclosing it. Nature **641**(8062), 290–291 (2025)

20. Laakso, M., Welling, P., Bukvova, H., Nyman, L., Björk, B.C., Hedlund, T.: The development of open access journal publishing from 1993 to 2009. PLoS ONE **6**(6), e20961 (2011)
21. Melumad, S., Yun, J.H.: Experimental evidence of the effects of large language models versus web search on depth of learning. Available at SSRN 5104064 (2025)
22. Naddaf, M.: AI linked to explosion of low-quality biomedical research papers. Nature **641**(8065), 1080–1081 (2025)
23. Petersen, A.M., Arroyave, F., Pammolli, F.: The disruption index is biased by citation inflation. Quan. Sci. Stud. **5**(4), 936–953 (2024)
24. Picazo-Sanchez, P., Ortiz-Martin, L.: Analysing the impact of chatgpt in research. Appl. Intell. **54**(5), 4172–4188 (2024)
25. Piwowar, H., et al.: The state of oa: a large-scale analysis of the prevalence and impact of open access articles. PeerJ **6**, e4375 (2018)
26. Price, D.D.S.: Science Since Babylon. Philosophy Sci. **30**(1), 93–94 (1963)
27. Price, D.J.D.S.: Little science, big science. Columbia University Press (1963)
28. Rovira, C., Codina, L., Lopezosa, C.: Language bias in the google scholar ranking algorithm. Future Internet **13**(2), 31 (2021)
29. Sage: Editorial Policies: Artificial Intelligence Policy. https://www.sagepub.com/journals/editorial-policies/artificial-intelligence-policy
30. Solomon, D.J., Laakso, M., Björk, B.C.: A longitudinal comparison of citation rates and growth among open access journals. J. Informet. **7**(3), 642–650 (2013)
31. Steele, C.: Digital publishing and the konwledge process. In: eLearning and digital Publishing, pp. 175–193. Springer (2006)
32. Strathern, M.: Audit cultures, vol. 146. Routledge, London (2000)
33. Suchak, T., Aliu, A.E., Harrison, C., Zwiggelaar, R., Geifman, N., Spick, M.: Explosion of formulaic research articles, including inappropriate study designs and false discoveries, based on the nhanes us national health database. PLoS Biol. **23**(5), e3003152 (2025)
34. Taylor & Francis: To slice or perish, vol. 38 (2023)
35. Thelwall, M., Sud, P.: Scopus 1900–2020: Growth in articles, abstracts, countries, fields, and journals. Quantitative Science Studies **3**(1), 37–50 (2022). https://doi.org/10.1162/qss_a_00177
36. To, W., Yu, B.T.: Rise in higher education researchers and academic publications. Emerald Open Res. **1**(3) (2023)
37. Van Vlokhoven, H.: The effect of open access on research quality. J. Informet. **13**(2), 751–756 (2019)

Designing Deliberative Digital Communication Platforms

Kian Schmalenbach[(✉)] [iD] and Bastian Brechtelsbauer [iD]

Institute of Information Systems, Friedrich-Alexander-Universität
Erlangen-Nürnberg, Nuremberg, Germany
{kian.schmalenbach,bastian.bb.brechtelsbauer}@fau.de

Abstract. Despite the enormous potential of digital communication platforms (DCPs) to disseminate information and facilitate deliberative public discourse without interference from traditional gatekeepers, they are subject to widespread criticism due to problems such as misinformation and societal polarization. While this criticism is supported by numerous empirical studies, current research lacks an alternative positive vision that integrates DCPs and normative ideals for public discourse. To this end, we develop design knowledge for deliberative DCPs according to the ideals of Habermas' theory of communicative action (TCA). Specifically, we develop TCA-based meta-requirements and utilize network gatekeeping theory to develop suitable design principles for their implementation. Thereby, we contribute design knowledge of a normatively grounded DCP that can assist researchers, system designers, and policy makers seeking a foundation for the conception, development, and regulation of DCPs.

Keywords: Digital Communication Platforms · Theory of Communicative Action · Network Gatekeeping

1   Introduction

Deliberative public discourse is essential for a functioning democracy and individual flourishing, enabling citizens to exchange ideas, challenge power structures, and make informed collective decisions. The quality and inclusivity of this discourse depend on the infrastructures through which communication is mediated. Historically, these infrastructures were shaped by institutional mass media and their editorial gatekeeping, grounded in structures of professional responsibility, journalistic norms, and legal regulation [14]. With the rise of Web 2.0, interactive applications enabled decentralized participation, allowing individuals to consume, create, and share content [26]. Initially seen as liberating—promising to dismantle editorial hierarchies and foster pluralism and freedom of expression [3]—this shift soon gave way to new centralized infrastructures: large-scale *digital communication platforms* (DCPs) that now serve as the sociotechnical foundations for online interaction [27]. Over time, a few privately owned platforms have come to organize much of online discourse through opaque and largely

© The Author(s) 2026
L. Hagedorn et al. (Eds.): DIGHUM 2025, LNCS 16319, pp. 499–514, 2026.
https://doi.org/10.1007/978-3-032-11108-1_37

unregulated governance systems [9]. This development marked the rise of the *platform economy*, where centralized intermediaries generate value by capturing attention, extracting behavioral data, and steering communication flows through algorithmic personalization [22]. Hence, although DCPs may appear as neutral spaces for expression, they are governed by architectures optimized for monetization and engagement rather than deliberation [5,12].

On modern DCPs, content visibility is shaped by data-driven recommender systems that personalize exposure based on behavioral patterns, a process referred to as *secondary gatekeeping* [27]. These systems operate in self-reinforcing loops that tie engagement to data extraction and personalization, creating powerful network effects between user attention and advertiser value [29]. As a result, platform governance becomes structurally complex and opaque, outpacing the assumptions of traditional editorial models [9] and creating a direct structural link between gatekeeping sophistication and platform value [4]. These new gatekeeping mechanisms are embedded in a broader model of *surveillance capitalism*, where platform design prioritizes profitability over democratic communication [38]. As a result, communicative power is concentrated in opaque systems optimized to capture attention [30]. This has become a central concern in academic and policy debates. Empirical studies show that such systems have far-reaching societal consequences, contributing to the spread of misinformation, the normalization of hate speech, and political polarization [1,23,34]. The erosion of shared understanding has even been described as the defining societal crisis of our time [7]. Yet, despite the urgency of these challenges, most critiques remain focused on identifying operational mechanisms through which these challenges emerge, such as algorithmic amplification, moderation failures, and filter effects, while overlooking the governance, power, and incentive structures that systematically produce them [5]. In this paper, we argue that research would benefit from moving beyond such operational critique toward a constructive, normative vision of how DCPs can be redesigned to foster democratic discourse.

In this vein, Jürgen Habermas' *Theory of Communicative Action* (TCA) [17], which outlines conditions for inclusive and rational deliberation, has already served as a foundation for system design in various academic disciplines [6]. In parallel, multi-actor frameworks such as the platform governance triangle provide structural tools for conceptualizing alternative governance configurations [11]. What remains missing, however, is design knowledge for DCPs that aligns these normative ideals with the realities of contemporary digital spaces. Under current shareholder-driven logics, DCPs are structurally incentivized to reward sensationalism, outrage, and emotionally charged content over thoughtful, inclusive, and rational communication [22]. The issue is not that DCPs perform gatekeeping—that is a necessary feature of any communication system—but that their prevailing logic is fundamentally misaligned with the requirements of democratic deliberation. If DCPs are to fulfill their societal role as enablers of informed and participatory discourse, their internal gatekeeping structures must be critically reexamined and reimagined.

In this paper, we therefore develop design knowledge for deliberative DCPs, grounded in gatekeeping theory and informed by Habermas' TCA. Using the TCA as a kernel theory, we derive four meta-requirements and 24 corresponding design principles for structuring platforms that support democratic discourse. This contributes to a design theory for deliberative DCPs grounded in a humanistic ideal and provides researchers, policymakers, and system designers with a foundation for the conceptualization, design, and regulation of such platforms.

2   Background

2.1   Theory of Communicative Action

Habermas' TCA centers on the processes and conditions of rational communication in social interactions, highlighting how individuals use different forms of action to influence collective decision-making [17]. It distinguishes *strategic action*, which is goal-driven and self-interested, from *communicative action*, which seeks mutual understanding and consensus [14]. This distinction parallels Habermas' division of society into the *system*, comprising institutions like the state and economy, and the *lifeworld*, the sphere of shared meanings and communicative practices [13]. Strategic action serves system imperatives, whereas communicative action grows from dialogue within the lifeworld. While formal systems are essential for society, Habermas envisions a democracy grounded in communicative action within the lifeworld [13].

Communicative action is vital to democratic functioning, allowing individuals to engage in discourse to shape collective outcomes. Rooted in Enlightenment ideals, its model of deliberative rationality depends on four validity claims:

- *Comprehensibility.* Expressions used in communicative actions must be clear, understandable, and have the potential to be grasped by all participants.
- *Truth.* The statements or propositions expressed in communicative actions correspond to objective, verifiable facts.
- *Normative rightness.* The moral and ethical principles embedded in communicative actions align with shared normative standards.
- *Sincerity.* Participants of communicative acts express their attitudes, intentions, and beliefs genuinely and without deception.

To conceptualize ideal conditions for such discourse, Habermas introduces the *ideal speech situation* (ISS), a theoretical environment free from coercion, distortion, or power imbalances, where participants can engage equally and express views without manipulation. In this space, norms are not imposed but emerge from collective agreement: "Only those norms can claim to be valid that meet (or could meet) with the approval of all affected in their capacity as participants in a practical discourse" [16, p. 66].

The ISS provides the normative foundation of the public sphere, defined as the realm where public opinion forms and access is guaranteed to all [15]. An open, inclusive public sphere aligns with the principles of communicative action.

A crucial enabler of this vision is unrestricted access to diverse, factual information. In theory, the internet and Web 2.0 platforms support this by decentralizing information flow and bypassing traditional journalistic gatekeepers. The widespread availability of digital tools enables broader participation in public discourse. Yet, this potential is undermined by algorithm-driven platforms that amplify hate speech [34] and misinformation [23] driven by commercial interests. This tension reflects a fundamental incompatibility between the deliberative ideals of communicative action and the strategic, profit-oriented logic embedded in today's platform architectures and governance models [24].

While the TCA represents a normative and idealized vision of discourse, its value for the digital age lies in providing guiding principles for how sociotechnical systems such as DCPs can be aligned with communicative action rather than commercial optimization. Accordingly, our research defines meta-requirements based on the TCA and develops corresponding design principles for DCPs that foster deliberatively rational, inclusive, and democratic discourse.

2.2 Gatekeeping in the Digital Sphere

We use gatekeeping theory as an abstract model to describe how information spreads through networked systems and to analyze information dissemination mechanisms in Web 2.0 platforms, independent of current business models and governance practices. While early definitions of gatekeeping focused on traditional, broadcasting-based media, later work expanded the concept to include online environments. Shoemaker and Vos observed that, "compared to other mass media, the internet provides much more opportunity for audience members to interact with news makers, news creators, and each other" [32, p. 6], emphasizing that this interactivity turns audience members into gatekeepers. Similarly, Barzilai-Nahon developed a comprehensive theory of networked gatekeeping tailored to technology-mediated networks such as the internet [2]. She defines the following constructs related to network gatekeeping:

- *Gate.* The entrance or exit from a network or its sections.
- *Gated.* The entity, e.g., a community, subjected to gatekeeping.
- *Gatekeeping.* The process of controlling information moving through a gate, including, selection, addition, withholding, channeling, shaping, manipulation, repetition, timing, localization, integration, and deletion of information.
- *Gatekeeping mechanism.* A tool, technology, or methodology used to carry out the process of gatekeeping, see Table 1.
- *Network gatekeeper.* An entity, e.g., people, organizations, or governments, that exercises gatekeeping through a gatekeeping mechanism in networks.

While all these elements are important parts of gatekeeping, the mechanisms are particularly significant, as they determine *which* and *how* information is disseminated, shaping discourse in interactive DCPs. These mechanisms are guided by strategies that, in current platforms, are often driven by commercial goals such as maximizing retention, time spent, or ad interaction. A humanistic design theory could instead inform alternative, normative principles to guide these mechanisms. We therefore draw on gatekeeping theory to develop design principles that fulfill the meta-requirements we derive from Habermas' TCA. Specifically, we refer to the gatekeeping mechanisms outlined by [2] (see Table 1) to structure how these processes should be designed to meet our normative criteria. We choose this framework because it (1) offers a comprehensive view of mechanisms whose mismanagement drives problems such as biased narratives and misinformation, and (2) provides an abstract lens that enables articulating design principles without the constraints of current commercial logics.

Table 1. Different network gatekeeping mechanisms [2, p. 1498]

Mechanism	Definition and Examples
Channeling mechanisms	Mechanisms that are designed to attract the attention of gated and convey or direct them. *Examples:* search engines, recommendation algorithms, hyperlinks
Censorship mechanisms	Mechanisms that suppress "undesired" information to prevent it from entering, exiting, or circulating in the network. *Examples:* filtering, blocking, and deletion of users or content
Internationalization mechanisms	Mechanisms that localize information, services, and products, according to characteristics of communities based, e.g., on customs, cultures, nationalities, languages, and religions. *Examples:* translation and localization of platforms and content
Security mechanisms	Mechanisms that manage confidentiality, availability, and integrity of information flow in the network. *Examples:* integrity, authentication, and access controls
Cost-effect mechanisms	Mechanisms that control the cost of gated to join, use, and exit a network. *Examples:* costs for infrastructure, learning, connecting to, and exiting the network
Value-adding mechanisms	Mechanisms that attract and retain gated through value offerings. *Examples:* lock-in mechanisms, personalization, customization, and integration
Infrastructure mechanisms	Infrastructure components and characteristics that are utilized to control information and behavior of gated. *Examples:* network access, technology channels, and network configuration
User interaction mechanisms	Mechanisms that reside at the interface layer and act as intermediaries between the gated and the network. *Examples:* add-on navigation tools, default homepage, content preferences
Editorial mechanisms	Mechanisms that are similar to traditional gatekeeping mechanisms used by editors. *Examples:* technical and content control, design tools for information content
Regulation meta-mechanisms	Regulation can apply to all other mechanisms. It refers to rules, treaties, agreements, or procedures for information control. *Examples:* governmental regulation, self-regulation

3   Deliberative DCPs as a Design Problem

Many challenges in the context of DCPs trace back to unequal, disproportionate, or discriminatory communication patterns. These patterns often emerge as platforms seek to enhance user engagement through algorithms that tolerate or promote content emphasizing homophily, sensationalism, or controversy. However, such patterns are not technologically inevitable; rather, they stem from underlying business models and governance arrangements. To move beyond analysis of existing systems and toward developing a normative vision of deliberative DCPs, we combine a critical, future-oriented perspective on technology [8] with the design science framework proposed by Jones and Gregor [20]. This allows us to conceptualize platforms as sociotechnical systems whose communicative structures can be deliberately designed to foster democratic discourse.

Following Jones and Gregor's anatomy of design theory, we first develop and iteratively refine *meta-requirements* for deliberative DCPs guided by the TCA, which serves as the kernel theory of our work [20]. The TCA provides the normative foundation for defining the conditions of inclusive, rational, and deliberative discourse in the digital public sphere and thus outlines the desired state that deliberative DCPs should achieve. Building on these normative requirements, we then develop *design principles* that operationalize them through the concept of network gatekeeping [2], which offers constructs of entities and mechanisms governing information flow and discourse formation on DCPs. Using these constructs, we articulate how the TCA-informed meta-requirements can be realized through concrete gatekeeping-related design principles.

As such, our approach differs from empirical or technical studies by adopting a sociotechnical perspective on DCPs. In line with information systems research, which views systems as interactions between humans, tasks, and technology, we understand DCPs as artifacts embedded in broader social, economic, and institutional contexts. Designing DCPs therefore requires not only technical considerations but also reflection on governance, management, and the normative frameworks that guide their operation. Our work thus takes one step back from implementation to re-examine the assumptions shaping today's digital communication infrastructures, reconceptualizing DCPs as sociotechnical infrastructures of public discourse and developing normative design knowledge. Despite its conceptual nature, this work can inform and foster a discussion about technological development, policy, and institutional decision-making toward aligning DCPs with democratic deliberation.

4   Designing Deliberative DCPs

In the following, we derive four meta-requirements (MR1-MR4) for deliberative DCPs from the TCA. These meta-requirements serve as foundational guardrails, guiding specific design aspects. By aligning with the TCA's normative claims, particularly the ideal of an ISS, our platform aspires to establish a deliberative and inclusive digital communication space, thereby overcoming the challenges posed by contemporary platforms.

4.1   Meta-Requirements for Deliberative DCPs

Firstly, in recognizing the risks associated with restricted access and unequal participation, we underscore the imperative for a deliberative DCP to provide unrestricted access and promote equal engagement among all members of the public. This principle aligns with the overarching goal of communicative rationality embedded in Habermas' TCA, envisioning an ISS fostering open and inclusive discourse. For Habermas, equal access in the ISS context means individuals, irrespective of social standing or affiliations, should have unimpeded entry into the public sphere and equal opportunities to participate in discussions. In the digital sphere, equal access implies removing social and technological barriers hindering individuals from expressing opinions or engaging in discourse, addressing issues like algorithmic biases and promoting digital literacy. Emphasizing the importance of a deliberative DCP that provides unrestricted access, promotes equal engagement, and mirrors the ISS ideals in fostering an inclusive online public sphere, we formulate our first meta-requirement as follows:

MR 1: *A deliberative DCP should provide unrestricted access to and promote participation among all members of the public.*

Secondly, we emphasize the crucial role of a deliberative DCP in systematically fostering communicative acts rooted in the principle of communicative rationality, building on Habermas' TCA and its ISS. This underscores the platform's commitment to fostering discourse characterized by openness, inclusivity, and a dedication to rational argumentation. These principles align with the validity claims associated with communicative rationality, as previously introduced in Sect. 2.1. For instance, the claims of comprehensibility and truth are pivotal in countering the spread of misinformation, underscoring the importance of honest and integral statements aligning with objective, verifiable facts. Additionally, ensuring normative rightness aids in mitigating polarization by aligning moral and ethical principles in communicative acts with shared normative standards. Simultaneously, the claim of sincerity plays a crucial role in fostering genuine dialogue, countering deceptive practices that contribute to a lack of trust in online discussions. In sum, through the incorporation of mechanisms that assess the quality of communicative acts based on adherence to norms of rational discourse, the platform aims to cultivate an environment where users are motivated to engage in meaningful, truthful, and ethically aligned conversations. Therefore, we propose our second meta-requirement as follows:

MR 2: *A deliberative DCP should promote and assess communicative acts based on the notion of communicative rationality.*

Thirdly, we underscore the importance of deliberative decision-making within a DCP, proposing a departure from prevailing practices observed in major social media platforms. In contrast to the current use of opaque algorithms for content dissemination, the principles advocated by the TCA call for transparency, traceability, and a strong emphasis on public consensus-building in governance decisions. The prevalent focus on monetization, often driving competitive advantages through secretive algorithms and commercially oriented user engagement mechanisms, is replaced by a model where the community of users actively contributes to decision-making processes. Unlike platforms that centralize decision authority, our envisioned design empowers voluntary users who have demonstrated expertise or merit to play a role in content visibility, moderation, and other governance aspects. This user-centric approach mirrors collaborative models such as open-source communities, promoting openness, inclusivity, and participatory governance. By shifting decision-making power to the user community, we aim to establish a deliberative digital communication space, fostering transparency and shared responsibility. Therefore, our third meta-requirement follows as:

MR 3. *A deliberative DCP should base its governance decisions on transparent processes and public consensus-building.*

Finally, we emphasize the critical need for our platform design to protect its autonomy and allow it to resist the sway of commercial interests or state interference, aligning it with the principles of communicative rationality as articulated in the TCA. Within the framework of the TCA, a fundamental distinction arises between the lifeworld, constituting the sphere of everyday human activities, interactions, and communicative actions, and the system, encompassing external forces like economic and political entities that hold the potential to dominate and distort the lifeworld. Translating these concepts into the realm of DCPs, it becomes imperative for their design to stand apart from conventional practices, where profit-driven motives or external political agendas might compromise the integrity of deliberative spaces. The platform, in this context, must ensure protection against external systemic influences, such as foreign entities or malicious agents. This requires robust defense mechanisms against the encroachment of the system into the lifeworld, guaranteeing a steadfast dedication to fostering open discourse, inclusivity, and user-driven decision-making. Such commitment fortifies the platform's role as a deliberative digital communication space, resilient against undue external pressures and devoted to the preservation of the autonomy, independence, and integrity of the lifeworld. Therefore, we formulate our fourth meta-requirement as follows:

MR 4: *A deliberative DCP should be protected from and resist domination by commercial interests or state interference.*

4.2   Design Principles for Deliberative DCPs

In this section, we explain how the previously introduced mechanisms of network gatekeeping can be designed to achieve our newly formulated meta-requirements. To this end, we considered for each meta-requirement if and how each gatekeeping mechanism can contribute to fulfilling it, resulting in the following design principles.

Unrestricted Access and Equal Participation (MR1). In order to provide unrestricted access and promote participation in discourse, channeling mechanisms play a crucial role in enabling users to navigate a network and its sections, and find content or discourses, e.g., through search functions. These mechanisms need to avoid isolating users in information-limiting environments and instead promote their participation in relevant discourse, e.g., through recommendations. Here, technology provides great potentials for serendipity to provide users with diverse and relevant content. Further, internationalization mechanisms can improve the accessibility of the platform, for example, through offering multilingual user interfaces and support services that offer equal accessibility independent of language restrictions. In this context, the motivation for internationalization should be inclusion itself, rather than mere calculus of accessing new market segments. Platform access is also directly related to the platform's cost-effect mechanisms because it simultaneously lowers the cost of joining and using the platform. This minimization of costs for joining, using, or exiting the platform is another important factor for unrestricted access, particularly for economically challenged individuals or groups. Other possible measures can be assistance for novice users and platform models that forgo direct monetary costs for the gated. Access similarly needs to be ensured on an infrastructure level. Although much of the technological infrastructure that is needed to access DCPs often lays outside their scope, platforms should aim to ensure global accessibility, e.g., by utilizing globally spread technical standards and designing the platform for an array of user devices. Finally, providing user-friendly interfaces in connection with effective support services is crucial for unrestricted access because it enables users with limited technical experience and skill to access and use the platform, receive information, and participate in discourse. The guiding principle, again, should be to maximize access rather than to minimize costs at only a limited level of access. To achieve unrestricted access and equal participation, we therefore propose the following design principles that relate to five different relevant gatekeeping mechanisms:

- DP 1.1: *Avoid informational isolation and promote discourse participation.*
- DP 1.2: *Provide multilingual user interfaces and support services.*
- DP 1.3: *Minimize costs for platform access, usage, and exiting.*
- DP 1.4: *Ensure equal access through global platform accessibility.*
- DP 1.5: *Provide open access with user-friendly interfaces.*

Promotion of Communicative Rationality (MR2). To promote communicative rationality as the foundational principle of discourse, channeling mechanisms, such as the prioritization of content in search and recommendation functionalities, form an integral part. When search engines and recommendation algorithms prioritize content that is well-supported, factually accurate, and representative of diverse viewpoints, they contribute to the creation of an environment where reasoned discourse can flourish and polarization and misinformation become less likely. Further, for extreme violations of the principles of communicative rationality, censorship mechanisms can be a last resort that provide the option to filter and remove objectionable content. Similarly to multilingual platform access, offering translation and localization of content enables all users to comprehend it and participate in a discourse. Here, for example, automated systems can efficiently provide great benefits but need to be used transparently. As another foundation for deliberative discourse, the authenticity of content needs to be ensured. This means, for example, that authentication mechanisms need to be able to differentiate between human users and artificial users such as bots. Moreover, value-adding mechanisms provide various possibilities to promote rational discourse, for example, by rewarding contributors for constructive contributions over attention grabbing content, that is often oversimplified or polarizing. Infrastructure mechanisms need to be designed in a way to avoid the unequal treatment of content or users through technical means, e.g., prioritization or limitations in platform access through infrastructure and based on criteria that are incompatible with the ideals of communicative rationality. Infrastructure should therefore generally be neutral to avoid intransparent gatekeeping. In order to enable discourse, user interaction mechanisms need to provide the necessary functions for users to interact with other users and their content, and to provide their own opinions on topics. These functions should themselves be designed based on the principles of communicative rationality. Finally, editorial mechanisms play a pivotal role in fostering rational discourse by upholding regulated standards that govern content curation and publication. These standards serve as guiding principles in ensuring the promotion of reasoned, well-supported, and factually accurate information. By adhering to such editorial benchmarks, platforms can actively encourage critical thinking, diverse perspectives, and informed dialogue, thereby nurturing an environment conducive to reasoned and meaningful exchanges of ideas. In summary, in order to promote communicative rationality, we derive these eight design principles:

- DP 2.1: *Promote content aligned with rational discourse.*
- DP 2.2: *Promote rational discourse by filtering objectionable content.*
- DP 2.3: *Offer transparent translation and localization of content.*
- DP 2.4: *Assure dissemination of authentic and sincere content.*
- DP 2.5: *Avoid prioritizing polarizing, sensational over constructive content.*
- DP 2.6: *Prevent biased and intransparent content prioritization by providing neutral infrastructure.*
- DP 2.7: *Enable users to provide feedback and interact with other users.*
- DP 2.8: *Promote deliberative discourse through regulated editorial standards.*

Consensus-Based Governance (MR3). The third meta-requirement demands that governance decisions on the platform should be based on public consensus. Consequently, this requirement applies to a number of gatekeeping mechanisms that realize platform governance. This means that the previously mentioned interventions, e.g., the prioritization of content through channeling need to be communicated transparently and be able to build consensus among the users. Similarly, decisions to enact censorship need to be based on an open and traceable process that is driven by collective agreement. By embracing this transparent model of censorship, platforms can establish accountability, foster trust, and promote a shared understanding of the standards. To achieve consensual governance, value-adding mechanisms such as attracting users to participate in governing activities can be utilized. Encouraging active user participation promotes ownership and involvement in decision-making processes. By inviting and facilitating the involvement of active users, platforms benefit from diverse perspectives and insights, ensuring that governance aligns with the community's collective interests. This inclusive approach strengthens community bonds, enhances accountability, and enriches the overall governance framework by tapping into the expertise of dedicated platform users. Furthermore, user interaction systems that afford the identification and reporting of inappropriate content or behavior are essential. Accessible mechanisms for flagging or reporting empower users to contribute to a desirable digital environment. Therefore, these systems are vital tools in upholding community standards, swiftly addressing inappropriate behavior or content. Further, consensus-based governance in editorial content control ensures that decisions on content publication, promotion, or moderation derive from collective agreements among various users and user groups, incorporating the perspectives of editors, moderators, and community representatives. Emphasizing transparent processes and inclusive decision-making integrates diverse viewpoints to develop policies that foster fair and community-driven editing. To implement consensus-based governance, we present the five design principles:

- DP 3.1: *Ensure transparent and consensus-capable content curation decisions.*
- DP 3.2: *Conduct transparent and traceable censorship based on consensus.*
- DP 3.3: *Encourage active users to participate in governance activities.*
- DP 3.4: *Provide mechanisms to report inappropriate content or user actions.*
- DP 3.5: *Implement transparent editing guided by consensual standards.*

No Domination by Commerce or State (MR4). In order for public deliberative discourse to develop freely, it is essential to avoid dominating influences by systemic, e.g., economic or governmental interests, on the platform and its users. This means that critical mechanisms need to be protected from certain influences. Firstly, this involves refraining from amplifying or endorsing content like advertisements for promotional purposes without regarding its value for the deliberative discourse. Similarly, this applies to censorship, which must avoid the suppression of content based on motives unrelated to meaningful deliberation, e.g., for political or commercial reasons. Moreover, it is important to safeguard users and their data from external interests for example through establishing robust security measures and ethical practices. Additionally, it entails creating transparent policies that prioritize users' control over their data, ensuring informed consent and empowering individuals to make decisions regarding the usage and distribution of their information. However, these measures simultaneously need to be compatible with legitimate, e.g., legal concerns, that do not aim to exert dominating influence. In connection to cost-effect mechanisms independent public funding can be a crucial factor to achieve minimal costs for users while upholding platform independence. Similarly, the platform's autonomy needs to be protected in regard to its infrastructure. Therefore, redundant and decentralized architectures that provide independence from singular business partners or governmental influences should be pursued. Regarding the editorial mechanisms, preserving integrity necessitates meticulous scrutiny and critical editing of third-party content to ensure accuracy and alignment with established standards. By rigorously reviewing and editing external content, the platform upholds its commitment to maintaining quality, reliability, and trustworthiness within its informational landscape. In conclusion, we present the following six design principles to avoid a dominating impact from commerce and state:

- DP 4.1: *Avoid promoting non-deliberative content for strategic reasons.*
- DP 4.2: *Avoid suppressing or deleting content for strategic reasons.*
- DP 4.3: *Protect users and their data from external interests.*
- DP 4.4: *Enable free participation through publicly funded infrastructure.*
- DP 4.5: *Protect autonomy through redundant and decentralized architecture.*
- DP 4.6: *Protect integrity through critical editing of third-party content.*

5   Discussion

The transformative potential of DCPs for fostering deliberative discourse lies in their capacity to facilitate broad participation, accommodate diverse perspectives, and enable dynamic interaction [3]. Yet, conceptual [25, 28, 35] and empirical research [1, 23, 34] highlight that current DCPs often foster selective exposure, misinformation, and polarization. While these studies have been crucial in identifying harms, they largely describe the absence of an ideal state rather than articulating positive visions for alternative designs [21]. The responses derived from such work typically focus on mitigating visible symptoms through technical or regulatory interventions, such as content moderation or algorithmic adjustments, without addressing the deeper sociotechnical foundations that produce these dysfunctions. To overcome this limitation, our research adopted a design science perspective [20] that regards DCPs as sociotechnical systems whose architecture, governance, and incentive structures can be reimagined to foster deliberative democratic discourse.

To this end, we employed Habermas' TCA to define a normatively desirable state of deliberative digital discourse and derived a design theory for deliberative DCPs grounded in communicative rationality. Our results comprise four meta-requirements as foundational conditions for deliberative communication and 24 corresponding design principles based on the concept of network gatekeeping [2].

By combining the normative insights of TCA with an operational understanding of gatekeeping in digital contexts, our work bridges philosophical ideals and design-oriented reasoning, offering a concrete and theoretically informed pathway for the development of DCPs. The resulting framework provides a theoretically grounded foundation for reimagining DCPs as infrastructures that align with democratic deliberation rather than commercial optimization.

By conceptualizing DCPs as sociotechnical infrastructures that interlink technological architectures with governance and incentive structures, our design emphasizes that fostering deliberation requires rethinking not only platform functionality but also the institutional logics that guide their operation. This sociotechnical perspective complements existing research on DCP regulation and design [10,18,25] and empirical perspectives [21,33,37], helping shift the research focus from documenting operational dysfunctions toward envisioning design elements that support inclusive and rational public discourse. Notably, our research is among the first to apply TCA to the context of DCPs, addressing a lack of theoretical grounding that has limited empirical studies on the causes of dysfunction in online discourse [31,36]. By articulating a digital communication environment rooted in humanistic and democratic ideals, our framework provides a conceptual foundation for future empirical and design research. It enables a shift from predominantly negative assessments, such as the identification of filter bubbles, fake news, or hate speech, toward the evaluation of concrete design elements that can help realize a positive vision of deliberative DCPs.

Our contribution also speaks to the growing practical relevance of DCP design and regulation. By providing theoretically grounded design knowledge, we outline a positive vision of how DCPs can be structured to promote deliberation rather than polarization. This normative foundation offers valuable orientation for system designers, policymakers, and researchers seeking to align technological infrastructures with democratic values. As such, it also emphasizes that deliberative ideals must extend beyond user interaction to encompass the broader institutional arrangements and incentive systems that shape platform governance. In doing so, it complements ongoing policy efforts such as the European Union's regulatory initiatives on digital markets [19], which primarily constrain harmful behavior but often lack positive design perspectives for the digital space.

While our work is conceptual and does not provide implementation guidance, its purpose is to establish a theoretically grounded normative foundation for future interdisciplinary research on how deliberative DCPs can be realized both technically and institutionally. We thus call for empirical, technological, and policy-oriented studies that explore how the proposed design principles can be instantiated, tested, and governed in practice. Beyond offering specific design ideas, our work aims to stimulate discussion on *what* normatively desirable DCPs should look like and *how* their sociotechnical realization can be achieved.

6   Conclusion and Outlook

DCPs hold immense potential to foster inclusive, deliberative discourse by enabling broad participation and dynamic interaction. Yet, contemporary DCPs often fall short of this potential, as their design and governance are shaped by commercial incentives rather than democratic ideals. Addressing this gap, we drew on Habermasâ' TCA to formulate a design theory for deliberative DCPs comprising four meta-requirements and 24 design principles that guide the configuration of network gatekeeping mechanisms. Advancing a sociotechnical perspective, our work emphasizes that supporting democratic deliberation requires rethinking both technical architectures and institutional logics. The resulting design knowledge outlines how deliberative DCPs could be structured and provides a normative foundation for future interdisciplinary research, offering valuable orientation for policymakers, designers, and researchers seeking to align the governance and development of DCPs with the principles of communicative rationality and democratic discourse.

Disclosure of Interests. The authors have no competing interests to declare that are relevant to the content of this article.

References

1. Bakshy, E., Messing, S., Adamic, L.A.: Exposure to ideologically diverse news and opinion on Facebook. Science **348**(6239), 1130–1132 (2015)
2. Barzilai-Nahon, K.: Toward a theory of network gatekeeping: a framework for exploring information control. J. Am. Soc. Inform. Sci. Technol. **59**(9), 1493–1512 (2008)
3. Birdsall, W.F.: Web 2.0 as a social movement. Webology **4**(2), 1–10 (2007)
4. Caplan, R.: Networked platform governance: the construction of the democratic platform. Int. J. Commun. **17**, 3451–3472 (2023)
5. Cornils, M.: Designing platform governance: a normative perspective on needs, strategies, and tools to regulate intermediaries (2020). https://algorithmwatch.org/wp-content/uploads/2020/05/Governing-Platforms-legal-study-Cornils-May-2020-AlgorithmWatch.pdf
6. Cukier, W., Ngwenyama, O., Bauer, R., Middleton, C.: A critical analysis of media discourse on information technology: preliminary results of a proposed method for critical discourse analysis. Inf. Syst. J. **19**(2), 175–196 (2009)
7. Dixson-Decleve, S., Gaffney, O., Ghosh, J., Randers, J., Rockstrom, J., Stoknes, P.: Earth for all: a survival guide for humanity. New Society Publishers, 1 edn. (2022)
8. Feenberg, A.: Transforming technology: a critical theory revisited. Oxford University Press (2002)
9. Flew, T., Martin, F., Suzor, N.: Internet regulation as media policy: rethinking the question of digital communication platform governance. J. Digit. Media Policy **10**(1), 33–50 (2019)
10. Geschke, D., Lorenz, J., Holtz, P.: The triple-filter bubble: Using agent-based modelling to test a meta-theoretical framework for the emergence of filter bubbles and echo chambers. Br. J. Soc. Psychol. **58**(1), 129–149 (2019)
11. Gorwa, R.: The platform governance triangle: conceptualising the informal regulation of online content. Internet Policy Rev. **8**(2) (2019)
12. Gorwa, R.: What is platform governance? Inf. Commun. Soc. **22**(6), 854–871 (2019)

13. Habermas, J., McCarthy, T.: Theory of communicative action, volume two: Lifeworld and system: a critique of functionalist reason. Beacon Press, Boston (1987)
14. Habermas, J.: Communication and the evolution of society. Beacon Press, Boston (1979)
15. Habermas, J.: The public sphere. In: Bronner, S.E., Kellner, D. (eds.) Critical theory and society: a reader, pp. 136–142. Routledge, New York (1989)
16. Habermas, J.: Moral consciousness and communicative action. MIT Press, Cambridge (1990)
17. Habermas, J., McCarthy, T.: Theory of communicative action, volume one: Reason and the rationalization of society. Beacon Press, Boston (1984)
18. Helberger, N., Karppinen, K., D'Acunto, L.: Exposure diversity as a design principle for recommender systems. Inf. Commun. Soc. **21**(2), 191–207 (2018)
19. Hučková, R., Semanová, M.: Various consequences of digital markets act on gatekeepers. EU and Comparative Law Issues Challenges Series (ECLIC) **7**, 295–314 (2023)
20. Jones, D., Gregor, S.: The anatomy of a design theory. J. Assoc. Inf. Syst. **8**(5), 312–335 (2007)
21. Kitchens, B., Johnson, S., Gray, P.: Understanding echo chambers and filter bubbles: the impact of social media on diversification and partisan shifts in news consumption. MIS Q. **44**(4), 1619–1650 (2020)
22. Lu, P., Zhou, L., Fan, X.: Platform governance and sociological participation. J. Chinese Soc. **10**(1) (2023)
23. McKay, S., Tenove, C.: Disinformation as a threat to deliberative democracy. Polit. Res. Q. **74**(3), 703–717 (2021)
24. Metakides, G.: Democracy in the digital era. In: Introduction to Digital Humanism, pp. 495–509. Springer Nature Switzerland, Cham (2024)
25. Moore, M.: Tech giants and civic power. The Policy Institute (2016)
26. Moreno, M., D'Angelo, J.: Social media intervention design: applying an affordances framework. J. Med. Internet Res. **21**(3), 1–9 (2019)
27. Napoli, P.M.: Social media and the public interest: governance of news platforms in the realm of individual and algorithmic gatekeepers. Telecommun. Policy **39**(9), 751–760 (2015)
28. Pariser, E.: The filter bubble: how the new personalized web is changing what we read and how we think. Penguin (2011)
29. Parker, G.G., Van Alstyne, M.W.: Two-sided network effects: a theory of information product design. Manage. Sci. **51**(10), 1494–1504 (2005)
30. Prem, E.: A brave new world of mediated online discourse. Commun. ACM **65**(2), 40–42 (2022)
31. Schmalenbach, K., Gengler, E., Schötteler, S., Laumer, S.: Unraveling information-limiting environments: an empirical review of individual, social, and technological filters in social media. In: Proceedings of the 18th International Conference on Wirtschaftsinformatik (2023)
32. Shoemaker, P.J., Vos, T.: Gatekeeping theory. Routledge (2009)
33. Shore, J., Baek, J., Dellarocas, C.: Network structure and patterns of information diversity on twitter. MIS Q. **42**(3), 849–872 (2018)
34. Silva, L., Mondal, M., Correa, D., Benevenuto, F., Weber, I.: Analyzing the targets of hate in online social media. In: Proceedings of the International AAAI Conference on Web and Social Media, vol. 10, no. 1, pp. 687–690 (2021)
35. Sunstein, C.: The law of group polarization. J. Polit. Philos. **10**(2), 175–195 (2002)
36. Terren, L., Borge, R.: Echo chambers on social media: a systematic review of the literature. Rev. Commun. Res. **9**(1), 1–39 (2021)

37. Tran, T., Valecha, R., Rad, P., Rao, H.R.: An investigation of misinformation harms related to social media during two humanitarian crises. Inf. Syst. Front. **23**(4), 931–939 (2021)
38. Zuboff, S.: The age of surveillance capitalism. In: Social theory re-wired, pp. 203–213. Routledge (2023)

Who Wants to Live Forever? AI-Centricity as Ex-centricity of Death

Alexandru Balasescu[✉] [iD]

Royal Roads University, Victoria, BC, Canada
alec.balasescu@royalroads.ca

Abstract. This essay propose an essay-meditation upon death as an "uneasy" phenomenon for digitised modernity. It analyses how AI changes constantly the view we have on our own selves, our forms of organisation, and our lives, and points to the tensions between an AI-centric immortal world and the finitude of our planet.

Keywords: Immortality · Artificial Intelligence · Limitless Growth

1 Preamble

The past decade have seen the rapid development of the vast domain of Artificial Intelligence (AI), with the diversification of both types of AI and their application domains. From healthcare to art, and from justice systems to education, AI technology all but revolutionised the fields it entered. This asymptotic growth engendered new fields of study, raised new ethical concerns, and generated the need of new governance policies and practices, most of them still in the making. While the AI economy is accelerating, societies rapidly adopt and adapt to these systems.

Within this context, concerns about the pedagogy, learning and educational practices appeared, particularly because the use of Large Language Models (LLM), Agentic, and Generative AI systems impact the very design of the learning processes, from producing and sharing knowledge to evaluating results. So much so that in a recent article in the New Yorker, Hua Hsu [8] proclaimed the death of the essay. This comes few years after Foer [6] lamented the death of the author.

I will propose an essay-meditation upon death as an "uneasy" phenomenon for digitised modernity. I will argue that one of the most important aspects of AI is not necessarily what it does to the objectual world, that is its technological capabilities, but the way it changes constantly the view we have on our own selves, our forms of organisation, and our lives. As it is already common place in philosophical debates that the construction of the self is a process situated historically and culturally, one may wonder what kind of self the digital era proposes. How does this self "behaves" in the world, and what are the worldviews embedded in it?

Precisely because the relation of self and technology is circular, the paper also argues that this type of technology itself is engendered by a certain type of view on the self

L. Hagedorn et al. (Eds.): DIGHUM 2025, LNCS 16319, pp. 515–521, 2026.
https://doi.org/10.1007/978-3-032-11108-1_38

and the individual, deeply embedded in modernity's paradigm, and that this is both "a blessing and a curse". In order to ensure that AI will empower, not overpower humans, we must understand its deep unquestioned premises, and we must question them whenever they push abstract development over concrete human needs. At the same time we need to reconsider the distinction between needs and wants, in order to gain heightened discernment in relationships with technology.

2   What Death has to do with It?

Subjectivities are relational and dynamic, they are the product of continuous interaction with the environment and one-selves. Thus, in an anthropological sense, humans are a technological creation [13]. This means that technology and humanity are co-creations, the very act of inventing and using technology re-creates not only the world that surrounds us, but also our subjectivities. At least partially, and within the limits of biology (up until recently), we are the subjects of our own (technological) creation. With AI, things promise to change dramatically. But how exactly, and what exactly is the promise that fascinates - consciously or not - brought about by digitisation? Let's briefly state what digitisation really means: it is the numerical re-interpretation of the world similar to a Leibnizian dream, in which every object or "thing" has a number attached to it that fixes its meaning. In this way, the re-interpreted world becomes a world of data that is subsequently treatable and imaginarily manipulable by automation systems, the AI. Leibniz proposed the data-isation of meaning at the end of the 30 Years War in order to avoid further misunderstandings and future conflicts. It is only few centuries after, with the series of inventions that made possible programmables computers and their binary language in the XIXth century, and their physical creation in the XXth, that the possibility of a completely "data-ified", perfectly digitised world appeared within reach. As history and recent events proves, this does not, alas!, save us from human conflicts, but it does, in the vision of many who invent and some who use it, offer a different salvation: a quasi-religious immortality.

In his principles of generalised economy initially published in the 1960s, Georges Bataille [3] postulated the necessity of "unproductive expenditure", that is of death, in order to secure the healthy life of any complex system. In other words, observing the two fundamental principles of thermodynamic, the French economist and philosopher made the argument that death is necessary, unavoidable, and it should be, yes!, desirable because it is the unproductive expenditure that secures the perpetuation of life. Death avoids the explosive accumulation of energy that, in conformity to his principles, will need to be consumed in an unproductive manner. This surplus constitutes "the accursed share" that, should it grow and accumulate without limit, would be "forced" to consume itself through an explosive event. In human experience this usually means war. In other words, in this paradigm, accumulation of unspent energy and multiplication of lives lead to catastrophic events.

3   Enters AI

The relatively long history of AI could be traced in the works of Al Khwarizmi, the polymath living in IXth Century, active in the House of Wisdom in Baghdad, who devised the procedure of solving any problem through a suite of logical step by step propositions. He was rediscovered by the scholars of Italian Renaissance and "baptised" with the easier for them to pronounce name Algoritmi. His method took his name. However, the algorithmic method was not suited for a possible automatic machine - it still worked with words. If one would assign numbers to words, and if one can create automatic machines to manipulate numbers using mathematical language, than a "thinking machine" would be possible. The first step was taken at the end of XVIth Century, when Paccioli published the guide for the double entry book of accountancy for merchants. With this technique of assigning value (numbers) to household or merchandise goods, numbers gained rhetorical qualities [11]. In other words, data started to speak. This is where Leibniz's idea probably came from—Paccioli published his work before Leibniz was even born, and the double entry book was well adopted when Leibniz wrote his treaties. However, the combination of merchants methods and the Enlightenment philosophical searches of objectivity made mathematics the privileged field of truth production. The exactitude of the mathematical system in which the observations upon the world were codified was confused (willingly or not) with the accuracy of the observations themselves. However, the process of this transfer itself was under-analysed or altogether obscured from view in order to allow the rhetoric of numbers to take effect and stand in for truth [11].

This process is known today as "codification". If one could create a simplified language based on numbers, and a machine to manipulate it, the exactitude of mathematical language could have been postulated as objectivity regarding the observations on the world. If the observations are accurate and the language used to manipulate them is exact, there would be no doubt about the value of truth of the results. That is, the automatic machine is also a truth machine - a double entry book that not only speaks through numbers, but also "understands" the world. Ada Lovelace came up with that language that allowed programming of automatic machines: the binary language of programming. Her scientific partner, Babbage, added his will and philosophy behind the idea of the creation of such machines. Electricity allowed the invention of the automatic machine herself, and the rest is recent history [5].

4   The Promise

The double book entry made also possible the modern financial and economic system known as capitalism. Its development coincided with that of modernity, the era of scientific, ideological, and material transformations that we are still living today to a great extent. One of the promise at the centre of this system is that of perpetual growth (and accumulation). It is both seductive and contradicting of Bataille's principles of general economy [3] - if not those of thermodynamics. It is a human system that promises the overcoming of human condition, that of mortality. Many may sustain that this is humanity's dream from the beginning of times. Maybe. Maybe not. The particularity of modernity is *where* immortality is achievable. If in premodern times it was achievable in symbolic realms of legends or in sacred realms of the afterlife, modernity promises material immortality. If one can create a perpetually cumulative system and apparently forever enduring objects and materials, why not also perpetual life? The shifting of the goal, from sacred to profane immortality, seems to be the ultimate dream of late modernity. Here and now. If one can conceptually transform the living world into a mathematical model, than immortality is at hand. This is the pervasive logic that appears in the search for perpetual life, individual and collective, promised by Silicon Valley (transhumanist) luminaries: from Kurzweil who postulates Singularity as the act of transcending the imperfect human condition [4] and daily consumes large quantities of pills in order to preserve his body, to Brian Johnson who experiments on himself, literal immortality is actively sought after in AI and connected realms. I would argue that this is the deep promise of AI: the technological alchemy of producing eternal life - through objectifying biology on the one hand, and through subjectifying mathematics on the other - as in endowing complex algorithms with anthropomorphic characteristics and subjectivity.

How is the former achievable? Despite the efforts, for the moment, biological bodies insist on dying. The unique event of the individual end of life remind the digitised system of its imperfections. It reintroduces both materiality of the ultimate referent, and its *memento mori*. "Solutions" are constantly proposed: cryogenics has been around for awhile, with different levels of offer: freezing the head only, or the entire body - with a different price tag. The head-only tier is tributary to the very cartesian view of cognition as measure of existence, and to the very modern derived idea that cognition is a brain function. The derived offer is that of "saving" one's cognition into an electronic system, eliminating thus any biological imperfection and promising 'sillicated' perpetuity; as long as there is an electric plug at hand. The most elaborated promise is that of eliminating altogether dying through bio-engineering. While medicine has a lot to gain from AI applications in terms of curing, the question remains: is dying a disease, too? It seems that transhumanists agree on considering death a curable illness, and this view is at least few decades old - see NPR's "Is Death a Disease to Be Cured?", aired in 2010 [7]. The quasi-religious aspects of AI become transparent. The way societies and cultures look at individual dying reveal many of their patterns. Understanding our view of death will enhance our understanding of technology, machines, nature, and intelligence (be it artificial or otherwise).

5   Do You have a Body, or are You a Body?

The entire pattern of individual salvation is transferred into the economy of well-being. Our bodies are data-generating nodes for a digital economy of addiction, desire, or intent - depends who and what you are reading. Through this mostly voluntary process (the desire to buy and own smart watches or phones, fit-bits and so on) we also change our perceptions of our bodies. They become vehicles of constant improvement; resources to be exploited in our attempt to "grow", get a better job, a better partner, or even a "better body" (a sort of self-reflexive improved state of wellbeing materially expressed through bodily engineering). Metabolism morphs into the economy of constant self-improvement that reflects back on productivity. The prevalent practices around body and wellbeing in Sillicon Valley became not only a sign of health but a criteria of acceptance into the tribe, so to speak. They are also projected upon the world as solutions for both individual and planetary well-being [12].

This type of economy comes to a sudden stop when facing death. The perception of finitude as "a problem" that gave us some medical currents that describe death as "disease" is a cultural particularity of Western modernity. The latest attempt at immortality either through digital transcendence as in the cyberpunk novels by Greg Egan, the blueprint of Singularity embraced by the likes of Kurzweil or Peter Thiel, or through biotech are embedded and expressed in both the philosophies and the practices of Sillicon Valley's luminaries briefly detailed above. The most prominent exponent of conquering death is Bryan Johnson, the Silicon Valley billionaire creator of the project "Don't Die". He put his money behind himself as a project of immortal human. He is using a patchwork combination of AI algorithms, bio-engineering and medicine including transfusions of bodily fluids from his own son, diets and other techniques in order to perpetually rejuvenate his body - or so he claims.

His approach is "to measure everything that can be measured in the body" parameters, including his nighttime erections in terms of intensity and duration, and to ameliorate these measurements constantly. The erectile measurement is particularly interesting, as it is double-fold. It indicates the masculine standardisation of measurements (still an issue in modern medicine), and it is also reminiscent of the aspirations of Immortan Joe, the character in the post-apocalyptic film "Mad Max 4". His idea of achieving immortality was by impregnating the most eligible women in the land he controlled. The metaphor couldn't be clearer. A decade after the movie came out, the public learned that Immortan Joe may have a real-life double in Elon Musk. Another problem is that these aspirations come with a certain political culture that emphasizes efficiency, mathematical organisation of society, and elimination of errors from this utopian society. Those later may be human lives themselves, as it recently turned out, with Sillicon Valley figures starting to play an important role in politics.

Perhaps the danger is not that machines will take over the world (to great degree this already happened in the process of industrialisation), but the taking over of our mind by the algorithmic method of thinking that promises to eliminate the effects of biology, life, emotions, and experiential unicity. This effacing of affection for the world through AI is the hoped-for future, the promise and aspiration of a large part of the champions of AI and certainly is a characteristic of the Silicon Valley culture. Why? Simply because, in Hannah Arendt's words, biology (and its materiality) is a reminder of death: "The mortality of men lies in the fact that individual life, with a recognizable life story from birth to death, rises out of biological life." [1: 19] If transhumanism aspires to transcend biological limitation and death, and if AI is seen as the means to this end, the ethical implications of the generalised use of AI as socio-cultural regulatory technology are well-beyond our conversations today. Individual immortality already operates within the postulate of differentiate access (not everyone will be immortal). Today already, access to cutting edge treatments based on bio-tech and gene therapy, not to speak about genetic design, raise important unanswered ethical questions. At the same time and perhaps existentially important, postulating immortality reifies the possibility of limitless growth and unlimited accumulation on a finite planet that already seems to have exhausted some of its resources.

6 New Bodies, New Souls

The illusions sold in the AI "packages" is this: to achieve optimal parameters of functioning is equivalent to achieving immortality. This desire is built into, and creep out of our handheld devices through the apps that we download compulsively, use obsessively, sometimes forget but never delete. This new form of subjectivation renders the mechanisms of power and subjectivation easier to understand. The use of wearables that "sense" our bodies and retransmit the information to our eyes under numerical form reform our sense of selves. Senses are not only a means to feel oneself, but also a means to think (of) oneself, and gain self-consciousness, as Merleaux-Ponty [10] emphasized. Senses are the constitutive part of both the thinking about oneself, and in thinking the self. The visualization of bodily function through apps generates new subjectivities by turning inside out the means of subjectivation. The disintegration of bodies in measurable parameters and their reintegration in data clouds reshapes our understanding of the body/self aggregate, and the perception of the physical world, speaking about our relationship with the environment.

"The world alienation", or "the escape from materiality" as Arendt [1] details it, comprises the attempt to escape one's own material conditions. Arendt pointed out to the deepest desire generated by this form of alienation: to "escape" the confinement of the Earth. The movement to space is also a movement that marks the "saving" from biological life. In an AI centric world death is ex-centric. It is an inconvenience, as Kneese [9] observes. It is a reminder of the false promise of techno-solutionism, the ultimate glitch in an otherwise "perfect" system [2]. The question remains: who wants to live forever? And how does a society of immortals would look like?

References

1. Arendt, H.: The Human Condition, 1st edn. The University of Chicago Press (2018 [1958])
2. Balasescu, A.: Climate Change in the Age of Artificial Intelligence. Nature, Culture, and the Politics of Technology. Springer, Cham (2025). https://doi.org/10.1007/978-3-031-90042-6
3. Bataille, G.: The Accursed Share, vol I. Zone Books. University of Princeton Press (1991)
4. Broussard, M.: Artificial Unintelligence: How Computers Misunderstand the World. MIT Press (2018)
5. Crawford, K.: Atlas of AI: Power, Politics, and the Planetary Costs of Artificial Intelligence, 1st edn. Yale University Press (2021)
6. Foer, F.: World Without Mind. The Existential Threat of Big Tech, 1st edn. Penguin Press – Penguin Random House LLC (2017)
7. Goodenough, U.: Is Death a Disease that Can Be Cured? NPR Radio (2010). https://www.npr.org/sections/13.7/2010/07/15/128536658/is-death-a-disease-that-can-be-cured. Accessed 15 Sept 2025
8. Hsu, H.: On the Demise of the English Paper. The New Yorker (2025). https://www.newyorker.com/newsletter/the-daily/hua-hsu-on-the-demise-of-the-english-paper
9. Kneese, T.: Death Glitch. How Techno-Solutionism Fails Us in This Life and Beyond. Yale University Press, New Haven (2023)
10. Merleau-Ponty, M.: Phenomenology of Perception. Routledge – Taylor & Francis Group (2013)

11. Poovey, M.: A History of the Modern Fact: Problems of Knowledge in the Sciences of Wealth and Society, 1st edn. University of Chicago Press (1998)
12. Sexton, A.E.: Food as Software: Place, Protein, and Feeding the World Silicon Valley–Style. Economic Geography (2020). https://doi.org/10.1080/00130095.2020.1834382
13. Warnier, J.-P.: Construire la Culture Materielle. L'Homme qui Pensait avec ses gts [Constructing material culture: The man who thought with his fingers] (French). Presses Universitaires de France (1999)

Paperwork vs. Paperplay

The Media History of Playing Cards as aLudological Critique of Contemporary Digital Culture

Simon Huber[(✉)]

Gumpendorferstr. 17/10, 1060 Vienna, Austria
simon@secondsunrise.at

Abstract. The presented project sets out to examine playing cards in a longitudinal media-historical study. These paper things thus appear as paradigmatic interfaces between legibility and playability: On the one hand, playing cards are toys – namely artefacts that allow for certain operations – and on the other they are cultural sign systems, from which meaning is extracted from in varying ways. This calls for a systematic ludology that has been conceptualized as scientific research into playful cultural techniques. The aim is to establish an independent academic perspective on games and game design that is not merely orientated towards existing disciplines, but develops from the materiality and logic of the game itself. Within the agenda of digital humanism, this project seeks to understand the relationship of computer science and digital culture of our age with regard to the ongoing rapid transformations and innovations. These technological advances need to be mediated to the individual ways of handling knowledge. Thus, there is a need to understand and critically examine the materiality and functionality of interfaces and media, their playful (mis-)use and hacks that are part of the actual transformation of our knowledge society. Games and play are entities in their own right that need to be discussed with regards to the complex social, psychological/biological and media-technological aspects at once, without favouring one of those aspects for methodological reasons. This short paper aims at presenting some results of the funded INTRA-research project of the university of applied arts ("Ludological Investigations. Game Design in Terms of Cultural Techniques"), while explaining why it matters and presenting an outlook of potential upcoming research focussing on the prototypical playing card. It stood out as a special artifact of high ludicity, exemplifying the ludic potential as a special appeal, but also a liberating force for empowering autonomy against bureaucratic oppression. We're looking forward to adapting in this early stage to the issues, topics and major problems pointed out in the field of digital humanism.

Keywords: Research in Cultural Techniques · Media Genealogy · Digital Games · Ludology · Interface Cultures

L. Hagedorn et al. (Eds.): DIGHUM 2025, LNCS 16319, pp. 522–528, 2026.
https://doi.org/10.1007/978-3-032-11108-1_39

1 Bureaucracy as a Central Problem

David Graeber (2015) explained that the all-encompassing bureaucratisation can be shown by the increase in the use of the term 'paperwork', although the term bureaucracy is not heeded with great academic consideration. Still, feelings of being overwhelmed by paperwork itself have increased – not to mention the countless application procedures that are processed now on screens. This primarily refers to the hypertrophic effects of current power relations. But taken literally, playing with cards also appears to be 'paperwork' and playing in general is, in Adorno's (2012) words, "the reproduction of unfree labour" – like the factory workers Roland Barthes (2017) observed: they were playing Pachinko in the same monotonous manner, like on production line.

To this end, an update of the media history of playing cards is proposed here: not only the provenance of the classic French set, its variations (e.g. Tarot) and design experiments (e.g. Edita Moser's designs). A cursory glance at current trends in game design reveals cultural relevance. A relatively new genre – "deckbuilding" – thrives on the constant adaptation of the card set; famously pioneered by *Dominion*. This could be understood as a cultural shift in analog gaming, rooted in algorithmic practices of the digital realm. In return players of computer games also virtually encounter computer-controlled characters who challenge them with their deck: where there are actually knightly quests to be completed, time is passed by playing cards (called "Gwent" in *The Witcher*).

A media-genealogical critique of contemporary digital culture (which permeates daily life with bureaucratic acts and processes) can be based on playing cards. Within the long history of playful knowledge transfer, the media archaeology of knowledge visualization (Huber 2022) can be supplemented by a longitudinal study, revealing potential of the 'epoch of paper' (Müller 2012). "White magic" not only echoes in literary history (the "dark arts" of typography), but is also part of our "infra-ordinary" everyday life (Perec 1989). The card playing table is the habitual setting, where societal structures and individual practices – media and messages – intertwine.

The overarching research question explores the feasibility of an independent science of games and play. As there are no trained ludologists, just sociologists, biologists, psychologists with interest in 'Game Studies' the subject matter might be difficult to grasp and not serious enough? Could the playing card be such a prototypical object for interdisciplinary research that 'belongs to no one yet' (Barthes 1972) – thus providing the basis for an autonomous ludology?

As Claus Pias noted in his media archaeological study *Computer Spiel Welten* (2010) the human-computer interaction is modelled along the cultural conventions. Pre-verbally we're working with machines, navigating data sets and reconfiguring simulations. Likewise, a critical framework for commenting on advances in knowledge communication tackles also the lack of consistency of the current research in games and play. Such is often about didactical potential (e.g. Salen Tekinbas 2008) or the problematic depictions of certain game titles. Instead the ideological implications of chatbots, VR-glasses, AR museums or other popular fancies need to be pointed out. In paperfree illusions the magical, play-like emergence of knowledge is imagined, while children in school actually need to get their phones taken away.

2   Relevance for Digital Humanism

In the paper material, knowledge of the card game, play, and work overlap in an exemplary way. As in documents, information is processed by filing, sorting, and revealing (Gitelman 2014, Valente & Marchetti 2015). Paperplay and paperwork coincide in the dating app Tinder: it turns the smartphone screen into the top card of the virtual stack to be sorted. This principle has been transferred to other areas, such as job adverts. Job seekers now work through questionable offers like a talon (i.e., the stockpile of cards in a deck). The boundaries between ludic behaviour and economic calculation are becoming blurred, as are those between fundamentally different matters such as choosing a partner and choosing a job.

This transformation particularly affects the popularisation of knowledge and education. A marketable image of embodied knowledge can be seen, for example, in packs of cards that condense entire bookshelves into 'tangible' learning media in analogue sets (e.g., *pipdecks.com* promise "Expert knowledge in your back pocket"). Here, complexity reduction, gamification, and the belief in experiential knowledge become central elements of a post-disciplinary concept of learning. This concept is no longer orientated towards educational canons or subject logic, but towards the 'user experience' (i.e., ease of use and entertaining engagement).

Such examples also offer opportunities for academic self-reflection on research practice, which is nowadays often organised in an iterative and game-like manner. The development of (artistic) scientific projects is similar to the logic of game design: testing, discarding, and combining ideas. Accordingly, research designs are also fragmented, application-orientated, temporarily financed and therefore less committed to established institutes—playing with knowledge, but also working on and with its conditions. This is especially problematic in matters of urban planning, when actually the knowledge of the inhabitants that is extracted and visualized in workshops, interviews and other participatory formats ('participitainment') have no impact on the actual construction of city-scapes. It is not taken seriously, as it looks and feels like play, thus an optional nice-to-have.

The playing card, as a condensation of work, play, and information exemplifies various ways of dealing with tacit knowledge (Polanyi 2016). According to Pias (2010, 12), we have all been computer players for a long time. The card game continues to test and refine the handling of information technology.

3   Stage of Research: Lacking Ludology

A central debate in (multidisciplinary) game studies is the controversy between ludology and narratology (Frasca 2003, Aarseth 1997, Mukherjee 2015). These camps are notional, but point to a struggle for disciplinary identity. Bogost's 'procedural rhetorics' (2007) leads to the end of the discussion, but is itself an inadequate explanation: The economic success of computer games legitimised the academic study of games, but also complicated the situation: a confusing number of audiovisual components and interfaces are interwoven into entertainment products. These are sometimes consumed by small children: pressing, controlling, clicking, etc. – all without recognising the significance of the presentations; without 'reading' the very games that are consumed, ignoring the encoded meaning.

Since pre-modern times, however, the playing card has been active as a toy, game interface and now also as a medium of exchange in trading card games. According to Roger Caillois' (2001) classification, their use oscillates easily between improvisational card tricks (paidia) and structured game rules (ludus). It can be used to modulate chance, dexterity and tactical skill at the same time. It combines simple game operations - stacking, picking up, placing, hiding in a hand of cards, turning over into complex game forms and variations. 'Paperplay' can be understood in its entirety as a cultural technique, which are in contrast to any techniques characterised by recursive pragmatics (Macho 2007): while you can't make fire by making fire, you can write about writing, draw pictures about drawing pictures, etc. In exactly this symbolic work game knowledge is processed: cards are used to play games – a suitable object of investigation that underpins Huizinga's thesis of the origin of culture in play with media-historical material. Playful performance is more than cultural representation. Such a ludology should not be distracted too much from the depicted output, but focuses on 'necessary nonsensicality' of material handling that precedes it.

4   Method and Epistemological Interest

How to deal historiographically with elusive, performative culture of play? Two kinds of movements are "constitutive for media genealogy: 'swimming' in the sea of 'necessary' conditions [that lead to any given case], as well as the courageous selection of 'sufficient lines'" (Apprich & Bachmann 2017, 418). The former (swimming) corresponds to the investigations into the field of playful 'abuse' of all material culture: hacks, tricks, testing and tinkering (1.). Secondly the playing card represents the lineage that produces a "sufficient" cultivation of playful use: by generating artificial conflicts (game design) in card format, knowledge is tacitly processed (3.), which is needed to participate in the game at all and thus provides empirical mass for investigation.

1. **Research into cultural techniques** allows systematic speculation along 'primitive techniques' (Siegert 2020) that are used in card games. Elementary operations (stacking, shuffling, picking, dealing, drawing, discarding; see also www.ludology.uni-ak. ac.at) as recursive processes of meaning generation in relation to bodies, space and collectives (Dünne et al., 2020)
2. **History of knowledge visualization**: In block printing, the playing card is created as a standardised artefact, in the distribution of which the potential of paper is revealed and thus its media development in areas such as typography, administration and academy - conventional play is handed down through the written-image composite of letters, numbers and images (Krämer et al. 2012).
3. **Supplemented by ethnographic field research**: analysing design practices in contemporary communities as a context-bound, situated embodied form of knowledge. We are particularly interested in how cards (as well as their improvised paper substitutes) are used by game designers to develop and test new prototypes in order to create new games.

The desired insight lies in the development of a heuristic for the description of game-based knowledge practices with a special focus on pre-verbal communication. All kinds of phenomena of game culture can be localised between play instinct (paidia), rule system (ludus) and simulation (strategic play) in order to be positioned as part of the research field with corresponding relevance. A pack of cards can be considered a toy for cardistry, a game interface or a probabilistic model for trial treatments.

5   A Knowledge Module between Matter and Data

At the intersection of media and cultural studies, history of knowledge, game studies and design research the presented approach paves a way to a consistent science of games and play instead of contouring a thematic focus. The need for a material grounding for the research in such cultural affairs is met with the focus on various forms of the paper artifact, the (playing) card. It is an object between bound books on the one hand, the central medium for academic knowledge: no matter whether the contained texts are considered a source for humanities, or whether they are conceptualized as text books introducing new engineers to their fields. On the other hand it is not a map that provides topographical context to a given object according to numerical coordinated data. Cards are neither bound to the typical linearity of typography, nor is it necessarily spaced out and aligned with the local circumstances. Its prototypical modularity makes it a perfect example to study the development of ludic cultures, hence their *ludicity* per se in modernity.

Political and communication-pragmatic consequences resulting from this interdisciplinary state must not be ignored: who is actually asked when concerns about games and play arise? What sort of expertise is provided and accepted as such? When set out to systematically investigate the feasibility of a critical ludology one should also consider the societal needs it caters to – not only the innovative potential. Therefore, in our project crossdisciplinarity is not emphatically stressed and met with a multitude of different perspectives (Zimmermann et al. 2020), assuming some synergies will emerge. Also in regard to its educational consequences such disciplinary claims need to be discussed: the curricular changes like new subjects – *Digitale Grundbildung* in Austria and the establishment of a critical vocabulary and methodologies of dealing with gameplay in the center of research interests.

Exemplary for a potential ludology, the materiality, order and embodiment of knowledge are traced to the ludicity of the playing card. It is understood as a versatile interface between play and seriousness, between contingency and system. Critical ludology appears as a contemporary form of reflection that equally problematises hierarchised, school-based institutions of mediation as well as the algorithmic, opaque knowledge architecture of digital platforms. Thus, looking out for a way of knowledge communication that is aligned with humanistic values. A thorough study of play allows innovative perspectives on knowledge as a culturally and technically produced relationship between body, space and collectives. Vice versa, profiling the culture-creating function of games would be advantageous for cultural studies by containing their 'boundlessness' – which in Aleida Assmann's account (2016) oscillates indecisively between archaeology of things and rules of narration, just like Game Studies.

Disclosure of Interests.   The author has no competing interests to declare that are relevant to the content of this article.

References

Aarseth, E.J.: Cybertext: Perspectives on Ergodic Literature. Johns Hopkins University Press, Baltimore (1997)

Adorno, T.W.: Ästhetische Theorie, 19th edn. Suhrkamp, Frankfurt am Main (2012)

Apprich, C., Bachmann, G.: Mediengenealogie. Zurück in die Gegenwart digitaler Kulturen. In: Koch, G. (ed.) Digitalisierung: Theorien und Konzepte für die empirische Kulturforschung, pp. 405–425. UVK Verlagsgesellschaft, Konstanz München (2017)

Assmann, A.: Die Grenzenlosigkeit der Kulturwissenschaften. Kulturwissenschaftliche Zeitschrift **1**(1), 39–48 (2016)

Barthes, R.: Jeunes chercheurs. Communications **19**(1), 1–5 (1972)

Barthes, R.: Im Reich der Zeichen. Suhrkamp, Frankfurt am Main (2017)

Bateson, G., et al.: Escape! Computerspiele als Kulturtechnik. Böhlau, Köln (2007)

Caillois, R.: Man, Play and Games. University of Illinois Press, Urbana (2001)

Collins, H.M.: Tacit and Explicit Knowledge. University of Chicago Press, Chicago (2010)

Dünne, J., Fehringer, K., Kuhn, K., Struck, W. (eds.): Cultural Techniques: Assembling Spaces. Texts & Collectives. De Gruyter, Berlin (2020)

Frasca, G.: Ludology meets Narratology. Similitude and Differences between (Video) Games and Narrative. http://www.ludology.org/articles/ludology.htm. Accessed 23 Sept 2025

Gitelman, L.: Paper Knowledge. Toward a Media History of Documents. Duke University Press, Durham (2014)

Graeber, D.: The Utopia of Rules: On Technology, Stupidity, and the Secret Joys of Bureaucracy. Melville House, New York (2015)

Huber, S.: Die Emergenz der Anschaulichkeit in Comenius' Orbis pictus (1658). University of Applied Arts, Vienna (2022)

Huizinga, J.: Homo Ludens: Vom Ursprung der Kultur im Spiel. Rowohlt, Hamburg (2009)

Krämer, S., Cancik-Kirschbaum, E.C., Totzke, R. (eds.): Schriftbildlichkeit: Wahrnehmbarkeit, Materialität und Operativität von Notationen. Akademie Verlag, Berlin (2012)

Macho, T.: Tiere zweiter Ordnung. Kulturtechniken der Identität. In: Schmidinger, H.M., Sedmak, C. (eds.) Der Mensch: ein "animal symbolicum"?, pp. 51–66. Wiss. Buchges., Darmstadt (2007)

Mukherjee, S.: Video Games and Storytelling: Reading Games and Playing Books. Palgrave Macmillan, Basingstoke (2015)

Müller, L.: Weisse Magie. Die Epoche des Papiers. Hanser, München (2012)

Perec, G.: L'infra-ordinaire. Seuil, Paris (1989)

Pias, C.: Computer Spiel Welten, 2nd edn. Diaphanes, Zürich (2010)

Polanyi, M.: Implizites Wissen, 2nd edn. Suhrkamp, Frankfurt am Main (2016)

Siegert, B.: Attached: the object and the collective. In: Dünne, J., Fehringer, K., Kuhn, K., Struck, W. (eds.) Cultural Techniques: Assembling Spaces, Texts & Collectives, pp. 131–140. De Gruyter, Berlin (2020)

Salen Tekinbaş, K. (ed.): The Ecology of Games: Connecting Youth, Games, and Learning. MIT Press, Cambridge (2008)

Valente, A., Marchetti, E.: Make and play: card games as tangible and playable knowledge representation boundary objects. In: Proceedings of the 15th International Conference on Advanced Learning Technologies (ICALT), pp. 137–141. IEEE, Washington (2015)

Zimmermann, O., Falk, F., Deutscher Kulturrat e.V.: Handbuch Gameskultur. Deutscher Kulturrat, Berlin (2020). https://www.kulturrat.de/publikationen/handbuch-gameskultur/

Vulnerability as a Design Ethics
for Digital Humanism

Erich Prem[1,2](✉) (iD)

[1] TU Wien, Karlsplatz 13, 1040 Vienna, Austria
`prem@eutema.com`
[2] eutema GmbH, Vienna, Austria

Abstract. The paper suggests vulnerability as a central ethical concept for Digital Humanism. In going beyond just a criticism of transhumanism, vulnerability is presented as a foundation of a Digital Humanist ethical theory and for designing a vision of a good digital life.

Keywords: Ethics · vulnerability · digital systems design · digital humanism

1 Digital Humanism and the Digital Good Life

The Spanish philosopher José Ortega y Gasset was one of the first philosophers of technology to focus on the intricate and intimate human relationship to technology [1]. Technical disciplines often stress technology's instrumental role as a means to meet human needs, a position[1] prominently held by Martin Heidegger [9]. Yet Ortega y Gasset and later philosophers claim that technology is more than a tool; it is a distinctly human way of shaping the environment, often reshaping our needs in the process [11]. Technology adapts nature to the subject and in this process of human rebellion against circumstance creates a *supra-nature* [1]. Today this *supra-nature* is often digital and raises a key question: how can we design the *supra-nature* to promote human and ecological flourishing?

Digital Humanism offers a response. It adopts a design stance, asserting that digital technologies are malleable and can be shaped through regulation and public engagement. It emphasizes individual rights—such as privacy and freedom of expression—and collective goals like democratic governance of technology and the protection of social achievements in a post-digital world. Digital humanism works to overcome privacy erosion, digital surveillance, technology monopolies, online power, and shifting concepts of human identity in the age of AI. Digital Humanism calls for human-centred AI, the preservation of agency, human dignity, and the environment [18]. However, to date it lacks specific design criteria or a compelling vision of the digital good life.

---

[1] Heidegger's analyses of technology, particularly in *The Question Concerning Technology (Die Frage nach der Technik)*, are widely cited and considered seminal for the philosophy of technology. At the same time, Heidegger's involvement with National Socialism requires a critical stance in any scholarly engagement with his work.

© The Author(s) 2026

L. Hagedorn et al. (Eds.): DIGHUM 2025, LNCS 16319, pp. 529–536, 2026.
https://doi.org/10.1007/978-3-032-11108-1_40

This paper proposes *vulnerability* as a central concept for such a vision. I argue that vulnerability should be a central focal point of the digital humanist agenda as a potential answer to a "program of technological humanism" [13]. It offers a vital ethical and philosophical framework for imagining *the digital good life*.

2   Vulnerability in the Philosophy of Technology

2.1   The Concept of Vulnerability

Initially tied to physical wounding, the Latin origin *vulnerare* evolved to encompass emotional, cognitive, and systemic dimensions. The philosophical work of Judith Butler [3] has reframed vulnerability as a political and ethical category, highlighting how our shared exposure to harm is the basis for solidarity and moral responsibility. Martha Fineman [7] expands this by positing the "vulnerable subject" as the normative subject of law and justice, emphasizing universal, ontological vulnerability over liberal notions of autonomy.

Today, we speak of economic, environmental, organizational, or digital vulnerability. It is applied to networks, infrastructures, and systems, yet its meaning shifts. A "cyber-security vulnerability" or "economic vulnerability" speaks more of systemic exposure to attack than the existential or relational openness that marks the human condition. We must be careful, then, not to conflate the vulnerability of systems with that of people. Only the latter involves pain, healing, care, and the moral demand they entail.

Vulnerability is not an incidental condition but a foundational characteristic of the human condition. To be human is to be exposed to harm. Vulnerability concerns the individual who is open to being wounded and ultimately mortal ('ontological vulnerability' [6, p. 219]). Also, vulnerability links with other beings and society. We rely on others to care for us – from being babies to being sick. There are also social wounds that can afflict us from vulnerable relationships to dependable positions in society ('social vulnerability'). In addition, as humans we know about our own fragility and hence dependability.

Alasdair MacIntyre was one of the first virtue ethicists to argue for vulnerability as a central concept that helps explain our human nature as *dependent rational animals* [14]. In his view, vulnerability is a source of a meaningful life and the ground for our fundamental dependence on others. Clearly, vulnerability is also central to bioethics starting with medical ethics. In fact the principlism of T.I. Beauchamp & F. Childess [19] strongly links with vulnerability in the ethics of care that originated in feminist ethics. As such, vulnerability should constitute a central starting point for any ethical reflection on the design of our lives and desirable environments. This paper explores the potential of vulnerability as a basic concept for developing visions of how to live well digitally. It challenges the dominant narratives in technology design that either ignore or seek to *overcome* human fragility and argues instead for a reorientation toward designing with, rather than against, vulnerability.

2.2   The Denial of Human Fragility

The focus of scholarly work on vulnerability in information technology has mostly been on transhumanism. This is because a rejection and denial of human fragility has been most clearly formulated in the transhumanist movement. It describes humanity as a phase to be transcended through technological enhancement. It advocates imagined futures where cognitive capacity, emotional stability, physical health, and even mortality are radically improved or eliminated through information technology such as AI, genetic engineering, or other forms of bioaugmentation. Less futuristic versions focus on the augmentation of humans with specific technological tools such as memory chips, devices to replace or assist sensory organs, or stronger or more durable limbs etc. Some of these ideas are no longer science fiction as the connection of certain types of electronic devices to human neural circuits has now become possible. Today, we can sometimes restore lost hearing with cochlear implants, for example. Such a neuroprosthesis thus partially realizes the idea of improving humans with the help of biocybernetics, although in this example the implants may not exceed or even reach average hearing capability [22]. More radical versions of transhumanism, however, promote a massive biocybernetical 'optimization' of humans to overcome what transhumanists present as 'limits' of our human biology. And even more radical transhumanist visions include the idea of eliminating human bodies completely by 'downloading' the human mind to computers. Such in-silico versions of human minds might then become practically immortal as they no longer depend on a biological substrate.

The most radical versions of transhumanism go beyond anthropocentrism, arguing that humans may be overtaken by technically implemented systems that outperform humans, e.g. in terms of intelligence. Such super-intelligence may or may not build on humans. It could mean a continued in-silico evolution of previously downloaded human minds or start with artificial 'superintelligence'. This version of transhumanism has also been labelled *technological posthumanism* or *posthuman transhumanism,* cf. [23]. It is important to distinguish it from *philosophical posthumanism,* which is often understood as the philosophical critique of humanism.[2] Philosophical posthumanism arises from a critique of the anthropocentric focus of humanism. Depending on the precise version of posthumanism it suggests including a more intersubjective perspective, the consideration of other living beings (e.g. animals), or even a broader all-encompassing creationist perspective. I have previously argued that, despite its name, digital humanism is indeed a form of philosophical post-humanism, given its focus on nature, the environment, anti-colonial emphasis, and societal concerns, c.f. [18].

Transhumanism champions technological advancement and mistakes it for progress. As it often remains unclear against which precise criteria the advancements should be considered also improvements, it is not convincing that purely technical improvements also constitute advances for individuals or for society. Transhumanists promote a reduction of the criteria against which to consider humans imperfect to illness and mortality or to 'shortcomings' of our memory and sensory organs. Hence, transhumanism fails to account for the moral significance of being limited or vulnerable. In its quest to improve or perfect humans, it risks obliterating the very qualities that make us morally valuable. By focusing on increasing isolated features or overall 'efficiency', transhumanist narratives overlook our dependency, our care relations, and the value of our limitations. Much of the philosophical debate argues against a transhumanist vision of a perfected

---

[2] Note that there are other meanings of the term 'post-humanism'. A complete conceptual analysis of different meanings of *post-humanism* is beyond the scope of this paper.

and ideally deathless existence. Hauskeller pioneered the idea of a *positive* account of vulnerability connecting human weakness, vulnerability, and mortality with making life valuable and meaningful [10].

A transhumanist program of immortality and invulnerability also fosters extraordinary individualism. The invulnerable individual does not depend on others and populates a world where care is not a central social concept. Science and technology then are efforts to make us less vulnerable [10 p. 16, 6 p. 221]. For the transhumanist research and innovation describe the path to a utopia where humans become invulnerable.[3] The idea that humans are imperfect erodes the ethical foundation of humanism and risks legitimizing forms of exclusion, elitism, and disposability.

By contrast, an ethics grounded in vulnerability affirms that our imperfections are not deficiencies, but conditions for solidarity and moral meaning. This critique echoes Hans Jonas' [12] imperative of responsibility, i.e. to constrain technological power by an ethics of care for the fragile human *and* the planet. For Jonas, this is particularly important with respect to future generations and due to the society-level effects of modern technologies as well as their often cumulative and unpredictable consequences. He proposes to act particularly cautiously when there is a risk that technology will negatively affect future generations. This could be seen as a generational type of vulnerability that I am addressing here.

So far, the transhumanist program is a vision, often linked to science fiction ideas about our future, but it also proposes directions for research and human development. There are also concrete trends and attitudes in current systems design that carry post- and transhumanist ideas and characteristics: Transhumanist ideals often prioritize optimization of people over empowering them in their current state and being. There is an idea of using digital systems to improve individuals towards an idea of perfection and similarly to enforce societal norms through rigid, inescapable infrastructures. Both seek to technologically overcome human and societal shortcomings. Such ideas underlie digital interventions from automation to censorship, from behavioural nudging to paternalistic control. However, automation contributes to de-skilling and alienation, sidelining human roles. Censorship limits expression and access to knowledge, often under the guise of avoiding harm, but aligned with commercial interests. An ethical future of technology, however, lies not in perfecting or overcoming humanity but in affirming it.

3 Designing with, not Against, Vulnerability

3.1 Digital Humanism and the Notion of Vulnerability

Digital humanism fundamentally relates to human vulnerability and notions of care, emerging largely as a response to the threats that digitalization poses to the human condition and individual self-determination. The movement arises from serious concerns about the way digitalization is developing and its detrimental impact on individuals and society. This critical awareness of human vulnerabilities focuses on documented

---

[3] Coeckelbergh provides a long list of reasons why the transhumanist program may not in fact realize invulnerability [4]. Whether versions of transhumanism exist that are compatible with vulnerability is subject of current philosophical debate [6].

shortfalls in digitization, including privacy infringements, power shifts, human alienation, and disownment. Digital humanism recognizes that digital technologies facilitate unprecedented intrusions into privacy, promote surveillance, and threaten fundamental rights, undermining the notion that digitization is inherently beneficial for humanity. The *Vienna Manifesto* [17] affirms that technology must serve human dignity, agency, and relationality, hence a vulnerability-aware Digital Humanism offers a contrast to technological determinism and uncritical transhumanist optimism.

A core aspect of this vulnerability is the threat to human authorship, which is the central concept underlying humanist philosophy. Digital humanism seeks to ensure that digitalization strengthens human self-determination, autonomy, and dignity [20, 21]. Vulnerability manifests when people become existentially dependent due to external circumstances (such as illness or unemployment), causing them to lose their status as life's authors. Consequently, digital humanism positions the concept of dignity as central, demanding that humans be protected even when not directly affected by computer-controlled actions. This stands in direct contrast to transhumanist perspectives which often hold a deficit view of human beings as weak, requiring technical improvement.

The concept of care in digital humanism can be associated with the Latin term *humanitas*, meaning humanity or kindness [18, 21]. Interpreted in this sense, digital humanism adopts a more relational view of human-machine interaction, moving away from a metaphysical search for the *essence* of humans toward a focus on acts of humanity [24]. This relational view results in a mandate for digital technology to actively protect people and the environment [18]. The resulting task for digital development is defined as caring for individuals and society affected by digitalization, necessitating constraints on the power of digital systems and their owners. This approach leads to a type of virtue ethics in digital development, emphasizing dignity, wisdom, and *praxis*. Ultimately, digital humanism calls for strengthening the social contract and ensuring fundamental rights, aiming to develop digital technology to support inclusion and guarantee these rights, especially for the disempowered.

3.2 From Paradoxical Vulnerability to Designing Systems

At the heart of the demand to embrace vulnerability lies a paradox. It consists in accepting vulnerability while at the same time emphasizing care and avoiding harm. To abolish vulnerability entirely would strip away an essential aspect of human life—an outcome neither possible nor worth pursuing. Vulnerability is essential both at the level of the individual and of society. Vulnerability constitutes a source of meaning—it shapes human values, fosters empathy, and draws our attention to the world and others within it. It drives curiosity, learning, science, and underpins play, sports, and leisure. Our capacity to be wounded opens our capacity to care, to relate to others, and to act responsibly. The desire to eliminate all suffering risks stripping life of meaning, reciprocity, and the communal dimension of healing [2].

Digital Humanism urges us to design not from fantasies of invincibility, but from the reality of shared vulnerability. We are not perfectible machines; we are fragile beings who seek justice, meaning, and connection. Honouring that we are the best humans that exist does not limit technological ambition. It reorients it toward human flourishing and aligns vulnerability with the *lessening* of harm.

Although perhaps a paradoxical idea, putting vulnerability centre stage is not without precedent. Medicine, for example, seeks to alleviate suffering, but not to erase our human condition [6, p. 221]. It reduces wounds without denying our fragility. It affirms care even where no cure is possible—where the aim is not perfection, but the alleviation of pain, and the practice of compassion.

Care ethics [8, 16] offers a framework centred on attentiveness, responsibility, and responsiveness. Rather than seeing vulnerability as a flaw to be engineered away, Digital Humanism opens a path to designing with responsibility and empathy. In the digital realm, this means:

- Designing systems that uphold human autonomy and dignity.
- Avoiding deceptive anthropomorphism and emotional simulation.
- Ensuring transparency about system capabilities and their limits.
- Including diverse perspectives in design.
- Preventing interfaces from reinforcing social vulnerabilities.

These principles challenge prevailing paradigms driven by efficiency and profit. They call for a relational ethics that treats the user as a moral subject. The goal of digital technology should not be to eliminate vulnerability, but to design with it in mind. Digital design must begin with *Being-as-it-is,* acknowledging people in their fragile conditions, not from visions of post-human perfection. Design must care for all, not exclude those deemed less desirable or labelled imperfect. This entails:

- Recognizing human fragility as a source of meaning, not a flaw.
- Empowering users by enhancing their autonomy, rather than limiting it.

    - Instead of restricting discourse, raise users' awareness and choice.
    - Inform users about norms and risks, rather than enforcing compliance.
    - Enrich interactions by enabling learning, creativity, and personal growth—rather than prescribing behaviour or automating judgment.

- Respecting diverse forms of vulnerability by supporting decision-making, not replacing it with automation.

The aim is not to perfect humanity, but to cultivate the strength and poise [9] to live with imperfection. The design of IT systems must not presuppose users as rational, efficient, and minimally flawed. We are emotional, dependent, and socially embedded beings. These traits are not weaknesses to be engineered away but conditions for the possibility of ethical life. We must ask: What kind of humans are we designing for? What kind of future are we building in the process? Digital humanist designs should support the courage to face adversity, not by erasing it, but by helping us navigate it with dignity.

3.3 Conclusions and Directions for Further Research

From the perspective of philosophical ethics, vulnerability can be considered a fundamental concept underlying different ethical conceptions. It links principlism with virtue ethics, consequentialism, and potentially deontology. Principlism as a normative ethical consideration of how to treat people in medical experiments originated from considerations of protecting vulnerable populations. More recently, the principles of autonomy, beneficence, and justice have also become central to AI ethics [25].

In addition, vulnerability can be regarded as a source of social virtues such as humility, responsibility, and solidarity [5, 13, 15]. These virtues would make little sense if it was not for others around us that require our support and attention for their vulnerability.

Recognizing human vulnerability can help us better understand some aspects of Kant's moral philosophy – particularly his emphasis on respect for people, autonomy, and duties to self and others. While Kantian deontology does not focus on vulnerability – a source of later critique especially from the position of care ethics – the duty to respect others as ends in themselves implies a recognition that others can be harmed or exploited, i.e., they are vulnerable to our actions. Without vulnerability, the moral weight of that duty would be diminished.

Finally, vulnerability forms an important foundation of utilitarian considerations. Focusing on pleasure and the absence of pain only makes sense where people are vulnerable to pain, deprivation, frustration, and harm. In this way, vulnerability gives utilitarianism its moral urgency.

Promoting the concept of vulnerability demands further clarification and a more systematic analysis, as Fernandez has also suggested [6, p. 217]. The vulnerability paradox requires research into which aspects of vulnerability we need to preserve for human flourishing, and which wounds can be eliminated without losing human nature and our dependence on and obligation to care. It also means to navigate the spectrum of possible digital designs from enforcing protection to paternalism, from nudging to full autonomy of human choice based on considerations of care. This is not an easy task that requires much more situational consideration and contextual awareness than a generalized solutionism that often prevails today.

Acknowledgments. Parts of this research were funded by the European Commission (Digital, Industry, and Space) as EU project EUDHIT, Grant Agreement ID 101212890.

Disclosure of Interests. The author has received a grant from the EC as stated above. Parts of this paper were edited using Generative AI for English grammar correction and style.

References

1. Alonso, M.: Ortega: a philosophy of technology pioneer. Ann. Univ. Bucharest LXIX **1**, 9–26 (2020)
2. Bovassi, G.: Vulnerability and resilience in the context of transhumanist an posthumanist provocations. Bioética **25**(1), 25–26 (2025)
3. Butler, J.: Precarious Life: The powers of mourning and violence. Verso (2004)
4. Coeckelbergh, M.: Vulnerable cyborgs: learning to live with our dragons. J. Evol. Technol. **22**(1), 1–9 (2011)
5. Facal, C.: Vulnerability theory and transhumanism: Helping the ontologically vulnerable. Ithaque **34**(Automne), 23–25 (2024)
6. Fernandez, B., Rueda, J.: In defense of posthuman vulnerability. Scientia Fides **9**(1) (2021)
7. Fineman, M.: The vulnerable subject and the responsive state. Yale J. Law Feminism (2008)
8. Gilligan, C.: In a Different Voice. Harvard University Press, Cambridge (1982)

9. Heidegger, M.: The question concerning technology. Technol. values: Essential Read. **99**, 113 (1954)
10. Hauskeller, M.: Ephemeroi – Human vulnerability, transhumanism, and the meaning of life. Scientia Fides **7**(2) (2019)
11. Ihde, D. Technology and the Lifeworld. Indiana University Press (1990)
12. Jonas, H.: The Imperative of Responsibility. University of Chicago Press (1984)
13. Llano F.H.: Transhumanism, vulnerability and human dignity. Deusto J. Hum. Rights 39–58 (2019)
14. MacIntyre A.: Dependent rational animals. Open Court (1999)
15. Sandel, M.: The Case Against Perfection. Harvard University Press, Cambridge (2007)
16. Tronto, J.: Moral Boundaries. Routledge (1993)
17. Vienna Manifesto on Digital Humanism, Vienna (2019). https://digitalhumanism.eu
18. Prem, E: Principles of digital humanism: a critical post-humanist view. J. Responsible Technol. 100075 (2024)
19. Beauchamp, T., Childress, J.: Principles of biomedical ethics. Edicoes Loyola (1994)
20. Nida-Rümelin J., Staudacher K.: Philosophical foundations of digital humanism. In: Werthner H., et al. (eds.) Introduction to digital humanism, 17–30. Springer, Cham (2024)
21. Nida-Rümelin, J., Winter, D.: Humanism and enlightenment. In: Werthner, H., Ghezzi, C., Kramer, J., Nida-Rümelin, J., Nuseibeh, B., Prem, E., Stanger, A. (eds.) Introduction to digital humanism, pp. 3–16. Springer, Cham (2024)
22. Loizou, P.C.: Introduction to cochlear implants. IEEE Eng. Med. Biol. Mag. **18**(1), 32–42 (1999)
23. Merzlyakov, S.S.: Posthumanism vs. transhumanism: from the "end of exceptionalism" to "technological humanism". Herald of the Russian Academy of Sciences, **92**(Suppl 6), 475–482 (2022). https://doi.org/10.1134/S1019331622120073
24. Prem, E.: Zur Verwirklichung eines digitalen Humanismus. (Realising a digital humanism.) In: Zukunft (2025). https://diezukunft.at/zur-verwirklichung-eines-digitalen-humanismus-von-erich-prem/
25. Prem, E.: Approaches to ethical AI. In: Werthner, H., et al. (eds.) Introduction to Digital Humanism. Springer, Cham (2024). https://doi.org/10.1007/978-3-031-45304-5_15

Unpacking the Tensions of Empowerment in Digital-Self Tracking: A Digital Humanism Perspective

Anke Schneider$^{(\boxtimes)}$ and Cornelia Gerdenitsch

AIT Austrian Institute of Technology GmbH, Vienna, Austria
{anke.schneider,cornelia.gerdenitsch}@ait.ac.at

Abstract. Data-driven tools, such as digital self-tracking technologies, are increasingly embedded in everyday life. However, their impact is ambivalent, as previous research has shown that they can simultaneously empower and disempower individuals. In this paper, we adopt a perspective from digital humanism to unpack key empowerment tensions at the intrapersonal, interactional, and behavioral levels that shape the effects of digital self-tracking: self-connectedness vs. self-alienation, social embeddedness vs. normative pressure, and agency vs. technological control. We argue that realizing the empowering potential of digital self-tracking requires careful design, implementation, and use. To support this, we offer guiding questions for each level of empowerment to help shape digital self-tracking towards empowerment rather than disempowerment.

Keywords: Quantified-Self Technology · Empowerment · Data-Driven System · Humanity-Centered Design · Digital Humanism · Interaction Design · Digital Self-Tracking

1 Ambivalent Effects of Digital Self-Tracking

The trend toward digital self-tracking has gained considerable attention in recent years [10]. An increasing number of individuals now use quantified-self technologies, such as smartwatches, fitness trackers, and health applications, to monitor and analyze data related to their bodies and behaviors. These tools promise to deliver personal insights, motivate lifestyle changes, and provide greater control over one's health, well-being, and performance, positioning themselves as instruments of self-optimization [15]. Previous research indeed highlights these potential benefits, showing that digital self-tracking can foster improvements in health and well-being [7], as well as enhance personal performance [2]. In this sense, quantified-self technologies can be seen as empowering tools that enable individuals to actively shape and optimize their lives [20]. However, there is also substantial evidence pointing to potential downsides. The pursuit of self-improvement through data can paradoxically create external pressures [11], self-exploitation [15], and increased stress and anxiety [12,14], ultimately transforming these tools into instruments of disempowerment. Thus, empowerment and

© The Author(s) 2026
L. Hagedorn et al. (Eds.): DIGHUM 2025, LNCS 16319, pp. 537–543, 2026.
https://doi.org/10.1007/978-3-032-11108-1_41

disempowerment are not mutually exclusive outcomes but often coexist within the same self-tracking practice.

This ambivalence, where digital self-tracking can simultaneously empower and disempower users, is characteristic of data-driven systems. The growing presence of data-driven technologies in general, and quantified-self technologies in particular, in everyday life raises pressing questions about how to design them to prioritize human needs and values. We argue that the extent to which digital self-tracking empowers or disempowers individuals depends critically on how these systems are designed, implemented, and integrated into daily practices over time. Only through careful conceptualization, thoughtful design, and use can the empowering potential of these technologies be fully realized. To unpack this, we identify three core tensions that shape the empowerment potential of digital self-tracking: *self-connectedness vs. self-alienation, social embeddedness vs. normative pressure,* and *agency vs. technological control.* Based on this analysis, we offer guiding questions to support a humanistic approach to technology design, implementation, and long-term usage.

2   Tensions of Empowerment in Digital Self-tracking

Zimmerman [23] conceptualizes psychological empowerment as a dynamic process that emerges across three interconnected levels: intrapersonal, interactional, and behavioral. This model highlights that empowerment involves not only individual experience but also social dynamics and structural participation. Applying this perspective to digital self-tracking highlights the simultaneous impact of these systems across the three levels, with three tensions emerging that shape empowerment. These three tensions are illustrated in the following Fig. 1.

The **intrapersonal level** refers to an individual's subjective perception of self-determination, motivation, and self-efficacy [23]. Research shows that digital self-tracking can strengthen users' self-image, enhance bodily awareness [4], increase self-efficacy [18], and support personal growth [8]. These benefits arise from reflective processes [2, 19], as self-tracking technologies provide insights into diverse aspects of the body and mind, such as behaviors, emotions, and habits, thereby deepening self-understanding. These reflective processes support self-connectedness, that is, a deeper awareness and connection to one's body and mind. A key design feature that enables this is the visualization of personal data. Indeed, studies show that visualizing individual progress can increase motivation and strengthen self-efficacy [18]. However, visualizations can also create new demands. Continuous self-monitoring encourages constant self-evaluation, pushing users to compare themselves with predefined standards or normative averages [11]. This can give rise to self-doubt, self-criticism, and feelings of inadequacy when such expectations are not met [11]. Moreover, it is important to carefully question whether the underlying data are valid and inclusive. Not all sensors used by self-tracking technologies capture data with equal accuracy and reliability [3], and reference values used for comparisons may be based on biased or limited population averages that fail to reflect diversity and context. In the

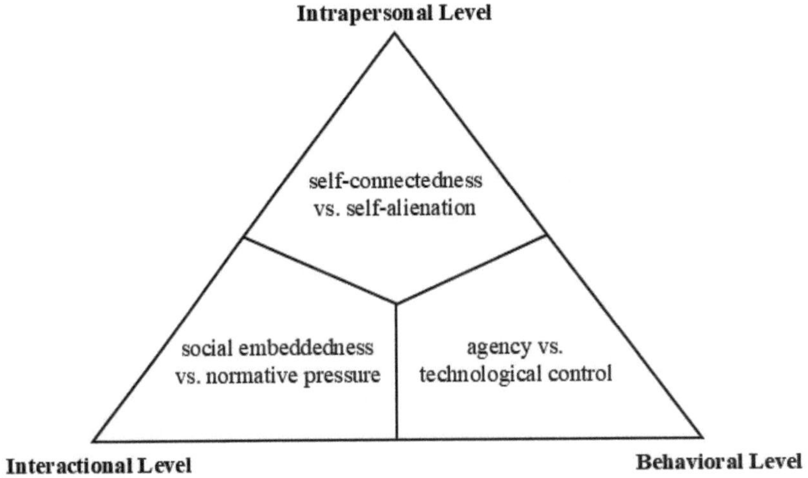

Fig. 1. Three empowerment tensions in digital self-tracking across the intrapersonal, interactional, and behavioral level.

worst case, inaccurate personal data are compared with biased or even artificial normative datasets, leading individuals to strive for artificial and unrealistic ideals. Additionally, when technological feedback increasingly overrides bodily awareness, users lose interpretative authority over their own experiences, resulting in disembodiment and alienation [4]. This ultimately raises the question of whether individuals, as datafied selves, become more oriented towards technologically constructed norms than towards their authentic selves. Consequently, rather than fostering a connectedness to oneself, digital self-tracking can have the opposite effect, leading to an alienation of oneself towards a technologically constructed ideal. Accordingly, a key tension at the intrapersonal level is between *self-connectedness and self-alienation.*

On an **interactional level**, empowerment emerges from social dynamics, social norms, and power relations [23]. Digital self-tracking is never a purely individual practice but is always deeply embedded within social contexts [21]. This embeddedness means that self-tracking acts within social networks, mutual evaluation, and institutional expectations. Users are influenced by interactions with peers, social groups, communities, or organizational structures. This social embeddedness can promote a sense of belonging, shared meaning, social exchange, and collective motivation [1,15]. Additionally, comparisons may help users to assess their progress and interpret their own data for optimizing themselves. On the other hand, comparative data can reinforce normative pressure by encouraging individuals to measure themselves against certain standards, which can lead to self-doubt, self-criticism, and feelings of inadequacy when expectations are not met. Constant comparison can become an emotionally charged experience that fosters a feeling of never being good enough, resulting in stress and exhaustion [11]. Over time, this can turn self-optimization into self-exploitation in pursuit of an idealized individual [8,15], enabled and reinforced by subtle or explicit monitoring from peers, supervisors, or platform algorithms [1,10,16]. Thus, sharing data can generate both social support and social pressure. While comparisons may help users to assess their progress and interpret their own data, they can also reinforce normative expectations. This reveals a tension at the interactional level between *social embeddedness and normative pressure.*

At the **behavioral level**, empowerment is understood as an individual's agency, which refers to the ability to take actions, participate, and influence systems and their rules [23]. In other words, it also includes the capacity to establish routines and deliberately adapt everyday practices. A sense of agency describes the feeling of having control of one's body and environment, and it is essential for understanding how individuals experience interactions with technology. It reflects the power to act self-effectively and make decisions that create change [13]. Digital self-tracking can foster this sense of agency by enabling users to define personal goals, monitor their progress, and receive feedback that supports self-directed action [15]. In this way, individuals can modify concrete behaviors such as exercise habits, dietary choices, sleep patterns, or stress management routines. These changes can strengthen feelings of competence by supporting individuals in managing different physical or mental states through adaptive behavior. However, the question arises of whether the behavior that emerges through the use of digital self-tracking is genuinely self-determined or whether it is guided externally, guided by the technology itself. Many applications shape behavior by embedding normative benchmarks (e.g. ideal step counts or hours of sleep) into visualizations and reinforcing them through design elements such as reminders, leaderboards, or gamification [8]. These mechanisms nudge individuals to align with predefined standards, thereby stabilizing certain routines but also driving more intensive technology use, ongoing engagement, and the purchase of monetized services. While these dynamics operate at the behavioral level, they are also shaped by broader structural conditions. Self-tracking technologies are developed and influenced by powerful organizations whose economic interests and values define what is considered optimized behavior. This concentration of influence is described by researchers as *technofeudalism*, which is a situation in which a small elite of corporate actors and technical experts dictate goals, benchmarks, and behavioral norms [9]. In line with that, King et al. [11] criticize that users of digital self-tracking tools have little influence over how their behavioral data is interpreted and visualized. Frequently, data becomes the exclusive property of technology companies or institutions, while users lose control over how their information is used [5]. As a result, behaviors that appear self-directed may reflect external guidance rather than self-determined agency. Accordingly, a key tension at the behavioral level concerns whether digital self-tracking supports genuine agency and self-directed routines, or instead reinforces external control through technologically steered practices. Thus, there is a tension between *agency and technological control.*

3   Design Questions

From the perspective of digital humanism, technology design should address human needs and values but also consider broader societal and ethical consequences [6], which aligns with the growing trend towards humanity-centered design in human computer interaction [17] and recent work on ethics of digital self-tracking in particular [22]. Taking this perspective, we formulated a set of guiding questions to realize the empowering potential of digital self-tracking (see Table 1). While the design questions focus on individual, social, and behavioral aspects separately, it is important to note that these levels are interconnected: challenges at one level may influence others. Thoughtfully addressing the questions can help mitigate tensions across levels, supporting empowerment in line with digital humanism principles.

Table 1. Questions to guide the design of digital self-tracking.

Intrapersonal level → empowerment through self-connectedness	- How can digital self-tracking support reflective self-connection over external self-optimization? - How can visualized feedback preserve personal meaning and embodied self-understanding? - How can users stay connected with oneself while engaging with quantified data of the self?
Interactional level → empowerment through social embeddedness	- How can digital self-tracking support meaningful social connection without promoting conformity or surveillance? - How can interfaces enable optional, contextual, and supportive social comparison? - How can users stay in control of when, how, and with whom their data is shared to avoid normative pressure?
Behavioral level → empowerment through agency	- How can digital self-tracking reflect diverse lifeworlds and avoid one-size-fits-all optimization? - How can interfaces ensure transparency and uphold user control over data use? - How can tracking stay voluntary, context-sensitive, and accessible, especially for marginalized groups?

These questions, concerning the conceptual framing, interface design, and real-world implementation, including both initial and long-term use, should be used to guide the design and usage of digital self-tracking. At the same time, they can also serve as evaluation criteria to assess whether systems in practice actually foster empowerment across the three levels. To unfold its full empowerment potential, it is essential to address the intrapersonal, interactional, and behavioral levels in an integrated way. In this vein, digital self-tracking can be crafted to reflect the values of digital humanism. To operationalize these guiding questions, designers can draw on methods such as reflective workshops, co-design sessions, scenario-based design, and iterative prototyping, while evaluating intrapersonal, interactional, and behavioral dimensions through user surveys, co-design feedback, or usage analytics. This approach provides a compact framework to assess whether systems enhance self-connectedness, meaningful social engagement, and user agency, thereby supporting complex ethical and practical considerations in line with the principles of digital humanism.

References

1. Ajana, B.: Digital health and the biopolitics of the quantified self. Digital Health **3**, 1–18 (2017). https://doi.org/10.1177/2055207616689509
2. Avrahami, D., Williams, K., Lee, M.L., Tokunaga, N., Tjahjadi, Y., Marlow, J.: Celebrating everyday success: improving engagement and motivation using a system for recording daily highlights. In: Proceedings CHI Conference, pp. 1–13 (2020)
3. Bieg, T., Gerdenitsch, C., Schörpf, P., Jahanjoo, A., Taherinejad, N.: Neurophysiological data collection at the digital workplace. In: NeuroIS Retreat, pp. 201–209. Springer (2024)
4. Boldi, A., Rapp, A.: Quantifying the body: body image, body awareness and self-tracking technologies. In: Michalos, A. (ed.) Quantifying Quality Life: Incorporating Daily Life Med., pp. 189–207. Springer, Cham (2022)
5. Cecchinato, M., Gould, S., Pitts, F.: Self-tracking & sousveillance at work: insights from human–computer interaction & social science. In: Augmented Exploitation: Artificial Intelligence, Automation and Work, pp. 127–137. Wildcat (2021)
6. Coeckelbergh, M.: What is digital humanism? a conceptual analysis and an argument for a more critical and political digital (post) humanism. J. Responsible Technol. **17**, 100073 (2024)
7. Feng, S., Mäntymäki, M., Dhir, A., Salmela, H.: How self-tracking and the quantified self promote health and well-being: systematic review. J. Med. Internet Res. **23**(9), e25171 (2021)
8. Gerdenitsch, C., Bieg, T., Gaitsch, M., Schörpf, P., Tscheligi, M., Kriglstein, S.: Tracking to success? a critical reflection on workplace quantified-self technologies from a humanistic perspective. In: Proceedings CHIWork, pp. 1–7 (2023)
9. Gilbert, J.: Techno-feudalism or platform capitalism? conceptualising the digital society. Eur. J. Soc. Theory **27**(4), 561–578 (2024)
10. Hepp, A., Alpen, S., Simon, P.: Beyond empowerment, experimentation and reasoning: the public discourse around the quantified self movement. Communications **46**(1), 27–51 (2021)
11. King, V., Gerisch, B., Rosa, H., Franz, R., Lindner, D., Salfeld, B., Stenger, M.: Self-optimization via figures and digital parameters-psychic repercussions of digital measurement and comparison. Hist. Soc. Res. **49**(3), 213–237 (2024)
12. Li, N., Hopfgartner, F.: To log or not to log? SWOT analysis of self-tracking. In: Selke, S. (ed.) Lifelogging: Digital Self-Tracking and Lifelogging: Between Disruptive Technology and Cultural Transformation, pp. 305–325. Springer (2016)
13. Limerick, H., Coyle, D., Moore, J.W.: The experience of agency in human-computer interactions: a review. Front. Hum. Neurosci. **8**, 643 (2014)
14. Lomborg, S., Langstrup, H., Andersen, T.O.: Interpretation as luxury: heart patients living with data doubt, hope, and anxiety. Big Data Soc. **7**(1), 2053951720924436 (2020). https://doi.org/10.1177/2053951720924436

15. Moore, P., Piwek, L., Roper, I.: The quantified workplace: a study in self-tracking, agility and change management. In: Ajana, B. (ed.) Self-Tracking, pp. 153–171. Palgrave Macmillan, Cham (2018)
16. Neff, G., Nafus, D.: Self-tracking. MIT Press, Cambridge (2016)
17. Norman, D.: Humanity-centered design. https://www.interaction-design.org/literature/topics/humanity-centered-design
18. Ong, E., Samson, B.: Exploring design opportunities for improved self-motivation in self-tracking and health goal achievement. Proc. MHCI **8**, 1–17 (2024)
19. Rivera-Pelayo, V., Fessl, A., Müller, L., Pammer, V.: Introducing mood self-tracking at work: empirical insights from call centers. Proc. TOCHI **24**(1), 1–28 (2017)
20. Swan, M.: The quantified self: fundamental disruption in big data science and biological discovery. Big Data **1**(2), 85–99 (2013)
21. Venturini, T., Acker, A., Plantin, J.C., Walford, T., Jethani, S.: The quantified self and beyond: Situated data practices and scope creep. In: The Sage Handbook of Data and Society. Sage Publications, London (2025)
22. Wieczorek, M., O'Brolchain, F., Saghai, Y., Gordijn, B.: The ethics of self-tracking. a comprehensive review of the literature. Ethics Behav. **33**(4), 239–271 (2023)
23. Zimmerman, M.A.: Psychological empowerment: issues and illustrations. Am. J. Community Psychol. **23**, 581–599 (1995)

Author Index

© The Editor(s) (if applicable) and The Author(s), under exclusive license
to Springer Nature Switzerland AG 2026
L. Hagedorn et al. (Eds.): DIGHUM 2025, LNCS 16319, pp. 545–546, 2026.
https://doi.org/10.1007/978-3-032-11108-1